MANY
PEOPLES,
ONE
LAND

ALETHEA K. HELBIG
AGNES REGAN PERKINS

MANY PEOPLES, ONE LAND

A Guide to New Multicultural Literature for Children and Young Adults

GREENWOOD PRESS
Westport, Connecticut • London

Library of Congress Cataloging-in-Publication Data

Helbig, Alethea.
　　Many peoples, one land : a guide to new multicultural literature for children and young adults / Alethea K. Helbig and Agnes Regan Perkins.
　　　　p.　cm.
　　"Successor to This land is our land (1994)"—Pref.
　　Includes bibliographical references and index.
　　ISBN 0–313–30967–1 (alk. paper)
　　1. Children's literature, American—Bibliography.　2. Ethnic groups—United States—Bibliography.　3. Young adult literature, American—Bibliography.　4. Children—United States—Books and reading.　5. Ethnic groups in literature—Bibliography.　6. Minorities—United States—Bibliography.　7. Folk literature, American—Bibliography.　8. Minorities in literature—Bibliography.　I. Perkins, Agnes.　II. Helbig, Alethea. This land is our land.　III. Title.
Z1232.H45　2001
[PS173.E8]
016.8108'09282—dc21　　　　　00–025111

British Library Cataloguing in Publication Data is available.

Library of Congress Catalog Card Number: 00–025111
ISBN: 0–313–30967–1

First published in 2001

Greenwood Press, 88 Post Road West, Westport, CT 06881
An imprint of Greenwood Publishing Group, Inc.
www.greenwood.com

Printed in the United States of America

The paper used in this book complies with the Permanent Paper Standard issued by the National Information Standards Organization (Z39.48–1984).

10 9 8 7 6 5 4 3 2 1

Contents

Preface   vii

Annotated Bibliographical Entries

  1   African Americans: Books of Fiction   1

  2   African Americans: Books of Oral Tradition   90

  3   African Americans: Books of Poetry   97

  4   Asian Americans: Books of Fiction   115

  5   Asian Americans: Books of Oral Tradition   147

  6   Asian Americans: Books of Poetry   174

  7   Hispanic Americans: Books of Fiction   180

  8   Hispanic Americans: Books of Oral Tradition   223

  9   Hispanic Americans: Books of Poetry   231

10   Native-American Indians: Books of Fiction   247

11   Native-American Indians: Books of Oral Tradition   294

12   Native-American Indians: Books of Poetry   326

Index of Titles   335

Index of Writers   347

Index of Illustrators   353

Index of Titles by Grade Level   357

Index of Subjects   367

Preface

Many Peoples, One Land: A Guide to New Multicultural Literature for Children and Young Adults, successor to *This Land Is Our Land* (1994), involves books of fiction, oral tradition, and poetry published from 1994 through 1999 suitable for young people from preschool through high school. It deals with four major ethnic groups within the United States: African Americans, Asian Americans, Hispanic Americans, and Native-American Indians. Contained are 561 entries on 541 books (a few are considered in more than one category, such as anthologies of both fiction and poetry). Also included in these entries is information about 130 other books by these writers or related books that help in identifying the writer or that amplify the description of a particular book. In addition, the entries are also expanded by references to more than 260 books that appear in the earlier volume. Since retellers and editors are represented as well as authors, we use the term "writer" throughout.

Many Peoples, One Land follows *This Land Is Our Land*, a critical reference that takes up books published from 1985 through 1993 of the same literary genres and same American ethnic groups. This earlier volume involves 570 entries on 559 books, along with information about 188 other books by their writers and 90 related books. Taken together, the two volumes offer 1,131 entries and information on more than 1,100 featured books and cover a span of fifteen years of multicultural literature for young readers. While *Many Peoples, One Land* is intended primarily for the use of librarians, teachers, and parents, scholars and researchers can find it a valuable springboard for insights into the development of multicultural literature during this period.

Since we have been involved with children's literature for more than thirty years, chiefly through teaching it to college students, most of whom are prospective teachers, we have long been concerned with the issue of quality in multi-ethnic books of imaginative literature. We ourselves have selected, read, and considered all the books included here (as well as those in *This Land Is Our Land*) and have judged them primarily on such literary values as plot development, style, and characterization. An example of how important evaluating such literary features can be appears with stereotypes. However sympathetically portrayed, stereotyped characters may engage the reader's emotions but do not promote real understanding. Similarly, plotting that is inept may catch the reader's attention, but when a writer romanticizes events and reaches illogical conclusions, the reader may be left feeling skeptical about the writer's honesty and about the real situation of the ethnic group as well.

For the most part, our choices have followed the practice of *This Land Is Our Land*. Since this bibliography also focuses on the American ethnic experience (including Puerto Rico), works set in other countries are excluded, except for the oral tradition of Asian and Hispanic peoples, because these latter groups within the United States have not developed extensive oral literature based in this country. This is not true of African Americans, however; a large body of folk material set mainly in the American South has grown up. It derives its roots from Africa, but the versions are distinctively American. Therefore, we have not included retellings directly from African oral tradition, even though many well-told and attractive books of that sort exist. Native-American Indian oral tradition, of course, has its origins in what is now the United States. We have also included originally oral material from such groups as the Aztecs and Maya because these relate to the Native-American Indian experience and to the Hispanic experience as well. We have grouped them under Native-American Indians.

In doing these volumes, we have discovered that deciding on what constitutes the particular ethnic experience is not a simple task. Distinctions are not clear-cut. Certainly, in each of the groups are people whose lives are like those of anyone in mainstream United States, and this very fact is a part of their ethnic experience and valuable for young readers to be exposed to. In recent years, many books reflect this situation, especially picture-story books.

Books about an ethnic group have not been included unless the book, in story or at least in the illustrations, is mainly about minority characters. A number of the books considered for inclusion have one or more characters from a particular ethnic group, but the story's protagonist is Anglo. We have chosen those in which the predominant problem or action of the story concerns the minority figures but not those in which they are merely incidental friends of the Anglo or in which the primary development in understanding has been for the white protagonist.

Since the scope of this volume includes high school students, much of the poetry and a number of the novels and short stories were originally published for adults. Where the material requires more than usual maturity or contains elements that might be objectionable, we have so indicated in the commentaries.

Although we have made every effort to include all the appropriate books from this time period, we could not secure a few in time to meet our deadline. We would have liked to have a better balance in the number of books from the four groups, but this was not possible. Not surprisingly, as we discovered with the previous volume, many more books about African Americans have been published than for any of the other groups. Increasingly, these reflect a broader spectrum of middle-class American life (as is also true with the other three groups), unlike books in earlier years, when the emphasis was more specifically on the inner-city experience or on discrimination from the dominant culture.

In the Hispanic section, bilingual stories and retellings of folktales continue to provide a special experience. Poetry is more richly represented among Hispanics than in the previous volume, and Latina writers are publishing more poetry and fiction, a welcome development. In fiction generally, Hispanic Americans and Asian Americans continue to contribute novels and short stories of high quality. Native Americans are well represented in all areas with laudable work, but poetry, the genre in which Native Americans have been especially prolific and skilled, is less extensive than before. Native-American fiction and poetry continue to be highly informed by oral tradition. Among all the groups, many of the books are accessible to later middle school, although aimed at adults. As we discovered in working on *This Land Is Our Land*, fantasy is sparsely represented. Picture-story books and illustrated books of oral tradition are often of extraordinary beauty, even though the pictures sometimes dominate the texts or are forced to compensate for or even bolster uninspired writing.

Entries appear in alphabetical order by writer within each ethnic group, with subsections within each group: fiction (including picture-story books of fiction), oral tradition, and poetry. Each entry includes standard bibliographical information; age and grade levels; a brief summary of content, incorporating themes; critical comments with a judgment of the book's value as an example of its genre; and, where pertinent, other books by the writer, if not given in separate entries, and related books of importance. Cross-references direct the reader's attention to books by the writers in *This Land Is Our Land*.

The length of an entry does not necessarily indicate the book's importance or quality, since plots can be summarized more briefly and critical judgments stated more succinctly for some books than for others. In a few instances when protagonists of different enthic groups are represented, bibliographic entries have been repeated. Readers are referred to the full annotations given by entry number. For example, Marie Lee's *Night of the Chupacabras* appears in both Asian-American and Hispanic-American fiction sections because the protagonists are Asian and Chicano children of equal importance. When books contain more than one genre, distinct entries have been included under both, depending on the book's emphasis. An example is *Daughters of the Fifth Sun: A Collection of Latina Fiction and Poetry*, by Bryce Milligan et al.

Occasionally the substance of a book can be classified under two genres. For example, Brian Swann's *Touching the Distance: Native American Riddle-Poems* is oral tradition material presented in the form of poetry. In such cases, the book appears under one genre; under the other genre only the bibliographical information is given, with a cross-reference to the full entry.

Sometimes several entries appear by the same writer. Various reasons governed our choices in such cases. Some writers, like Laurence Yep and Harriette

Gillem Robinet, have been more prolific in this period than others. In instances in which the works by a writer are similar, they have been included in a single entry, for example, Sandra Belton's books about Ernestine and Amanda. The book featured may be the first in the series, as with Belton's book, or the most recent, or in some cases the most highly regarded from this period. Sometimes, however, the works of a writer fit into more than one genre or subgenre, and these have been given separate entries. For instance, Gary Soto has written picture-story books of fantasy and realism, novels of domestic adventures for younger readers, problem novels for middle school and above, and collections of short stories and poems for a broad age range.

With respect to age and grade-level designations, in most cases we have followed the suggestions of the publishers, except where our experience with children and young people leads us to judge differently. Particularly in oral tradition, suggested levels should not be followed rigidly. Since folktales, myths, hero tales, and fables were intended for all ages, the retellings can usually be treated with flexibility, and depending upon the proposed use, may have no age limits. Even with the other genres, age and grade-level designations should not be adhered to slavishly. Children differ greatly, and their receptivity to books depends on the skill and enthusiasm of the adults working with them.

Most users will be familiar with the terms we employ, but a few may need explanation. By realistic fiction we mean books in which events could have happened in the world as we know it, as opposed to an imaginary or fantastic world, and not necessarily that the action is convincing or plausible. Historical fiction includes those books in which actual historical events or figures function in the plot or in which the specific past period is essential to the action and in which the story could not have occurred at any other time. Books that are merely set in the past time, like *To a Widow with Children* by Lionel G. Garcia, we have called period fiction. By picture-story books, we mean those highly illustrated books of a single original short story. Books from oral tradition are often single stories highly illustrated; these are included under oral tradition. Books of rhymes and songs are included with poetry, as are picture-story books of verse.

Several indexes appear. In all these, items are keyed to entry numbers: a title index (with writers' names in parentheses); an index of writers, editors, and retellers; an illustrator index; a grade-level index; and a subject index. The subject index includes genres by ethnic group; subgroups within the larger ethnic group, for example, Puerto Ricans, Ojibway Indians; settings, for example, Fresno, farms; and such general subjects as friendship, women's concerns, basketball, culture shock, prejudice against Hispanics, and so on.

We ourselves have done all the selecting, reading, research, and writing for *Many Peoples, One Land*, as we did for *This Land Is Our Land*. We have had valuable suggestions from many sources, especially our librarian friends.

We express our appreciation to the Bruce T. Halle Library at Eastern Michigan University, the Ann Arbor, Michigan, District Library, and the Ypsilanti,

Michigan, District Library for the use of their extensive collections and inter-library loan services and for their ongoing encouragement and support as well. Specifically, we thank Brian Steimel, Margaret Best, and Carolyn Kirkendall of the Halle Library for the many ways in which they have helped.

The assistance of the Ann Arbor District Library has been invaluable, in establishing lists, securing books, and ferreting out information. We thank the reference librarians, the adult fiction and nonfiction librarians, and the clerical and library staff of the Youth Department at the Main Library, especially the following: Sherry Roberts, Paula Schaffner, Laura Raynor, Betsy Baier, Cynthia Chelius, and Linda Powers, and at the Loving Branch, Ieva Bates and the circulation staff.

Our appreciation also goes to Margaret Davis and the circulation staff of the Ypsilanti District Library for helping in a variety of ways.

1

African Americans: Books of Fiction

1 Ackerman, Karen, *By the Dawn's Early Light*, illus. Catherine Stock, Atheneum, 1994 (hardcover), ISBN 0–689–31788–3, $14.95, unp.; Aladdin, 1999 (paper), ISBN 0–689–82481–5, $5.99. Ages 4–8, grades PS–3.

Narrated by Rachel, a young African-American schoolgirl, a picture-story book about a fatherless family whose mother works the night shift at a factory. Nana, evidently the grandmother, fixes supper for Rachel and her little brother, Josh, as Mom hurries off to work. Through the evening, as she does her homework, dries the dishes, takes her bath, and goes to bed, Rachel thinks of what her mother is doing: punching the time clock, working on the assembly line, taking her coffee breaks, eating lunch in the cafeteria, and finally heading home. Rachel hears her unlock the front door and wakes Josh so they can both have a little time with their mother, eating an early breakfast, cuddling with her on the sofa, telling her about their evening, and watching the sun come up. The warm story is enhanced by watercolor illustrations in soft hues, showing details of home, city, and factory life.

2 Baldacci, David, *The Simple Truth*, Warner, 1998 (hardcover), ISBN 0–445–52332–1, $25.00, 470 pp. Ages 14 up, grades 9 up.

Mystery-detective novel set mostly in and near present-day Washington, D.C., and involving the criminal justice system, military justice system, and Supreme Court intrigue and power struggles. Physically large and powerful African-American Rufus Harms has been incarcerated in the Fort Jackson Military Prison in Virginia for twenty-five years, doing hard time for murdering a little white girl, a crime he freely admits. When Rufus receives a letter from the Army, the contents of which are revealed only late in the novel, he contacts Samuel Rider, the JAG (judge advocate general) attorney who had defended him, and instructs Rider to file an appeal on his behalf with the U.S. Supreme Court, to convey to the highest court in the land "the simple truth" of what really happened that night long ago. Michael Fiske, considered the most brilliant of the law clerks at the court, finds the appeal papers, realizes they are potential dynamite, and visits Rufus in prison to verify the facts. He unwittingly precipitates events that lead to his own murder, as well as those of another clerk and Rider, and plunges several people, including his older brother, John, also an attorney, and his former sweetheart and fellow law clerk, Sara Evans, into great danger, as the power of the military and CIA brass conspire to prevent them from discovering the truth about what caused Harms, a highly religious, innately gentle man, to break out of the military stockade in which he was confined and commit murder. Also involved are Supreme Court Justice Elizabeth Knight, a woman of great principle and concern for the underdog, who is the wife of long-time Senator Jordan Knight; Chief Justice Harold Ramsey, a hard-bitten conservative incessantly concerned about the court's reputation; Buford Chandler, of the D.C. Police Department, a tough, determined, fair-minded African-American detective, who allows John, a former policeman, to assist in investigating his brother's killing; Josh Harms, a highly decorated Vietnam vet, determined to help his brother evade the officials out to kill him; and FBI Agent Warren McKenna, a loud, authoritative official, who seems obsessed with proving that John killed Michael to get the five hundred thousand dollars in insurance money. Eventually it is learned that because Rufus's dyslexia was never diagnosed, he was unable to read the orders he was punished for disobeying. Officers and soldiers, jealous and angry because they thought he was a slacker, administered a drug the Army was testing at that time. The drug caused him to go berserk, a condition the top brass and top civilian authorities in the know have been hiding all these years. Jail scenes, hospital scenes, various court scenes, numerous tight spots and nick-of-time rescues; chases, in particular that of Josh and Rufus across the country-side in Josh's camper truck after Josh helps Rufus break out from the hospital, because both know the brass will see to it that Rufus will never emerge alive— such conventions of a nail-biting, potboiler thriller by a lawyer-turned-novelist produce a just-plain-good read from start to finish. Scenes from the personal life of John and his estranged brother, his father, and his Alzheimer's-patient mother, on Sara's sailboat, and of lovemaking with Sara provide the personal element and enough respite from the tension to make the conspiracy more intense. The reader is carefully given just enough information to figure out along with the "good guys" what must be going on. The Supreme Court scenes and those involving Senator Knight are cold and technical enough to cause one to question the bases upon which American justice rests.

3 Bang, Molly, *One Fall Day*, illus. Molly Bang, Greenwillow, 1994 (hardcover), ISBN 0–688–07015–9, $15.00, 24 pp. Ages 4–8, grades PS–3.

A simple bedtime story reviews the day rhythmically, ending with a promise of a new day to play tomorrow. The illustrations are photographs of the activities of one day enacted by an African-American doll and a stuffed gray cat, as the child wakes, eats breakfast, plays outdoors in the sun and the rain, paints, prepares for bed, and goes to sleep, while gray cat curls close and watches all night. This low-key book may appeal to children just beyond the board-book stage and to older youngsters interested in the unusual way to tell a story.

4 Banks, Jacqueline Turner, *Egg-Drop Blues*, Houghton, 1995 (hardcover), ISBN 0–395–70931–8, $13.95, 120 pp. Ages 8–12, grades 3–7.

Amusing, lightweight, present-day, realistic novel of family and school life set in the mixed-ethnic, middle-class town of Plank in western Kentucky. Sequel to *Project Wheels* (1993), this novel focuses on African-American Judge Jenkins, the narrator twin of Jury. Both boys are in sixth grade at Faber School and members of the mixed-ethnic group who call themselves the posse. Judge learns that he is dyslexic, a diagnosis that explains, he thinks, why he cannot answer the teacher's "trick questions" on tests and is getting a very low grade in science. Since his teacher says he can elevate his grade if he participates in the Einstein Rally, he agrees and also volunteers Jury, to Jury's dismay, because Jury would much rather engage in the forbidden game of pom-pom tackle. Much of the story is taken up with their efforts to prepare for the egg drop, that is, they must devise a way of dropping a raw egg from a roof without breaking it. Another problem, introduced late, revolves around their divorced father's new girlfriend, whom the boys have difficulty accepting. They are pleased at the end, however, when she is present along with their father and mother to cheer them on in the contest and celebrate their being among the three teams tied at the finish. The book examines in a limited way the importance of family, the meaning of friendship, and relationships between siblings and parents. Jury is chiefly defined by his jabs at Judge and his almost constant use of clichéd expressions, and Judge by his need to see himself as worthy and capable in spite of his learning disability. The gentle humor, credible problems, extensive, real-sounding dialogue, demanding but not rigid parents, helpful teachers, and convincing relationships between the members of the posse, make for an entertaining, upbeat story in which the plot turns out as hoped. The tension between the boys is credible, as are their mother's attempts to keep them in line and at their duties and their perceptions of her as being much older than she is and hence unable to appreciate contemporary music and situations. Judge's description of how dyslexia limits him—trouble concentrating and focusing and not being able to follow the action of a football game on television without turning off the sound, for example—is an especially good feature. *The New One* (1994) revolves around narrator Jury's interest in Ayreal, a new African-American classmate, whom Judge and the posse do not like, and the possibility that their mother might marry Frank, her new boyfriend, whom neither boy likes. A description of *Project Wheels* appears in *This Land Is Our Land* (1994), no. 5.

5 Battle-Lavert, Gwendolyn, *Off to School*, illus. Gershom Griffith, Holiday House, 1995 (hardcover), ISBN 0–8234–1185–0, $15.95, unp. Ages 4–8, grades PS–3.

Amusing realistic picture-story book of family life, in which a young girl learns that she must live up to her responsibilities. Wezielee's father is a share-cropper farmer, who moves his family from state to state as the crops mature. His children never attend school as long as there is work to be done and are used to taking turns cooking the meals while the others work with their parents in the fields. When it is time for Wezielee, the youngest, to cook, she ruins all the meals, because she does not keep her mind on her work. She thinks about the school down the road all the time and wishes she were there. Sometimes she even leaves for school, but each time Dad catches her before she gets there. She finally settles down and makes a good meal, what Dad calls the "hottest soup this side of Texas." Then, to her joy, he tells her it is now time for her to go to school. All the members of Wezielee's family are depicted in the representational paintings as tall and goodlooking, happy, smiling, and spotless, in spite of the long, hard hours in the fields. The story is well told and gives some sense of the hardships of migrant life in a lighthearted way.

6 Belton, Sandra, *Ernestine & Amanda*, Simon & Schuster, 1996 (hardcover), ISBN 0–689–80848–8, $16.00, 149 pp.; Aladdin, 1998 (paper), ISBN 0–689–80847–X, $3.99, 157 pp. Ages 8–12, grades 3–7.

Realistic novel of friendship and family life set in an upper middle-class neighborhood in an unnamed city in the 1950s and lasting one school year. African-American Ernestine Harris and Amanda Clay, both eleven, tell in alternating chapters how, although at first determined antagonists, they rise above their mutual dislike and become friends. Ernestine thinks of Amanda as Miss Stuck-up, while Amanda regards overweight Ernestine as Fatso. They meet at Miss Elder's piano studio, where Ernestine, who plays by ear, has just begun taking lessons. Soon, Alicia Raymond, another pupil and Amanda's best friend, has become friends with Ernestine, to Amanda's disgust, and about the same time, Amanda learns that her older sister, Madlyn, is romantically attracted to Ernestine's older brother, Marcus, a situation that disgusts both girls. Miss Elder has planned a special competition: the one of her pupils that famous pianist and composer Camille Nickerson thinks has played the best will be allowed to play with Miss Nickerson in the class's spring recital at the high school. The girls choose their pieces, discuss dresses—the recital is a major topic of conversation. Scenes of family life provide many warm and lighter moments, except that home life deteriorates for Amanda and Madlyn, and in the spring, just before the recital, their parents decide to separate. Neither Amanda nor Ernestine wins the competition, but when Ernestine sees that Amanda is miserable, although she does not know why, she tries to cheer her up. She tells her that she thinks that Amanda played the best and wishes her the conventional "break a leg" before the recital. Both girls agree that having the opportunity to meet and hear Miss Nickerson was a marvelous experience. The girls are individualized in broad strokes, tone is intimate, dialogue moves naturally with childhood patois, like dropped g's and elided words ("whachu lookin' at"), and bickering and teasing are commonplace. Alicia and her twin, Edna, are pleasant peacemakers, and adults for the most part let the girls solve their own problems. This novel is the first in a series, the next books being *Ernestine & Amanda: Summer Camp: Ready or Not!* (1997); *Ernestine & Amanda: Members of the C.L.U.B.* (1997); and *Ernestine & Amanda: Mysteries on Monroe Street* (1998), further adventures of two girls who are not really friends, but not enemies either, learning how to get along with and accommodate to each other. For a picture-story book by Belton, see *From Miss Ida's Porch* in *This Land Is Our Land* (1994), no. 7.

7 Belton, Sandra, *May'naise Sandwiches & Sunshine Tea*, illus. Gail Gordon Carter, Four Winds, 1994 (hardcover), ISBN 0–02–709035–3, $14.95. Ages 4–9, grades PS–4.

Contemporary realistic picture-story book, in which a little girl and her Big Mama (grandmother) stretch out together on Big Mama's bed and look through Big Mama's book of "rememberies"—shots of relatives, celebrations, and graduations—a family history in photographs. Little Miss loves Big Mama's "wraparounds," the stories that go with the pictures, especially the one about Big Mama and her good friend, Bettie Jean, whose parents were teachers and at whose house the two girls would play dress-ups and have an elegant tea. When Bettie Jean comes to play at Little Miss's house, her mother serves all she has—may'naise sandwiches and sugar water in glasses that catch the beauty of the dancing sun. Bettie Jean says this is the best lunch she has ever had. The pastel-colored illustrations are "wraparounds," too; they flow around the framed text on each page and realistically depict situations and characters. Their slight mistiness adds to the nostalgia of this warm slice of family life and special relationship between generations. For an earlier picture-story book, see *From Miss Ida's Porch* in *This Land Is Our Land* (1994), no. 7.

8 Bledsoe, Lucy Jane, *The Big Bike Race*, illus. Sterling Brown, Holiday House, 1995 (hardcover), ISBN 0–8234–1206–7, $13.95, 90 pp.; Camelot, 1997 (paper), ISBN 0–380–72830–3, $3.99, 96 pp. Ages 7–12, grades 2–7.

Contemporary sports novel set in Washington, D.C. Orphaned, African-American Ernie Peterson yearns to make the world take notice of him. He has asked for a racing bike for his tenth birthday and is exceedingly deflated when his Grandma gives him a big, yellow, clunky machine with baskets over the wheels. To compensate for his disappointment, he begins to think of himself as Ernest Peterson III and dreams big dreams of becoming president or winning an important race. One day near the White House, he meets a young black man riding on just the kind of bike Ernest would like and dressed in appropriate racing gear. Ernest becomes friends with Sonny King, one of the city's best male competitors. Sonny helps Ernest streamline the clunker and coaches him in training and riding. Encouraged by Sonny, Ernest competes in the Citywide Cup junior race, in which he makes mistakes and comes in thirtieth but does well considering the limitations of the yellow clunker. Sonny, however, wins the adult male Citywide Cup race and gets a brand-new bike as his prize. In front of the TV cameras afterward, Sonny thanks Ernest for being his chief supporter and gives his old bike to Ernest in appreciation. Ernest is a likable if typical boy in his yearnings, disgust for his sister, and attempts to understand his struggling Grandma's motivations and financial constraints. The book stresses doing one's best and competing fairly. An especially good feature is that the story deals with a sport little taken up in sports books for boys. Only a few references and the realistic black-and-white, full-page illustrations indicate the protagonist's race.

9 Bolden, Tonya, *Just Family*, Cobblehill, 1996 (hardcover), ISBN 0–525–65192–6, $14.99, 151 pp. Ages 8–14, grades 3–9.

Realistic novel of family life in Harlem in the 1960s, as seen from the vantage of the second daughter in a middle-class, inner-city, African-American family. Life changes drastically for Beryl Nelson, ten, during the elegant dinner that she and her older sister, Randy, thirteen, have prepared with their grandmother's help for their parents' anniversary. She learns to her dismay that Randy is her half-sister, the child of her mother but not of her father. Her shock and anger are soon replaced by fear and numerous questions. Suppose Randy's real father, who lives not far away, took her with him to keep? Suppose he is rich? Why won't Randy show her his picture? Shouldn't Daddy love her more than Randy? A big fight breaks out between the two sisters when Beryl opens Randy's keep-sake box and finds the picture of Rusty, their mother's long-ago sweetheart and Randy's birth-father. Beryl gradually learns the facts: her mother became pregnant at a young age, and since the parents-to-be were very young, their parents decided that it would be better if they did not marry. Beryl's grandmother helped her mother raise Randy, and when Daddy came along and fell in love with Ma, he happily made Randy his own. At the family reunion "Down South" in South Carolina, Beryl discovers that everyone seems to know about Randy and loves her like family anyway. Aunt Bunny remarks to Beryl that "it's not the blood. It's the love" that is important and makes a family a family. Beryl concludes that while wanting to know about Randy and Randy's place in the family was all right, she handled the matter badly. She prays that God forgive her poor behavior. Beryl's feelings and questions seem genuine, as do Randy's at not wanting to discuss the matter. The bickering, teasing, and sibling rivalry are typical of the age, as are playground and other social behavior and the girls' and their friends' conversations about boys and Beryl's discovery. The family reunion is well drawn, lots of people milling around, mounds of delicious food, and personal conversations between various adult relatives and the girls. Beryl's decision to consult aged Uncle Lemuel about the matter without having sounded him out previously seems a stretch, but may be forgiven because Beryl is pre-sented as stubborn and assertive. The plot problem is slow in developing, but once set in motion is presented in literate, sensitive style, and period details add texture. Bolden has also published another novel with Vi Higginson, *Mama, I Want to Sing*, which is described in *This Land Is Our Land* (1994), no. 52.

10 Bolden, Tonya, ed., *Rites of Passage: Stories about Growing Up by Black Writers from Around the World*, Hyperion, 1994 (hardcover), ISBN 1–5628–2688–3, $16.95, 209 pp.; 1995 (paper), ISBN 0–786–81076–9, $7.95. Ages 10 up, grades 5 up.

Anthology of seventeen stories, twelve of which are by American writers, "about turning points and forks in the road . . . happenings in the lives of girls and boys that journey them one step closer to being women and men." Although every story of the twelve concerns African-American young people and looks at life from the standpoint of blacks, at the same time the episodes transcend race and culture, and even age. As a result, readers from middle grades to mature adults can connect with the protagonists and appreciate the discoveries they make about life and themselves. In the opening story, "Raymond's Run," by Toni Cade Bambara, a top girl runner sees possibilities for friendship in rising above the demands of competition. Two young boys discover that color is the defining feature that makes them prime suspects in a robbery in "The Mountain," by Martin J. Hamer. John Henrik Clarke describes the agony and the triumph of a talented black youth and his black principal-mentor when the white school supervisor discovers that the boy has painted a picture of Jesus as black and fires the principal. A girl is ushered into womanhood in a moving, celebratory ritual conducted by her closest female relatives in "BigWater," by Charlotte Watson Sherman, and another learns a hard reality at the welfare office in "Getting the Facts of Life," by Paulette Childress White. A boy learns that adults are also sometimes confused about life in "My Mother and Mitch," by Clarence Major; and another youth discovers that his dream girl is just that—an illusion— in "My Lucy," by Howard Gordon. Styles, which range from the colloquial to the storytelling to the lyrical and formal, and a variety of moods, as well as the range of substance, give this collection holding power. A foreword by Charles Johnson, an introduction by the author, and information about the writers complete the book.

11 Bond, Adrienne, *Sugarcane House and Other Stories About Mr. Fat*, illus. Leuyen Pham, Harcourt, 1997 (hardcover), ISBN 0–15–201446–2, $16.00, 86 pp. Ages 7–12, grades 2–7.

Six stories about Mr. Fat, the African-American trickster figure similar to High John (see *This Land Is Our Land*, 1994, no. 185, *The Adventures of High John the Conqueror*), an impudent, clever figure who manages to come out on top in most trying situations. These stories are embedded in a frame story of little DeWayne, who hears them from his wheelchair-bound great-grandmother, Ma Minnie, in her trailer home where he stays while his busy parents are working or going to college. Mr. Fat has the ability to talk with his mule, Brownie.

He bests the con-artist raffle man at the fair, and runs off with a tent show, where he is pressed into playing the part of Willie Winkle, the midget dancer. He even escapes from the chain gang. His age and period vary with the stories. Some are set when the country belonged to the King of England; some appear to be within the lifetime of Ma Minnie. Ma Minnie tells them in Southern colloquial language, with the feel of folktale, though the book is listed as fiction. The frame story adds some nice touches: first-grader DeWayne thinks that when he is old enough to drive, he'll take Ma Minnie to school for show-and-tell.

12 Boyd, Candy Dawson, *Fall Secrets*, Puffin, 1994 (paper), ISBN 0–14–036583–4, $3.99, 216 pp. Ages 9–15, grades 4–10.

Realistic novel of family and school life and career preparation set in Oakland, California, in 1992, about a year after the fire that devastated the Oakland/ Berkeley region. African-American Jessie Williams, eleven, is overjoyed at being accepted at Oakland Performing Arts Middle School. She plans to become a dramatic actress and open a drama school for girls like her grandmother, Mamatoo. Immediately, problems develop: piles and piles of homework, auditions, handling the attentions of handsome Jamar, and getting along with the three girls in her school Home Base. Julie, a white girl, has a problem she does not want to talk about and studies violin; black, angry, bossy Addie Mae, a dancer, wishes to be called Obidie and refuses to talk about her home life; and Mexican-American Maria hopes to become a concert pianist. The four girls gradually grow together as they plan and carry out a project for Home Base credit. They perform for and eventually become friends with the elderly residents of a nursing home. They all win parts in various school performances, Jessie mostly winning parts as old women, whom she plays well. She keeps her grades up and attends social events, too, among them a dance with Jamar. A big problem concerns her older sister, Cass, with whom she often has spats, partly because she has a secret—she feels inferior because she overheard her fourth-grade teacher speak disparagingly of her by comparing her with Cass, denigrating her darker skin and calling her dumb. When Cass has a falling out with her boyfriend because he is pressuring her for sex, the two girls begin to confide in each other and also in their mother. Jessie learns that Julie lost her beloved cat in the big fire. Obidie suggests they distribute flyers, and the pet is recovered through help from a nursing-home resident. The girls also start a support group for those who lost family, friends, or property in the fire. The book overflows with the sort of detail that middle-grade girls enjoy—fashions, career, boys, makeup, club secrets—and there is plenty of opportunity for readers to identify with Jessie. Pace is fast; some tension arises, with respect to whether or not Jessie's grades will be high enough to continue and whether or not Jamar really likes her; there is just enough theatrical detail; and having Mamatoo in the Williams household to provide ballast and encouragement is a good touch. Jessie's life continues in a sequel, *A Different Beat* (1996). Other novels by Boyd are described in *This Land Is Our Land* (1994), no. 10, *Charlie Pippin*, and no. 11, *Chevrolet Saturdays*.

13 Bunting, Eve, *Smoky Night*, illus. David Diaz, Harcourt, 1994 (hardcover), ISBN 0–15–269954–6, $15.00, unp.; 1999 (paper), ISBN 0–15–201884–0, $6.00. Ages 5 up, grades K up.

The Los Angeles riots, seen through the eyes and the experience of a young African-American boy named Daniel. From their apartment window he watches with his mother the vandalism and looting in the street and stores below, including that of Asian-American Mrs. Kim, with whom they do not like to trade because she is not one of "our own people." That night they are awakened when their building is burning and flee to shelter in a church hall. Daniel's chief worry is about his cat, Jasmine, who has disappeared, but no one else seems interested. Later a firefighter appears with two cats, Jasmine and Mrs. Kim's, saying he found them hiding together under the stairs. On the strength of the new friendship of the cats, who have always fought before, and of their common predicament, Daniel's mother makes a tentative overture of friendship to Mrs. Kim. The unusual illustrations are bold, in strong colors heavily outlined in black and set, as are the inserted rectangles of the brief text, on varied backgrounds, some textured paper, some with other patterns like the spilled dry cereal from the store and the plastic bags from the dry cleaner's. While they are striking enough to justify the Caldecott Medal awarded the book, the rather stylized pictures of the characters make Daniel look several years older than he is depicted in the text. In *This Land Is Our Land* (1994), no. 344, *How Many Days to America?*, is also a picture-story book; no. 13, *Summer Wheels*, is a chapter book for early readers.

14 Bunting, Eve, *Your Move*, illus. James Ransome, Harcourt, 1998 (hardcover), ISBN 0–15–200181–6, $16.00, 32 pp. Ages 4–8, grades PS–3.

An African-American boy proves himself to his gang, but decides that protecting his little brother is more important than belonging. James, ten, who cares for his brother Isaac, six, while their mother works at night, sneaks out to accomplish whatever feat is required to join the K-Bones, not a gang or a crew, their leader Kris insists, but just a bunch to have fun with. Kris complains when James brings Isaac along and directs James to climb a highway sign and spray-paint their name over that of the Snakes, a major gang of the area. Secretly terrified, James does this, then runs with the others until they are confronted by a group of threatening Snakes. James pulls Isaac away, hears a shot, and for an awful minute thinks his brother has been hit, but Isaac has just fallen, ripped his jeans, and skinned his knees. At home they find their mother, alerted by a neighbor, deeply disappointed that they have sneaked out. The next night Kris arrives with brand-new Lakers caps for both boys to welcome them into the K-Bones. First James, who knows the caps have been shoplifted, and then, reluctantly, Isaac, say, "Thanks. But no thanks." The text, which is longer than that of most picture books, is faced through the whole story by full-page paintings of the realistic night scenes, with characters well differentiated and not overly idealized. One especially effective picture shows five Snakes, older boys menacing enough to strike fear in anyone. In *This Land Is Our Land* (1994), no. 344, *How Many Days to America?*, is also a picture-story book by Bunting; no. 13, *Summer Wheels*, is a chapter book for early readers.

15 Burgess, Barbara Hood, *The Fred Field*, Delacorte, 1994 (hardcover), ISBN 0–385–31070–6, $14.95. 181 pp.; Dell, 1995 (paper), ISBN 0–440–41067–3, $3.99, 192 pp. Ages 10–14, grades 5–9.

Humorous novel of African-American family life set in Detroit's inner city in the mid-1980s, sequel to *Oren Bell* (1990). School is out, and a lively summer is just beginning for Oren, thirteen, his family, and friends. Oren and the Friends of Fred intend to make the empty lot next door, with the "evil house" in which their friend Fred Lightfoot was murdered, into a ballfield as a memorial to their fallen friend. Oren's twin, Latonya, a practiced organizer, helps Oren with the project and also skillfully arranges the July 4 wedding of Mama and Jack Daniels, the veterinarian whom Mama met the previous year and the children have also come to love. A talented artist, Brenda helps with a beautification project a few blocks over—painting and decorating with found-art the abandoned, boarded-up houses there. The twins also perform in their music teacher's high school symphonic band on Belle Isle in the Detroit River. After the field has been made ready for baseball and hoops, Oren turns his attention to solving the mystery of who killed Fred, an enterprise in which he is assisted by the Friends of Fred and also by a formidable young thug called Goon Eye, who it turns out actually witnessed Fred's murder. In bringing the unlikely murderer to justice, which involves a series of childlike comic routines, Goon Eye reforms and then devotes himself to helping a family of foster children so they will not suffer abuse as he did. At the end, the Bells-Daniels family learn that, since the city is going to tear down their long-condemned house and build low-income housing units in the area, they must move to an apartment. Oren is upset that the units will be placed on the Fred Lightfoot Memorial Field but is comforted by learning that a statue of Fred will stand at the entrance and appreciates having a room and bed of his own for the first time in their new place. The principal characters are well drawn and distinct, and, as in its predecessor, the emphasis is upon a warm, loving, close family confronting problems and working together with like-minded friends in a positive spirit to solve them. Life can be good in spite of neighborhood deterioration, crime, drugs, and gangs. Goon Eye reforms too quickly, and Brenda's genius and quirky nature are overdone, but the Bells-Daniels family are the kind of people any neighborhood would welcome. For a description of *Oren Bell*, see *This Land Is Our Land* (1994), no. 14.

16 Butler, Octavia, *Blood Child and Other Stories*, Four Walls Eight Windows, 1995 (hardcover), ISBN 1–56858–055–X, $18.00, 146 pp.; Seven Stories, 1996 (paper), ISBN 1–888–36336–3, $10.00. Ages 14 up, grades 9 up.

Two novellas and three short stories, all futuristic fantasies, and two essays, previously published but here put together for the first time, by a prominent African-American woman writer who has won major awards for this genre. In "Blood Child," humans, or possibly humanoids, called Terrens, serve wormlike masters, who implant them with eggs. The protagonist human male agrees to be implanted, giving the author the opportunity to explore such matters as the relationship between rulers and ruled and a situation in which a male becomes pregnant. "The Evening and the Morning and the Night" examines the moral issue of to what extent, if at all, one with an incurable, debilitating disease is obligated to help relieve the suffering, even perhaps arrest the progress of the disease, of others who are afflicted. "Near of Kin" tells of a young woman who discovers that her uncle is also her father and gains a new understanding of the mother she has despised. In a society in which law and order have broken down and disease has left many people speechless, the woman protagonist of "Speech Sounds" discovers that helping some children restores in part her ability to speak as well as her self-respect. Whether she is hallucinating or diseased by alcohol, the protagonist of "Crossover" finds her dull, repetitive-action job and private life extremely painful. Although these well-crafted and suspenseful stories seem pessimistic and depressing, in each case, when the protagonists forget self and reach out with love or charity, the possibility that their lives will be better becomes more real. Here is provocative reading for older readers who can appreciate the entertainment value in suspense without high action, as well as plenty to think about for those who enjoy stories with meanings on more than one level.

17 Butler, Octavia, *Parable of the Talents*, Seven Stories, 1998 (hardcover), ISBN 1–888363–81–9, $24.95, 365 pp. Ages 14 up, grades 9 up.

Futuristic fantasy set almost entirely in northern California beginning in 2032 and lasting some fifty years, sequel to *Parable of the Sower* (1993). The novel extrapolates skillfully on current dire social, economic, political, and ecological predictions. The United States has changed drastically: arid climate; rampant looting, vandalism, murder, and rape; inoperable schools; extremes of wealth and poverty; millions of homeless on the move; pervasive drugs; corrupt governments; and increasing emigration to Canada and Alaska. Young African-American Lauren Olamina, her elderly husband, Dr. Bankole, and a few of their friends have made their way north from Los Angeles to Bankole's "safe haven," a remote, abandoned family property, where they have set up a "back to the earth" farming commune called Acorn. They live under Lauren's humanitarian philosophy of Earthseed. She displays the traits that distinguished her in the previous book: toughness, persistence, and integrity; hyperempathy syndrome or "sharing," a condition under which she can physically feel other people's pain; and the need to define God for herself and record her ideas about God and life in her journal as her Earthseed beliefs. Although Earthseed is prospering, in human relationships if not in wealth, its inhabitants are disquieted by news from the outside world, in particular, the election for president of Texas Senator Andrew Steele Jarret, a minister of the Church of Christian America, a right-wing, racist, sexist extremist, who calls groups like Earthseed Satanist cults. Not long after Lauren and Bankole have a child, a girl named Larkin, a band of Jarret's Crusaders descends on Earthseed, killing many, including Bankole, abducting the children, among them Larkin, and enslaving the adults, whom they control by means of wired collars. For more than a year, Lauren and others endure rape, torture, beatings, starvation, and numerous indignities, until they destroy their captors and Acorn and leave. Lauren and a friend reach Portland, Oregon, where Lauren believes Larkin lives with an adopted family. Although she never finds Larkin, she builds another Earthseed community. In later life, she meets Larkin, now in her early thirties, who has left her abusive adoptive family and found and moved in with her mother's brother, Marcus. Curious about the cult, Larkin seeks out its leader and learns that the woman is her mother. At the end, Earthseed has become a powerful force, which many, antagonized by the extremism of Jarret's followers, are joining. Setting, atmosphere, and ideas take precedence over character and plot. The book's structure is complex and demands careful attention. Larkin, in first person, supplies the bridge material between mostly her mother's journals (which are so intriguing that the reader forgets that it must have been almost impossible to maintain them) and Bankole's and Marcus's accounts. Violence appears, rapes occur but are never explicitly described, and the Biblical aspect appears only on the last two pages, where the parable is presented, the idea being, apparently, that Lauren has made the most of the talents she has been given. Numerous passages from Lauren's Earthseed writings give a good sense of the philosophical foundation. The writer's skill in exploiting the possibility that such painful conditions might come to pass is what most keeps the reader engrossed.

18 Campbell, Bebe Moore, *Brothers and Sisters*, Putnam, 1994 (hardcover), ISBN 0–765-10630-2, $26.95, 476 pp.; Berkeley, 1995 (paper), ISBN 0–425-14940-4, $6.99. Ages 15 up, grades 10 up.

Realistic sociological problem novel set in Los Angeles in the early 1990s just after the Rodney King riots and involving racial and gender discrimination and corporate duplicity. Angel City National Bank is the catalyst for intertwining several lives: Esther Jackson, thirty-four, well-educated, capable, African-American regional manager; blonde Mallory Post, thirty-six, loan officer and Esther's confidant; Preston Sinclair, fifty-three, white, tough, opportunistic bank president; Kirk Madison, white ambitious head of lending operations; and Humphrey Boone, suave, intelligent black man hired by Preston for a newly created executive position to promote diversity. When Sinclair hires Humphrey, he un-wittingly stimulates emotions and actions that threaten the bank's stability. Kirk, in particular, is resentful and conspires to scuttle both Humphrey and Sinclair; Esther's and Mallory's hopes for promotions diminish. Humphrey and Sinclair grow close when Humphrey helps Sinclair's son out of a depressed mental state, and Sinclair tells Humphrey that he is grooming him for the presidency. Al-though both Humphrey and Esther hope that each can help the other, being a "brother" and a "sister," and Esther has romantic feelings toward him, Hum-phrey only sees her as one of the black women who in the past scorned him for his big lips and very dark skin. Humphrey resigns under allegations of sexual harassment toward Mallory and accepts the position of president at Solid Rock National Bank, an institution newly established by a local minister specifically to help minorities, later to be joined by Esther. Paralleling this professional plot line are several private-life stories, among them Esther's on-off love affair with a Western Express deliveryman and Humphrey's desire to provide for his family and his guilt over not helping Esther as he thinks a "brother" should. Characters are well drawn, even minor ones. At 550 pages, the book is long and detailed in emotions and motivations and contains many explicit love scenes. Especially well-depicted are the lingering sense of racial tensions in the city; the search for love, success, and happiness on the part of all major figures; the resentments and hopes that affirmative action engenders; and the reader's understanding that the main players share certain common traits and that it is these traits that make them brothers and sisters in spite of the divisions presented by color, back-ground, or ambition.

19 Campbell, Bebe Moore, *Singing in the Comeback Choir*, Putnam, 1998 (hardcover), ISBN 0–399–14298–3, $24.95, 372 pp.; Berkeley, 1999 (paper), ISBN 0–425–16662–7, $7.50, 400 pp. Ages 15 up, grades 10 up.

Contemporary realistic novel set in Los Angeles, California, and Philadelphia, Pennsylvania, of how an intelligent, successful African-American career woman copes with her grandmother's aging, her husband's infidelity, and her own threatened job. Thirty-something Maxine Lott McCoy seems to have everything: a well-paying position as executive producer of a popular television talk pro-gram, The Ted Graham Show; a beautiful house; a successful lawyer husband, Satchel, whom she loves very much; a baby on the way; and a host of supportive friends. Several matters, however, worry her: her husband's past infidelity, which she has forgiven but cannot forget; the show's slipping ratings; and con-cern for her grandmother, once-brilliant pop singer Lindy Walker, who raised her but who has been injured in a fall and is ruining her already poor health with drink and cigarettes. Although Maxine knows that she is jeopardizing her job, she flies to Philadelphia, intending to find someone to care for Lindy or to bring her back to Los Angeles. Lindy, however, is unyieldingly determined to remain in her deteriorating house in the junk-filled neighborhood of addicts, trashtalking resentful teenagers, and fearful elderly. Encouraged by Maxine, by neighbors, by her old boyfriend, Mr. Bootsy, and by a pianist she long ago fell out with, Mr. Worthington Spencer, Lindy practices diligently to regain as much of her old singing form as possible in order to perform in an upcoming music festival. The practice is arduous, but Lindy succeeds, proving that while she is not as good as she once was, she can still give pleasure. At the same time, she revivifies the choir of the nearby Baptist Church. Heeding Lindy's admonition that people must love and rejoice in what they have, Maxine tries hard to accept her husband's efforts to make up for his indiscretions, and to take him at his word that he will henceforth remain faithful. The show is canceled for low ratings, but Ted Graham says that he has something else in mind and will make a place in it for Maxine. Lindy stands out in the large cast—determined, petty, sneaky, prevaricating, wise, stalwart, and unstinting in her love for Maxine. Lindy's long-time neighbors, choral characters barely distinguishable from one another, whom Maxine calls The Tongues; Maxine's professional friends, similarly unindividualized but functional; a group of teens and almost-teens, one of whom, the rebellious C. J., happens to have a marvelous singing voice; the prima donna Ted Graham—all play roles of varying importance in solving both Lindy's problems and Maxine's. That Maxine has trouble forgiving Satchel because she felt abandoned in her childhood when her parents died seems a stretch but possible. Sex scenes are explicit, and some conversation is trashy and earthy. Good passages capture the old musical days and give a fine sense of the convoluted world of talk shows and TV ratings.

20 Chambers, Veronica, *Amistad Rising*, illus. Paul Lee, Harcourt, 1998 (hardcover), ISBN 0–15–201803–4, $16.00, unp. Ages 8 up, grades 3 up.

Historical fiction in picture-story form of the mutiny aboard the slave ship *Amistad* in 1830 that eventually led to the freedom of a group of Mende people from Sierra Leone. Although taking slaves from Africa and selling them in the Western Hemisphere is no longer legal, the trade continues. Among those captured and transported is a young man man named Singbe but called by the Spaniards Joseph Cinque. After reaching Cuba, the slaves are transferred to another ship, the *Amistad*, which runs into a terrible storm. When the ship's cook, playing a cruel joke, indicates that the Africans will be eaten, Cinque leads a rebellion and captures the ship, keeping three of the sailors to navigate them back to Africa. Although they obediently steer toward the rising sun, at night they turn west again and eventually land in New London, Connecticut. The Africans are sent to prison, but abolitionists take up their cause, with the defense led by aging John Quincy Adams. The case goes all the way to the Supreme Court, which rules in favor of the slaves. Abolitionists raise enough money to sail the ship and the surviving captives back to freedom in Africa. Although presented in oversized format with dramatic acrylic paintings filling at least every other page, the serious story is more appropriate for children and young adults beyond the usual picture-book age.

21 Clair, Maxine, *Rattlebone*, Farrar, 1994 (hardcover), ISBN 0–374–24916–1, $19.00, 213 pp.; Penguin, 1995 (paper), ISBN 0–1402–4825–0, $9.95. Ages 12 up, grades 7 up.

Eleven interconnected short stories, all set in the African-American community of Rattlebone, on the edge of Kansas City, Kansas, in the 1950s. Most of them are from the point of view of Irene Wilson, eight years old in the first story, graduating from high school in the last one. During these ten years she copes with her parents' failing marriage, her own growing awareness of boys and sex, and a number of tragedies in the close-knit community. A few stories are from the viewpoints of others: one is her father, one her mother, one a widower, a deacon of the church, who marries Irene's best friend, Wanda, and one the manager of a boarding house for teachers. Wanda, a couple of years older than Irene, is considered a "fly" girl, wild by Rattlebone standards, but touchingly she twice saves her retarded brother, Puddin, once from his mother's attempted euthanasia and once, later, from the state institution to which he has been sent, when she marries the older man who, she knows, will take him in to live with them. Other characters are sharply drawn, notably Miss October Brown, Irene's third-grade teacher who has an affair with her father and, some ten years later, is one of the panel that examines and awards Irene a scholarship to college. Partly because they are constructed as separate stories, each piece has a strong, individual impact, yet they add up to a novel-like picture of the neighborhood and the period. Sensitively written and true to the developing understanding of the young protagonist, this is a superior book for perceptive teenagers.

22 Coleman, Evelyn, *The Foot Warmer and the Crow*, illus. Daniel Minter, Macmillan, 1994 (hardcover), ISBN 0–02–722816–9, $14.95, 32 pp. Ages 4–8, grades PS–3.

Clever Hezekiah, a slave dwarf in size but not in spirit or intelligence, wins his chance for freedom from heartless Master Thompson in true trickster fashion. An object of ridicule and fun, Hezekiah is forced to turn flips and stand on his head to amuse guests, but he hides his skill at understanding and communicating with birds. After one escape attempt, for which he is severely punished, he is tipped off by a crow, the only survivor of a youthful cruelty by Thompson, and volunteers to become the master's foot warmer, sleeping at the foot of his bed. There he listens to the man talking in his sleep and learns many of his secrets. One after another, he reveals these to Thompson, then bets him that he can tell the man the one thing that really scares him. In return, he demands his freedom. Thompson, an inveterate gambler who thinks no one can guess his secret fear, agrees to give Hezekiah a full night's start at escape if he wins the bet. Hezekiah says his master is haunted by the fear that the one nestling that escaped his cruelty will return and peck his eyes out. While the man is howling at the memory, Hezekiah slips away. That night, Master Thompson, waking to see a crow clawing at the windowsill, suffers a seizure and dies. The illustrations, in bright, clear colors and imaginative perspectives, are slightly cartoonish but not demeaning to the little slave.

23 Coleman, Evelyn, *What a Woman's Gotta Do*, Simon & Schuster, 1998 (hardcover), ISBN 0–684–83175–9, $23.00, 319 pp.; Dell, 1999 (paper), ISBN 0–4402–3500–6, $6.50. Ages 15 up, grades 10 up.

Fast-paced thriller featuring African-American Atlanta journalist Patricia Conley, who unwittingly becomes involved with scientists planning, through cloning and gene altering, to wipe out all but white males to achieve a "pure" world population, not dependent on women and including no people of color. This extravagant plot is further complicated by fantasy elements of the Dorgon people of Africa, who have advanced understanding of many scientific principles and are apparently descended from people of outer space and who need a diamond that has come into Conley's possession to avert a catastrophe to the whole world. From the opening scene, in which Conley is stood up at the wedding court by the man she expects to marry, to the final scene, in which an elderly Dorgon appears to her in spirit and explains the meaning of life, the action is frenetic, with shootings, betrayals, abductions, and sexual encounters following each other breathlessly. Despite some annoying flaws (she repeatedly says she does not cry, but tears stream down her face in situation after situation, for instance), this is a page-turner that should appeal to young readers steeped in science fantasy and looking for an African-American protagonist in their chosen genre.

24 Collier-Thomas, Bettye, comp. and ed., *A Treasury of African-American Christmas Stories*, illus. James Reynolds, Holt, 1997 (hardcover), ISBN 0–8050–5122–8, $20.00, 254 pp. Ages 12 up, grades 7 up.

Ten stories and one poem published in the late nineteenth and early twentieth centuries, all occurring on or having to do with Christmas. Of the nine authors represented, all but two are women and their pieces are, on the whole, better stylistically, less stilted, and less sentimental than those by the men, though all have some dated language. Several of the stories give some insight into the internal politics of Negro churches of the time, in particular "Bro'r Abr'm Jimson's Wedding: A Christmas Story" by Pauline E. Hopkins and "A Christmas Party That Prevented a Split in the Church" by Margaret Black. In "After Many Days: A Christmas Story" by Fannie Barrier Williams, a lovely young woman soon to be married, who has been raised as a privileged white, discovers that an old ex-slave woman is her grandmother. In this case her suitor realizes that her true worth is not tainted, and there is a happy ending (though how they treat the grandmother in the future is not pursued), but in another story about a black-white affair, "Three Men and a Woman" by Agustus M. Hodges, the African-American man from New York is almost lynched by "the best citizens of the community" in a small South Carolina town where the woman grew up, and he is saved only because they prefer not to burn him alive on Christmas day. Except for this story, in which both lovers are reprehensible until reformed and parted forever, most of the characters are worthy people of the educated middle class. The collection has more interest for its historical insight into attitudes of the period than for its rather quaint fiction. Each story is preceded by three or four pages giving biographical information about the author and analyzing, rather too simplistically, the contents of the piece.

25 Cooper, J. California, *Some Love, Some Pain, Sometime*, Doubleday, 1995 (hardcover), ISBN 0–385–46787–7, $22.95, 273 pp.; Amazon, 1996 (paper), ISBN 0–385–46788–5, $10.95. Ages 14 up, grades 9 up.

Ten short stories, all starring African-American women, most of whom have made bad choices in men. They all come to realize, eventually, that they can succeed and be happy if they take charge of their own lives, sometimes alone, sometimes by turning to decent, hard-working men, and sometimes by reforming the ones they already have. Narrated in a conversational dialect, usually by an observer though occasionally by the protagonist, the stories have a certain sameness, but they also detail hardships and longings of those caught in poverty that ring true, with a good deal of humor despite the grim reality. None of the characters starts in the middle or professional class socially, but a few pull themselves out of the ghetto or hardscrabble rural areas, overcoming their early foolishness and achieving some material and emotional stability. Although the language is earthy and the discussion of sex frank, the central theme of the collection is the importance of using the head while not forgetting the heart and of opting for education and independence, not flashy and momentary pleasure.

26 Cosby, Bill, *The Meanest Thing to Say*, illus. Varnette P. Honeywood, Scholastic, 1997 (hardcover), ISBN 0–590–13754–9, $13.95, unp.; (paper), ISBN 0–590–95616–7, $3.99, unp. Ages 6–9, grades 1–4.

Chapter book for early readers in the "Little Bill" series, in which the main character, his family, and some but not all his friends appear to be African American. The narrator, Little Bill, is challenged by Michael, the new boy in class, to a game called "Playing the Dozens." Each player gets twelve chances to say something mean, with the meanest thing winning. So worried that he starts making a list, Little Bill can think of nothing else until his father remarks that they used to call it "ranking." When Little Bill repeats the insults Michael has already thrown at him, his father just replies, to each, "So?" The next day Little Bill tries the same technique on Michael, effectively defeating him, and then becomes his friend. Brightly illustrated with what look like paper cutouts, the book has brief chapters and simple sentences but not a severely restricted vocabulary. Other books in the series include *The Best Way to Play* (1997), *The*

Treasure Hunt (1997), *Money Troubles* (1998), *Shipwreck Saturday* (1998), and *Super-Fine Valentine* (1998).

27 Crews, Nina, *One Hot Summer Day*, illus. Nina Crews, Greenwillow, 1996 (hardcover), ISBN 0–688–13393–2, $15.00, 24 pp. Ages 4–8, grades PS–3.

On one sweltering summer day, a very young African-American girl tries to fry an egg on the sidewalk, plays with her shadow, draws chalk pictures on the concrete, eats two grape popsicles, and, when the sky clouds up and it starts to sprinkle, catches big drops in her mouth and dances in the rain. The illustrations are photographs of a pretty child with her hair in cornrows playing on city sidewalks and in the park. A few of the backgrounds have been embellished with drawings and added collage elements. The text is extremely simple, with only about 125 words, leaving the pictures to capture the heat and the pleasure of early childhood.

28 Cummings, Pat, *Carousel*, illus. Pat Cummings, Bradbury, 1994 (hardcover), ISBN 0–02725512–3, $14.95, unp. Ages 6–9, grades 2–4.

Picture-story book of a birthday party, spoiled by the rude behavior of African-American Alex, possibly seven or eight, to her mother and aunts, because she is disappointed that her father is not present. In the night the animals from the toy carousel her father left for her come alive in her dream, and she rides them through the night skies. In the morning her father returns, and so does Alex's good humor. The lavish illustrations, done in colored pencil, watercolor, and gouache, are stronger than the story. Cummings is also author of a picture-story book described in *This Land Is Our Land* (1994), no. 198, *Jimmy Lee Did It*.

29 Curtis, Christopher Paul, *The Watsons Go to Birmingham—1963*, Delacorte, 1995 (hardcover) ISBN 0–389–32175–9, $15.95, 210 pp.; Bantam, 1999 (paper), ISBN 0–440–22836–0, $2.99. Ages 9–12, grades 4–7.

Situation-comedy, episodic family novel with period aspects, set mostly in a middle-class neighborhood in Flint, Michigan, the first six months of 1963. African-American Kenny Watson, ten, describes those months for the "Weird Watsons," his warm, happy, active family: Dad, a goodnatured, solid-citizen autoworker; loving Momma; sweet, pretty, kindergarten-aged sister, Joetta; and his older brother, By (Byron), as Kenny presents him a mean, self-centered bully. The chapters in the first half of the book are largely self-contained but linked by the same characters. Some deal with Kenny's problems, but most events involve By. In the book's most hilarious scene, By plays with matches, in spite of Momma's repeated warnings, and is caught setting fire to the parachutes of his toy Nazi soldiers. Momma furiously decides to teach him a lesson by burning his fingers. The escapade that precipitates the family trip to Birmingham is By's getting a "conk," that is, bleaching and straightening his hair.

After Dad angrily shaves By completely bald, he and Momma decide that By should live with Grandma Sands in Alabama. They set out down I-75 in the Brown Bomber, which Dad has outfitted with a brand-new Ultra-Glide record player. They arrive ahead of schedule, Dad having decided he can drive nonstop. Since Grandma Sands, although frail, has a "Wicked Witch of the West" tongue and attitude, By behaves for the most part. The family returns to Flint when the Baptist Church to which Joetta has gone for Sunday School is bombed and four girls killed. In Flint, Kenny is made so distraught by his memories of what he saw at the church that he can find solace only in hiding in the "World-Famous Watson Pet Hospital" behind the livingroom couch, until By persuades him to rejoin life. Although the action is disjointed and the conclusion abrupt, the family's decision to return to Flint bringing By with them seems reasonable. Since only a few aspects of racial discrimination are mentioned and then only briefly, the reader is not prepared for the bombing, and the book's title does not fit with what happens in the bulk of the book. Characters have dimension, and the family might live next door, so real do they seem. By often uses trash talk, and the children's behavior seems true to their ages. A disturbing aspect is the idiosyncratic use of commas, which produces ungrammatical comma splices. An epilogue summarizes some events in the Civil Rights Movement to establish the setting for the bombing, which is historical.

30 Curtis, Gavin, *The Bat Boy and His Violin*, illus. E. B. Lewis, Simon & Schuster, 1998 (hardcover), ISBN 0–689–80099–1, $16.00, unp. Ages 4–10, grades PS–5.

Realistic picture-story book set in 1948, the year after Jackie Robinson joined the Brooklyn Dodgers. Although young Reginald is good on the violin and practices faithfully for his next recital, his father, manager of the Dukes baseball team, gives him little credit for his skill. Papa's mind is on the Dukes, the worst team in the Negro National League, because, Papa says, now that baseball has become integrated, all the good players are joining white teams. Papa says the Dukes need Reginald as bat boy and that he can practice between innings and on his travels with the players. Reginald tries to do his job well, but everything goes wrong. Papa takes over the bats, and Reginald practices his violin on the bench while the game is going on. Ironically, his music inspires the team to win their first game in four months, and they embark on a winning streak that lands them an invitation to play against the Monarchs, the best team in the league. Although the Dukes lose, Papa assures Reginald that his music was good for the team, that he loves Reginald more than winning, and that he is impressed by his son's ability. The whole team attends the recital and applauds Reginald. Although the text is strong enough to stand by itself, the plot limps. Soft-toned watercolors, some single-page, some doublespreads, provide a needed dimension. They depict events and convey character. Reginald is a sober child with an earnest face and strong arms and hands. Papa and his players are also intense and engrossed in their work. They are tall, powerfully built, goodlooking, well-muscled young men, and the playing scenes are so believably portrayed that one can almost hear the crack of the bat with the long swings. For another book by Curtis, see *This Land Is Our Land* (1994), no. 22, *Grandma's Baseball*.

31 DeBerry, Virginia, and Donna Grant, *Tryin' to Sleep in the Bed You Made: A Novel by and about Best Friends*, St. Martin's, 1997 (hardcover), ISBN 0–312–15233–7, $24.95, 374 pp.; (paper), ISBN 0–312–96313–0, $6.50. Ages 14 up, grades 9 up.

Realistic, romantic novel of two African-American women, long, tangled, and filled with twists and melodrama, set in the New York–New England area. Pretty, popular Gayle Saunders and plain, chubby, intellectually advanced Patricia Reid are raised as sisters but go separate ways in their teens when Pat wins a scholarship to an exclusive school. Gayle tries to trap aspiring major-league ballplayer Marcus Carter (a childhood friend of both girls) into marriage, then marries fast-talking, free-spending, gambler-businessman Ramsey Hilliard, with whom she has a daughter, Vanessa, and lives lavishly before debts and the fast life catch up with Ramsey, who commits suicide, leaving her penniless and in a homeless shelter, after her little apartment burns, severely injuring Vanessa. After college, Pat lands a job with an advertising agency, rises rapidly to a high executive position, and falls in love with another executive, who spurns her. She aborts their child, seeks to make contact with her newly discovered father, a prominent civil rights leader and political figure, Turner Hughes, who also spurns her. She gets together with Marcus, whose star baseball career has been ended by injury, who has become a sports scout, and whom she marries. After being let go from her well-paying position during a merger, Pat visits a homeless shelter her father has started, where she discovers Gayle and Vanessa living and takes them home. More problems transpire, including the reappearance of Ramsey, who is not dead as supposed. Eventually, all the principals decide to make the best of life together, helping one another out and letting bygones be bygones, including Turner, who has indicated that he acknowledges Pat as his daughter. This is pure soap-opera fiction, a fast-moving story of pride, dreams, deception, lust, and treachery. Some sex scenes appear, as are typical of the genre.

32 DiSalvo-Ryan, DyAnne, *City Green*, illus. DyAnne DiSalvo-Ryan, Morrow, 1994 (hardcover), ISBN 0–688–12786–X, unp. Ages 5–12, grades K–6.

Contemporary realistic picture-story book with an ecological slant, set in an urban area. An empty lot now exists where once a dilapidated apartment stood, so that the block "looks like a big smile with one tooth missing," according to African-American schoolgirl Marcy, the narrator. In the spring, she and her neighbor Miss Rosa have a bright idea—planting seeds so there will be flowers and greenery. Before long, other neighbors join in, clear away the junk, rake, plant, and cultivate, even grouchy Old Man Hammer, typically down on everything. By summertime, the lot is vibrant with vegetables and flowers, and way in the back, shining their golden heads over everything are Old Man Hammer's sunflowers. Upbeat, slightly cartoonish, watercolor, pencil, and crayon pictures, varied in size, present before-and-after views of this example of community cooperation. Especially striking are those illustrations in which the mixed-ethnic neighbors confer about procedures and celebrate their success. The last page gives directions about starting a community garden.

33 Draper, Sharon M., *Forged by Fire*, Atheneum, 1997 (hardcover), ISBN 0–689–80699–X, $16.00, 160 pp.; Aladdin, 1999 (paper), ISBN 0–689–81851–3, $3.99, 156 pp. Ages 12–15, grades 7–10.

Novel of a boy's role as protector of his young half-sister in a dysfunctional African-American family in Cincinnati. Gerald Nickelby's own life almost ends when he is three and caught in a fire while his irresponsible mother is out looking for drugs. While she is in jail, her great-aunt, Aunt Queen, though confined to a wheelchair, takes him in, and they live happily. When he is nine, his mother reappears with a husband, Jordan Sparks, and a frail six-year-old daughter named Angel. Athough Aunt Queen wants to keep both children, she dies of a heart attack. When Gerald realizes that Jordan is sexually abusing Angel, he resolves to protect her and, with the help of a school friend's father, is able to get Jordan arrested and sent to prison. Six years later Jordan returns, supposedly rehabilitated. Although Gerald tries to watch over Angel, Jordan eventually gets her alone and once more attacks her, ignoring the smoke that is filling the apartment from a pan boiled dry in the kitchen. In the resulting fire, Gerald saves Angel, but Jordan is killed. The grim and dramatic story is marred by one-dimenstional characters and a reliance on narration rather than drama-tized scenes of action. An earlier young adult novel by Draper, *Tears of a Tiger* (1994), avoids this problem by having no direct narration whatever. The story of a high school basketball player who is drinking and driving in an accident that kills his best friend and of his resulting depression and sense of guilt, it is told entirely through dialogue, letters, newspaper stories, and pieces written for class assignments.

34 Duncan, Alice Faye, *Willie Jerome*, illus. Tyrone Geter, Macmillan, 1995 (hard-cover), ISBN 0–02–733208–X, $15.00, unp. Ages 4–8, grades PS–3.

Realistic picture-story book set in recent years in an inner city. African-American Judy starts "to feel sorta blue" because no one in their family or neighborhood appreciates her little brother Willie Jerome's trumpet playing, not big brother Earl or Mr. Jackson, the storekeeper, or Miss Alversa Lee, their neighbor, or even Mama, who says that he should come down from the roof on which he practices. But Judy, who enjoys "bopping" to his rhythms, insists Mama sit on the steps and listen while the sun goes down and let his music speak to her spirit. Mama apologizes, agreeing that Willie Jerome has a special talent. The cool greens and blues and the indistinct, almost smudgy pictures have a sense of movement that complements the rhythmical portions of the text, so that periodically they "bop" and "jazz" along together to produce a warm family story about a little girl's abiding faith that her brother is exceptionally talented.

35 England, Linda, *The Old Cotton Blues*, illus. Teresa Flavin, McElderry, 1998 (hardcover), ISBN 0–689–81074–1, $16.00, unp. Ages 4–8, grades PS–3.

Realistic, contemporary picture-story book. Young Dexter loves three things: his mother, the smell of pork chops cooking, and the sound of his friend Johnny Cotton's blues clarinet. When he tells Johnny that he would like to play, too, Johnny suggests that he ask his mother to buy him a clarinet. But Dexter's mother says they simply do not have the money. Johnny suggests that Dexter might dream of playing harmonica music as Johnny's daddy did, and gives the boy his daddy's old "silver Mississippi harp." He teaches Dexter how to play it, and before long the two are "swaying and playing" the Old Cotton Blues together. Dexter has one more item to add to his list of loves: playing on his silver harmonica. The text is remarkably euphonious, its cadences and use of assonance in particular catching various jazz and blues rhythms in phrases like "razzle-dazzle," "blue-down blues," and "mishamasha music." The gouache illustrations exude a liveliness and energy that enhance the text and move it along, catching its repetition and vigor. Johnny Cotton is a rotund, elderly gentleman, who puts his whole being into his music, and Dexter is a small, round-faced, sober shadow of his mentor. A particularly evocative picture is that in which, near the end, both are leaning into their music, literally, their bodies in parallel lines as they play side by side on the sidewalk at the foot of the steps leading up to Dexter's front door. In the pictures the characters are African American, but no mention of race appears in the text.

36 Fenner, Carol, *Yolanda's Genius*, McElderry, 1995 (hardcover), ISBN 0–689–80001–0, $17.00, 211 pp.; Aladdin, 1997 (paper), ISBN 0–689–81327–9, $4.50. Ages 9–14, grades 4–9.

Light, contemporary, girl's growing-up novel in a family context. Fed up with Chicago's drugs and violence, widowed African-American Josie Blue moves her family—heavy, tall, inventive fifth-grader Yolanda and sweet, thin Andrew, six—to the small, predominantly white town of Grand River, Michigan. When some kids call her "whale," disparaging her size, Yolanda responds with a long discourse of information about that mammal, arousing the admiration of white classmate Shirley Piper, who wonders if Yolanda is a genius. Yolanda decides the term describes Andrew, whose musical ability on a small wooden pipe and on the harmonica his deceased father gave him she feels is truly exceptional. Her sometimes humorous, occasionally poignant efforts to get his musical talent recognized drive the meager plot. Eventually, her family visit Aunt Tiny in Chicago at the time of the annual blues festival at Grant Park. Yolanda arranges to get herself and Andrew "lost" on stage, where they meet the famous B. B.

King, among other stars. King listens to Andrew play, calls him the "little dude" and a "mean harp man" and encourages him to pursue his playing. A subplot revolves around Yolanda's relationship with white Shirley, with whom she would like to be friends but to whom she does not, in the interest of promoting herself, always tell the truth. Yolanda dominates the book, not always sympathetically or credibly, and Andrew is a winning child, one-dimensionally developed. The book's best feature lies in its warm, close family life, and the best section revolves around the festival, where the noise, crowds, and confusion come through with strength and vigor.

37 Flournoy, Vanessa, and Valerie Flournoy, *Celie and the Harvest Fiddler*, illus. James E. Ransome, Tambourine, 1995 (hardcover), ISBN 0–688–11457–1, $15.00, unp. Ages 5–12, grades K–7.

Picture-story fantasy, set on Halloween. Young African-American Celie is eager to win the contest for the best costume in the community parade. She has heard stories about a mysterious Fiddler who turns up at celebrations and wonders whether the musician fiddling for the parade is he. When her too-quickly constructed costume fails to hold together, she flees in embarrassment, then finds the musician awaiting her by a brook. He gives her an unusual mask, which is only for her, he says. Although her costume is clearly the best, she does not win the prize. The mask enables her to get something much better: her two brothers, who have been transformed into wolves, back in their human form. The powerful, deep-palette, often brooding oils follow the course of the story. They extend it with details of setting and costume, contribute atmosphere, and reveal character. The text, with its echoes of folklore, is strong enough to stand by itself. For an earlier book by Valerie Flournoy, see *The Patchwork Quilt*, in *This Land Is Our Land* (1994), no. 30.

38 Forrester, Sandra, *Sound the Jubilee*, Lodestar, 1995 (hardcover), ISBN 0–525–67486–1, $15.99, 184 pp.; Puffin, 1997 (paper), ISBN 0–140–37930–4, $4.99, 192 pp. Ages 9–14, grades 4–10.

Historical novel with girl's growing-up story aspects set in North Carolina for three years during the American Civil War, beginning in 1861, as seen from the viewpoint of Maddie, eleven, a spunky, bright slave girl. Almost all characters are fictitious, but events are based on little-known actual history. Because Yankee soldiers threaten River Bend Plantation, Mistress McCartha, wife of the owner, is sent for safety to the McCartha summer home on Nags Head on the coast. Accompanying her are Maddie's family, Titus, her father and the plantation foreman, who sees this as the opportunity for the freedom for which he has yearned; Ella, her capable mother; Angeline, her hardworking older sister, who marries Royall Tate, a responsible slave from a farm nearby; and Pride, the little brother. Not long after the family arrive at Nags Head, Yankee soldiers take the area. Mistress flees with her maid, but the rest cross to Roanoke

Island, where Union soldiers help them and hundreds of other refugee and run-away slaves set up homes on acre lots plotted out by a surveyor. Titus adopts the surname Henry, lends his considerable physical and organizational talents to the building and socializing effort, and, when the call comes for enlistments in the Union Army, joins up, along with Royall. Royall is brought wounded to the Roanoke Island hospital some months later, but Titus has been killed and buried in Tennessee. Maddie, who can read and write, sets up a school for the slave children, but adults also enroll, to Maddie's gratification. She continues to teach even after an adult teacher, historical Miss Elizabeth James, arrives, sent by the American Missionary Society to prepare the ex-slaves for employment and society after the war. Early April, 1965, brings the good news of Union victory but also the sad news that the freed slaves must leave the island, the homes they have built, and the land they believe is theirs, since the government has pardoned the pre-war landowners. In May, they leave for North Carolina, hoping to buy land. Maddie hopes to go North and get more education. History and private events are skillfully blended, producing a clear picture for young readers of what life must have been like on Roanoke during this brave but ill-fated social and economic attempt to give the self-freed slaves a start on a better life. Characters are individualized, style is sufficiently detailed, and the family are good people, with whom it is easy to identify. The book shows that the road to freedom and self-sufficiency was difficult and that many Yankees were as prejudiced and spiteful in their way as were the Southerners before them. A preface and an afterword contribute valuable background information. Maps are lacking; they would be welcome aids to understanding. Forrester's first novel, it is followed by a sequel, *My Home Is Over Jordan* (1997), in which Maddie and her family find that establishing a home in post-war North Carolina is also harsh, disappointing, and challenging.

39 Golden, Marita, *The Edge of Heaven: A Novel*, Doubleday, 1998 (hardcover), ISBN 0–385–41507–9, $22.95, 242 pp.; Bright Mountain, 1997 (paper), ISBN 0–914–87527–2, $14.95. Ages 14 up, grades 9 up.

Contemporary, realistic novel of African-American domestic life and a girl's growing up. Lena comes home from four years in prison to confront the hostility of her twenty-year-old daughter, Teresa, who, in turn, is confronted with the necessity of acknowledging she has told lies to cover up her mother's absence. The reader is confronted with the task of determining why Lena has been in prison and why Teresa is so angry at her mother. The story is told in shifts, beginning with Teresa in the "I" person, and then also in third person from the perspectives mostly of Lena but occasionally of Teresa's father, Ryland. Teresa, now a college student who aspires to a law degree, and her younger sister Kenya were living happily in Washington, D.C., with Lena, a highly successful corporate accountant, and Ryland, a handsome, dashiki-clad, bearded painter. Dif-ficulties arose between the parents, stemming from the pressures of Lena's career and Ryland's sensitivity to her greater success. One day, when Kenya was eleven, Lena struck her in a fit of anger and then shoved her down the stairs, killing her accidentally. Scenes occur variously, in the home, in Ryland's studio, before and after the death. The prison scenes are sympathetic to Lena and to the other incarcerated women, who are shown with children and other visiting relatives, but never with their men. Teresa and her grandmother, who has raised her since the murder, visit regularly, and although Teresa is angry, they converse civilly. Confronted with her mother's release, however, Teresa's anger becomes so great that she can barely speak to Lena. Having to live with the woman she holds accountable for loss of both father and sister is almost too much to bear. Gradually, however, since Lena makes no demands on her and confident that her boyfriend, Simon, feels strongly for her, she accepts her mother and looks ahead to a good future with Simon. Through flashbacks and internal musings the mystery of what happened to Kenya and to the marriage is gradually revealed, making this a top-notch, if low-key, murder mystery as well as a study in how a marriage can go awry. The pace is fast, the emotion restrained, and the writer carefully avoids placing the blame on either parent, but the idea that a successful woman may encounter special problems is clear. There are some explicit sex scenes. Golden has also written a feminist novel, *A Woman's Place*, described in *This Land Is Our Land* (1994), no. 32.

40 Gray, Libba Moore, *Little Lil and the Swing-Singing Sax*, illus. Lisa Cohen, Simon & Schuster, 1996 (hardcover), ISBN 0–680–80681–7, $16.00, unp. Ages 4–8, grades PS–3.

Picture-story book about a little African-American girl who restores her uncle's prized possession. Little Lil, the narrator, lives in a city with her mama, Big Lil, and her Uncle Sudi Man, who drives a steam shovel during the day but plays a "low-moaning" saxophone at a jazz club at night. One evening Big Lil gives her daughter the gold ring with the blue stone that had been her grandmother's, and they take her "red ribboned and patent leathered" to hear Uncle Sudi make the sax sing. But when Big Lil gets sick and needs expensive medicine, Uncle Sudi pawns his horn. Little Lil knows that her mother will not get really well until she hears the saxophone again. She draws a picture of a Christmas tree with all three of them dancing to the horn music, and she tries to trade her art for the saxophone. Honest Don, the pawnbroker, sees her ring, and reluctantly Little Lil offers it for the horn. Honest Don hands her the saxophone, then, winking, returns the ring and hangs her picture in his window. On Christmas Day they dance on the flat tar roof of their building while Uncle Sudi plays his swing-singing sax. The simple story is distinguished by memorable phrases—the "shelf-piled" pawnshop, Uncle Sudi's "silver-keyed horn" that fills the air with "velvet notes," the neon lights "blink blink blinking like an upside-down, cold electric sky." The acrylic illustrations are in bright, flat planes with figures outlined with heavy, black lines in a pseudo-primitive style.

Gray is also author of a picture-story book, *Miss Tizzy*, in *This Land Is Our Land* (1994), no. 33.

41 Greenfield, Eloise, *Easter Parade*, illus. Jan Spivey Gilchrist, Hyperion, 1998 (hardcover), ISBN 0–7868–2271–6, $14.95, 42 pp. Ages 4 up, grades PS up.

Nostalgic picture-story book in four short chapters. Two young girl cousins, Leanna in Chicago and Elizabeth in Washington, D.C., prepare for the Easter Parade in April of 1943, during World War II. Leanna looks forward to the parade, excited about her new clothes and knowing that her father, brother, and mother will be with her to celebrate the holiday. Elizabeth and her mother, on the other hand, are alone. Elizabeth's father is away fighting in the war, and Elizabeth and her mother are worried because they have not heard from him in weeks. On the day before Easter, the mailman delivers a letter from Father. Knowing that he is safe adds to the peace and joy of their celebration. Both families find Easter a day of beauty and excitement. Both join the Easter parade on the street, where they feel the happiness and inspiration of the holiday. The simple, poetic text, the book's smaller-than-average size, and the antique type combine with the oval, brown-toned realistic illustrations to project the sense of a bygone era and family love. Although the text is nonspecific about race, the illustrations show the families as handsome African Americans. For other books by Greenfield, see *Grandpa's Face*, no. 34, *Koya Delaney and the Good Girl Blues*, no. 35, and *William and the Good Old Days*, no. 36 (fiction), and *I Make Music*, no. 206, and *Night on Neighborhood Street*, no. 207 (poems) in *This Land Is Our Land* (1994).

42 Grimes, Nikki, *Jazmin's Notebook*, Dial, 1998 (hardcover), ISBN 0–8037–2224–9, $15.99, 102 pp. Ages 11–15, grades 6–10.

Girl's growing-up story of a young African-American teenager in Harlem in the 1960s. Jazmin Shelby lives with her sister, CeCe, who is only six years her senior, their mother, an alcoholic, being now in a mental hospital with depression and their father, a jazz musician, killed in a car crash a couple of years after their divorce. Jazmin spends much of her time sitting on the front steps of their building, observing life on Amsterdam Avenue and writing poetry. Interspersed among the chapters, each presented as an entry in her journal or notebook, are poems she writes, all free verse, some with striking insights. Jazmin experiments with the popular modes of rebellion of the period, once skipping school and going to a party in the apartment of an older man where she smokes too much pot, lies down dizzily in the bedroom, and has to fight off an intended rape. Another time, on an errand at night, she is accosted by a man and saved by a big, tough-looking friend of CeCe's. Throughout the notebook, Jazmin has refused to visit her mother, even though her sister tries to persuade her. Finally, on December 31, she agrees to go to the hospital and is surprised to find her mother coherent, even, to her astonishment, somewhat affectionate. Jazmin is tough-minded, a survivor, and determined to make something of herself, but CeCe is the real heroine of the novel, a nurturing, sensible, hard-working woman who cannot be more than twenty but has taken on her younger sister's care with devotion and good humor. The period setting is not particularly important; with a few minor alterations, the novel could be set today.

43 Hamanaka, Sheila, *Bebop-A-Do-Walk!*, illus. Sheila Hamanaka, Simon & Schuster, 1995 (hardcover), ISBN 0–689–80288–9, $15.00, unp. Ages 4–8, grades PS–3.

Realistic, period, picture-story book of New York City in the 1950s. The narrator, Japanese-American Emi, and her best friend, African-American Martha, beg Emi's father, an artist, to take them on one of his long walks. He says that this time he will visit friends and then do some sketching in Central Park. They walk with him past the delicatessen into the candy store, where the owner gives them nuts for the squirrels, past the bakery to Washington Square Park, Union Square, and the Flatiron and Empire State buildings, through "swinging" Fifty-Second Street, where Bob plays a mean trumpet for them, into the Museum of Modern Art, and on to Central Park. After they ride the carousel and reach the pond, Emi's father makes paper boats and hats for them and the other children. Before they know it, the sun is starting to set, and Emi's father says it is time for them to board the bus for home. On board, Emi's father makes paper cranes for everyone on the bus. The text of this simple story emphasizes love of family and friends and the joy that one can find in different situations. The evocative acrylic illustrations offer varied perspectives, some being more conventional interior and street scenes, but most are less usual: angled shots of the girls and the father in crowds, the Empire State building turned on its side with the girls lying across it at the left as one views the picture, a jazzy dark-toned glimpse of Fifty-Second Street, and the girls sitting in front of a large abstract, expressionist painting, as the rotund guard tiptoes up to them and gives them peppermints. The view of Central Park pond is more impressionistic, although the girls are rendered in flat planes of color. The boats on the pond are abstract, details pulled out, and close to the viewer's dimension. See *This Land Is Our Land* (1994), no. 298, *Screen of Frogs*, for another book by Hamanaka.

44 Hamilton, Virginia, *Second Cousins*, Scholastic, 1998 (hardcover), ISBN 0–590–47368–9, $14.95, 168 pp. Ages 9–14, grades 4–9.

Sequel to *Cousins* (see *This Land Is Our Land*, 1994, no. 42), occurring a year later. The extended family of Cammy Coleman is having a reunion, with relatives arriving from all over the country, in particular two girls from New York, GiGi, daughter of Cammy's Uncle George, and Jahnina Madison, who prefers to be known as Fractal and is introduced as living with Uncle George's family. Cammy is confused and hurt when Elodie, the poor-relation cousin who has been Cammy's best friend and companion all summer, immediately pairs up with GiGi. Fractal, about a year older than Cammy, is also a puzzle, sometimes cold and rude, then suddenly friendly and willing to share the secrets of her laptop computer. They hook up the laptop along with the computer of Cammy's father, who is separated from her mother, and are both lost in cyberspace when he arrives. Fractal, surprised, calls him Daddy, and Cammy suddenly realizes why so many relatives have been ill at ease seeing the girls together. Instead of quietly explaining to Cammy, he insists that the two girls work it out, and leaves. While Fractal is willing to accept her as a half-sister, Cammy is devastated, mostly because so many others seem to know and no one has told her the truth. By the end of the reunion, however, the general family good will has infected her, and she has grown up enough to try to understand. The action is slowed by elementary lessons in the use of computers, detailed at length by Fractal. While there is some explanation of what happened in *Cousins*, so many characters reappear and so many references to the last summer's tragedy are made that readers who have not read it may be confused. Among Hamilton's other books are, in *This Land Is Our Land* (1994), no. 41, *The Bells of Christmas*, no. 43, *Drylongso*, no. 44, *The Mystery of Drear House*, and no. 45, *A White Romance* (all fiction), and no. 180, *The People Could Fly*, a collection of folktales. She is probably still best known for her early novels, notably *M. C. Higgins, the Great* (1974).

45 Hansen, Joyce, *The Captive*, Scholastic, 1994 (hardcover), ISBN 0–5904–1625–1, $13.95, 195 pp.; Apple, 1995 (paper), ISBN 0–5904–1624–3, $4.50. Ages 9–12, grades 4–7.

Novel of a twelve-year-old African boy captured, smuggled into New England, and sold illegally in the early nineteenth century. Kofi, son of an Ashanti chief, is made a captive through a series of betrayals and sales in Africa and is transported on a slaver, where he meets Tim, an indentured British boy, and Joseph, a slave held as a worker by the brutal captain. In Salem, Massachusetts, the three are sold to an abusive farmer named Browne, who rents Joseph, despite illness that nearly kills him, to a baker and works the other boys mercilessly. Kofi, the youngest, is taught housework by Master Browne's wife, who also teaches him English and his letters, although her husband forbids this as a waste of time and inappropriate for a slave. After a year of grueling labor, interrupted by beatings and long sessions on their knees while Master Browne prays for them, the three run away, although Tim has only four more years on his contract and Joseph is hesitant, more afraid of the poverty of a free black than of Browne's cruelty. They hide aboard a schooner owned by a free black named Captain Paul Cuffe, where they are discovered by Browne and a bailiff. When Captain Cuffe stands up for them, they are sent to prison to await trial. Cuffe makes a good case for their freedom, since importing, selling, and holding slaves in Massachusetts is illegal. Although Browne protests that he did not buy them but was merely giving them a home and his cowed wife backs him up, the judge decides that he has no right to Joseph and Kofi, but sends Tim back to work out his contract. Captain Cuffe takes the other two to his Quaker home, where his Native-American wife treats them as part of the family and, best of all, Kofi finds Ama, a girl he met in Africa, whom Captain Cuffe rescued from slavery the year before. An author's note says that while the story is fiction, Captain Cuffe was a real person, son of a slave who had bought his freedom and a Native-American woman, a man dedicated to saving illegal and escaped slaves and starting a freed-slave colony in Africa, a goal he never reached. Other novels by Hansen include, in *This Land Is Our Land* (1994), nos. 46, *Which Way Freedom?*, and 47, *Yellow Bird and Me*.

46 Hansen, Joyce, *I Thought My Soul Would Rise and Fly: The Diary of Patsy, A Freed Girl*, Scholastic, 1997 (hardcover), ISBN 0–5908–4913–1, $10.95, 202 pp. Ages 9–12, grades 4–7.

Novel in the form of diary entries set on Davis Hall Plantation, Mars Bluff, South Carolina, starting on April 21, 1865, and telling how the end of the Civil War gradually changes the lives of those who live there, both black and white. Although the slaves have heard rumors of the Emancipation Proclamation, they still live and work as they always have for Master and Mistress in the house or the fields. Patsy, twelve or thirteen, has no idea of her parentage, and since one of her legs is shorter than the other, she limps. She also stammers so badly that she is thought to be dim-witted, but she actually is highly intelligent and has taught herself to read and write by listening to the lessons of Master's niece and nephew. As word of freedom is confirmed, some of the former slaves begin to leave, and those remaining take over their duties. With some help from the Freedman's Bureau, the fieldhands bargain with Master to bring in the cotton crop for a share of the profit, an allotment of five acres each, and a school for their children. In the meantime, Patsy starts teaching the others and reads aloud the *Colored American* newspaper designed to teach freedmen and women about the government. When Master dies and Mistress reneges on the contract, the remaining workers leave the plantation. An epilogue tells how Patsy, now known by her chosen name, Phillis Frederick, gets further education, marries the young man from Davis Hall she has long admired, and eventually joins others to found Libertyville, South Carolina. A long historical note tells about Reconstruction and includes photographs, etchings, recipes, and a song from the period. Hansen is also the author of two novels described in *This Land Is Our Land* (1994), no. 46, *Which Way Freedom?*, and no. 47, *Yellow Bird and Me*.

47 Havill, Juanita, *Jamaica's Blue Marker*, illus. Anne Sibley O'Brien, Houghton, 1995 (hardcover), ISBN 0–395–72036–2, $13.95, unp. Ages 4–8, grades PS–3.

Another realistic contemporary picture-book story about Jamaica, depicted in the illustrations as African American, and her friends in a school setting. Jamaica is a polite and obedient little girl, who tries to please her teacher and get along well with her classmates. When her teacher asks her to share her markers with

Russell, she agrees, but is more than a little taken aback when he grabs her blue one and scribbles all over her picture of a fall tree. The teacher punishes Russell, but Jamaica complains to her parents, calling him a "mean brat." They agree with her that Russell behaved badly. The next day, while Russell is outside for recess, the teacher confides to the class that Russell will soon be moving to another city. They will be having a going-away party for him on Friday, his last day. She asks the class to make cards for him to remember them by. Jamaica at first is reluctant to do so. At dinner, Dad's comments about how Russell feels about moving start her thinking. The next day, Jamaica is making a card when the teacher asks for help in preparing the party. After the party, the students give their cards to Russell. Having no card, Jamaica gives him the blue marker instead. He thanks her and says she is lucky because she does not have to move. Now Jamaica knows how Russell has been feeling and tells him she will miss him. This simple story of a child's learning to look for reasons behind behavior and practicing forgiveness is less moralistic in tone than it might seem, the didacticism mitigated by the cheerful, realistic watercolors. The illustrations are static views of various school and home situations and show the class as mixed racially and Russell as white. Also in the Jamaica series are *Jamaica and Briana* (1993), *Jamaica's Find* (1986), *Jamaica Tag-Along* (1989), and *Jamaica and the Substitute Teacher* (1999). Books by Havill are described in *This Land Is Our Land* (1994), nos. 50 (*Jamaica Tag-Along*) and 357, *Treasure Nap*.

48 Haynes, David, *The Gumma Wars*, illus. David Zinn, Milkweed, 1997 (hardcover), ISBN 1–57131–610–8, $6.95, 110 pp. Ages 8–13, grades 3–8.

First of a series of novels for middle-grade readers about St. Paul's mixed-racial West 7th Wildcats, a club, not a gang, as the six boys insist. Narrator is sixth-grader Lawrence Jackson Underwood, known as Lu, one of two African-American Wildcats, along with Bobby Samson. There are also two Hmong boys, Tou Vue and Johnny Vang, one Mexican American, Tony Rodriguez, and one "regular white kid," Kevin Olsen. Lu is looking forward to Tony R.'s twelfth birthday party, an all-night-and-all-the-next-day event, but his parents remind him that he must spend the afternoon with his grandmother, Gumma Jackson, since it is her birthday and she wants to take him out to buy him a present, an annual rite. Because his parents are going out of town, they have asked his Gumma Underwood to stay with him and then quickly ducked out, knowing what a difficult woman she is. Lu knows the two old ladies do not get along, and he enlists Tou Vue to go along to the store and help him, but controlling his Gummas is beyond their best efforts. After a series of slapstick episodes, they all end up at the Rodriguez house in time for the party, where the grand-mothers are welcomed and the boys gladly shuck off their responsibility. While the humor is mostly fourth-grade level, the two very different elderly African-American women trying to outdo each other in insults, both plying the reluctant boys with gifts, is genuinely amusing. Also in the series is *Business As Usual*

(1997), about a sixth-grade project in marketing and finance, starring Bobby Samson.

49 Haynes, David, *Live at Five*, Milkweed, 1996 (hardcover), ISBN 1–57131–009–6, $21.95, 267 pp.; Harcourt, 1997 (paper), ISBN 0–156–00503–4, $12.00. Ages 14 up, grades 9 up.

Humorous and insightful novel of an African-American news anchor who, as part of a gimmick to boost ratings, discovers a world of black people in St. Paul, Minnesota, of whom he was literally unaware. When the new station manager decides that Brandon Wilson is not "black" enough, he hits on the brilliant idea that Brandon will move to the inner city and broadcast a series of human-interest stories from his home, thereby wooing the African-American viewing audience from reruns of "The Facts of Life" in the same time slot. Reluctantly, Brandon rents an apartment in an aging building managed by Nita Sallis, a single mother of three who also works a full-time job and goes to night school. In a series of broadcasts, Brandon (now "Brad") interviews people from the building and the neighborhood, introducing him to a hard-working, decent segment of the population and, to his surprise, increasing the show's ratings greatly. At night he usually goes back to his other world with his light-skinned, sophisticated girlfriend, Sandra, but he also becomes sexually involved with Nita. The situation is complicated by a rather amateurish drug dealer named Sipp, who has moved into the apartment above Nita's and whose ambition is to make one more big deal, then return to Mississippi with enough cash to start a legitimate business. He tries to get sexually involved with Nita and persuade her to come south with him, but though she is attracted, she has better sense than to believe him. Just when it looks as if she has no choice but either to link up with him or to betray him, she takes charge and comes up with a solution where they all win. In addition to some hilarious scenes, the novel explores the ignorance of upper-middle-class African Americans about how most of their brothers live and the prejudice of those who are educated and light-skinned against the darker and less well-off blacks. Haynes has also written other adult novels, notably *Somebody Else's Mama* (1995), a family story set in Missouri.

50 Herron, Carolivia, *Nappy Hair*, illus. Joe Cepeda, Knopf, 1997 (hardcover), ISBN 0–679–87937–4, $17.00, unp.; Dragonfly, 1998 (paper), ISBN 0–679–89445–4, $6.99. Ages 3–8, grades PS–3.

Exuberant picture-story book about how God decided to make a little girl whose hair has eight complete circles per inch, a story related by Uncle Mordecai at the backyard picnic, his story interrupted by comments from other relatives in a call-and-response pattern. The voices from the listeners are in varying styles and sizes of type, to indicate different people and attitudes. At first they are critical: "Brother, you ought to be ashamed," and "Now, why's he got to come back to that?," but as he reaches the part where God says, "This sweet little brown baby girl chile. She's going to have the nappiest hair in the world!," they change to "That's what he said," and "Ain't it the truth." The illustrations show a cheerful, lively little girl with a head of wildly uncontrollable hair amid a crowd of African-American relatives, painted with bright colors in mostly flat planes. The book has been controversial, with some critics objecting to the use of the word "nappy" and the emphasis on that characteristic and other readers welcoming the frank and joyous tone.

51 Holt, Kimberly Willis, *Mister and Me*, illus. Leonard Jenkins, Putnam, 1998 (hardcover), ISBN 0–399–23215–X, $13.99, 74 pp. Ages 9–12, grades 4–7.

Novel of African-American family life set in a sawmill town in Louisiana in 1940. Since her father's death when she was a baby, Jolene Johnson's family has been her mother, Ruby, who sews for the well-to-do white people in town, and Grandpa, who works in the mill. When Leroy Redfield begins courting Ruby, Jolene is resentful and scared of change. She refuses to use his first name, as he suggests, and instead starts calling him "Mister." Tactfully, Leroy woos both the Johnson women, successfully with Ruby but meeting considerable resistance with Jolene. He shows Jolene the length of beautiful red velvet he plans to give Ruby when she agrees to marry him and the blue velvet he bought for Jolene's dress, and he asks her to keep them for him until the big day. Angrily, Jolene cuts both into many pieces and hides the bag. After her mother accepts a ring from Leroy and Jolene is forced to produce the bag, Grandpa is ashamed of her and Ruby is furious, but Leroy says, "It ain't the end of the world." News of the illness of Grandpa's sister takes both him and Ruby to New Orleans while Leroy stays with Jolene, cooks for her, introduces her to Louis Armstrong's music, and takes her to the movies and to the family valentine dance. Contrite, Jolene digs out the bag of velvet scraps and the fabric pieces she has saved for doll clothes and starts a crazy quilt, like one she has seen at a white lady's house, as a wedding gift for Ruby and Leroy. The quiet story is told simply and convincingly and should appeal to youngsters about the age of Jolene, who may be eight to ten years old.

52 Houston, Gloria, *Bright Freedom's Song: A Story of the Underground Railroad*, Harcourt, 1998 (hardcover), ISBN 0–15–201812–3, $16.00, 145 pp. Ages 8–12, grades 3–7.

Historical novel set from 1853 to 1862 in the Blue Ridge Mountains, overlooking South Carolina, the southern portion of the middle route of the Underground Railroad. From the time she is six years old, white Bright Freedom Cameron knows there is something special about the small farm and smithy of her father and mother. She knows that occasionally strangers, black people, appear, are fed and clothed, kept strictly hidden, and then disappear. One of these is Marcus, a tall, well-muscled, kind, black man, who is her father's dear friend and helper and who once was a slave. She also learns that her father was once an indentured servant from Scotland, whom after a long servitude Marcus helped to gain freedom. She knows that her mother and father have strong beliefs that slavery is wrong and eventually is told that their farm is a safe house on the route northward. After she sees firsthand instances of the slavecatchers' brutality and the callousness of slave holders, she helps in every way she can to advance the cause except transport the slaves to the next safe house, because her father thinks that is far too dangerous for her to attempt. When he falls ill of fever and overwork after the Civil War breaks out, Bright and Marcus must drive a "bundle" of runaways by night in their horse and wagon. In an exciting passage that both opens the book and ends it, they manage to satisfy Southern soldiers that they are on a neighborly errand and reach safety. The hackneyed plot holds no surprises, characters are well drawn if also well-known types, style is appropriately descriptive and never sensational, and tone is earnest and often didactic. The historical Quaker abolitionist Levi Coffin makes a cameo appearance. The story found its source in the author's interest in the indentured servants who were used as slaves and who often ran away to the hills to freedom. She speculates that many of these yeoman farmers helped other servants and slaves escape. A lengthy bibliography concludes the book.

53 Howard, Elizabeth Fitzgerald, *Papa Tells Chita a Story*, illus. Floyd Cooper, Simon & Schuster, 1995 (hardcover), ISBN 0–02–744623–9, $15.00, unp.; (paper), ISBN 0–689–82220–0, $5.99. Ages 4–8, grades PS–3.

Historical picture-story book, loosely based on and embellishing the experiences of the writer's uncle in the Spanish-American War. Chita loves the stories Papa, a doctor, tells after supper and before bedtime. Tonight, Papa tells how, a soldier in Cuba fighting Spain, in order to secure reinforcements for his fellow soldiers, he carries a secret message across the island, riding his big black horse named Majestic past a huge brown snake. When Majestic balks at going through a green and slimy swamp, Papa evades an immense alligator by swimming beneath the creature, climbs a very high hill covered with brambles, and, exhausted, falls asleep in an eagle's nest, before arriving at the American camp. After finishing the account, Papa says that some of the story is true and some is not, but what is true is that he won a medal for bravery. The excitement of the tall tale is caught and extended by the realistic, muted oil washes. Another warm and affectionate story about Chita is described in *This Land Is Our Land* (1994), no. 57, *Mac and Marie and the Train Toss Surprise*.

54 Howard, Elizabeth Fitzgerald, *What's in Aunt Mary's Room?*, illus. Cedric Lucas, Clarion, 1996 (hardcover), ISBN 0–395–69845–6, $14.95, 32 pp. Ages 4–10, grades PS–5.

Realistic picture-story book of affectionate family life and history. When little Susan and Sarah visit their Great-Great-Aunt Flossie, they are delighted when she allows them to enter the room of their ancestor, Aunt Mary, who died at ninety-eight. Flossie always keeps the room locked, because in it she has placed "things to save, things to keep." The girls help her search for the key, unlock the door, and stepping carefully around the furniture and other keepsakes, find the big, precious, old family Bible. Because Susan's writing is so neat and clear, Flossie allows her to write hers and Sarah's names in it. Soft full-, half-page, and doublespread representational pastels depict the girls, Flossie, and the setting, the mistiness evoking the sense of yesteryear and family closeness. They show the children with chubby faces and tight braids and Aunt Flossie as gentle and indulgent. Another book by Howard appears in *This Land Is Our Land* (1994), no. 57, *Mac and Marie and the Train Toss Surprise*.

55 Jackson-Opoku, Sandra, *The River Where Blood Is Born*, One World/Ballantine, 1997 (hardcover), ISBN 0–345–39514–X, $25.00, 401 pp.; Ballantine, 1998 (paper), ISBN 0–345–42476–X, $12.95. Ages 16 up, grades 11 up.

Panoramic novel tracing the women in an African-American family for more than 200 years in realistic scenes and narrative. Alternately it follows the battle of wits between the women spirits of the village of the Great Beyond, especially the Queen Mother of the River and the Gatekeeper, and Ananse, the spider trickster and taleteller, over who will control the stories of their lives. Portions of the novel deal with each of the nine women in the direct line, but most prominently featured are Allie May (Alma) Peeples, originally of Chicago, her great-grandmother, Big Momma, of Cairo, Illinois, and *her* great-grandmother, Ama Kash or Proud Mary, a "saltwater" woman, that is, one who was captured in Africa and transported in a slave vessel. Although a feminist novel in the sense that it concentrates on female lives and draws the women as strong survivors, it does not picture them as good role models. Except for Lola, one of Big Momma's granddaughters, who has a hard-working though unappreciated husband, all the women bring about their own disasters by attaching themselves to irresponsible, exploitive, and usually abusive men. In the end, Alma, who has returned to Africa to find her roots, seems to have found a good man in Kwesi Omobowale, but only after years of being the third simultaneous wife to bigamist Trevor Barrett, a college professor much older than she is. The individual stories are mostly interesting and usually ring true, but the scenes in the Great Beyond are pretentiously written and tedious. Although it has won some prestigious acclaim, only a highly motivated high school student is likely to finish the lengthy novel.

56 Jenkins, Beverly, *Through the Storm*, Avon, 1998 (paper), ISBN 0–380–79864–6, $5.99, 368 pp. Ages 14 up, grades 9 up.

Historical romance novel set during and immediately following the American Civil War. Sable Fontaine, daughter of a white planter and a black woman descended from African queens, has been raised as a house slave and educated with her father's legitimate daughter, but when hard times during the war hit the plantation in Georgia, she learns that she is to be sold to a man named Morse whom she loathes. With the help of Harriet Tubman, here known as Araminta, she escapes to a "contraband" camp, a large settlement of newly freed slaves. There, she comes to the attention of Major Raimond LeVeq, a free black from a wealthy New Orleans family originally from Haiti. LeVeq, a man who has always had his way with any woman he sees, is attracted to both Sable's beauty and her independence, and from their first meeting their stories are entwined, with Morse also in deadly pursuit of Sable, whom he considers his property despite emancipation. The novel is a curious mixture of extensive research into the historical facts and social conditions of the period and the wildly implausible conventions of the popular romance novel. No effort is made to use lauguage of the period, even for the plantation African Americans, and Sable is endowed with a saucy and challenging personality, highly unlikely in an ex-slave. Through many twists of the plot, misunderstandings, partings, and coincidental reunions, Sable and LeVeq are finally married, and their acquaintance turns to physical love, with sexual scenes full of words like "pulsing" and "throbbing," "his ebony manhood," and "her lush golden breast," explicit descriptions but couched in euphemistic terms. The novel is notable mainly for being in one of the earliest series of popular romances to feature African Americans. Others by Jenkins in the series include *Night Song* (1994), *Vivid* (1995), *Indigo* (1996), and *Topaz* (1997).

57 Johnson, Angela, *Gone from Home*, DK Ink, 1998 (hardcover), ISBN 0–7894–2499–1, $15.95, 112 pp. Ages 12 up, grades 7 up.

Twelve short stories all capturing young people at moments that are important or decisive to their development of understanding. Most are set in Ohio, although Venice, California, and George, Kansas, are also mentioned. Most of the characters appear to be African American, though some could be of any ethnic background. A few of the pieces are very brief sketches, a couple of pages, while others are more developed stories, like "Starr," about an unconventional babysitter who wins the hearts of a girl and her father before hopping on her Day-Glo mountain bike and riding off to where cancer will soon end her life. In "A Handful" a young boy is rescued from falling off a bridge by his brother Kevin and saved from hysterical fear every time he must cross any bridge by Kevin's story of "the flying boy." Yet the narrator remains wild, a real handful, until he, too, rescues a hyperactive toddler and develops responsibility, even repeating the flying-boy story for the child he has saved. Perhaps the most poignant story is "Home," in which Pearl dresses as a boy and sets off to find her mother, Ruby, who takes her into her squat at an abandoned warehouse, shows her true love, and leaves again. Despite the bittersweet endings, even of "Sweetness," who dies of a police bullet, the well-written stories have an upbeat tone with decent characters concerned for each other, even those engaged in illegal activities, and a sense of hope through understanding, even in the least promising situations. For other books by Johnson, see *This Land Is Our Land* (1994), no. 63, *The Leaving Morning* (picture-story book) and no. 64, *Taming the Sweep* (novel).

58 Johnson, Angela, *Heaven*, Simon & Schuster, 1998 (hardcover), ISBN 0–689–82229–4, $16.00, 138 pp. Ages 10–14, grades 5–9.

Life in Heaven, Ohio, has been idyllic for Marley Carroll, fourteen, with her loving parents, her younger brother, Butchy, and her best friend, Shoogy Maple. Although she is not fond of Shoogy's too-perfect parents, most of the people in the small town are friendly, and life is pleasant. She baby-sits for Feather, the infant daughter of artist Bobby Morris, and admires his single-minded devotion to the baby, even though he tells her little about his past life in Brooklyn and nothing about Feather's mother. All this changes after her parents receive a letter from the minister of a church burned in Alabama, trying to reconstruct parish records and asking for information about Monna Floyd. This prompts her parents to reveal that she is actually their niece, daughter of her father's twin brother, Jack, and a woman named Christine. The news upsets Marley terribly. At first she is furious, feels betrayed and lied to, and she fends off her parents' attempts to help her. For years her "Uncle Jack" has written her letters telling about his wanderings and his dog, Boy. Gradually she begins to understand that, in his grief over Christine's death, he gave her to the couple he knew would give her a good, loving home. She also sees that Shoogy's family is far from perfect and that Bobby is an unconventional but ideal single father. By the time Uncle Jack arrives to meet her again, she has accepted her new knowledge. Although all the characters seem to be African Americans, nothing is made of their race except for the concern about the church burnings and occasional mentions of skin shade. If Heaven has any white residents, they are not identified. The conflict is all in Marley's mind and emotions, believable but not very compelling. For other books by Johnson, see *This Land Is Our Land* (1994), no. 63, *The Leaving Morning* (picture-story book), and no. 64, *Toning the Sweep* (novel).

59 Johnson, Angela, *Humming Whispers*, Orchard, 1995 (hardcover), ISBN 0–5310–6898–6, $15.95, 121 pp.; Scholastic, 1995 (paper), ISBN 0–590–67452–8, $3.99. Ages 9–12, grades 4–7.

Sensitive novel of the overwhelming effect of mental illness on a family. Sophy, eleven, adores and at the same time fears and even hates her older sister, Nicole, twenty-four, a beautiful, intelligent, graceful dancer who suffers from schizophrenia. Since their parents were killed in an accident when Sophy was four, they have lived with their Aunt Shirley in Cleveland, Ohio, where Nicole sometimes takes her medicine and attends college classes, sometimes is hospitalized, and sometimes wanders off and disappears, unable to cope with the voices in her mind. Sophy's greatest fear is that the whispers will start in her own head and she will follow Nicole into mental illness, a fear she knows Aunt Shirley shares. Other characters affected by Nicole's condition are her faithful boyfriend, Reuben Harding, an artist, and Miss Onyx Phelps, Reuben's aging neighbor, who was once a professional dancer and who encourages Sophy, a more promising dancer even than Nicole was before her illness. The sisters are very close and devoted. Sophy is aware of the slightest change in her older sister's condition. Nicole tries to help Sophy rid herself of her fear of storms, which they both understand is an unspoken fear of insanity. Reuben, Aunt Shirley, and even less involved persons are supportive, but unable to provide a solution. The reader is left believing that Sophy will not become schizophrenic but that she will never escape her worry and responsibility for Nicole. Although the two girls are pictured as African Americans on the book's cover, nothing in the text is race specific. For other books by Johnson, see *This Land Is Our Land* (1994), no. 63, *The Leaving Morning* (picture-story book), and no. 64, *Toning the Sweep* (novel).

60 Johnson, Angela, *Songs of Faith*, Orchard, 1998 (hardcover), ISBN 0–531–30023–4, $15.95, 103 pp.; Knopf, 1999 (paper), ISBN 0–6798–9488–8, $4.99, 108 pp. Ages 9–12, grades 4–7.

Novel for middle-school readers set in Harvey, Ohio, in 1975, dealing with the pain and loneliness caused to families by divorce and the absence of fathers. Doreen and her brother, Bobo, now wanting to be known as Robert, face a summer with their father gone and Mama Dot so involved with her college classes, in order to get a job to support them, that she seems also absent. Next door a family moves in headed by Miss Mary, an ex-forger of documents who has "got religion," with her two little boys and her stepdaughter, Jolette, whose father is a disturbed Vietnam veteran now departed for parts unknown. When her best friend, Viola, moves away and Robert, upset by his father's abandonment, stops talking, Doreen feels really alone and only gradually, and not very convincingly, finds faith that her life will once more become bearable. Presumably, all the characters are African Americans, although this is not of any particular significance in the plot and the situation could apply to any ethnic group. Doreen's voice is frank and appealing. The misery felt by both children and adults is well evoked, as are the sorts of bargains with fate that they try: Robert will not speak until his father returns; Jolette will jump a million times with her rope so that her father will come back. For other books by Johnson, see *This Land Is Our Land* (1994), no. 63, *The Leaving Morning* (a picture-story book), and no. 64, *Toning the Sweep* (a novel).

61 Johnson, Charles, *Dreamer*, Scribner, 1998 (hardcover), ISBN 0–684–81224–X, $23.00, 236 pp.; 1999 (paper), ISBN 0–684–85443–0, $12.00, 240 pp. Ages 15 up, grades 10 up.

More homage to the memory of Martin Luther King than a biographical novel, covering the last months of his leadership in Chicago and, finally, in Memphis. In the voice of Matthew Bishop, one of the young workers in his organization, the book tells of the discovery and training of a double for King, a man who looks so much like the minister that he is often mistaken for him, but whose own checkered background is very different from that of the dedicated man. Chaym Smith is highly intelligent, a talented artist, and well read, though not formally educated. He has traveled widely, including spending a year in a Buddhist monastery in Japan, but he also has violence and possibly murder in his past. His motive for posing as King is never clear. Sometimes he seems genuinely to desire a change and redemption in his life; at other times he is cynical and derogatory about the aims of the Civil Rights Movement. At King's direction, Bishop and Amy Griffith, a girl he greatly admires, take Smith to an isolated house in southern Illinois where they help him practice his impersonation and study King's sermons. Shortly before the Memphis march in support of sanitation workers, two men, probably from the FBI, show up at the house and blackmail Smith, with threats about revealing his past, into leaving with them to "cooperate" in whatever plan they have to discredit King. Whether he really contributes to the disasters in Memphis is not clear. While most of the action is narrated by bookish Bishop, long passages are ostensibly in the mind of King, who struggles with weariness and the difficulties of organizing and unifying his followers. Although the idea of a double is intriguing and Bishop, who seems to speak for the author, is devoted to King's ideals, the novel is damaged by pretentious language and continual references to works of philosophy and theology, not just by Bishop, where it might be excused as characterization, but by all the main figures. Though young people interested in a picture of King's last days would find this book useful, only a dedicated few will enjoy it as a novel. See *This Land Is Our Land* (1994), no. 65, *Middle Passage*, for another novel by Johnson.

62 Johnson, Dolores, *Papa's Stories*, illus. Dolores Johnson, Macmillan, 1994 (hardcover), ISBN 0–01–74847–5, $14.95, unp. Ages 5–8, grades K–3.

Picture-story book of a little African-American girl who discovers her father cannot read. Every night, Kari waits for her father to come home from work and read to her, liking especially the way the stories are different every time he reads them. When a girl from her school points out that her favorite book is *Little Red Riding Hood*, not *Little Miss Too-Big-for-Her-Red-Britches*, as her father has always told it, she begins to suspect the truth. At first she is hurt, thinking she has been lied to, but when her father confesses that he never had a chance to learn, she offers to teach him, as soon as she herself learns. He admits that he has begun to realize the need to read and that Kari's mother has been teaching him. The realistic illustrations picture a warmly loving family, not overly idealized in appearance. For other picture-story books written and illustrated by Dolores Johnson, see *This Land Is Our Land* (1994), no. 66, *The Best Bug to Be*, no. 67, *Now Let Me Fly: The Story of a Slave Family*, and no. 68, *Your Dad Was Just Like You.*

63 Johnson, Dolores, *Seminole Diary: Remembrances of a Slave*, illus. Dolores Johnson, Macmillan, 1994 (hardcover), ISBN 0–02–74848–3, $14.95, unp. Ages 7–12, grades 2–7.

Historical picture-story book of slaves who escape and live with Seminole Indians in the 1830s. With a frame story of a modern African-American child whose mother finds the journal of an ancestor, the story is told in diary form by Libbie, about nine or ten, who with her father and little sister, Clarissa, seven, joins a group of slaves making their way south through thickets and marshes, until they are met by Seminoles, who welcome them, give them food, and take them to their village. Although technically now slaves of the Indians, the blacks are treated with respect. Clarissa, in particular, fits in and is adopted by Honey Flower, whose baby died. The government's decision to drive the Seminoles to a reservation in Oklahoma splits up the village. Honey Flower, taking Clarissa, flees south into the deep swamps; some young warriors, including Wild Jumper, whom Libbie loves, vow to fight the U.S. army; Libbie and her father start the long walk west under armed guard. Based on actual records of escaped slaves, the story is moving if a little too preachy. The illustrations, done in oils, make the most of the gorgeous Seminole clothing and the rich greens and blues of the lush vegetation and waters. For other picture-story books written and illustrated by Dolores Johnson, see *This Land Is Our Land* (1994), no. 66, *The Best Bug to Be*, no. 67, *Now Let Me Fly: The Story of a Slave Family*, and no. 68, *Your Dad Was Just Like You.*

64 Johnston, Tony, *The Wagon*, illus. James E. Ransome, Tambourine, 1996 (hardcover), ISBN 0–688–13457–2, $16.00, unp.; Mulberry, 1999 (paper), ISBN 0–688–16694–6, $5.95. Ages 5–10, grades K–5.

Historical picture-story book set in one of the Carolinas just before, during, and at the very end of the American Civil War. The narrator, a boy, tells how he was born into a loving slave family on the farm of a sometimes cruel master. The narrator's father, a skilled carpenter, builds a wagon, which the boy imagines is the chariot that will carry them away from slavery. Before Emancipation, however, the wagon and the boy see slaves borne to market or brought to the farm, slaves beaten, and unending drudgery. At the war's end, the little family leave the farm in the wagon, joyfully free at last, only to learn that President Lincoln has been shot and killed. The boy, now twelve, asks to go to the funeral to say goodbye to Lincoln. The fairly ordinary text is much uplifted by the magnificent, powerfully executed paintings in mostly brooding colors, which subtly extend the action and the symbolism of the wagon. Perspectives vary from head-on views to overhead shots to broad-view silhouettes. Contrast is effectively employed; for example, near the end of the book, the picture in which the ex-slaves dance in "jubilee" is followed by the more serious one of the family in the sturdy wagon, happy but sober, seemingly anticipating the sad conclusion, which is depicted two pictures later with the family in the dark, dark wagon silhouetted against the setting sun, deep sadness on the face of the boy, whose face is the only one depicted. For an earlier book by Johnston, see *This Land Is Our Land* (1994), no. 304, *The Badger and the Magic Fan: A Japanese Folktale.*

65 Jones, Gayl, *The Healing*, Beacon, 1998 (hardcover), ISBN 0–8070–6314–2, $23.00, 283 pp.; 1999 (paper), ISBN 0–8070–6325–8, $12.00, 296 pp. Ages 15 up, grades 10 up.

Novel of the changes in the life of a young African-American woman who starts as a beautician and becomes, to her own surprise, a faith healer, traveling to small towns and restoring both believers and skeptics to health. Essentially moving backward through her life, Harlan Eagleton tells of her girlhood in Louisville with her mother and grandmother, her father having decided to stay with his Korean woman after his war service. So shy at first that she is known as Possum, Harlan develops through a series of relationships. She marries Norvelle, a professor of medical anthropology, and goes with him to Africa, where she wearies of his neglect as he follows a Masai medicine woman from village to village. Back in the United States, she becomes first a makeup artist, then business manager for a rock singer, Jane Savage, a woman educated as a research chemist. She also has brief flings with Jamie, Jane's ex-husband, and with Josef, a mysterious, wealthy black man from Germany, whom she meets at the Sarasota races. Her healing powers become apparent after an attempt on her own life. More distinctive than what happens is the unusual style, a first-person stream of consciousness intertwined with dialogue, all using Southern black dialect in the repetitive pattern of a person mentally or orally chewing over an idea or a memory and all without quotation indicators so it is not always clear what is said and what is thought. Also running under the events is the question of the African American's relationship to the United States, exemplified in Jane's great success in Europe and Japan, which means little to her because she craves American fame, Josef's phalanx of bodyguards, which may indicate that he is really an American gangster, not the wealthy German horse breeder he claims, and Norvelle's ultimate return from Africa to find at home what he has been seeking. The action may be slow for most young readers, but it is relieved by humor and clever allusions, as Harlan educates herself and refines her natural intelligence by reading Jane's books.

66 Klass, David, *Danger Zone*, Scholastic, 1996 (hardcover), ISBN 0–590–48590–3, $16.95, 240 pp.; (paper) ISBN 0–590–48591–1, $4.99, 282 pp. Ages 9–12 up, grades 4–7.

Sports novel of an international junior basketball tournament in Italy with complications of racial misunderstandings and threats of terrorism. Although the narrator, Jim Doyle, is a white boy from Minnesota, he is chosen for a team of mostly African-American players to be trained on the UCLA campus. Almost immediately he runs into hostility from the star, Augustus LeMay, who resents his midwestern naivete, what he perceives as Jim's privileged background, and especially his inclusion on the team that knocked out Augustus's cousin. Before they leave Los Angeles, Augustus, his cousin, and a friend newly out of prison hijack Jim and forcibly give him a tour of the rougher parts of the city in a stolen car. In Italy a skinhead neo-Nazi group threatens the American team, and tension makes Jim's game deteriorate. In the last minutes of the final game, against Spain, he and Augustus are both in a "zone," a dreamlike state of superb play. After Jim's final, incredible game-winning basket, a man with a gun rushes the floor and aims at Augustus, but his arm is jarred by a policeman and the bullet hits Jim in the leg. In a later scene, in a Los Angeles hospital where Jim is awaiting a second operation, Augustus arrives and finally shakes Jim's hand, an understanding having been achieved. Games are described vividly, and action is exciting, but, although Augustus's initial resentment is understandable, the speeches he delivers as they drive through the city at night are didactic and implausible.

67 Koller, Jackie, *A Place to Call Home*, Atheneum, 1995 (hardcover), ISBN 0–6898–0024–X, $16.00, 204 pp.; Aladdin, 1997 (paper), ISBN 0–6898–1395–3, $4.50. Ages 10–14, grades 5–9.

Novel of a dysfunctional family in rural Connecticut that the half African-American high school-aged daughter tries desperately to hold together. When her alcoholic mother disappears, Anna O'Dell is left to cope with her little blond half-siblings, Mandy, six, and Casey, seven months, not for the first time, but when she sees her mother's station wagon submerged in the deep lake, she realizes she is on her own. Just as the money her mother left is almost gone, she gets an envelope in the mail, postmarked Sunnydale, Mississippi, and containing two hundred dollars but no note. As that runs out, she moves the children to a tumbledown cabin that she learns belongs to her nearest neighbor, Nate Leon, a classmate who has always treated her well and who now, against his better judgment, helps her hide out. When Casey develops an ear infection, she gives up and takes him to a doctor. A social worker finds them a foster home that is far from welcoming, and when she overhears the woman say she will keep Casey but not the other two, she dresses like a boy and starts for Mississippi, hoping to find family to take them in. Instead, she meets frigid rejection from her white maternal grandmother, who denies that her daughter left because her father and her older brother abused her sexually, facts that a helpful African American confirms, along with the suspicion that they also killed Anna's father. Back in Connecticut, she finds that the social worker has moved Mandy and

Casey to a new home, where the young couple are hoping to adopt them. At first devastated, Anna sees how happy the children are and agrees to their placement, then accepts the offer of a home with the owners of a convenience store she has often patronized. Essentially a story of a child forced into an adult role, the novel does a good job of portraying Anna's conflicting emotions. While her African-American paternal side is not the major element in the plot, it is a factor, since most foster parents do not want a black child and her grandmother in Mississippi is horrified that the neighbors might see her.

68 Krishner, Trudy, *Spite Fences*, Delacorte, 994 (hardcover), ISBN 0–395–32088–4, $14.95, 283 pp.; Laurel Lee, 1996 (paper), ISBN 0–4402–2016–5, $4.50. Ages 10–14, grades 5–9.

Historical novel of the early Civil Rights Movement in the small Georgia town of Kinship, narrated by Maggie Pugh, thirteen, a poor white girl caught up unintentionally in events because she has a friendship with Zeke Freeman, an African American with a secondhand trading cart. Although she has known all her life that whites and "colored" do not mix, she is appalled when she witnesses a vicious attack on Zeke after he has entered the white restroom in the drugstore. Naively thinking that he made the mistake because he is illiterate, she offers to teach him to read, an offer he takes up quickly. He soon gets her a job cleaning a small house nearly hidden by trees owned by a professor of mathematics whom she never sees, although they correspond by notes. When she discovers he is African American, she is shocked, but she continues because he has been nice to her and because her family badly needs the money she earns. After she overhears plans for a drugstore sit-in, she and her adventurous friend, Pert Wilson, hide in a tree to watch the Independence Day celebration of the black community, are discovered, and then welcomed to the picnic, where she takes pictures of the festivities with a camera Zeke once gave her. These pictures, shown around town by the clerk in the drugstore, get her into trouble with both her family and the white community, but pictures she takes of the sit-in, which turns into a riot, she sells to *Life* magazine, and she is persuaded to testify against the hoodlums who beat Zeke. Although Maggie's involvement in many of the events is not entirely believable, the picture of social tensions in Kinship, both racial and economic, is convincing. A sequel, *Kinship* (1997), focuses on Pert Wilson.

69 Kroll, Virginia, *Can You Dance, Dalila?*, illus. Nancy Carpenter, Simon & Schuster, 1996 (hardcover), ISBN 0–689–80551–9, $15.00, unp. Ages 4–8, grades PS–3.

Realistic, contemporary picture-story book, in which a little African-American girl learns what type of dancing is right for her. When Dalila is ill and Gramma lets her watch TV, she sees a dance show that inspires her to learn to dance. Gramma takes her to watch Irish dancing, country-western line dancing, ballet, and tap, all of which Dalila tries without success. She cannot seem to make her arms, legs, and feet work correctly together for any of them. Then Gramma takes her to a performance of the West African Troupe, whose dances imitate the movements of animals and forces of nature. When the dancers invite the audience to participate, Dalila joins in and right away knows she has found the best dance form for her. Spirited oil paintings, lively with movement and color, catch the sense of dance as an art form and Dalila's joy in participating. The bodies of the performing artists are so carefully rendered that the viewer easily picks up the essential differences between the forms. See *This Land Is Our Land* (1994), no. 73, *Masai and I*, for another book by Kroll.

70 Lasky, Kathryn, *True North: A Novel of the Underground Railroad*, Blue Sky Press, 1996 (hardcover), ISBN 0–590–20523–4, $14.95, 208 pp.; Scholastic, 1998 (paper), ISBN 0–590–20524–2, $4.99, 266 pp. Ages 9–12, grades 4–7.

Set in 1858, *True North* departs from the usual formula by having two protagonists, a slave girl named Africa and white Lucy Bradford, the fifth daughter of a prominent Boston family, who share the story about equally in alternating chapters. Africa has run away after being brutally whipped because she refused to lie again with Master Thompson, who has gotten her with child. Although at first part of a group led by Harriet Tubman, she is left behind when her baby is born months prematurely and she insists on staying with it until it dies. From there on she is alone, making her way with the help of various "conductors" until she arrives in Boston, feeling her way through an underground passage and ending in the empty grandfather clock in the study of Lucy's grandfather. Grieving over his recent death, Lucy discovers her and takes on the obligation to accompany her to Canada. Very different in background but alike in spirited personality, the two girls, both about fourteen, are attractive characters, and the suspenseful plot is fast-paced. A lesser-known problem of the abolitionist movement, the spies and false safe houses established by bounty hunters, is an integral part of the story and adds depth.

71 Levy, Marilyn, *Run for Your Life*, Houghton, 1996 (hardcover), ISBN 0–395–74520–9, $14.95, 217 pp. Ages 10–15, grades 5–10.

Realistic novel of contemporary neighborhood life set for about a year in Oakland, California, and based on actual people and incidents. Kisha Clark, thirteen, the narrator, lives on welfare with her mother, unemployed father, and younger brother, Ty, nine, in a cramped but tidy apartment in the almost completely African-American poverty-, violence-, and drug-ridden Walt Whitman housing project. In August, Darren Hayes, a young, black social worker, reopens the local community center and picks Kisha to help him organize a track team. Kisha gets her best friend, Natonia, to help, and soon Darren has six girls for his team, which he says is Olympics-bound. Although he lays down strict rules—good grades, no liquor or drugs, and no pregnancies—and works the girls hard, they thrive and think of themselves more as a family than a team.

The team helps Kisha to think beyond her homelife problems and abusive father, and at the end she is relieved that her parents agree to see a counselor. Natonia flees sexual abuse at home, first taking refuge with Darren and his family and then finding a home with a woman teacher. The girls do poorly in their first meet, but in a national one in March they take several awards. Kisha, who had felt she could never overcome her physical awkwardness, sets a new record in the 800-meter event. Darren has helped the girls to see a way out of the project and to a better life through learning good habits, making wise choices, and possibly gaining scholarships. He calls them all winners because they have picked themselves up and done their best. The problems the girls encounter in the project and in competing—particularly racial prejudice—are the expected ones. Darren is the most compelling figure. Adding force to the narrative is the information, given on the book jacket, that Darren has an actual counterpart in the Oakland area and that the girls are composites of real girls with whom he worked.

72 Lyons, Mary E., *The Poison Place*, Atheneum, 1997 (hardcover), ISBN 0–689–81146–2, $16.00, 165 pp.; Aladdin, 1999 (paper), ISBN 0–689–82678–8, $3.99. Ages 12 up, grades 7 up.

Biographical novel about Charles William Peale, one of America's first scientists and portrait painters and owner of Peale's Museum in Philadelphia. The story of Peale's ambiguous nature is told on the night of his death by his ex-slave, Moses Williams, to Moses's eleven-year-old daughter, Maggie, as he leads her through the deserted museum. As a child, Moses lives in the kitchen of Peale's house with his slave parents, even though Peale publicly denounces slavery. In his early years Moses is a playmate and companion to Peale's eldest son, Raphaelle, two years his senior. When Moses is nearly ten, Peale decides to free his parents, but he keeps the little boy, promising to free him when he is twenty-eight or earlier, if he shows "industry and perseverance," an incentive that Moses soon sees is hollow. Peale has a number of other children, his favorite being Rembrant, a spoiled and unpleasant boy. Peale has an antipathy to Raphaelle, though the boy as he grows up tries hard to please him. Having a grand idea for a museum of natural history, Peale begins to preserve birds and animals through a process of taxidermy that involves arsenic, a process he knows is dangerous, yet he demands that his eldest son work continually in the preserving process, which he avoids himself. Moses escapes partly by being relegated to the lower jobs of feeding and cleaning up after the many animals Peale collects, and partly by skillfully working the "physiognotrace," a device Peale acquires to trace a silhouette of those who cannot afford a painted portrait. When he is twenty-seven, largely at the insistence of Raphaelle, Moses is freed, but he continues to work at the museum. The entire book is in the voice of Moses, who blames Peale with some bitterness for Raphaelle's death and for his own long servitude. An author's note discusses historical fact and supposition. For other books by Lyons, see *This Land Is Our Land* (1994), no. 77, *Letters from a Slave Girl*, another biographical novel, and no. 184, *Raw Head, Bloody Bones*, a collection of folktales.

73 McKissack, Patricia C., *Ma Dear's Aprons*, illus. Floyd Cooper, Atheneum, 1997 (hardcover), ISBN 0–689–81051–2, $16.00, unp. Ages 3–8, grades PS–3.

Realistic picture-story book of single-parent, African-American family life in rural Alabama at the beginning of the twentieth century. David Earl, three or four years old, can always tell what day it is and with what work he will be helping his mother, a laundress, by the color of the apron Ma Dear wears. On Monday, she puts on her fresh blue apron, the one with the long, front pocket in which she puts clothespins for hanging out the wash. Tuesday's apron is yellow like the sun, the one she covers David Earl with when he falls asleep after they have finished ironing. Wednesday's apron is green for shopping, Thursday's a cheerful pink for visiting the sick and shut-ins, Friday's brown for housecleaning for a neighboring family, and Saturday's flowered for baking, after which Ma Dear puts on an "over-the-head gray" one to give David Earl "a good scrubbing from head to toe." There is no apron for Sunday, however, since on Sunday both put on their best clothes for "service," which is followed by a picnic down by the creek. The story is based on the life of Leanna, the author's great-grandmother, a strong, independent woman affectionately known as Ma Dear. The straightforward text is accompanied by full-page, representational paintings, which depict situations and characters, their misty outlines and muted colors enhancing the sense of memoir. For earlier books, see *This Land Is Our Land* (1994), no. 79, *The Dark Thirty*, no. 80, *Flossie and the Fox*, no. 81, *A Million Fish . . . More or Less*, no. 82, *Mirandy and Brother Wind*, and no. 83, *Constance Stumbles* (all fiction), and no. 215, *Messey Bessey* (verse).

74 McKissack, Patricia C., *A Picture of Freedom: The Diary of Clotee, a Slave Girl*, Scholastic, 1997 (hardcover), ISBN 0–590–25988–1, $9.95, 203 pp. Ages 9–15, grades 4–10.

Historical novel of slavery and the Underground Railroad set on Belmont Plantation, Virginia, for about one year, beginning in March, 1859. Most figures are historical, including the African-American narrator, Clotee, twelve, who describes the events of that momentous year in a diary she surreptitiously keeps. A reliable and intelligent house slave, Clotee fans her mistress, Miz Lilly Henley, while she teaches her son, William, twelve, his lessons. By listening and observing carefully, Clotee learns to read and write, but she is careful not to let any but her most trusted friends among the slaves know of her ability. In addition to telling of the routinely hard work, poor living conditions, frequent whippings, and other degradations the slaves must endure, even on this fairly well-run and prosperous plantation, Clotee describes two events that change the lives of everyone on the place. Mas' Henley buys a champion race horse, ostensibly for his son but in reality so that he can increase his gambling winnings through the expert riding of his talented young slave jockey, Hince. Although ordered not to, William rides the spirited horse by himself and has an accident that leaves him partially paralyzed. When he recovers enough to resume his lessons, the Henleys hire a tutor for him, a young white Southerner named Mr. Ely Harms, who, Clotee soon discovers, has ties to the abolitionists. Through him, she learns that Belmont has a station on the Underground. When Mr. Harms's abolitionist role is discovered, Clotee, Hince, and Spicy, Hince's sweetheart, pull off a clever ruse to save him. Clotee then helps the others flee for freedom, but she herself stays at Belmont in order to help still other slaves escape by maintaining the plantation's station. An epilogue indicates that the idea for the story came from the life of a McKissack ancestor, that the details of the book are inferred from historical documents collected and recorded almost a century later, and that the plot is fiction. Clotee, Spicy, Hince, and Aunt Tee, the cook, are good characters, Mr. Harms and most of the other slaves are functional types, and the master and mistress are one-dimensionally evil. To say that most events are the familiar ones of slave stories is not to diminish their importance in the black experience. That Clotee, who has only begun to form letters and read with some ease, can write a diary with so much connected narrative, telling detail, and organized dialogue strains credibility, as does her ability to conceal the book from the prying eyes of fellow slaves. Once into the story, which has many tense moments, however, that narrative difficulty is overcome, and the lives of these people are foregrounded. Historical information, maps, and archival pictures add credibility. For other books by McKissack, see *This Land Is Our Land* (1994), nos. 79, 80, 81, 82, and 83 (all fiction), and 215 (verse) (see preceding entry, no. 73, for titles).

75 McKissack, Patricia C., *Run Away Home*, Scholastic, 1997 (hardcover), ISBN 0–590–46751–4, $14.95, 160 pp. Ages 8–12, grades 3–7.

Historical novel set on a farm near and in the village of Quincy in the Alabama piney woods for a few weeks in 1888 against the notorious Jim Crow laws intended to deny African Americans such privileges of citizenship as voting and property rights. Native-American Apaches are being moved from their Florida prison to another in Alabama prior to being relocated in Oklahoma. One Sunday after church, the narrator, Sarah Jane Crossman, twelve, daughter of a hardscrabble black farmer born in slavery, observes a railroad car of Apaches, among them the historical leader Geronimo. She spies a boy of about fifteen as he slips away from the group and knows from Geronimo's attitude that she must be silent. Later, the Crossmans find the boy, Sky, at their farm, burning with swamp fever. Mama and Sarah nurse him to health, and the family agree to inform George Wratten, the historical Indian agent, when Sky has recovered. Life becomes precarious for the Crossmans when Papa discovers boll weevils in the cotton crop for which he has borrowed seed money from Sheriff Johnson, who covets the Crossman land. Proud, determined, a skilled carpenter, Papa arranges to pay off the debt in thirty days by making desks for the school that historical Booker T. Washington (who appears briefly) is founding, Tuskegee Institute. When night riders threaten and it seems as though the farm will be lost, Mr. Wratten, some Apaches, and United States Army soldiers arrive in time to complete the desks, and the debt is paid. The Crossman parents and Sarah are well drawn, and Sky emerges as the most interesting figure, but except for Mr. Wratten (upon whose journals and writings the story is loosely based), the white characters are stereotypically racist. The historical matters involving blacks and Indians of the time are cleverly combined, and if the racism seems too laid on and conclusion too pat, the reader applauds the victory of the Crossmans and Sky, who casts in his lot with his benefactors. The plot moves fast with many tight spots, and the tension that develops between only-child Sarah and Sky, because Sarah is jealous of the attention Sky gets from her father, is credible. The story is based on the African-American writer's great-great-great-grandfather, a Native American found in the woods and reared by blacks, who married a black woman and became a carpenter. The rest is based on research and imagination. While there are too many complications and the plot is fragmented, the book offers a credible if simplistic glimpse of the period for middle readers. For other books by McKissack see *This Land Is Our Land* (1994), nos. 79, 80, 81, 82, 83 (fiction), and 215 (verse) (see previous entry no. 73 for titles).

76 McMillan, Terry, *How Stella Got Her Groove Back: A Novel*, Viking, 1996 (hardcover), ISBN 0–670–86990–2, 368 pp.; Signet, 1997 (paper), ISBN 0–451–19200–1, $6.00, 448 pp. Ages 14 up, grades 9 up.

Realistic, contemporary novel set near San Francisco, California, and in a resort in Jamaica, West Indies. Independent, divorced Stella Payne, forty-two, has everything—beauty, brains, degrees, well-appointed house, fine-paying job as a "fancy smancy analyst" for a major investment house, BMW and a truck to boot, high-fashion clothes, handsome son of eleven—and still laments that "nobody has rocked" her world or made her "heart flutter like it did" when she fell in love with her ex. On vacation, she books a reservation at a posh Jamaican resort, where she meets a handsome, sweet, young Jamaican college student half her age. A torrid romance begins, during which, while the sex is terrific and the company exhilarating, her thoughts repeatedly return to the difference in their ages. Back in California, she discovers she has been terminated from her job, deals with a mixed response about her romance from her sisters, and eventually decides to attempt to make the most of the opportunity that seems to have presented itself. This long story of a woman's December romance with a May man, or what's sauce for an aging gander may also be sauce for a mid-life goose, gets tedious, especially in the midsection, after Stella's situation is established and she has met and pants like a teenager for her Jamaican boyfriend. Characters and plot are vapid, sex scenes are explicit, accompanying sex talk and yearnings become adolescent, and her hedonistic, self-serving, stream-of-consciousness monologues occupy seemingly dozens of pages. Best are the descriptions of the lazy days and activities at the resort and in the mountains of the island's interior. Another good item—indeed a gem—is the writer's brief passage of self-criticism on page sixty. Although on the whole the book is a bore, devotees of McMillan's fiction will like it. For an anthology of African-American fiction McMillan earlier published, see *This Land Is Our Land* (1994), no. 84, *Breaking Ice*.

77 Medearis, Angela Shelf, *The Adventures of Sugar and Junior*, illus. Nancy Poydar, Holiday, 1996 (hardcover), ISBN 0–8234–1182–6, 32 pp. Ages 4–9, grades PS–4.

Realistic picture-story book of the domestic adventures of a present-day urban Hispanic-American boy and an African-American girl. Junior Ramirez is excited when Sugar Johnson moves in next door, because now he has someone to play with. Each of the four short chapters describes an adventure. They discuss their names while they play follow-the-leader, bounce the basketball, turn cartwheels, swing, and climb the jungle gym, all the while Sugar showing Junior that she is his equal at each of these. They mix cookies at Sugar's house, making substitutions in the recipe as they think necessary. When the cookies turn out to be hard and tasteless, Junior suggests they use them for rocks. Junior invites Sugar to attend a monster movie with him, assuring her that he will comfort her during the scary parts. When Junior screams and hides under the seat, Sugar consoles him and holds his hand all the way home. Their adventures conclude with a trip to the ice cream man. Sugar selects chocolate, but Junior cannot make up his mind. While Sugar gets a drink at the water fountain, she leaves her cone with Junior, who licks it all up to keep it from dripping. They buy a two-scooper chocolate cone, which they take turns licking all the way home. Although some might quarrel with the health aspects of the final story, the adventure, like the others, is mostly dialogue and moves fast to conclude with a twist. The way of looking at life is childlike, and the characters are credible, likable, and inventive. The bright, cheerful, active watercolors are located in exactly the right places to illuminate the children's activities and emotions. This is an entertaining, smoothly written, first chapter-book for those who are just reading. For other books by this prolific writer, see *This Land Is Our Land* (1994), no. 216, *Dancing with the Indians*, no. 217, *Picking Peas for a Penny*, and no. 218, *The Zebra-Riding Cowboy*.

78 Medearis, Angela Shelf, *Haunts: Five Hair-Raising Tales*, illus. Trina Schart Hyman, Holiday House, 1996 (hardcover), ISBN 0–8234–1280–6, $15.95, 37 pp. Ages 8–14, grades 3–9.

Suspenseful fantasies with folklore and Old South motifs and flavor, involving a phantom fiddler, whose magical tune lures a little boy away; a headless horseman, the memory of whose wild and threatening ride turns a young girl's hair white; a murdered husband who rises from the grave as a skeleton and forces his wife to dance the night away, after which his rolling head pursues her relentlessly; a witch who demands that the town mayor tell her his age as the price of stopping the flood that threatens to wipe out his town; and a pastor who watches as the body parts of a dead man drop down the chimney and reassemble, while dozens of mewling cats watch. Capturing the spookiness of each tale is a full-page, black-and-white, surrealistic illustration, which depicts important scenes and main characters. Other books by Medearis appear in *This Land Is Our Land* (1996), no. 216, *Dancing with the Indians*, no. 217, *Picking Peas for a Penny*, and no. 218, *The Zebra-Riding Cowboy*.

79 Medearis, Angela Shelf, *Our People*, illus. Michael Bryant, Atheneum, 1994 (hardcover), ISBN 0–689–31826–X, $14.95, unp. Ages 4–8, grades PS–3.

Contemporary, realistic, picture-story book, in which a daddy tells his little girl about the "glorious past" of the African-American people and their race's contributions to human history and asserts that she has a "glorious future" in store for her. Daddy says that their people built the pyramids, were African kings, queens, and artists, crossed the ocean with Columbus and the continent with Lewis and Clark, farmed, went west, and became inventors and scientists, among other achievements. As he describes each contribution, the little girl wishes she had been there at that time, too. Strongly composed, detailed, colorful, off-the-page paintings wrap themselves around the text and extend it, so that text and illustrations together tell more than either text or pictures alone. Although the book is a serious look at history, humor plays an important role. For example, after a two-page spread of slaves being led to freedom through a swamp by a red-shawled woman, perhaps Harriet Tubman, the next two-page spread shows the little girl, shawl-clad, pulling a wagon filled with her stuffed toys and saying that if she had lived then she would have led her people to freedom, too. For other books by Medearis, see *This Land Is Our Land* (1994), nos. 216, 217, and 218 (see preceding entry, no. 78, for titles).

80 Medearis, Angela Shelf, *Poppa's New Pants*, illus. John Ward, Holiday House, 1995 (hardcover), ISBN 0–8234–1155–9, unp. Ages 4–8, grades PS–3.

Humorous family picture-story book of African Americans. While Poppa and George are shopping in the local store, Poppa spies just the pants—gray with red plaid—he longs for. They are much too long, even for tall Poppa, but he is sure than one of the visiting women relatives in the household can shorten them in time for him to wear them to church the next morning. During the night, which George spends on the kitchen floor because all the beds are taken up by visitors, he observes three ghosts come one after another and shorten the pants. The next morning, Poppa's pants are much too short, good only for everyday, sporting wear, so he passes them along to George. The fun of the text is caught and extended by full-color, representational paintings. They depict the family so realistically that the people almost take life and move off the page. A later adventure of George and Poppa and their female relatives is *Poppa's Itchy Christmas* (1998), in which gifts that George does not really like, with Poppa's help, turn out to be just the ones he needs to make the Christmas special. The illustrations, also by Ward, bring situations and people to life and make the humor palpable. For other books by Medearis see *This Land Is Our Land* (1994), nos. 216, 217, and 218 (see entry 78 for titles).

81   Meyer, Carolyn, *Jubilee Journey*, Gulliver/Harcourt, 1997 (hardcover), ISBN 0–15–201377–6, $12.00, 271 pp; (paper), ISBN 0–15–201591–4, $6.00, 256 pp. Ages 10–14, grades 5–9.

Sequel to *White Lilacs* (1993). This novel picks up the story of Freedomtown in Dillon, Texas, when Rose Lee Jefferson is eighty-seven and has lived for seventy-five years in the Flats, as that section was called when all the African Americans were forcibly moved there to make room for a city park. Most of the narration is in first-person chapters by Emily Rose Chartier, thirteen, her great-granddaughter. Interspersed are chapters in third person from the point of view of Mother Rose, as the old woman is now known to most of the town. Emily Rose, her mother, Susan, and her two brothers, handsome black Steven, seventeen, and white, French-looking Robby, about eleven, have come from their Connecticut home at Mother Rose's invitation for the Juneteenth celebration of the seventy-fifth anniversary of the move from Freedomtown. The visit reawakens and ultimately lays to rest traumatic childhood memories for Susan and opens the eyes of the three youngsters, who have been raised as "doubles, au lait," half black, half white, of French-Canadian ancestry, unaware of the strong racial biases of the South. Mother Rose lives with her undertaker cousin, Uncle James Prince, in quarters attached to his funeral home. The occasion is complicated by the death of Cornelius Overton, a man who courted Mother Rose when she was a girl and whom she despises as an Uncle Tom, and by the arrest and police beating of Steven by a redneck sheriff, essentially for dating a wealthy white girl. After the celebration, which is highlighted by the first display of the many brilliant paintings of Freedomtown and its people by Mother Rose, Emily Rose decides to spend the rest of the summer in Dillon, getting to really know that side of her heritage. Although the novel can stand alone, much of its impact comes from the earlier book, where the threats to the African-American community were more menacing and their recourses more limited. For books by Meyer, see *This Land Is Our Land* (1994), no. 86, *Danny's Tapes*, no. 87, *White Lilacs*, and no. 447, *Where the Broken Heart Still Beats*.

82   Miller, William, *Bus Ride*, illus. John Ward, Lee & Low, 1998 (hardcover), ISBN 1–880000–60–1, $15.95, unp. Ages 4–8, grades PS–3.

Picture-story book of a little girl who emulates Rosa Parks by refusing to sit in the back of a bus. Sara rides the bus daily with her mother, always sitting in the back as required by law and tradition. One day, after her mother gets off, leaving her to ride on to school, Sara wonders what is so special about the seats in front and decides to find out. Her action gets her removed from the bus and taken to the police station, where her mother is called to retrieve her. In the meantime, a reporter takes her picture, and the next day her story makes head-lines. As she and her mother walk rather than board the bus, many other African Americans follow their example. Soon the rule is changed, and they can ride wherever they wish. The dramatic story of the real bus boycott is simplified and watered down with a child protester, losing its historic authenticity. Stubborn Sara has some character in her face, but all the other African Americans are idealized and generic.

83 Mitchell, Margaree King, *Granddaddy's Gift*, illus. Larry Johnson, BridgeWater, 1997 (hardcover), ISBN 0–8167–4010–0. $14.95, unp.; Troll, 1998 (paper), ISBN 0–8167–4011–9, $5.95. Ages 5–10, grades K–5.

Realistic picture-story book set in pre-integrated Mississippi. African-American Little Joe tells about an incident that happened when she was eight years old. She enjoys more than anything else accompanying Granddaddy as he does his farm work. Although Granddaddy only finished the eighth grade, he worked hard and saved his money to buy the farm, and he loves to read to his grandchildren. The books he reads are better than the tattered ones the children have in school, which are hand-downs from the white children's schools. When Little Joe skips school, because she does not see why she should continue to attend, Granddaddy drives her past a cottonfield of workers, some of them Little Joe's age, and that night to a meeting at the church. When a lawyer asks for volunteers to register to vote, Granddaddy raises his hand, the only one to do so because everyone else is afraid. The next day he is told by the white man in the Court House that he must pass a test on the Constitution before he can be registered. The lawyer helps Granddaddy study and accompanies him to take the test. He passes the test, but that night the church is burned down. The incident, however, spurs other African Americans to register. Little Joe realizes that her grandfather has given her a great gift, not just the right to vote without harassment, but also the example of standing up for her rights and of making her voice heard. The story is told in straightforward language without flourishes. Magnificent realistic, deep-toned paintings picture incidents, extend the plot, and establish the reality of events. More memorable than the text, they show the children as goodlooking and well cared for, and Granddaddy as physically strong but gentle, hardworking, and determined, clearly a force for good among his family and friends. Earlier, Mitchell published another picture-story book, no. 90, *Uncle Jed's Barber Shop* described in *This Land Is Our Land* (1994).

84 Mosley, Walter, *Black Betty*, Norton, 1994 (hardcover), ISBN 0–393–03644–8, $19.95, 255 pp.; Pocket, 1995 (paper), ISBN 0–671–88427–1, $6.50. Ages 15 up, grades 10 up.

Fourth in a series of mysteries starring Easy (Ezekiel) Rawlings, an African-American tough, unlicensed private investigator, who is often called upon by both blacks and whites, and sometimes even the police, to hunt through sleazy bars, dangerous alleys, and ratty tenements of Los Angeles where they dare not go themselves. *Black Betty* is set in the early 1960s and involves the search for a woman Easy knew as a prostitute when he was a child in Houston, who has since worked for a wealthy family in southern California. As in his other novels, there are corrupt and brutal cops, murders, betrayals, and tender scenes, all wound into an intricate plot. Once again he must care for the two children he has rescued and unofficially adopted, for whom he would willingly kill if necessary—Jesus, a Mexican boy sold as an infant into prostitution, and little Feather, whose white grandfather murdered her mother for bearing a black child. He must also cope with his crazy friend, Mouse (Raymond) Alexander, newly out of prison and determined to kill whoever sent him there. The world has changed in some ways since his earlier mysteries, *Devil in a Blue Dress* (1990), set just after World War II, *A Red Death* (1991), set in 1953, and *White Butterfly* (1992), set a few years later, reflecting the beginnings of the black pride and Civil Rights Movements, but Easy's streets are no less racist and violent. A more recent prequel, *Gone Fishing* (1997), deals with Easy's life in Texas and Louisiana as a very young man, before he came to California. These books give exciting and graphic pictures of the dangerous life of a black man, by an African-American writer.

85 Mowry, Jess, *Babylon Boyz*, illus. Eric Kinyer, Simon & Schuster, 1997 (hardcover), ISBN 0–689–80839–9, $16.00, 188 pp.; Aladdin, 1999 (paper), ISBN 0–689–82592–7, $8.00. Ages 12 up, grades 7 up.

Novel of African-American teenaged boy friendships, set in the tough wharf neighborhoods of the San Francisco Bay area. Dante, thirteen, a motherless Rastafarian, has a congenital heart problem because his mother was addicted to crack cocaine. His two close friends also have problems. Wyatt Brown is obese; Pook, a handsome, athletic boy who hopes to become a doctor, is gay. The three befriend a homeless youngster named Radgi, who is an Australian aboriginal, and, later, a classmate named Jinx, an addict now in rehab. When Dante and Pook see a youthful drug dealer, Air Touch, throw a bundle from his car before being chased down by police, they retrieve the package, hoping it is money that will pay for Dante's needed operation and Pook's education. Their discovery that it is pure cocaine, worth a great deal on the street, poses a dilemma for them. Wyatt, whose strong mother runs a restaurant for dockworkers and truck drivers, has the most stable background and least direct need. He points out that drugs are ruining his community and favors flushing the content of the package down the toilet. Dante wants to try to sell the dope. Pook is torn between Wyatt's logic and Dante's need. In the end, Dante is lucky to escape with his life, but in the ensuing events he discovers that Radgi is actually a pregnant girl and finds in her the love he needs to continue, while Pook develops a reciprocated love for Jinx. The novel's strength is in its convincing, earthy dialogue and street scenes. Its weakness lies in the overdrawn pictures of insensitive rehabilitation workers, police, and school personnel and in belaboring the moral decency of the oddly assorted boys. For earlier writings by Mowry, see *This Land Is Our Land* (1994), no. 96, *Way Past Cool.*

86 Myers, Walter Dean, *The Glory Field*, Scholastic, 1994 (hardcover), ISBN 0–590–45897–3, $14.95, 375 pp. Ages 12 up, grades 7 up.

Historical novel in six parts telling the story of an African-American family with the focus on the land they work and later own on Curry Island, near Johnson City, South Carolina. Early sections are set in Africa, on a Curry Island plantation during the first days of the Civil War, and on the island in 1900, when one young man earns the money for taxes by a daring rescue of the blind son of a wealthy white man, who tries to cheat him out of the promised reward. One is set in Chicago in the 1930s, when his daughter, longing to go to college, is unable to borrow the necessary money but rallies to start a hair-styling business. Another is set during the Civil Rights protests in the early 1960s, and the last is again on Curry Island, where the family is assembling to bring in the last crop before turning it into a resort, financed by the hair stylist who has become highly successful. In this last segment, a young musician in New York is designated to find and bring his cousin, who is addicted to crack cocaine, to the gathering, and after a terrible journey, watches the family's concern and help for the cousin and comes to understand their closeness. Although events, especially in the early segments, are predictable, many strong details give a picture of life for African Americans in both the South and the northern cities. Earlier books by Myers are described in *This Land Is Our Land* (1994), no. 97, *Crystal*, no. 98, *Fallen Angels*, no. 99, *The Mouse Rap*, no. 100, *The Righteous Revenge of Artemis Bonner*, no. 101, *Scorpions*, no. 102, *Somewhere in the Darkness*, and no. 103, *Sweet Illusions* (all fiction).

87 Myers, Walter Dean, *Slam!*, Scholastic, 1996 (hardcover), ISBN 0–590–48667–5, $15.95, 266 pp.; (paper), ISBN 0–590–48668–3, $4.99, 272 pp. Ages 12 up, grades 7 up.

Sports novel set in Harlem in the 1990s, following Slam, a basketball player, through his junior year in a mostly white school to which he has transferred, leaving behind his friends, including his long-time buddy, Ice. The new school poses many problems: Slam is behind most of the other students academically, his teachers seem to scorn him, the coach will not put him in as a starter, and most of the other team members are hostile. All this is exacerbated by Slam's truculent attitude. In a crucial game against his old school, Slam is pitted against Ice, and, largely because of his play, his team wins. Ice invites him to a party, which sours when Slam realizes that his old friend is dealing drugs. A dying grandmother and other family problems add to his worries. Gradually, however, he learns to deal with his new life and in the end seems destined to win a basketball scholarship to college. The strongest element in the novel is the detailed description of several basketball games, revealing Slam's skill and love for the sport. Most of the cliches of inner-city stories are avoided. Earlier books by Myers are described in *This Land Is Our Land* (1994), nos. 97, 98, 99, 100, 101, 102, and 103 (all fiction) (see preceding entry, no. 86, for titles).

88 Myers, Walter Dean, *Smiffy Blue, Ace Crime Detective: The Case of the Missing Ruby and Other Stories*, illus. David J. A. Sims, Scholastic, 1996 (hardcover), ISBN 0–590–67665–2, $14.95, 75 pp. Ages 8–11, grades 3–6.

Four deliberately silly stories, in which the supposedly great and brilliant detective blunders about in a wild goose chase, eventually solving the crime more by accident than acumen. In each story, the obvious solution is given away in the illustrations, so that any observant reader can reach the correct conclusion before Detective Smiffy Blue and his sidekick, Jeremy Joe, do. Working with them is Smiffy's brave and trusty dog, Dog. The stories are printed in large, well-leaded type to make easy reading for children ready for their first chapter books. The age levels suggested by the publisher may be a little high; most eleven year olds would find them too elementary, though the slapstick humor might attract some fifth and sixth graders. Earlier books by Myers are described in *This Land Is Our Land* (1994), nos. 97, 98, 99, 100, 101, 102, and 103 (all fiction) (see entry no. 86 for titles).

89 Nolen, Jerdine, *Harvey Potter's Balloon Farm*, illus. Mark Buehner, Lothrop, 1994 (hardcover), ISBN 0–688–07887–7, $15.00, unp.; Mulberry, 1998 (paper), ISBN 0–688–15845–5, $4.95. Ages 4–10, grades PS–5.

Exuberant, highly colorful tall tale in picture-story form, set in the United States rural south "in the summer of '59." The narrator, a pigtailed African-American girl, learns the secret of eccentric farmer Harvey Potter's ability to grow balloons on the corn stalks on his farm—balloons of all colors—"Pleasin' Purple, Orange-Ray Sun, Yellin' Yellow . . . Rip-TwoShot Red, and Jelly-Bean Black, Bloomin' Blue, and Grassy Green"—and in all shapes and sizes, from animals to clowns and even monsters. Everyone in the area is proud of Harvey's success, except for crotchety old Wheezle Mayfield, who calls the Government. The Government men investigate, find nothing wrong, and give Harvey the right to grow balloons. Because she is "a-hankering to know" how he does it, the girl climbs the big old sycamore outside Harvey's house one night and in the moonlight is witness to an amazing sight involving Harvey's "conjure stick." The next day, the girl returns to Harvey's farm to see if anything has happened. When he sees her inspecting the tiny, sprouting balloons, Harvey tells her she can have all the plants she wants. She selects three, which form the basis of her own burgeoning farm in years to come. The bold realism of the full-page, calendar-art pictures suspends the reader's disbelief, as do the narrator's straight-forward tone and matter-of-fact use of detail. Some illustrations are close-ups, others panoramic and aerial views of the region and Harvey's farm, with its thousands of brilliant, glowing balloons. Small details add to the fun: the animals real and fantastic hidden amid the balloons or in the clouds, among them a rhinoceros, a dinosaur, rabbits, and chickens and, at the end, the girl being carried off in a balloon basket, powered by one of Harvey's balloons. Some touches will probably delight the adult reader more than the child, for example, the four Government inspectors, shrouded in white hoods, bulky uniforms, and oversized gloves, seriously examining a balloon, one of them about to prick an orange clown-balloon to see if it pops.

90 Oppenheim, Shulamith Levey, *Fireflies for Nathan*, illus. John Ward, Tambourine, 1994 (hardcover), ISBN 0–688–12147–0, $15.00, unp.; Puffin, 1996 (paper), ISBN 0–140–55782–2, $4.99, unp. Ages 3–8, grades PS–3.

Contemporary picture-story book, in which African-American Nathan, six, visits his father's mother and father in their modest countryside home, catches fireflies with them in early evening, and puts the insects in the very same jar that his father used when he was little. Feeling satisfied after a pleasant evening, loved, and wanted, he goes to bed with the jar glowing on his pillow, asking his grandparents to let the fireflies out while he is sleeping, just as his father did. The text of this warm, loving family story is aptly extended by framed-with-white, full-page, representational acrylics. They depict the country setting, portray interiors, and characterize the principals as affectionate, caring people. Handsome little Nathan wears the only bright colors, which stand out in the mist as the sun sets, and the grandparents are shown as goodhearted, solid citizens, willing and happy to spend time with this special grandson.

91 Patchett, Ann, *Taft*, Houghton, 1994 (hardcover), ISBN 0–395–69461–2. $21.95, 305 pp.; Ivy, 1995 (paper), ISBN 0–8041–1388–2, $5.99. Ages 15 up, grades 10 up.

Moving novel of an African-American father's love for his nine-year-old son and his involvement with a young white girl, a waitress in the Memphis bar he manages, and her drug-dealing brother. A devoted father, John Nickel has suf-fered when Marion Woodmoore, the boy's mother whom he did not marry when he had a chance and who now refuses to marry him, took little Franklin out of his reach to Miami. He has sent Marion to nursing school, supported Franklin, and given up his career as a drummer to please her, to no avail. When Fae Taft, seventeen, applies for work, John doubts that she is the twenty she claims, but something in her vulnerable, East Tennessee mountain manner draws him to her. Soon he is embroiled in her difficulties, as she lives since the death of her father with an aunt and uncle she despises, tries to cope with her slightly younger brother, Carl, who is on drugs, and falls deeply if naively in love with John. Through it all, John imagines the life of Fae's father, Taft, with whom he identifies in long, realistic passages. Written with skill, the picture of a decent, caring man, trying to help without getting overwhelmed by the problems of Fae and her brother, is convincing and compelling, as is his strong commitment to his son.

92   Pate, Alexs D., *Losing Absalom*, Coffee House, 1994 (hardcover), ISBN 1–56689–017–9. $19.95, 204 pp.; Berkley, 1995 (paper), ISBN 0–4251–5013–5, $7.50. Ages 15 up, grades 10 up.

Novel of the last day in the life of Absalom Goodman, hard-working husband and father, respected African-American homeowner on deteriorating Whither Street in North Philadelphia. As he lies dying of cancer, Absalom's spirit roams in both time and place, to the North Carolina of his boyhood, around the hospital, to his years of working as a deliverer of bakery goods, to his wife, Gwen, whose strength keeps him going, to his son, Sonny, now working for a corporation in Minneapolis, and to his daughter, Rainy, who is living with a drug dealer in the old Whither Street house. Overwritten and prone to pretentious passages, the novel still gives a good picture of the disintegrating black community and family, as violence takes over the neighborhood and as Absalom's children, for whom he worked so hard, either flee to the white world or succumb to the fast-buck culture of the drug scene.

93   Paterson, Katherine, *Jip His Story*, Lodestar/Dutton, 1996 (hardcover), ISBN 0–525–67543–4, $14.99, 209 pp.; Puffin, 1998 (paper), ISBN 0–1403–8674–2, $4.99. Ages 10–14, grades 5–9.

Historical novel set just before the Civil War. Jip, a foundling about eleven years old, raised on a Vermont poor farm, discovers he is not the gypsy he has been led to believe but a fugitive slave being hunted by the white master who fathered him. Ironically, it is his resemblance to this man, recognized by a slave catcher passing through the neighborhood, that puts him in jeopardy. Although life at the poor farm, where he has gradually assumed all the work with the help of a retarded inmate and a mentally ill man, is hard and he is not appreciated by the drunken manager and his greedy wife, Jip has been happy and is especially pleased when the new teacher encourages him and introduces him to a local young Quaker man. When the slave catcher returns with the owner, Jip flees to the Quaker farm. Hunted down, he is locked in jail where the teacher proposes she will say she is his mother while the young Quaker volunteers to claim to be the father. Realizing that this will ruin the reputations of both of them, Jip escapes and makes his way to Canada. The irony of a father attempting to find his son so that he can enslave him drives the story, but also sweet-natured Jip and other characters are well drawn, and the Vermont landscape is beautifully evoked. For a retelling by Paterson from oral tradition, see *This Land Is Our Land* (1994), no. 313, *The Tale of the Mandarin Ducks*.

94 Pinkney, Andrea Davis, *Bill Pickett: Rodeo-Ridin' Cowboy*, illus. Brian Pinkney, Harcourt, 1996 (hardcover), ISBN 0–15–200100–X, $16.00, unp. Ages 5 up, grades K up.

Biographical fiction picture-story book of one of the greatest of all African-American cowboys. Born in Texas in 1860 the son of a farmer and former slave, Bill Pickett early develops a love of the out-of-doors and the cowboy life. While still a boy, he learns the peculiar hold, biting and hanging onto the upper lip of a steer, that later enables him to become the greatest of all the steer wrestlers, or bulldoggers. His fearless riding and feats at rodeos earn him recognition throughout the West and a coveted place in the largest of all the shows, the 101 Ranch Wild West Show, with which as the show's star he tours the United States, Canada, Mexico, South America, and England. In later life, he settles on the 101 Ranch with his family. He dies in 1932, famous to the end as the Dusky Demon. The text can stand by itself. Powerful scratchboards in mostly dark tones, some doublespread, some full page, some partial page, picture scenes and establish Bill as muscular and dignified, daring but skillful. Their static nature emphasizes the enduringness of his legend. One picture is especially striking; it stretches across two pages, isolating the five lines of text at upper left, and shows a red-shirted youth leaping from his black, racing horse to grasp the horns of an equally hard racing steer. Unlike most of the pictures, this one exudes action and speed. The intensity of the expression upon Bill's face and in his eyes reflects the danger of his feat and clutches the viewer's emotions. Information about black cowboys and a short list of references concludes the book. Another book by Andrea Pinkney appears in *This Land Is Our Land* (1994), no. 111, *Seven Candles for Kwanzaa*.

95 Pinkney, Andrea Davis, *Hold Fast to Dreams*, Morrow, 1995 (hardcover), ISBN 0–688–12832–7, $15.00, 112 pp. Ages 10–15, grades 5–10.

Novel of home and school life set in Wexford, Connecticut, in the 1980s, dealing with the problems of a professional African-American family when they move into an all-white, upper-middle-class community. The book pairs with the view of modern African-American life presented in *Raven in a Dove House*, no. 96, about the problems of modern blacks in a black community. Bennett Willis, now the vice president of a major corporation, and his wife move their family of two daughters, narrator Deirdre, twelve, and her younger sister, Lindsay, so that, as their mother explains, their daughters can have a better life than their parents had. All experience homesickness for their cramped but companionable neighborhood in Baltimore and meet racial prejudice in various forms. Bennett is especially hurt when he is "hassled" by a security guard at his corporate headquarters. In addition, Mother gave up her second-grade teaching position in the move, and the two girls feel lonely, unwanted, and put down. After an elderly English teacher validates Deirdre's proud support of Langston Hughes's work, an anonymous note warns her to stay away from the "gross" teacher. Lindsay, who is great at lacrosse, the local sport of choice, is ostracized rather than acclaimed. A locker room conversation after Deirdre fails to make the lacrosse team results in a friendship of sorts with the writer of the note, a white girl named Web. Web admires Dee's ability with the camera and suggests that Dee enter the June Founders Day Assembly contest at school. While Lindsay talks up to the girls in her school, demanding respect, Dee earns hers by taking second place with a small but well-executed photographic exhibit, which she presents to the school along with recitations of two Hughes poems, one of which is the poem of the book title. Interesting characters, restrained emotion, skillful dialogue, an appealing style, and a clear but never overdone presentation of the problem combine for a story that transcends race and examines what it means to be an outsider in a closed society. Another book by Andrea Pinkney appears in *This Land Is Our Land* (1994), no. 111, *Seven Candles for Kwanzaa.*

96 Pinkney, Andrea Davis, *Raven in a Dove House*, Gulliver, 1998 (hardcover), ISBN 0–15–201461–6, $16.00, 208 pp. Ages 10–15, grades 5–10.

Contemporary realistic novel of family life and a girl's growing up set in sleepy, economically depressed Modine, New York, where a small group of freed blacks settled after the American Civil War. Pretty, butterscotch-brown Nell Grady, twelve, daughter of successful New York City lawyer, Wes Grady, arrives for her yearly August visit with her religious, overprotective Great-Aunt Ursa. Soon several problems confront her: the estrangement between Ursa and Wes, which arose when Wes left for the city; her intense dislike for her widower father's girlfriend, Brenda; her infatuation with Slade Montgomery, fourteen, a handsome, "boppin'," sweet-talking youth, the best friend of Foley, fourteen, who is her father's cousin and Ursa's only child; and the two boys' desire to leave Modine for New York City. Matters become critical after the two boys give Foley's Raven .25 gun to Nell for safekeeping, one of two weapons that Slade purchased from a local ring. Guiltily, she hides the gun in her dollhouse, Dove Haven, where it stays until after Slade is found, shot dead by the railroad tracks, and Foley takes it and runs away. The family and town are devastated by these events, which resolve themselves at the time of the celebration of the town's founding, when Wes, having broken up with Brenda, brings repentant Foley back from New York and gives moral support to brokenhearted Ursa, and local police are on the way to apprehending the gun-selling ring. Events proceed much as expected, and most aspects for anticipating the conclusion lie on the surface. Nell's attraction to Slade is natural and understandable, and people of Ursa's generation are warm, wholesome, likable figures. While some dialogue seems inept, with the author's voice seemingly superimposed upon those of the speakers, the book's strength lies in its clear, vivid depiction of the close family and community. The symbolism of the title is obvious. For another novel by Andrea Pinkney see *This Land Is Our Land* (1994), no. 111, *Seven Candles for Kwanzaa.*

97 Pinkney, Andrea Davis, *Solo Girl*, illus. Nneka Bennett, Hyperion, 1997 (hardcover), ISBN 0–7868–2265–1, $14.40, 51 pp.; (paper), ISBN 0–7868–1216–8, $3.95. Ages 7–9, grades 2–4.

Short, realistic, contemporary novel of neighborhood and family life, set in an urban community. The newest girl in the area, second-grader Cass yearns to jump double Dutch (two ropes spinning at the same time) like the girls over on Haskins Row, who call themselves the Fast Feet Four. Her twin brothers, Jackson and Bud, say that she just needs a beat and make up a catchy rhyme for her that soon keeps her feet in line for one rope, but while she does well as Solo Girl, she cannot manage two ropes. Then Cass, who Ma Lettie says has been "blessed with the numbers gift," discovers that Pearl, one of the Four, is having trouble with her summer math homework. Cass helps Pearl with math, and in return Pearl helps Cass learn to double Dutch. Cass practices and becomes so good that the Fast Feet Four invite her to join them. The group becomes known as the Fast Feet Five, and Jackson and Bud compose a jump rhyme especially for them. Although the plot holds no surprises, the dialogue is accurate, the girls' hopes and wishes are typical and appealing, the brothers are pleasingly helpful, supportive, and not domineering, the fast pace holds the attention all the way, and the whole book (one in the set called Hyperion Chapters) is the kind of story that just-reading girls find enjoyable. The text is not race or ethnic specific, but the illustrations show Cass and her brothers and most of the other children as African Americans. Another book by Andrea Pinkney appears in *This Land Is Our Land* (1994), no. 111, *Seven Candles for Kwanzaa*.

98 Pinkney, Brian, *The Adventures of Sparrowboy*, illus. Brian Pinkney, Simon & Schuster, 1997 (hardcover), ISBN 0–689–81071–7, $16.00, 40 pp. Ages 4–9, grades PS–4.

Comic book–like adventure story of Henry, an African-American newspaper boy who discovers that, like his hero, Falconman, he can fly after an encounter with a bird. He swoops through the neighborhood righting wrongs, giving bullies their comeuppance, and saving the friendly sparrow from a cat, before returning to his bicycle and the rest of his paper route. A number of the pages are sectioned off into small squares like a newspaper comic page, and the language is straight from the funnies: "Zap!," "Whoosh!," "Rrrrrrp!," "Sit, doggie," as he captures and ties up Wolf, the vicious German shepherd; "I don't get it," when the sparrow seems unable to fly; and smart rejoinders to the bad guys' taunts. The illustrations are in bold, heavily outlined scratchboard, gouache, and transparent dyes. This is a fantasy sure to appeal to youngsters weaned on popular culture.

99 Pinkney, Brian, *JoJo's Flying Side Kick*, illus. Brian Pinkney, Simon & Schuster, 1995 (hardcover), ISBN 0–689–80283–8, $15.00, 32 pp.: Aladdin, 1998 (paper), ISBN 0–689–82192–1, $5.99. Ages 5–8, grades K–3.

Picture-story book about a little girl overcoming her fears and winning her yellow belt in karate. Master Kim, the Tae Kwon Do insructor, tells JoJo that tomorrow will be her test for promotion, for which she will have to break a board with a flying side kick. She begins to worry. Grandaddy tells her that before his boxing matches, he used to do a little shuffle step to quell his jitters. Her friend P. J. says she must yell louder as she kicks. Mother says she should visualize a perfect side kick. JoJo knows that what she really fears is the creepy bandit tree in her front yard that seems to move back and forth across her window, trying to climb in. The next day she shuffles her feet, visualizes the bandit tree, and side kicks with all her might, screaming as she cracks a board. That evening, for the first time, she confidently tries the swing in the bandit tree. The very simple story is greatly enhanced by richly colored, double-page illustrations, in a scratchboard technique, with text superimposed on the pictures. Although the text is not ethnic specific, Master Kim has Oriental features, and all the other characters are African Americans.

100   Pinkney, Brian, and Andrea Pinkney, *I Smell Honey*, Harcourt, 1997 (board book), ISBN 0–15–100640–0, $4.95, unp. Ages 6 mo.–3, grades PS.

Very simple board book of a young African-American girl helping her mother cook dinner. The text is minimal: "I smell honey in a sweet potato pie. Hear catfish cracklin' as they fry," takes up the first four pages. The meal is of ethnic food: catfish, red beans, collard greens, and pie. The happy-faced family gathers to eat, three adults, the narrator, and a sibling in a high chair. Illustrations are simple, in broad, flat colors enclosed in heavy black lines with each two-page spread surrounded by another black line and a half-inch-wide white border. The book is six and a half inches square and appears solidly bound, a must for this age group. Others in the series (all 1997) include *Watch Me Dance, Shake Shake Shake*, about a shekere, an African percussion instrument, and *Pretty Brown Face*, which shows a father and son admiring their visages and ends in a reflective sheet that acts as a mirror.

101   Pinkney, Gloria Jean, *The Sunday Outing*, illus. Jerry Pinkney, Dial, 1994 (hardcover), ISBN 0–8037–1198–0, $14.99, unp. Ages 4–10, grades PS–5.

Realistic picture-story book about an African-American family, companion to *Back Home* (1992), set probably in the 1930s. Young Ernestine loves taking the trolley to North Philadelphia with her great-aunt Odessa on summer Sunday afternoons to see the trains going south. She loves the stories Odessa tells about their family in North Carolina and imagines herself riding the train to Lumberton, the town where she was born. One Sunday, when she tells Odessa that her parents have told her that they cannot afford a ticket because they are saving for a house, Odessa suggests that she give up something to save her parents money. Later, when she sees her mother about to make her new clothes for school, she insists she does not need new ones. Her parents give up getting some new things, too, and a couple of days later she is on the train to North Carolina and her relatives. The indistinct, impressionistic watercolors are more memorable than the pleasant, undistinguished text. They show Ernestine as a pinafore-clad, earnest child, Odessa as a large, comfortable, understanding woman, the parents as nice-looking, caring people, and Ernestine's classmates as skeptical of her hoped-for trip. Details of dress, home furnishings, and trains establish the period, and the importance of the railroad to Ernestine is emphasized by the appearance of a train in some form on almost every page. *Back Home* is described in *This Land Is Our Land* (1994), no. 112.

102 Polacco, Patricia, *Pink and Say*, illus. Patricia Polacco, Philomel, 1994 (hardcover), ISBN 0–399–22671–0, $15.95, unp. Ages 4–9, grades PS–4.

Historical novel in picture-book form, telling of the friendship between two young Union soldiers, a white farm boy from Ohio and an ex-slave from Georgia, during the Civil War. Sheldon "Say" Russell Curtis, fifteen, has been wounded while running from battle and left for dead until, two days later, he is found and rescued by Pinkus Ayles, who has become separated from his outfit. Pink takes Say to the cabin of his mother, Moe Moe Bay, who has managed to stay on by scrounging from the remains of the burned big house and the nearby woods. She nurses Say back to health and is heartbroken when Pink quietly insists that they must try to return to the Union army. Before they can get away, she is shot by marauders while the boys hide in the root-cellar. As they try to find Pink's outfit, they are captured by Confederate soldiers and taken to Andersonville. Pink is hanged, but Say survives illness and near starvation to tell the story to his daughter, who passes it on to the family. In a nice reversal of the Civil War story, the African-American boy is the leader, better educated and more knowledgeable about the principles of the war. Oversized and highly illustrated, the book is better developed and has more text than most picture books. For two other picture-story books written and illustrated by Polacco, see *This Land Is Our Land* (1994), no. 113, *Chicken Sunday*, and no. 455, *Boat Ride with Lillian Two Blossom*.

103 Porte, Barbara Ann, *Chickens! Chickens!*, illus. Greg Henry, Orchard, 1995 (hardcover), ISBN 0–531–06877–3, $14.95, unp. Ages 4–8, grades PS–3.

Picture-story book about a man who lives on a chicken farm and paints chickens. When he goes to the city, he continues to paint chickens, only now he puts them in city settings—on elevators, driving cabs, riding buses. In an art store he meets a woman, and they fall in love. They marry, have children, and move back to the country to run a chicken farm, and he continues to paint chickens. His wife traces his chicken pictures onto pillow cases, stuffs them with feathers and down, and puts up a sign announcing pictures and pillows for sale, country style. She invites all her friends in the city to come to the grand opening. They all exclaim at the "folk art" and buy paintings and pillows. Although the text says nothing about the ethnicity of the characters, the brightly colored illustrations, painted, a note says, with oil-based house paint, show all the people as African Americans and have the naive charm and exuberance of the best folk art. Porte is also the author of no. 114, *I Only Made Up the Roses* (novel), and no. 260, *Leave That Cricket Be, Alan Lee* (picture-story book), in *This Land Is Our Land* (1994).

104 Porte, Barbara Ann, *Something Terrible Happened*, Orchard, 1994 (hardcover), ISBN 0–531–06869–2, $16.95, 214 pp.; Troll, 1996 (paper), ISBN 0–816–73868–8, $4.50. Ages 12–15, grades 7–10.

Novel of the child of an interracial family, her mother an African American of West Indian heritage, her father a white man who died when she was four of a drug overdose. After her mother becomes ill from AIDS, Gillian Hardwick, ten, is sent from New York to live with her father's older brother, Uncle Henry, in Oak Ridge, Tennessee. He and his wife, Aunt Corinne, are kind and try to be helpful, but the relationship is strained except for their little daughter, DeeDee, who adores Gillian. After her mother's death, Gillian confidently plans to stay in New York, but her grandmother refuses to let her, and she returns unhappily to Tennessee. Gradually, she adjusts to her new life. A group of African-American young people from nearby Scarboro, where all the non-white workers at Oak Ridge traditionally have lived, include her in some of their activities, and she does well in school and is chosen for a special program at Oak Ridge National Laboratory with a scientist studying fish. A visit from Cousin Antoine, adopted son of Aunt Corinne's sister, helps her gain perspective and understand Uncle Henry better, since Antoine is of Filipino heritage and can also provide some information about her uncle's traumatic childhood. When her grandmother is offered a job at the University of Tennessee, Gillian realizes that, although it will be nice to be within easy visiting distance, she really wants to stay in Oak Ridge. The novel has a strangely complex structure, being told partly through narration by a friend of Gillian's grandmother, a woman who never appears as a character, and partly through letters to her from Gillian. The action is constantly interrupted by stories told to or by Gillian, some fact, some folklore, connected tangentially with the main plot. Although Gillian's mixed heritage is central to her feeling of alienation, its problems are not explored at length. Other books by Porte include, in *This Land Is Our Land* (1994), no. 114, *I Only Made Up the Roses*, a novel, and no. 260, *Leave That Cricket Be, Alan Lee*, a picture-story book.

105 Poydar, Nancy, *Busy Bea*, illus. Nancy Poydar, McElderry, 1994 (hardcover), ISBN 0–689–50592–2, $14.95, unp. Ages 4–8, grades PS–3.

With minimal text, a picture-story about a little African-American girl who keeps losing her possessions because she is so active and too busy to remember them. She loses her lunch box, her jacket, her raincoat, her father's umbrella, her new sweater, and the note from her mother to the teacher. On the other hand, she is always good at finding things for her grandmother, like her glasses and her knitting basket. Her teacher points out the lost-and-found, and Bea retrieves all her lost things. The illustrations are bright and lively, slightly cartoonish.

106 Reeder, Carolyn, *Across the Lines*, Atheneum, 1997 (hardcover), ISBN 689–81133–0, $16.00, 220 pp.; Camelot, 1998 (paper), ISBN 0–380–73073–1, $4.50, 224 pp. Ages 8–12, grades 3–7.

Historical novel of the last year of the Civil War, set in and near Petersburg, Virginia, a rail hub south of Richmond, told alternately from the points of view of two twelve-year-old boys, Edward, son of a plantation owner, and Simon, his companion and slave. When the boys watch from a tree as the Yankee troops swarm onto their landing, both are astonished to see that many of the soldiers are black. While the family packs frantically to go to relatives in Petersburg, Simon hides out, realizing for the first time that he is free to go or stay as he pleases. Edward is crushed to think that the boy he considered his friend would desert him, but the Union officer has given them only an hour to get out. Simon retrieves the field glasses that Edward left in the tree and hires himself out to various Yankees, finding that he is working harder and with less security than when he was a slave. At the home of his Aunt Charlotte in Petersburg, Edward and his family suffer increasing shortages of food and fuel. Except for one daring trip behind enemy lines to get quinine for his older brother, Edward spends the rest of the war in Petersburg, mostly lonely and worried about his father, his cousin, and his uncle, who are all serving the Confederacy. At one point Simon comes upon his brother Ambrose, now a Union soldier, and spends some time with him until Ambrose is killed. Working as a water boy, he is taken in by Corporal Gabriel Jackson, a free black from Philadelphia, who offers to take him home to his family if they come out of the war alive. Eventually, Gabriel is wounded and loses an arm, but at last Petersburg is taken and a week later the war ends. Edward, his father and cousin dead, returns with his family to almost ruined Riverview, where Simon secretly brings them supplies from the Yankee field kitchen and, just before he heads north with Gabriel, leaves the field glasses for Edward. In a story rich with detail and character, the novel gives a good picture of the military blunders, the squalor, the suffering, and the bravery on both sides and of the difficulties the newly freed African Americans have to achieve decent treatment in either camp.

107 Rinaldi, Ann, *Cast Two Shadows: The American Revolution in the South*, Gulliver, 1998 (hardcover), ISBN 0–15–200881–0, $16.00, 281 pp. Ages 12 up, grades 7 up.

Historical novel of two months in the American Revolution during the British occupation near Camden, South Carolina. The summer of 1780 is filled with distressing events for Caroline Whitaker, fourteen, daughter of a wealthy Patriot landowner and businessman. Caroline watches helplessly as British soldiers hang her dear friend, Kit Gales. Then British Colonel Rawdon commandeers her family's plantation for his headquarters; her father is imprisoned for his anti-Tory leanings; her Loyalist brother, Johnny, runs away from the British army after he is whipped by the British for refusing to give up his blooded horse to a British officer; her sister, Georgia Ann, becomes Rawdon's sweetheart; and her mother is forced to cook for the man. When word comes that Johnny is hiding out nearby and needs help, only Caroline and her black grandmother, the slave healer Miz Melindy, are able to make the journey to rescue him. On the way, Caroline learns why she has a black ancestor, why Johnny really fled from the British army and turned Patriot, and how she herself has reserves of strength and determination she never dreamed possible. Although this long and complex novel overflows with incidents and characters, the linear structure eliminates problems. Filled with historical and cultural information, scenes occur in the plantation house, on the often terrifying journey, and variously on the plantation. If some happenings seem trite—a young British private helps Caroline and her mother escape from the plantation house by shinnying down a rope he throws up to their bedroom window, after which they set fire to the place by shooting a flaming Indian arrow through the window—they serve the plot well and provide excitement. Caroline's coming to terms with her heritage seems credible given the times. Some figures are historical, for example, Just Agnes, the pathetic, bedraggled, misused woman who was Cornwallis's abandoned mistress and who dies of malaria after wandering destitute through the area. Some people, like Miz Melindy, are composites of real persons, and several are based on actual people, like Caroline's father and the women of nearby plantations who were left to fend for themselves and their children after their men were executed by the British and their slaves shipped off to be sold in the West Indies. The book is solidly anti-British, the young private being the only British soldier painted with a positive brush. The sense of the confusion, terror, and disaster the war brought, the conflicts that caused it to become in effect a civil war, and the secrets it may have unwittingly uncovered are strongly presented. A map would be welcome, but an extensive author's note and a bibliography provide a useful conclusion to the book. For an earlier book about African Americans by her, see *This Land Is Our Land* (1994), no. 116, *Wolf by the Ears*.

108 Rinaldi, Ann, *Hang a Thousand Trees with Ribbons: The Story of Phillis Wheatley*, Harcourt, 1996 (hardcover), ISBN 0–152–00876–4, $12.00, 352 pp.; (paper), ISBN 0–152–00877–2, $6.00. Ages 12 up, grades 7 up.

Biographical novel set in Boston, Massachusetts, in the mid-1700s about the historical first African-American woman poet (1753–1784). The novel adds incidents, dialogue, and some characters but for the most part stays to the facts of Wheatley's life as they are known. Kidnapped by rival tribesmen from her home in Senegal, Keziah, seven, her mother, and her good friend, Obour, a year older, are sold to the captain of the slave ship, *Phillis*. The Atlantic crossing is graphically described—filled with horrors for her and the other captives. Keziah's mother is thrown overboard because she resisted the advances of the first mate. Only Obour's tender care keeps the terror- and grief-stricken child alive. In Boston, Keziah is bought at auction by John Wheatley, a kind and affluent merchant, who names her Phillis after the ship and gives her as maid to his spoiled, intolerant, and sometimes cruel only daughter, Mary, ten years older than Phillis. Phillis is quick and attentive, and when Mary is allowed to sit in on her twin brother Nathaniel's lessons, Phillis soon reads and writes English and excels in Greek and Latin. Noting her precocity, the elder Wheatleys treat her as their own child, indulge her variously, and even dress her in the finest attire. While she grows to be a good woman, Phillis has few practical skills, is inclined to be saucy, stubborn, frivolous, and affected, is easily impressed by appearances, and generally lacks good sense, even falling in love with Nathaniel. She composes poetry, which is published, first in England and later in America, where she must go before a committee of eminent Boston citizens to testify that she has indeed written the poems. She accompanies Nathaniel to England, where she meets London elite and Benjamin Franklin. She returns to Boston, where as the colonies move closer to the Revolution and times become hard, she cares for the Wheatleys and meets and falls in love with John Peters, a greengrocer, who tides the family over pre-Revolution tough times and whom she eventually marries. Rinaldi's story stops with Phillis's marriage, and in an epilogue the author briefly describes the rest of Phillis's short, hard life. While Rinaldi's account follows the facts, the novel fails to engage the emotions as one would expect, perhaps because it is hard to warm up to self-centered Phillis, except when she is a child and abused. The account of the Middle Passage holds the interest, even though the horrors described are familiar from other such accounts. The picture of Boston and London life and the political thought of the day are fascinating. For another novel by Rinaldi, see *Wolf by the Ears*, no. 116 in *This Land Is Our Land* (1994).

109 Robinet, Harriette Gillem, *Forty Acres and Maybe a Mule*, Atheneum, 1998 (hardcover), ISBN 0–689–82078–X, $16.00, 144 pp. Ages 8–12, grades 3–7.

Historical novel set during Reconstruction at the end of the American Civil War, mostly in Georgia. In April, 1865, impulsive Gideon, seventeen, the older brother of steady Pascal, twelve, returns to the South Carolina plantation from which he had run away. He informs Pascal that all the slaves are now free and persuades the boy to leave with him to claim the "forty acres and maybe a mule" that every family of freed slaves can now receive under the law. Taking with them little Nelly, eight, a newly arrived slave girl, they walk many miles, avoiding "night riders" whose aim is to return them to their former masters, seeking a Freedmen's Bureau office to make their claim, and collecting fellow travelers along the way, notably an old carpenter who calls himself Freedman, a beautiful young black woman named Gladness, and the Bibb family, poor whites also seeking land and a better life. Arrived at a town in Georgia across the Savannah, they adopt the last name of City so that Gideon can apply and also discover a newly formed school for ex-slaves and illiterate whites, which the children later attend. Their forty acres, whose landmark is the Ghost Tree, lie a few miles away by a lake. Under Gideon's leadership and with the help of various people, sheer faith, and much hard work, they plant cotton, build a house, dig a well, and look forward to better times at Green Gloryland. In the fall, however, white men come and put them out, the land having been given by law to whites. With gold coins they discover under the Ghost Tree, they head east to start over on the Georgia Sea Islands. Characters are types, and the story is mostly dialogue. Best is the setting. The hardships the ex-slaves faced during Reconstruction—hangings, fires, shootings, and threats, as well as the vagaries of the laws and the chicanery of those who executed those laws—come alive as epitomized by this little family. They start with nothing but hopes, dreams, and longings, at the same time trying to define what freedom really means. Pascal concludes that freedom is doing what is good and right. An author's note and a bibliography appear at the end of the book. For another historical novel by Robinet, see *Children of the Fire*, in *This Land Is Our Land* (1994), no. 118.

110 Robinet, Harriette Gillem, *If You Please, President Lincoln*, Atheneum, 1995 (hardcover), ISBN 0–689–31969–X, $15.00, 149 pp. Ages 8–12, grades 3–7.

Historical novel about the unfortunate expedition to relocate freed slaves on tiny Isle a Vache (Cow Island) off Haiti in early 1864. Slave to a Maryland priest, who has taught him to read and write, Moses, fourteen, flees to Washington, D.C., hoping to get more education, make something of himself, and get away from the servitude he hates. He falls in with a young blind man, Goshen, who also has some education. While on the docks, the two are impressed aboard a ship bound to colonize Cow Island, in what is later revealed as a scam. To their dismay, they discover the ship crammed with 400 people, mostly men, and the expedition led by historical Bernard Kock, an arrogant German charlatan. He has a contract, signed but later rescinded by President Lincoln, to pay him for founding a settlement for African Americans in Haiti. Lincoln had originally hoped thus to avoid ill feelings that might arise against the freed slaves but later dropped the plan as unwise. During the two-week voyage down the coast to the Caribbean, the people suffer from lack of food and water, cold, filthy, cramped quarters, dysentery, and smallpox. At Port-au-Prince, they learn that Kock has no lease for Cow Island, but the ship sails there anyway. They discover that the island has no fresh water and is ill-suited for planting, that Kock lacks supplies, like seed for cotton and food crops, and implements, like hoes, for planting; and that no dwellings await them. When Kock becomes demented, Moses and Goshen assume leadership. The Haitian authorities inform the United States government about the settlers' plight, and eventually a ship arrives to take the 300 survivors to Baltimore. Goshen finds work as a barber, and Moses gets his long-awaited opportunity for schooling. Moses and Goshen are well depicted, gradually revealed, and dynamic. The fast-moving plot, in which the slaves' hopes so quickly turn to despair, holds many exciting episodes. The book's strength lies in its graphic revelation of a little-known and shameful episode in American history. An author's note and a bibliography conclude the book. For an earlier book, see *This Land Is Our Land* (1994), no. 118, *Children of the Fire*.

111 Robinet, Harriette Gillem, *Mississippi Chariot*, Atheneum, 1994 (hardcover), ISBN 0–689–31960–6, 117 pp.; Aladdin, 1997 (paper), ISBN 0–689–80632–9, $3.99. Ages 8–12, grades 3–7.

Period novel set in the very small town of Sleepy Corners in the Delta region of Mississippi for two weeks in May of 1936. His sharecropper, laundress mama often tells her youngest of five children, mischievous, plucky Shortening Bread (Abraham Lincoln) Jackson, twelve, to "watch his mouth." On his twelfth birthday, however, Shortening decides to free his innocent daddy from the chain gang, where he has been sent for car theft by a vindictive sheriff. He loves his gentle, religious, hardworking father, and besides, the Jacksons live on the verge of starvation and need him to help provide. Since Rufus Jackson was convicted on hearsay alone, Shortening ironically decides to start a rumor that the FBI are coming to Sleepy Corners to investigate the conviction. At about the same time, he saves fat, disliked Hawk Baker, son of the white postmaster, from drowning. After some days of near discoveries and the fortuitous arrival of a stranger thought to be from the FBI, Mr. Baker quietly takes up Rufus's cause, secures his release, and makes it possible for the Jacksons to leave Sleepy Corners and head for a new life in Chicago. The sense of small-town racial prejudice; the need for the African Americans to remain "invisible" against retaliation of several sorts, including the Ku Klux Klan; the difficulty of the black sharecroppers to make a living since the landowners "cook the books" to keep them in debt; and the whites' desire to keep blacks subservient since they fear that the blacks, who outnumber them about seven to one, will rise up against them—these factors, plus a well-drawn central character, outweigh the improbable plot and make for a fast-moving, gripping period novel that illuminates the African-American migration northward in the thirties. The title comes from a slavery-times code phrase to warn of danger. A bibliography concludes the book. For an earlier book, see *This Land Is Our Land* (1994), no. 118, *Children of the Fire*.

112 Robinet, Harriette Gillem, *The Twins, the Pirates, and the Battle of New Orleans*, Atheneum, 1997 (hardcover), ISBN 0–689–81208–6, $15.00, 138 pp. Ages 8–12, grades 3–7.

Historical novel set in late December 1814 and early January 1815, during the Battle of New Orleans in the American War of 1812 against the British, involving some historical figures. Fictional twins, Andrew and Pierre Alexandre, twelve, the first inventive and precipitous, the second cautious and wise, slaves of a large Southern Louisiana landowner, are helped to run away to the deep swamps southeast of New Orleans by their father, Jacques. The twins face several problems: wondering what has happened to their father, who has not joined them; freeing their mother, Isabel, and their three-year-old sister; staying alive, since supplies are meager; and evading slave catchers and others eager to claim the posted $1,000 reward. They observe the British, the Americans, and pirates, who occupy a small, nearby island, and inevitably become involved in the war. During one battle, they help the Americans, an activity observed by General Andrew Jackson. They also go several times to the island where the pirates live, among whom are some African Americans, and are detected by one of them, Evil Eye, who turns out to be the half-brother of their father, whom they learn is dead. The pirates, under the leadership of historical Jean Lafitte, join the Americans, in return for Jackson's promise of amnesty. Eventually, the twins inform the Americans about British ship movements in return for the freedom of their mother and sister and thirteen other slaves. The twins are well depicted and change as a result of their experiences, and the little mystery about their parentage is cleared up believably. Their involvement in the war is credible given the context and their personalities. Although their being trusted to such an extent by Jackson and Lafitte strains belief, it works in context. Excitement is often high, tight spots and near encounters being frequent, and humor lightens some dark passages, usually arising out of Andrew's not always sensible escapades. The rigors of life in the swamps, on the run and always on the edge, explicitly detailed, and their comments and memories about slave life are other assets. Here is history and adventure rolled into one for enticing reading for middle graders. An earlier historical novel by Robinet appears in *This Land Is Our Land* (1994), no. 118, *Children of the Fire*.

113 Robinet, Harriette Gillem, *Washington City Is Burning*, Atheneum, 1996 (hardcover), ISBN 0–689–80773–2, $16.00, 149 pp. Ages 8–12, grades 3–7.

Historical fiction set during the American War of 1812 in Washington, D.C., in which a fictitious young black girl, Virginia, a slave belonging to President Madison and his wife, Dolley, is brought to the President's House to serve Miss Dolley. While in Washington, Virginia's comings and goings give the reader glimpses of what the city was like physically; what the First Couple's life was like, especially the numerous social events, from the point of view of the female slaves; and, to a more limited extent, what the political climate was like, in particular, attitudes toward the British and slaves. The book contrasts with the writer's *The Twins, the Pirates, and the Battle of New Orleans* (no. 112), which, while involving the war to some degree, is more a period boy's adventure story.

Virginia travels to Washington, the reason for her trip from Madison's Montpelier home a mystery to her, until Tobias, the black humpbacked coachman enlists her help in weekly surreptitious transports of runaway slaves to the Potomac. She encounters another mystery, too, why some of the house slaves should behave so spitefully toward her, a circumstance never fully explained but perhaps due in part to the sale months previously of the young daughter of Rosetta Bell, the meanest of them all. Another mystery involves the capture and execution of a group of slaves Virginia has transported: who informed the slave catchers? The spy turns out to be Rosetta Bell, a matter of no surprise to the reader. Virginia sees war, terrifyingly close, when the British attack the city and burn public buildings and dwellings, among them the President's House. The Madisons' evacuation, during which they save the Declaration of Independence, is well described, as are other events during the attack, and the efforts of the British admiral to be as lenient as he can, especially to the common people caught in the conflict, is a good inclusion. Virginia is staunch, nervy but mostly level-headed, and the reader has no doubt that she will acquire the education she longs for and make a worthy contribution to her race and times. Lots of action and dialogue keep the book lively and the reader involved. The author provides background information and a bibliography to end the book. An earlier book, *Children of the Fire*, is described in *This Land Is Our Land* (1994), no. 118.

114 Rosen, Michael J., *A School for Pompey Walker*, illus. Aminah Brenda Lynn Robinson, Harcourt (hardcover), ISBN 0–15–200114–X, $16.00, unp. Ages 7 up, grades 2 up.

Realistic picture-story book, in which, at the dedication of a school named for him, a ninety-year-old ex-slave tells the story of how, with the help of a white friend, he received freedom, came to Ohio, and accumulated enough money to build a school for black children. Born into slavery in 1832 on a plantation, Pompey Bibb keeps the master's stable, until one day he angers the overseer and is put on the sales block. He is purchased and freed, ironically, by his master's former son-in-law, widower Jeremiah Walker from Cincinnati. They outwit "paddyrollers" (slave catchers) by hiding Pompey in a secret compartment under Jeremiah's buggy. They finance the trip north by selling Pompey back into slavery, from which he then runs away with Jeremiah's help. On the trip north, Jeremiah teaches Pompey numbers and letters. In Madisonville, Ohio, Pompey, now sixteen, yearns for a school for the black children and suggests to Jeremiah that they employ the same ruse to raise money—selling Pompey over and over. They venture south almost forty danger-fraught times before they have enough money to build the four-room school they name Sweet Freedom. In 1923, a larger school is named for Pompey Walker, who adopted the last name of his benefactor. The suspenseful text, which is longer than that of most picture-story books, does not spare some of the more sordid aspects of slave life but does not dwell on them either. The stunning, full-color, strongly composed, two-dimensional paintings arrest the attention and extend the story. Although on occasion they seem overly dramatic, they catch the temper of Pompey's narrative from his emotional perspective. The story was inspired by a newspaper clipping about a similar figure and the recollections of slaves. For another unusual picture-story book by Rosen and Robinson, see *Elijah's Angel*, in *This Land Is Our Land* (1994), no. 120.

115 Sanders, Scott Russell, *A Place Called Freedom*, illus. Thomas B. Allen, Atheneum, 1995 (hardcover), ISBN 0–689–80470–9, $16.00, unp. Ages 5–8, grades K–3.

Picture-story book, based (according to the book jacket) on the true story of the founding of Lyles Station, Indiana. In 1832, when young African-American James Starman, who tells the story, is seven and his father, Joshua, is freed, Joshua moves his family north from the Tennessee plantation, where James was born, following the drinking gourd (Big Dipper) to the Wabash River. There the family works hard, buys a piece of land, and builds a sturdy cabin. Time after time, Joshua returns to Tennessee to lead north relatives and friends, both free and slave, who are joined by others from far and wide in the South, until a small town results. James's simply told, straightforward story, which reflects the courage and perseverance of many African Americans who sought good lives for themselves, is eloquently complemented by mostly full-page, expressive pictures done in muted bluish tones with an occasional striking touch of color. They extend the story and, especially in the carefully modeled faces, convey the strength of the people they celebrate.

116 Sapphire, *Push*, Knopf, 1996 (hardcover), ISBN 0–679–44626–5, $27.95, 179 pp.; Vintage, 1997 (paper), ISBN 0–679–76675–8, $11.00, 192 pp. Ages 15 up, grades 10 up.

Gritty realistic novel of an abused African-American girl in Harlem and her struggle to escape her past and become a good mother. At sixteen, Precious Jones is grossly overweight, illiterate, and pregnant with her second child by her father. Since her home life is that of a slave to her mother, a woman so obese that she seldom moves, only occasionally summoning energy to beat or kick the girl, Precious is devastated when she is expelled from school for being pregnant. In her junior high, however, she mostly just sat in the back row, unable to see the blackboard or do the assignments. Only her math teacher has a good word for her, and on his recommendation she is entered in an alternative school, "Each One Teach One," where she finds her first friends and first real help. In the following months she shows phenomenal achievement and begins to hope to enter the GED program. After her mother, furious because her welfare allowance for Precious has been cut off because the girl is not registered in regular school, throws Precious out, she is found a place in a halfway house and eventually has her baby, a boy she calls Abdul and to whom she is devoted. Just as it seems that she may pull herself from the misery of her first sixteen years, her mother shows up at the halfway house, the first time she has left her apartment for years, to tell Precious that her father has died of AIDS and to try to persuade her to return to her apartment so she can get welfare allowances for both Precious and Abdul, having given Precious's first child, a Down's syndrome girl they call Mongo, to her mother, although she still collects the welfare allowance for her. Precious by now has enough self-esteem and knowledge to refuse her mother and to get herself and her little boy tested. She is positive for HIV, but Abdul is not. A true survivor, Precious pulls herself out of her depression, determined to last as long as she can and give Abdul the love and good start in life that she never had. The novel may be objectionable for its crude language and horrifyingly explicit scenes of sexual abuse by both Precious's father and mother, but there is nothing titillating, and Precious ultimately is an admirable character.

117 Schertle, Alice, *Down the Road*, illus. E. B. Lewis, Harcourt, 1995 (hardcover), ISBN 0–15–276622–7, $16.00, unp. Ages 4–8, grades PS–3.

Realistic picture-story book of African Americans. Papa thinks Hetty is big enough to walk down the road all by herself to Mr. Birdie's Emporium to buy fresh eggs so that they can have scrambled eggs for breakfast. She promises to come straight home and not dilly-daddle. She practices holding the basket and crossing the stream carefully and feels so grown up with coins in her pocket. She even remembers to say "thank you" to Mr. Birdie. On the way home, she crosses the stream carefully and repeats her "walking words" to herself. Except that she stumbles a little on a rock, everything goes well until she spies an apple tree in a meadow and decides it would make Mama and Papa happy to have some "sweet, juicy, crackly-crisp" apples. The egg basket tips while she is reaching up, and the eggs tumble out and break. She climbs the tree and just sits there, feeling sad and not wanting to go home. Papa comes hunting for her and climbs the tree, too, and then Mama joins them, and they all three sit there for a while, enjoying the comfort of being together and seeing the world from high inside an apple tree. Although there are no scrambled eggs for breakfast in the morning, there is warm, fresh apple pie. Accompanying and extending this delightful, warm family story are fresh impressionistic watercolors. They picture incidents, show the family as strong and goodlooking and Hetty as an earnest little girl with pigtails, overalls, and sneakers. They shine and shimmer and emphasize the beauty of life. The tree is not identified by owner. Thus the issue of whether or not the apples were for them to pick is not addressed. Nevertheless, this is a charming family story for the very young, with echoes of oral tradition.

118 Schroeder, Alan, *Carolina Shout!*, illus. Bernie Fuchs, Dial, 1995 (hardcover), ISBN 0–8037–1676–1, $14.99, unp. Ages 4 up, grades PS up.

A recording and celebration of the street sounds of Charleston, South Carolina, in particular the many, varied shouts of the vendors calling attention to their wares and services. Delia, a young African-American girl, cannot believe that her sister Bettina does not hear the music of the streets. To dancing Delia, everything makes music, the raindrops, the milk delivery, even the bullfrogs. All through the day the workmen sing at their jobs—the carpenters and the chain gang repairing the railroad track—or cry their wares—the charcoal man, the oyster man, the chimney sweep. Even the children playing hopscotch or jumping rope have their rhymes and chants. The oversized book is stunningly illustrated with full-page oil paintings on canvas in muted tones of early morning or late evening sunlight. Particularly striking are the paintings of the track workers, their prison stripes echoed in the cross-ties of the railroad, and the Pepper-Sauce Man, who is almost hidden under his hanging bunches of peppers except for his smile, the whitest teeth ever seen.

119 Schroeder, Alan, *Minty: A Story of the Young Harriet Tubman*, illus. Jerry Pinkney, Dial, 1996 (hardcover), ISBN 0–8037–1888–8, $16.99, unp. Ages 5–9, grades K–4.

Biographical fiction in picture-book form, telling of what might have been the childhood of the famous escaped slave who returned to the South repeatedly to lead others to freedom. Minty (Araminta) at eight is known as a "difficult" slave, not docile and subservient, on the Brodas plantation on Maryland's Eastern Shore in the 1820s. She is punished for her clumsiness by being sent to work in the fields and is whipped for freeing the animals when she is assigned to collect the muskrats caught in steel traps set in the river. Her parents, Old Ben and Old Rit, warn her that she may be sold South if she doesn't mend her ways. Repeatedly she vows to run away. When Old Ben sees that she really means it, he shows her the North Star and teaches her all he can about survival in the woods. An author's note at the end points out that she did not achieve this goal until 1849, when she was nearly thirty. At the opening a note by the author gives an idea of how much is actually known about Tubman's childhood and how much is fiction, and one by the illustrator describes his research into details of plantation life, dress, and food in the area and period of the story. Illustrations are highly realistic, full double-page spreads with insets of text. Colors are mostly soft, muted shades with occasional vivid spots in the slave women's head covering and the bright red door of the log plantation house.

120 Sinclair, April, *Coffee Will Make You Black*, Hyperion, 1994 (hardcover), ISBN 1–5628–2796–0, $19.95, 239 pp.; Avon, 1997 (paper), 0–380–72459–6, $10.00, 256 pp. Ages 12 up, grades 7 up.

Convincing, humorous coming-of-age novel set on Chicago's South Side in the 1960s. Stevie (Jean Eloise Stevenson), eleven at the opening, learns to understand and come to terms with her feelings about race and her own sexuality in a series of incidents that take her through her high school years. Daughter of a rigid, unsympathetic mother, Stevie longs to belong among her more worldly friends and turns, in need, to her maternal grandmother, who owns and operates a successful fried chicken stand but still has a social view so dated that it is not much help to Stevie. The novel explores prejudice not only of white against black, but also of black against white and lighter- against darker-skinned people. The language is distinctively African American, and Stevie's voice rings true. Often hilarious but never condescending, this is one of the better recent novels of a girl growing up. A sequel, *Ain't Gonna Be the Same Fool Twice* (1996), which follows Stevie through college in southern Illinois and to San Francisco, where she experiments with sex and tries to decide whether she is a lesbian, is more polemic and lacks the spontaneity of the earlier book.

121 Smalls-Hector, Irene, *Ebony Sea*, illus. Jon Onye Lockard, Longmeadow, 1995 (hardcover), ISBN 0–681–00679–x, $12.95, unp. Ages 8 up, grades 3 up.

Historical fiction in picture-story form based on a real incident in the Georgia Sea Islands during the period of American slavery. When a shipload of African Americans, in chains, arrives, the slaves already working the land watch sadly as they are unloaded. They make no sound, as they move, following the lead of one woman, turn directly into the deep Watteree River, every man, woman, and child, and drown themselves. Because they were believed to be Ebo people, the place became known as Ebo Landing. Because of the grimness of their heroic response to enslavement, the book is more suitable for older children than the usual pre-school picture-book age. Other historical picture-story books by Smalls-Hector present a gentler view of slavery, among them *Jenny Reen and the Jack Muh Lantern* (1996), *Irene Jennie and the Christmas Masquerade: The Johnkankus* (1996), and *A Strawbeater's Thanksgiving* (1998). Other books by Smalls-Hector include *Irene and the Big, Fine Nickel* and *Jonathan and His Mommy*, in *This Land Is Our Land* (1994), nos. 129 and 130.

122 Smalls-Hector, Irene, *Louise's Gift or What Did She Give Me That For?*, illus. Colin Bootman, Little Brown, 1996 (hardcover), ISBN 0–316–79877–0, $15.95, unp. Ages 4–8, grades PS–3.

Picture-story book about a little girl in Harlem whose exciting day, as the family gathers to greet a new baby cousin, is marred when Nana, the oldest relative, gives all the other children gifts with predictions that they will be rich or strong or pretty, but gives Louise a blank piece of paper saying she can put on it "whatever you wish." Although she is miserable, Louise goes out to play with the other children and saves them from disaster when they lose a ring among large rocks, and she thinks of a way to move a stone with a lever so they can retrieve it. On the way home they see a big truck stuck under a bridge, with important-looking men trying to pry it out with machines. She runs up to the man with the fanciest clothes and shouts, "Mister, take the air out of the tires." Her solution saves the truck and wins her the word for her piece of paper,

"Creativity." The realistic pictures, with individualized children and older people, give a feeling of warm family life and the busy city area where they live. Among many other picture-story books about African-American children by Smalls-Hector are *Father's Day Blues: What Do You Do About Father's Day When All You Have Are Mothers?* (1995) and *Kevin and His Dad* (1999). Other books by Smalls-Hector include *Irene and the Big, Fine Nickel* and *Jonathan and His Mommy*, in *This Land Is Our Land* (1994), nos. 129 and 130.

123 Smothers, Ethel Footman, *Moriah's Pond*, Knopf, 1995 (hardcover), ISBN 0–679–84504–6, $14.00, 111 pp. Ages 8–12, grades 3–6.

Autobiographical novel of African-American family life and a girl's growing up set in the Piney Woods of rural Georgia in the 1950s. Free-spirited, independent narrator Annie Rye, ten, and her two older sisters, Maybaby, fourteen, and Brat, twelve, also feisty and life-loving, are spending the summer with their sturdy, wise great-grandmother, Moriah. Moriah does housework and washing for white people in the neighborhood, including Mr. Daniels, who now owns Moriah's land, and Miz Riggs, whose daughter Betty Jean, always dressed like a princess, is lonely and wishes to be friends with the three girls. Annie Rye, however, does not trust Betty Jean, and it seems her fears are confirmed when Mr. Daniels, who saw Betty Jean offer Brat a drink of her soda water, insists that Brat be beaten for sharing a bottle with a white girl. The pond serves as a catalyst for a better relationship with Sally Jean. Although warned not to swim in there after some diseased hogs have been in it, the girls disobey, and Brat gets very sick, even losing her eyesight for a while. It is touch and go for her, especially since the other two girls will not admit they were all in the pond. Visiting after Brat recovers, Betty Jean brings bottles of soda water as a peace offering and apology for not having spoken up about her part in Brat's beating. Characters are individualized, and if all the white figures are types in attitude, they are true to the times in which whites expected certain behaviors from the "coloreds" who lived near them and worked for them. Moriah's sensibleness and warmth are good features, and Uncle Curry, really the girls' great-uncle, Moriah's brother who lives with her, provides a small note of mystery—how did he come to be lame?—the story of which is an important element in Annie Rye's decision to accept Betty Jean. One of the book's best features, in addition to the closeness of the family and Moriah's good sense, is how it shows that in a racist society even very small matters (sharing a pop bottle) can assume undue importance. Colloquial speech establishes the setting well but occasionally seems overdone. For an earlier autobiographical book by Smothers, see no. 133, *Down in the Piney Woods*, in *This Land Is Our Land* (1994).

124 Steptoe, John, *Creativity*, illus. E. B. Lewis, Clarion, 1997 (hardcover), ISBN 395–68706–3, $15.95, 32 pp. Ages 4–8, grades PS–3.

Picture-story book about a new boy in school. Hector from Puerto Rico seems strange at first to Charles, because, although he looks much like the African Americans in Charles's family, he has straight hair and speaks Spanish. Charles's mother explains that they share much the same heritage, and his father says that "saying what you mean in your own special way—that's being creative." The next day in gym class, Hector is ridiculed for having the wrong sort of sneakers. Charles takes his extra pair of sneakers to Hector's house, and in return Hector gives Charles his favorite shirt, one with a picture of a palm tree on the front, and they decide that their trade is creative. Although didactic in its information about racial mixing and its moral message, the story has a pleasant tone, and the watercolor illustrations, picturing the boys as about ten or eleven, are realistic and individualized, not idealized or cartoonish.

125 Stolz, Mary, *Cezanne Pinto: A Memoir*, Knopf, 1994 (hardcover), ISBN 0–679–84917–3, $15.00, 252 pp.; 1997 (paper), ISBN 0–679–88933–7, $4.99. Ages 11 up, grades 6 up.

Historical novel of a young slave's flight to freedom in Canada and his efforts to build his life, beginning in 1860 and related in first person from the vantage point of ninety years of age. Deucy grows up on Gloriana, the Virginia plantation of Ol' Massa Clayburn, where he develops a fine way with horses. Deprived of his beloved Mam, who has been sold into Texas, Deucy runs away when he is about twelve, accompanied by tall, intelligent, determined Tamar, the cook, who taught him to read, write, and improve his English. He calls himself Cezanne Pinto, the first name from a child of the legendary black founder of Chicago and the last name from a horse he has cherished. Following the North Star, they connect with the Underground Railroad and arrive in Philadelphia. Worried that they will be caught and returned under the Fugitive Slave Law, they leave for Canada. Sheltered for four years by a kind and affectionate Canadian couple for whom Cezanne is stableboy, he feels compelled to join the Union forces. He takes the train to Washington, D.C., and falls in with a cavalry detachment, fortunately near the war's end. He makes friends with brash Cal Trillo, a Mex-Texan corporal, with whom, the war over, he returns to the Trillo ranch near the Brazos River in the southern part of Texas, where he works and also searches unsuccessfully for Mam. After five years of "trailing," he leaves for Chicago and becomes a family man. Told eighty years after events, the book succeeds as the memoir of a very old man, since incidents can convincingly remain undeveloped, because many years have elapsed, and Cezanne can credibly comment on the progress of African Americans in their quest for civil rights. The small cast of characters provides scope for developing them in dimension—especially Tamar, Cal, and steady, sensible, proud Cezanne himself. The first part of the book recalls plantation and runaway slave narratives but offers few new views. The last part gives a limited but keen sense of the difficulties and challenges of rebuilding the western South, the beginning of the cowboy era, and the part the freed blacks played in both and is clearly the book's strength. For other books by Stolz, see *Stealing Home* and *Storm in the Night*, in *This Land Is Our Land* (1994), nos. 139 and 140.

126 Straight, Susan, *The Gettin Place*, Hyperion, 1996 (hardcover), ISBN 0–7868–6186–3, $22.95, 488 pp. Ages 14 up, grades 9 up.

Long, powerful novel of an African-American family's attempts to hang on to their land in an area called Treetown in Rio Seco, some sixty miles east of Los Angeles, as urban sprawl surrounds them and developers greedily eye their semirural island. Framed by two riots, the story centers on the Thompson family, whose father, Hosea, as a young child lost his own father in the 1921 Tulsa violence, when police and white citizens murdered and burned to wipe out the Negro area and then falsified records to hide the truth, and ends with the riots in Los Angeles after the police who beat Rodney King are acquitted. The immediate threat to their land, where they grow citrus, apricots, and olives and operate a towing service, starts when the bodies of two young white women are found in a burning car on the property, followed not long afterward by the body of a man dressed as a woman, who has been bludgeoned to death. To the Thompsons it is clear that someone wants to make them look bad, drive them to a violent reaction, and get them arrested or driven away. Marcus, youngest of the five Thompson sons, known to his brothers as Sissyfly or Ba-by boy because he has not faced the outside world with his fists or guns as the older ones have, is forced into the position of trying to unravel the complicated situation because as a history teacher he has negotiated with the white world. The novel is rich in characters: Alma, Hosea's half-Mexican wife; Oscar, Hosea's blues-singing brother, who runs the Blue Q, a rough nightspot next door to the used car lot, where he dispenses chitlins and home brew; Finis, the fourth brother, whose brain has been destroyed by angel dust and who wanders, sweet-tempered, singing bits of old songs and new words that drift through his mind; Sofelia, the only daughter, who has hidden away from the family for more than twelve years after being raped, drugged, and brutalized, afraid her brothers will kill the resulting child; that son, hardened by his life in Los Angeles and his fascination with guns; and their women and friends. Although the novel contains both sex and violence, they are not gratitous or sensationalized, but shown as part of the life the Thompsons and their neighbors are forced to live. Straight's earlier novel, *Blacker Than a Thousand Midnights* (1994), about an African-American firefighter, is also set partly in Rio Seco, and some of the same characters appear in minor roles.

127 Tate, Eleanora E., *A Blessing in Disguise*, Delacorte, 1995 (hardcover), ISBN 0–385–32103–1, $14.95, 185 pp.; Yearling, 1996 (paper), ISBN 0–440–41209–9, $3.00. Ages 8–12, grades 3–7.

Realistic novel of family and community life set among African Americans in recent years in the dying town of Deacons Corners, the third in the author's books about Calvary County near the coast of South Carolina. The narrator, Zambia Renelda Brown, twelve, calls Deacons Corners an "ole country town" and thinks it no fun at all. She would like to live in Gumbo Grove with her father, Vernon "Snake" LaRange, a smooth-talking, fancy-dressing high roller, who owns a popular night club. Her mother has been in a Charleston hospital for years. Since she was four, Zambia has lived with Snake's sister, Aunt Limo, her Uncle Lamar, and cousin Aretha, hardworking, pillar-of-the-community, blue-collar people. She knows they love her but yearns for her own father's approval, comforting embrace, and upscale lifestyle and for the friendship of her always-in-fashion, older half-sisters, Seritta and Meritta. When Snake opens Paradise Two just down the way on Silver Dollar Road, Zambia seizes every opportunity to ingratiate herself with him, even though she is told he is involved in drugs and other illegal activities, had abandoned her mother, and has never, in all these years, even so much as bought her a pair of shoes. Within only a few weeks after the club opens, the street becomes the scene of robberies, assaults, and drug-dealing. The police arrive at all hours, ambulances roam the area, and radios blare from long, fancy cars and SUVs. Unsavory figures, many elegantly dressed, others shady, frequent the club, streets, and green areas, make themselves at home, and exchange money and merchandise surreptitiously. After Zambia gets enticed into helping Potsey, a neighbor youth, with a drug scam, a drive-by shooting leaves Seritta dead and Zambia and others wounded. Zambia comes to her senses about her father and participates when the Reverend Reed organizes a community protest to drive out Snake and his crime-ridden operation. Zambia sees that these unfortunate occurrences have been a blessing in disguise to herself and her neighbors and friends, since they were forced to clarify their values on a personal and collective basis. Although Zambia seems slow in accepting her father's true nature and appreciating the relatives who have raised her, her need for a father's validation is in keeping with her age and stage in life. The book seems didactic, tailored to speak to problems of the times, and dialogue occasionally reflects the author's voice, but on the whole, the teen talk, topical references, and interactions among the youth and between the youth and the earlier generation seem accurate. The small-town atmosphere is strong, the book's best feature. Tate has also written no. 141, *Front Porch Stories at the One-Room School*, and no. 142, *The Secret of Gumbo Grove* (fiction) in *This Land Is Our Land* (1994).

128 Tate, Eleanora E., *Don't Split the Pole: Tales of Down-Home Folk Wisdom*, illus. Cornelius Van Wright and Ying-Hwa Hu, Delacorte, 1997 (hardcover), ISBN 0–385–32302–6, $14.95, 140 pp.; Yearling, 1999 (paper), ISBN 0–440–41322–2, $4.50, 144 pp. Ages 8–12, grades 3–7.

Seven humorous stories by a prominent African-American writer, illustrating folk sayings and proverbs, most with a fantasy element, among them two talking animal stories, and involving a mix of both African-American and white characters. Maggie, the fat old basset hound, puts false to "You Can't Teach an Old Dog New Tricks" when she accompanies a one-legged seagull down to the water and learns how to catch fish. When two brothers violate the old folk rule "Don't Split the Pole," they find themselves in another, scary dimension and, once back in reality, in a new place for happy skateboarding. In "What Goes Around Comes Around," psychic Mother Gratify (really Taneshia's grandmother disguised) gives advice on how Taneshia can get a handsome boyfriend—be polite, be a good citizen, and help around the house. Mudslider, the young snapping turtle, whose growth has been stunted by insect sprays that have poisoned his pond, is helped by Gran Snappy, the head of the turtles, to use his gift of common sense in "Slow and Steady Wins the Race." The extensive, lively dialogue is peppered with contemporary expressions and terms, which may seem incongruous given the stories' titles but which help make the old sayings seem more current. The plots are inventive, if overlong, the characters interesting, and the humor engaging, and the result is good reading entertainment, moralistic but nondidactic in tone. A list of recommended books about proverbs and folk sayings appears at the end. Tate has also written other books, *Front Porch Stories at the One-Room School* and *The Secret of Gumbo Grove*, also fiction, described in *This Land Is Our Land* (1994), nos. 141 and 142.

129   Taylor, Mildred D., *The Well: David's Story*, Dial, 1995 (hardcover), ISBN 0–803–71802–0, $14.99, 92 pp. Ages 9–14, grades 4–9.

Short period novel set in rural Mississippi during the hot, dry summer of 1910, another in the cycle of novels and short stories about the African-American Logan family, the best known of which is the Newbery Award–winning *Roll of Thunder, Hear My Cry* (1976). Polite, timid David Logan, ten, who grows up to become the much-respected Papa in *Roll of Thunder*, looks back on this summer of his childhood and starts his story: "Charlie Simms was always mean." Charlie, a neighboring white boy of fourteen, son of sharecroppers, and proud, self-assured Hammer, David's brother, thirteen, are the catalysts for the trouble that afflicts the landowning Logans that summer. A prolonged drought has dried up most of the area's water. The only well with sweet water belongs to the Logans, who generously share it with everyone. One dawn, when Charlie and his younger brother, Ed-Rose (sic), come for water, Hammer stands proud, refusing to behave obsequiously. Mama (Caroline, later known as Big Ma) intervenes before there is trouble. After breakfast, David and Hammer take the cows to the Creek Rosa Lee, a shared watering place, where they meet several youths, black and white, including the Simms boys. The white boys are racially insulting, and tension accelerates. Later that week, the Logan boys encounter Charlie by the side of the road, his wagon minus one wheel. Charlie orders the "niggers" to give him a hand in replacing it. David quickly agrees, to keep the peace, although on a crutch from a broken leg. He tries but cannot hold the wagon up long enough for Charlie to put the wheel back on. When the wagon falls, Charlie strikes David. Temper flaring, Hammer attacks Charlie, who hits his head against a stone. Afraid that Charlie is dead, the Logan boys flee, rush home, and tell Mama. When the white sheriff comes, Mama tells him what her sons told her happened. Although he is sympathetic, he realizes the Simmses and other whites must be placated and arranges for the Logan boys to work for Mr. Simms, and Mama whips the boys to satisfy Mr. Simms. Even after Papa (Paul Edward) returns from working along the Natchez Trace, the boys labor for Mr. Simms, Hammer's resentment increasing all the while. After Papa heads back to the Trace, Hammer goes to the Simms place and knocks Charlie down. A couple of days later, the Logan well is fouled with dead animals. Hammer accuses the Simms boys, and eventually it is proved that Charlie and Ed-Rose are guilty. They are forced to clean the well, but the water is spoiled for weeks. Based on stories told in the author's family dating back to the early part of the twentieth century, the book's strongest point is its picture of racial tension deriving from the whites' attitude that they are inherently superior to blacks and in particular from their resentment of landowning, independent blacks. Several short anecdotes about slave and just post-slave days appear within the larger story. Although Hammer is too prickly and Charlie too mean, independent, resourceful Mama and sensible, sturdy Papa are good figures. Many of the characters appear in the other Logan books, and encountering them here lends depth to the other stories. Other books by Taylor, *The Friendship* and *The Road to Memphis*, are described in *This Land Is Our Land* (1994), nos. 143 and 144.

130 Thomas, Joyce Carol, *I Have Heard of a Land*, illus. Floyd Cooper, HarperCollins, 1998 (hardcover), ISBN 0–06–023478–4, 14.89, unp. Ages 6–12, grades 1–6.

Lyrical, realistic, picture-story book of the African-American pioneer experience, based upon the author's own family history and focusing upon the women who made the trek westward and claimed land. Each two-page spread has from four to eight lines of text in deep, dark print, enclosed and extended by the off-the-page brown-toned, soft-edged paintings, which picture situations and add details. Each text-set starts with the title line and then contributes some facet of that wonderful western land of promise of which the once-enslaved pioneers have heard. The first picture shows a determined, sturdy woman observing a poster, which proclaims free land in Oklahoma, and dreaming of being there. A covered wagon, on the next spread, shows a family starting out, and subsequent spreads show a woman pounding in the stake that marks the land, preparing to eat flapjacks covered with honey, leading worship under an arbor on Sunday, sleeping in a sod hut, and helping neighbors who are building her a cabin, among others. The last double-spread shows her and her family clustered together in anticipation of a bright future, whose possibilities extend "as far as our imaginations can carry us." Although anyone even somewhat knowledgeable about history knows that things were not always so rosy for the pioneers, the book captures the courage and cooperative spirit of the African Americans who went west and celebrates in particular the special determination, strength, and vision of the women. For other books by Thomas, see *A Gathering of Flowers, Journey, Water Girl,* and *When the Nightingale Sings,* in *This Land Is Our Land* (1994), nos. 146 (also no. 274), 147, 148, and 149.

131 Turner, Glennette Tilley, *Running for Our Lives,* illus. Samuel Byrd, Holiday House, 1994 (hardcover), ISBN 0–823–41121–4, $15.95, 198 pp. Ages 9–13, grades 4–8.

Escaping slave story, starting in New Franklin, Missouri, and ending in Canada. Luther, evidently about eleven or twelve, and his sister Carrie, one year younger, with their mother and a toddler, Tilly, whom they have taken in, plan an escape in the fall of 1855, when Kansas and Missouri are torn by conflict between pro- and anti-slavery forces, but they must wait until their father, a coachman on a neighboring plantation, can join them. Luther, who has been exercising his master's horses, has discovered a cave where the family can hide the first night. They make their way north, narrowly avoiding slave catchers and other obstacles, even crossing the ice-covered Mississippi on their bellies, until they reach a sawmill that is an Underground Railroad station. There they, and a young couple who have joined them, are put into three separate lumber wagons, Luther and Carrie separated from their parents, and sent for safety to a different destination. From there on, Luther and Carrie make their way with help from various abolitionists, until they reach Detroit, where, fortuitously, they meet their aunt from Virginia, who has escaped with her husband. With these relatives they go to Buxton, Ontario, where they farm, always looking for their missing parents. In 1860, after they have almost given up hope, they come upon their father in Windsor and return to live with their parents, Tilly having died on the way. The novel contains much information about the Underground Railroad in the Midwest, including a useful map and an author's note reviewing the history of the period, and has about twenty attractive full-page charcoal drawings. Unfortunately, the story never comes alive. The characters speak in standard twentieth-century English, with no discernible difference between slaves and the people they meet, and the plot is dependent on coincidence. The terrible suffering of their trip in the cold, with very little food, and the constant danger are told but never made real for the reader.

132 Walter, Mildred Pitts, *Second Daughter: The Story of a Slave Girl,* Scholastic, 1996 (hardcover), ISBN 0–590–48282–3, $15.95, 214 pp. Ages 10–14, grades 5–9.

Historical novel, most major characters historical, set in Sheffield, Massachusetts, focusing on efforts of slaves to be declared free during and just after the American Revolution. The fictitious narrator, Aissa (Second Daughter), is the younger sister of the historical woman, Bett, who sued her owner, wealthy John Ashley, for her freedom under the Massachusetts Constitution and won, setting a precedent for others. The novel starts while the two girls are still young and enslaved to a wealthy New York Dutchman. Their master's daughter, Annetje, marries Ashley and takes the girls to Massachusetts, where although treated well by most standards of the day, they suffer repeated humiliation and punishment because their mistress is demanding, selfish, and easily angered, regarding them as barely above animals. Much of the story involves their daily lives—the work, the humiliations, the shifting grounds of their servitude, and the constant fear that they might be sold. Bett, an herbalist, marries Josiah Freeman, a free black highly regarded in the area, but is only allowed to spend weekends with him on their farm. When they have a child, the child is also a slave to the Ashleys because the mother is. During the war, the slaves' hard labor intensifies, because the men are away fighting. Bett also reports that discussions take place in an upper room in the Ashley mansion, during which the declaration of grievances against the British government and demand for independence are worked out. When the mistress loses her temper at Aissa, grabs a hot shovel from the fire, and inadvertently strikes Bett with it, maiming her, she provides Bett's lawyer with the evidence he needs to persuade the jury to free her. Didacticism over-shadows storytelling in describing the condition of the slaves, the slave trade, and the slaves' yearning for Africa, the right to use their language and retain their culture, and the common human rights of forming family units and caring for one another. Annetje and Ashley are stereotypically cruel and unfeeling, in particular Annetje, who has no saving graces. Bett is long suffering and selfless, an ideal, and Aissa is a strong figure in her own right. The best part of the novel, in addition to its making known the events of the litigation that started the abolitionist movement, is the trial, which grips with tension and suspense. Other books by this writer, *Justin and the Best Biscuits in the World, Mariah Loves Rock, Trouble's Child*, and *Two and Too Much*, are described in *This Land Is Our Land* (1994), nos. 158, 159, 160, and 161, all fiction.

133 Wesley, Valerie Wilson, *Easier to Kill*, Putnam, 1998 (hardcover), ISBN 0–399–14445–5, $23.95, 193 pp.; Avon, 1999 (paper), ISBN 0–380–72910–5, $6.99, 304 pp. Ages 14 up, grades 9 up.

Fifth in a series of mysteries starring African-American Tamara Hayle, an ex-cop, now private investigator in her thirties, with a teenaged son, Jamal. Like all except the third, *Where Evil Sleeps* (1996), which occurs almost entirely in Kingston, Jamaica, this is set in Newark, New Jersey, a city that is just beginning to recover from the devastating 1967 riots. Tamara is hired by the popular black talk-show host, Mandy Magic, to find out who is sending the crudely printed notes that seem to threaten her for rising above her past, a background she and Tamara partly share, since they both grew up in the Hayes Homes housing project. Mandy's hairstylist, who has been blackmailing her, has been murdered, and before Tamara reaches the truth, two of Mandy's other associates are dead. Clearly, the threat has something to do with Mandy's past when she was Starmanda, a teenaged prostitute, a past she has been trying to put behind her and conceal. Suspicion focuses on her associates, until they are murdered, then on her former pimp and her adopted daughter, a tough little cookie, before Tamara discovers the real killer. Like most mysteries, the plot is convoluted, though plausible, and the pace is unrelenting, a good read, but the strength of the series is in the picture of smart, sassy Tamara, a survivor against long odds, as is the grimy, disintegrating city she loves. In the first novel of the series, *When Death Comes Stealing* (1994), someone is systematically killing the five sons, all by different mothers, of her no-good ex-husband, and Tamara becomes involved to save Jamal. In the second, *Devil's Gonna Get Him* (1995), a wealthy man who has hired her to watch his stepdaughter's lover dies of an allergy to peanut butter stirred into the bean dip at a major fundraiser. In the fourth, *No Hiding Place* (1997), a poor woman stakes her total savings to discover the real killer of her son, a small-time hood. In each of the novels, at least one of the characters has a connection with Tamara's past.

134 Wesley, Valerie Wilson, *Freedom's Gifts*, illus. Sharon Wilson, Simon & Schuster, 1997 (hardcover), ISBN 0–689–80269–2, $16.00, 32 pp. Ages 8 up, grades 3 up.

Set in 1943, a picture-story book of how the Juneteenth picnic makes two young girl cousins friends and helps them appreciate their freedom. June does not look forward to the visit of her cousin Lillie from New York, who always finds fault with the "old-timey" ways of Texas, is shocked by the "Whites Only" signs on drinking fountains, and brags about the superiority of northern ways. June's great-great-Aunt Marshall, who was born in slavery, insists that Lillie and June sit with her at the picnic and tells them about the first Juneteenth, the day in 1865 when the slaves of Texas learned of the Emancipation Proclamation signed more than two years earlier and for her the wonderful return of her freedom-loving sister Sophie, who had been sold away earlier and had come back to find her. Lillie, who had never heard these stories before, decides that she would like to return to Texas every June for the celebration, and both girls are sure they can expand freedom's gifts in their lifetimes. Although there is more text than in most picture books, the soft-hued illustrations cover at least every other full page and capture the antagonism between the girls, the excitement, music, and good food of the picnic, and the ancient lady's fragility. An author's note briefly tells the history of Juneteenth.

135 West, Dorothy, *The Richer, the Poorer: Stories, Sketches, and Reminiscences*, Doubleday, 1995 (hardcover), ISBN 0–385–47145–9, $22.00, 254 pp. Ages 12 up, grades 7 up.

Seventeen stories and a handful of other pieces by the African-American author who was the youngest member of the Harlem Renaissance of the 1920s and early 1930s. Although most of the stories have been published previously, some as early as 1926 and 1928, they were confined to the Negro newspapers and magazines of the time and have not been collected before for the general market. Remarkably, except for the differences in buying power of the money mentioned (a fifty-dollar prize in a movie drawing is a fortune in "Jack in the Pot," and a little boy's despair and happiness stem from the loss and return of a single cent in "The Penny"), the stories have a contemporary ring, and most of them could have been written in the last decade. The subjects include the dread of welfare workers' calls, the tensions between middle-class and poorer African Americans and between lighter- and darker-skinned people, and family conflicts as well as family love. All are set in the North. West, herself an educated member of the Boston elite black society, was a welfare investigator and WPA relief worker in Harlem during the Depression. While not about the current inner-city crime and violence, her stories have the ring of authenticity.

136 West, Dorothy, *The Wedding*, Doubleday, 1995 (hardcover), ISBN 0–385–47143–2, $20.00, 240 pp.; Anchor, 1996 (paper), ISBN 0–385–47144–0, $10.95. Ages 15 up, grades 10 up.

Novel of five generations of family relationships, culminating with the wedding of Shelby Coles at the Martha's Vineyard enclave of the elite African-American community commonly called the Oval. Characters include Gram, white great-grandmother of the Cole girls whose "old-maid" daughter, Josephine, married the son of an ex-slave, a man who has through persistence become the first black president of the leading Negro college in Washington. After Josephine rejects her daughter, Corinne, Gram moves in and raises the child, who later marries Clark Cole, a doctor, and becomes the mother of Shelby and her sister, Liz. Shelby is engaged to a white jazz musician, Meade. Although both Corinne and his family disapprove, the wedding promises to be the biggest social event of the season. Complicating the situation is the presence of Lute McNeil, an uneducated but highly successful black entrepreneur, who is spending the summer on the Oval with his three little daughters, each by a different white wife. A confident stud, he sets out to seduce Shelby, seeing her as a way into the highly desirable upper-class society of the Oval. A complex study of prejudice, the novel explores not just white prejudice against African Americans, but the pervasive prejudice of the lighter skinned against the darker skinned and the unacknowledged but haunting desire of the light for sexual experience with the dark. Although badly overwritten in places, especially in the elaborate language used to explain the emotions of the characters, it is a fascinating study of class distinctions within a subclass.

137 Williams-Garcia, Rita, *Like Sisters on the Homefront*, Lodestar, 1995 (hardcover), ISBN 0–525–67465–9, $15.99, 165 pp.; Puffin, 1998 (paper), ISBN 0–140–38561–4, $4.99, 176 pp. Ages 12–18, grades 7–12.

Girl's sociological problem novel set in recent years, first in South Jamaica, Queens, New York, and then in a rural area near Columbus, Georgia. When selfish, barely literate, trash-talking, unwed African-American Gayle Ann Whitaker, fourteen, gets pregnant for the second time, her baby boy, Jose, only seven months old, Mama hustles her off to an abortion clinic. She then puts grumbling and protesting Gayle and Jose on a plane to Mama's brother, the Reverend Mr. Luther Gates, in Georgia. Uncle Luther openly disapproves of Gayle, but his wife, Miss Auntie, a college professor working for her Ph.D., and cousin Cookie, sixteen, are welcoming. They remain sweet and nonjudgmental in spite of Gayle's sassy, snide remarks and continual complaints about having to help about the house and care for Great, the senile, bedridden great-grandmother, who is expected to die before summer is out. Gayle looks down on Cookie for doing social service work, for singing in the church choir, where she is a soloist, and for the spirituality of her religion. Gayle's frank talk about sex embarrasses Cookie, as do her general rebelliousness and insensitivity to others. Gayle learns from Cookie that Great will "Tell (sic) before she dies," that is, pass along the family history, and that she will "tell" to Cookie. Great seems to like Gayle and occasionally confides bits of family history and old lore. She predicts that Gayle will some day "lay down her deviling" and that Jose will join the long line of preachers in the family. Gayle discovers that Cookie is sweet on Stacey Alexander, a handsome college freshman and football player. Gayle is offended when Cookie talks with her mother about her feelings toward Stacey instead of discussing them with Gayle, since she considers herself an expert on sex. Angry and jealous, she gets Cookie in trouble with the church and her father. When Cookie is "grounded," Great "tells" to Gayle instead, going all the way back to slave-ship days, then dies. Having heard the story, Gayle has a new appreciation for her family. She keeps Cookie from sneaking out to join Stacey, insisting that she wants to save her cousin and acknowledging that she needs the family to save her. From an epilogue letter Gayle writes to an unnamed homegirl, the reader learns that Great has had a large funeral and that Gayle plans to return to school in the fall. The conclusion is abrupt and unconvincing, and the often explicit sex talk may offend some. The contrast between Gayle's New York life and street talk and the Gateses' Georgia life and proper Southern speech is noticeable, the style employs both dialect and standard English, Gayle whines and sasses too much and seems too self-absorbed and lazy, and the main characters are stereotypes. Great, however, arouses admiration and rises above the other figures. Other novels by Williams-Garcia, *Blue Tights* and *Fast Talk on a Slow Track*, are described in *This Land Is Our Land* (1994), nos. 168 and 169.

138 Willis, Meredith Sue, *The Secret Super Power of Marco*, HarperCollins, 1994 (hardcover), ISBN 0–06–023558–6, $14.00, 104 pp. Ages 8–12, grades 3–7.

In a tough inner-city neighborhood where Marco has moved with his single mother and his little sister, Ritzi, there are lots of things to be afraid of—big guys who hang around the basketball court, drug dealers in the abandoned build-ings down the hill, wild kids from the Other Side of the Park, Crazy Wee-wee, a mentally ill homeless man—but most immediately he is afraid of Tyrone, a large, "hyper" kid mainstreamed into his class, where he bullies everyone. Then Marco remembers that he has secret super powers and can often see clearly what is going to happen or two alternative possible outcomes to any situation. With his new little dog, Lucy, he convinces Tyrone of his special powers and suddenly finds he has a friend, almost a shadow, who follows him everywhere. Tyrone helps him get Lucy back from Crazy Wee-wee after she escapes and the home-less man appropriates her, and he helps find Ritzi when she is bored with playing house at nursery school and walks out. In a sequel, *Marco's Monster* (1996), Tyrone gets the part of the Main Monster in the fourth-grade play, and Marco goes to great lengths to keep his friend out of trouble so he will not be barred from performing. While neither book mentions the ethnic background of the boys, it is clear from context and the cover pictures that at least Tyrone is African American, while Marco could be of Puerto Rican or Italian extraction. Tyrone, a neglected child who acts tough but shows his true side in his affection for Ritzi, is the most interesting character.

139   Woodson, Jacqueline, *From the Notebooks of Melanin Sun*, Blue Sky, 1996 (hard-cover), ISBN 0–590–45880–9, $14.95,160 pp.; Point, 1997 (paper), ISBN 0–590–45881–7, $3.99. Ages 11–18, grades 6–12.

Boy's growing-up novel set at the time of publication in a mixed-ethnic part of Brooklyn, New York. African-American Melanin Sun, almost fourteen, tells the story partly in direct discourse to the reader and partly in notebooks he writes to himself. A tall, introspective young man, Melanin lives with his smart, never-married Mama in a small fifth-floor apartment. She named him Melanin, because his skin is dark, and Sun, because she could see "the sun right there in the center of him, shining through." School out for the summer, Melanin is confronted by three concerns: awareness of his developing sexuality, especially when he gets a "hard-on" while thinking about pretty Angie, whom he is too shy to call, and when he worries that people might consider his stamp collecting "faggoty"; his changing relationship with his mother, after he learns that she is gay; and his overall attitude toward gays and whites. Early in July, Mama an-nounces that she will be bringing home someone for him to meet. Since he and his "homeboys," Sean and Raphael, confidently expect that the guest will be a man, Melanin is shocked, even disgusted, when the visitor turns out to be a young lawyer, Kristin, who has "shimmery white-people" blonde hair. Later, on the way home from Jones Beach, Mama announces to Melanin that she and Kristin are lovers. Melanin is furious, resentful of Kristin for taking Mama away just when he wants to talk to Mama about how to interact with Angie and fearful that the lesbian relationship will become known. He learns from Sean and Raphael that people already know about Kristin and Mama. One day at the beach, Kristin confides to him that she has been cut off from her family for being gay and that the only family she has now are Mama and Melanin. Melanin warms toward her and Mama. He says that he keeps his notebooks to "get it [his worries] out of me," a statement that seems in character for a bright, highly introverted boy his age. His fragmentary ruminations are not as angst-laden as those in many teen novels, but his wish to consult his mother about starting a relationship with Angie does not ring true. Their discussions about tolerance are believable, as is his anger at learning he has a "dyke" mother and his hopes that one of his pals' mothers is lesbian, too. The conversation with Kristin seems fabricated, and the ending is too pat, but the reader happily believes that Melanin is progressing toward intellectual and emotional maturity during this "growing time" in his life. For other books by Woodson, see *The Dear One* and *Last Summer with Maizon* in *This Land Is Our Land* (1994), nos. 174 and 175.

140 Woodson, Jacqueline, *I Hadn't Meant to Tell You This*, Delacorte, 1994 (hardcover), ISBN 0–385–32031–0, $15.95, 115 pp.; Laurel Leaf, 1995 (paper), ISBN 0–440–21960–4, $4.50. Ages 11–18, grades 6–12.

Realistic sociological problem novel set for about four months in recent years in a predominantly middle-class African-American suburb of Athens, Ohio. Telling the story is African-American Marie, thirteen, daughter of a professor at Ohio University, whose manic-depressive wife walked out two years before the story begins. Marie describes how, three days after school begins in the fall, a poorly dressed, unkempt, aloof white girl named Lena Bright enrolls. Lena lives with her father and younger sister, Dion, down by the dump, where the blacks say "white trash" live, and says that her mother died from breast cancer. Marie feels close to Lena, because of their mutual losses, but her father has misgivings about the girls' friendship, being a former civil rights worker who was assaulted by whites. Lena's slovenliness puzzles Marie, as do some statements, like her remark that sometimes there can be too much love. Lena says that she and Dion have to get out of the house as fast as they can in the morning and then elaborates on that by saying that she has no privacy and her father "does things" to her. She also says that she often feels as though she is "the dirtiest, ugliest thing in the world" but makes Marie promise not to tell anyone. She fears that the authorities will find out and send the sisters to separate foster homes, as they did once before. Lena and Dion have hot chocolate and take bubble baths at Marie's house, which Dion says is the "most beautifulest house" she has ever seen. Since Marie knows that Lena feels hopeless, she suggests that Lena work hard and get a scholarship to college. Lena replies that she cannot keep her mind on schoolwork, that her mind "goes off and does what it feels like." Lena begins missing classes, then one day tells Marie that her father is "touching" Dion now and that she and Dion are leaving but will write to Marie some day. Later Marie finds outside their empty house a piece of notebook paper on which is written in Lena's handwriting: "Elena Cecilia Bright and her sister Edion Kay Bright lived here once." Marie imagines the two walking happily hand-in-hand to-gether. One morning, after dreaming about Lena, Marie feels that Lena is telling her that it is all right to tell Lena's story so that other girls can go through life not being afraid as Lena has been. Characters are one-dimensional, and the story's memoir-like quality supports the retrospective narration but lessens the emotional impact. The nature of the molestation is never specified, but Lena's behavior seems clinically correct and emphasizes the novel's didactic nature. When Marie asks Lena if she is afraid she will get pregnant, Lena replies that her father "doesn't do that." Even the girls' intimate conversations seem too brief and superficial to hold the interest as they should. The open-ended con-clusion is troubling. Does Lena's whole family move away together? If so, is the reader to expect that the problems will continue? Or do the girls run away? If so, is that to be taken as the best way out of such a predicament? For other books by Woodson, see *The Dear One* and *Last Summer with Maizon*, in *This Land Is Our Land* (1994), nos. 174 and 175.

141 Woodtor, Dee Parmer, *Big Meeting*, illus. Dolores Johnson, Atheneum, 1996 (hardcover), ISBN 0–689–31933–9, $16.00, unp. Ages 5–8, grades K–3.

An annual family reunion in the South, narrated by Ethelene, known as Sweet Pea, possibly eight or ten, who comes from somewhere up north with her parents and her younger brother, Bubba, to Oakey Streak, where relatives are gathering from all over. They arrive at Grandma Bessie's house, listen to Grandpa Ques-sie's ghost stories, and spend the first night in a strange bed. The next morning, all dressed up, they attend the Little Bethel A.M.E. church, where Aunt Hester sits the children in the front row and keeps them firmly in order. Then they spill out with more relatives than they can count into the church yard, meeting new ones, slipping off to the cemetery to renew acquaintance with old ones, eating from the mountain of food, and finally riding back to Grandma's for a whole week of playing in the woods and stream. The simply told story catches the nostalgia of such gatherings, and the illustrations, which fill each page opposite the text—etchings and aquatints with watercolor and colored pencils—are in soft hues echoing the mood.

142 Worley, Demetrice A., and Jesse Perry, Jr., eds., *African-American Literature: An Anthology*, NTC, 1998 (paper), ISBN 0–8342–5924–1, $32.65, 495 pp. Ages 14 up, grades 9 up.

Large, comprehensive anthology of contemporary and historical writings by African Americans, intended as a textbook. The first eight selections are from oral tradition, including two anonymous spirituals (no. 157), fifty-four poems (no. 192), and the remainder, the bulk of the book, are prose pieces, short stories, excerpts from longer fiction, memoir, and autobiography, and essays from the late 1700s to the present. The intent is "to present . . . an insight into the richness of African-American literature, and African-American culture." All are preceded by short biographical essays (but in almost every case no commentary about the selection itself) and followed by discussion questions and suggestions for writing. The selections are arranged in eleven sections, each illustrating some aspect of the African-American experience—The Blues, Slavery, Identity, Women, Men, Relationships, Family and Ancestors, and so on—with each section introduced by a short, helpful essay. The book opens with a historical overview and concludes with an author-title index. Included under the section entitled Language and Literacy is Mary Elizabeth Vroman's "See How They Run," in The Blues is Ann Petry's "Solo on the Drums," and Arna Bontemps's "A Summer Tragedy" appears under Standing Ground. Among the excerpts are "Epilogue" from Ralph Ellison's *Invisible Man* and "1927" from Toni Morrison's *Sula*. This large and varied anthology accomplishes its objective in giving historical and cultural insights into the genres of African-American literature in addition to providing much fine reading entertainment.

143 Wright, Courtni C., *Wagon Train: A Family Goes West in 1865*, illus. Gershom Griffith, Holiday, 1995 (hardcover), ISBN 0–8234–1152–4, $15.95, unp. Ages 5–9, grades K-4.

Picture-story book of ex-slaves crossing the great plains to California just after the Civil War. The African-American family, Ma, Pa, Ben, baby Molly, and the narrator, Ginny, pack up their meager belongings and leave in a twelve-wagon train made up of those who were slaves on Master John's plantation and a neighboring one, including Grandma Sadie, who is eighty-three, and Grandpa Williams, who is even older. Their wagon train, led by black Mr. Turner, suffers various difficulties: Pa is bitten by a rattlesnake, Indians terrify them but prove harmless, drought and mile after dry mile almost defeat them, but they reach California with high hopes. The illustrations, covering almost every large-sized page with text overprinted, give a good feel for the landscape, but the people are somewhat idealized, looking too light, young, and clean for the life they have led and the arduous journey. Other picture-story books by the same author-illustrator team include *Jumping the Broom* (1994), about a slave wedding, and *Journey to Freedom: A Story of the Underground Railroad* (1994), about a successful escape to Canada.

144 Wyeth, Sharon Dennis, *The World of Daughter McGuire*, Delacorte, 1994 (hardcover), ISBN 0–385–31174–5, $14.95, 167 pp.; Yearling, 1995 (paper), ISBN 0–440–41114–9, $3.99. Ages 9–12, grades 4–7.

Girl's growing-up novel of a mixed-blood girl, eleven, trying to find where she belongs in a new neighborhood, a new school, and a family of very mixed origins. Daughter has one African-American grandmother, married to an Italian, and one Jewish grandmother whose husband was Irish. Her friends unkindly say she's a "mixed-up" or a "nothing," and the story bounces from that worry to her other troubles. A gang of tough boys who call themselves the Avengers do some mild terrorizing. Her father has run off to Colorado to write a novel, and her mother has started going out with a man named Jim Signet, whom Daughter doesn't like. All her problems are resolved predictably. Her father returns and, after some on again, off again attempts, her parents reconcile. Daughter makes two good friends, and they start an explorers' club. She stands up to the head of the Avengers when he is bullying one of his followers and wins their admiration. Jim Signet, who she has decided is a drug dealer, turns out to be starting a laundromat. For a school project, she interviews her grandparents and learns something of the background of all her progenitors and achieves pride in her mixed origins. While the story is pleasant and the happenings believable, there is little tension in the plot, and Daughter, the narrator, never seems to come alive.

145 Young, Al, ed., *African American Literature: A Brief Introduction and Anthology*, HarperCollins, 1995 (paper), ISBN 0–363–99017–6, $19.95, 363 pp. Ages 14 up, grades 9 up.

Anthology of fiction and poetry (no. 193) by African Americans, arranged by order of authors' birth dates, with a few autobiographical selections and a play, in the HarperCollins Literary Mosaic Series of which Ishmael Reed is general editor, intended primarily for college classes. The book, which is the largest of the four in the series, opens with a history of African-American writing and concludes with a thematic arrangement, list of readings, index of titles and first lines, and acknowledgments. Each writer's selection is preceded by a short introduction with biographical information and selected publications. Unfortunately, the editor seldom indicates whether the fiction piece is a short story or an excerpt from a longer work. The anthology has a generous representation of twenty-seven fiction writers, ranging from Charles W. Chestnutt, the earliest, to Jerome Wilson, the youngest. In between, appear Jean Toomer, Richard Wright, Zora Neale Hurston, Chester Himes, Amiri Baraka, Alice Walker, Brenda Flanagan, Jamaica Kincaid, Terry McMillan, and Trey Ellis, among others. Chestnutt's well-known, revealing "The Wife of His Youth" opens the collection of fiction; the poignant "Almost A Man" represents the work of Richard Wright; the contribution from John Williams's work is the resentful "Son in the Afternoon"; and Kristin Hunter's amusing, elucidating "The Jewel in the Lotus" provides a sample of her work. Clarence Major's "Five Years Ago" is a sad father-daughter story, and "The Only Man on Liberty Street" comments on nineteenth-century marriages. The anthology's best attribute is its great variety. The selections are invariably interesting, occasionally are in dialect, reveal how diction and attitudes have changed throughout the century, range from funny to wry tongue-in-cheek to pensive and reflective and intermingle the familiar with the less familiar. For other publications by Young, see no. 177, *Seduction by Light* (fiction), and no. 221, *Heaven: Collected Poems, 1956–1990*, in *This Land Is Our Land* (1994).

2

African Americans: Books of Oral Tradition

146 Faulkner, William J., coll. and ret., *Brer Tiger and the Big Wind*, illus. Roberta Wilson, Morrow, 1995 (hardcover), ISBN 0–688–12985–4, $15.00, unp. Ages 4 up, grades PS up.

Humorous trickster tale, in which Brer Rabbit and his friends teach selfish Brer Tiger a lesson when, during a famine, he refuses to share the pears from the tree under which he lives. Hints of African-American speech rhythms and bits of dialect enliven and distinguish the text, and framed, realistic, full-color, textured, quarter-page, full-page, and double-spread paintings retell the story, depict the animals in various situations, and enhance the action. Their use of emotion and comic touches reveals a good deal about human nature that older readers and viewers will especially appreciate. A note about the writer indicates that the late Faulkner, a respected African American folklorist, storyteller, pastor, and teacher, heard this story as a child from Simon Brown, a former slave who worked on the Faulkner farm.

147 Hamilton, Virginia, sel. and ret., *Her Stories: African American Folktales, Fairy Tales, and True Tales*, illus. Leo and Diane Dillon, Blue Sky, 1995 (hardcover), ISBN 0–590–47370–0, $19.95, 114 pp. All ages, grades 1 up.

Nineteen mostly old oral tradition stories and a few from personal experience, "about females from the vast treasure store of traditional black folklore," collected and retold by a prolific reteller of folk stories and myths and novelist. The pieces "focus on the magical lore and wondrous imaginings of African American women" (book jacket). "Little Girl and Buh Rabby" is a trickster tale about the figure better known as Brer Rabbit. In "Miz Hattie Gets Some Company," the Lord God creates the cat out of his glove to give the old woman relief from the hordes of mice that are bothering her. "Woman and Man Started Even" tells how, at the very beginning of the world, the devil helps the woman get power from the Lord God to counterbalance man's greater physical strength. "Annie Christmas" is a tall tale about a legendary, very powerful, and enterprising African-American woman keelboat operator on the Mississippi River. While some tales seem more fluently told than others, all retain the important oral quality, many employ dialect but never ponderously, and all suggest black speech cadences. Some stories are serious, some humorous, some cautionary, some downright funny. They vary in tone, atmosphere, and intent; most seek to entertain, while some convey morals or teach but in a nondidactic tone. All claim the attention well. Like Hamilton's other folklore anthologies, this has a helpful introduction that gives valuable background to the stories as well as section introductions, an important "Comment" that closes each story, and a list entitled "Useful Sources" at the end of the book. The attractively framed, strongly composed, full-color paintings—dramatic, suspenseful, or funny as needed—and framed, cream-toned text pages produce a remarkably handsome volume. For other books by Hamilton, see *The Bells of Christmas, Cousins, Dry Longso, The Mystery of Dream House*, and *A White Romance* in *This Land Is Our Land* (1994), nos. 41, 42, 43, 44, and 45, all fiction, and *The People Could Fly*, no. 180, oral tradition.

148 Hamilton, Virginia, ret., *A Ring of Tricksters*, illus. Barry Moser, Blue Sky Press, 1997 (hardcover), ISBN 0–590–47374–3, $19.95, 112 pp. Ages 4–8, grades PS–3.

Highly illustrated, large-format retelling of eleven animal trickster tales, four from the United States, three from the West Indies, and four from Africa. As an introductory note explains, the original tales came from Africa to the Caribbean islands and the American South with slaves, and the last four tales developed from those taken back to Freetown, the capital of Sierra Leone in West Africa, by former slaves, forming a ring of trickster tales crossing the seas in both directions. Among the American tricksters are Buh Rabby (Brer Rabbit); Bruh Wren, who tricks Bruh Buzzard; Fox, who fools both Cat and Rat; and Bruh Rabbit, who gets the best of Bruh Wolf. All three West Indies stories concern Anansi, the spider-man figure. In the African tales the tricksters are Cunnie Rabbit (a water deerlet or small gazelle), spider, Old Mister Turtle, and Shulo, the hare. All are in interesting language echoing oral tellings, the African tales employing an especially interesting dialect. Each section is introduced by a page explaining characteristics of tales from that area, and the book ends with notes on each story giving sources and additional information. Each tale is preceded by a full-page watercolor, and additional large illustrations are scattered through the text, many of them dramatic like the picture of a brooding buzzard talking to a perky wren. In *This Land Is Our Land* (1994) are nos. 41, 42, 43, 44, and 45 (all fiction), and no. 180, a collection of folktales (see entry 147 for titles).

149 Hamilton, Virginia, ret., *When Birds Could Talk & Bats Could Sing*, illus. Barry Moser, Scholastic, 1996 (hardcover), ISBN 0–5904–7372–7, $17.95, 72 pp. Ages 4–8, grades PS–3.

Eight highly illustrated African-American tales collected by Martha Young, originally in slave-era black dialect, retold in more accessible colloquial speech. All feature birds or bats, with one human, Alcee Lingo, pictured as a young boy who can talk with them and with other animals, sometimes helping them out, sometimes being helped by them, as when Blue Jay and Swallow steal fire for him. Most of the tales are in the *cante fable* style, which includes verses and ends with a moral, here printed in italics. They also tell how some creature, usually a bird or bat, got its characteristic look or song. An Afterword by the author tells about sources. The lavish watercolor illustrations picture the birds and bats realistically except that most wear hats. Among Hamilton's other books are nos. 41, 42, 43, 44, and 45 (all fiction) and no. 180, a collection of folktales, in *This Land Is Our Land* (1994) (see entry 147 for titles).

150 Harris, Joel Chandler, ret., *The Last Tales of Uncle Remus*, ed. Julius Lester, illus. Jerry Pinkney, Dial, 1994 (hardcover), ISBN 0–8037–1303–7, $10.99, 156 pp. Ages 10 up, grades 5 up.

Fourth in a series of retellings of the African-American folktales originally written down by Joel Chandler Harris as though told by a slave, Uncle Remus. In these thirty-nine tales, most but not all with animal characters, Lester frequently uses modern idioms and allusions: a diet of tofu and bean sprouts "will certainly swunk you up"; animals once "could read and write and do arithmetic, slam dunk a basketball and anything else you can think of"; a woman makes sheep's-head stew that they do not have at McDonald's. The spelling of the Harris versions is standardized and the dialect modified, but enough is retained to give a flavor of Southern oral tradition. Illustrations include three double-page watercolors and occasional black-and-white drawings. Another collection of the Harris stories, *Further Tales of Uncle Remus*, edited by Lester, is described in *This Land Is Our Land* (1994), no. 181.

151 Hudson, Wade, and Cheryl Hudson, sels., *How Sweet the Sound: African-American Songs for Children*, illus. Floyd Cooper, Scholastic, 1995 (hardcover), ISBN 0–590–48030–8, $15.95, 48 pp.; 1997 (paper), ISBN 0–590–96911–0, $9.95. Ages 4 up, grades PS up.

Impressive collection of twenty-three African-American songs and poems. Fourteen are "traditional," that is, from the oral tradition, like "Kum Ba Ya" and "Miss Mary Mack," some are spirituals, like "Go Down Moses" and "Swing Low, Sweet Chariot," and others are by known writers. The collection is intended to give readers "a glimpse at the history of Blacks in America through their music" by including "songs from Africa, spirituals, work songs, gospels, jazz, blues songs, play songs, chants, soul, and popular music of our own time." Other spirituals include "Over My Head" and "Get on Board, Little Children." "Sweet Oranges" and "Blueberries" are street cries, while "This Little Light of Mine," "Hambone," "Freedom's Comin'," and "We Shall Not Be Moved" are

traditional chants and songs. The double-spread, suffused-with-brown-tones illustrations flow around and over the texts and picture situations under which
the songs might have been sung or were inspired. For example, the illustration
accompanying "Over My Head" depicts a family laboring in a cotton field, with
the foregounded child longingly looking upward, imagining she hears music and
singing in the air and yearning for the "God somewhere," who represents a
better world. An introduction about African-American music and song opens
the book, and acknowledgments, an index of writers, titles, lines, and topics, a
list of Recommended Reading and Listening, and a particularly valuable section
with notes about the songs, composers, and music conclude the book. For earlier
books by Wade Hudson and Cheryl Hudson, see *Jamal's Busy Day* and *Pass It
On*, nos. 60 and 209 (Wade), and *Afro-Bets ABC Book, Good Morning, Baby*,
and *Bright Eyes, Brown Skin*, nos. 58, 59, and 208 (Cheryl), in *This Land Is
Our Land* (1994).

152 Lester, Julius, ret., *John Henry*, illus. Jerry Pinkney, Dial, 1994 (hardcover), ISBN
0–8037–1606–0, $16.95, unp. Ages 4–8, grades P–3.

Prose retelling of the story of the steel-driving hero of African-American
legend, best known in ballad form. Lester starts with John Henry's birth and
unusual infancy, when he leaps from his mother's arms and grows up in one
day, and includes several episodes exhibiting his great strength and physical
ability before he starts work on the West Virginia tunnel and his contest against
the steam drill. The large format and illustrations, done in watercolor and colored
pencil, most larger than full page, make this a lavish book. Most interesting are
pictures of the old steam drill and details of rural and small town life. Lester is
also the editor of no. 181 *Further Tales of Uncle Remus*, by Joel Chandler
Harris, in *This Land Is Our Land* (1994).

153 Medearis, Angela Shelf, ret., *The Freedom Riddle*, illus. John Ward, Dutton, 1995
(hardcover), ISBN 0–525–67469–1, $14.99, unp. Ages 5 up, grades K up.

Folktale drawn from the collection of noted folklorist William Faulkner, a
tale based on a true story told to Faulkner by a former slave. On Master Brown's
Virginia plantation, whenever two people meet for the first time on Christmas
day, whoever says "Christmas Gift" first receives a present. Jim, a clever young
overseer, sets about turning this custom to his advantage to gain his freedom
from his master. He catches Master Brown unaware, says the phrase first, and
asks that the man either guess a riddle that Jim will pose to him or give Jim
his freedom. Master Brown reluctantly agrees, and a year passes while Jim
concocts his riddle, which he does from various events that occur. The riddle
consists of several clues tucked in a ten-line verse, which ends, "I'm innocent,
now set me free." Master Brown puzzles and puzzles over the riddle, walks
back and forth in deep thought, ventures one answer after another, and finally
concedes defeat. Jim throws his hat in the air, wishes everyone a Merry Christ-

mas, and rides off, a free man at last. The story combines elements of the classic underdog tale and the ancient riddling form, which, among others, recalls the puzzlers posed by Samson of biblical story. The text is solid, longer than those of most picture-story books, well told, and lively with a little dialect, and the full-color, deep-toned paintings reveal character and picture the elements of the riddle as it develops. Jim is shown as a bright, strong, handsome young man. Earlier books, *Dancing with the Indians, Picking Peas for a Penny*, and *The Zebra-Riding Cowboy*, all verse, appear in *This Land Is Our Land* (1994), nos. 216, 217, and 218.

154 Meaderis, Angela Shelf, ret., *Tailypo: A Newfangled Tall Tale*, illus. Sterling Brown, Holiday House, 1996 (hardcover), ISBN 0–8234–1249–0, $15.95, unp. Ages 4–10, grades PS–5.

Retelling of a classic Southern folk tale, here presented with African-American characters in the illustrations. A little boy, Kennie Ray, and his parents live on a hardscrabble farm in the Texas hill country. Kennie Ray's best friend is his dog, Fang, the "roughest, foulest, fiercest, most vicious chihuahua" ever. One night, a monstrous composite creature, with sharp ears, yellow eyes, a long pointy nose, and lion's teeth, enters Kennie Ray's bedroom and sets about eating the family's last remaining beans and greens. Kennie Ray chases it with a broom, and Fang grabs its tail, pulling so hard that the furry tail breaks loose. After Kennie Ray sells the tail for food money, he is accosted by the creature, which demands its "tailypo." After more scary adventures, Kennie Ray gets rid of the monster by shouting so loudly that he does not have the "tailypo" that he scares the creature away. While the retelling fails to engage the emotions as much as it might, the full-color, off-the-page, realistic paintings give the story life and ground its fantasy in reality. They effectively contrast the ugly monster with the brave little dog and the handsome boy, who triumph because of perseverance and courage. Earlier books appear in *This Land Is Our Land* (1994), nos. 216, 217, and 218 (see entry 153 for titles).

155 San Souci, Robert D., ret., *The Hired Hand*, illus. Jerry Pinkney, Dial, 1997 (hardcover), ISBN 0–8037–1297–9, $14.95, unp. Ages 5–10, grades K-5.

Lively retelling of an African-American folktale, which has counterparts in European lore going back to ancient times. Old Sam, a charitable black miller, father of lazy selfish Young Sam, hires willing, able, and forgiving New Hand. When Young Sam secretly observes New Hand cure an arthritic farmer in ways involving magic actions and verses, making the farmer young and sprightly again, Young Sam tries to do the same thing with the farmer's wife, with disastrous results. While Young Sam is on trial for the woman's murder, New Hand turns up, having brought the woman back to life, and calls for Young Sam's release. Freed, Young Sam mends his evil, lazy ways, an ending that gives a twist to the normal story pattern, in which the evildoer is punished or exiled. Hints of unschooled speech create the Southern setting of an earlier period, which is splendidly evoked by Pinkney's pencil-and-watercolor paintings. The carefully controlled, seemingly spontaneous artwork flows off the pages and around the boxed texts, just soft-colored and soft-edged enough to give the sense of far earlier times in which magical beings walk the earth and the supernatural often occurs. The paintings recreate important events, portray character, and extend the setting well beyond what is stated in the text. A note indicates that the story is given a free black milltown setting, like that of Waterford, Virginia, which was developed in the 1700s by antislavery Quakers. A writer's note gives sources and interesting information about the story. For other books by San Souci, see *The Boy and the Ghost, Sukey and the Mermaid, The Talking Eggs, The Enchanted Tapestry*, and *The Samurai's Daughter*, in *This Land Is Our Land* (1994), nos. 187, 188, 189, 316, and 317.

156 Stevens, Janet, ad., *Tops & Bottoms*, illus. Janet Stevens, Harcourt, 1995 (hardcover), ISBN 0–15–292851–0, $15.00, unp. All ages, grades PS up.

Lively retelling of an African-American trickster tale, in which clever Hare and his family outwit lazy Bear. After Hare's land falls to Bear through a lost bet, Hare wins it back by persuading Bear to let him harvest and plant on Bear's property, splitting the profits each time as Bear chooses. The first time, sleepy, slow-witted Bear chooses tops as his share of the profits, so Hare plants carrots, radishes, and beets. The second time, Bear, still not fully awake, chooses bottoms, so Hare plants lettuce, broccoli, and celery. The third time, exasperated Bear chooses both tops and bottoms, thinking he finally has bested Hare, but Hare plants corn. No longer sleepy and thinking more clearly, Bear angrily announces he will do his own planting and harvesting henceforth. Using his considerable profits, Hare buys back his land and prospers. This classic underdog tale is perfectly complemented by detailed, full-color, humorous illustrations that wrap around the framed text and flow off the pages. The book works vertically rather than horizontally, that is, it opens from the right side, as do most books, but the tops of the pages are along the left-hand side, a method of presentation that emphasizes the tops-bottoms idea and adds to the humor. The opening picture, in which Bear lies sprawled asleep in his porch easy chair sets the mood and perfectly characterizes him. The nose of a tiny rabbit peeks out from the text-box, foreshadowing what lies ahead. Good fun all the way, the book was named a Caldecott honor book. For an earlier book by Stevens, see *This Land Is Our Land* (1994), no. 537, *Coyote Steals the Blanket: A Ute Tale.*

157 Worley, Demetrice A., and Jesse Perry, Jr., eds., *African-American Literature: An Anthology*, NTC Publishing, 1998 (paper), ISBN 0–8342–5924–1, $32.65, 495 pp. Ages 14 up, grades 9 up.

Large, comprehensive anthology of contemporary and historical writings by African Americans intended as a textbook. The first eight selections are from folk literature, among them, two anonymous spirituals, "Motherless Child" and "Swing Low, Sweet Chariot." Others include a retelling of the story of John Henry, "The Steel Drivin' Man," retold by A. Philip Randolph and Chandler Owen, and the vigorous, tall-tale adventures of "Stagolee," retold by Julius Lester. Most of the pieces are short but distinctive and serve as a fine introduction to the material to follow, since, as the anthologists point out, some writers like Zora Neale Hurston often incorporate folk material into their writings. The anthology is intended to "present . . . an insight into the richness of African-American literature, and African-American culture." Other genres included are short stories, excerpts from longer fiction, memoir, and autobiography, and essays from the late 1700s to the present. All are preceded by short biographical essays (but in almost every case no commentary about the selection itself) and followed by discussion questions and suggestions for writing. The selections are arranged in eleven sections, each illustrating some aspect of the African-American experience (The Blues, Slavery, Identity, Women, Men, and Family and Ancestors, etc.), with each section being introduced by a short but helpful essay. The book opens with a historical overview and concludes with an author-title index. For the poems and fiction, see nos. 142 and 192, this book.

3

African Americans: Books of Poetry

158 Barnwell, Ysaye M., *No Mirrors in My Nana's House*, illus. Synthia Saint James, Harcourt, 1998 (hardcover), ISBN 0–152–01825–5, $18.00, unp. Ages 3–7, grades PS–2.

Brief, realistic, contemporary picture-story book, in which a little girl, whose house has no mirrors, recalls how she saw her own beauty reflected in the warmth and approval of her loving grandmother's eyes. The little girl remembers that, since Nana's house was without mirrors, she did not know that her skin was very dark, that her nose was too flat and broad, or that her clothes were ill-fitting. Nor was she aware of the cracks in the wall, the excessive dust, or the rubbish and noise in the hallway outside. The look in Nana's eyes reflected beauty, because the beauty intrinsic to everything about her was all that Nana allowed herself to perceive. The book concludes with Nana asking the little girl to look deep into her eyes, the better to experience her own beauty and the beauty of life. The spare, rhythmical, repetitive text moves like the song it is, being one recorded by the musical group, Sweet Honey in the Rock, and composed by a member. The brilliantly colored acrylic paintings are equally minimalist, the faces of the two-dimensional figures lacking features, for example, and the sparsely detailed settings. This "cuddle-up" book, stunningly decorated and keen with emotion, demands to be savored, preferably in a one-on-one situation. Although the lack of facial features universalizes the story, it is also a sophisticated technique that may disturb some children. A CD in which the author reads the text and Sweet Honey in the Rock sings the song is included.

159 Boyd, Candy Dawson, *Daddy, Daddy, Be There*, illus. Floyd Cooper, Philomel, 1995 (hardcover), ISBN 0–399–22745–8, $15.95, unp.; Paper Star, 1998 (paper), ISBN 0–698–11750–6, $5.00. Ages 4–9, grades PS–4.

Sixteen short, free-verse poems, or perhaps one long poem in sixteen stanzas, in which a child lists occasions in which it is important for father to be there: in scary crowds, on first days of school, with storybooks and nursery rhymes,

on picnics and birthdays, in tough times and good times—situations special for
a child—face to face and not just on the telephone or for just a few hours a
week. The feelings are poignant, and while the words may not be those that a
child would use because of inexperience, they are ones that children probably
feel. The soft-edged, full-page paintings are done in brown and yellow tones
and show close-up frontals and back views. Although the text is not ethnic
specific, most of the illustrations show African Americans. Other races appear
also, a feature that supports the universality of the feelings. Although sometimes
sentimental, this is a pleasant book to which most children can relate, but it
should be used with discretion. Fiction by Boyd appears in *Charlie Pippin* and
Chevrolet Saturdays in *This Land Is Our Land* (1994), nos. 10 and 11.

160   Bryan, Ashley, ed., *Ashley Bryan's ABC of African American Poetry*, illus. Ashley
Bryan, Atheneum, 1997 (hardcover), ISBN 0–689–81209–4, $16.00, unp. All ages,
grades PS up.

Twenty-six poems, or selections from poems, by twenty-five African-
American poets, and one black spiritual, organized by the letters of the alphabet.
Included are tightly patterned, more traditionally rhythmical, and free verse poems, poems in earlier voices like Paul Laurence Dunbar, Langston Hughes, and
Countee Cullen, but many are by more recent writers—Maya Angelou, Audre
Lord, Haki Madhubuti (Don Lee), and Rita Dove. A principle of selection was
that the line containing the letter of the alphabet inspire a particular image to
illuminate the black experience or belief. For example, the letter "A" verse is
from James Weldon Johnson's "God's Trombones" and shows God sweeping
through space, sun in hand, about to create the world. The illustration for Dudley
Randall's "Black Magic" depicts a strongly drawn, dignified black girl with full
red lips, around whose sculptured head are grouped luscious cherries, blackber-
ries, and grapes. The full-page, firmly composed, framed tempera and gouache
pictures exude deeply paletted, vibrant color. Each picture and poem forms an
integrated whole, each poem leads naturally into the next, and all together constitute a rich viewing and listening experience. For earlier books by Bryan, see
All Night, All Day, Sing to the Sun, and *Sh-Ko and His Eight Wicked Brothers*,
in *This Land Is Our Land* (1994), nos. 195, 196, and 291.

161   Bryan, Ashley, sel., *Carol of the Brown King: Nativity Poems by Langston
Hughes*, illus. Ashley Bryan, Atheneum, 1998 (hardcover), ISBN 0–689–81877–7,
$16.00, unp. All ages, grades PS up.

Five short poems about Christmas by Langston Hughes, which reflect different experiences with the Christ Child, all from the African-American perspective, "Shepherd's Song at Christmas," "On a Christmas Night," "On a Pallet of
Straw," "The Christmas Story," and the title poem, along with a short, expressive, anonymous, four-couplet piece, powerful in its simplicity, translated from
a Puerto Rican Christmas card. Accompanying the poems are vibrantly colorful,

sophisticated, geometrically patterned illustrations, framed in themselves and themselves framing the verses. The concluding picture of Mary gazing at the baby is a Madonna-and-Holy-Child gem. This is an exceptionally beautiful book with which all ages can celebrate Christmas. For other books by Bryan, see *This Land Is Our Land* (1994), nos. 195, 196, and 291 (see preceding entry, no. 160, for titles).

162 Burleigh, Robert, *Hoops*, illus. Stephen T. Johnson, Harcourt, 1997 (hardcover), ISBN 0–15–201450–0, $16.00, unp. Ages 4 up, grades PS up.

Realistic picture-story book that speaks to the essence of basketball, the brief, economical, alliterative text and accompanying pictures presenting a fast-moving game in progress. Full-page, muted pastels, whose indistinct lines seem to move before the viewer's eyes, focus mostly on portions of bodies in typical, critical game positions—eyes hypnotized with intent, hands holding or dunking a ball, feet in motion or poised under legs outstretched, faces caught in solid determination—all scenes that resonate with the sparse poetic words, whose consonance and assonance echo the bouncing of the ball and the tromping of the feet. The figures of speech extend the poetry of a sport well played. This is an unusually handsome and effective book, one that explores the nature of what the sport truly means to the young people who play it with all their hearts and skill. The text makes no racial or ethnic references, but the illustrations depict mostly strong, well-muscled, goodlooking African Americans.

163 Clinton, Catherine, comp., *I, Too, Sing America: Three Centuries of African American Poetry*, illus. Stephen Alcorn, Houghton, 1998 (hardcover), ISBN 0–395–89599–5, $20.00, 128 pp. Ages 5 up, grades K up.

Anthology of three dozen poems by twenty-five African-American poets from colonial times to the present, arranged by order of birth and accompanied by biographical sketches, brief introductions to the poems, and afterwords by the compiler and artist. Most poets are familiar, like Langston Hughes, with four pieces in addition to the title poem, James Weldon Johnson, Arna Bontemps, Gwendolyn Brooks, Maya Angelou, and Rita Dove, the first African-American Poet Laureate of the United States, who concludes the collection. Others less well known include Lucy Terry, whose "Bars Fight," which deplores an Indian attack on two white families on the Massachusetts frontier, was the first poem composed by an African American, preceding Phillis Wheatley (also represented) by some years, and is bitterly ironic when read in the climate of the late twentieth century. Topics include protest and activism, the contributions of black women, demands for political and economic justice, the "outsider" experience, indictment of bigotry, friendship across racial lines, celebration of the natural beauty of the South, the slave experience, and the need for focusing on the needs of black children. Although few new poems are included, most pieces being those usually associated with the writers, they eloquently express the intellectual and emotional ideas intended. Forms vary from tightly patterned to free verse, mostly the rhythmical and structural patterns that prevailed in the poets' periods. The illustrations are muted-color, full-page, mixed-media, highly stylized paintings, whose fluid, circular patterns subtly pick up and extend the matter of each poem. Introducing each poet is a full-page, brown-toned reproduction of an African textile. Altogether this is a coffee-table volume of exceptional beauty.

164 Dove, Rita, *Mother Love: Poems*, Norton, 1995 (hardcover), ISBN 0–393–03808–4, $17.95, 77 pp.; 1996 (paper), ISBN 0–393–31444–8, $10.00. Ages 14 up, grades 9 up.

Thirty-five poems by the former Poet Laureate of the United States that take their inspiration from the story of Demeter and Persephone from Greek mythology. The poems vary in form, some being strictly structured fourteen-lined sonnets, others less tightly bound by rules, but all displaying rhythm, lyricism. In her foreword, the poet explains that she is probing the ramifications of the violated world, such as that in which Demeter and Persephone found themselves, a world the opposite of that prescribed by the sonnet, which assumes an "intact" world. She adds that the sonnet is ideal for exploring the story, since "all three— mother-goddess, daughter-consort and poet—are struggling to sing in their chains." The personas shift from young daughter to young mother to older child and older mother, to daughter looking ahead to motherhood to those who are witnesses of their circumstances—the different perspectives of universal motherhood and daughterhood. Settings move from schoolyard and childhood to Paris to the Mexican pyramids and ancient temples. Some poems retell the ancient myth, or stay very close to the tale; most apply it to contemporary situations. The voice and viewpoint remain strongly feminine throughout; these are a woman's poems directed at women of an age to understand or to begin to have some comprehension of generational women's experiences. *The Poet's World* (1995), a book of lectures delivered during Dove's term as Poet Laureate, includes some previously published poems, while *The Darker Face of the Earth* (1994) is a play in blank verse set on a southern plantation and based on the story of Oedipus from Greek mythology. More recently published poems appear in *On the Bus with Rosa Parks* (1999), some of which address universal experiences, while others deal with the civil rights movement and reflect African-American women's perspectives. For earlier publications by this versatile, much-honored writer, see *This Land Is Our Land* (1994), nos. 25, *Fifth Sunday* (short stories), 26, *Through the Ivory Gate* (novel), and 199, *Thomas and Beulah* (poems).

165 Feelings, Tom, comp., *Soul Looks Back in Wonder*, illus. Tom Feelings, Dial, 1994 (hardcover), ISBN 0–8037–1001–1, $15.99, unp.; Puffin, 1999 (paper), ISBN 0–1405–6501–9, $6.99, 40 pp. Ages 4 up, grades PS up.

Short poems by thirteen African-American writers, all composed specifically to go with art work by Feelings, all celebrating the beauty and strength of being black. Frankly assembled to raise the self-esteem of children, the poems are stronger on uplifting spirit than on technique, although they are written by such well-known authors as Walter Dean Myers, Langston Hughes, Margaret Walker, Maya Angelou, and Lucille Clifton. Each accompanies or is superimposed on a striking double-page or nearly double-page illustration. These use a variety of techniques, including collage, spray painting, and colored pencils. The art work dominates.

166 Gershator, Phillis, and David Gershator, *Greetings, Sun*, illus. Synthia Saint James, DK, 1998 (hardcover), ISBN 0–789–42482–7, $15.95, unp. Ages 3–7, grades PS–2.

Very simple picture-story book in rhyme. Throughout a day, two African-American children welcome the day and familiar objects in their lives, including parts of their bodies ("Greetings, toes. Greetings, knees."), clothes, food, sky, clouds, ants, and bees. At school they greet girls, boys, books, and toys. At home, they have dinner, prepare for bed, and end by sending greetings to the moon. The illustrations are equally simple, in brilliantly colored flat planes with almost no detail. The boy and girl, as well as the other characters, are featureless, with brown heads, black hair, arms and legs but no fingers. Perhaps because both text and illustrations are reduced to essentials, this is an attractive book.

167 Giovanni, Nikki, *The Genie in the Jar*, illus. Chris Raschka, Holt, 1996 (hardcover) ISBN 0–8050–4118–4, $15.95, unp.; 1998 (paper), ISBN 0–805–06076–6, $6.95. Ages 4–8, grades PS–3.

Poem by a highly acclaimed African-American woman poet, previously published in *Re: Creation* (1970), here presented in picture-book form. Short, free verse, one line per page, the poem celebrates the joy and power of music, song, dance, and heritage. It invites the hearer, a small child, to become a participant by choosing a note and then sporting with it, giving it all the happiness and movement she can summon. The poem also celebrates the black musical experience and the contributions of black performers. Raschka's simple, cartoonish line drawings, done in India ink, oil sticks, and watercolors, expand the rhythmical sensation with their swirling movements, pie-shaped faces, rounded bodies, and encircling arms. The chocolate-brown figures are presented on mostly tan-toned pages, otherwise without detail, and with occasional red, yellow, and turquoise garments. The genie in the jar is the small child, whose female relatives and friends are teaching her to "sing a Black song our Black song" from the traditions that are the peculiar treasure of black people.

168 Giovanni, Nikki, *Knoxville, Tennessee*, illus. Larry Johnson, Scholastic, 1994 (hardcover), ISBN 0–590–47074–4, $14.95, unp. Ages 4 up, grades PS up.

Bright, colorful picture-book version of a poem from this celebrated writer's first published collection, *Black Feeling, Black Talk, Black Judgement* (sic) (1968). Perhaps Giovanni's best-known poem and one that has frequently been anthologized, it is a short, sensory celebration of remembered summer joys with family and friends—eating succulent seasonal products like fresh corn, okra, greens, and cabbage, enjoying barbecue, buttermilk, homemade ice cream, and gospel music on the lawn at the church picnic, walking to the mountains with grandmother and running barefoot there, and, best of all, feeling warm and loved. Deep, vibrant greens predominate, capturing not only the sense of summer but also of being young and eager for life. The first two-page spread, off the page as are all the pictures, depicts a young African-American girl wearing a white dress and sitting on a blanket on a broad expanse of green lawn, the large family house gleaming white in the background and bordered by lush, green trees. The girl savors brilliant yellow corn on the cob, while a long brown dog, face uplifted toward her, lies patiently in front of her, awaiting his share of the summer treat. The combination of medium and dark tones, of horizontal and slanting lines, and of powerful, discernible brush strokes adds meaning to the line, "you can eat fresh corn," and at the same time prepares the reader for more of summer's pleasures to come. Forms are smudgy around the edges and faces featureless, a technique that contributes to the sense of nostalgia. Although illustrating the poem line by line detracts from its impact as a verbal creation and focuses the reader upon the pictured scenes, this is a remarkably handsome book, one that readers of all ages can enjoy alone and together time and again.

169 Giovanni, Nikki, *The Selected Poems of Nikki Giovanni*, Morrow, 1996 (hardcover), ISBN 0–688–14047–5, $22.00, 292 pp. Ages 12 up, grades 7 up.

A collection of 150 poems by a leading African-American woman poet, chosen from her previously published collections, presented in the chronological order in which the books were published, *Black Feeling, Black Talk, Black Judgement* (sic) (1968), *Re: Creation* (1970), *My House* (1972), *The Women and the Men* (1975), *cotton candy on a rainy day* (1978), and *Those Who Ride the Night Winds* (1983), and supplemented by four occasional poems. Introducing the collection is a lengthy, detailed critical analysis of Giovanni's work by Virginia C. Fowler, in which she makes this significant, summary judgment: "The development of a unique and distinctive voice has been perhaps the single most important achievement of Giovanni's career . . . [and even a quick reading] will reveal many changes in tone, in ideas, and in subjects . . . what remains consistent . . . is the voice speaking to us from the page" (3). Also included are a chronology, a title index, and an index of first lines. Many of the poems are the ones that easily come to mind and have often been anthologized, like "Nikki-Rosa," "Knoxville, Tennessee," "Ego Tripping," "Poem for Aretha," "Legacies," "Mothers," "The Funeral of Martin Luther King, Jr.," "A Poem on the Assassination of Robert F. Kennedy," and the militant "The Great Pax Whitie," which brought her a great deal of attention. There are many other poems here, however, that are less well known and are worth additional readings. Most of the poems are free, some having internal rhymes and chimes, and some, especially those in the last book published, *Those Who Ride the Night Winds*, are more demanding prose-poems. Reading the collection straight through supports Fowler's observation; Giovanni's voice is still intimate and sharp but less self-conscious and overtly angry, and her world view has broadened. While some of these poems have appeal to young children, like "Knoxville, Tennessee," most will be best apprehended by older readers. Of the fifty-four mostly short poems in the thematic compilation *Love Poems* (1997), almost half also appear in *Selected Poems*. While most are mature, some, like "Love Is," can be appreciated by children. A collection of completely new poems is *Blues: For All the Changes: New Poems* (1999), which explores various facets of blues and other forms of music, and, as is usual with Giovanni, different facets of life as well. Many of these poems are easily appreciated on a surface level of meaning and thus can be used with younger readers.

170 Giovanni, Nikki, ed., *Shimmy Shimmy Shimmy Like My Sister Kate: Looking at the Harlem Renaissance Through Poems*, Holt, 1996 (hardcover), ISBN 0–8050–3494– 3, $16.95, 191 pp. Ages 11 up, grades 7 up.

Anthology "that looks at the Harlem Renaissance through poems," according to the editor, Renaissance being the term used "for the flowering of the arts in Harlem [in New York City] between 1917 and 1935," the period into which she classifies her own early work. The fifty poems by twenty-three writers, mostly men, are accompanied by insightful, helpful, and very readable critical and informative essays on both poets and poems. The essays comment on individual poems, relate the poems of one writer to others of the writer and to the poems of other writers, and place the poets' works within the literary movement. Introducing the volume is a lengthy, valuable, critical essay on the movement and on some of the poets, and concluding it are biographical sketches, lists of related anthologies and collections and of biographies and other studies on the Harlem Renaissance, a general index, and an index of first lines. The poets are arranged in order of birth, beginning with W.E.B. Du Bois, although Giovanni asserts that she feels the movement really began with Paul Laurence Dunbar, because he was "a popular poet" whose poems were widely published and hence well known. The most recent poet included is Ntozake Shange (b. 1948), whose poem "it's not so good to be born a girl/sometimes" Giovanni says not only reflects the problems of black women but of all girls, and of blacks in general. In between, are the familiar writers of the period, most represented by their best-known, and perhaps for that reason, most important poems. Ten of Langston Hughes's pieces appear, among them "Harlem"; "I, Too," from which comes the well-known line, "I am the darker brother"; and "The Negro Speaks of Rivers." Other selections include "Incident" by Countee Cullen (represented by six poems), "Those Winter Sundays" and "The Whipping" by Robert Hayden, "The Creation" by James Weldon Johnson, and "Nikki-Rosa" by Giovanni herself. Among the other poets are Gwendolyn Brooks, LeRoi Jones/Amiri Baraka, Sonia Sanchez, and Ishmael Reed. The anthology is intended as an introduction to the work of these writers, to the period, and to themes that occupied their minds and that continue to appear in black writers' work, like the relationship between the races, the dignity of the black appearance, black self-respect, and the importance to African Americans of their African heritage—objectives ably achieved.

171 Giovanni, Nikki, *The Sun Is So Quiet*, illus. Ashley Bryan, Holt, 1996 (hardcover), ISBN 0–8050–4119–2, $14.95, 32 pp. Ages 4–10, grades PS–5.

Brilliant, rainbow-colored, highly patterned illustrations decorate and extend the substance and atmosphere of thirteen short poems mostly about nature and the seasons intended for younger children. Some poems are rhymed, some are free, all move along well to convey the substance of what the poet desires, albeit the end-rhymed form is not one the poet uses effortlessly and as a result some images seem strained. An occasional condescending tone intrudes, as in "Rainbows," in which the boy persona describes his rainbow boat as "oh so big," pretends to be the captain, and ruefully remarks that he is "just a little boy" who "wonder[s] why" there are "rainbows steering" past him. A few poems exhibit a keen, entertaining sense of verbal play, like "Prickled Pickles Don't Smile"; "Covers" evokes a warm, cozy feeling that courts sleep; and "Racing Against the Sun" captures youthful aspirations for a bright, unlimited future. Children tiptoe through strawberry patches, lick chocolate from their fingers, and cherish books just because books bring joy. While many of the less complex poems that appear in Giovanni's adult collections are better crafted than these and are well within the scope of children to appreciate when they are read to them, this beautiful book can bring a measure of reading and hearing pleasure.

172 Greenfield, Eloise, *Angels*, illus. Jan Spivey Gilchrist, Hyperion, 1998 (hardcover), ISBN 0–7868–0442–4, $14.95, unp. Ages 4–8, grades PS–3.

Seventeen original poems inspired by Gilchrist's evocative pencil drawings of angels and adults, who behave like angels, comforting, protecting, and guiding children in their everyday lives. A stepfather brings flowers on the occasion of his daughter's first solo, telling her she sings like an angel; babies lie securely sleeping, while angels hover overhead; big sister plays the angel role by buttoning shirts, playing games, and comforting little brother; and Kamali wonders if the angel he sees in the bubble he blew will disappear forever if the bubble pops. Some poems have the quality of prayer, others are pensive, reflective, or more active in describing children's pursuits. Among the best is "Daniel in Snow," in which the poet describes how the little boy seems called out into the snow, where he trudges a "million long miles from Daddy" while "invisible angels" walk protectively beside him. The poems capture the small child's perspective about matters important to the age in short, to-the-point stanzas, structured, occasionally rhymed. Although the book's illustrations and overall design are stunning, the poems are not as well conceived and executed technically as those in such earlier books of Greenfield's as *Honey, I Love* (1978). For other books by Greenfield, see in *This Land Is Our Land* (1994), *Grandpa's Face, Koya Delaney and the Good Girl Blues,* and *William and the Good Old Days,* nos. 34, 35, and 36 (fiction), and *I Make Music* and *Night on Neighborhood Street,* 206 and 207, poems.

173 Greenfield, Eloise, *For the Love of the Game: Michael Jordan and Me,* illus. Jan Spivey Gilchrist, HarperCollins, 1997 (hardcover), ISBN 0–06–027298–8, $19.89, unp.; 1999 (paper), ISBN 0–064–43555–5, $5.95. Ages 3 up, grades PS up.

Short, free-verse poem divided into two sections. The first celebrates the achievements of Michael Jordan, the African-American basketball star, and the second part describes two eleven-year-old (according to an author's note) children, who see possibilities in life because of Jordan's choice to make the most of the talents he was given. Full-page, off-the-page paintings in mainly brown tones, some, particularly those of Jordan, strongly composed, others soft edged and touched with the mystical, depict the characters, extend the poem with basketball action scenes, and capture the children's emotions. While the poem moves adequately, rhythms and devices approximating the game, the illustrations greatly overpower the text, and it is they that linger in the memory. Greenfield has published fiction and other books of poems. See in *This Land Is Our Land* (1994), nos. 34, 35, and 36 (fiction) and nos. 206 and 207 (poems) (see preceding entry, no. 172, for titles).

174 Grimes, Nikki, *A Dime a Dozen,* illus. Angelo, Dial, 1998 (hardcover), ISBN 0–8037–2227–3, $15.99, 56 pp. Ages 10–14, grades 5–9.

Short, personal poems describing the life of the author in three sections, Genius, The Secret, and A Dime a Dozen. The first twelve, telling about her childhood, her parents, and her sister, are mostly loving, though sometimes showing slight irritation at her mother. The Secret's nine poems are about the family breakup, the drinking, the divorce, and the times alone with her father. The third section is about asserting herself and sticking to her desire to be a writer, even if, as her mother says, writers are a dime a dozen. The poems are easily accessible, some in free verse, some in regular rhyme and meter, more in a combination with pattern and occasional rhyme. Only a couple indicate that the writer is African American, but the attractive black-and-white illustrations, which look like pencil drawings with charcoal shading, show all the people as dark skinned.

175 Grimes, Nikki, *It's Raining Laughter,* illus. Myles C. Pinkney, Dial, 1997 (hardcover), ISBN 0–8037–2003–3, $14.99, unp. Ages 4–8, grades PS–3.

A dozen poems celebrating the joys of childhood, all simple and all but one, "The Laughing Bug," unrhymed free verse. The book is illustrated by exuberant color photographs of African-American children, mostly in lively action, running, jumping, wading, swinging, and laughing, though a few are in quieter pursuits, reading or playing the piano. This is an attractive book, more notable for its illustrations than for its poems.

176 Grimes, Nikki, *Meet Danitra Brown*, illus. Floyd Cooper, Lothrop, 1994 (hardcover), ISBN 0–688–12073–3, $15.00, 32 pp.; Mulberry, 1997 (paper), ISBN 0–688–15471–9, $4.95. Ages 4–8, grades PS–3.

Thirteen verses celebrating the friendship between the narrator, Zuri Jackson, and Danitra Brown, the "most splendiferous girl in town." Danitra is an independent spirit, not cowed by insults about her glasses from the neighborhood boys or criticism of her always purple clothes, which she insists on wearing because it is a royal color and she might just be a princess. Together the two jump rope, go for wild bicycle rides, and do the housework when Danitra's mother is ill. Like most best friends of their age, which appears to be about nine to eleven, they have a falling out when Zuri blurts out a secret Danita has told her, but they make up. Although the text does not specify racial identity, illustrations with brown-toned city backgrounds show them to be African Americans, well individualized and realistic, in double-page spreads on which the type is superimposed. The book is attractive and catches some of the delight of close friendship, but the verses are just a step up from doggerel, not a good introduction to poetry.

177 Hudson, Cheryl Willis, comp., *Hold Christmas in Your Heart: African-American Songs, Poems, and Stories for the Holidays*, illus. Anna Rich, Cal Massey, Eric Battle, James Ransome, Ron Garnett, Sylvia Walker, and Higgins Bond, Scholastic, 1995 (hardcover), ISBN 0–590–48024–3, $10.95, 32 pp. Ages 3–8, grades PS–3.

Anthology of traditional and contemporary writings about Christmas: ten poems; three stories, one a retelling of a Brer Rabbit story; and three songs with music, "Go Tell It on the Mountain," adapted and arranged by John W. Work, "Children, Go Where I Send Thee," a black traditional carol, and "Christmas Is A'Comin'," by Huddie Ledbetter (Leadbelly). Of the poems, two are by Langston Hughes, "Carol of the Brown King" and "Shepherd's Song at Christmas," and others are by such writers as Angela Shelf Medearis ("Snow"), a stanza from Lucille Clifton's "Everett Anderson's Year," "Christmas Kittens" by Cheryl Willis Hudson, and "Christmas Valentine" by Nikki Grimes, mostly easy, pleasing, innocuous, undistinguished in technique but filled with the sights and sounds of Christmas. Vibrantly colored illustrations of families in various situations, ornaments, Christmas trees, snow activities, the Three Kings, and the like with African-American figures, if calendar-artish, give the book a festive air. Other books by Cheryl Hudson, *Afro-Bets ABC Book; Good Morning, Baby;*

and *Bright Eyes, Brown Skin* appear in *This Land Is Our Land* (1994), nos. 58, 59, and 208.

178 Hudson, Wade, and Cheryl Hudson, sels., *How Sweet the Sound: African-American Songs for Children*, illus. Floyd Cooper, Scholastic, 1995 (hardcover), ISBN 0–590–48030–8, $15.95, 48 pp.; 1997 (paper), ISBN 0–590–96911–0, $9.95. Ages 4 up, grades PS up.

Attractive, useful collection of twenty-three African-American songs and poems. Fourteen are "traditional," that is, from the oral tradition, like "Kum Ba Ya" and "Miss Mary Mack," and some are spirituals, like "Go Down Moses" and "Swing Low, Sweet Chariot." These traditional pieces are described in no. 151. The nine other selections are by known writers. Represented are "Lift Ev'ry Voice and Sing," which is known as the Black National Anthem and was written by J. Rosamond Johnson and his brother, poet James Weldon Johnson, "in tribute to the hopes, courage, and triumphs of the African-American people." The syncopated beat of ragtime marks "That's How the Cake Walk's Done," by J. Leubrie Hill, which was featured in a black musical in the very early 1900s. "Bring Me Li'l Water, Silvy," composed by Leadbelly (Huddie Leadbetter), is a work song, while "The Boll Weevil," by the same composer, is blues; "Take the 'A' Train," by Billy Strayhorn, is jazz; and James Brown's "Say It Loud, I'm Black and I'm Proud" and Stevie Wonder's "Happy Birthday," in honor of Martin Luther King, Jr., are soul songs. The entire collection is intended to give readers "a glimpse at the history of Blacks in America through their music" by including "songs from Africa, spirituals, work songs, gospels, jazz, blues songs, play songs, chants, soul, and popular music of our own time." The double-spread, brown-toned illustrations flow around and over the texts and picture situations under which the songs might have been sung or were inspired. For example, the illustration accompanying "The Boll Weevil" depicts a young guitar player coaxing the melody from his instrument, and the picture for "Bring Me Li'l Water, Silvy" shows a man laboring with a hammer awaiting little Silvy's arrival with a bucket of water. An introduction about African-American music and song opens the book, and acknowledgments, an index of writers, titles, lines, and topics, a list of Recommended Reading and Listening, and a particularly valuable section with notes about the songs, composers, and music conclude the book. For earlier books by the Hudsons, see *This Land Is Our Land* (1994), nos. 60 and 209 (Wade), and 58, 59, and 208 (Cheryl) (see entry 151 for titles).

179 Johnson, Angela, *The Other Side: Shorter Poems*, Orchard, 1998 (hardcover), ISBN 0–531–33114–8, $16.99, 46 pp. Ages 9–12, grades 4–7.

Thirty-four brief poems, all in unrhymed free verse, about life in the African-American town of Shorter, Alabama, which is being torn down to make way for a dog track. The narrator comes back from the North to see the town before it is gone and remembers her early years in Shorter—the other children, the old people, the good smells of cookies and magnolias and the "soap clean" Wash-a-Teria. Not all the memories are pleasant. There are the red ants, the heat, and "twenty miles / to any mall." Taken together, the poems give a picture of a close-knit community that will soon be gone forever, preserved only in a box of the "red, red dirt of Alabama." The book is illustrated with photographs of the author's family and friends and places in and around Shorter. A novel by Angela Johnson, *Toning the Sweep*, is no. 64 in *This Land Is Our Land* (1994). A picture-story book is no. 63, *The Leaving Morning*.

180 Johnson, James Weldon, *The Creation*, illus. James E. Ransome, Holiday House, 1994 (hardcover), ISBN 0–8234–1069–2, $15.95, unp.; 1995 (paper), ISBN 0–823–41207–5, $6.95. Ages 4 up, grades PS up.

Retelling in poetry of the story of the creation of the world and the first man from Genesis 1 and 2 of the Bible, done with conviction, deep reverence, elegance, verve, and touches of humor. Auditory and intimate in style, the story is presented as told by a storyteller, who is depicted only in the illustrations and whose phrases and rhythms resonate with the force and flavor of southern African-American storytelling and preaching. One of the poetic sermons from Johnson's *God's Trombones: Seven Negro Sermons in Verse* (1919, 1927), the poem is accompanied by expressive, deep palette, full-color paintings. The double-page, wide landscapes are truly magnificent, like murals, while in the pictures containing people the facial expressions and body language are arresting and set the mood. This is a stunning book that appeals to the intellect as well as the emotions and can catch and hold readers and viewers of all ages, particularly when shared aloud as the poem was intended.

181 Johnson, James Weldon, *Lift Ev'ry Voice and Sing*, illus. Jan Spivey Gilchrist, Scholastic, 1995 (hardcover), ISBN 0–590–46982–7, $14.95, unp. All ages, grades PS up.

Poem written by the eminent African-American poet (1871–1938) and set to music by his brother, composer J. Rosamond Johnson, now often referred to as the African-American National Anthem. The poem describes the history of blacks in America, celebrates liberty, and issues a strident and stirring call for rising above past vicissitudes and maintaining faith in God and hope for the future. The words and music appear at the end. Extending the verses, providing a setting for them, and in particular enhancing the atmosphere are magnificent full-color, off-the-page paintings, luminescent and sometimes brooding, occasionally realistic as heads and bodies, and occasionally exhibiting touches of surrealism. Puffy clouds swirl through hazy dark skies to accompany the lines that speak of the tears that have watered the people's progress, shadowy faces peer from a dark, misty background behind the lines that speak of the "chast'ning rod," and dark figures move toward or stand silhouetted against a mellow, pale yellow moon in the prayer-lines that ask God to keep his people forever on his pathway. This is an especially handsome book, one that extracts new meanings from the familiar poem.

182 Jones, Patricia Spears, *The Weather That Kills*, Coffee House, 1994 (paper), ISBN 1–56689–029–2, $11.95, 75 pp. Ages 12 up, grades 7 up.

Thirty-five poems, mostly about contemporary African-American life, although a few go back to the writer's youth, like "Glad All Over," about the Civil Rights Movement of the sixties. A number concern music, especially that of Billie Holiday, Miles Davis, and Sly and the Family Stone. Other well-known figures are the subject or occasion for poems, among them Rita Hayworth and Magic Johnson. Several are evocative pictures of cities—jazz and heat in New Orleans, Boston in winter, the homeless in Manhattan, Halloween and the Day of the Dead in Brooklyn, April rain in New York, AIDS in San Francisco, violence in black districts. One, both sad and moving, is "In My Father's House," which describes a day with her father when she is young and longing for "twilight's too slow descent," when she can return home to her mother. The poems are all in free verse, a few employing occasional rhyme. While much of the work is difficult and needs explanation to be completely understood, even the least easily explicable have lines that resonate and linger in the memory.

183 McKissack, Patricia, and Fredrick McKissack, *Messey Bessey's School Desk*, illus. Dana Regan, Children's, 1998 (hardcover), 0–516–20827–6, $17.00, 32 pp.; (paper), ISBN 0–516–26361–7, $4.9. Ages 4–8, grades PS–3.

A Rookie Reader present-day school story told in verse. Messey Bessey's desk is in terrible shape with dirty tissues, dried-up markers, a rotten sack lunch, overdue library books, an old apple core, and several other pieces of useless and unwanted items. After Bessey cleans up, she realizes that the other children's desks are messy, too, so she organizes a classroom cleanup. The children are so impressed with her energy and organizational ability that they elect her class president. The text does not specify race, but the illustrations show Bessey as African American. Gentle humor arises from the long list of "messy" items in the narrative and from the views inside Bessey's cluttered desk and the expressions on the children's faces. The poetry lacks distinction but works in the context of the illustrations. Rookie Reader companions to this pleasant book for just-readers are *Messey Bessey* (1987), *Messey Bessey's Closet* (1989), *Messey Bessey's Garden* (1991), *Messey Bessey and the Birthday Overnight* (1998), and *Messey Bessey's Holidays* (1999). For other books by Patricia McKissack individually, see *This Land Is Our Land* (1994), nos. 79, 80, 81, and 82, and by both Patricia and Fredrick McKissack, see nos. 83 and 215 (for titles, see entry 73, this book).

184 Medearis, Angela Shelf, *Rum-a-Tum-Tum*, illus. James E. Ransome, Holiday House, 1997 (hardcover), ISBN 0–8234–1143–5, $16.95, unp. Ages 4 up, grades PS up.

Narrative poem in picture-story book form set in New Orleans at the beginning of the twentieth century, in which a young, nightgown-clad, African-American girl opens her balcony window and describes the sights and sounds of early morning on Market Street in snappy, four-line verses. Interspersed between the verses are the street cries of fruit and vegetable vendors she sees peddling their wares. After dressing, she joins the teeming crowd, which in addition to shoppers includes mourners singing "Nearer My God to Thee" and a high-stepping marching band playing jazzy rhythms. The bold, full-color paintings bring figures and scenes close up to the viewer's plane and in unusual perspectives. They flow off the page and pull out and exaggerate details; for example, two-thirds of a double-page spread presents a strongly conceived banana vendor shouting his cry, while dominating the white space in the remaining third of the spread is a bunch of five yellow life-sized bananas, brilliantly golden above the brief black italicized banana cry below. The narrative verses are catchy if ordinary, but the illustrations make this book stunning, a viewing delight for all ages with its slice of old New Orleans. For earlier books, *Dancing with the Indians, Picking Peas for a Penny*, and *The Zebra-Riding Cowboy*, see *This Land Is Our Land* (1996), nos. 216, 217, and 218.

185 Medearis, Angela Shelf, *Skin Deep and Other Teenage Reflections*, illus. Michael Bryant, Macmillan, 1995 (hardcover), ISBN 0–02–765980–1, $15.00, 48 pp. Ages 10 up, grades 5 up.

Forty short, free-verse poems in the "I" person, about matters of concern to present-day American preteens and teenagers. Some poems are race specific, like the title one, where the persona wishes for a zipper in order to slip out of his/her dark skin so that hateful attitudes toward black people can be avoided and where the speaker laments having missed big events in the push for civil rights. Some are gender specific, as when the narrator deplores thinking about boys all the time or regrets being tied down with a baby, although she knows that having a baby was her own choice. Most of the poems deal with thoughts, feelings, and situations common to the age both universally—like lost sweethearts, coping with parental restrictions, dealing with the physical changes of puberty, and acknowledging the feeling of being immortal and invulnerable— and more specifically of today—like worrying about whether one's expensive shoes will be stolen, the pressure not to excel in school, and the very important rite of passage of getting a driver's license. The poems are prosy and occasionally trite, but many project an eloquence that comes from the writer's remembering accurately and observing keenly the hopes, fears, disillusionments, and joys of the ten-to-twenty age range. For earlier books by Medearis, see *This Land Is Our Land*, nos. 216, 217, and 218 (titles given in entry 184).

186   Myers, Walter Dean, *Angel to Angel: A Mother's Gift of Love*, illus. photographs, HarperCollins, 1998 (hardcover), ISBN 0–060–27721–1, $15.95, unp. Ages 4 up, grades PS up.

Eight poems accompanying more than forty photographs of African Americans from the nineteenth or early twentieth centuries. Predominantly they are of mothers and children, some dressed up for formal portraits, some in snapshots taken on the front steps or even in the woods and fields. The poems have a wide variety of verse forms and seriousness, from the nonsense verse, "A Serious Poem About Something" to "Furniture," about a sparsely filled square room that holds love, "enough furniture for a small room." Although a few of the verses border on the sentimental, the collection as a whole is saved by the lively, ballad-like "Don't Mess With Grandmama and Me," which should be a favorite of children, and "Sunday," with an appeal more to adults in the complaints about mushy greens and a "preacher without a plan." The book is lavishly produced, printed on heavy, creamy paper with end pages backed in silver to match the silver type of the subtitle and the decorations at head and foot of most pages. This follows two other books of poems and old photographs by Myers, *Brown Angels* (1993) and *Glorious Angels: A Celebration of Children* (1995), which contains pictures of children from many cultures around the world. Earlier books by Myers are described in *This Land Is Our Land* (1994), nos. 97, 98, 99, 100, 101, 102, and 103 (all fiction) (for titles, see entry 86, this book).

187   Myers, Walter Dean, *Harlem*, illus. Christopher Myers, Scholastic, 1997 (hardcover), ISBN 0–590–54340–7, $16.95, unp. Ages 4–8, grades PS–3.

Free-verse poem celebrating the diversity and vitality of Harlem. Citing real names and places—the uptown A train "rattles past 110th Street," a radio announces the triumphs of Jack Johnson, Joe Louis, and Sugar Ray—the lines mix past and present, children and adults, the joyful and the despairing. More striking than the quality of the verse are the illustrations, filling large-format pages with a vivid mixture of painting and collage, showing street scenes, fire escapes, and storefront churches but more notably faces, ranging from deep black to light tan, portrayed far more realistically than in most book illustrations. *Harlem* was named a Caldecott Honor book. Earlier books by Myers are described in *This Land Is Our Land* (1994), nos. 97, 98, 99, 100, 101, 102, and 103 (all fiction) (for titles, see entry 86).

188   Parks, Gordon, *Arias in Silence*, illus. photographs by Gordon Parks, Bulfinch/ Little Brown, 1994 (hardcover), ISBN 0–8212–2120–5, $40.00, 128 pp. Ages 10 up, grades 5 up.

Primarily an art book, this lovely volume also contains twenty-six previously unpublished poems by Parks, all in unrhymed free verse celebrating, as do the photographs, the beauty of nature as found in such little things as leaves, stones, shells, flowers, snow. The titles give clues to the nature of the poems: "Watching

a Memory," "Fallen Petals," "I Will Be All Light," "That's the Way Things
Go"—musings on beauty and a life spent in seeing beyond the surface. Published in his eightieth year, the book is a departure from the realistic shots of
crime, racism, and poverty usually associated with this renowned photographer.
Most are fragmentary objects pictured against abstract watercolor backgrounds:
a shiny black stone against a cloudy sky, fallen leaves making a landscape of
mountains and valleys before a red sunset, a single white blossom looking like
a bird in flight across a blue seascape. The most moving of his poems, accompanied by a picture of leaves on what might be a shoreline, is "Two Traveling
West," which ends on a note of mourning, not for the leaf he describes but for
himself, a "fellow traveler" going west "through time growing thin."

189 Temple, Charles, *Train*, illus. Larry Johnson, Houghton, 1996 (hardcover), ISBN
0–395–69826–X, $14.95, unp. Ages 4–10, grades PS–5.

Narrative poem in picture-book form of the progress of a C&O train. After
the whistle sounds and smoke puffs from the stack, the train moves through
town and country, picking up speed as it goes. A man in jail watches it pass, a
smile on his face; a little girl pauses in her hoeing to watch; and cows stop their
grazing as it rumbles by. Most of the narrative describes activities inside the
train—passengers dealing out a card game, children dancing down the aisle,
grownups snoozing or chatting, diners in the dining car, riders lurching, moving,
and swaying in response to the train's movements. Although here and there the
verse is strained, on the whole it conveys euphoniously and rhythmically with
participial forms, repetition, and onomatopoeia the sense of the train's sound
and progress. Paintings in full, deep colors depict scenes the train passes and
show the passengers as mixed racial but focus mostly on African Americans.
Their slightly distorted facial features contribute to the sense of movement. An
especially effective doublespread shows the black-toned train completing a curve
as it comes almost directly at the viewer, and another has striking closeups of
black-and-white cows, one of which is staring directly at the viewer.

190 Thomas, Joyce Carol, *Cherish Me*, illus. Nneka Bennett, HarperFestival, 1998
(hardcover), ISBN 0–694–01097–9, $9.95, unp. Ages 3–5, grades PS–K.

Poetry picture book for the very youngest, with large, full-color, representational, sculptured, foregrounded illustrations, one for each of the poem's nine
lines, the whole of which celebrates African-American ethnicity and reinforces
positive self-esteem. The little girl in the pictures is told in the poem that she
springs from earth, in whose colors she was clothed, and nourished by the sun,
who gave her pottery-colored skin. She (and by extension every black child) is
beautiful and should be cherished. The pig-tailed, large-eyed little girl is strikingly attractive, happy, thriving, healthy, loved, and well cared for. The picture
of the little girl cuddled in the arms of her handsome, doting father is especially

memorable for its warmth. In *This Land Is Our Land* (1994), see nos. 146, 147, 148, 149, and 274, all for older readers.

191 Thomas, Joyce Carol, *Gingerbread Days*, illus. Floyd Cooper, HarperCollins, 1995 (hardcover), ISBN 0–06–023472–5, $14.89, unp.; HarperTrophy, 1997 (paper), ISBN 0–06–446188–2, $5.95. Ages 4–10, grades PS–5.

Twelve short poems, one for each month of the year, that celebrate the seasons, family love and togetherness, and African-American history, pride, and identity—going to church, baking gingerbread men, starting school in the fall, hearing Grandpa talk about Buffalo Soldiers, sending a prayer-letter to God for the fall pumpkins, knowing that Daddy will keep his child safe from storms, and feeling Mother's soothing touch. The poems are uneven in technique, with some rhyming seeming forced and scanning falling short, but images are powerful on occasion, and the overall tone is warm, comforting, and uplifting. The powerfully executed paintings show strongly sculptured faces and hands, convey emotion well, and catch the essence of each poem in mostly foregrounded figures and situations. While the poetry is average, this is still a fine "lap book," great for sharing with one or two cuddled-up children on a comfy sofa. Earlier books appear in *This Land Is Our Land* (1994), nos. 146, 147, 148, 149, and 274 (fiction) (for titles, see entry 130, this book).

192 Worley, Demetrice A., and Jesse Perry, Jr., eds., *African-American Literature: An Anthology*, NTC Publishing, 1998 (paper), ISBN 0–8342–5924–1, $32.65, 495 pp. Ages 14 up, grades 9 up.

Large, comprehensive anthology of contemporary and historical writings by African Americans intended as a textbook "to present . . . an insight into the richness of African-American literature, and African-American culture"—folk literature, short stories, excerpts from longer fiction, memoir, and autobiography, poems, and essays—from the late 1700s to the present. Represented are 34 poems by 29 writers and two anonymous spirituals, all of which are preceded by short biographical essays (but in almost every case no commentary about the selection itself) and followed by discussion questions and suggestions for writing. The selections are arranged in eleven sections, each illustrating some aspect of the African-American experience (The Blues, Slavery, Standing Ground, Women, Men, etc.) with each section being introduced by a short but helpful essay. A historical overview opens the book, which concludes with an author-title index. The selections are arranged not in chronological order but as they inform the particular theme. The poems are short and usually those that are the writers' best known. James Weldon Johnson, for example, is represented by "Lift Every Voice and Sing" and "The Creation" and Langston Hughes by four poems, among them "I, Too" and "Mother to Son." Nikki Giovanni's "Nikki-Rosa," bell hooks's "the woman's mourning song," Robert Hayden's "Runagate Runagate," and Rita Dove's "Canary" are also familiar. But most of the rest appear less often in mainstream anthologies. Other writers represented are Audre Lorde, Arna Bontemps, Alice Walker, Al Young, Joyce Carol Thomas, Mari Evans, and Haki Madhubuti.

193 Young, Al, ed., *African American Literature: A Brief Introduction and Anthology*, HarperCollins, 1995 (paper), ISBN 0–363–99017–6, $19.95, 363 pp. Ages 14 up, grades 9 up.

Anthology of fiction (no. 145) and poetry by African Americans arranged by order of birth, with a few autobiographical selections and a play, in the HarperCollins Literary Mosaic Series, of which Ishmael Reed is general editor, intended primarily for college courses. The book, which is the largest of the four in the series, opens with a history of African-American writing and concludes with a thematic arrangement, list of readings, index of titles and first lines, and acknowledgments. The poems by each writer are preceded by a short introduction with biographical information and selected publications. The anthology has a generous assortment of eighty-nine poems from forty-eight writers, with most writers being represented by their best-known pieces. For example, Robert Hayden's "Frederick Douglass" and "The Whipping" appear, as do "Lift Every Voice and Sing" and "The Creation" by James Weldon Johnson, "We Wear the Mask" by Paul Laurence Dunbar, and seven very familiar poems by Langston Hughes, including "Mother to Son," "Birmingham Sunday," and "I, Too," without which no anthology presuming a historical overview would be complete. Recent poets are represented by Nikki Giovanni (with "Nikki-Rosa," her best-known poem and a single representation); United States Poet Laureate Rita Dove; Joyce Carol Thomas; and the minimalistic, highly oral, pop-culture and rap influenced, sometimes very imagistic, often narrative work of Cecil M. Brown, Quincy Troupe, O. O. Gabaugh (also strongly influenced by folk rhythms and strident in tone), Kofi Natambu ("For Billie Holiday"), Kool Moe Dee, and Kevin Young, whose nostalgic "The Preserving" concludes the section. The editor, himself a noted African-American writer, has chosen well to acquaint readers with the depth and breadth of African-American literature available at the end of the twentieth century. For other publications by Young, see no. 177, *Seduction by Light* (fiction) and no. 221, *Heaven: Collected Poems 1956–1990*, in *This Land Is Our Land* (1994).

4

Asian Americans: Books of Fiction

194 Bunting, Eve, *So Far from the Sea*, illus. Chris K. Soentpiet, Clarion, 1998 (hardcover), ISBN 0–395–72095–8, $15.00, 32 pp. Ages 4–8, grades PS–3.

A picture-story book of a Japanese-American family's return to the site of the World War II internment camp of Manzanar in eastern California where the narrator's grandfather, a fisherman, died in 1943. Laura's father tells her and her little brother, Thomas, something of the relocation of the west coast Japanese and of life in the camp. When Laura protests at the unfairness, he says they have to put it behind them and move on. He has previously told Laura that when the soldiers came to take them, his father told him to put on his Cub Scout uniform, so they would know he was an American, but it made no difference. Laura has brought his old Cub Scout scarf to put on her grandfather's grave. Illustrations of the present-day family are in color, while those of the camp are in shades of sepia, an effective way to mark the emotional difference. An afterword tells briefly the historical background and a few facts about Manzanar. For other books by Bunting, see *Summer Wheels* and *How Many Days to America?*, in *This Land Is Our Land* (1994), nos. 13 and 344, all fiction for pre-school and early grades.

195 Chang, Lan Samantha, *Hunger*, Norton, 1998 (hardcover), ISBN 0–393–04664–8, $22.00, 191 pp. Ages 14 up, grades 9 up.

Novella and five short stories about Chinese-American family relationships, the heart-wrenching pain as the children pull away from the older generation, and the ties that bind them even as they try to escape. In the title piece, the longest, a very talented violinist destroys, by his obsessive desire to succeed, first his own chance of a permanent teaching position and then the love and happiness of both his daughters, while the narrator, his wife, watches helplessly. Her English is so limited that she cannot express the depth of her feeling to the girls, and their understanding of Mandarin is not sufficient when she tries to tell them in Chinese. Their father relentlessly tutors the older girl, who wants desperately to please him, until he discovers that she doesn't have the perfect natural pitch he believes is necessary. He rejects her summarily and turns to her rebellious younger sister, who, after tears and continual battles of wills, becomes a brilliant violinist, and then rejects him and music completely. Each of the shorter stories echoes similar problems in different family settings, reflecting the anguish of the immigrant experience. All this is written with clarity and intense emotion but no sensationalism or sentimentality. The result is a haunting book.

196 Chao, Patricia, *Monkey King*, HarperCollins, 1997 (hardcover), ISBN 0–06–018681–X, $24.00, 310 pp. Ages 14 up, grades 9 up.

Novel of incest and suicide attempts in a seemingly perfect Chinese-American family. Talented artist Sally Wang, divorced from her husband, Carey Acheson, finds herself in the posh Willowridge mental hospital after trying to take her life with a pill overdose. As she gradually pulls herself out of her depression and confronts her past life, the reader learns about her long-held secret, the nocturnal visits from her father in her childhood that she equates with the evil tricks of the Monkey King, a figure in Chinese mythology. At family therapy night at the hospital, both her mother and her sister, Marty, who had shared a room with her and witnessed the attacks, deny that they happened, driving Sally almost to a renewed suicide attempt and further self-mutilating slashes of her forearm. After her release, she visits her Aunty Mabel and Uncle Richard in Florida, where her recovery is aided by their friendship and her uncle's frank admiration, by a visit from Mel, an attractive man several years her junior who was also a patient at Willowridge, and most of all by her aunt's admission that her mother told her of the incest. She returns to her studio-apartment in New York and, eventually, forces Marty to admit that she knew but was jealous, because their father never paid any attention to her. At the end, Sally has begun to paint again, and her future seems brighter, although not assured. What could be an ordinary novel on a sensational subject is made extraordinary by skillful use of detail, vivid description, and startling characterization. Each member of the family is individualized—her parents, both of whom teach at Yale, her father a cold, unhappy man, her mother a stylish, decisive woman; her sister, a beauty who manipulates men; her grandmother, an aristocrat from Shanghai. Minor figures are also fully rounded characters. The family's denial for the sake of appearances, even at the cost of Sally's mental health, is at least partly the result of their immigrant experience. Although devastating things happen and descriptions are graphic, there is nothing smutty or scatological in the tone.

197 Chin, Frank, *Gunga Din Highway*, Coffee House Press, 1994 (hardcover), ISBN 1–56689–024–1, $24.00, 404 pp.; 1995 (paper), ISBN 1–56689–037–3, $14.95. Ages 15 up, grades 10 up.

Highly amusing novel of a Chinese-American father and son who despise each other but whose lives are inextricably bound together and to Hollywood's image of the Asian experience. A handsome womanizer, Longman Kwan is known in Chinatown as Charlie Chan's Number 4 son, a part he played long ago, and as The Chinaman Who Died, for all the movies in which he has been cast as Chinese, Japanese, Mexican, Indian, or Indo-Chinese and in all of which he dies dramatically. His great ambition is to be the first man of Chinese extraction to play Charlie Chan in a revival of the series. The novel follows his youngest son, Ulysses Kwan, who becomes a movie writer, and several of Ulysses's friends, through the protests of the sixties, a hippie commune experience in Hawaii, and into his middle years. Both father and son see their lives as various movies, one running as reality, the version gleaned from Hollywood, and the imaginary "Movie About Myself" that rewrites events into more palatable stories. Raucous, highly irreverent, and very clever, the novel explodes conventional ideas of Chinese Americans and gives memorable caricatures of a wide variety of friends and family members of both generations. For an earlier novel by Chin, see *This Land Is Our Land* (1994), no. 225, *Donald Duk*.

198 Choi, Sook Nyul, *The Best Older Sister*, illus. Cornelius Van Wright and Ying-Hwa Hu, Delacorte, 1997 (hardcover), ISBN 0–385–32208–9, $13.95, 48 pp.; Bantam, 1998 (paper), ISBN 0–440–41149–1, $5.99. Ages 4–8, grades PS–3.

A "Yearling First Choice Chapter Book," a present-day story of Korean-American family life set up in four chapters and big print for early readers. Little Sunhi resents her baby brother. Her parents and especially her beloved grandmother, Halmoni, seem completely occupied with him. As his first birthday approaches and she knows he will have a big party in the Korean way, she becomes even more resentful. Sensitive Halmoni, however, suggests that she invite her friends, Robin and Jenny, to come over and help decorate. When Sunhi apologizes for her jealous behavior, Halmoni tells her that she knows that Sunhi will be the "best older sister" she can be for Kiji. Jenny and Robin (who are African American and white) help Sunhi plan and decorate. At the party, Sunhi's father takes a picture of the three girls with Kiji, all four dressed in their finery. The cheerfully colored illustrations extend the story with details of character, setting, plot, and atmosphere and help to distinguish this account of a girl's discovery of how she fits into the scheme of things. Diction is less stilted and sentences smoother and more idiomatic than in many books of this type. Other publications by Choi include no. 226, *Echoes of the White Giraffe*, in *This Land Is Our Land* (1994).

199 Choi, Sook Nyul, *Gathering of Pearls*, Houghton, 1994 (hardcover), ISBN 0–395–67437–9, $13.95, 163 pp. Ages 10–18, grades 5–12.

School novel set from 1954–55 in New York State, sequel to *Year of Impossible Goodbyes* (1991) and *Echoes of the White Giraffe* (1993), both of which take place in Korea. Fresh from her home in Korea, Sookan Bak, 18, enrolls as a scholarship student at Finch College, filled with excitement and apprehension about being in a strange country where she knows no one. She is grateful for the hospitality shown her by the nuns and soon makes friends with her room-mate, outgoing Ellen, and with the almost reclusive girl across the hall, Marci. She worries about not knowing English, about conforming to a culture so different from her own, and about lack of money. She elects a heavy course load, soon is studying almost all the time, and babysits on weekends for Professor Bennett's two children, whom she enjoys greatly. Her limited social life includes visits with Ellen's and Marci's families. The tension between the two generations surprises and concerns her, but she is able to give sound advice and encouragement to both girls. She also feels some estrangement from her own family, especially from her older sister, Theresa, who is a nun and expects Sookan to join her in the convent. At the end of the book, Sookan mourns the loss of her mother, who has died of a cerebral hemorrhage, and cherishes her mother's words about making the most of opportunities and challenges: "Tough times are the times when one gathers pearls." Sookan resolves to gather pearls: she will forgive her imperious sister and "finish college and figure things out from there." The story seems true to Sookan's stage in life and background, moves with just enough complications to hold the interest, reveals some contrasts between the two cultures, and, although the style jolts occasionally with unusually formal diction, offers pleasant and consistently entertaining reading matter for girls and young women. See *This Land Is Our Land* (1994), no. 226, *Echoes of the White Giraffe*, for information about the two earlier novels.

200 Choi, Susan, *The Foreign Student*, HarperFlamingo, 1998 (hardcover), ISBN 0–06–019149–X, $23.00, 325 pp. Ages 14 up, grades 9 up.

Unconventional love story set in 1955 of a Korean student at the University of the South in Sewanee, Tennessee, and a young, well-to-do southern woman living idly in her family's summer home in the town. Chang (Chuck) Ahn has lived through horrors during the Korean War and has acquired, largely to escape the memories, a scholarship at the very conventional, religious college, where he is treated as an exotic specimen, to be examined from a distance and to be proof of local generosity and tolerance. One of the few people to see him as an individual is Katherine Monroe, daughter of a New Orleans businessman who used to come to the mountain town of Sewanee every summer to recapture the youthful thrill of his college years and to see his former roommate, Charles Addison, now a lionized professor at the college. Both Chang and Katherine have demons in their pasts that they must exorcise. Chang has suffered betrayal, terror, near starvation, torture, and guilt, all of which keep him from reaching out to make friends. Katherine has a secret in her past, her seduction at fourteen and her continuing love affair with Addison, a man who long carried on a flirtation with her mother and now casually admires and uses Katherine without any attempt at commitment. Their stories are told through long flashbacks, those in Korea being especially devastating and graphic. The way these two damaged young people find their way to emotional understanding and love is a compelling story, told with an exquisite sense of detail and ironic pictures of the American involvement in Korea and life in the self-congratulatory Southern culture, but without explicit sex scenes or sentimentality.

201 Derbyshire, John, *Seeing Calvin Coolidge in a Dream*, St. Martin's, 1996 (hardcover), ISBN 0–312–14044–4, $22.95, 273 pp.; 1997 (paper), ISBN 0–312–15649–9, $11.95, 288 pp. Ages 14 up, grades 9 up.

Very clever novel of Chai, a Chinese immigrant, now a banker in New York with a beautiful wife and an infant daughter. The setting skips back and forth between the present and various periods of Chai's life: his orphan childhood in Northern China, his activities as a Red Guard, his disillusion with the Communists, his swim across Deep Water Bay to Hong Kong, his love for a girl named Selina he meets there, and his terrible sense of loss when she departs for San Francisco to marry the young man to whom she has been engaged all the time. Chai is given to intense enthusiasms—for English words, for various Chinese scholars, for Dr. Samuel Johnson, and now for Calvin Coolidge, whose plain honesty and respect for hard work seem to epitomize the best in American life. He reads everything he can by and about Coolidge. His young wife, Ding, is tolerantly amused by this new interest and accompanies him on a weekend in Vermont to tour Plymouth Notch and the Coolidge Foundation's visitor center. Chai is disappointed that a performance by a Mr. Ruggles, a Coolidge impersonator, has been canceled. By chance he discovers that Selina is living in Boston, looks her up, discovers that she is a buyer for a department store and that she visits New York often. Moreover, he catches a glimpse of her oldest child, now a young man of twenty, and realizes instantly that he is the boy's father. His obsession switches to having an affair with Selina. She is attracted but resists. He persists. Then Ding, who is a smart girl, secretly takes a hand and with the help of Mr. Ruggles convinces Chai that Calvin Coolidge does not approve of this adultery, and Chai subsides back to his humdrum but really very satisfactory life with Ding. Chai's comments on life in both China and America, on language, and on love and disappointment are lively and highly amusing.

202 Fenkl, Heinz Insu, *Memories of My Ghost Brother*, Dutton, 1996 (hardcover), ISBN 0–525–94175–4, $23.95, 271 pp.; Plume, 1997 (paper), ISBN 0–452–27717–5, $11.95, 288 pp. Ages 14 up, grades 9 up.

Autobiographical novel of a Korean-American grade-school boy's growing up, set in Pupyong, South Korea, for several years during the early part of the Vietnam War, in which the mix of cultures and the culture-clash are so strong the setting is almost a character in its own right. Insu, son of a South Korean mother and a German-American Army sergeant, lives with Mahmi, her sister, and the sister's husband, who is often drunk and talks dirty to Insu, their two children, and Mahmi's country niece. Insu grows up knowing he is loved by his Korean relatives. He also grows up on the streets, where he observes prostitutes soliciting soldiers and soldiers seeking pleasure, sees black marketeers in action, and associates with assorted young ruffians, some of them the unwanted offspring of the GIs. He engages in petty thievery, is sometimes bullied by the older boys, and early experiences death as part of everyday life. Mahmi's pregnant niece commits suicide because her GI lover has spurned her, and later his best school friend, James, is found dead in a drainage ditch, perhaps killed by his own mother because he is half black and she wishes to marry a white GI. Insu both fears and admires his stern, ill-tempered father, who visits infrequently, shows Insu around the demilitarized zone, enrolls the boy in an American school (where he is punished for speaking Korean), and brings him books to read so that he will be acquainted with important literature. Insu is increasingly haunted by a picture, which he learns is of his older brother, whom Mahmi gave away because Insu's father did not want to have the son of another man around. The book concludes with Insu's father having left for the United States for cancer treatment and Mahmi, Insu, and Insu's baby sister, Anna, leaving to join him. The detail-filled prose transmits sights and sounds with remarkable clarity. Best is the impression the book conveys of a country in turmoil, still reacting to the former Japanese occupation and now absorbed with the Americans, who also dominate every facet of the people's lives.

203 Garland, Sherry, *My Father's Boat*, illus. Ted Rand, Scholastic, 1998 (hardcover), ISBN 0–590–47867–2, $15.95, unp. Ages 4–8, grades PS–3.

Realistic, contemporary picture-story book set on a Vietnamese-American shrimp boat on the Gulf of Mexico. Before dawn, a little boy, perhaps six, and his father go shrimp fishing. Out on the waters, far away from shore, the boy watches his father get the nets ready, launch them, haul them in, and separate the crabs from the shrimp. As he works, the father's mind returns to the land of his youth. He sings songs he learned before he emigrated during the war and recalls the mountains, the sea, and his father, a shrimp fisherman on the South China Sea, whom he has not seen in twenty years. He promises the boy that sometime they will go back so that he can meet his grandfather and fish on the South China Sea. They spend the night on the boat and return with their catch early the next morning as the stars fade into day. The poetic, nostalgic text is extended by full-page, full-color, evocative watercolor, acrylic, and chalk paintings. They create the wildlife, the fog, the dawn, the sun's rays, and the misty atmosphere of the water, and show the closeness of the father and the son and the love the father feels for the boy and his now old father. Some perspectives are unusual, for example, the scene in which gliding, greenish-blue dolphins observe the boat in the background, on which the boy and his father watch the dolphins. For other books by Garland, see *The Lotus Seed* and *Why Ducks Sleep on One Leg*, in *This Land Is Our Land* (1994), nos. 231 and 296, both also highly illustrated books for younger readers and viewers.

204 Guback, Georgia, *Luka's Quilt*, illus. Georgia Guback, Greenwillow, 1994 (hardcover), ISBN 0–688–12154–3, $14.00, unp. Ages 4–8, grades PS–3.

Contemporary, realistic picture-story book about the special relationship between a little Hawaiian-American girl, Luka, and her grandmother, Tutu. Tutu says that she would like to make a quilt for Luka, as she did for Luka's mother years before. She and Luka go to a fabric store, where Luka picks out her favorite color, green, for the quilt. One day, at last, Tutu puts the quilt on Luka's bed. To Luka's dismay, no colorful flowers adorn it, only white flowers ranging across the green. For days, she can barely speak to Tutu. One day, Tutu suggests they declare a truce and go together to the Lei Day celebration in the park. They have a fine picnic, along with hordes of other happy people. When Luka makes a lei of different colored flowers, Tutu decides to make a circular lei quilt to place on top of the green-and-white one. Luka is delighted—she now has two quilts, a beautifully colored lei one and a white flower-garden one. Brightly colored, cut-paper primitives depict flower-filled gardens, yards, and park. They decorate the book and immediately attract the reader's eye. They also extend the text of the simple, not completely logical family story with a wealth of details of the natural beauty of the islands and of the interiors of houses, stores, and Luka's house and bedroom. Luka and her grandmother are comfortably round, as are the flower motifs on the green-and-white quilt, their circularity emphasizing the warmth and security that the characters and reader feel at the end of the story.

205 Guterson, David, *Snow Falling on Cedars*, Harcourt, 1994 (hardcover), ISBN 0–15–100100–6, $21.95, 345 pp.; Vintage, 1995 (paper), ISBN 0–6797–6402–X, $13.00, 460 pp. Ages 14 up, grades 9 up.

Subtly written novel of a murder trial of a Japanese-American gill-netter in Puget Sound set in 1954, when emotions from World War II fears and prejudices are still raw and easily enflamed. When the body of Carl Heine, young father and native of San Piedro Island, is found entangled in his net as his boat drifts, evidence at first seems to point to accident, then to Kabuo Miyomoto, a young man his own age, also a fisherman, although both have hoped to return to the strawberry raising with which they grew up. Courtroom scenes are interrupted by long flashbacks from the point of view of Kabuo, his wife, Hatsue, and Ishmael Chambers, publisher of the local newspaper, who has loved Hatsue since childhood. Woven in are the stories of the devotion all three have for the island, of the forced removal early in the war of all the local people of Japanese ancestry, of their difficult time in internment camps, of the war service of both Kabuo, who volunteered and served in Europe, and of Ishmael, who served and lost an arm in the Pacific. Suspicion of Kabuo is based on circumstantial evidence and the well-known dispute over seven acres of strawberry land, which his father had bought from Heine's father, all but the final payment, when he was arrested by the FBI and which Heine's mother cheated the Miyomoto family out of while they were interned. Although some of the islanders are bigoted and vicious, others are appalled at the discrimination their neighbors have suffered. Characters are strongly realized, and the island setting is beautifully evoked.

206 Hamanaka, Sheila, *Bebop-A-Do-Walk!*, illus. Sheila Hamanaka, Simon & Schuster, 1995 (hardcover), ISBN 0–689–80288–9, $15.00, unp. Ages 4–8, grades PS–3. See entry 43.

207 Heo, Yumi, *One Afternoon*, illus. Yumi Heo, Orchard, 1994 (hardcover), ISBN 0–531–06845–5, $15.95, unp.; 1998 (paper), ISBN 0–531–07103–0, $6.95. Ages 3–7, grades PS–2.

Very simple picture-story book telling in about 150 words of an afternoon in a city. Minho and his mother go to the laundromat, the beauty salon where she gets her hair cut, the ice cream store, the shoe repair shop, and the supermarket. They see puppies and other animals in the pet store window, the heavy traffic and construction on the street, a fire engine, the El train, and children playing stickball. Minho is so tired when he gets home that he falls asleep on the couch. The illustrations, in oil paint, pencil, and collage, dominate the book with bright colors and strong action in a pseudo-primitive style, with plenty of detail for young children to identify. The little boy and his mother have a slightly Oriental look, probably Korean-American, since that is the author-illustrator's ethnic group.

208 Hogan, James P., *Bug Park*, Baen, 1997 (Hardcover), ISBN 0–671–87773–9, $22.00, 405 pp.; 1998 (paper), ISBN 0–671–87874–3, $6.99, 416 pp. Ages 14 up, grades 9 up.

Adult science fiction and mystery novel set in recent years in and around Seattle and Tacoma, Washington. Two teenaged scientists, Kevin Heber, 15, and his closest friend, Japanese Taki, are instrumental in foiling a grand scheme of corporate intrigue and saving Kevin's father's burgeoning business, Neurodyne. Much of the early part of the novel is devoted to explaining micro-robots, or micromecs, of humans and insects that Kevin and Taki have further miniaturized and manipulate by direct neural connection, or DNC. The boys have come up with an inventive virtual reality setup, Bug Park, which Ohira, Taki's uncle, considers viable for theme park exploitation and other commercial uses. Soon after Ohira and his lawyer, Michelle Lang, initiate business discussions, trouble starts. Someone seems intent on scuttling Neurodyne by releasing to the media erroneous information that DNC will detrimentally affect the mind of the user. Doug Corfe, an electronics expert, joins the boys and Michelle in unmasking the culprits, who include Kevin's father Eric's former employer, Martin Payne. A micromec inadvertently placed among the bags of Vanessa Heber, Eric's wife and chief financial adviser and Kevin's stepmother, reveals that Vanessa is in league with Martin to get Eric to change his will in her favor, kill him, take over the company, and exploit the new commercial possibilities. After various nefarious events and tight spots, Taki and his Japanese relatives help the "good guys" escape Martin's minions, and Vanessa and Martin drown in a channel as they attempt to flee authorities. An epilogue shows Kevin and Taki busily helping Ohira with their new corporation. The plentiful action and mystery offer potent draws for non-sci-fi–oriented readers, but computer age "tech stuff" abounds for the "tech set." As with most novels of this genre, characters are flat, well-known types, and expectedly Kevin and Taki, like two peas in a pod, are intelligent, inventive, brave, and decisive. Although the story mostly follows Kevin's family's fortunes, Taki is equally as important as Kevin.

209 Jen, Gish, *Mona in the Promised Land*, Random House, 1996 (hardcover), ISBN 0–679–44589–7, $24.00, 320 pp.; Vintage, 1997 (paper), ISBN 0–679–44589–7, $12.00, 304 pp. Ages 15 up, grades 10 up.

Rollicking, farcical novel of growing up and family life set in the late 1960s in upscale Scarshill, New York. Asian-American, high school–aged Mona Chang gets on fairly well with her parents, Ralph and Helen, who are especially proud of her older sister, Callie, a student at Harvard-Radcliffe; are determined that their daughters remain dutiful and respect the Chinese ways; and own a pancake-house restaurant, in which Mona works part time. Roman Catholic, they are taken aback by Mona's conversion to Judaism (she becomes a "more or less genuine Catholic Chinese Jew"). She gains the affections of Seth Mandel, pseudo-philosopher, espouser of causes, and occasional pot-smoker, who lives in a teepee in his parents' backyard and with whom she has her first intercourse. She helps to hide African-American Alfred, a cook at the pancake house on the outs with his wife, in an episode that leads eventually to Alfred's being fired and his filing a lawsuit for racial discrimination against her parents. She has a big blow-up with Helen over the lawsuit and runs away to Callie's dormitory room, where Helen finds Mona, who has obviously been in bed with Seth. Protracted sets of episodes revolve around her infatuation with Japanese-American Sherman Matsumoto, whom she met when she was eleven and he thirteen, and around some mysterious phone calls. An epilogue finds her and Seth getting ready for their wedding. Mona has given birth to a daughter, Io, whose existence Helen finds hard to accept. Seth has become a college professor, and Mona has held various social-welfare and volunteer-organization positions. The pleasure of the book comes mainly from the humor of wit, wordplay, strik-ing turns of phrase, insights into human nature revealed through the conversa-tions, the omniscient narrator's observations, and for adult readers, also from a look back upon a turbulent period. An eccentric, occasionally almost surrealistic exploration into race, ethnicity, religion, and family relationships, there is much here to reward the persevering and mature reader. For another novel by Jen, see *This Land Is Our Land* (1994), no. 238, *Typical American*.

210 Johnston, Tony, *Fishing Sunday*, illus. Barry Root, Tambourine, 1996 (hardcover), ISBN 0–688–13458–0, $16.00, unp. Ages 4–10, grades PS–5.

Realistic picture-story book of Japanese Americans on the coast of California. The narrator, who is shown in the illustrations as a Japanese-American boy of about six or seven, hates Fishing Sunday. His old, stooped grandfather gets them up early to go to the fishing boat for sport on the water. The narrator is ashamed of Grandfather, in his too-short pants and bare feet with their sharp, split, black toenails and his fishhooks made of bones. The worst is that Grandfather talks to the fish, asking them politely to let him catch them and thanking them when he brings them in on his bamboo pole. When the boy follows suit but is unsuccessful, Grandfather says that "fish talk takes time," and gives the boy one of his bone fishhooks. The boy examines it carefully, notes that it is beautifully made and polished, and sees the old man in a new light. He is beautiful, too. Although the conclusion is abrupt and not clearly motivated, this is a tender story of a boy's growing appreciation of his grandfather's true nature and worth. The realistic paintings of the seacoast and on the boat catch the magnificence of the setting and the camaraderie of the mixed-ethnic fishermen. A breathtaking view of the fishing boat on the broad, rippling waters appears on the endpapers.

211 Keller, Nora Okja, *Comfort Woman*, Viking, 1997 (hardcover), ISBN 0–670–87269–5, $21.95, 213 pp.; Penguin, 1998 (paper), ISBN 0–1402–6335–7, $12.95, 224 pp. Ages 15 up, grades 10 up.

Intense, complex novel of the relationship of a Korean-born mother and her Korean-American daughter, set in Hawaii with scenes shifting continually to earlier times, especially to the World War II period in Korea. As a twelve-year-old, Soon Hyo, youngest of four daughters, is sold for her eldest sister's dowry to become a "Comfort Woman" or prostitute for the Japanese occupation troops. For at least two years, she is confined to a stall where the soldiers line up for her services, until, after a doctor performs a brutal abortion with a sharp stick and no anesthetic, she escapes to a missionary compound, unable to speak, even to give her name. They call her Akiko, the name stenciled on her clothes, actually the name the Japanese gave Induk, the previous occupant of her stall, who was executed for rebellion and whose clothes were passed along to her. The missionary, an American man many years her senior, marries her but makes no attempt to understand her even after she regains her speech, only congratulating himself on saving a fallen woman. Almost twenty years later, to everyone's surprise, she has a daughter, whom her husband names Rebeccah and whom Akiko calls Beccah, a girl she cherishes and defends jealously from dangers real and imagined. Nearly half the novel is told from Beccah's point of view, as she grows up, her father having died when she was a young child, alone with a mother often mentally ill, in trances talking to Induk and fighting off malevolent spirits. A restaurant owner, Auntie Reno, who has employed

Akiko, sees the possibility of promoting her as a spirit-medium and becomes her manager. Although Beccah suffers because of her mother's strangeness, they are very close, and it is not until Akiko's death that Beccah, now grown up, discovers her mother's real name, the terrible secrets of her past, and the depth of her devotion to her daughter. Only mature students will master the continual shifts in time and place of the narrative and be able to see the beauty in the story that includes horrible incidents but also strong mother-daughter love and survival strength. For those who do, this is a compelling novel.

212 Kline, Suzy, *Song Lee and the Hamster Hunt*, illus. Frank Remkiewicz, Viking, 1994 (hardcover), ISBN 0–670–84773–9, $11.99, 52 pp.; Puffin, 1996 (paper), ISBN 0–140–76831–3, $3.99. Ages 7–10, grades 2–5.

Easy chapter book, one in a series about activities in multiethnic Room 2B of South School. Her classmates are delighted when Korean-American Song Lee brings her hamster, Yi (rhymes with Lee), to school. One morning they discover that his cage is empty. Sidney forgot to latch the cage-hook, and Yi has escaped. The children search diligently without success. When Song Lee makes a poster advertising for him, Miss Mackle suggests that they all follow suit. The children plaster the school walls with wanted posters, and a great hamster hunt ensues. Mr. John, the custodian, turns out to be the hero; he discovers Yi in the boiler. Although the story is told by the keenly observant Caucasian classmate, Doug Hurtuk, Song Lee is at the story's center. As a whole, the class seems real. The narrative is almost all dialogue, the tone is warm and intimate, and the reader is brought close to the action also by the cartoonish, black-and-white drawings. Song Lee has dimension—a goodhearted peacemaker, the inventive one whose idea leads to the recovery of Yi and whose knowledge of languages and quick thinking help to solve a classmate's personal problem. This lively story conveys an authentic sense of contemporary classroom life for early readers. Kline's Horrible Harry series involves the same children. For an earlier Song Lee book, see *Song Lee in Room 2B*, in *This Land Is Our Land* (1994), no. 241. More recent ones include *Song Lee and the Leech Man* (1995) and *Song Lee and the "I hate you" Notes* (1999).

213 Lee, Gus, *Honor and Duty*, Random House, 1994 (hardcover) ISBN 0–679–41258–1, $24.00, 425 pp.; (paper), ISBN 0–8041–1004–2, $6.99. Ages 15 up, grades 10 up.

Autobiographical, Chinese-American boy's coming-of-age novel, set in California and in New York State from 1964 to 1968, sequel to *China Boy* (1991). Now seventeen, Kai Ting, son of a former colonel in the Chinese Nationalist Army, leaves his mixed-ethnic neighborhood in San Francisco for West Point Military Academy. He endures with good heart the deprivation, brutalizing, and bullying handed out to plebes, determined to succeed for the family honor, and catches the eye of commanding officers for his spirit, dedication to duty, and ability to lead. The days pass into years: his classmates and friends become so many that their names become almost impossible for the reader to keep track of. Among his staunchest supporters is Major H. Norman Schwarzhedd, a Vietnam veteran and son of the U.S. Army officer his father had most admired. Kai also works through his infatuation with beautiful Christine and falls in love with Pearl Yee, the attractive daughter of a wealthy Chinese-American shipping magnate. His single biggest challenge at the Point involves his being asked to smoke out cadets engaged in cheating, an increasingly dangerous endeavor Kai embarks upon with misgiving but with the eventual certainty that it is the right and honorable course. In spite of being tutored and given three opportunities to achieve, he fails math at the end of his third year and is expelled. He becomes a sergeant in the Airborne Infantry (in spite of acrophobia) and is accepted at the University of California to complete his degree. A few subthemes include his coming to terms with his abusive stepmother and seeking out and learning to know his older sister, Janie, whom Edna had placed in a Canadian foster home simply because she did not want the girl. The book is overly long and suffers from the author's self-indulgence with incident and detail and is sometimes stylistically self-conscious. Dialogue exudes authenticity, often including trash talk and in-terms, most of which are explained in a glossary. Since the narrative is laced with humor, irony, poignancy, sorrow, elation, and suspense (some often in juxtaposition), the reader is enticed to continue and admires this plucky, thoughtful, intelligent, hardy young man, who has had a difficult childhood and now experiences a trouble-laden youth. As in the first book, Kai shows that he can roll with the punches and come out a true winner, reconciling the best of his Chinese and American heritages. For *China Boy*, see *This Land Is Our Land* (1994), no. 244.

214 Lee, Gus, *No Physical Evidence*, Ballantine, 1998 (hardcover), ISBN 0–449–91139–X, $24.95, 387 pp. Ages 15 up, grades 10 up.

Contemporary detective novel set in Sacramento, California, in which a deputy prosecuting attorney, whose career and personal life are on the skids, takes on a rape case fraught with political ramifications. Asian-American Joshua Jin is assigned what appears to be a hopeless case—an assault on a white girl who lives in Chinatown, an area whose votes the incumbent District Attorney sorely needs. The case is uphill all the way, because there is no physical evidence to implicate the accused, Chico Moody, a grubby ex-convict. The victim, schoolgirl Rachel Farr, 13, has been so traumatized by living in an abusive home and the events of the rape that she cannot discuss the incident. Since Jin's daughter, Summer, 11, died recently of heart disease, he feels a strong attachment to Rachel, takes her into his own home, and determines to bring Moody to justice. He is aided by a large number of public and private figures and agencies and by his ex-wife, Ava Pascal, herself an attorney. As the preliminary investigations wear on, Josh realizes that he has been set up for failure by persons unknown. In spite of an antagonistic judge and the defense lawyer's eloquence and cleverness, Jin secures a conviction, but shortly discovers that physical evidence does exist and forensic tests prove Moody innocent. Other discoveries, however, implicate Moody in a children-for-pornography-and-prostitution ring, a well-organized operation involving people in high places. In rousing action scenes, Jin breaks the ring wide open and at the same time solidifies his position within the Chinese community. Caring for Rachel before and during the trial brings Jin and Ava together again, and at the end things look hopeful for them, although not so much for Rachel, who has many psychological problems to overcome. The plot is complicated by not only the lawyerly material but also the many ingenious, enthralling twists and turns. Jin is a well-drawn and sympathetic protagonist—a man of duty, honor, intelligence, and compassion—and while he functions mostly in white society and world of work, he is still motivated by his heritage. Language is frank, earthy, and naturally contains sexual references, and the rape details are explicit. The lengthy trial scenes are filled with professional detail, which may put off some readers not dedicated enough to persevere. As in Lee's other novels, and in *China Boy*, in *This Land Is Our Land* (1994), no. 244, events are based on his personal experience.

215 Lee, Gus, *Tiger's Tail*, Knopf, 1996 (hardcover), ISBN 0–679–43855–6, $24.00, 298 pp.; Ivy, 1997 (paper), ISBN 0–804–11326–2, $6.99, 370 pp. Ages 15 up, grades 10 up.

Mystery-adventure novel with detective-story aspects set in Korea for one week in 1974. Asian-American Jackson Hu-chin Kan, West Point graduate, attorney, former paratrooper, and United States military prosecutor, is sent to Camp Casey in the Demilitarized Zone (DMZ). He is to investigate the disappearance of another military investigator, Captain Jimmy Buford, who was looking into irregularities in the office of Colonel Frederick LeBlanc, the Staff Judge Advocate, or top lawyer, for the American soldiers. LeBlanc is a white-haired, dignified, Bible-reading man, with, it turns out, a remarkable propensity for graft, deviousness, and cruelty. Kan's quest leads him in surprising directions, including a local whorehouse; a filthy, inhumane South Korean jail, where LeBlanc has imprisoned Sergeant Major McCrail, a huge Irishman, to prevent him from blowing the whistle; to a dopehouse, where Kan finds Buford near death from frequent injections of narcotics; and to a mountain on which stands an orphanage for Asian-American children presided over by a woman shaman of great respect and wisdom. Kan is assisted by, among others, Captain Levine, a beautiful, tough, woman weapons expert, who deduces that LeBlanc plans a suicide mission into North Korea with small, portable, nuclear bombs; and Min, a tiny South Korean noncommissioned, pidgin-speaking jeep driver of great audacity behind the wheel, who turns out to be a high-level officer in the Korean CIA. Another unusual figure is Song Sae Moon, a Korean woman who frequents whorehouses patronized by American soldiers, hoping to interest them in the plight of Asian-American orphans. Events reach their climax at the mountain orphanage, where LeBlanc is prevented in the nick of time from blowing up everyone with a portable bomb. After a slow start, the plot becomes complex, filled with action, intrigue, and duplicity, its linearity interrupted by flashbacks to Kan's Chinese childhood, his father's advice, and his mother's admonitions, which show clearly that in spite of his American upbringing he is still a child of China in his attitudes toward life, family, duty, and country. Trash talk, army jargon, and sex talk and references abound, but no explicit sex occurs. Kan's personal life and problems are well blended into the plot. Other novels by Lee include, in *This Land Is Our Land* (1994), no. 244, *China Boy*.

216 Lee, Marie G., *Necessary Roughness*, HarperCollins, 1996 (hardcover), ISBN 0–060–25124–7, $14.95, 280 pp.; 1998 (paper), ISBN 0–064–47169–1, $4.95, 240 pp. Ages 11–17, grades 6–12.

Contemporary novel of Korean-American family life in a sports-story format. Chan, the narrator, 16, describes the year the immigrant Kim family, his father Abogee, his mother O-Ma, and his twin sister, Young, pull up roots, sell their Los Angeles grocery store, and move to Iron River, Minnesota, to take over Abogee's brother's failed convenience store. Chan immediately notes that the school is a "complete whiteout"; the Kims are the only nonwhites in this sleepy town of tall, northern European–descended blondes. Chan gains partial acceptance through football. He works hard, endures what near-sadist Assistant Coach Kearny calls the "necessary roughness" of practices, and becomes the Miners' main kicker and all-round utility player. Prejudice and bigotry lessen as Chan contributes more and more to the team's success and the town's pride. Throughout, Chan yearns for the approval of his father, who strongly disapproves of football and Chan's new friends. When Coach Larson learns that Mr. Kim will not attend the football banquet at which Chan will receive his letter-sweater, he persuades the man to change his mind. Another catalyst for solving family problems and gaining them acceptance is, ironically, Young's death in a car accident just after the team wins the big game. The town responds with many expressions of sympathy, gifts of food, and other offers of friendship. At the end, the Kims have experienced many instances of seemingly necessary roughness, but their lives in this community go on. Characters and events offer few surprises. Young's death, however, seems gratuitous, and the concluding scene, in which Chan places the winning trophy on her grave, oozes sentimentality. Projected well are the sense of small-town provincialism and the importance of football and school events. Football practices are especially well described. Strongest is the tension between generations, arising from conflict between old-world, traditional perceptions and the pull the children feel toward American life. The parents, in particular Abogee, insist that associating with the opposite sex should wait until college, and then only with Koreans, and feel that studies, achievement, and getting well-paying jobs are the only things, other than family, that really matter. For other novels by Lee, see *Finding My Voice* and *If It Hadn't Been for Yoon Jun*, in *This Land Is Our Land* (1994), nos. 245 and 246.

217 Lee, Marie G., *Night of the Chupacabras*, Avon, 1998, ISBN 0–380–9706–0, $14.00, 120 pp. Ages 8–13, grades 3–8.

Light, contemporary mystery-thriller, which starts in New York City and soon moves, for the bulk of the action, to Sonora, Mexico. Mexican-American Lupe, 13, invites her best friend, Korean-American Mi-Sun, and Mi-Sun's brother, Ju-Won, 8, to join her for the summer on her Mexican uncle's goat ranch. At the ranch, Tio Hector allows the children a good bit of freedom, and they often visit Tierralinda, the little town nearby where they sample the delicious bread and the luscious, fruit-filled popsicles and buy huaraches. Alarming things happen right away. Ju-Won, who is addicted to horror novels, says the area is spooky; they hear unearthly cries; a wild dog attacks Tio Hector's dog; they glimpse a strange, black-garbed woman at the door of the adobe house; and, especially, an old man in town warns them to beware of the chupacabras—goat suckers, vampire-like creatures that kill goats. A goat is soon found dead, and fruit is found mashed and punctured in the kitchen sink. It turns out that the wild dog that attacked Tio Hector's dog has also been killing goats and that the new housekeeper, the black-garbed woman, is a widow who has been preparing a surprise for the children of fruit-juice ices. Good features include the descriptions of the terrain, the stores, the small-town ethic, the extensive use of Spanish and Korean words (explained by context or in the glossary), the foods, for example, the mouth-watering tamales the children love, the fruits, and the ices, and the carefully controlled point of view; that is, everything is seen from the naive child's vantage so that the children's overreacting seems credible. Characters are distinguished by one main feature, style is easy, pace is fast, and, while the sophisticated or discerning reader soon suspects what is happening, the story offers undemanding entertainment from start to finish. Other books by Lee appear in *This Land Is Our Land* (1994), no. 245 *Finding My Voice*, and no. 246, *If It Hadn't Been for Yoon Jun*.

218 Lee, Marie, *Saying Goodbye*, Houghton, 1994 (hardcover), ISBN 0–395–67066–7, $14.95, 219 pp. Ages 12–17, grades 7–12.

Realistic sociological problem novel set about the time of publication at Harvard University, Cambridge, Massachusetts, sequel to *Finding My Voice* (1992). Korean-American, pre-med student Ellen Sung finds her new surroundings exciting and fulfilling. She likes her roommate, assertive, intelligent, African-American Leecia Thomas, although she finds Leecia's race-sensitive attitude troubling. She faces the usual freshperson's decisions: choosing courses; conserving study time; pursuing her interest in creative writing in a class with author Marianne Stoeller; investigating extracurricular activities like tae kwon do (Korean martial arts), which she enjoys, and KASH (Korean-American Students at

Harvard), whose militancy she also finds troubling; and dating Jae-Chun Kim, another Korean-American freshperson, who is a good student, works to support himself because his parents' store was burned in the Los Angeles riots, teaches her Korean, excels in tae kwon do, and helps her to a greater appreciation of her heritage. Two racist experiences involving Leecia at Korean-American stores foreshadow the difficulty to come between the two girls, which is triggered by the clash between KASH and the African-American student group, of which Leecia is a leader. The African-American students promote the campus appearance of a rap star whose lyrics are highly anti-Korean, a residue of the riots. To forestall the appearance, Ellen initiates what Leecia thinks is a dirty trick. Their enmity, while short, results in greater understanding for both, but not in the resumption of their friendship. The book captures the atmosphere of campus life, the strains of being on one's own and of making important decisions for which one is totally responsible, and of Ellen's growing appreciation of her family and heritage. Her relationship with sensible Jae is sweet and tender and requires sexual decision making. While occasionally the author's voice intrudes, Ellen's first-person narrative seems true to this stage in her life. Other novels by Lee, *Finding My Voice* and *If It Hadn't Been for Yoon Jun*, are described in *This Land Is Our Land* (1994), nos. 245 and 246.

219 Mochizuki, Ken, *Heroes*, illus. Dom Lee, Lee & Low, 1995 (hardcover), ISBN 1–880000–16–4, $14.95, unp.; 1997 (paper), ISBN 1–880–00050–4, $6.99. Ages 6–13, grades 1–8.

Period picture-story book set somewhere in the United States in the 1960s during the Vietnam conflict. Donnie Okada, perhaps ten, tells how, when he and his pals get together, they always insist that they play war and that Donnie be the enemy because as a Japanese-American he looks like the enemy. Donnie replies that, since his father served in Italy and France in World War II and his Uncle Yosh fought in Korea, Japanese-Americans cannot be the enemy. When he asks his father for war medals to show as proof, his father simply says that the kids should play something other than war, and Uncle Yosh says that real heroes do not brag. One day, while Donnie is playing alone in the woods, the guys chase him, and almost in a panic, he flees for safety to his father's gas station. The next day, Dad and Uncle Yosh meet Donnie after school, Dad wearing his veteran's cap covered with medals and Uncle Yosh dressed in his medal-laden officer's uniform and hat. The boys, suitably impressed, accept Donnie as one of them. The predictable plot gains credibility and distinction from the understated, straightforward style and accompanying realistic, scratchboard-and-oil paintings. Done mostly in brown tones, they pick up just enough of Donnie's apprehensions and the kids' teasing attitudes. The painting of Dad and Uncle Yosh in their military garb is particularly impressive, depicting them as capable, broad-shouldered, serious men. In the next scene, Uncle Yosh throws the football in a perfect spiral right at Donnie, his action leading into the final spread, which shows Donnie, football in hand, leading the boys off to play football, a game more suitable than war. A note about the contribution of Japanese-Americans in World War II introduces the book and sets the tone. Mochizuki earlier published *Baseball Saved Us* (1993), set in a Japanese-American internment camp in World War II; see *This Land Is Our Land* (1994), no. 254.

220 Molnar-Fenton, Stephan, *An Mei's Strange and Wondrous Journey*, illus. Vivienne Flesher, DK, 1998 (hardcover), ISBN 0–7894–24477–0, $15.95, unp. Ages 4–9, grades PS–4.

Realistic picture-story book set in recent times, in which An Mei, 6, tells how she is born on a train in China, is placed on the stone steps of the Wuhan orphanage, is adopted as a baby by a light-skinned man with a bushy black beard, and travels with him to the United States. At the end of the long trip, she is warmly welcomed by the man's wife and lovingly nurtured into early childhood by both her new parents. Since An Mei describes her babyhood experiences as though she herself recalls them and not as described to her by someone else, the narrative is not entirely credible. The story, however, is told with such tenderness and conviction and is supplemented by powerful impressionistic illustrations in warm and enticing pastel tones that this narrative flaw can easily be forgiven. The story is based on the author's own experiences in adopting An Mei from a Chinese orphanage, a circumstance that he briefly describes in an afternote. He says that he intends the account to represent the journeys of all adopted babies wherever they take place. A particularly meaningful section in the afternote explores why parents put their children up for adoption and concludes that it usually happens because they want better lives for their children than they themselves can give them.

221 Namioka, Lensey, *April and the Dragon Lady*, Browndeer Press, 1994 (hardcover), ISBN 0–15–276644–8, $10.95, 214 pp.; (paper), ISBN 0–15–200886–1, $3.95. Ages 12 up, grades 7 up.

Novel of intergenerational and intergender conflict in a Chinese-American family in late twentieth-century Seattle. Since her mother's death two years earlier, April Chen has become more and more responsible for her father's mother, who lives with her family and seems to be getting forgetful. Her brother, Harry, Grandma's favorite, studying at the university, manages to slide out from any duties of watching over her, pleading upcoming tests or projects that must be finished. April's father, Gilbert, is seeing Ellen Wu, a divorced, strong-minded young woman who would like to marry him but balks at moving in as Grandma's daughter-in-law. Until April joined the high school Rock Hounds and met Steve Daniels, a red-haired classmate, she accepted her subordinate role submissively, but now chafes at the assumption that she is worth less than her brother and should give up her plans for college study of geology to care for her grandmother. She also delays introducing Steve to Grandma, for fear he will be insulted. To complicate matters, Grandma is discovered to have diabetes. As events unfold, it becomes apparent that Grandma is not so much senile as manipulative, timing her wandering episodes to thwart any move toward independence in the family and to burden them with feelings of guilt. A visit to a nursing home, considered a possible solution, is a disaster when Grandma cheats all the old people out of their valued possessions at mah-jongg. A solution is finally reached when Gilbert moves out to live with Ellen, Harry becomes man of the house, a widowed Chinese woman is hired as housekeeper, and April is free to go to college. The different expectations of the older generation and the Americanized youth are brought into sharp focus, and although a reader's sympathies are always with April, Grandma's desire for ease and deference in old age after having been a virtual slave to her husband and mother-in-law is also understandable. For a book by Namioka in a lighter vein, see no. 255, *Yang the Youngest and His Terrible Ear*, in *This Land Is Our Land* (1994).

222 Namioka, Lensey, *Yang the Third and Her Impossible Family*, illus. Kees de Krefte, Little Brown, 1995 (hardcover), ISBN 0–316–59726–0, $15.95, 143 pp.; Yearling, 1996 (paper), ISBN 0–440–41231–5, $3.99. Ages 9–12, grades 4–7.

Novel of a musical Chinese-American family in Seattle, sequel to *Yang the Youngest and His Terrible Ear* (see *This Land Is Our Land*, 1994, no. 255). Third Sister Yingmei has changed her name to Mary and tries in every way to become like her American friends, but her family consistently embarrasses her. Her mother compliments Mrs. Hanson, mother of Holly, whom Mary desperately wants for a friend, on being old and fat, qualities admired in China. Second Sister misses her old home and insists on wearing Chinese pajamas and cloth shoes. Eldest Brother, a talented violinist, refuses to play sports for fear of hurting his hands and is derided by his schoolmates as a nerd. Even Father humiliates her by being unable to pronounce the "th" sound and mixing his "l"s and "r"s. When Mary sees a chance to ingratiate herself with Holly by giving a home to one of the Hansons' kittens, Fourth Brother helps her smuggle the cat into their basement, since Father absolutely bans pets, for fear the family's instruments will be scratched or their sheet music torn up. With great difficulty they manage to keep the kitten, named Rita Hayworth, concealed until events conspire to show Mary that Holly is cold and shallow and that her own family, despite their mistakes, are more genuinely human. In the end Rita is adopted by neighbors, who think she is a stray, Mary has a new friend in Kim, and Eldest Brother has risen in the estimate of his peers by a daring rescue of Rita watched by Kim's brother. The story is light, with considerable humor, and family love, if not understanding, prevails. A third book in the series is *Yang the Second and Her Secret Admirers* (1998).

223 Narahashi, Keiko, *Is That Josie?*, illus. Keiko Narahashi, McElderry, 1994 (hardcover), ISBN 0–689–50606–6, $14.95, unp. Ages 3–7, grades PS–2.

Question-and-answer picture book of a child's day, the realistic question pages alternating with scenes of the same actions in the child's imagination. The little girl peeking out of bed is a sly fox hiding in her den; the child thumping down the stairs with her doll is a kangaroo with her baby in her pouch; the child making waves in her bath is a dolphin diving deep. Although there is no mention of ethnic origin, the illustrations picture little Josie and her mother with straight black hair and a slightly Oriental cast of features. This is a warm story for the very young that celebrates the power of make-believe. For another picture-story book by Narahashi, see no. 256, *I Have a Friend*, in *This Land Is Our Land* (1994).

224 Nunes, Susan Miho, *The Last Dragon*, illus. Chris K. Soentpiet, Clarion, 1995 (hardcover), ISBN 0–395–67020–9, $14.95, 32 pp. Ages 5–8, grades K–3.

Picture-story book in which young Peter Chang is reluctant to spend his summer with his great aunt in Chinatown, probably Honolulu, until he spots a decrepit dragon hanging in the window of a trading company on Jefferson Street, "Our last dragon," the shopkeeper tells him. Peter decides he must have it. His reluctant great aunt finally agrees, and so starts a concerted effort to restore the dragon to its former glory. Peter gets help from the tailor, who mends the moth-eaten body; from his aunt's mah-jongg group, who rebuild its horns; from the kite maker, who, in exchange for odd jobs by Peter, restores the tail; from the herbal apothecary, who supplies milky-white balls for eyes; and from the street artist, who paints sharp teeth and new color in the face. At a farewell dinner for Peter at the Golden Palace Restaurant, with all his new friends in attendance, the assembled dragon appears, along with a Buddhist priest who blesses the creature and paints black dots on the blind eyes so it can see. On ten pairs of silken black legs, it prances about the room and parades down the street with Peter proudly carrying the tail. Intensely detailed watercolor illustrations capture the diversity and teeming life everywhere in Chinatown, all the characters having well-differentiated Oriental faces and the glorious dragon dominating all.

225 Okimoto, Jean Davies, *Talent Night*, Scholastic, 1995 (hardcover), ISBN 0–590–47809–5, $14.95, 161 pp. Ages 12–16, grades 7–11.

Novel of a biracial boy, who hopes that by getting in touch with his Japanese side he will be given some money by his great uncle. Until the letter from Uncle Hideko arrives, Rodney Suyama has two main concerns, his rap music and Ivy Ramos, a half-Filipino, half African-American girl in his language arts class. When Uncle Hideko indicates that he is thinking of giving the money he has received as reparation for being interned during World War II to either Rodney or his sister, Suzanne, if they should prove to have retained enough of their Japanese culture, the siblings first vie then join forces to learn and display something of their ethnic roots. Since their father departed from the family, they have dropped his Polish name but otherwise are thoroughly assimilated American teenagers. Their mother, born in an internment camp, has been reluctant to say much about her background and is ambivalent about her uncle's proposed visit. When he arrives, the traditional dinner the two cook for him is a fiasco, and his rudeness infuriates them. To his own surprise, Rodney has become the boyfriend of beautiful Ivy, and with her encouragement he signs up for Talent Night, preparing a rap about anti-Japanese discrimination. Their act, in which Ivy takes the part of the energizer rabbit, turns from serious to comic after a couple of blunders, but it is a great hit, and they pretend that is how they planned it. The whole experience with Uncle Hideko has brought Rodney and Suzanne no money but has taught them something about their roots and also how important acceptance of diversity is. The novel is more notable for the authentic picture it gives of high school social life than for any statement about Japanese culture. For an earlier novel by Okimoto, see *Molly by Any Other Name*, in *This Land Is Our Land* (1994), no. 258.

226 Revoyr, Nina, *The Necessary Hunger*, Simon & Schuster, 1997 (hardcover), ISBN 0–684–83234–8, $23.00, 365 pp.; St. Martin's, 1998 (paper), ISBN 0–312–18142–6, $13.95, 365 pp. Ages 14 up, grades 9 up.

Sports novel about high school girls' basketball in Los Angeles. Nancy Tarashiro is living with her father, a teacher and assistant coach, in a run-down but not seriously dangerous area when his African-American woman friend, Claudia, and her daughter, Raina, move in with them. Both Nancy and Raina, who attend different schools, are basketball stars, being recruited in their senior year by a number of colleges, and both are lesbians. Nancy is deeply attracted to Raina, but she conceals her emotion for fear of rejection. Their living arrangement and their common obsession with basketball throw them together, and an unspoken rivalry goads both of them into greater effort, harder practice, and ultimately better performance than either would achieve alone. The novel follows their final high school year, detailing their fortunes on and off the basketball court. Some of the other players are gay; some are not. Their sexual orientation is treated very decently, in a matter-of-fact way. Nancy's insecurity and yearning are not unlike those of any straight seventeen-year-old girl for a much-admired and unobtainable boy. Since they live in a black area of the city and almost all their school friends are African American, the prejudice Nancy occasionally encounters is anti-Asian, a difficulty Claudia also suffers because she lives with a Japanese-American man. The language the girls use is rough, as is the brand of ball they play, but they are passionately dedicated to the sport and to their fellow team members. The length of the novel may discourage young readers, but it could be the ideal book for girls equally consumed by basketball or trying to sort out their own sexual identity.

227 Rumford, James, *The Island-below-the-Star*, illus. James Rumford, Houghton, 1998 (hardcover), ISBN 0–395–85159–9, $15.00, 32 pp. Ages 5 up, grades K up.

Story of the discovery of the Hawaiian Islands by early Polynesian explorers more than fifteen hundred years ago. Four brothers, seeking adventure, set off to find the island below the star Arcturus. Soon they find their fifth brother, little Manu, stowed away among the calabashes of food, and though they teasingly pretend they will throw him overboard, they really welcome him. Hoku, the eldest, loves the stars; Na'ale loves the sea; 'Opua loves the clouds; Makani loves the wind, and Manu loves birds. Each brother uses his special talents to cross the huge expanse of the Pacific, but when they are blown off course by a bad storm and clouds hide the stars, it is Manu who spots a bird that guides them to land. The wide pages are a series of lovely watercolor seascapes evoking distance and open space around the frail canoe and giving an idea of the immense journey and the courage of these early sailors.

228 Salisbury, Graham, *Jungle Dogs*, Delacorte, 1998 (hardcover), ISBN 0–385–32187–2, $15.95, 183 pp. Ages 9–13, grades 4–8.

Realistic, sociological problem novel of family and school life set in recent years in a coastal village somewhere in the Hawaiian Islands. Mixed-ethnic (Hawaiian-Filipino-Chinese-Portuguese) Boy (James) Regis, 12, has two problems, in addition to being small for his age and wearing glasses: his brother, Damon, 14, and the jungle dogs he is sure lurk in the trees along his early-morning paper route. Damon is the leader of a school gang called the Cudas, is increasingly a problem in their home, and refuses to help with the route. He is on the outs with Dad, is obnoxious to his siblings, and belittles his older sister's boyfriend. Although very late one night he comes home badly cut up from a fight with an older gang, his "tough guy" attitude grows, especially since the leader of the gang is Crowboy, the older brother of a classmate who constantly bullies Boy. After Damon slashes the tires of Crowboy's truck, the story reaches a climax with a violent fight on the beach. Dad breaks it up, dealing easily and authoritatively with the antagonists and assuring Crowboy that Damon, regardless of motives, will reimburse him for his loss. Damon seems chastened at the end and accompanies Boy on the route, but one is left to wonder how long Damon's about-face will last. Fine scenes in the home of this decent, hardworking, troubled family, good school scenes, where Boy tries to do his best and struggles with a written assignment that reveals much about his thinking, the carefully paralleled look at "jungle dogs," a well-realized setting, and the author's ear for adolescent male dialogue and eye for teen attitudes offset the inconclusive ending, while the insights into Boy's feelings, the fast pace, and just-enough action hold the interest all the way. Earlier Salisbury published *Shark Bait* (1997), in which a twelve-year-old boy in a small Hawaiian town is torn between obeying his police-chief father and being with his friends, who plan to view a fight between an island boy and a sailor.

229 Salisbury, Graham, *Under the Blood-Red Sun*, Delacorte, 1994 (hardcover), ISBN 0–385–32099–X, $15.95, 246 pp.; Yearling (paper), ISBN 0–440–41139–4. Ages 11–18, grades 6–12.

Historical novel of the Japanese attack, December 7, 1941, on Pearl Harbor in Honolulu, Hawaii. The first half of the book sets the social and political milieu, and the last half tells about the bombing and the events leading out of it. The main concerns in late 1941 of narrator Tomi (Tomikazu) Nakaji, 13, are school; his mixed-breed dog, Lucky; being the man of the family while his fisherman father, Taro, is on his sampan; taking care of Taro's prize racing pigeons; baseball; hanging with his best friend, Billy Davis, a haole (white) boy his age; and staying out of the reach of the bullying haole kid, Keet Wilson, on whose wealthy father's lands the Nakaji shack stands. Tomi and his friends are barely aware of the wars that are raging in Europe and the Far East, but they know that anti-Japanese sentiment has increased greatly. Tomi is often embarrassed by Grampa's great pride in being a first-generation Japanese immigrant. Starting with that fateful Sunday morning, life gets tough for the Nakajis. Tomi is catching Billy's practice pitches when the boys become aware of planes zooming and circling. At first they think the planes are American, then realize they bear the Japanese blood-red sun emblem. When they see immense black clouds of smoke, Tomi remembers that Taro is in the harbor fishing. Frightened, Mama insists that all Grampa's Japanese heirlooms be buried immediately. They soon learn that the region is under military control. Near-turmoil ensues. School is canceled indefinitely, and soldiers force Grampa and Tomi to kill Taro's pigeons, because someone has reported that the birds are messenger pigeons. They learn that Taro was shot in the leg, his helper, Sanji, killed, and the fishing boat scuttled. Tomi discovers that Taro is being held prisoner on Sand Island in the harbor and bravely swims out to visit him, after which Taro is interned somewhere on the mainland. Without Taro's income and with food and supplies running low, times get very hard. Two FBI agents arrest Grampa and take him away to a place unknown. Eventually, they learn that Taro is imprisoned in Texas, but they cannot find out where Grampa is. Mama bravely assures Tomi and Kimi that they will be strong and survive, and Tomi is sure that, while his family are ashamed of what Japan has done, some day he will bring Grampa's heirlooms out and again display them with pride. Characters are well drawn, even minor ones like Keiko, Sanji's widow, who returns Mama's generosity by sharing some crawfish, and Mr. Ramos, the law student, who became a teacher because he feels he can do more good as a teacher and discusses such issues of the war as freedom of choice with his students. Tomi's narrative, with Tomi always and credibly at the center, moves steadily. Best is the sense of chaos and tension the bombing arouses among the unsuspecting, ordinary people and the irrational actions of some citizens and authorities.

230 Tan, Amy, *The Hundred Secret Senses*, Putnam, 1995 (hardcover), ISBN 0–399–14114–6, $24.95, 358 pp.; 1998 (paper), ISBN 0–375–70152–4, $13.00, 368 pp. Ages 14 up, grades 9 up.

Contemporary, realistic novel with fantasy aspects of Chinese-American family life. Olivia Bishop, the narrator, has mixed feelings toward her much older half-sister, Kwan, the child of Olivia's father by a woman whom he left behind in China when he emigrated to the United States. On his untimely death, while Olivia and her brothers were still small, he asked that Olivia's mother bring Kwan to America. Since Olivia's mother has neglected Olivia in favor of various projects and boyfriends, Kwan has virtually raised Olivia. Although grateful to Kwan, Olivia is often embarrassed by her eccentric older sister, who says she (Kwan) has yin eyes, that is, can see ghosts. Kwan often tells Olivia stories of a previous existence in China in the mid-1800s. During the strife with the Manchus and the coming of the missionaries, as Nunumu or Miss Moo from the tiny, out-of-the-way village of Changmian, she associated with people who are now ghosts. She also tells Olivia stories of her this-century childhood and youth in the small village, a jumble of accounts intermingled with those of the previous century and highly colored by Kwan's lively imagination and personality. Olivia and her husband, Simon, are having marital problems, since Olivia is convinced that Simon, even after nearly twenty years of marriage, is still in love with his old sweetheart. Kwan sets out to rectify their situation, apparently seeing them as destined for each other based on the earlier century's experiences. When Simon and Olivia are encouraged to get information and photographs to do an article on present-day China for a magazine story, Kwan engineers a trip to Changmian and eventually a reconciliation. Olivia gains tangible, if amazing, proof of Kwan's previous-century existence. She and Simon return to the United States without Kwan, who has mysteriously disappeared. Olivia has learned much about her need to forgive and accept, about unconditional love, and about what "believing in ghosts" of the kind that Kwan believed in means—that people we love are never lost, since we can always find them "with our hundred secret senses." A large set of amazing figures; fine pictures of Chinese small-village life; many humorous scenes, mostly arising out of Kwan's view of life and people that seems extraordinary to Olivia's westernized eyes; and a poignant conclusion—all these seem just right considering that the book sometimes outruns itself. A slow pace picks up when the trio reaches China and the various threads come together. For other books by Tan, see *The Joy Luck Club* and *The Kitchen God's Wife*, in *This Land Is Our Land* (1994), nos. 271 and 272, also of the Chinese and Chinese-American experience.

231 Wang, Ping, *American Visa*, Coffee House, 1994 (paper), ISBN 1–56689–025–X, $11.95, 179 pp. Ages 14 up, grades 9 up.

In graceful, unsentimental prose, eleven stories tell of a girl's childhood in China during the Cultural Revolution and her early years as a new immigrant in New York City. Eldest of three daughters in what had been an upper-middle-class family—her father a naval officer, her mother a musician—Seaweed suffers not only the demotion in social status for intellectuals of the period, but also her mother's unexplained hostility and abuse, apparently singling her out from the three girls to do all the housework and scorning her as ugly and stupid, even though she gets top marks in school. Because she hopes to go to college and only those who have spent two years being "reeducated" in the country can be recommended, she volunteers to go to an extremely poor and remote village. The backbreaking labor and physical hardships are bad enough, but the casual cruelty of the peasants stuns her. After three years she is allowed to enter not the university, as she has hoped, but a second-rate language school to prepare to be a teacher. Eventually, she is able to get to New York, where she is lonely but, with persistence, achieves a little independence, only to be besieged by demands from her family in China for money, for aid in getting to this country, and for other favors, all of which, in the Chinese family tradition, she feels duty bound to honor. A later novel by Wang, *Foreign Devil* (1996), tells much the same story of a girl's early life in an expanded version but ends before she leaves for the United States.

232   Wartski, Maureen, *Candle in the Wind*, Fawcett Juniper, 1995 (paper), ISBN 0–449–70442–4, $4.50, 185 pp. Ages 10–18, grades 7–12.

Novel of trauma and eventual understanding in a Japanese-American family after the shooting of their promising elder son on the night of his high school graduation party. After Harris Muzuno is killed when he approaches a house to ask to use the phone after a car breakdown, the family suffers debilitating anger and discrimination. The narrator, Terri, 15, who was closest to Harris emotionally, is filled with hate for Rodney Waring, the older man who shot her brother in panic, thinking he was being attacked. The rest of the family breaks apart, each obsessed by his own grief. A couple of hotheaded Japanese-American boys join with some West Coast young men in an Asian Power organization, and are countered by a white supremacy group until the town of Westriver, Massachusetts, divides into two camps. To their surprise, Mr. Mizuno's mother, whom they call Obaachan, announces that she is coming from Japan to "light incense over Harris's ashes." At first their Japanese grandmother seriously increases the family's problems. She carps incessantly at Terri and her mother, thinks her son can do no wrong, and dotes on the younger brother, Mitch. The only relief Terri has is her friendship with the son of the enlightened editor of the local newspaper, Nick Kawalsky, who lost his mother in an accident caused by a drunken driver and understands her fury. On the night when the newspaper office is firebombed, Terri hunts for Mitch in a darkened park and comes upon Waring, who turns out to be not the villain she has pictured but a guilt-ridden, shambling old man. At a huge march for nonviolence in Boston, where the Mizuno family are show-pieces, Obaachan insists on seizing the microphone and averting a major confrontation by giving an impassioned speech, with Terri's help, against hate. In addition to the central theme, the novel has many insights into cultural differences and the difficulties of children growing up products of a mixed marriage.

233 Watanabe, Sylvia, and Carol Bruchac, eds., *Into the Fire: Asian American Prose*, Greenfield Review, 1996 (paper), ISBN 0–912678–90–9, $17.95, 389 pp. Ages 15 up, grades 10 up.

Large and varied collection of short stories, excerpts from novels, and personal-experience or autobiographical pieces by thirty-two Asian-American writers, with small biographical sketches of each, several interviews of prominent writers, and reflections on the development of Asian-American literature by Chinese-American Shawn Wong, as well as introductory essays by the two collectors. Divided into five sections, Origins, Islands, Survival, Heartland, and Full Circle, the selections offer a broad range of Asian-American voices, Hawaiian, Chinese, Korean, Japanese, Filipino, Asian-Indian, and Vietnamese, in a variety of moods. Taken together, they are an always interesting array of perspectives on the Asian-American experience, cultures, intergenerational attitudes and tensions, intercultural attitudes and tensions, and the history of Asian Americans in the United States. The persona of Lovey, a child growing up in Hawaii, describes her joys and sorrows with raising rabbits in "Dominate and Recessid Jeans" from Lois-Ann Yamanaka's novel *Wild Meat and the Bully Burgers* (sic; 1996), a sometimes funny, always telling piece that proves that children, wherever they live and from whatever background, are much alike. Garrett Hongo (Japanese-Hawaiian) tells of the vicissitudes of buying a used car in "Sunbird," while Wakako Yamauchi describes the extremely tough times a Japanese-American family (perhaps her own) have during the Great Depression and the subsequent relocation during World War II. In "Over Here Is Where I Am," Joseph Won gives word-picture views of a group of Hawaiian expatriates in Seattle, as bohemian, sophisticated intellectuals. Darrell Lum shows how confusing certain cultural customs can be for a child in "Giving Tanks," in which in a kind of Chinese-Hawaiian pidgin English a boy describes his confusion about celebrating the American holiday of Thanksgiving. While most of the stories demand a high level of maturity or skill with interpretation, the opening one, which deals with Korean women taken as prostitutes by Japanese soldiers, may put off even some mature and sophisticated readers. For other books by these editors, see *Talking to the Dead and Other Stories* and *Home to Stay*, in *This Land Is Our Land* (1994), nos. 281 and 282.

234 Wong, Shawn, ed., *Asian American Literature: A Brief Introduction and Anthology*, HarperCollins, 1996 (paper), ISBN 0–673–46977–8, $19.95, 462 pp. Ages 14 up, grades 9 up.

Anthology of Asian-American fiction and poetry (see no. 300), with some autobiographical selections and a play, one in the publisher's Literary Mosaic Series, of which the general editor is Ishmael Reed, intended primarily for college classes. Twenty short stories by as many Asian-American writers of various backgrounds present divergent views of what it means to be Asian American earlier in the century and today. Among the issues reflected are yearning for homeland, adapting to new mores and a new language, nostalgia for homeland or original culture, conflict between generations after immigration, and the discrepancies between the values of homeland and culture and the perceived ones of America. The writers are arranged in chronological order by birth, with earlier writers represented by, among others, Toshio Mori (Japanese) and Bienvenido Santos (Filipino), in whose story, "Quicker with Arrows," the culture conflict appears in the ill-fated romance between an American girl and a young Filipino man of a wealthy family, and the most recent ones by Fae Myenne Ng (Chinese), T. C. Huo (Laotian), and Monique Thuy-Dung Truong (South Vietnamese). Tones vary, but most stories are serious explorations of whatever issue the writer has in mind, although humor is not absent, as in the ironically funny "Nobody's Hero," by Lonny Kaneko, in which two schoolboys in a Japanese relocation camp during World War II, who think they will be regarded as heroes for beating the system, become school laughingstocks. O. Wini Terada's (Hawaiian) "Intermediate School Hapai" is a tender brother-sister story. Several of the stories display interesting structural forms, combining memories, flashbacks, and snatches of poetry and mixing American and pidgin English and original language for striking cross-cultural effects. A valuable historical overview of Asian-American literature introduces the book, and highly informative introductions precede each writer.

235 Yamanaka, Lois-Ann, *Blu's Hanging*, Farrar, 1997 (hardcover), ISBN 0–373–11499–4, $22.00, 260 pp.; Bard, 1998 (paper), ISBN 0–380–73139–8, $12.00, 261 pp. Ages 12 up, grades 7 up.

Poignant, sometimes amusing, family novel, with growing-up story aspects, involving a Japanese-American-Hawaiian family in a mixed-ethnic village in Hawaii, probably in the 1970s. Ivah Ogata, 13, describes how life is for her father, Bertram; brother, Blu, 9; sister, Maisie, 5; and herself, after the death of their mother, Eleanor. Bertram, a janitor, becomes moody, maudlin, and often irascible. Ivah cooks, mostly Spam and rice, cleans, cares for her siblings without complaint, diligently keeps up her grades, and tries to overlook her father's increasing reliance on marijuana to ease his emotional pain. Maisie does poorly in kindergarten, wets her pants, and is practically mute. Blu has a fine singing voice, which he puts to good use in church programs; yearns for his father's approval; and overeats to compensate for his feelings of loss and inadequacy. Passages deal with the children's memories of Mama (Eleanor); their efforts to make money; Blu's kindnesses toward Maisie, and toward Ivah, for whom he buys a sanitary belt and pads when he realizes she has begun to menstruate; their acquiring a dog; and their friendship with Miss Ito, Maisie's teacher, who helps Ivah acquire a scholarship to Mid-Pacific Institute. A powerful scene describes Poppy (Bertram) confiding a deep secret to Ivah: he and Mama met at a lepers' institution at the beginning of World War II and, deemed cured by sulfa drugs, married. Mama, afraid of relapsing, continued to take sulfa, which destroyed her kidneys. The episodes are united by the themes of coping, family love and concern, and common compassion, but as the novel nears its conclusion, two other problems emerge. When Poppy objects to Ivah's leaving for boarding school, Blu assures him that he, Blu, will be the second man in the family. Ivah leaves, hoping also to make it easier for Blu and Maisie in their turn to get more education. The second matter concerns Blu's relationship with nearby, disliked Portuguese-Hawaiians. Needy for love, Blu becomes involved in oral sex with twenty-year-old Uncle Paulo, who is also having sex with his younger girl cousins. Blu realizes the activity has been a coping mechanism and determines never to let the behavior happen again. At the end he is hanging on but in a more responsible way. A palpably conceived multiethnic atmosphere, strong emotional tension, clearly drawn characters, and a pidgin-English style that contributes to the setting—these add to this engrossing, sympathetically presented if discursive story of a family in crisis. Yamanaka has also written *Wild Meat and the Bully Burgers* (1996), a humorous maturation story with a girl protagonist, who wishes she were a haole (white), and *Saturday Night at the Pahala Theatre* (1993), a book of "poetic novellas." More recent is *Heads by Harry* (1999), an amusing girl's growing-up novel also set in Hawaii.

236 Yamauchi, Wakako, *Songs My Mother Taught Me: Stories, Plays, and Memoir*, Feminist, 1994 (hardcover), ISBN 1–55861–086–3, $35.00, 257 pp.; (paper), ISBN 1–55861–086–3, $14.95. Ages 14 up, grades 9 up.

Nine short stories, two plays, and five short memoirs by a Japanese-American writer, edited by Garrett Hongo, who contributes a helpful introduction about her background and factors that influenced her work. The stories revolve around the Japanese immigrant experience, and are strongly marked by the hardscrabble attempts to wrest a living from the arid desert of California's Imperial Valley; the vicissitudes of family life under those conditions; the disruption of families because of World War II relocations; anti-Japanese sentiment before and after the war; attitudes of the immigrants toward the mother country; and the woman's point of view and concerns. The stories gain power not only from Yamauchi's precise use of detail, mostly visual, but also of emotion and situation selectively and understatedly described. The stories are divided into two sets: Country Stories and City Stories. The first group reflects desert agrarian life before the war, the most heartrending being that of the drowning death in a tub of a baby during a terribly hot, dry summer (in a story reminiscent of Southern American regional writers). The second group includes a story set in Tokyo during the war, memorable for its pictures of the bombing, the lack of food and other necessities, and the attempts to keep family life going and cling to heritage on the part of Japanese-Americans who have returned to Japan for an education and are caught in events. In some stories, intruders bring trouble to marriages, among them a Japanese priest, who was relocated and who, after the war, lives a dissolute life, begging, mooching, squandering, and using people. In another story, a mother leaves home, ostensibly to help her sister, her son finding consolation briefly in the handkerchief she gave him, until he learns that she is never coming back. In others, wives discarded for younger women are forced to gain work skills. Many of the stories deliberately leave questions unanswered. Yamauchi knows how to move the reader; her stories tease the intellect and touch the heart as well.

237 Yep, Laurence, *The Case of the Lion Dance*, HarperCollins, 1998 (hardcover), ISBN 0–06–024447–X, $14.95, 214 pp. Ages 10–14, grades 5–9.

Yep's second San Francisco Chinatown mystery, starring Lily, 12, and her great aunt, the famous Chinese-American actress Tiger Lil, following *The Case of the Goblin Pearls* (1997). At the opening of a new restaurant owned by friends, Auntie Tiger Lil is managing the publicity, including a contest between rival karate schools, each team, dressed in an elaborate lion costume, dancing through a maze to reach the "lettuce," a large ball of two hundred green hundred-dollar bills hung from the restaurant sign, which will then be donated to charity. When an explosion disrupts the celebration and puts the lion dance winner, Lily's friend Barry, in the hospital, Lily and her aunt start an investigation to trace what has happened to the lettuce. This leads to a variety of red herrings and complications, including an unlikely corrupt slum landlord. Many of Auntie Tiger Lil's ideas come from movies in which she acted and which are well known to her Chinatown admirers, an element that provides considerable humor. An interesting sidelight uncovered in their search is the prejudice and resentment felt by the China-born residents toward the American-born, especially toward those who, like Lily, can speak little Chinese. A third in the series is *The Case of the Firecrackers* (1999). For earlier books by Yep, see *American Dragons, Dragon War, Mountain Light, The Star Fisher, The Man Who Tricked a Ghost, The Shell Woman and the King,* and *Tongues of Jade* in *This Land Is Our Land* (1994), nos. 285 (also 338), 286, 287, 288, 330, 331, and 332.

238 Yep, Laurence, *The Cook's Family*, Putnam, 1998 (hardcover), ISBN 0–399–22907–8, $15.99, 184 pp.; Paper Star, 1999 (paper), ISBN 0–698–11804–9, $5.99, 192 pp. Ages 12–16, grades 7–11.

Novel of family relationships and obligations in Chinese-American culture, set in San Francisco, sequel to *Ribbons* (1996). Daughter of a Chinese-American mother and an Anglo father, Robin Lee is mostly interested in her dancing, an activity supported by her father, a producer of artistic films, and her grandmother, recently arrived from Hong Kong, who is a friend of the ballet teacher. On a visit to Chinatown, Robin and her grandmother inadvertently become involved in the fantasy of an unhappy cook named Wolf, who pretends that they are his wife and daughter, his own, he believes, having starved during one of China's disastrous periods. The pretense supplies Robin with a diversion from her parents' constant quarrels since her mother has begun acting as bookkeeper for a new business enterprise of Robin's uncles as well as continuing her full-time job. For Grandmother, it is a link to her youth, because Wolf remembers many of the same places, stories, and songs. After several weeks, during which Wolf becomes an ardent admirer, they come upon a scene of chaos at the restaurant, where Wolf's real daughter, having survived and arrived illegally, vents her fury on her father. Father and daughter both flee the police, but Robin has begun to understand her Asian roots, and both Grandmother and Mother have reappraised their obligations to family. The sad, lonely cook is a touching character, but Grandmother, with her feet crippled from binding and her spirits suppressed from long practice, is the most interesting character as she blooms in the unaccustomed admiration. Earlier books by Yep are described in *This Land Is Our Land* (1994), nos. 285, 286, 287, 288, 330, 331, 332, and 338 (for titles, see entry 237, this book).

239   Yep, Laurence, *The Ghost Fox*, illus. Jean Tseng and Mou-sein Tseng, Scholastic, 1994 (hardcover), ISBN 0–590–47204–6, $13.95, 70 pp.; Apple, 1997 (paper), ISBN 0–590–47205–4, $2.99, 80 pp. Ages 9–12, grades 4–7.

Fantasy based on an ancient Chinese ghost story, collected in the seventeenth century by a scholar and preserved in both literary and oral versions. Little Lee, only nine, helping his father load his trading boat, accidentally bumps into a young gentleman in a red robe, who takes offense and hurries off vowing revenge. After the boat leaves, Little Lee is bothered by what appears to be a fox scrabbling at his window. One night he wakes to find the window broken and his mother lying in the kitchen. After that, she is changed in personality, mean and critical of him. With great effort he repairs the window and stays awake at night until he sees the fox and, swinging a big kitchen knife, cuts off a chunk of its tail. He follows the drops of blood to a deserted mansion, where he sees the red-robed gentleman with a servant brushing the bandaged tail hanging below his robe. He overhears them say that in one more night the ghost fox will have stolen his mother's soul, and then they will celebrate with sweets. Little Lee devises a plan, walks to the village where his aunt lives, borrows poison, swipes the foxtails his uncle has hanging on the wall, and accepts a package of sweets from his aunt. By using the tails he tricks the fox's servant into thinking he is a high-ranking ghost fox and gives him the sweets, which he has poisoned. The next day, they find the two ghost foxes dead at the old mansion, and his mother returned to her former loving self. Both the story and the black-and-white, line-drawing illustrations say much about life in a seventeenth-century

Chinese village. Earlier books by Yep described in *This Land Is Our Land* (1994) are nos. 285, 286, 287, 288, 330, 331, 332, and 338 (for titles, see entry 237, this book).

240   Yep, Laurence, *Hiroshima*, Scholastic, 1995 (hardcover), ISBN 0–590–20832–2 $9.95, 56 pp.; Apple, 1996 (paper), ISBN 0–590–20833–0, $4.50. Ages 9–12, grades 4–7.

Historical novel of the dropping of the atomic bomb on Hiroshima, Japan, in August, 1945. The incident is seen partly from the point of view of Colonel Tibbets, who piloted the *Enola Gay*, the plane that carried the bomb, and partly that of a little girl named Sachi, who is one of the few survivors in the area close to where the bomb fell and whose sister, Riko, is killed. Although Sachi is horribly disfigured, she is eventually taken to the United States as one of the "Hiroshima Maidens," who receive medical treatment. After many operations, she returns to Japan. Although the book is subtitled "A Novella," it is far more straight history. Sachi is a composite figure, but otherwise the facts are as close as possible to the actual incident. Yep makes an effort to argue both sides of the controversy about the use of the bomb, but clearly comes down against its further use. The book ends, "It must not drop again." It is followed by an afterword by the author and a several-page bibliography of sources. Earlier books by Yep are described in *This Land Is Our Land* (1994), nos. 285, 286, 287, 288, 330, 331, 332, and 338 (for titles, see 237, this book).

241   Yep, Laurence, *The Imp That Ate My Homework*, illus. Benrei Huang, Harper-Collins, 1998 (hardcover), ISBN 0–060–27688–6, $14.95, 87 pp. Ages 8–12, grades 3–7.

Lighthearted fantasy set in San Francisco's Chinatown. United States–born Jim has always been bored with traditional Chinese stories of demons, ghosts, and goblins and has avoided his grandfather, known as the meanest man in Chinatown, until he has to write a biography of him for a school assignment. Instead of interviewing Grandpop, he builds a dull paper out of the only nice things his parents can think of about the cantankerous old man: Grandpop is always honest, and he never fought with Grandmom. Watching the Chinese newscast that evening, Grandpop is inexplicably disturbed to learn that construction workers have uncovered a sealed ancient vase in the ruins of a temple with writing on it cursing anyone who opens it. That night, Jim is awakened by a strange green apelike creature with four arms and huge red eyes who taunts him and teasingly eats his homework. This is just the first encounter with the imp, whose real quarrel is with Grandpop, in a former life Chung Kuei, the famous demon fighter who imprisoned it in the vase. Since the imp is very quick and invisible to everyone except Jim and Grandpop, it causes trouble in both regular and Chinese school and in the workplaces of both Jim's parents, all of it blamed on the boy. Finally, it appears in Portsmouth Square where Grandpop is playing chess, and the old man takes off after it, with Jim panting behind. They tear through Chinatown, creating havoc in stores and restaurants, ending in a building that was once a theater, where they all become characters in a traditional play. Finally, Grandpop traps the imp, using the stone lions guarding a bank entrance, and with Jim's help binds it again. The humor is mostly slapstick, middle-school variety, but the pictures of Chinatown, both in the text and in the frequent black-and-white drawings, are vivid, and the new alliance between grandfather and grandson is satisfying. Earlier books by Yep are described in *This Land Is Our Land* (1994), nos. 285, 286, 287, 288, 330, 331, and 338 (for titles see entry 237, this book).

242 Yep, Laurence, *Later, Gator*, Hyperion, 1995 (hardcover), ISBN 0–786–80059–3, $13.95, 122 pp.; Disney, 1997 (paper), ISBN 0–786–81160–9, $4.50. Ages 9–12, grades 4–7.

Humorous realistic story of family life in San Francisco's Chinatown. The narrator, Teddy, resents his sweet-tempered little brother, Bobby, whom everyone praises and loves. When his mother insists that he buy Bobby something special for his birthday and suggests a turtle, Teddy has an inspiration and buys, instead, a baby alligator. In the resulting series of disasters and slapstick misunderstandings, the two brothers bond for the first time, and Teddy discovers that, although it is not the Chinese way to praise children or to show affection openly, his parents and other relatives really admire his imagination and his initiative. The extended family who gather for Bobby's birthday party show that the same sort of strain existed between the boys' father and his brothers. Earlier books by Yep are described in *This Land Is Our Land* (1994), nos. 285, 286, 287, 288, 330, 331, and 338 (for titles, see entry 237, this book).

243 Yep, Laurence, *Thief of Hearts*, HarperCollins, 1995 (hardcover), ISBN 0–06–025341–X, $14.95, 197 pp.; Harper Trophy, 1997 (paper), ISBN 0–06–440591–5, $5.95, 208 pp. Ages 10–14, grades 5–9.

Sequel to *Child of the Owl* (Harper, 1977), this novel featuring Casey's daughter Stacy, who is blond like her non-Chinese father. Her great-grandmother, Tai-Paw, with whom Casey stayed in *Child*, lives with them in Almeden, some miles from San Francisco's Chinatown. Both parents are busy professionals and Stacy is well liked in her middle school, where she has never considered herself Chinese, although her mother clings to some of her old friends, with whom she speaks Cantonese. Stacy is drafted into being companion to Hong Ch'un Wang, newly arrived from China, although she speaks little Cantonese and no Mandarin, the Wangs' language. Moreover, Hong Ch'un acts superior and calls Stacy *t'ung chung*, half breed. That afternoon, friends of Stacy discover some of their possessions missing, little things treasured for their sentimental value. The missing articles are found in Hong Ch'un's backpack, and she is accused of being a thief. Stacy goes home with her friend Karen, who comes from a troubled family and whom she has been neglecting lately. By evening, Hong Ch'un has fled, evidently to the city. Tai-Paw and Stacy, driven by Casey, go to Chinatown to hunt for her and, with the help of Mr. Jeh, Tai-Paw's old friend, find her, but not before Stacy has a tour of Chinatown by night and learns much about her mother's childhood and her great-grandmother and comes to appreciate them both more than before. The next day, with the help of her father, she sets a trap and discovers that the thief is Karen, who has resented her new friend. Inserted is a long folktale about the Thief of Hearts, which fits symbolically but awkwardly into the narrative. Earlier books by Yep are decribed in *This Land Is Our Land* (1994), nos. 285, 286, 287, 288, 330, 331, 332, and 338 (for titles, see entry 237, this book).

5

Asian Americans: Books of Oral Tradition

244 Armstrong, Jennifer, ret., *Wan Hu Is in the Stars*, illus. Barry Root, Morrow/ Tambourine, 1995 (hardcover), ISBN 0–688–12457–7, $15.00, unp. Ages 4–8, grades K–3.

Retelling of a Chinese legend explaining the formation of the constellation known as the lotus. Wan Hu, a poet, is so absent-minded that people ridicule him, but he is undeterred in his determination to reach the stars and wanders about in his blue robe patterned with lotus thinking of ways to achieve this goal. He tries climbing the mountain, but that does not get him high enough. He tries harnessing geese and cranes to fly him there, but only becomes entangled in the silk bands of their harnesses. Then a fireworks display inspires him. He binds forty-seven great fireworks rockets to a chair and, as evening falls and a crowd gathers, sets them off and soars upward. The villagers look everywhere for him and find no trace, but they notice a new group of stars in the shape of a lotus. The oversized book is illustrated lavishly with gouache paintings showing rural Oriental houses, people, and landscape. A novel by Armstrong is described in *This Land Is Our Land* (1994), no. 4, *Steal Away*.

245 Bodkin, Odds, ret., *The Crane Wife*, illus. Gennady Spirin, Harcourt, 1998 (hardcover), ISBN 0–15–201407–1, $16.00, 32 pp. All ages, grades PS up.

In one of the most beautiful of recent illustrated books, a retelling of the Japanese tale of the sailmaker Osamu, a poor and lonely weaver of sails, lives on a hilltop overlooking a green marsh, often dotted with white cranes. A storm drives a crane against his house. He brings the stunned creature inside and nurses it back to health, then watches it fly away. In another terrible storm, he finds a lovely woman knocking on his door. He takes her in, falls in love, and marries her. When food becomes scarce, she offers to weave a magic sail, as long as he does not watch her at work. He sells that sail for enough gold to live half a year. When that money runs out again, he begs her to repeat her weaving, promising never to ask again, and she reluctantly agrees. Later the captain of a trading ship promises enough gold for a lifetime in exchange for a sail. Osamu's wife at first refuses, but, when he orders her to make another sail, she sadly agrees. After a long time he can no longer contain himself and peers around the screen where she is weaving. He sees the great crane he saved from the storm, weaving her own white feathers into a sail. Realizing that she has been observed, she spreads her wings and flies away. Though clearly a tale of the dangers of greed, this attractively retold version draws no morals. The stunning paintings, mostly filling two large double pages, are delicate and artistic and exploit the beauty of the lovely birds.

246   Bouchard, David, ret., *The Great Race*, illus. Zhong-Yang Huang, Millbrook, 1997 (hardcover), ISBN 0–7613–0305–7, $21.40, unp. Ages 4 up, grades PS up.

Retelling in picture-story book form of an ancient version of how the animals in the Chinese zodiac came to be in their present order. A grandmother tells her granddaughter how the Great Buddha summoned the dragon and eleven animals. Dog and pig end up last because pig's stoutness slows him down and dog will not leave him behind in the desert. Rooster elects to protect some hens and thus ends tenth. Monkey and goat choose to remain by a small, clear pond with lush grass. Horse and snake argue and lose their way in a woods. Tiger, rabbit, ox, and rat travel through the cold, windy mountains. Rat and ox arrive first at the Jade City, followed by tiger and rabbit, with dragon turning up much later. The story is fluently and mellifluously told, with the moralistic elements played down in favor of narrative. The diction is descriptive, making it easy to visualize situations and creatures, and extensive dialogue enlivens the whole. The illustrations are splendid with color and action, sometimes panoramic, sometimes upfront, sometimes more decorative than pictorial, but always with a sense of the Chinese culture in arrangement, motifs, or framing. The book concludes with an explanation of the characteristics and years associated with each animal. Also by Bouchard is *The Dragon New Year: A Chinese Legend* (1999). In no. 249, Demi presents another account of the Chinese zodiac, as does Ed Young in no. 285. Still other versions of the Chinese zodiac story appear in *The Rooster's Antlers: A Story of the Chinese Zodiac* (1999), retold by Eric Kimmel, and in *The Animals of the Chinese Zodiac* (1997), retold by Susan Whitfield.

247   Chang, Margaret, and Raymond Chang, rets., *The Beggar's Magic: A Chinese Tale*, illus. David Johnson, McElderry, 1997 (hardcover), ISBN 0–689–81340–6, $16.00, unp. Ages 4–9, grades PS–4.

Folktale also known as "Planting Pears," retold from a gathering of stories of magic and the supernatural made in Shandong province in China in the seventeenth or early eighteenth century and published in English in 1908. A gentle, old stranger appears in young Fu Nan's small village. Believing he is a priest under the vow of poverty, the villagers give him a hut in which to live and share their rice and vegetables freely with him. His magical powers, which the children are the first to detect, are verified for the entire village when stingy Farmer Wu refuses to share even one pear from his cartload of luscious fruit with the thirsty old man. Generous Fu Nan uses the few coins he has saved for a kite to buy one and gives it to the old man, who gratefully eats it all, except for one tiny black seed. This he plants in the village square. A magnificent pear tree sprouts and grows to maturity before their astonished eyes, loaded down with perfect golden-brown fruit, enough for everyone in the village. Then Farmer Wu is horrified to discover that his pears and even the cart that bore them are completely gone. The old man has conjured away the stingy farmer's pears to punish him for his greed. The story is well told in the fashion of folklore, with simple, direct, to-the-point style. Soft, earth-toned, full-page watercolors with objects and figures done in fine, delicate lines depict scenes and reveal character. Some views are frontal; others have an overhead perspective; all have a strength that belies their seeming fragility. The Changs have also capably retold *The Cricket Warrior: A Chinese Tale* (1994), another story from the Shandong collection and illustrated in watercolors by Warwick Hutton. Also moral in intent, the story describes the trouble that a self-indulgent, unthinking emperor brings upon his people and the sacrifice of a brave young man to save them. Both stories contain the motif of the mysterious, wandering man who intervenes to help those who are worthy. Notes on the stories are included. A more recent retelling from oral tradition, its source explained in an endnote, is *Da Wei's Treasure: A Chinese Tale* (1999). In this story of the "mysterious housekeeper" type, a kitten, actually an enchanted woman, rewards the youth who befriended her. Lori McElrath-Eslick's watercolors evoke the spirit of the story and make this an unusually handsome book.

248 Demi, ret., *Buddha*, illus. Demi, Holt, 1996 (hardcover), ISBN 0–8050–4203–2, $18.95, unp. Ages 8–12, grades 3–7.

Version of the life of the prince who becomes known as the Buddha, skillfully told, in slightly formal language, stunningly illustrated in delicately crafted pictures tinged with gold, and presented in an oversized format appropriate to the importance of the central figure. Before Siddhartha is born, holy men predict that he will either become a mighty king and rule the world or leave the household, find truth, and become the savior of the world. Determined to keep his son with him, his father the king surrounds the prince with every luxury. Meditative from his early years, however, aware of the suffering around him, precocious, intelligent, although married at sixteen and soon a father, the boy realizes that a different destiny calls him. On a quest for truth, he spends six years with hermits living a life of deep austerity, but, still feeling unfulfilled, he leaves to pursue a path of moderation. He sits under a large bodhi tree, from which he refuses to leave until he has found truth, life over death, and the means to end suffering for everyone. Afflicted by a variety of evils, he resists them all. As the Buddha, he acquires disciples and hundreds of followers from all levels of society. He helps those in need and teaches widely, often speaking in parables. In spite of opposition, his reputation grows, and at the age of eighty, after preaching for forty-five years, he dies and enters nirvana, the state of eternal peace. He has been to the very end of his life the teacher and comforter of his followers. Demi, herself Buddhist, compiled the details of the story of the man who became one of the world's great religious leaders from a wide variety of oral and written sources. Demi's *Buddha Stories* (1997) contains Jataka stories about the Buddha. Demi has also published *A Chinese Zoo, The Magic Boat,* and *Dragon Kites and Dragonflies*, nos. 294, 295, and 334 in *This Land Is Our Land* (1994). For another version of the story of the Buddha, see no. 268, this book.

249 Demi, ret., *The Dragon's Tale and Other Animal Fables of the Chinese Zodiac*, illus. Demi, Holt, 1996 (hardcover), ISBN 0–8050–3446–3, $16.95, unp. Ages 4 up, grades PS up.

Twelve animal fables based on the Chinese zodiac. Each short, linear, unadorned narrative moves straight to the moral, which is set off at the end of the story in red print that matches that of the story's title. Each story is surrounded by a circular frame about two inches wide, in which appear tiny animals, sea creatures, solar features, or whatever is appropriate to the story. The scene on the facing page, also circular in form, picks up an important episode in the story. In each story, anthropomorphized animals learn important lessons about life. The rat wishes to assume one form after another, until he finally realizes that it is best to be oneself. Oxen, who allow themselves to be divided by gossip, fall prey to tigers. A spotted snake learns not to judge by appearances. A frog learns there is more to the world than his narrow well. Silly monkeys learn the futility of trying to fish the moon out of a well. A proud boar learns humility, and a young dog teaches an old dog something about life. The stories are pleasingly told, but the colorful illustrations, as is usually the case with Demi's work, steal the book. The small delicate figures are fashioned with exquisite precision to approximate Chinese art. The tiniest lines were produced by a brush made of a single mouse whisker. Although this is a picture book, readers of all ages will find much to interest them, among other aspects the obvious similarity to the pure fable type attributed to Aesop of Greek tradition. For other versions of the Chinese zodiac, see nos. 246 and 285. For other books by Demi, see *A Chinese Zoo* and *The Magic Boat*, nos. 294 and 295, oral tradition, and *Dragon Kites and Dragonflies*, no. 334, poems, in *This Land Is Our Land* (1994).

250 Demi, ret., *The Stonecutter*, illus. Demi, Crown, 1995 (hardcover), ISBN 0–517–59864–7, $15.00, unp. Ages 4–8, grades PS–3.

Retelling of a Chinese folktale, one that appears in different forms around the world. A poor stonecutter envies the rich man on whose house he works, dreams of similar wealth, and finds his wish to be rich granted by a kind angel. Not satisfied, he envies the governor, then a farmer, the sun, the cloud, the wind, and a huge rock, and each time the angel hears and grants his wish to be that person or object. As a rock, feeling the pain of being cut by stonecutters, he wishes he were a stonecutter again and is changed back into his first form. He never again wishes to do anything else than to carve the "biggest and most beautiful stones in the world." Extending this story about being satisfied with who you are and what you have are pen-and-ink drawings and paints on gold backgrounds. Figures are composed of delicate lines in mainly reds and royal blues with touches of yellow and orange and planes of white in imitation of old Chinese art. The red-winged angel swooshes across the top corner of the left-hand page, observing intently with serious face and granting the increasingly selfish wishes with upraised arms. Slightly comic red dragons, which are woven together to make the intricate orb of the sun, constitute a particularly striking full-page design. No source is given for the story. Two other books of Chinese folklore by Demi, both also distinguished by clear writing and exquisitely detailed and vibrantly colored illustrations are *The Magic Tapestry* (1994), about a son who bravely tackles impossible tasks to find and return to his mother the elegant tapestry she has woven, and *The Greatest Treasure* (1998), in which both a rich man and a poor man ultimately agree on the truth of the old Chinese proverb that claims, "Gold and silver have their price, / but peace and happiness are priceless." Demi has also published *A Chinese Zoo* and *The Magic Boat*, nos. 294 and 295 (both oral tradition) and *Dragon Kites and Dragonflies*, no. 334 (poems), in *This Land Is Our Land* (1994).

251 Fang, Linda, ret., *The Ch'i-lin Purse: A Collection of Ancient Chinese Stories*, illus. Jeanne M. Lee, Farrar, 1995 (hardcover), ISBN 0–374–31241–9, $16.00, 127 pp.; 1997 (paper), ISBN 0–374–41889–1, 160 pp. $4.95. Ages 6–12, grades 1–7.

Nine pleasing stories retold from classic Chinese novels and operas, which themselves had their origin in ancient folktales. The stories are romantic in tone, an attitude extended by the misty, fluid, gray-and-white pictures; underscore the importance of generosity, helpfulness, and the need to use one's wits; and move along with an intimate storytelling flavor. A haughty, wealthy young bride forgets herself long enough to give her purse to a poor bride and is later helped by the other woman in her time of need. A carp-fish spirit changes herself into a woman because she has sympathy for a young man and ironically retains that form forever. A clever prime minister settles the dispute when a valuable jade becomes the source of difficulty between two warring kingdoms. A doctor makes sacrifices in order to find a remedy for a strange, seemingly incurable disease, and a clever magistrate helps a poor farmer who has lost his coat and teaches a hardfisted shopkeeper a lesson at the same time.

252 Farley, Carol, ret., *Mr. Pak Buys a Story*, illus. Benrei Huang, Whitman, 1997 (hardcover), ISBN 0–8075–5178–3, $15.95, unp.; 1999 (paper), ISBN 0–807–55179–1, $6.95. Ages 4–8, grades PS–3.

Lively retelling of a humorous Korean folktale, built around the old practice of "buying" stories from wandering reciters. The story is introduced by the ages-old formulaic phrase, "When tigers smoked long pipes," which indicates that it is a make-believe tale. An elderly Korean couple, lonely and bored in their countryside home, send their slow-witted servant, Mr. Pak, to buy them a story to entertain them and give him 100 gold coins with which to pay for it. Mr. Pak encounters a man walking by himself and, thinking the man must be a wandering storyteller, offers him the 100 coins for a tale. Really a cunning thief, the man simply describes the problems a stork is having with a fox in a nearby field. Mr. Pak goes home and teaches the tale to the couple, who repeat it with enjoyment night after night. It so happens that the thief and his gang come to rob the couple, but as the thief climbs over the wall and draws near the house, he hears the tale and thinking that the action in it refers to him, flees with all his fellows. The colorful, comic illustrations follow the action, catch the emotion, and play up the ironic humor. The picture of the foregrounded thief trying to scramble back over the wall, almost transfixed by fear and calling to his gang to leave because there is "terrible magic here," is hilarious.

253 Giskin, Howard, coll. and ret., *Chinese Folktales*, NTC, 1997 (paper), ISBN 0-8442-5927-6, $23.95, 271 pp. Ages 12 up, grades 7 up.

Highly entertaining collection of ninety-three Chinese tales told to Giskin and his wife by his students while he was teaching at Northeast University in China. Since the students came from various places, Giskin and his wife were able "to gather stories from every region of the country except the Tibetan High Plateau," tales that are representative of "cities, towns, or villages that are scarcely known outside of China." The book resulted from the Giskins' conviction "that there are many Chinese tales that have yet to be made available to the English-speaking world." The stories are divided into seven sections: Dragon Tales; Love; Magic; Ghosts, Monsters, and Evil Spirits; History and Legend; Fairy Tales and Fables; and Human Nature. Each category is defined in the excellent introduction that opens the book. The stories are preceded by brief introductions in the words of the students who contributed them, each of whom is identified. Most stories are simple, unembellished narratives, one or two pages long, without dialogue. The style is literate and projects respect for the past and those relatives and friends who shared them with the student collectors. The accounts in the Dragon Tales section sometimes portray the dragons as helpful, at other times as hostile to humans. The opening story, "The Legend of the Two Islands," describes the latter sort, an angry, vindictive monster, whom two brave young men kill while riding on his back. They fall into the sea, where they become two islands upon which the teller's neighbors now live. In "Dragon Pond," people help a suffering dragon and henceforth find that their pond is never dry or devoid of fish. Many of the stories in the Love section portray lovers who come to grief, because romantic love is discouraged in the culture. Some stories tell how features of the landscape or the natural environment came to be. Among the others, "Madame Qin" contains a fine picture of the world of the dead, while "Castles in Air" is a didactic story that exalts filial devotion. Some recall tales of other cultures, among them "The Magic Pot," which tells of the magical object that is stolen and refuses to stop producing because the thief does not say the controlling words correctly. This is a delightful collection, a fine source for storytelling material to use with younger audiences as well as for older ones to read to themselves. Since the book's format is scholarly, it is not likely to appeal to less dedicated or younger readers.

254 Granfield, Linda, ret., *The Legend of the Panda*, illus. Song Nan Zhang, Tundra, 1998 (hardcover), ISBN 0–88776–421–5, $15.95, unp. Ages 4 up, grades PS up.

Very impressively retold and illustrated picture-story book version of the ancient Chinese legend of how the giant panda originated. Doloma, a brave, young shepherdess, lives with her three sisters deep in the mountains of Sichuan province, where every day she leads her small flock out to graze. One morning a white bear cub joins her flock, and, welcomed and happy, comes every day thereafter to feed and play. One day a snow leopard leaps from a tree and attacks the cub, wounding it, and then attacks Doloma when she comes to the cub's defense, killing her. The white cub, recovered, leads the bear kind at Doloma's funeral, and, like the villagers, the bears smear themselves with ashes in mourning. Everywhere they touch their bodies, the ashes stain their fur, causing it to become black forever. The story has all the elements of a successful tale— stalwart characters, villain, tension, irony, sorrow—and the illustrations extend the enjoyment. The full-page, colorful panoramic scenes of mountains and valleys are alive with movement (one can almost hear the squirrel skitter up the tree trunk) and emotion (the eyes of the sheep and the little cub are wide with fear as the leopard leaps). The scent of flowers can almost be detected and the sound of the water heard as it plunges over the waterfalls. The woeful expressions on the pandas' faces at the end seem to foretell the book's additional purpose, to call attention to the World Wildlife Fund's efforts to keep the popular mammal from diminishing further in numbers. A commentary about the panda concludes this stunningly beautiful book.

255 Greene, Ellin, ret., *Ling-Li and the Phoenix Fairy: A Chinese Folktale*, illus. Zong-Zhou Wang, Clarion, 1996 (hardcover), ISBN 0–395–71528–8, $14.95, 32 pp. Ages 5 up, grades K up.

Chinese folktale, which underscores the importance of virtue and explains the origin of a wildflower known in the United States as jewelweed. In the mountainous part of China, Ling-Li, a pretty, industrious young woman of a poor family, works diligently for months to make a dress for her wedding to an equally diligent young farmer named Manchang. A selfish, wealthy girl in the same village, envying her, steals it, and, when pursued, throws the dress onto a wall, from which a flock of magpies carry it off. Ling-Li traps the magpies in a net and, lifted into the air by the flock, is transported to a high mountain. There, a spirit maiden, wearing the dress, approaches Ling Li and gives it to her. Shortly thereafter, Ling-Li sees a gorgeous phoenix fly out of the woods and realizes that the woman was the Phoenix Fairy, the Queen of the Birds. Home again, Ling-Li marries Manchang and they live happily until the wealthy girl again steals the dress. Magpies encircle her and peck at her, until the dress is torn to shreds and the girl is permanently scarred. Eventually the fragments of cloth become brilliantly colored wildflowers that cover the countryside. The story is adequately retold, although one must pay close attention to grasp motivations, and the descriptions sometimes impede the story. Strongly composed, deep-toned, colorful, three-quarter-page acrylics establish the setting and depict events, but facial features are not individualized. The paintings reveal the glorious coloring and magnificence of the mythological phoenix. A detailed afterword gives information about the phoenix, and indicates the sources of the tale. See *This Land Is Our Land* (1994), no. 505, *The Legend of the Cranberry*.

256 Hamilton, Morse, ret., *Belching Hill*, illus. Forest Rogers, Greenwillow, 1997 (hardcover), ISBN 0–688–14561–2, $15.00, unp. Ages 5 up, grades K up.

Based on the Japanese folktale, "The Old Woman Who Lost Her Dumpling," this version featuring a sweet-faced but indomitable old woman and ugly but never scary ogres. When she drops a dumpling that she intends to share with her pig, Hanako, and it rolls downhill, the old woman chases it even into a tunnel full of a large community of ogres. With threats if she fails, they supply her with a few grains of rice and a large pot, into which she dips a large, magic wooden spoon that makes the rice thicken and grow into enough for dumplings for even the greediest ogres. Sated, they settle down for a nap. The old woman rolls the pot to the edge of an underground river, climbs in with Hanako, and sails off. When she emerges into daylight again, she lands and drags the pot up the hill, cleverly retaining the spoon, with which she makes rice dumplings for her neighboring farmers, soon, as her fame spreads, earning a handsome living. The full-page illustrations have an Oriental feel, but are more wildly colored than most Japanese paintings, with the ogres in deep shades of green, blue, and purple and the old woman and her pig in bright orangish red.

257 Han, Oki S., and Stephanie Haboush Plunkett, ads., *Kongi and Potgi: A Cinderella Story from Korea*, illus. Oki S. Han, Dial, 1996 (hardcover), ISBN 0–8037–1571–4, $14.99, unp. Ages 4–8, grades PS–3.

With a few cultural variations, this follows the well-known version of the Cinderella story, with long-suffering, hard-working Kongi abused and scorned by her stepmother, Doki, and her stepsister, Potgi. Kongi gets aid from a bull, which helps her clear a rocky hillside, a toad, which stops up a hole in the water jar she must fill, and a flock of sparrows, which help her separate grains of rice from chaff, all tasks Doki has assigned her, thinking them impossible. Her beautiful clothes for the prince's party are supplied by angels descending from the heavens. Her slipper is not glass, but magically adjusts to fit only Kongi when the prince's men arrive to try it on all the young women. After she is married, Kongi is forgiving and loving to both Doki and Potgi, who reform under her good influence. The slightly stylized illustrations are rich watercolors, packed with details of Korean village life, with both exterior and interior scenes of the farmhouses and the palace and a view of the market, showing the thatched stalls where grains, fish, vegetables, pottery, and fabrics are displayed. A long note precedes the story, telling "Some Facts About Korean Culture," not essential to understanding the tale but adding another dimension that may attract readers older than those designated by the publisher. For another Korean folktale retold and illustrated by Han, see *Sir Whong and the Golden Pig*, in *This Land Is Our Land* (1994), no. 299.

258 Ho, Minfong, and Saphan Ros, *Brother Rabbit: A Cambodian Tale*, illus. Jennifer Hewitson, Lothrop, Lee & Shepard, 1997 (hardcover), ISBN 0–6881–2552–2, $16.00, unp. Ages 4–8, grades PS–3.

A folktale from Cambodia starring the clever trickster figure, Brother Rabbit, similar in many respects to the American Brer Rabbit. When Brother Rabbit spots a patch of tender rice seedlings on the other side of the river, he persuades the crocodile to carry him across by promising to help him get rid of his rough skin. Once on the other side, he runs away, shouting insults back at the crocodile. He eats his fill of seedlings, then, by playing dead, tricks a woman carrying a basket of bananas to sling him into the basket, where he eats all her bananas. He fools the elephant into helping him escape when he is stuck to the resin of a stump, and he fools the crocodile twice more. Even when he has been swallowed whole, he pretends to be delighted because he has always wanted to eat a crocodile's insides, and the terrified croc lets him stroll out of his mouth unharmed. The lively illustrations, done with watercolor paint and ink, make the most of the fierce, many-toothed crocodile and the sassy rabbit with backgrounds depicting traditional Cambodian farming and marketplace. Each page is bordered by a strip of motifs of the region.

259 Ho, Minfong, ad., and Saphan Ros, trans., *The Two Brothers*, illus. Jean Tseng and Mou-Sian Tseng, Lothrop, 1995 (hardcover), ISBN 0–688–12550–6, $15.00, 32 pp. Ages 5 up, grades K up.

Cambodian folktale exploring the conflict between predestination and free will. When two orphan brothers, who have grown up in a Buddhist monastery, wish to leave, the abbot, consulting his astrological charts, predicts that Kem, the elder, will become a wealthy merchant and that the younger, Sem, will eventually become a king. He advises Sem: "When in love, look at the girl's mother. When in pain, don't sleep. When in bed, don't talk." Kem sails for

China and soon fulfills the prophecy. Sem falls in love and marries a village girl with a shrewish mother, and is soon ragged and poverty-stricken. He sails for China, finds Kem, and is well treated, but when he leaves he is given only a new pair of trousers and a bolt of cloth. On the return trip, full of disappointment and pain, he vows not to sleep. During the night, a sea ogre attacks the junk. Sem holds him fast until the ogre gives him three wonderful gifts, a magic stick to beat his enemies, a magic rope to tie them up, and a magic pot to cook whatever he wishes. Back in his village, his wife has taken a boyfriend. Because Sem forgets the injunction against talking in bed, they learn about the marvelous gifts and steal them. Ignored by the local judges, Sem goes to the king to complain, and together they trick the adulterous couple. Sem donates the gifts to the king, who, astonished at his generosity, allows him to wed his daughter and eventually succeed to the throne. The illustrations, mostly in bright shades with red and gold predominating, show scenes from the monastery, sea voyages, and village and court life and give a good idea of Cambodian culture.

260 Jaffe, Nina, ret., *Older Brother, Younger Brother: A Korean Folktale*, illus. Wenhai Ma, Viking, 1995 (hardcover), ISBN 0–670–85645–2, $14.99, unp. Ages 3–8, grades PS–3.

Korean folktale showing how kindness and respect for all creatures, and especially one's elders, may be repaid manyfold. Two brothers, very different boys, live with their father. The older, Nolbu, is cruel and greedy, while the younger, Hungbu, is considerate of even the smallest living thing. When the father dies, Nolbu turns Hungbu and his family out of the house. They leave without complaint and find an empty house, where they settle down, work hard, and eke out a living. One day Hungbu rescues a baby swallow with broken wings. It recovers under his care and flies away. Later it returns and drops three seeds into Hungbu's hand. He plants and cares for them. On the vines that sprout from them three gourds appear. When Hungbu and his family start to harvest them, they break open, revealing shimmering silk, golden coins, enough rice to feed them for years, and seven carpenters who build a magnificent new house. When Nolbu hears, he stomps angrily to Hungbu's house and demands an explanation. Wanting the same good fortune, Nolbu knocks a young swallow from its nest and breaks its wing. It, too, returns with three seeds that produce gourds, but the first of these is filled with mud and manure, the second with snakes, scorpions, and spiders, and the third with evil spirits and howling demons that destroy his house and all he owns. Contrite, Nolbu and his family go to Hungbu, who welcomes them to live with him. The illustrations are gentle watercolors employing Korean settings and clothing.

261 Kimmel, Eric, ret., *Ten Suns: A Chinese Legend*, illus. Yongsheng Xuan, Holiday House, 1998 (hardcover), ISBN 0–8234–1317–9, $15.95, unp. Ages 4 up, grades PS up.

Highly illustrated retelling of a Chinese sun myth, one of a number in world mythology that tell how the sun came to be as it is. At the eastern horizon stands a giant mulberry tree, in whose topmost branches rests the magnificent jade palace of Di Jun, the great emperor who rules the region where the sun rises. Each day, one of his ten sons walks across the sky, bringing light and warmth to the earth. Bored with their daily routine, however, one morning all ten decide to make the journey together. So bright is their collective light and heat that crops shrivel, forests catch fire, lakes dry up—there is disaster all over the earth. Saddened by the carnage they are causing, Di Jun summons Hu Yi, the Archer of Heaven, to whom he gives ten arrows with which to kill his ten sons. One by one Hu Yi does so, exploding them and transforming them into crows. The great emperor of the world intervenes, however, before all the suns have been destroyed. He sends his fastest messenger to remove one arrow from Hu Yi's quiver. That is why, to this day, only one sun lights the skies, and why, also, every morning as the sun rises, the sun's brothers gather, as crows, to greet the dawn. Sweeping paintings, predominately in yellows, oranges, and reds, retell the story and emphasize its drama and importance. The sons are presented as chubby-faced boys, too young to realize the consequences of what they are about to do, while the archer is a well-muscled, determined, young athlete. Di Jun's dilemma is clear, but he decides to act in favor of humanity, which he also loves. The pictures have a cartoonish aspect that keeps the story from being overly serious, but the narrative is dignified and dialogue befits the heavenly order. Sources are given. For other books by Kimmel, see *The Greatest of All* and *The Witch's Face: A Mexican Tale*, in *This Land Is Our Land* (1996), nos. 306 and 509.

262 Kraus, Robert, and Debby Chen, rets., *The Making of Monkey King*, illus. Wenhai Ma, Pan Asian, 1998 (hardcover), ISBN 1–57227–043–8, $16.95, unp. Ages 5–10, grades K–5.

Retelling of the early life of Monkey King, the brave, mischievous, cocky trickster-hero, one of the best-known and most-loved figures in Chinese folklore. Born magically from a mysterious rock atop Flower Fruit Mountain, he becomes the king of the monkey people by bravely jumping through a vast waterfall. There he discovers a huge cave to which he leads his people and where they live peacefully for 400 years. Aware suddenly of his mortality, he searches for the secret of eternal life and finds a wise man, Subodhi, with whom he studies for twenty years. Banished for disobedience and vanity, Monkey King returns to the cave, where he finds that his people have been enslaved by the Demon of Chaos, whom he bravely conquers. A retellers' afternote indicates that Monkey King is the protagonist of a multitude of further adventures in which he "wreaks havoc in heaven, hell and everything in between," a robust, colorful character, whose story dates back to the thirteenth century. Toned-down, doublespread paintings, filled with small monkey and human figures, sweep across the text and move the reader/viewer onward, often depicting more than one episode within the same spread. The illustrations catch both the majesty and the humor of the Monkey King figure.

263 Martin, Rafe, sel. and ret., *Mysterious Tales of Japan*, illus. Tatsuro Kiuchi, Putnam, 1996 (hardcover), ISBN 0–399–22677–X, $19.95, 74 pp. Ages 9 up, grades 4 up.

Spirited, straightforward, dignified retellings of ten stories from Japanese oral tradition, some collected by the reteller, long a student of Japanese tales, but most adapted from such printed sources as those of the well-known collector Lafcadio Hearn. All are "ghost stories," whose purpose, according to Martin, "is not to horrify . . . [but to] distill the essence of what is mysterious in life . . . to remind us of the dreamlike—'ghostly'—reality of all things." In "Urashima Taro," a simple fisherman marries his dream princess and travels with her to the Island Where Summer Never Dies. They live happily there until he becomes curious about his homeland, returns, and finds he has been gone for hundreds of years. Some stories reveal a closeness to nature, like "Green Willow," where a samurai falls in love with a tree-woman, and "The Pine of Akoya," in which a young man, the incarnation of a pine tree, gives his life for his people. "The Snow Woman" and "The Crane Woman" emphasize the importance of keeping one's promises; in both cases, those who forget to keep their word lose the people they love. Some involve talking animals, but most revolve around the activities of humans and are tender, poignant, and delicate in tone, more so than the European tales that they sometimes resemble. Transformations are frequent, and occasionally there is a moral note. Full-page, full-color, luminescent paintings accompany each story, depicting significant situations. An introduction, story notes, and a bibliography add to the value of this pleasing collection. Other books by Martin are described in *This Land Is Our Land* (1994), nos. 518 and 519, *The Boy Who Lived with the Seals* and *The Rough-Face Girl*.

264 Martin, Rafe, and Manuela Soares, sels., ads., and rets., *One Hand Clapping: Zen Stories for All Ages*, illus. Junko Morimoto, Rizzoli International, 1995 (hardcover), ISBN 0–8478–1853–5, $16.95, 47 pp. Ages 8 up, grades 3 up.

Eighteen retellings from the Zen Buddhist tradition, some about the Buddha but most featuring the Zen masters of China and Japan who helped to pass on the Buddha's teachings. All are intended for "awakening the Mind." Martin, a student of Zen for more than twenty-five years, says that these stories are "for the tender heart that children and adults naturally share." Most of the stories are short, a page in length, and are decorated and extended by colorful illustrations done in different media, mostly in what is commonly thought of as an Oriental style and placed variously to make the most of the situations or catch subtle nuances of narrative or character. The stories take unexpected twists, often feature animals, and are similar to fables. Unlike those of Aesop, however, they carry implicit morals that must be deduced and in some cases are vague or capable of different interpretations. Virtues stressed are patience, enjoying or making the most of the moment, practicing silence or contemplation, generosity, simple kindness, being oneself, and not judging by appearances or making unwarranted assumptions. "The Fish in the Sea" conveys the idea that one is an integral part of one's surroundings, while in "The Cherry Blossoms," a nun, refused lodging, sleeps under a tree, which bursts into gorgeous bloom during the night, causing her to thank the village that spurned her. In "The Zen Master and the Samurai," Zen Master Hakuin demonstrates to a skeptical samurai the difference between heaven and hell. This is an unusually attractive book, with a valuable introduction by Martin about the Zen Buddhist tradition. For other books by Martin, see *This Land Is Our Land* (1994), nos. 518 and 519, *The Boy Who Lived with the Seals* and *The Rough-Face Girl*.

265 Namioka, Lensey, ret., *The Loyal Cat*, illus. Aki Sogabe, Browndeer, 1995 (hardcover), ISBN 0–15–200092–5, $15.00, 40 pp. Ages 5 up, grades K up.

Folktale in which a modest but very holy priest named Tetsuzan saves a kitten called Huku from monkeys and takes it to live with him. Huku discovers he has the magical abililty to raise objects into the air and suspend them there, but he tells no one. The priest's temple becomes poorer and poorer, so that even the mice leave, and Huku sees he must take action. A serving girl from the lord's castle tells them that the old lord has just died and his son wants to impress everybody with a magnificent funeral. All the popular priests from wealthy temples have been invited to come and pray, but not Tetsuzan. As the lord's casket is being carried to the cemetery, Huku makes it rise from the cart and stay in the air. The frantic young lord sends for his warriors and his wrestlers, who cannot pull it down, then the famous priests, who cannot pray it down. The serving maid suggests the very holy priest, and Tetsuzan is summoned. As soon as he begins to pray, Huku lets the coffin slowly return to the ground. Although the young lord offers a great reward, Tetsuzan, seeing Huku hold up three toes, asks for only three gold pieces. Huku is appalled, since he had meant three hundred gold pieces. There is enough, however, to repair the deteriorating temple and buy food, and Tetsuzan is happy as before, quietly tending his garden. The story is attractively retold, and the cut-paper illustrations, bordered by frames of heavy black lines, with many of the features similarly outlined in heavy line, are reminiscent of Japanese paintings and evoke a strong sense of traditional rural temple life. An earlier novel by Namioka, *Yang the Youngest and His Terrible Ear*, is described in *This Land Is Our Land* (1994), no. 255.

266 Porte, Barbara Ann, *Hearsay: Strange Tales from the Middle Kingdom*, illus. Rosemary Feit Coven, Greenwillow, 1998 (hardcover), ISBN 0–688–15381–X, $15.00, 136 pp. Ages 10 up, grades 5 up.

Fifteen stories about ancient China, about half retellings from the oral tradition, the rest original stories using folklore motifs and cultural elements. Subjects include ghosts, dragons, crickets, trained eels, foot binding, sorcerers, peddlers, and bandits. Three of the pieces feature a Jewish child whose mother tells her the tales of their Chinese Jewish ancestors, a group that existed before the journey of Marco Polo. A series of long notes at the end lists sources and discusses elements in the stories, adding immensely to the value of the collection. The writing is unpretentious and occasionally humorous, making this a charming book. Earlier books are described in *This Land Is Our Land* (1994), no. 114, *I Only Made Up the Roses*, a novel, and no. 260, *Leave That Cricket Be, Alan Lee*, a picture-story book.

267 Rappaport, Doreen, ret., *The Long-Haired Girl: A Chinese Legend*, illus. Yang Ming-Yi, Dial, 1995 (hardcover), ISBN 0-8037-1411-4, $14.99, unp. Ages 4–8, grades PS–3.

A legend of how a girl saves her village at the risk of her life. In the drought Ah-mei, like all the other villagers, carries water two miles and still has scarcely enough to water her pigs and the seedlings she has planted. Gathering herbs on the mountain one day, she reaches for green leaves growing in a crevice and pulls out a turnip. From the hole runs fresh, cold water. The sky rumbles, and she is swept up to a cave where Lei-gong, the God of Thunder, lives. He threatens to kill her if she tells anyone about his secret spring. As the drought continues, she worries until her long raven hair turns white. When an old man stumbles in front of her house and spills the water he is carrying, she knows she must act. She summons the villagers and leads them to the spring, where they chop up the turnip and start a lovely waterfall. Lei-gong again sweeps her to his cave and promises her a slow, painful death lying on the cliff with the water falling on her. She begs for a chance to bid her mother goodbye, and as she returns as promised she meets the old man again. He has made a statue looking just like Ah-mei, but he needs her hair to complete it. With a pass of his hand, he sweeps her hair from her head to the statue, where it takes root. At the same time, her black hair begins to regrow until it is as long as before. The gentle story is handsomely illustrated with woodcuts printed on rice paper and painted with watercolor and ink. Another tale from the oral tradition retold by Rappaport is described in *This Land Is Our Land* (1994), no. 314, *The Journey of Meng*.

268 Roth, Susan L., ret., *Buddha*, illus. Susan L. Roth, Doubleday, 1994 (hardcover), ISBN 0-385-31072-2, $15.95, unp. Ages 4–9, grades PS–4.

Pleasing picture-story book version of the legendary early life of the man who became known to history as the Buddha. When beautiful Queen Maya dreams she is pregnant with a milky-white elephant, a wise man predicts that her child will become a very holy man. The prince's father, the king, however, wishing to spare his son that hard life, surrounds him with only beautiful objects and fine music. When Siddhartha is sixteen and marries a lovely princess, his father thinks he has averted the prediction. The young man becomes aware of the problems of life nevertheless, old age, illness, and death among them, and decides to become a holy man to seek inner peace and find a way to end suffering in the world. He leaves behind everything he has and eventually becomes known to the world as the Buddha, the religious leader called the Enlightened One. An afterword summarizes the rest of the Buddha's story and the impact of Buddhism on Chinese and Japanese culture. Brilliantly colored, highly patterned, two-dimensional, static collages depict episodes and characters. While they give some sense of the Asian-Indian culture and the story is gracefully told, this version is overall less successful than that of Demi, no. 248, which, however, is aimed at a somewhat older audience. For other books by Roth, see *Another Christmas, Kanahena,* and *The Story of Light,* in *This Land Is Our Land* (1994), nos. 375, 530, and 531.

269 Rumford, James, ad., *The Cloudmakers,* illus. James Rumford, Houghton, 1996 (hardcover), ISBN 0–395–76505–6, $15.95, unp. Ages 4–8, grades PS–3.

Adaptation of an ancient legend about the way paper, invented more than two thousand years ago in China, became known in the West. An old Chinese grandfather and his grandson are taken prisoner by Arab warriors. Dragged before the Great Sultan from Samarkand, Young Wu blurts out, "My grandfather can make clouds!" Thinking perhaps they are magicians, the Sultan gives them seven days to make good on the boast, before being sold into slavery. The first day, they soak their shoes of hemp and beat them (the noise is thunder for clouds); the next they strain boiling water through ashes (stinging raindrops); then they boil the beaten shoes in this water (billows of fog-like steam). On the fourth day, they fish the hemp fibers from the water, wash them, and dry them in the sun. For the next two days, they continue to bleach the fibers. On the last day, they make a frame, cover it with worn sacking (a net to catch clouds), dip it into a large tub containing the hemp fibers, and raise it aloft (a cloud!). When dry, the thin sheet is caught in a gust of wind and floats like a cloud. Although the crowd laughs derisively, the Sultan recognizes it as Chinese paper, and asks the old man and the boy to teach the Arabs the secrets of the art. From Samarkand, the skill spreads to the Western world. Alternating pages, wider than they are high, hold text and illustrations, both framed by a thin red line. The paintings, done in predominantly blues and reds, are handsome and dramatic. An afterword tells of the historical spread of papermaking westward from China.

270 Sanfield, Steve, ad., *Just Rewards or Who Is That Man in the Moon & What's He Doing Up There Anyway?,* illus. Emily Lasker, Orchard, 1996 (hardcover), ISBN 0–531–08885–5, $14.95, unp. Ages 4–10, grades PS–5.

Adaptation, based on stories found in Chinese collections (sources specified), of how the man got into the moon. The version is sprightly and lively with dialogue, and proceeds directly to the moralistic conclusion, the didacticism of which is relieved by the humor. The dramatic, full-color, mostly doublespread illustrations are distorted for comic effect and work well with the humorous tale. The figures in the pictures, however, are not identifiable as Oriental, or, perhaps better put, do not look as Asians are commonly thought to appear, but seem Caucasian. One day, a farmer finds a sparrow whose wing has been injured, takes it home, and nurses it to health. When he releases it, the bird gives him a seed with instructions to plant it. He does so, and a magnificent watermelon vine grows, producing fruit filled with so many precious jewels that he becomes one of the wealthiest men in the land. Envious of his friend's good fortune, his neighbor deliberately wounds a sparrow and nurses it to health, all the time reminding the bird to give him his reward. Upon release, the bird gives him a seed, which he duly plants. A prolific vine sprouts up, without fruit, however, and stretches high into the sky. The greedy man climbs it in search of his reward, and when he reaches the moon, is sure he is intended to receive all that heavenly body's riches. He climbs from the vine onto the moon, and as he does so, the vine withers, leaving the greedy man there for all time to come. For African-American tales retold by Sanfield, see *The Adventures of High John the Conqueror* and *A Natural Man: The True Story of John Henry*, in *This Land Is Our Land* (1994), nos. 185 and 186.

271   San Souci, Robert D., ret., *Fa Mulan: The Story of a Woman Warrior*, illus. Jean and Mou-Sien Tseng, Hyperion, 1998 (hardcover), ISBN 0–7868–0346–0, $15.95, unp. Ages 5 up, grades K up.

Retelling of an ancient Chinese legend about a courageous and intelligent woman warrior. When, during an invasion by the Tartars, young Fa Mulan sees her frail, elderly father's name on the list of men conscripted for the Khan's army, she persuades her family to let her fight in his place. She cuts her hair, puts on her father's armor, buys a horse, fastens his weapons to the horse's saddle, and rides to the encampment at the Yellow River. In terrible fighting, the Khan's forces break the Tartar lines. As the months, then years, pass, Mulan proves herself in battle as a warrior and rises gradually to the rank of general, where she wins acclaim as a brilliant tactician. For twelve years, no one has suspected that the greatest warrior and general of the Khan's army is a woman. The battles won, the enemy defeated, Mulan returns home, escorted by her "fire companions." She exchanges her armor and boots for a woman's robe and slippers, ready and hoping to assume the woman's role of wife and mother. Brightly colored, vibrant scenes of home life and battles sweep across the pages, retelling and extending the story with additional drama and pageantry, small decorative borders at top and bottom revealing that story and illustrations are to be viewed as an unrolling, extended manuscript. This is an exceptionally well-told and compatibly illustrated book, one that although a picture book and intended for the young, holds appeal for all ages. An author's note at the end specifies sources and discusses the historicity of the figure. Other versions of Mulan's story appear in *China's Bravest Girl: The Legend of Hua Mu Lan* (1993), retold by Charlie Chin and dramatically illustrated by Tomie Arai, with the Chinese calligraphy by Wang Xing Chu skillfully integrated into the artwork, in Maxine Hong Kingston's novel *The Woman Warrior* (1976), and in *The Ballad of Mulan* (1998) by Song Nan Zhang. For other books by San Souci, see *This Land Is Our Land* (1994), nos. 187, 188, 189, 316, and 317, all oral tradition (for titles, see entry 155, this book).

272 San Souci, Robert D., ret., *Pedro and the Monkey*, illus. Michael Hays, Morrow, 1996 (hardcover), ISBN 0–688–13744–X, $15.95, unp. Ages 4–10, grades PS–5.

Amusing retelling of a Filipino folktale, a trickster narrative similar to the "Puss in Boots" story from European tradition. Pedro, a poor, young Filipino farmer, traps a monkey who has been stealing his corn. When the monkey bursts into tears, because Pedro threatens to sell him as a pet, kindhearted Pedro releases him. In return for his kindness, the monkey promises to arrange his marriage to the daughter of Don Francisco, the wealthiest landowner in the district. Through a series of clever moves, the monkey persuades Don Francisco that his master is rich and suitable as a son-in-law, then tricks a wealthy cannibal giant out of his lavish manor. Pedro moves in, Don Francisco and his daughter visit, Pedro asks for the girl's hand, and her father immediately agrees to the wedding. The monkey spends half his time advising Pedro and the other half helping Don Francisco. All live happily ever after. The smooth text is amplified by muted, tropical-colored, acrylic-on-linen paintings. The yellow cornfields, tan, reed-roofed huts on stilts, tile-roofed mansions, deep green, tropical vegetation, and loose-fitting, southern Asian garments establish the setting, and the facial expressions, especially the sly looks of the clever monkey, contribute to the fun. An author's note at the end of this delightful book identifies the source material. For other books by San Souci, see *This Land Is Our Land* (1994), nos. 187, 188, 189, 316, and 317, all oral tradition (for titles, see entry 155, this book).

273 Schroeder, Alan, ret., *Lily and the Wooden Bowl*, illus. Yoriko Ito, Doubleday, 1994 (hardcover), ISBN 0–385–30792–6, $14.95, unp.; Yearling, 1997 (paper), ISBN 0–440–41294–3, $5.99. Ages 4–8, grades PS–3.

Japanese folktale relating how a lovely young girl, faithful to her dying grandmother's wishes, hides her beauty by wearing a wooden bowl on her head and still wins the heart of a good and wealthy young man. Lily's poor grandmother leaves her only a folded paper crane, a wooden rice paddle, and the direction to wear a bowl on her head at all times. After laboring in the fields, where the jeering workers are driven off by the paper crane, Lily is spotted by the farmer who owns the fields and asked to help his ailing wife in his house. The wife, however, is a mean and spiteful woman who immediately hates the lovely girl. When her son is curious about Lily, his mother says that her face is horribly scarred by disease. He is still attracted by Lily's quiet grace and begs her to let him remove the bowl. She refuses, but the young man, after a brief glimpse of her face, is so entranced that he wants to marry her. His father is pleased, but his furious mother devises a task to trick Lily into leaving. Giving her one grain of rice, she directs Lily to cook enough rice for one hundred wedding guests and locks her in a room. Near despair, Lily remembers the rice paddle, and when she stirs the pot, the rice multiplies magically until there is more than enough. The vindictive wife sends a plague of rats to eat all the rice and starts to beat Lily and drive her away. The farmer, knowing the natures of the two women, drives his wife away instead, and the wedding proceeds. As she raises the wine cup in the ceremony, the bowl on Lily's head cracks and splits, releasing a shower of precious jewels and revealing her beautiful face. The illustrations, using traditional Japanese motifs, picture Lily as a truly lovely young woman.

274   Schroeder, Alan, ret., *The Stone Lion*, illus. Todd L. W. Doney, Scribner's, 1994 (hardcover), ISBN 0–684–19578–X, $14.95, unp. Ages 5 up, grades K up.

Tibetan folktale of two brothers who receive very different rewards for their contrasting attitudes in life. The elder brother, Jarlo, is a greedy goldsmith who cheats his customers and cares little for his elderly mother. Drashi, the younger brother, is too clumsy to be a good craftsman, but he is kind, devoted, and always honest. When his forthrightness costs Jarlo a sale, the older brother drives him and their mother out of the village to the foot of a large mountain, where they settle in an old hut and eke out a Spartan existence. When Drashi climbs high on the mountain to find deadwood, since he will not cut a living tree, he comes upon a huge statue of a fierce-looking lion, which astonishingly speaks to him. The lion directs him to place his bucket under the stone chin and stroke his mane, but to stop before the bucket overflows. To Drashi's amazement, gold coins pour from the lion's mouth. Drashi and his mother wisely use the money to buy pastureland and sheep. Soon news of their change in fortune reaches Jarlo, who with his wife tries to copy his brother's actions. He lets the bucket overflow, then reaches into the lion's mouth to extract one large coin, and the stone jaws clamp down on his arm. After many nights of suffering, while his wife brings him blankets and food, Jarlo admits that he has been a fool and that Drashi deserves his good fortune. At that, the lion's jaws spring open, and Jarlo flees to Drashi's house, asking forgiveness from his brother and mother. Dramatic illustrations take full advantage of the gorgeous scenery of Tibet and the typical village scenes and costumes, making the book of interest to older readers as well as those to whom the tone of the Oriental tale will appeal.

275 Shepard, Aaron, ret., *The Crystal Heart: A Vietnamese Legend*, illus. Joseph Daniel Fiedler, Atheneum, 1998 (hardcover), ISBN 0–689–81551–4, $16.00, unp. Ages 6–9, grades 1–4.

Gently sad tale of a mandarin's daughter, who falls in love with a song and learns too late that the simple man who sang it was worth her love. Shut away from the eyes of men in her room at the top of a tower, Mi Nuong hears a lovely song from a fishing boat on the river below. Romantically, she decides it must be a mandarin's son in disguise, and impatiently awaits his arrival. Finally, pining away, she takes to her bed, and her devoted maid approaches the mandarin and tells him of the song. He commands that the singer be found and is astonished when a simple fisherman named Truong Chi is brought before him. When he sings the song, as ordered, Mi Nuong, dressed in her finest, opens her door, stares, and bursts out laughing at her folly. Truong Chi, however, having caught a glimpse of her beauty, is stricken with love and soon dies. His fellow villagers find a large crystal, his frozen heart, on his chest. They put it in his boat and push it into the river, expecting it to float out to sea, but instead it stops by the mandarin's palace. He has it made into a cup for his daughter. As she starts to drink tea from it, she sees Truong Chi's face and hears the beautiful song. When Mi Nuong realizes the cruelty of her laugh, one tear drops onto the cup and melts it, releasing the spirit of Truong Chi, and she hears the song one last time. The gorgeous illustrations, which a note says are rendered in Winsor & Newton alkyd, glow with rich tones in pictures of a beautiful girl and lovely but simplified settings with little detail.

276 Spagnoli, Cathy, ret., *Asian Tales and Tellers*, August House, 1998 (hardcover), ISBN 0–87483–527–5, $24.95, 202 pp.; 1998 (paper), ISBN 0–874–83526–7, $14.95, 224 pp. Ages 9 up, grades 4 up.

Fifty stories of different lengths, but mostly one or two pages, from China, Japan, Burma, Pakistan, India, Bangladesh, Korea, Vietnam, Cambodia, the Philippines, Laos, Tibet, Sri Lanka, Indonesia, Taiwan, and Nepal, collected by the reteller from both oral and printed sources. They are arranged in nine sections by topic: Harmony and Friendship; Filial Piety and Respect for Elders; Charity and Simplicity; Hard Work and Study; Nature and Humans; Faith and Belief; Fantasy and the Supernatural; National Identity and Pride; and Wit and Wisdom, which is itself divided into four sections: Tricksters and Fools (a particularly entertaining set), Word Play, Wisdom, and Modern Jokes and Stories. Each major section contains from three to six tales, except for the last one, which has thirteen very short ones. An introduction precedes the stories in each section. Characters range from peasants to kings to animals to inanimate objects, settings from hovels, forests, and streams to palaces, tones from poignant and sad to wry or amusing and funny. Unexpected turns of plot are frequent, and most stories examine the vagaries of human nature. In the opening tale, "Two Friends," from the Hmong of Laos, a bear warns a youth against believing that someone is a friend when that person does not help him in time of danger. In "Banh Day, Banh Chu'ng," from Vietnam, a youngest son proves he is worthy to rule by preparing a rice cake for his father instead of presenting the monarch with rich and exotic foods as do his brothers. "Three Charms" from Japan describes how a monk helps a boy outwit a yamanba, a fierce, clever, shapechanging monster. Trickster tales include stories of the popular Hodja (India), Si Kabayan (Indonesia), and Xieng Mieng (Laos), and several stories show women as particularly clever and one even as being a judge in a court of law. The overall tone is warm and intimate, and wit and wordplay abound. Helps include an introduction about sources; chapters on storytellers and styles and storytelling tools; notes on the stories significant for the folklorist (e.g., tale types and motifs) as well as for the casual reader; works cited; a glossary of terms; and a section of additional resources, which include "helpful books," publishers and resource centers, and Internet sites by country. Here is a valuable resource for storytellers. Two other books by Spagnoli with tales from Laos and Cambodia are described in *This Land Is Our Land* (1994), nos. 290 and 326, *Nine-in-One, Grr! Grr!* and *Judge Rabbit and the Tree Spirit.*

277 Uchida, Yoshiko, ret., *The Wise Old Woman*, illus. Martin Springett, McElderry, 1994 (hardcover), ISBN 0–689–50582–5, $14.95, unp. Ages 5 up, grades K up.

Japanese folktale about the value of wisdom acquired with long life. When his mother becomes seventy, the age at which his cruel lord has ordered that useless old people must be taken to the mountain to die, a young farmer cannot bear to leave her there, but carries her back home and, for two years, hides her in a secret cave beneath his house. A proclamation from mighty Lord Higa announces that in three days he will conquer the village unless someone there accomplishes three impossible tasks. Although wise men and even wise animals think of no solutions, the old woman solves the problems, and the village is saved. Thereafter, the lord respects the wisdom of the old and rescinds his cruel order. With a graceful prose style and handsomely patterned full-page and double-page illustrations, made with ink and airbrush, this is an elegant book for all ages. Books by Uchida in *This Land Is Our Land* (1994) are *The Bracelet, The Happiest Ending*, and *Picture Bride*, nos. 278, 279, and 280, fiction, and *The Magic Purse* and *The Two Foolish Cats*, 323 and 324, folktales.

278 Waite, Michael P., ret., *Jojofu*, illus. Yoriko Ito, Lothrop, 1996 (hardcover), ISBN 0–688–13660–5, unp. Ages 4 up, grades PS up.

Elegantly illustrated Japanese picture-book retelling based on a story from the ancient scrolls known as the *Ages Ago Stories*, collected in India, China, and Japan from 500 A.D. to 1075 A.D. The stories are known from the way they begin, and this set is no exception, being introduced with the words "Ages ago." A young hunter in the province of Mutsu keeps thirty hunting dogs. Although he loves all of them, Jojofu is his favorite because of her bravery and intelligence. Two times her instinct for danger saves her master and the rest of the dogs. A short while later, at night while the hunter sleeps in a tree and she lies beneath it, she awakens him with raging snarls and desperate leaps. Thinking her mad, he is about to kill her with his sword when he sees an immense snake preparing to attack. Jojofu leaps for the snake, her jaws grasping its throat so tenaciously that the hunter can easily dispatch the creature with his sword. Henceforth, the hunter never travels without Jojofu and relies on her judgment without reservation, calling her his eyes and ears. The text tells the story with drama and vigor, the bond between dog and man established early and reinforced in the first illustration, where the love and trust they hold for each other are immediately apparent. The richly colored illustrations have an impressionistic cast and an occasional delicacy of line that recall oriental art. Although the dog is not identified by breed in the story, the pictures show her as all white and sturdily built, like dogs of the Samoyed or American Eskimo breeds. The two double-page spreads in which she battles the snake are filled with action, movement, and ferocity. The snake's head alone in the close-up shot is almost half the dog's size, its upper fangs wider than her head and its rough, green-toned scales a menacing contrast to her soft, white fur. The last picture shows her rounded head and soft, black eyes on a scroll, like the smiling portrait of a beloved relative. An author's note introduces the story.

279 Wang, Rosalind C., ret., *The Treasure Chest: A Chinese Tale*, illus. Will Hillenbrand, Holiday House, 1995 (hardcover), ISBN 0–8234–1114–1, $15.95, 32 pp. Ages 5 up, grades K up.

A Chinese folktale showing that kindness to a dumb creature may be repaid in life-saving gifts. A poor fisherman named Laifu frees a rainbow-colored fish caught between two rocks along the seashore, although he knows he could sell it for much money. An evil ruler named Funtong sees and covets Pearl, the beautiful girl whom Laifu loves and plans to marry. Laifu rejects his offer of one thousand gold pieces for the girl. Enraged, Funtong wants to kidnap Pearl, but he realizes that act would arouse the villagers against him. He proposes, therefore, three contests, all rigged so that the advantage is clearly his. A sea turtle appears to Laifu, takes him to the Ocean King, whose son is the fish that Laifu saved, who gives Laifu a reward of a box containing three magic bamboo sticks with instructions to break one when he is in great danger. In each contest, the broken stick produces a giant monk who provides whatever help is needed, and Laifu wins them all. The last is a chest containing thousands of toy soldiers, who, after winning the contest for Laifu, turn on Funtong and defeat him and his entire army, so the fisherman and his Pearl can marry and all the villagers can live happily ever after. An illustrator's note says that the setting and costumes of the pictures are "taken from the introspection and lyricism of southern Sung paintings (A.D. 1200)." They clearly have an Oriental quality, especially in the green demon face of Funtong and the stylized mountaintops emerging above the clouds in one especially attractive double-page spread. Another re-telling of a folktale by Wang is no. 327, *The Fourth Question*, in *This Land Is Our Land* (1994).

280 Wells, Ruth, ret., *The Farmer and the Poor God: A Folktale from Japan*, illus. Yoshi, Simon & Schuster, 1996 (hardcover), ISBN 0–689–80214–5, $16.00, 26 pp. Ages 4–8, grades PS–3.

A poor farmer and his wife, beset by troubles, are convinced that their bad fortune is caused by the Poor God, who lives in the attic of their small hut. They decide to move, sneaking off before dawn to start a new life away from him. In the moonlight, the farmer finds the Poor God waiting to accompany them, weaving straw sandals for the journey. Each day he waits, weaving more sandals of various colored straw with attractive patterns. When passersby admire the sandals, the Poor God gives them away, until the farmer advises him to say they cost a bag of rice or a chicken. The farmer takes the extra sandals and sells them in the village. Soon the farmer's wife and children are busy collecting more straw for the Poor God, and the farmer learns to make sandals, discovering an artistic talent he has not suspected. At the New Year, the Poor God appears to say goodbye, since their fortune is so good that his place will be taken by the Rich God, who is arriving. The farmer, his wife, and his children, having grown fond of the Poor God, push this newcomer out, realizing they are truly wealthy as they are. The illustrations mostly spread across two pages in rich hues. While the story can be understood by the very young, the language is not oversimplified, and the picture of rural Japanese life will interest older children as well.

281 Williams, Carol Ann, ret., *Tsubu the Little Snail*, illus. Tatsuro Kiuchi, Simon & Schuster, 1995 (hardcover), ISBN 0–671–87167–6, $15.00, unp. Ages 4 up, grades PS up.

Japanese folktale demonstrating the importance of kindness to even the most insignificant beings. A poor rice farmer and his wife want a baby above all things. When the wife prays to the Water God, they are sent a snail, which they care for and love as a son. Twenty years later, as the farmer, now an aging man, struggles to load the rice bales for his yearly tax to the choja, his overlord, he hears a voice volunteering to help. His son, the snail, assures him that he can take the bales to the choja, and riding on the front bale he directs the horses, singing to them as they go. The choja is so impressed that he offers the snail marriage to one of his daughters. Although the farmer and his wife are poor, the high-born girl works hard and is happy and carries her husband in the fold of her sash to the festival, but at his request puts him down by the side of the path when she goes into the temple to pray. Returning, she cannot find him, and she searches frantically on her hands and knees until she hears a cracking sound. Thinking she has killed her husband, she is ready to drown herself when she discovers that the snail has changed into a handsome young man, the child of the Water God. The story is illustrated beautifully with realistic paintings in subtle tones, predominantly shades of brown, filling every facing page.

282 Yep, Laurence, ret., *The Dragon Prince: A Chinese Beauty and the Beast Tale,* illus. Kam Mak, HarperCollins, 1997 (hardcover), ISBN 0–0602–4381–3, $14.95, unp.; 1999 (paper), ISBN 0–0644–3518–0, $5.95. Ages 4 up, grades PS up.

The seventh daughter of a poor farmer one day saves a little water serpent from her sister, Three. That afternoon a dragon springs from a nearby cave and seizes her father, demanding one of his daughters as a wife. After the older girls all refuse, Seven agrees to save his life by going with the dragon. They fly through the Milky Way and under a sea, to a beautiful palace. Stroking the dragon's cheek, she says that before this "my hand has never touched wonder." The dragon changes into a handsome prince, and they live happily in luxury, but Seven pines for her family. The dragon prince allows her to go home for ten days, taking gifts to ensure that they will never have to work or go hungry again. Jealous Three persuades Seven to change clothes with her, then knocks her on the head and pushes her into the river. Masquerading as Seven, she tells the dragon she has been ill and lost her beauty, but he suspects that something more is wrong, and he looks everywhere for his lost love. Seven has not drowned and now lives with an old woman, embroidering beautiful dragons on shoes for sale in the marketplace. When the dragon prince sees the shoes, he buys them and follows the old woman home, reunites with Seven, flies with her back to his palace, and sends Three home in disgrace. Although marketed to a very young audience, the book has value to older students as a comparison with European versions of the tale and as an example of gorgeous illustrations, luminous paintings that glow with rich colors. Other books by Yep are, in *This Land Is Our Land* (1994), nos. 285, 286, 287, 288, 330, 331, 332, and 338 (for titles, see entry 237, this book).

283 Yep, Laurence, ret., *The Khan's Daughter: A Mongolian Folktale,* illus. Jean Tseng and Mou-sien Tseng, Scholastic, 1997 (hardcover), ISBN 0–590–48389–7, $16.95, unp. Ages 4–8, grades PS–3.

Folktale in which a poor man predicts that his son, Mongke, will some day be rich and marry the Khan's daughter. Taking this prediction literally, Mongke sets off for the city of the Khan, where he finds a great swarm of people preparing for war. To amuse his captains, the Khan lets his wife set two impossible tasks for the young man: he must defeat the seven demons of the mountains and return with their wealth, and he must drive the enemy from the land. More by luck than cleverness, Mongke succeeds. The Khan's daughter, Borte, then sets her own condition: he must conquer Bagatur the Clever and Mighty. When he meets a horse and rider clad all in black, Mongke is terrified, and after one wild shot he tumbles off his horse and begs for mercy. Bagatur turns out to be the Khan's daughter in disguise, teaching him some caution and humility before she accepts him for a husband. The lavish watercolor illustrations depict Mongolian faces, clothes, way of life, and scenery, making the book of interest to an older audience as well as the young group for which it is published. Earlier books by Yep described in *This Land Is Our Land* (1994) are nos. 285, 286, 287, 288, 330, 331, 332, and 338 (for titles, see entry 237, this book).

284 Yep, Laurence, ret., *Tiger Woman*, illus. Robert Roth, BridgeWater, 1995 (hardcover), ISBN 0–8167–3464–X, $15.95, unp.; 1996 (paper), ISBN 0–8167–3465–8, $4.95. Ages 4–8, grades PS–3.

A retelling of a Shantung Chinese folk song, cautioning against selfishness. A greedy old woman, eating on her doorstep on market day, is approached by a beggar and rebuffs him, saying, "I'm a tiger when I'm famished," to which he replies, "You will be what you say you are!" Almost immediately, she turns into a tiger, terrorizing those around her. When she sees soldiers with spears, she dives into a sedan chair, where she finds a piece of steamed bread. Saying, "I'd be a dumb ox to waste a snack," she chomps it down and becomes an oriental ox. And so, by not paying attention to what she says, she becomes a bird, an elephant, and then a pig, until she repents of her niggardly ways and returns to human shape. Her speech, and that of the other characters, is given in verse form, but the rest of the text is in prose. Illustrations are lively, humorous watercolors in keeping with the tone of the song. An earlier, more lavishly decorated picture book retold by Yep also comes from the oral tradition in a round-about way. *The Junior Thunder Lord* (1994) was collected and published in the seventeenth century, a fable extolling the virtue of those at the top helping those at the bottom. The brilliant and dramatic illustrations of the thunder god by Robert Van Nutt far outweigh any didactic purpose of the story. Earlier books by Yep described in *This Land Is Our Land* (1994) are nos. 285, 286, 287, 288, 330, 331, 332, and 338 (for titles, see entry 237, this book).

285 Young, Ed, *Cat and Rat: The Legend of the Chinese Zodiac*, illus. Ed Young, Holt, 1995 (hardcover), ISBN 0–805–01977–X, $15.95, unp.; 1998 (paper), ISBN 0–805–06049–9, $6.95. Ages 4–8, grades PS–3.

Legend of how the twelve animals of the Chinese zodiac were chosen by the Jade Emperor of Heaven. He invites all the animals to enter a race, each of the winners to be chosen to represent one year in a cycle of twelve. Rat and Cat, who are great friends, start out together, and at the suggestion of resourceful cat, climb on the back of early-rising buffalo. As they cross the wide river, tricky rat pushes cat into the water and, as soon as they reach shore, races ahead of buffalo to be the first. While cat struggles in the river, each of the other animals reaches shore and claims a place. When cat realizes that he is thirteenth and will have no place in the zodiac, he tries to attack rat. He is prevented, but they have been enemies ever since. The handsome illustrations are strange, almost expressionistic portraits of each animal in turn, mostly on dark backgrounds, with wide black strips down the sides on which the text appears in white. At the opening the twelve zodiac animals are listed, with the years from 1900 to 2007 to which they give their names and the characteristics of people born in those years. For other versions of the Chinese zodiac origin, see nos. 246 and 249. Another book by Young is *Lon Po Po: A Red-Riding Hood Story from China*, in *This Land Is Our Land* (1994), no. 333.

286 Young, Ed, ret., *Little Plum*, illus. Ed Young, Philomel, 1994 (hardcover), ISBN 0–399–22683–4, $15.95, unp. Ages 4–8, grades PS–3.

Chinese variant on the widespread folktale in which a much desired child emerges from a fruit stone and goes on to do great deeds. In this version, the tiny boy is normally born but is no bigger than a plum seed, hence his name. He is a delight and a great help to his parents, and manages the family mule by riding in its ear and shouting encouragement. When drought comes and the villagers cannot pay their taxes, the lord of the city sends soldiers who loot and beat the peasants and drive their livestock off to the city. Little Plum promises to bring them back, and through clever use of his small size he is able to retrieve all the stolen animals and restore happiness to his parents and his village. Young's pastel paintings, which cover every page with text overprinted in white, make the most of the dramatic size differences; for instance, one with Little Plum standing in what looks at first like a grass-lined cave is in reality the boy in the mule's hairy ear. For a variant on the same folktale see no. 281. Another book by Young is *Lon Po Po*, in *This Land Is Our Land* (1994), no. 333.

287 Young, Ed, ret., *The Lost Horse: A Chinese Folktale*, illus. Ed Young, Harcourt, 1998 (hardcover), ISBN 0–15–201016–5, $18.00, unp. Ages 5–8, grades K–3.

Picture-story of a Chinese tale based on a proverb. A man named Sai has little wealth but a fine horse, which is terrified in a thunderstorm and escapes. When friends commiserate, Sai says, "You know, it may not be such a bad thing," and sure enough, the horse returns with a fine mare. When friends congratulate him, Sai says, "Perhaps it is not such a good thing." His son, riding the mare, is thrown and breaks his leg. Again friends try to console Sai, and he says, "It could be this is not such a bad thing." When all able-bodied men must go off to fight invaders, Sai's son is spared. And so, trusting in the ever-changing fortunes of life, father and son live in harmony. The illustrations, in collage with pastel and watercolor, show details of life in northern China of the past. In addition, the story is written in Chinese calligraphy facing the title page, and on the inside back cover is a plastic pocket containing jointed cardboard puppets of the father, son, and horse, clever additions but not likely to last long if the book is used by children. Another book by Young is *Lon Po Po*, in *This Land Is Our Land* (1994), no. 333.

288 Young, Ed, ret., *Mouse Match*, illus. Ed. Young, Harcourt, 1997 (hardcover), ISBN 0–15–201453–5, $20.00, 26 pp. Ages 3–8, grades PS–3.

In an elaborate format, the Chinese version of the widely known folktale of the mouse bride, whose parents, seeking the greatest husband for their beloved daughter, approach first the sun, then the cloud, then wind, then mountain, only to learn that even the great mountain can be undermined and made to crumble by the simple gnawing mouse, truly the greatest of all. Young's book is in accordion folds, with text superimposed in white on richly colored illustrations done in collage, pastel, and watercolor. The mice characters are in black silhouette on broad bands and patches of variously textured backgrounds, giving an expressionistic quality to the pictures. On the reverse of each panel is a large black oblong with the text in white Chinese lettering. Tapes attached to front and back cover tie the book together like an Oriental carrying case. While the book may be impractical for the hard use of a school or library, it is a work of art that should appeal to an older audience than that specified by the publisher. Another book by Young is *Lon Po Po*, in *This Land Is Our Land* (1994), no. 333.

289 Young, Ed, ret., *Night Visitors*, illus. Ed Young, Philomel, 1995 (hardcover), ISBN 0–399–22731–8, $15.95, unp. Ages 3 up, grades PS up.

Chinese folktale promoting respect for all forms of life and kindness to even the smallest living things. When ants invade the storehouse and eat the rice, Ho Kuan's father orders that his servant find their nest and drown them. His son begs that instead they seal the walls and floor. Angrily, the father agrees to give him one month to seal the place before flooding it. That night Ho Kuan is wakened by soldiers in black armor, urging him to accompany them to the palace. After many days, they come to a great mountain city, where the king gives Ho his only daughter in marriage. They are very happy until red warriors invade and kill Ho's wife. Ho, though a man of peace, trains the army and defeats the invaders, but misses his wife so much he decides to go home and wakes to find himself at his own desk. Although he thinks it all a dream, he notices a line of ants crossing his papers. He follows them outside to the hollow of a cassia tree, where he finds an earthen jar full of silver coins, enough to pay for sealing the storehouse. The illustrations are in misty grays and sepia tones, with color subtly added to suggest mood. An author's note lists the earliest written sources for this ancient tale. Another book by Young is *Lon Po Po* in *This Land Is Our Land* (1994), no. 333.

290 Zhang, Song Nan, ret., *Five Heavenly Emperors: Chinese Myths of Creation*, Tundra, 1994 (hardcover), ISBN 0–88776–338–3, $19.95, 36 pp. Ages 5–12, grades K–7.

Collection of twelve Chinese myths of creation and origins and decorated by an equal number of full-page, doublespread, highly colorful paintings, whose motifs are taken from ancient Chinese pottery, sculpture, and other graphic arts.

After being born from the giant cosmic egg, the god Pangu separates earth from sky and then becomes features of the earth itself. After other gods come to be, the sister of one of them, Nuwa, looking for something interesting to do on earth, picks up yellow clay and creates humans. The gods give humans homes to live in, teach them to grow food, make fire, and hunt, and give them the rules that govern the universe. A minor god, Cangjie, a kind of scribe or accountant, comes up with the complicated set of figures that constitute the Chinese alphabet. The stories are pared down and incisive, without narrative adornment, decorative elements abounding in the illustrations, which with their many intricate details evoke a decidedly ancient Chinese flavor. While this picture-book edition is intended for young readers and viewers, older readers and adults will appreciate the subtlety of the retellings and the lavishness and intricacies of the pictures.

6

Asian Americans: Books of Poetry

291 Carbo, Nick, ed., *Returning a Borrowed Tongue: An Anthology of Filipino and Filipino American Poetry*, Coffee House, 1995 (paper), ISBN 1–56689–043–8, $14.95, 238 pp. Ages 12 up, grades 7 up.

Large, comprehensive, rich collection of the work of forty-nine contemporary poets, about two-thirds of them Filipino-American, most represented by three or four poems and speaking in a broad array of voices and almost entirely in free verse. Brief biographical notes after each poet's set of poems identify the writer's nationality. The best make highly skillful use of language—alliteration, consonance, assonance, repetition for good effect, and the like, and mind-altering images that in themselves are marvelous experiences. The less successful pieces are overextended, pretend what they do not deliver, and use language for inscrutable effect. While some demand an experiential or educational background that younger readers cannot be expected to bring to the selections, there are enough here for them and for the ones who are in love with poetry to find satisfaction. Subjects include the immigrant experience, alienation, longing for home in the Philippines and the old language, struggles with English, struggling to join a culture that looks down on brown skin, love and romance, the church and religion, and politics. Carlos Angeles's poems reveal powerful use of words, although the meanings of the poems may be obscure. Nerissa Balce's "Pizza and Pretense" is a playful love poem, while Regie Cabico complains that the government asks him to "Check One," race, that is, on forms. In "Little Brown Brother," the persona imagines that he is the little brown boy who aids John Wayne in fighting against the Japanese. In a set of family poems, Virginia Cerenio celebrates her baby and her mother, while Elsa E'der laments a simpler era, one before hunger, in "Once We Were Farmers." These are just a few of the eloquent voices in this surprising collection, one that may seem too esoteric on first perusal but that is rewarding when given a chance.

292 Chin, Marilyn, *The Phoenix Gone, The Terrace Empty*, Milkweed, 1994 (paper), ISBN 0–915943–87–5, $11.95, 97 pp. Ages 14 up, grades 9 up.

Collection of forty-four poems of the Chinese-American experience by a poet known for her sharp intellect, keen eye, wit, vigor, and clever use of language. Although some of the poems seem to lose their way or fail to make their points clearly, most of them speak expressively and cogently about what it is to be a Chinese person from Hong Kong who still feels an affinity for China; an American of Chinese background who sometimes meets, and whose people have long met, antagonism and prejudice in the land of the "Golden Mountains"; and varying combinations of the two. Family also occupies her thoughts, and she deals not gently with her father, who called her Marilyn after the sex-goddess actress; speaks wryly and sometimes bitterly of what is expected of a Chinese daughter and woman and gender discrimination; comments sarcastically or perhaps forlornly of lovers enjoyed, relied upon, and lost; and speaks of friends, dwellings, some real, some imagined; and remains aware of the effects of such episodes as the Tiananmen rebellion and similar events upon the Chinese and Chinese-American psyche. Images are mostly drawn from nature, although city life appears, back in China and also in urban America.

293 Dabydeen, Cyril, ed., *Another Way to Dance: Contemporary Asian Poetry from Canada and the United States*, TSAR, 1996 (paper), ISBN 0–920661–59–9, $19.95, 251 pp. Ages 14 up, grades 9 up.

Anthology of forty poets arranged in alphabetical order, eleven of whom are of Japanese, Chinese, Hawaiian, or other East Asian origin and residents of the United States. All are represented by from three to five poems, except for Garret Hongo, Hawaiian, with one. The editor remarks that "regardless of age or experience, the poets . . . are often loyal to their disparate Asian roots and ancestry in adding to the richness of the literature and cultural life around them." Poems speak of homeland, pride in culture, dealing with prejudice, and the generation gap and accompanying tension—themes common to Asian Americans, as well as touching on more universal matters. Mei-mei Berssenbrugge writes with an architect's sharp eye for detail of structure and the nuances and uses of space as she describes dwellings and buildings in what might be classed as prose-poems but have a more ordered form. Marilyn Chin writes of Tiananmen Square, of Chinatown residents, and in an amusing, almost rhyming piece, of eating turtle soup while engaging in a wide-ranging philosophical discussion. Wing Tek Lum painstakingly describes his father making tea for himself after dinner, a solid defender of family love and oneness against the "chaos of the world." David Mura speaks ruefully of life in just-pre–World War II when his father "was a boy . . . was a Jap. In America." Although vision is limited, forms are loose, and diction and point of view are often self-conscious, the poems offer insights into the lives of these poets and the America they live in.

294 Gotera, Vince, *Dragonfly*, Pecan Grove, 1994 (hardcover), ISBN 1–877603–25–2, 44 pp.; 1997 (paper), ISBN 1–877–60325–2, $10.35. Ages 14 up, grades 9 up.

Twenty-eight poems varied in substance and form, though most are free, as well as in mood, by a Filipino-American poet. Some poems talk about the Vietnam War he did not fight in, some about his Filipino background and family activities, like fishing with his father, or playing music on a guitar. In "First-Hand Plant: Skiing the Petaluma Ramp," he describes his son, Marty, skateboarding, the swooshing rhythms recreating the sweeping moves and movement of the sport. In another poem, "Tutankhamun, September 1979," he takes Marty, a small boy, to the museum, where the child falls asleep, his small body creating a headdress about the writer's neck almost like that Tutankhamun wears. He talks about terrorists and about his Uncle Ray shooting craps with a drunken Elvis Presley in Las Vegas. He jive-talks about imagining he is black in the poem of that name, and in "Gawain's Rap," he raps about how Sir Gawain encounters a green horseman. Two funny sonnetinas recreate the perspectives of Ferdinand Marcos and his wife, Imelda. In the first, Ferdinand reviles the United States for wanting to steal his billions, insisting Imelda has "got more brains in her right shoe" than anyone in the U.S. justice system. In the second poem in the set, Imelda throws a birthday party for Ferdinand, present as a frozen cadaver. The poems are sharp in craft and idea and keep the reader's interest through their imaginative insights, unusual perspectives, and wide-ranging subject matter.

295 Ho, Minfong, trans., *Maples in the Mist*, illus. Jean Tseng and Mou-sien Tseng, Lothrop, Lee & Shepard, 1996 (hardcover), ISBN 0–688–12044–X, $15.00, unp. Ages 5 up, grades K up.

Sixteen poems from the Tang Dynasty (618–907 A.D.), all by known authors but memorized and chanted by children for so long that they are recognized as part of the Chinese oral tradition. All are simple and short, but even in translation, many of the images are striking or evoke a mood: a traveler remembering his mother patiently mending his coat before he left home, a visitor from the speaker's hometown being asked for news, not of people or politics but whether the plum tree by the window is in bloom. Each poem is accompanied by a page or double-page watercolor painting, with the poem in Chinese characters printed down the side. At the end are brief biographical notes about the authors, though for some the writer can only say that not much is known. This beautiful book seems to span the gulf between the literary and oral traditions.

296 Merwin, W. S., *The Folding Cliffs*, Knopf, 1998 (hardcover), ISBN 0–375–40148–2, $25.00, 331 pp. Ages 14 up, grades 9 up.

Long, dramatic narrative poem of nineteenth-century Hawaii, recounting the exploitation by Europeans and Americans and especially the abusive practice of arresting and forcibly exiling victims of leprosy to a remote area with no effective medical treatment and few of the basic necessities of life. After a rather slow start, the poem becomes a gripping tale of a young couple, Pi'ilani and her husband, Ko'olau, who with their little boy resist the deportation and hide out successfully in an almost inaccessible valley for years. When both Ko'olau and the child are discovered to have the disease, the three make the arduous trip to Kalalau, an area known to be sheltering lepers, where the healthy Hawaiians and the less severely ill welcome and help them until an implacable minor official named Stolz decides, in hope of his own political advancement, to root out all the disease victims. In self-defense Ko'olau shoots Stolz, and the three escape the ensuing efforts of soldiers and Provisional Government police to arrest or kill them, hiding even from their friends until first the boy and then Ko'olau die and Pi'ilani returns to the home of her mother. Many of the characters are historical figures, and the arrogance, cruelty, and disregard for native culture of both officials and missionaries is shocking, but the courage and love of the little family is the most memorable part of the story. The verse is in epic form, with fact, action, dialogue, and stream of consciousness running together, often without punctuation; but after the opening portion, in which similar and unfamiliar names are confusing, the power and rhythm of the narrative carries a reader along without difficulty. Highly motivated high school students will be fascinated by this revelation of a shameful episode in the treatment of native peoples.

297 Mori, Kyoko, *Fallout*, Tia Chucha, 1994 (paper), ISBN 1–882688–04–X, $7.95, 95 pp. Ages 12 up, grades 7 up.

Collection of thirty-two poems, one or two pages in length, divided into four sections, Family Pictures, In an American Landscape, Every Woman, and Returning to the Land of Gold. They mostly set forth this Japanese-American poet's reflections on her family and on her life in the United States and in Japan, and on the contrast between the two. Forms are free, with mostly two- or three-line stanzas, but occasionally haiku patterns occur, and rhythm and movement result from careful choice of verbals and internal rhymes or echoes. On the whole, the effect is static and placid, but not unpleasingly so, more visual than auditory, and individual poems have less impact than does the cumulative effect: a rich tapestry of family life remembered in Japan and the writer's new American existence. The poems are largely autobiographical: her relationships with her distant father, her harridan stepmother, and her exiled brother, an importer constantly on the move; traveling in the United States; and Wisconsin, where she received her degrees and now teaches, at different times of the year. Nature or objects in nature play an important role in substance and metaphor. Little social commentary appears, but a poem about the influence Amway and Avon saleswomen have on their women customers' pocketbooks and perception of themselves is telling. Also particularly notable in this regard is the final poem, "Fallout," in which a park memorial inspires her to ask serious questions not just about the attack on Hiroshima but about war and human nature.

298 Wang, Ping, *Of Flesh & Spirit: Poems*, Coffeehouse, 1998 (paper), ISBN 1–566–89068–3, $12.95, 102 pp. Ages 14 up, grades 9 up.

Curious but compelling poems by a young woman who grew up in Communist China and has lived at least a decade in New York City. While not dependent upon images alone, many of the poems reflect the imagistic tradition of Oriental poetry, with variations. Only the three haiku are in formal verse form. Many of the others switch within the piece from poetic lines to paragraph form; some have interesting stanza patterns, while others are in free verse. Subjects are equally varied. Several, including "Crossing Essex" and "Summer Rain," are pictures of New York. Other are concerned with places to which the poet has traveled, the American Southwest in "This Land" and "Unnamed," a return to China and trip to Tibet in "Ultimate Passage." A number of them concern relationships with her parents; a particularly moving one about her dying father is "Flag Signal." Also varied is tone. "In Touch with America" and the title poem, "Of Flesh & Spirit," display ironic humor. The strongest emotion is saved for those about the position of women in China, "Female Marriage" and, notably, "What Are You Still Angry About," in which, in response to the fury she feels when she bows to the all-male family tree in the clan hall, she traces the lives of her female progenitors, a horrifying series of stories of sales into marriage or brothels, of physical and emotional abuse, of the rejection and chamberpot drownings of female babies. Although some of the poems are obscure, most are understandable in whole or part by good high school readers, and many passages are memorable and strikingly powerful.

299 Wong, Janet S., *Good Luck Gold And Other Poems*, McElderry, 1994 (hardcover), ISBN 0–689–50617–1, $13.95, 42 pp. Ages 8 up, grades 3 up.

Pleasing collection of forty-two mostly short, one page or less, free-verse poems. Some speak of general experiences, like the five-lined "Home," in which, although the house needs a lot of work, the speaker still feels it is the best place of all, because it is home. Most pieces, however, are ethnic or child specific, or both, or speak to a different-from-normal multicultural experience, that of a Korean-Chinese-American child. The speaker goes to Chinatown and thrills to seeing so many Chinese faces; she resents not being waited upon at the railroad cafe, where all the white kids have been served; she is grateful at not living in the China of old where the girls' feet were bound; and she struggles not to let the taunt "Ching chong Chinaman" hurt. Some poems are funny, like "Chow Time," where she is sure that in another life she was a dog, because on a hot morning she wakes up "so doggone" tired she will only move for food; while others are pensive, like "Rich," where the speaker says she will work hard when she is old enough in order to buy material things for her mother, like a warm coat; or poignant, like "Stroke," where the persona reflects on her Grandpa lying in bed, extremely ill, and "Funeral," where she laments seeing her dead grandmother prepared for the funeral, lying there looking so different from real life that she can barely be recognized. The speaker ruefully points out that she is loud and not good at numbers, unlike the stereotypical Asians that her teacher holds up for her to emulate. Although some of the poems are slight, taken together this is a spirited and varied collection that presents perspectives on a mixed-ethnic, multicultural experience. *A Suitcase of Seaweed and Other Poems* (1996) continues Wong's observations on her experiences, presented in three sections to reflect her Korean, Chinese, and American backgrounds. Altogether the poems seem less effective than those in the first book, but they do have a particular interest in that the three heritages are compared and contrasted with one another in sometimes poignant, sometimes dramatic, and frequently humorous ways. Wong has also written the more tightly thematic *The Rainbow Hand: Poems About Mothers and Children* (1999), a collection of eighteen emotionally moving poems from the point of view of both mothers and children, exquisitely illustrated in scratchboard and watercolors by Jennifer Hewitson.

300 Wong, Shawn, ed., *Asian American Literature: A Brief Introduction and Anthology*, HarperCollins, 1996 (paper), ISBN 0–673–46977–8, $19.95, 462 pp. Ages 14 up, grades 9 up.

Anthology of fiction (no. 234) and poetry by Asian Americans, with a few autobiographical pieces and a play, intended primarily for college classes, in the HarperCollins Literary Mosaic Series, Ishmael Reed, general editor. The twenty poems are the product of nine poets, arranged by year of birth. Each author's set of poems is preceded by an informative introduction about the writer and his/her work. Some poems are long, esoteric, or difficult to apprehend by less sophisticated readers. Others, however, like those of Cathy Song (Chinese-Korean), strike immediate chords, being family poems of interpersonal relationships that reach across cultures. Marilyn Chin (Chinese) speaks of the trauma of emigrating through Angel Island and of assimilation concerns; Lawson Fusao Inada (Japanese) contributes a telling set of poems called "Legends from Camp," about life during the relocation of World War II, a frequent topic among Japanese-American writers; Woon Ping Chin (Malaysian) speaks of the ironic Americanization and fading Asian recollections of "Seven Vietnamese Boys"; Vince Gotera (Filipino) recalls his father's admonition to him during the Vietnam conflict to "be a good son" and "do your job," if he is sent to the war. Myung Mi Kim (Korean), in "Into Such Assembly," speaks sometimes poignantly and sometimes lightly about learning a new language, swearing allegiance to a new land, and answering seemingly pointless questions for Americans about her homeland. Other writers included are Russell Leong (Chinese), Li-Young Lee (Chinese-Indonesian), and Kimiko Hahn (Japanese). A helpful introduction about Asian-American literature opens the book, and such additional helps as a thematic arrangement of selections, a list of selected readings, and an index conclude the book.

7

Hispanic Americans: Books of Fiction

301 Ada, Alma Flor, *Gathering the Sun: An Alphabet in Spanish and English*, trans. Rosa Zubizarreta, illus. Simon Silva, Lothrop, 1997 (hardcover), ISBN 0–688–13903–5, $16.00, 40 pp. Ages 4–8, grades PS–3.

A dual-language alphabet book with simple descriptions for each letter inset in framed oblongs on highly colored double pages of scenes from Mexican-American farm life. The Spanish words are given first, with the English translation following, not always starting with the same letter. "D," for example, is for Duraznos, Peaches, described briefly: "Juicy, golden peaches, honey-sweet, like a gentle caress in the palm of my hand." Illustrations are in strong colors, predominantly oranges and reds, with figures outlined as if drawn and filled in. Family life is featured. "O," for instance, is for Orgullo, Pride; and "Q" is for Querer, Love, for friends, grandparents, parents, brothers, and sisters. Many scenes show children working with older family members. For a folktale by Ada, see *This Land Is Our Land* (1994), no. 390, *The Rooster Who Went to His Uncle's Wedding*.

302 Alcala, Kathleen, *The Flower in the Skull*, Chronicle, 1998 (hardcover), ISBN 0–8118–1916–7, $22.95, 180 pp.; Harvest, 1999 (paper), ISBN 0–156–00634–0, $12.00, 192 pp. Ages 14 up, grades 9 up.

Realistic novel of Mexican-Indian and Mexican-American family life as seen through the lives and words of three related women, starting in northern Sonora, Mexico, in the last third of the nineteenth century and continuing to the late twentieth century. Harassed repeatedly by Apache Indians and the Mexicans, who covet their farmlands, the Opata Indians flee from their village. Chiri, Concha's mother, sends her three daughters north into Arizona. Separated in a terrible storm from her pretty, younger twin sisters, tall, plain Concha arrives in Tucson where she finds work as a maid with the Moreno family. The kind merchant and his wife treat her almost like a daughter, caring for her and her baby, Rosa, when she is raped and impregnated by the spoiled son of an Irish business associate. Concha later marries a physician, who abandons her and Rosa. Just after Rosa, fifteen, marries Gabriel, a young Mexican-American Presbyterian minister, Concha dies, only about thirty years old. Gabriel's work takes him and Rosa and their four children many places throughout the United States. Years later, the story focuses on Shelly Rios, Rosa's career-woman granddaughter. Shelly, with a Los Angeles publishing house, interviews an Arizona woman and discovers that she is a direct descendant of Concha, is raped by her boss, and then quits her job, even though she knows that he will keep her from getting another as good. She intends to grasp her destiny, as did Concha, even though the way, like Concha's, may be hard. Shelly learns some family details in what seem to be visionary sequences, as do some of the other figures, a narrative feature that strains credulity but is explained by a family streak of clairvoyance. Concha is the most compelling figure, Rosa is less interesting, and Shelly's story seems foreshortened. Best are the descriptions of life in the Opata village and in southern Arizona at the same time. Gabriel appears briefly in an earlier novel, *Spirits of the Ordinary*, no. 303, which takes place partly in Mexico.

303 Alcala, Kathleen, *Spirits of the Ordinary: A Tale of Casas Grandes*, Chronicle, 1996 (hardcover), ISBN 0–811–81447–5, $22.95, 245 pp.; Harvest, 1997 (paper), ISBN 0–156–00568–9, $12.00. Ages 14 up, grades 9 up.

Period novel, companion to *The Flower in the Skull*, no. 302, set in the city of Saltillo and in the mountains of northern Mexico and variously in the southwestern United States in the 1870s. Less a plotted book than a study in character, the book excels in conveying the picture of family life among those who might be termed middle-class Mexicans. For thirteen generations, the Jewish Caravels have been observing their faith secretly. An herbalist and pharmacist in Saltillo, Julio, the current patriarch, and his mute wife, Mariana, treasure all things Hebraic, especially the old writings. Their only child, Zacarias, a gold prospector, marries Estela, daughter of an affluent merchant and trader. Estela throws Zacarias out because she resents his long absences and believes he squanders family money she needs to send their brilliant young son, Gabriel, to college in the United States. Zacarias searches for gold in the north among friendly Indians, where he comes upon an abandoned pueblo, Casas Grandes, a city that shines golden, discovers that he has a hunk of ore that seems to cure, and becomes known as a holy man, around whom many Indians both Mexican and American and insurgents gather, until subdued by the Mexican army. Julio and Mariana flee Saltillo for Texas, where Zacarias eventually finds them. Among the many other characters who flesh out this substantial novel are Magdalena, successful businesswoman and Zacarias's lover, and Gabriel, whose account appears in an epilogue, leaves to study in Michigan, decides to become a minister, and forms the bridge to the sequel, which focuses on women. In spite of being almost plotless, the novel grips with increasing intensity, because these intertwined characters are made so appealing.

304 Anzaldua, Gloria, *Prietita and the Ghost Woman/Prietita y la Llorona*, illus. Christina Gonzalez, Children's Book, 1996 (hardcover), ISBN 0–89239–136–7, 14.95, unp. Ages 5–8, grades K–3.

Realistic picture-story book with a visionary sequence set in modern Texas, which improvises on the old Mexican–United States Southwest legend of La Llorona, the weeping ghost-woman, who travels the countryside looking for her lost children and stealing other children. Here La Llorona compassionately helps a young girl find an herb so that a curandera (healer woman) can cure the girl's ailing mother. Confident that Dona Lola can heal anyone, young Prietita consults the elderly healer, who sends Prietita for a certain plant called ruda (rue). The girl sets out in the afternoon fearfully, because she has heard that the owners of King Ranch, where the herb grows, shoot trespassers. Toward night, she thinks she hears crying, sees a ghostly woman, whom she follows to where the plant grows, plucks the plant, turns to thank the ghost-woman, and finds that the woman has disappeared. She looks forward to working with Dona Lola to cure her mother the next day. Dramatic, full-color, mural- and poster-like paintings extend the strong text, which is presented in English followed by Spanish, enhancing the emotional aspects and recreating the Texas desert landscape of cactus and mesquite. The paintings of the women have a marvelous portrait-like quality and bring out the Indian part of Mexican-American heritage. For an earlier book by this writer, see *Friends from the Other Side*, in *This Land Is Our Land* (1994), no. 341.

305 Belpre, Pura, *Firefly Summer*, Pinata, 1996 (hardcover), ISBN 1–55885–174–7, $14.95, 205 pp.; (paper), ISBN 1–55885–180–1, $7.95. Ages 10–15, grades 5–10.

Realistic, episodic novel of family and plantation life in Puerto Rico at the turn of the twentieth century. Schoolgirl Teresa Rodrigo, thirteen, is delighted to learn that her high grades have exempted her from final examinations and she can return to the finca, her father's tobacco plantation, in time for the May Feast of the Cross. The activities and celebrations surrounding this annual festival for everyone who works at the Rodrigo house and the peasants on the plantation are just the beginning of a delightful summer for Teresa and her best school chum, Mercedes. The girls visit friends, especially Sixta, a young neighbor woman who plans to become a teacher. She shows them how to make bobbin lace; feed the animals and do other chores; go shopping in town; attend a birthday celebration; and help prepare the plantation house for a hurricane, among other activities. Linking the episodes is the mystery of the identity of Ramon, Don Rodrigo's sixteen-year-old ward, the orphan who has lived on the plantation for ten years and is now its capable foreman. Teresa and Mercedes discover his identity with persistent and lucky sleuthing. The girls return to school in the fall, elated at the joyful news that Mercedes's father has bought the plantation adjacent to Teresa's. Events are typical of family and domestic-adventure stories written in the thirties and forties, and characters are one-dimensional stereotypes. The book's strength lies in its vivid descriptions of the countryside of trees, flowers, tobacco fields, and sheds; the work of the trades-people in town and the women on the plantation; the celebrations, with their singing, dancing, and mouthwatering arrays of food; closeness to the church and the land; and the keen sense of the closeness of the owner's family and of the owner and the people who work for him. The novel was found among the papers of the African–Puerto Rican author, who died in 1982, and was published post-humously.

306 Bernardo, Anilu, *Fitting In*, Arte Publico, 1996 (hardcover), ISBN 1–55885–176–3, $14.95, 200 pp.; (paper), ISBN 1–55885–173–9, $7.95. Ages 8–15, grades 3–10.

Five entertaining and revealing short stories of home and school life (two of which might more properly be termed novellas, each being about fifty pages long) about the efforts of Cuban immigrant schoolgirls to fit in and be accepted by their American peers. Sari is ashamed of her Spanish-speaking, outgoing grandmother, who she thinks humiliates her before her friends, until in a heart-to-heart talk she learns Grandma had similar feelings when she was Sari's age ("Grandma Was Never Young"). In the most suspenseful story, "Hurricane Friends," Clari and Papa make a friend of their dour, complaining, elderly Amer-ican neighbor, when Papa boards up her prized picture window and Clari saves her beloved cat, Midnight, during hurricane Andrew. Mari learns she can star among her American classmates when she produces the winning diorama in her biology class in "A Do-It Yourself Project." Chari is faced with a dilemma when the principal asks her to befriend Yvette, a Haitian girl new in school, and her duties to Yvette conflict with her growing social life with her American friends in "Multiple Choices." In "American Girls," Tere deplores her poor pronunciation and inability to make friends until she reaches out to her worst tormentor in that girl's time of need and turns her enemy into her staunchest ally. The stories excel in portraying the feelings and problems of the outsider, especially those at that critical age when they need the approval of peers, at the same time that they feel the need to retain pride in and of their families and in their heritage.

307 Bernardo, Anilu, *Jumping Off to Freedom*, Pinata, 1996 (hardcover), ISBN 1–55885–087–2, $14.95, 198 pp.; (paper), ISBN 1–55885–088–0, $7.95. Ages 11–15, grades 5–10.

Realistic novel of contemporary Cuban political oppression and the flight of refugees to the United States. Soon after his son, David, fifteen, is detained and held incommunicado by police for three days for allegedly slaughtering a cow, Miguel Leal declares, "Cuba is a prison," and decides to "jump off to freedom" in the United States. After he painstakingly and surreptitiously gathers building materials and basic food supplies, he and David construct a raft under cover of night. Joined at the last minute by two acquaintances who have provided essential help, timid, easily confused Luis and surly, mean-spirited Toro, they slip away by night on the tiny, unstable craft, evading the border guards, hoping to take advantage of the Gulf Stream, and leaving behind David's mother and younger sister. Five days later, after surviving seasickness, a harrowing storm, blistering heat, threats from sharks, and Luis's bouts of irrationality, their meager supplies almost exhausted, disappointed at not being picked up by a passing ship, Miguel unconscious on the floor of the now-rickety raft, they reach the Florida Keys and are able to call home that they have arrived alive if not in good shape. Cliches mar the style, and dialogue is occasionally inept, for example, sometimes conveying information that is necessary for the reader's understanding of motives and situations but which the characters would already be expected to know. The story is filled with suspense and tight spots, although overforeshadowing spoils some of the tension. After Miguel falls ill, Toro expectedly rises to the occasion and proves a brave and unselfish leader. David realizes that quick judgments can be false and that bad situations can bring out the best in people. Adventure and action remain high throughout, and the picture of conditions that would drive people to such desperate measures, even to separate themselves from those they love most dearly, is made very clear.

308 Bertrand, Diane Gonzales, *Alicia's Treasure*, Arte Publico, 1996 (hardcover), ISBN 1–55885–085–6, $14.95, 125 pp.; (paper), ISBN 1–55885–086–4, $5.95, 125 pp. Ages 10–15, grades 5–10.

Girl's growing-up novel of a visit to the seashore near Port Aransas in Texas, in which ten-year-old Alicia learns something about herself and about family life. Tagging along on a vacation trip with her older brother, Sergio, and his girlfriend, Carmen, Alicia has high hopes for beach life, gleaned from movies and books. What she finds is quite different and in some ways disappointing. Food tastes sandy, oil stains her new bathing suit, and jellyfish scare them all out of the water. She also learns some new skills: how to build a sand castle, catch a fish, and clean it herself. More important, she learns that life with Carmen's family, the Sandovals, is more relaxed and accepting than with her own, where her mother is an excellent and very fussy housekeeper. Above all, she learns that Sergio, who has always treated her with scorn and with whom she automatically fights on every occasion, can be kinder and more supportive than she would have guessed. This is a gentle story in which not much happens, but the characters and the area are pleasantly described.

309 Bertrand, Diane Gonzales, *Sweet Fifteen*, Arte Publico, 1995 (hardcover), ISBN 1–55885–122–4, $12.95, 296 pp.; (paper), ISBN 1–55885–133–X, $7.95. Ages 12–16, grades 7–11.

Feminist novel of three Mexican-American women, each of whom manages to escape the protective restrictions of her culture and express her own creativity and abilities. Ostensibly about the quinceanera, the fifteenth-birthday celebration when the young girl is presented to her father's society, of Stephanie Bonilla, it is mostly from the point of view of her dressmaker, Rita Navarro, who sees that the girl is troubled and tries to make her uncle, Brian Esparza, understand how he can help her. Brian is trying to take the place of Stephanie's recently deceased father by continuing the elaborate party he had planned and she no longer wants, but he persists in treating the girl like a child. Rita, in the meantime, has been swindled by her business partner who absconded with all their funds, and, though she has a thriving business, she needs a new shop and partner. Stephanie's mother, Iris, has been so shocked by the sudden death of her husband, who was twenty years her senior and very much the dominating Hispanic male, that she is unable to cope. Rita offers Stephanie a temporary job in her shop, begins dating Brian, and woos Iris from her depression. In the process, Stephanie develops her innate artistic sense, and Iris, who has never done anything on her own but is intelligent, educated in business, and has great style sense, decides to become Rita's partner. There are various problems, mainly because with the best intentions Brian, who has become infatuated with Rita, wants to control and manage them all. Finally, they persuade him that his role is to give moral support but not to interfere. Their extended families, especially both Rita's and Brian's great-grandmothers, who were childhood friends, figure in the story. Rita's desire for independence does not preclude romance and eventual marriage, very likely to Brian. Although there are many stumbling blocks to their happiness, the novel is predictable and strangely without tension.

310 Bunting, Eve, *A Day's Work*, illus. Ronald Himler, Clarion, 1994 (hardcover), ISBN 0–395–67321–6, $14.95, 32 pp.; (paper), ISBN 0–395–84518–1, $5.95. Ages 4–8, grades PS–3.

Francisco, a young Mexican-American boy, stands in the parking lot with his grandfather among the other men waiting hopefully for jobs. When a man with a truck drives up looking for a gardener, Francisco assures him that his grandfather is a fine, experienced gardener, and since the old man speaks no English, he will work with him and charge no extra. Goodnaturedly, the man shows them a bank to weed and leaves them to it. They neatly pull out all the plants except those with flowers and are as appalled as the man when he returns and says they have removed all the young ice plants and left the chickweed. The grandfather, insisting on a translation, offers to return the next day, remove the chickweed, and replant what they removed by mistake. The man offers to pay half the agreed amount that night, but the grandfather refuses, saying that their extra work and missing tomorrow's ball game is the price of a lie. Their employer, admiring his attitude, says there is other work also for such an honest man. The simple story is illustrated appealingly with watercolors in subdued shades filling all the wide right-hand pages, spilling over onto the left side on a few. Francisco's pride in finding a job for his grandfather and working with him is a strong enough element to overpower the didacticism of the message. Another picture-story book by Bunting, *How Many Days to America?*, is described in *This Land Is Our Land* (1994), no. 344, and a chapter book for early readers, *Summer Wheels*, no. 13.

311   Calhoun, Mary, *Tonio's Cat*, illus. Edward Martinez, Morrow, 1996, (hardcover), ISBN 0–688–13314–2, $16.00, unp. Ages 5–10, grades K–5.

Realistic, contemporary picture-story book of the friendship between a lonely boy and an equally lonely cat. Immigrant Tonio, whose family have come to California for work, misses his dog, Cazador, who had to remain in Mexico. Lonely for the dog, unable to converse in English, Tonio notices a skinny, old, limping cat with a torn ear, whom he feeds and plays little games with. When he asks to keep the cat, Mama says pets are not allowed in their apartment building. One day, after the cat has been missing for a while, Tonio sees two little kids poking sticks at something inside a cage—it is Toughy, the lost cat. Tonio makes them stop and calms the cat. Happily, things work out well for both boy and cat. Guadalupe, who helps to serve breakfasts at the church to children whose parents work, tells Tonio the church needs a cat. That night, when Tonio shares leftovers with Toughy on the front steps, both are content. Full- and three-quarter-page representational oils in muted browns, tans, yellows, and greens, with only occasional touches of brighter colors, picture scenes and depict Tonio and his family as handsome, pleasant people and the orange-yellow cat as a little scruffy but enduring.

312   Castillo, Ana, *Loverboys: Stories*, Norton, 1996 (hardcover), ISBN 0–393–03950–5, $21.00, 224 pp.; Plume, 1997 (paper), ISBN 0–452–27773–6, $11.95. Ages 15 up, grades 10 up.

Twenty-three short stories, one an anecdote barely a page long, the last a novella, about loves in progress, lost, or newly gained, most of the lovers being men, and most of the important figures Hispanic. Some stories speak with cynical tones, some bemused, others hopeful or taciturn or satirical or sorrowful, but taken together they capture a range of emotions that this aspect of human experience can encompass. The woman narrator of the title story reminisces about a young lover just lost, as well as about several others that did not pan out, in sometimes alcohol-influenced style. In the funny "Vatolandia," the narrator and her friend, Sara, classify Sara's lovers, who "have been far too numerous for Sara to recall just off the top of her head," into two groups roughly by age, Veteranos Vatos and Junior Vatos, in the process musing about her experiences with them and concluding that lovers are not what they used to be. The last story, the novella, "La Miss Rose," revolves around a "loca" soothsayer/curandera dispenser of advice and aphrodisiacs, a woman of many words and talents, enormous energy, and unlimited ideas. While the language and style are not difficult or complex and there is no explicit sex, vulgar language, or trash talk, the levels of appreciation demand a more mature audience. Castillo has also written novels and poetry, some described in *This Land Is Our Land* (1994), no. 346, *So Far from God* (fiction), and no. 400, *My Father Was a Toltec* (poems).

313 Chambers, Veronica, *Marisol and Magdalena: The Sound of Our Sisterhood*, Hyperion, 1998 (hardcover), ISBN 0–7868–0437–8, $14.95, 141 pp. Ages 9–12, grades 4–7.

Novel of the friendship of two Panamanian-American girls, both born in New York, which is strained when one of them is sent to Panama to live with her grandmother. The narrator, Marisol Mayaguez, 13, is almost like a sister to her best friend, Magda (Magdalena) Rosario, whose mother, Tia Luisa, is best friend of Marisol's mother, Inez, and whose father, Tio Ricardo, has tried to act as a father to Marisol, whose own father returned to Panama when she was a baby and has not been heard from since. Because Inez is taking college classes at night, trying to qualify for a better job, she worries about leaving Marisol alone a great deal, and decides to send her to Panama to stay with her grandmother, her *Abuela*, for a year. Marisol is appalled at the idea of leaving her school, her best friend, and everything she knows, especially since her Spanish is elementary, she has never met her grandmother, and school in Panama City will start only two weeks after she arrives, in the middle of what she thinks of as summer vacation. Her one consolation is that she may be able to hunt up her father, Lucho, about whom her mother tells her nothing except that he is worthless. In Panama, after initial homesickness, Marisol finds life better than she expected. Shy and awkward in New York, she blossoms in the new environment, where she is sought out as the new American student and soon has a good friend in Ana, the daughter of Abuela's next door neighbor, and a boyfriend, Reuben Romero, who has been assigned to tutor her in Spanish. Her attempt to find her father is less successful. When she and Ana go to the apartment where he used to live, they find a man who looks much like the only picture Marisol has of him, but coarser and fat. He says he is Lucho's brother, Oscar, and he has no idea where Lucho is. By the end, Marisol's obsession with finding her father has cooled, and she looks forward to a visit from her mother and Magda for Christmas. The "best friend" angle is not compelling enough to bear the whole weight of the plot, and the question of Marisol's father is left hanging. It is not clear whether the man they talked to really was Oscar or whether he was Lucho, lying his way out of responsibility. The strongest elements of the novel are Marisol's fear of changes in her life over which she has no control and the pictures of the closely knit Panamanian communities of both New York and Panama City.

314 Chavez, Denise, *Face of an Angel*, Farrar, 1994 (hardcover), ISBN 0–3741–5204–7, $23.00, 467 pp.; Warner, 1995 (paper), ISBN 0–4466–7185–1, $12.95. Ages 14 up, grades 10 up.

Novel of Mexican-American family life in New Mexico, centered on Soveida Dosamantes, from the time she is a young girl until, after two marriages, one divorce, and the suicide of her second husband, she is soon to become a single mother. After many years of working in the El Farol Mexican Restaurant, she is writing *The Book of Service*, giving advice to beginning waitresses, and in doing so she reviews her own life and those of her mother, grandmother, and other women she knows. She concludes that the woman's place in her culture has been one of service, a role she accepts. At the same time, she is determined not to let herself be oppressed and with her child to break the pattern of abuse so common in the machismo society. A long book, it stays lively with vivid pictures of many family members, neighbors, and fellow workers at the El Farol and is full of earthy sex, humor, and compassion.

315 Ciavonne, Jean, *Carlos, Light the Farolito*, illus. Donna Clair, Clarion, 1995 (hardcover), ISBN 0–395–66759–3, $14.95, 28 pp. Ages 5–10, grades K–5.

Realistic, contemporary picture-story book of how a young Mexican-American boy in the American Southwest participates in the old Mexican custom of Las Posadas, the nine-day reenactment of the Christmas story in which Joseph and Mary, accompanied by pilgrims, seek shelter in an inn. While Carlos Castillo waits for his parents and his grandparents to come home on Christmas Eve, the ninth night of Las Posadas, he and Aunt Romelia put the finishing touches on the food for the party that will take place after the procession comes to the Castillo house. He regrets not being old enough to go to midnight mass with the family afterward but feels good about the little crèche in the living room, the delicious food smells, and being asked to light the farolito, or lantern, that will guide the procession to their house. When the procession arrives, Grandfather will sing the part of the innkeeper who refuses to accommodate the Holy Couple and then changes his mind and admits them. When Carlos's mother phones that they are late because their car broke down and the procession reaches the Castillo door, Aunt Romelia persuades the frightened boy to sing Grandfather's part. Everyone is proud of him, so proud that after the party, he is allowed to join them for mass. The story is simply told, everything for predicting the conclusion being on the surface, but effective at portraying the traditional custom and its importance in the people's lives. Carlos is a charming, self-effacing little fellow, willing and able. The pictures capture well the southwestern setting, their primitive style, colors, and motifs reflecting traditional Mexican-American arts and crafts. The illustrations of the procession are especially effective at explaining the tradition and catching its spirit.

316 Cisneros, Sandra, *Hairs: Pelitos*, illus. Terry Ybanez, Knopf, 1994 (hardcover), ISBN 0–629–86171–8, $15.99, unp.; Dragonfly, 1997 (paper), ISBN 0–679–89007–6, $6.99, unp. Ages 4–8, grades PS–3.

Bilingual picture-story book based on a brief chapter in Cisneros's *The House on Mango Street* (1984). Each person in the family has his or her own type of hair, one stiff and straight, one wild and untameable, one silky, one like fur. But mother's hair, curly like "little rosettes," is the best. It smells like bread dough rising as she welcomes the child narrator into her side of the bed while the father snores on the other side. It is a warm, loving picture of family life, with the single line of text at the top of each page repeated in Spanish at the bottom. Illustrations look like collage, though they might be semi-primitive paintings, with decorative borders around each central picture. Two other books are described in *This Land Is Our Land* (1994), nos. 349 and 401, *Woman Hollering Creek and Other Stories* and *My Wicked Wicked Ways*.

317   Cohen, Miriam, *Down in the Subway*, illus. Melanie Hope Greenberg, DK, 1998 (hardcover), ISBN 0–7894–2510–6, $16.95, unp. Ages 3–8, grades PS–3.

An amusing, lighthearted, picture-story fantasy, lively in text and illustration, which takes place in a New York City subway. Young Oscar, his mother, and his baby brother, who are either Puerto Rican Americans or African Americans (or possibly mixed), to judge by the pictures, are riding on the hot, hot subway, when Oscar spots the Island Lady, a woman from Puerto Rico, who is carrying a large shopping bag. When she asks whether he would like to see what is in the bag, he shyly replies that he would. She pulls out a cooling blue Island breeze, the green Caribbean Sea, a luscious picnic of Caribbean foods, the Calypso Man, a steel band, and finally an entire Island town. Everyone eats, sings, and dances, while the train rackets along the track, all the way home to the 125th Street Station. The Caribbean rhythms and the exuberance of the text as well as the narrative details are beautifully extended by the bright gouache illustrations, done in mainly tropical greens, reds, and yellows.

318   Cordova, Amy, *Abuelita's Heart*, illus. Amy Cordova, Simon & Schuster, 1997 (hardcover), ISBN 0–689–80181–5, $16.00, unp. Ages 4–9, grades PS–4.

Realistic picture-story book of the special relationship between a grandmother and a granddaughter. The narrator's grandmother, Abuelita, lives in the enchanted desert of the American Southwest. One night the little girl, whom Abuelita calls Corazoncito, dear heart, visits. After a delicious supper of pinto beans and green chiles, a happiness meal, the grandmother calls it, and as the sun goes down, Abuelita takes Corazoncito out into the desert and shows her the herbal remedies she uses. They enter a cave on whose wall appears a big heart carving, which shines in the glow of the candle Abuelita carries. She points out how the heart extends outward in spirals and says that by reaching out like the heart everyone creates something beautiful and lasting. The sentimentality is tempered by the powerful paintings, done in acrylics, oil pastels, and colored pencils. The figures are close to the viewer's plane, a technique that pulls the viewer in. The grandmother's facial features are bold and strong, and even her silver dog exudes the strength and wisdom that come from living close to nature. Such details as cacti, turquoise jewelry, the adobe house, the clay stove, sagebrush, and numerous Spanish words additionally establish the setting.

319 Danticat, Edwidge, *Breath, Eyes, Memory*, Soho, 1994 (hardcover), ISBN 1–56947–005–7, $20.00, 234 pp.; Random House, 1998 (paper), ISBN 0–37570–504–X, $11.00. Ages 14 up, grades 9 up.

Moving growing-up novel of a Haitian girl named Sophie, the product of a rape, who, after being raised by her devoted aunt, Tanta Aite, is sent to New York to join her mother, Martine, who has never recovered from the trauma of her assault. In the pattern of Hispanic culture, Martine watches Sophie relentlessly, never allowing her to go anywhere alone, guarding her virginity, and seeing that she does not even speak to boys. At eighteen, however, Sophie falls in love with Joseph, a black musician from New Orleans, a man considerably older than she is. Her marriage to him totally estranges her mother, who refuses to answer her letters or talk to her on the phone. Twice, Sophie returns to Haiti, once with her infant daughter, until Martine, summoned by Sophie's grandmother, comes to reconcile with her, and once with Martine's body, after she has become pregnant by her lover and killed herself, thinking the baby is bringing back the recurring nightmares of her rape. The novel reveals both the problems created by the Haitian culture—Sophie's bulimia and sexual dysfunction, Tante Aite's dismay that life has passed her by as she cares for her mother, and Martine's personal demons, as well as the violence and poverty in the society— and the beauty of the country and the love among the four generations of women. Danticat has also written several novels set entirely in Haiti.

320 Delgado, Maria Isabel, *Chave's Memories: Los Recuerdos de Chave*, illus. Yvonne Symank, Arte Publico, 1996 (hardcover), ISBN 1–55885–084–8, $14.95, 32 pp. Ages 4–8, grades PS–3.

In very simple language, a story of a girl's trip from Texas to visit her grandparents' ranch in Mexico. There are descriptions of the ranch house, Grandma's garden, the games Chave and her brother, Rafa, play with their cousins, the goatherd and his dogs, and the stories the hired man, Venancio, tells about playing his violin at night and how the wild animals would gather and join in singing to the music. Each paragraph is repeated in Spanish at the bottom of the page. The illustrations give a good idea of the dusty, cactus-covered hills and the ranch house, but the characters all have generic, idealized faces, not Latino in appearance.

321 Garcia, Lionel G., *To a Widow with Children*. Arte Publico, 1994 (hardcover), ISBN 1–55885–069–4, $9.50, 263 pp. Ages 12 up, grades 7 up.

Amusing realistic family novel of home and community life. Everyone in the little 1930s Mexican-American town of San Diego, Texas, a short railroad ride south of San Antonio, knows everybody else and everybody else's business as well: Don Bruno, the tax collector who never has any taxes to collect because everyone is too poor to pay any; his assistant, exceedingly plain Herminia, who is madly in love with Lupito, the telegrapher, who spurns her because he is madly in love with a woman at the end of the railroad/telegraph line named Flor, whom he has never seen; Pedro, the fat old sacristan, who is belabored verbally with regularity by sharp-tongued, raffle-loving Father Non, the village priest, and is madly in love with the town widow, Maria, who is also courted by Benjamin Argumedo, a gentlemanly former Mexican Revolution soldier, now a soldier of fortune turned farrier, who is madly in love with Maria but is too tongue-tied in her presence to tell her so and who yearns to be the stepfather of her four children, Cota, Juan, Frances, and Matias, aged twelve to nine, who early decide that their mother should marry Argumedo, who manipulate matters to that end behind the scenes, and who face possible placement in an orphanage, because curmudgeon Sheriff Manuel, certain that his wife, Ines, has been unfaithful with the children's now-deceased father and has decided to take his anger out on Maria and the children and destroy their family in revenge; and the ubitiquitous, rumor-mongering old men known familiarly as the codgers, who eagerly report all this and more scuttlebutt throughout the community— this long, involved sentence gives some sense of the highly tangled and thoroughly entertaining plot, in which all works out fine in the end, with the children being hailed as heroes for a truly brave deed and the adults appropriately matched and with even the chastised and mellowed Sheriff forgiving and taking back his wife. Some scenes are absolutely hilarious, a few are poignant, the sense of community is strong, and characters slowly develop and grab, in particular, Maria and the four neatly individualized children. Garcia has also published *I Can Hear the Cowbells Ring* (1994), aubiographical vignettes; and *Hardscrub* (1990) and *A Shroud in the Family* (1994), also about Mexican Americans in the southern part of Texas.

322 Garcia, Pelayo "Pete," *From Amigos to Friends*, Pinata, 1997 (paper), ISBN 1–55885–207–7, $7.95, 242 pp. Ages 11 up, grades 6 up.

Period and boy's growing-up novel set for several years, beginning in Havana, Cuba, on New Year's in 1960 and moving later to Miami, Florida, based loosely on the author's own experiences as part of the Peter Pan Program that aided youths in leaving Cuba. The Cuban Revolution changes the lives of twelve-year-old, long-time schoolboy friends, David Oviedo, Carlos Fernandez, and Luis Rodriguez. David's father, an architect, and Carlos's, an auto dealer, barely manage to keep going. Luis's father, however, has long supported Fidel Castro, in whose regime he has a high position. At first, the boys continue to enjoy their usual pastimes of swimming and ogling girls, but as shortages worsen and police grow more repressive, David's and Carlos's parents and Luis's mother discuss leaving for Miami. After Mr. Oviedo is interrogated by police, the Oviedos send David to Miami and hope to follow soon. Carlos's mother decides to follow suit. David leaves first, in Miami living in a camp run by the Catholic Church. Previously the steadiest of the three boys, he soon loses focus, his grades drop, and he has brushes with the law. When he learns that he is to be sent to a foster home in Cleveland, he drops out of the program. After Carlos leaves for the United States, Luis apparently commits suicide. At first, Carlos shares David's high life with liquor and women, but when David is nearly arrested after a wild party at the hotel where he is a lifeguard, he decides to turn over a new leaf, finish high school, and persuade Carlos to do the same. Life in Havana is depicted in fine detail, and the political aspects are presented sufficiently for appreciating the families' dilemmas. The problems and temptations for the young refugees, when they are not given enough caring supervision, are also clearly shown. Sex talk occurs, and sexual activity appears especially in the hotel scenes. Although the boys eavesdrop too often for credibility and occasional stylistic awkwardness would have been eliminated by more careful editing, the book tells with suspense the story of a period in Western Hemisphere history that deserves to be better known from the human perspective.

323 Garcia-Aguilera, Carolina, *Bloody Waters*, Putnam, 1996 (hardcover), ISBN 0–399–14157–X, $21.95, 274 pp.; Berkley, 1997 (paper), ISBN 04251–5670–2, $5.99, 292 pp. Ages 12 up, grades 7 up.

First in a series of mystery novels featuring Lupe Solano, Cuban-American private investigator based in Miami, Florida. From a well-to-do and socially prominent family, Lupe, though she was born in the United States, considers herself Cuban and has to fight conservative ideas of what women should do before she can start her own business, but, with her body-builder cousin, Leonardo, as her assistant, she has achieved modest success. A wealthy couple turn to her in desperation when their daughter, adopted illegally four years before, suffers from an illness fatal unless she can get a bone marrow transplant from her birth mother. Investigating the prominent lawyer who engineered the adoption, Lupe soon uncovers a web of corruption that eventually leads her to a daring trip by sailboat with a grossly overweight and pregnant woman involved in the baby-selling operation to Cuba, where they are captured and held at the direction of the doctor involved, make a desperate escape during which the woman kills their two guards, and discover the connection to a nunnery that takes in pregnant girls. Although the events are highly unlikely, the pace is breathless, and Lupe is a lively, sexy protagonist. This novel is followed by *Bloody Shame* (1997) and *Bloody Secrets* (1998), both also dealing with problems in the Cuban-American community of Miami.

324 Gonzalez, Ray, ed., *Currents from the Dancing River: Contemporary Latino Fiction, Nonfiction, and Poetry*, Harcourt, 1994 (hardcover), ISBN 0–15–123654–2, $26.95, 573 pp.; Harvest, 1994 (paper), ISBN 0–15–600130–6, $15.05. Ages 14 up, grades 9 up.

Extensive, varied compendium of short stories, excerpts from novels, essays mostly of personal experience, a few short retellings from oral tradition, and poems by seventy-one Latino/a practitioners of prose and poetry currently writing and living in the United States. The anthology "showcases Latino literature" by writers "who are not afraid to blend their native language with English to create new ways of speaking" and allows "these voices to express their timeless struggle for social justice [and recognition] at a time when there are more options and more advocates for progress" for these people in the increasingly multicultural atmosphere of the United States, according to the editor. Seventy-nine of the some 130 selections are poems that are intermingled among the prose pieces. These are discussed in no. 396 in this book. Some stories are by well-known writers, like Gary Soto, Judith Ortiz Cofer, Nicholasa Mohr, and the editor himself, but many are by lesser known or newer voices. Some demand concentrated attention, while in others the meaning is more easily apprehended. The immigrant experience, the pull of "La Isla" (Puerto Rico), street gangs, religion, trying to get a foothold on the ladder in a country that has not always welcomed Latinos, poverty, crowded conditions, too many children, the joys of family life—these are just a few of the many themes that enrich the book. In "What We Don't Know About the Climb to Heaven," by Julio Marzan, Daisy marries an illegal immigrant so that he can get a green card. Alejandro Murguia's "Lucky Alley" turns out to hold little of good fortune for the narrator, who yearns to be a filmmaker and have a theater of his own but has trouble spotting con men. In "My Grandfather's Eye," by Jack Lopez, young Rey seeks to avoid going to Vietnam, while in Marisella Veiga's "The Graduation" Glori decides she will attend the graduation of an extended family member whether her own family likes it or not. Biographical information about the writers concludes the book. For other books by Gonzalez, see in *This Land Is Our Land* (1994) nos. 355 (story anthology), 404 (poetry anthology), and 405 (poems by Gonzalez).

325 Guy, Ginger Foglesong, *¡Fiesta!*, illus. Rene King Moreno, Greenwillow, 1996 (hardcover), ISBN 0–688–14331–8, $15.00, unp. Ages 4–8, grades PS–3.

Counting book from one to ten, in which each short phrase is repeated in both Spanish and English. After each number-phrase, the question "¿Que mas?," meaning "What else?," appears to lead the reader on to the next part of the story. In detailed, soft-toned, slightly smudgy watercolor, pencil, and pastel two-page spreads, the brief narrative tells how children collect in one basket such objects as two horns, three little animals, four toy airplanes, and so on, until the basket is filled with ten items for a pinata, and they have a party. This is a joyful book, in which mixed-ethnic children enjoy a great time together.

326 Haugaard, Kay, *No Place*, Milkweed, 1998 (hardcover), ISBN 1–57131–616–7, $15.95, 187 pp.; (paper), ISBN 1–57131–617–5, $6.95. Ages 10–18, grades 5–12.

Realistic, contemporary novel of family, neighborhood, and school life in a mixed-ethnic, but mostly Spanish-speaking, area of Los Angeles, California. Arturo Morales, twelve, yearns to join the gang called Los Vatos Locos to which his brother, Francisco, fourteen, belongs. He is tired of school, of not having any money since his parents barely make ends meet, of the crowded apartment house in which they live, and of the gang-ridden, crime-driven, drug-pushing, junk-filled community, where kids play in the streets, on roofs, and in trash and where no trees, grass, or flowers are to be seen. A young student teacher, Mr. Moreno, changes Arturo's outlook by proposing that the students sponsor a community project. When Arturo suggests a park, the sixth graders eagerly agree. Led by Mr. Moreno and their regular teacher, they find an empty lot across the street from Arturo's place, draw up plans (which Arturo excels at), secure earnest money through fundraising events, interest a local businessman who organizes a meeting with the City Commerce Club, which donates $30,000, through him obtain matching funds from a community philanthropic foundation, and purchase the land. Since Mr. Moreno gets a good price for cash, there is enough money to buy equipment. The lot is stripped of junk and debris, and the park is ready for the little kids by the time the students graduate from sixth grade in the spring. One big factor complicates Arturo's life outside of South-wood Elementary School—Francisco is severely wounded by a gunshot but for days refuses to name the shooter. Eventually, he reveals that it was the leader of the Vatos, because he openly disapproved of their illegal activities. The boys inform the police; the Vato gangbanger is apprehended. Arturo feels good about the way things have turned out. Although success is a foregone conclusion, the details of the way in which the park comes about are fascinating. The students gain self-confidence and self-respect, learn to plan and work together, and come to value one another as people and for the special quality or talent each brings to the effort. The novel is based on an actual project of California inner-city youngsters to create a neighborhood park.

327 Heide, Florence Parry, and Roxanne Heide Pierce, *Tio Armando*, illus. Ann Grifalconi, Lothrop, 1998 (hardcover), ISBN 0–688–12107–1, $15.00, unp. Ages 5–10, grades K–5.

Realistic picture-story book, in which the narrator, little Lucitita, learns what family love and togetherness mean. The year that Tio Armando, Lucitita's great-uncle, a kind and gentle old man, lives with her and her family is filled with happy, fulfilling activities: listening to the story he tells about the silver ring on his finger that he made for his dear, now-dead wife, Tia Amalia; just talking, talking about ideas and not definite, ordinary things, like lists of groceries; visiting and leaving gifts for patients in the hospital; calming her little brother's night fears; going to the library; planning the menu for a party for him and his friends; and making snowmen. After Tio Armando dies, Lucitita knows the secret that he said his wife passed on to him: that he will always be with Lucitita and that the love they have for each other will endure forever. This calm, affectionate family story is augmented by soft, warm watercolor, brush-and-pencil illustrations, which depict white-haired, gentle-appearing Armando in various situations, mostly with Lucitita but sometimes with her brothers, other members of the family, and friends.

328 Hernandez, Irene Beltran, *The Secret of Two Brothers*, Pinata, 1995 (hardcover), ISBN 1–55885–141–0, $14.95, 181 pp.; (paper), ISBN 155885–142–9, $7.95. Ages 12–17, grades 6–12.

Realistic contemporary novel of family life and growing up. When Beaver (Francisco) Torres, 21, returns to his old, run-down neighborhood in West Dallas on parole after three years in prison for armed robbery, he faces troubling problems—the temptation to return to his former life; handling his grief for his mother, who died while he was away; coping with his abusive, alcoholic father, who now lives with a girlfriend; and, most important of all, finding a job and making a decent life with his beloved, fragile younger brother, Cande, fourteen, a talented painter. The two boys have a place to live, the old, run-down house their mother left them. Several people help—Joe Columbus, the Native-American Seminole supervisor at the youth center; elderly widower Jack Miller, who gives Beaver a job at his tire shop; old Mrs. Chavarria, who lives next door; and Ms. Rodriguez, his parole officer, who comes to his aid especially when Cande is injured in a car accident. Adding an additional complicating element is Mr. Torres's (the boys' father) conviction for child abuse after hospital personnel examine Cande following the accident. The conclusion promises a better future: Cande is doing well at the home and is enrolled in a magnet school for promising young artists, and Beaver has completed two semesters of culinary school at the local community college. Although Ms. Rodriguez privately has doubts, both boys are certain that they will soon be together again in the house that Beaver has fixed up. Although there are many suspenseful moments, especially at the beginning when Beaver is terrified of the prison guards and while he is trying to locate his brother after the accident, this is mostly the story of a young man who is trying very hard against great odds to overcome his past and make a good life for himself and the brother he dearly loves.

329 Herrera, Juan Felipe, *Calling the Doves/El Canto de las Palomas*, illus. Elly Simmons, Children's Book, 1995 (hardcover), ISBN 0–89239–132–4, $14.95, 32 pp. Ages 4–12, grades PS–7.

Realistic picture-story book based on the migrant-farmworker childhood of the writer, a poet, told in both English and Spanish, often on the same page. The writer's family has come from Mexico to California, where he is born, to pick grapes, melons, lettuce, and broccoli along with the other campesinos (farmworkers). His father drives them from labor camp to labor camp in an old army truck, and they live in a tent of thick green canvas. His mother cooks in the open, and the family bathes in a giant tin tub in the yard. At lunch, his father makes dove calls, which often attract the birds. At dinner, his mother sometimes entertains them by reciting poetry and his father by playing the harmonica and telling stories. The simple, poetically told understated narrative conveys the warmth of their life in spite of hardship and their respect for the people with whom they work and for the land. The illustrations are deep earth-toned, decorative, two-dimensional scenes of family life and work. Some resemble murals and are sparse with detail, while others have small animals or fruits or interesting patterns that create setting and the sense of Hispanic life or emphasize the meaning of the accompanying text. Two are stunning portraits of the parents. Herrera has also recently published, for older readers, a book of poems, *Border-Crosser with a Lamborghini Dream* (1999).

330 Hurwitz, Johanna, *School Spirit*, illus. Karen Dugan, Morrow, 1994 (hardcover), ISBN 0–688–12825–4, $14.00, 139 pp. Ages 9–11, grades 4–6.

Humorous novel, fourth in a series about Edison-Armstrong School in a southern California town. When the school board considers closing the eighty-year-old building and busing all the students to other schools, fifth-grade class president Julio Sanchez rallies the other kids to prove the value of history and continuity by displays of their school spirit. Although sixth-grader Jennifer Harper seizes control and ends up getting the credit, most of Julio's ideas prevail, and the board decides to abandon its plan. Earnest Julio persuades his mother and even his grandmother from Puerto Rico, who understands little English, to attend meetings to show support. He gets his brother, Nelson, to take pictures of Lucas Cott's four-year-old twin brothers for a poster to plead that Edison-Armstrong remain open for these pre-schoolers, and he initiates the idea of inviting everyone in town over eighty to attend their Christmas program. Interspersed among these events are amusing episodes when Nelson gets a camera and becomes a frenzied photographer, when Julio accidentally sets off a fire alarm, and when, thinking his grandmother is ill, he almost scares her to death by climbing through a window to save her. For a description of an earlier book in the series, see *This Land Is Our Land* (1994), *Class President*, no. 361.

331 Jimenez, Francisco, *La Mariposa*, illus. Simon Silva, Houghton, 1998 (hardcover), ISBN 0–395–81663–7, $16.00, unp. Ages 5–12, grades K–7.

Realistic picture-story book of an immigrant child's slow acclimation to American school life, in which the text is longer and plays a more important role than in most highly illustrated books. In his first year of school, earnest Francisco, son of migrant laborers, finds it hard to adjust, because customs and rules are strange and he knows no English. His one friend is Arthur, who knows both Spanish and English but is forbidden by the teacher to speak Spanish to Francisco. Francisco withdraws into a world of his own, often watching a yellowish-green and black caterpillar in a jar under the window by his desk. He enjoys art, however, and draws a picture of a large black-and-orange butterfly, which is tacked up on the board. One cold morning, when he needs a coat, the principal gives him one from a cardboard box of found clothes. The next day, Curtis, the biggest kid in the class, attacks him for the coat, and both are punished. Near the end of the school year, Francisco has learned a few English words and phrases, and he also notices that his caterpillar friend has spun a cocoon. Then two important things happen: Francisco wins a blue ribbon for his caterpillar drawing, and a magnificent butterfly, like the one in his drawing, emerges from the cocoon. When Curtis admires the drawing, Francisco gives it to him as a gesture of goodwill and friendship. This is a pleasing story of a boy's trying to keep to the traditional values his parents have taught him in a society that is strange and frightening. The story also points up the need for schools to, in some way, bridge the gap between cultures, as the butterfly symbolically does. Sweeping paintings suffused with browns, oranges, and brownish-yellows show Francisco as a mannish little fellow, sober and mature for his years. The paintings have the flavor of murals and thus contribute a universality to the story that goes beyond the literal. A glossary at the end of the book helps with unfamiliar Spanish words.

332 Kanellos, Nicolas, ed., *Hispanic American Literature: A Brief Introduction and Anthology*, HarperCollins, 1995 (paper), ISBN 0–673–46956–5, $19.95, 339 pp. Ages 14 up, grades 9 up.

Anthology of mainly Hispanic-American fiction and poetry (see no. 398), with a few autobiographical selections and a play, in the publisher's Literary Mosaic Series, of which the general editor is Ishmael Reed, intended primarily for college classes. The book opens with a history of Hispanic-American writing and includes at the end a short list of additional writings, a thematic arrangement, index of titles, writers, and first lines, and acknowledgments. Each writer's work is preceded by an informative introduction about the writer and the selection. The pieces speak of biculturalism, problems of assimilation, language difficulties, pride in culture and self in spite of prejudice from the dominant culture, and the importance of family—themes common in Hispanic-American writing. The eleven writers are mostly Mexican American, among them Rolando Hinojosa and Lionel G. Garcia, both of whom tell rollicking good stories in tall-tale style. Nicholasa Mohr (Puerto Rico) speaks about Puerto Rican women in New York City; Ed Vega, also Puerto Rican-American, contributes a story of a son's making peace with his ailing, elderly father; while Virgil Suarez (Cuban American) relates the account of a son-in-law coming to terms with his wife's mother. Other writers include Roberta Fernandez, Tomas Rivera, Alejandro Morales, Denise Chavez, and Helena Maria Viramontes, all Mexican American, and Roberto Fernandez, Cuban American. The stories move well, reveal cultural concerns, connect with broader human matters, and indicate that if Hispanics have been late in moving into the mainstream of American literature, they are now doing it with skill, invention, and conviction.

333 Lachtman, Ofelia Dumas, *The Girl from Playa Blanca*, Arts Publico, 1995 (hardcover), ISBN 1–55885–148–8, $14.95, 259 pp.; (paper), ISBN 1–55885–149–6, $7.95. Ages 10–14, grades 5–9.

Mystery novel set in Los Angeles involving land in the Mexican state of Tamaulipas owned by a Mexican-American family, the theft and smuggling of ancient Indian artifacts, kidnapping, and other skullduggery. With her seven-year-old brother, Carlos, Elena Vargas, seventeen, comes from the seaside village where both have been living since the death of their mother when Carlos was an infant. She is seeking their father, who has stopped writing or sending money for their support. She has the address where he lived five months ago, a letter from an American woman whom she has known in Playa Blanca to Ana Montalvo, a friend in Los Angeles, and a sealed envelope marked "Tamaulipas," which her father entrusted to her years ago. When no one at her father's address has heard of him, they find their way to La Fonda, a restaurant owned by Juan Otero, who knew her father but gives them no recent information. He does get his sulky daughter, Luisa, to drive them to the palacial Montalvo home where, after some misunderstandings, Doctor Montalvo sees the word "Tamaulipas" and suddenly becomes welcoming and hires her as companion to his wife, who is losing her sight. Carlos will live there, too, attend school with Mario, Montalvo's son about his age, and teach the boy Spanish. Although Ana is lovely to Elena and Carlos soon becomes friends with Mario, it is clear that something is not right in the household. Ana's son, David, by a previous marriage, gets involved, helps Elena in her search for her father, investigates suspicions of Doctor Montalvo's actions, and becomes chastely romantic with Elena. As a reader suspects early in the novel, Doctor Montalvo is the villain, Elena's father is hiding in fear for his life, and the mystery is connected to land his father owned in Tamaulipas which contains pre-Columbian Indian artifacts and, it develops, oil. While the plot depends partly on coincidences, the pace is rapid, Elena's predicament gains a reader's sympathy, and the difficulties of new arrivals from Mexico add interest.

334 Lachtman, Ofelia Dumas, *Leticia's Secret*, illus. Roberta C. Morales, Arte Publico, 1997 (hardcover), ISBN 1–55885–208–5, $14.95, 128 pp.; (paper), ISBN 1–55885–209–3, $7.95, 126 pp. Ages 8–12, grades 3–7.

When Leticia, cousin of Rosario Silva, eleven, begins to come for frequent visits to their home in the San Fernando Valley district of Los Angeles, all the youngsters in the family resent the attention and special favors she gets. Rosario must give up her bed and sleep on the sofa, and Mama and Grandmother, Nina Sara, go out of their way to cook special treats and to pamper the pretty cousin. Gradually Rosario comes to like Leticia, but she cannot find out what is going on, why Tio Felipe disappears with Leticia early in the mornings but no one will say where they go. Rosario's best friend, Jenny Gregg, believes that Leticia is trying out for movies, a supposition that seems reasonable because the girl is so beautiful that even raucous Lalo Ortega, who usually torments girls, becomes quite a different character around her and secretly writes a poem about her. The truth finally comes out one night when Papa's pickup is stolen with Rosario and Leticia sleeping in the back, where they have taken blankets so they can talk without the grown-ups knowing. Rosario's daring saves them and foils a burglary, but Leticia, weak and unable to participate, confesses that she is ill, suffering from cancer for which she is taking treatments and which she has promised not to talk about. Though all seems well the next day, Leticia is weaker, and not long afterward they get word that she has died. An old neighbor who gardens gives Rosario a rose bush which she, Jenny, and Lalo together plant in her memory. Leticia's illness is shown through the eyes of Rosario, whose concern for her cousin is mixed with ordinary worries and rivalries of sixth-grade girls. Other than the Hispanic names, the only element that might be ethnic specific is the reluctance of the adults to tell the young people of Leticia's cancer. Another novel by Lachtman for the same age group is *Call Me Consuelo* (1997), also a junior mystery set in the Los Angeles suburbs where orphan Consuelo comes to stay with her Anglo grandmother, adjusts gradually to the new life, and with school friends uncovers a burglary ring.

335 Lachtman, Ofelia Dumas, *Pepita Talks Twice/Pepita Habla Dos Veces*, illus. Alex Pardo DeLange, Arte Publico, 1998 (hardcover), ISBN 1–55885–077–5, $14.95, unp.; 1998 (paper), ISBN 1–55885–240–9, $7.95. Ages 4–8, grades PS–3.

Spanish-English picture book about little Pepita, who tires of having to translate for all the neighbors, since she is the only one who speaks both English and Spanish fluently. She decides she will no longer speak Spanish, even changing the name of their new dog from Lobo to Wolf and calling herself Pete. Her family points out that this will cause her difficulties, but she vows she will find a way. However, when the dog runs into the path of a car and will not respond to her calls of "Wolf!," she switches to "Lobo," and he escapes being hit. She realizes that knowing two languages is great. The text is in English at the top of each page, with the Spanish translation below. Illustrations are lively, colorful, and somewhat cartoonish. A later book about Pepita by the same author-illustrator team is *Pepita Thinks Pink/Pepita Y El Color Rosado* (1998).

336 Lattimore, Deborah Nourse, *Frida Maria: A Story of the Old Southwest*, illus. Deborah Nourse Lattimore, Harcourt, 1994 (hardcover), ISBN 0–152–76636–7. $15.00, unp.; Voyager, 1997 (paper), ISBN 0–152–01515–9, $6.00. Ages 4–10, grades PS–5.

Amusing, action-filled, period picture-story book set in probably the very early nineteenth century on a rancho along the Camino Real, Royal Highway, in old Spanish California. Frida is her mother's despair; she cannot sew, cook, or dance as a well-brought-up girl should. She loves to ride, too, but Mama forbids her to ride Diablo, Tio Narizo's big fast horse, at the coming fiesta. Tio Narizo is so proud of Diablo that he accepts the challenge of Don Ramon that whoever's horse loses in the fiesta race will pay the taxes of the entire city for one year. When by accident Mama gives the signal for the race to begin before Tio Narizo has mounted Diablo, Frida leaps astride and chases with the other competitors around and around the city. She prods Diablo to a great lunge so that the big horse crosses the finish line first. When Frida apologizes to Mama for disobeying, Mama replies that, although Frida is not the kind of young lady that she herself was raised to be, she is very proud of her, since she has made this fiesta glorious for the family. The watercolor and pencil pictures are brilliant with the colors that establish the California setting and also support the joy of the occasion. Their slightly comic attitude adds to the fun and makes convincing the antics and escapade of this iconoclastic girl. One illustration in particular epitomizes Frida's character, that in which she sits astride Diablo with the confidence and spirit of an Annie Oakley. The costumes, interior details, and background views of haciendas and missions establish setting. An author's note and a glossary of Spanish words and terms complete the book. For an earlier book by Lattimore, see *Why There Is No Arguing in Heaven*, no. 511 in *This Land Is Our Land* (1994).

337 Lee, Marie G., *Night of the Chupacabras*, Avon, 1998, ISBN 0–380–9706–0, $14.00, 120 pp. Ages 8–13, grades 3–8. See entry no. 217.

338 Martinez, Victor, *Parrot in the Oven: Mi Vida*, HarperCollins, 1996 (hardcover), ISBN 0–660–26706–2, $15.95, 216 pp.; 1998 (paper), ISBN 0–064–47186–1, $5.95. Ages 12 up, grades 7 up.

Boy's contemporary growing-up novel set in central California among Mexican Americans. Each chapter contributes an episode that portrays an early adolescent boy's sometimes tempestuous life. Manny (Manuel) Hernandez, the first-person narrator, enjoys good times and endures bad ones with his older brother, tough guy Nardo (Bernardo); his alcoholic, unemployed Dad; his Mom, who is always worried about money; his pretty, older sister, Magda; and little sister, Pedi. To get money for a baseball glove, he accompanies Nardo to the chile pepper fields, where he witnesses immigration agents round up illegals. When Mr. Hart, a teacher who recognizes Manny's ability as a student, gives the boy $20 for school expenses, Dad takes the money, blows it on liquor, goes on a rampage with his rifle, gets arrested, and is jailed briefly. Shortly after Manny and Nardo do chores for their Grandma, the old woman dies. When Magda leaves Manny to babysit Pedi while she steals out to be with her boyfriend, Manny fondles Dad's rifle, which accidentally discharges, almost hitting Pedi. Manny has romantic thoughts about girls and also about a teacher, pretty Miss Van der Meer. He acts as equipment manager and trainer for a boxing tournament and helps Mom take Magda to the hospital when she miscarries. At a birthday party, a red-headed boy makes it clear to Manny that being Mexican-American he is not wanted. Manny takes a terrible beating to pass the Test of Courage for initiation into the Callaway Projects gang so he can "make out" with a certain girl but does not invoke the "privilege." After he observes Magda's boyfriend rob a woman of her purse, he returns home appreciating his family, flawed as they are. The book is unified by characters and community, which seems a character in its own right. The novel's strengths derive from pride in heritage and family that form the core of Mexican-American culture. The title comes from a statement of Dad that implies that Manny is too trusting.

339 Marzollo, Jean, *Soccer Cousins*, illus. Irene Trivas, Scholastic, 1997 (hardcover), ISBN 0–590–74254–X, $6.95, unp. Ages 4–8, grades PS–3.

A Level 4, Hello Reader!, realistic story of two cousins, one Mexican American, the other Mexican. Because he froze at a critical point in the last soccer game and his team lost, David, about ten, vows he will never play soccer again. When he is feeling lowest, Miguel, his cousin in Mexico, calls to invite him to watch his team, the Eagles, in the big tournament. David discovers that Miguel's city is getting ready for the Day of the Dead, the annual, two-day celebration on November 1 and 2 to honor friends and relatives who have died. This year Miguel's family is especially honoring Abuelito, Miguel's grandfather, who was a famous soccer player. Miguel's team wins their next tournament game, but the one that follows is trouble. The Eagles early lose three players to injuries and cannot field enough players to continue. The coaches decide that the game can go on if David plays. Reluctantly he agrees, and each time he encounters a point of decision and wonders whether he should make a critical play or kick, he seems to hear a low voice saying, "Si!" Each time he performs, he gains confidence, and eventually he makes the game-winning play. Home again, David proudly displays to his parents the championship trophy he has been given. The next year, he plays with confidence, and his team is the best in the league. The plot is trite. Whether or not the low voice is supposed to be that of Abuelito is left open, but certainly David learns that he can perform in tight places. The toned-down pictures are filled with interesting and lively details: busy Mexico City, the glorious Day of the Dead festivities, and the game excitement. David and Miguel are happy, average, active boys. The diction is sometimes stilted, as is often the case with easy-reading material, but the story is enticing and fast-moving and overflows with wish-fulfillment appeal. A few Spanish words appear. For an earlier book by Marzollo, see *Soccer Sam*, no. 362 in *This Land Is Our Land* (1994).

340 Medearis, Angela Shelf, *The Adventures of Sugar and Junior*, illus. Nancy Poydar, Holiday, 1996 (hardcover), ISBN 0–8234–1182–6, 32 pp. Ages 4–9, grades PS–4. See entry no. 77.

341 Medina, Pablo, *The Marks of Birth*, Farrar, 1994 (hardcover), ISBN 0–374–20296–6, $22.00, 276 pp. Ages 14 up, grades 9 up.

Novel of family life and loosely disguised history that begins with the birth of Anton Garcia-Turner in 1949 on an unnamed Caribbean island that sounds much like Cuba and concludes about thirty years later with the death of Felicia, his grandmother, in Miami. The respected but not affluent Turner-Garcias live comfortably until Anton is about fifteen and the current dictatorial regime is toppled by Nicolas Campion, a communistic tyrant from whom the intelligentsia and upper middle class flee as soon as they can to the United States. Anton's father becomes a businessman in the New York area, Felicia gathers hopeful expatriates about her in Miami, and Anton completes college, fails at all vocational pursuits, and when his marriage also fails, drifts toward revolutionaries intent on liberating their homeland. At the end, he evades radar and flies over the island to sprinkle Felicia's ashes, after which, according to the author, he is never seen or heard of again. Both eulogy and satire, the story is filled with colorful figures and good detail of family life on the island and in the United States, where the expatriates never feel completely at home. The scenes of Anton's nuclear family's flight for freedom are intensely gripping, if cliche, and Felicia's outspoken anti-Campion brother, Antonio, who becomes a martyr, is a memorable figure. Although some sex and sex talk appear, such matters are mild on the whole. The birthmark that Anton bears on his back that flares up at critical moments is an obvious symbol, but the wordplay—birthmark and marks of birth—is more subtly humorous.

342 Milligan, Bryce, Mary Guerrero Milligan, and Angela de Hoyos, eds., *Daughters of the Fifth Sun: A Collection of Latina Fiction and Poetry*, Riverhead, 1995 (hardcover), ISBN 1–57322–009–4, $23.95, 284 pp. Ages 12 up, grades 7 up.

Anthology of thirty-two short stories, selections from longer prose, and poems (see no. 400) by as many contemporary Latina writers of various backgrounds. The "first anthology of Latina writing to be issued by one of the 'major New York publishing houses,'" the book is entitled *Daughters of the Fifth Sun*, meaning children of the present age, to underscore its emphasis on the contemporary experience. The seventeen prose pieces, two of which are translated, range in length from three to thirty pages. Attitudes embrace the serious and reminiscent to pensive to comic to melancholy to joyful with an occasional note of mysticism thrown in, but all make their points in mostly direct, nonfigurative, easily grasped (at least on the immediate level) prose. They speak of home, family, faith, ethnicity, lust, love, squabbles, quarrels, parties, hard work, play, squalid, crowded apartments, migrant fields, and churches, a bubbling pot of material in which to dip. The amusing "The Wedding," by Denise Chavez, and "Uncle Teo's Shorthand Cookbook," by Margarita Engle, tell of situations gone awry; "The House of Quilts," by Enedina Casarez Vasquez, describes a company of migrant workers, like pieces in a family quilt. Lucha Corpi contributes the charming account of an underage child's being given an exemption to attend school with her reluctant older brother in "Four, Free, and Illegal." Other writers include Sandra Cisneros, Ana Castillo, Julia Alvarez, and Ines Martinez, all of whom, along with those mentioned earlier, make this a pleasing, enlightening, and often surprising reading experience. A fine foreword, excellent introduction about Latina writing, and notes on the contributors enhance the book's value.

343 Mohr, Nicholasa, *The Magic Shell*, illus. Rudy Gutierrez, Scholastic, 1995 (hardcover), ISBN 0–590–47110–4, $13.95, 90 pp. Ages 6–10, grades 1–5.

Simple story of a young boy's difficulties at being transported by his family from the Dominican Republic to New York City, where he has no friends and where language, weather, traffic, and everything else seems alien. Before Jamie Ramos leaves, his great uncle, Tio Ernesto, gives him a conch shell, telling him it will bring back their mountain village when he really needs it. After lonely weeks in a high-rise apartment in New York, Jamie tries listening to the shell and finds that his uncle is right; he is back among his good friends and all the familiar sights and sounds that he misses so much. At the playground of their apartment complex, he is too shy to join the other children, but soon a red-haired boy named Peter makes overtures, and Jamie makes friends and learns English. When vacation comes, the other children are going to Discovery Summer Day Camp, but Jamie and his family are returning for the summer to the Dominican Republic. Again he feels displaced, worried that his old friends will not welcome him, and sad that he cannot go to camp with the others. Back at his old home in Montana Verde, he fits in immediately. When it becomes time to leave, he again worries about being accepted. Tio Ernesto reminds him of the shell, and when he tries it, he is transported to the New York playground with Peter and the others. He realizes that the true magic is being happy in both places. While the moral is too bluntly stated and Jamie's friends and family in both places idealized, the book still gives a good picture of the difficulties a child feels when he is ripped from a familiar environment and culture and expected to find his way in a new place. Mohr is the author of *Going Home*, no. 363 in *This Land Is Our Land* (1994).

344 Mohr, Nicholasa, *A Matter of Pride and Other Stories*, Arte Publico, 1997 (hardcover), ISBN 1–558–85163–1, $19.95, 164 pp.; 1997 (paper), ISBN 1–558–85177–1, $11.95, 191 pp. Ages 14 up, grades 9 up.

Seven stories about women of Puerto Rican or Dominican heritage, most in abusive marriages or relationships with men trained by their culture to think they have a right to dominate and demand devotion and faithfulness without practicing those virtues themselves. In most of the stories the women have freed themselves and in a couple have exacted revenge. In the title story a New York bride, honeymooning in Puerto Rico, learns from observing the perfect, submissive wife of a cousin that her own recent marriage was a mistake, one she will get out of as soon as possible. In "Memories: R.I.P." a young woman returns to the site of her former family home in the South Bronx barrio after the funeral of her older brother and remembers how his drug sales from their apartment and his subsequent arrest and prison term brought on her mother's illness and death and how her other brothers have continually applied to her to pay his fines and bail and now will not share her resentment. The only happy relationship is in "Rosalina de los Rosarios," a twenty-year adulterous love affair. All have a feminist point of view with, in most, an undercurrent of anger. Mohr is the author of *Going Home*, no. 363 in *This Land Is Our Land* (1994).

345 Mohr, Nicholasa, *Old Letivia and the Mountain of Sorrows*, illus. Rudy Gutierrez, Viking, 1996 (hardcover), ISBN 0–670–84419–5, $14.99, 30 pp. Ages 3–8, grades PS–3.

Original fantasy picture book in a folktale pattern, set in Puerto Rico. Old Letivia is a healer who lives alone with her whistling turtle named Cervantes. One day in the river they find a gourd containing a baby not much bigger than a chestnut. When Cervantes whistles a tune, the baby smiles, so they know he can hear, but he makes no sound. They take him home, name him Simon, and care for him lovingly. The three are happy except that no other children will play with the tiny boy. A great and continual wind strikes the village, and after much discussion the townspeople decide to consult Old Letivia, although they fear she is a witch. They learn that the Wild Wind hides in a big cave at the top of the Mountain of Sorrows. With many trials, Letivia, Cervantes, and Simon reach the Wind, who tells them he is lost and under the spell of the mountain. Old Letivia works out a way for him to escape the spell by hiding in Cervantes' shell, and she bargains that Simon will become normal sized and be given speech and that she will be given a large house and farm. She does not foresee, however, that the Wild Wind will be stuck in Cervantes' shell and he will be blown into the sky, where he becomes a star. The grateful villagers erect a statue of him. Like many other attempts to write a "folktale," this story is more complicated and has a different quality from those in oral tradition, but it is pleasant and the illustrations are striking and original. Mohr is the author of *Going Home*, no. 363 in *This Land Is Our Land* (1994).

346 Mora, Pat, *Tomas and the Library Lady*, illus. Raul Colon, Knopf, 1997 (hardcover), ISBN 0–679–80401–3, $17.00, unp. Ages 4–8, grades PS–3.

Picture-story book about a migrant-worker child who discovers a new world through the library. Tomas and his family call Texas home but travel to Iowa in the summers to pick fruit and vegetables. Tomas plays with his little brother, but best of all he likes to hear his grandfather tell stories. Papa Grande suggests that Tomas could get more stories at the library. The big library intimidates the little boy, but the library lady gives him a drink of water and finds books to interest him, then lets him check out a couple on her own card. At night he reads aloud to Papa Grande and the rest of the family. All summer he goes to the library and teaches the library lady words in Spanish, until it is time to go back to Texas. His mother sends *pan dulce* to the library to say thanks, and the library lady gives Tomas a big hug and a new book to keep. The illustrations depict, in quiet colors, Tomas's life, the library, and the exciting dinosaurs and cowboys he is reading about. For a slightly younger audience, Mora has also published *Pablo's Tree* (1994), about a five-year-old whose doting grandfather planted a tree the day he was adopted and each year decorates it for Pablo's birthday. The brightly colored illustrations are done with cut paper and dyes. Mora is also the author of a picture-story book, *A Birthday Basket for Tia*, no. 365, in *This Land Is Our Land* (1994), and a book of poems, *Communion*, no. 406.

347 Nye, Naomi Shihab, *Benito's Dream Bottle*, illus. Yu Cha Pak, Simon & Schuster, 1995 (hardcover), ISBN 0–02–768467–9, $15.00, unp. Ages 4–8, grades PS–3.

Picture-story fantasy, in which a little Hispanic-American boy helps his grandmother dream. When Benito learns that his grandmother has not had a dream in a long time, he thinks she must be sick. He asks everyone he knows where dreams come from in order to make her well again, but everyone tells him something different. Benito decides, however, that dreams come from a Dream Bottle that is inside everyone's body and pours dreams into their heads at night. When his grandmother says that she thinks her bottle is empty, Benito says they must think hard to fill it up. So they think and think and think about memories and wishes and imaginings, and Benito's friends think and think and think, too, until one morning his grandmother tells Benito she dreamed the previous night. Benito knows her bottle is full again. This is an imaginative, poetic story, tender in the concern the boy has for his grandmother and in the loving way in which everyone cooperates to help him solve his problem. The story also addresses the matter of what dreams are: memories, imaginings, concerns, and questions—the stuff of real life itself. The fluid, patterned watercolors are filled with details, often surrealistic, and pick up the story's emotional aspect as well as extend the exploration of dreaming. In some of the pictures, the facial features look more Oriental than Hispanic; perhaps some, at least, of these people are biracial, or perhaps the artist intends to extend the story's application by mingling the races.

348 Ortiz Cofer, Judith, *An Island Like You: Stories of the Barrio*, Orchard, 1995 (hardcover), ISBN 0–531–08747–6, $15.99, 165 pp.; Puffin 1996 (paper), ISBN 0–140–38068–X, $4.99. Ages 10–18, grades 5–12.

Twelve funny, sad, bittersweet, growing-up short stories of the full, active, sometimes puzzling everyday lives of mid-adolescents in a Paterson, New Jersey, Puerto Rican barrio. The epigraph poem, "Day in the Barrio," sets the tone; it concludes with the idea that in the midst of the activity and confusion of the streets, everyone "is an island," with needs, sorrows, perplexities, and joys that are individual yet the same for all. Each of the stories is distinct and can stand

alone, but characters recur in stories other than those in which they are protagonists, displaying different facets of their personalities as they do. Diffident
Doris of "The One Who Watches" seems caught in a spell woven by bold,
brash, glib Yolanda, until Yolanda is caught shoplifting and Doris decides to
take responsiblity for her own life. Later on, in the book's concluding story,
"White Balloons," a more self-assured Doris organizes a posthumous birthday
party in honor of a gay young man, who, dying of AIDS, returned to the barrio,
where he was despised for his homosexuality, and organized a theater group for
the young people. Other stories concern youths who are changed by association
with their grandparents; a boy who gets new perspectives on life from a chance
encounter with a church janitor; a girl who decides that the traditional Hispanic
idea of feminine beauty requires too much effort; and a boy who sees that the
price he must pay to be part of an older boy's social set is too high after he
wakes up in an emergency room, having unwittingly ingested some kind of
drug. Consistently interesting, fast-paced, these stories show that the pleasures
and perils of life in the barrio have some distinctly Hispanic-American aspects,
like waning bilingualism and a strong tie to "the island" of Puerto Rico, but on
the whole growing up for Puerto Rican Americans is not much different from
that of most young people in contemporary America. Herself Puerto Rican
American, Ortiz Cofer has also written *The Line of the Sun*, no. 367 (novel),
and *Triple Crown* and *Terms of Survival*, nos. 403 and 407 (poems), in *This
Land Is Our Land* (1994).

349 Ortiz Cofer, Judith, *The Year of Our Revolution: New and Selected Stories and
Poems*, Pinata, 1998 (hardcover), ISBN 1–55885–224–7, $16.95, 101 pp. Ages 10–18,
grades 5–12.

Collection of ten short stories and a few poems about growing up Puerto
Rican American in Paterson, New Jersey, from the girl's point of view and in
the "I" person. Ortiz Cofer catches the eye, feelings, and expressions of the
sixties teens, re-creates the outlook of that revolutionary period, and shows the
turmoil it brought, in this case to Puerto Rican immigrant mothers, still close
to the mores of their culture, and also to the second-generation Puerto Rican
American youth, in conflict with both parents and tradition. Several stories are
connected by the same protagonist, Mary Ellen (Maria Elenita), who affects the
garb and behavior of the counterculture, discovers love with a hippy poet, and
learns that nothing, not even love, comes without a price. In other stories, Isabel,
whose father was a janitor by day and a nightclub MC by night, learns that love
can be expressed in other than romance-novel ways; and in the only pieces set
in Puerto Rico, Maria Sabida uses love and wit to tame the man who is terrorizing her village, and Nina is awakened to sexual pleasures by a maimed Vietnam veteran. The poems have much less power than the simple, straightforward,
unadorned prose. For other books by Ortiz Cofer, a leading Latina writer, see

This Land Is Our Land (1994), *The Line of the Sun*, no. 367 (fiction), and *Triple Crown* and *Terms of Survival*, nos. 403 and 407 (poems).

350 Paulsen, Gary, *The Tortilla Factory*, illus. Ruth Wright Paulsen, Harcourt, 1995 (hardcover), ISBN 0–15–292876–6, $14.00, unp.; Voyager (paper), ISBN 0–15–201698–8, $7.00. Ages 5 up, grades K up.

Realistic picture-story and mood book that celebrates the earth's bounty. The uncomplicated text consists of two sentences. The first, in six words, establishes setting in place and time: California's rich agricultural land in the winter. The second sentence, the action of which begins in spring with the awakening earth, follows the agricultural year, picking up tempo as it proceeds. Mexican-American brown hands work the land, plant the corn seeds, which grow into tall green stalks, and prepare the ripe corn for the tortilla factory, where others work the dough and prepare the tortillas, which give strength to the brown hands that work the ground—the cycle repeats. Sweeping oils on buff-colored linen cloth make best use of earth tones and just enough detail to keep the overall effect of the book powerful in its expressive simplicity. Some pictures are land-scapes; one shows a boy and his dog standing in front of the tortilla factory and eating; some are closeups of hoeing the ground or of ears on the stalks. Most striking are those of hands, lovingly cupping the cornmeal, spooning beans into a tortilla, or squeezing and working the dough. For other books by Paulsen, see *Nightjohn*, *The Crossing*, and *Sisters/Hermanas*, in *This Land Is Our Land* (1994), nos. 109, 369, and 370.

351 Reiser, Lynn, *Tortillas and Lullabies/Tortillas y cancioncitas*, illus. "Corazones Valientes," Greenwillow, 1998 (hardcover), ISBN 0–688–14628–7, $16.00, 40 pp. Ages 4 up, grades PS up.

Highly illustrated picture-story book containing four very short chapters, in which four generations of women in succession give lovingly and joyously to one another. They make tortillas, gather flowers, wash clothes, and sing lullabies. Each page depicts two generations together, for example, the great-grandmother making tortillas for the narrator's grandmother, and so on, with the brief English text at the top of the page and the corresponding Spanish below. In between are detailed, two-dimensional, colorful pictures, which exude a warm family atmo-sphere and depict a lush tropical setting. Each little chapter concludes with the same words, "Every time it was the same, but different," as each generation puts its stamp on the family's combined lives. Concluding the book is a lullaby set to music and an author's note describing the origin of the book's illustrations: through a Peace Corps volunteer in Costa Rica. This is an unusual book, one that says something different and yet the same to women and girls who share it. For another English/Spanish book by Reiser, see *Margaret and Margarita/Margarita and Margaret*, in *This Land Is Our Land* (1994), no. 372.

352 Rosa-Casanova, Sylvia, *Mama Provi and the Pot of Rice*, illus. Robert Roth, Atheneum, 1997 (hardcover), ISBN 0–689–31932–0, $16.00, unp. Ages 4–9, grades PS–4.

Amusing, family picture-story book, set in an urban high-rise apartment building. When Lucy, who lives on the eighth floor, falls ill with chicken pox, her immigrant Puerto Rican grandmother, Mama Provi, who is used to cooking for a large family, prepares her a big pot of arroz con pollo, chicken with rice, and starts up the stairs from her first-floor apartment. On the way, she smells delicious aromas and stops at the apartments from which they come, trading bowls of her delicious rice and chicken for whatever the tenants have to offer. When she arrives at Lucy's, she has accumulated freshly baked white bread, black beans, green salad, collard greens, tea, and apple pie. Mama Provi and Lucy sit down to enjoy a marvelous multicultural feast. The soft, impressionistic, watercolor illustrations extend across the pages, wrap themselves around the text, and flow off the page to draw the reader to the next scene. The tenants are characterized well, the distance Mama Provi climbs is intensified by the distorted stairwells, and the feast on the round table with its colorful tablecloth looks scrumptious.

353 Roybal, Laura, *Billy*, Houghton, 1994 (hardcover), ISBN 0–395–67649–5, $14.95, 256 pp.; 1999 (paper), ISBN 0–395–96062–2, $5.95. Ages 12–15, grades 7–10.

Psychological problem novel of a boy kidnapped by his father when he is ten and his difficult adjustment to his adoptive parents when he is returned six years later. Billy Melendez, nicknamed Coyote, has a good, if somewhat freewheeling, life with his Hispanic father, former rodeo rider, in New Mexico, and has put out of his mind and almost forgotten his abduction from the Campbells, who adopted him after he was born to Mrs. Campbell's younger sister. His father has told him that the Campbells took him out of a sense of obligation and were relieved when he was gone, moving soon after so he would have no way to trace them. When Billy gets into a ruckus and is arrested with several of his friends, authorities run his fingerprints through state files and discover that he is William James Campbell, missing from Davenport, Iowa. To save his father from being charged with kidnapping, he agrees to go back with Dave Campbell to Iowa, although he deeply resents the way he is whisked away with no chance to say goodbye to his father, his friends, and his girlfriend. In Iowa he feels little connection with his mother or his sister, Cecilia, and an outsider at high school. Immediately he runs afoul of the restrictive rules imposed by Dave, and misunderstandings increase until he is expelled and reinstated only after Dave and he finally air their misconceptions about each other and reach some understanding. Still, Billy looks forward to returning to New Mexico when he is eighteen and can resume his life in the Spanish-American community there. Since much of his trouble in Iowa stems from the Campbell family's view of Mexicans as inferior, the novel is a study in prejudice; although Billy's Hispanic father is shown as clearly wrong to kidnap him, their relationship is healthier than any Dave Campbell can fashion in his narrow-minded insistence on discipline.

354 Santiago, Esmeralda, *America's Dream*, HarperCollins, 1996 (hardcover), ISBN 0–06–017279–7, $24.00, 325 pp.; (paper), ISBN 0–060–02826–3, $14.00, 325 pp. Ages 14 up, grades 9 up.

Novel of a battered Puerto Rican woman who finds her way to freedom and independence. Since she ran away with Correa, her love, when she was fourteen and returned a month later, pregnant, to live with her alcoholic, unmarried mother, America Gonzalez has lived in fear of the man. Correa, considerably older than America, has never been faithful and has a wife and children on another island, but he professes to love only America and their daughter, Rosalinda, now fourteen, who has run off with her boyfriend. His love is expressed sometimes in sweet talk but more often in blows and kicks. When he takes Rosalinda to live with his aunt, America is devastated. She seizes the opportunity to leave secretly for New York, to work for a Westchester County couple who have vacationed at the hotel where she is a maid. Although she knows little English and has never before been away from her home in Viques, America is soon running the large house, cooking, cleaning, caring for the children, driving them to and from school, play dates, and swimming and karate lessons, while the busy young parents are working or at social events. America has carefully told no one her address or phone number, but Correa finds out where she lives, and after stalking her by phone for some time, he arrives at the house one night. America screams a warning to the children to run, and as he tries to kill her with a kitchen knife, she fights back for the first time, kicking him in the groin and knocking him against the granite-topped coffee table. When she wakes in a hospital, Rosalinda and her mother are with her. She learns that Correa broke his neck and is dead, and her young employer visits, giving her back wages and, in effect, firing her. At the end America is again a maid, this time in a large Manhattan hotel, but she now is free of her fifteen-year fear of Correa, and Rosalinda, shocked out of her sullen resentment, is once more her daughter. The novel's strength is in showing America's genuine love for the children, and in evoking her fear and helplessness to face Correa's machismo assumption that he has a right to abuse her.

355 Soto, Gary, *Big Bushy Mustache*, illus. Joe Cepeda, Knopf, 1998 (hardcover), ISBN 0–679–88030–5, $17.00, unp. Ages 4–8, grades PS–3.

Amusing, realistic picture-story book about a special relationship between a Hispanic-American father and son. Everyone says little Ricky looks just like his mother, but Ricky wants to look like his father, a handsome man with a big, bushy, black mustache. When the teacher hands out costumes for the class Cinco de Mayo play, Ricky chooses only a big, bushy, black mustache, which he proudly wears home at the end of the day to surprise his father. Once home, he realizes that he lost the mustache somewhere along the way. He hunts for it without success, then tries to approximate it with various materials. Papi saves the day, however; he shaves off his big, bushy, black mustache, and, as he and Mami present it to Ricky, he tells Ricky that he (Papi) now looks just like Ricky. But he also tells Ricky that he should have listened to his teacher and left the mustache at school along with the other costume pieces. The framed, full-color, somewhat abstract paintings depict situations, play up the humor, reveal emotion well, and especially show the special bond between father and son. *The Cat's Meow* (1995), in which a third-grade girl becomes convinced that her cat can speak Spanish, is a chapter book aimed at a slightly older audience. For other books by Soto, see *Baseball in April and Other Stories, The Cat's Meow, Pieces of the Heart, The Skirt*, and *Taking Sides*, nos. 376, 377, 378, 379, and 380 (fiction), and *Neighborhood Odes* and *Who Will Know Us?*, nos. 409A and 409B (poems), in *This Land Is Our Land* (1994).

356   Soto, Gary, *Boys at Work*, illus. Robert Casilla, Delacorte, 1995 (hardcover), ISBN 0–385–32048–5, $14.95, 134 pp.; Dell, 1996 (paper), ISBN 0–440–41221–8, $3.00. Ages 8–12, grades 3–7.

Amusing, realistic novel of boys' domestic adventures set at the time of publication in Fresno, California, companion to *The Pool Party* (1993). The problem is early introduced. As Mexican-American Rudy Herrera, ten, deep into a game of baseball, rounds third base, he trips and lands on a pile of equipment belonging to an older boy, smashing the boy's Discman and plummeting himself into a peck of trouble because Slinky, the owner, is known to be a vato loco "as big as King Kong and just as mean." Rudy and his best pal, Alex Garcia, set about making money to replace the broken Discman before Slinky vents his wrath upon them both. Among other things, they comb cats of fleas for an eccentric old woman, roof a doghouse, sell a door and then must buy it back at a loss, play in Rudy's uncle's mariachi band, and analyze the handwriting on their boyfriends' love letters for Rudy's sister's girlfriends. Their final odd job involves locating and returning to its owner a lost cat, Pudding, a very successful activity that nets them $65. By this time, to their further consternation, they have discovered that Slinky does not own the Discman; he borrowed it from an even tougher older kid, Trucha Mendoza, who is known to be an "honest-to-goodness" tattooed gangster. At the end, Trucha snatches the money with "a greedy sneer" and says he is going to use it to buy a moped. The lively adventures, related with almost tongue-in-cheek humor, remain true to the boys' point of view throughout. The boys are admirable for their perseverance and ingenuity, and that Slinky is not the true owner of the Discman and is himself already in trouble with Trucha over a girl is an unexpected twist. Slinky and Trucha are types expanded larger than life but credibly so because events and people are tinged by the younger boys' overwrought imaginations. Except for a scattering of Spanish words and phrases and a few references, the book is not ethnic specific.

Black-and-white, full-page, realistic illustrations depict scenes and show the boys and their friends, and enemies, in various situations. The novel offers lively, escapist, intelligent reading for those who are just beyond chapter books. For earlier books, see *This Land Is Our Land* (1994), nos. 376, 377, 378, 379, and 380 (fiction), and 409A and 409B (poems) (for titles, see entry 355, this book).

357 Soto, Gary, *Buried Onions*, Harcourt, 1997 (hardcover), ISBN 0–15–201333–4, $17.00, 149 pp.; HarperCollins, 1999 (paper), ISBN 0–064–40771–3, $10.00, 160 pp. Ages 12 up, grades 7 up.

Contemporary, realistic novel of urban, Mexican-American family life and a boy's growing up set for a few weeks in Fresno, California. The narrator, Eddie, nineteen, a City College dropout, yearns for a worthwhile, peaceful life, away from the poverty, gangs, knifings, and drugs of his southeastern Fresno neighborhood. His father and uncles are dead, his mother is old beyond her years, many of his friends are in jail, and just recently his friend Jesus was knifed to death. Eddie's main problem is survival—keeping away from the gangbangers and finding a job to pay the rent on his roach-infested apartment and buy food. The odds are against him. The Anglos from whom he begs jobs distrust him, and police run him in for a robbery he did not commit in a truck they think he stole. After his friend Jose comes home briefly from the Marines before being shipped out and is knifed, Eddie confides in Coach, the ex-Vietnam vet and former gangbanger who runs the recreation program at the local playground. Coach tells him that because of his military service he was able to get a college education and suggests that Eddie try the same route out of this depraved area. The conclusion finds Eddie newly enlisted in the Navy and on his way to a training camp in the desert. The book is most notable for its strong depiction of Eddie's plight, involving the tangled web of family and neighborhood values that demands settling scores with bloodshed and dealing with a friend's enemy regardless of the consequences—standards that imprison the young people literally and figuratively. Although the conclusion is hopeful for Eddie, overall the book offers a bleak outlook for Mexican-American youth. The title comes from Eddie's observation that there must be a giant onion buried beneath Fresno because the city is so filled with tears. For earlier books, see *This Land Is Our Land* (1994), nos. 376, 377, 378, 379, and 380 (fiction), and 409A and 409B (poems) (for titles, see entry 355, this book).

358 Soto, Gary, *Chato's Kitchen*, illus. Susan Guervara, Putnam, 1995 (hardcover), ISBN 0–399–22658–3, $15.95, unp.; Paper Star, 1995 (paper), ISBN 0–698–11600–23, $5.95. Ages 4–10, grades PS–5.

Humorous, contemporary, picture-story fantasy, in which Chato, a Spanish-speaking, "cool, low-riding cat" with "a twinge of mambo in his hips," who thinks he owns the East Los Angeles barrio and plans on eating some newly arrived mice, discovers he has bitten off more than he can chew. When he learns five mice the "color of gray river rock" have moved in next door, he mails them a paper airplane invitation to dinner at his house that night. Papi mouse accepts, asking if they may bring a friend, Chorizo (Sausage), along. Certain that his dinner will now consist of six mice, instead of five, Chato hurries into his kitchen to prepare frijoles, guacamole, arroz, and other dishes perfect for mice. His best friend, flashy-dressing, green-eyed Novio Boy, helps with the tortillas. The mice prepare quesadillas with plenty of cheese to share with their host. The ratoncitos (little mice) climb onto Chorizo's furry back and cruise out of their yard over to Chato's place. When they open the door to their guests, Chato and Novio Boy confront a "low, road-scraping dog," a furry dachshund type, whose presence sends them scampering up the curtains. Assured by Mami mouse that Chorizo is totally nice, they descend, and everyone enjoys a fine meal—Chato, too, even if the menu does not include mice. Carefully calculated suspense, good characterizations, and the surprise ending make for a fine story, and the mix of contemporary terms and Spanish words add zest and create setting. The illustrations are an invaluable part of the narrative—splashy, tropical colors; figures outlined in black and foregrounded, whose faces exude emotion; highly textured; delightfully detailed and humorous—a perfect extension to the story. The mice parents and children are individualized, the cool cats are stereotypical Hispanic street gangbangers, and Chorizo is decked out in a little multicolored jacket and pinky-red artist's beret (which a jacket note says is one like the illustrator wears). Here is marvelously good tongue-in-cheek fun, a folkloric-based fantasy done up in modern garb. A glossary at the beginning of the book helps with the Spanish words. For earlier books, see *This Land Is Our Land* (1994), nos. 376, 377, 378, 379, and 380 (fiction), and 409A and 409B (poems) (for titles, see entry 355, this book).

359 Soto, Gary, *Crazy Weekend*, Scholastic, 1994 (hardcover), ISBN 0–590–47814–1, $13.95, 144 pp.; Scholastic, 1995 (paper), ISBN 0–590–47076–0, $3.50, 160 pp. Ages 8–14, grades 3–9.

Fast-moving, amusing boy's adventure novel set in central California in recent years. Mexican-American Hector Beltran and his best pal, Mando Tafolla, both thirteen, from East Los Angeles, spend a three-day weekend in Fresno visiting Hector's Uncle Julio Silva, an eccentric commercial photographer of limited means and good spirits. While on a shoot in Uncle Julio's business partner's small, decrepit Cessna, they spot two men robbing an armored truck, and Uncle Julio quickly takes pictures. He develops the film and rushes off to *The Fresno Bee*, hoping to sell the pictures to the paper. While they are at the newspaper office, a reporter, Vicky Moreno (with whom Uncle Julio immediately falls in love), interviews the boys, and the published article sets in motion a series of events in which the two robbers, Three Stooges–type ex-convicts Freddie and Huey, set out to find and destroy the pictures and eliminate the three so that they cannot testify against them. Although they do put Uncle Julio and the boys in some precarious situations, the bumbling robbers manage to trip themselves up repeatedly. Using the unlikely weapons of salad dressing, marbles, and a bowling ball, the boys capture the thieves, tie them up, and hold them for the police. At book's end, they, Uncle Julio, and Vicky are planning to spend the $5,000 reward money on a vacation in Acapulco. Good fun, the book has the tone and attitude of a television sitcom, sometimes tense, frequently amusing in a comedy of errors sort of way. The style employs many Spanish words and phrases, which can mostly be deduced from context, although a glossary concludes the book. A sequel is *Summer on Wheels* (1995), in which, when school is out, Hector and Mando enjoy a bike trip from Los Angeles to the beach in Santa Monica, visiting their relatives and having adventures along the way, among them making a television commercial and humanizing Hector's egghead cousin, Bentley. Soto, a native of Fresno, has written many poems, stories, and other novels with Hispanic-American settings. For earlier books, see *This Land Is Our Land* (1994), nos. 376, 377, 378, 379, and 380 (fiction), and 409A and 409B (poems) (for titles, see entry 355, this book).

360 Soto, Gary, *Jesse*, Harcourt, 1994 (hardcover), ISBN 0–15–240239–X, $14.95, 166 pp.; (paper), ISBN 0–590–52837–8, $3.99. Ages 12 up, grades 7 up.

Period novel set in Fresno, California, in the 1970s, of two brothers, Jesse, seventeen, the diffident narrator, and his stalwart, supportive, nineteen-year-old brother, Abel. The story operates on two levels: the two boys' struggles to survive during one school year, and the broader struggle of the Mexican-American young people, whom they represent, to exist in the face of poverty, racism, and classism. Knowing he battles against the odds, Jesse drops out of high school in his senior year, hoping to rise above his disturbing family life of drunken stepfather and despairing mother. After he persuades Abel, already in City College, to help him enroll, the two pool their meager resources, supplemented occasionally by gifts of food from their mother, and by picking in the fields, take a dingy, run-down apartment near downtown, and help each other achieve academically so that they will not have to spend their lives for barely subsistence wages. Jesse is talented in art, and Abel thinks he will major in either Spanish or forestry, but both would like to get good jobs and see something of the world. Because they want to avoid the trouble with society and police that snares many of their age-mates and also lack money, they have little social life. Jesse, a religious boy, is saved from several possibly troubling situations by his strong sense of right and wrong and an aversion to physical aggression, while Abel has common sense and a cool head. Both boys would like steady girls, but Jesse is shy, and only Abel strikes up a friendship, a low-keyed one, with Maureen, whose father makes prosthetic devices and, fortunately for the boys' finances, hires Abel part time. Jesse becomes good friends with Leslie, a white Vietnam veteran, whose artwork Jesse appreciates and who becomes the sweetheart of their kindly landlady's daughter, Glenda. Moments of high tension occur, as when the boys attend protest rallies organized around Cesar Chavez's efforts to improve working conditions for the field workers and when Jesse is accosted and beaten by drunken white boys. While there are a few lighter moments, the novel's poetic style, which eloquently portrays Jesse's inner yearnings, mostly conveys the intense despair and disillusionment these boys feel at a world that seems to find them, as Mexican Americans, of value only for what their hands can accomplish to keep big landowners wealthy. At the end, Jesse faces a bleak summer in the fields, sweating under the hot sun and yearning for the company of Abel, who has been drafted into the Army. For earlier books, see *This Land Is Our Land* (1994), nos. 376, 377, 378, 379, and 380 (fiction), and 409A and 409B (poems) (for titles, see entry 355, this book).

361 Soto, Gary, *Off and Running*, illus. Eric Velasquez, Delacorte, 1996 (hardcover), ISBN 0-385-32181-3, $15.95, 136 pp.; Bantam, 1997 (paper), ISBN 0-440-41432-6, $4.50. Ages 8-12, grades 3-7.

Amusing, realistic school novel with a feminist slant, set in Fresno, California, companion to *The Pool Party* (1993) and *Boys at Work* (1996; no. 356). As usual in Soto's books for young readers, the story starts fast. Miata Ramirez, ten, is seeking election as class president, with Ana Avila as her running mate, and against popular, obstreperous, and often gross Rudy Herrera and his running mate, Alex Garcia. While Rudy's platform includes working for longer recesses and ice cream every day, Miata advocates beautifying the school by erasing graffiti and planting lots of flowers, taking more school trips, and getting computers with CD-ROMs. She and Ana prepare campaign posters and buttons, but it seems that they are facing an uphill battle. When Miata seeks advice from her parents, her mother tells her about an elderly woman relative who had been mayor of a city in Mexico. The old woman promises to help with flowers and encourages Miata to conduct a forward-thinking campaign. Most of the scenes involve school events, like a baseball game in which Miata slams out a long ball, an assembly, and a visit to the San Diego Zoo. A note of mystery involves unsettling phone calls, which are surprisingly cleared up at the end of the book. Early in the campaign, Miata's mother gives her and Ana new permanents, which go awry, leaving both girls with frizzy, very curly hair. To their amazement, as the campaign quickens, their girl classmates, some of the boys, and even Rudy and Alex adopt the new style, as does their teacher, Mrs. Diaz, who tells Miata it is because Miata is universally admired. On election day, voting is soon over, and the girls are elated to learn they have won, 32-30. Miata is soon informed, by Rudy himself, that both he and Alex had voted for her and Ana, because Rudy says they would rather spend their time playing soccer. Miata soon initiates her beautification program, to the pleasure of school, parents, and community. Although the picture is mainly of life among Mexican-

American schoolchildren, there are views of warm, happy family life at Miata's house, her parents being especially supportive and pleasant, goodnatured people, and at a friend's quinceanera (girl's fifteenth-birthday celebration), during which even Rudy behaves. Miata is a solidly drawn figure, a sensible, considerate, and persevering good citizen, for whom the reader cheers, but Rudy is too exaggeratedly bad for belief, particularly in comparison to the characters in *Boys at Work*. Later elementary girls who seek lighthearted reading beyond the primer and chapter-book stage will applaud Miata all the way. For earlier books, see *This Land Is Our Land* (1994), nos. 376, 377, 378, 379, and 380 (fiction), and 409A and 409B (poems) (for titles, see entry 355, this book).

362 Soto, Gary, *The Old Man and His Door*, illus. Joe Cepeda, Putnam, 1996 (hardcover), ISBN 0–399–22700–8, $15.95, unp.; Paper Star, 1998 (paper), ISBN 0–698–11654–2, $5.95. Ages 4–8, grades PS–3.

Humorous story of family life reminiscent of folk tales involving foolish husbands. An old Mexican-American man grows fine tomatoes and green chiles but is terrible about listening to his wife. As his wife leaves for a neighborhood barbecue, he is more concerned about bathing his dog than in paying attention to his wife's reminder to bring the pig, the puerco. Later, when he remembers about the barbecue, he thinks she told him to bring the door, the puerta. Puzzled, but not disposed to argue with her, he unscrews the front door, puts it on his back, and starts out. He soon comforts a crying baby by playing peek-a-boo with her around the door, for which he gets a kiss; hides under the door when he accidentally bumps a beehive, then collects the honey after the bees leave; lets a tired goose rest on the door, for which he gets an egg as reward; uses the door as a raft to save a boy who is drowning, in the process catching some fish; and helps a young man load some furniture into a truck by using the door as a ramp and receives some watermelons in thanks. When, at the barbecue, his wife complains about his never listening to her, he gives her the kiss he received from the baby. Then everyone sits down to a good meal of the foods he has collected with the door. The good humor of this version of the battle between the sexes is amplified by brightly colored paintings with lots of circular designs, the well-fleshed, round-faced husband and wife, the chubby-faced children, the fat fish, the round hat in which he places the honey, the watermelons—all these contribute to the feeling that in spite of his silliness, he is loved, and all is right with the world. The story is based on an old Mexican song that says that door and pig sound the same to an old man. A glossary of Spanish words and terms appears at the beginning of the book. For other books by Soto, see *This Land Is Our Land*, nos. 376, 377, 378, 379, and 380 (fiction) and 409A and 409B (poems) (for titles, see entry 355, this book).

363 Soto, Gary, *Petty Crimes*, Harcourt, 1998 (hardcover), ISBN 0–15–201658–9, $16.00, 157 pp. Ages 10–14, grades 5–9.

Ten realistic short stories of middle-grade young people in and around Fresno, California, most involving "petty" crimes, that is, shoplifting and schoolboy scams. Except for the Hispanic names, occasional Spanish words, and references to immigration from Mexico, relatives there, and Mexican-American customs or dishes, the narratives might concern the offspring of any United States working-class families in any highly populated area. Gang intimidation, or the possibility of it, drives several stories. Adults appear mostly on the fringes, usually too tired, overworked, and beaten down by life to care enough to become involved with their children's concerns. The stories are not bleak, however, or despairing, although such moments occur; rather, they are enduring and resigned in tone. Several are ironically humorous, for example, that in which Laura attempts to give her failing grandfather memory lessons and the one in which Jose Luis's pet rooster, Frankie, mysteriously disappears after costing the family $100 in vet bills. In still other stories, Norma appeals for help in saving from female gang terrorists her already broken doll, Alma, which is in her care for a social-studies project; Mario scams fast-food merchants by placing bugs in their food and steals bills from a bride's dress during a dance; and Rudy tries unsuccessfully to show off for a girl during his very first boxing lesson. The stories move fast, contain a wealth of telling details of character and situations, exhibit Soto's strong sense of place and time, and feature interesting if not always likable protagonists. For earlier books, see *This Land Is Our Land* (1994), nos. 376, 377, 378, 379, and 380 (fiction), and 409A and 409B (poems) (for titles, see entry 355, this book).

364 Suarez, Virgil, *Going Under*, Arte Publico, 1996 (hardcover), ISBN 1–55885–159–3, $18.95, 155 pp. Ages 14 up, grades 9 up.

Realistic novel set in Miami, Florida, in the late 1980s, companion to *Havana Thursdays* (1995; see no. 365) in that it examines life for one young Cuban-American man, who might be taken as representative of many of his kind. Xavier Cuevas, successful insurance man, finds life a hassle. Traffic jams prevent him from keeping appointments on time, and his playboy partner is not holding up his end of the business. His mother is marrying again, a far different man from Xavier's extremely successful businessman father; his secretary is robbed of the $6,000 a client has paid for a lucrative policy; and his marriage is on the rocks. When Xavier suffers a panic attack, his father takes him to a Cuban santera, a faith healer, who combines African and Cuban beliefs and approaches. She summons the spirit of a deceased musician, Sonny Manteco, to help him out. Occasionally hearing Sonny's voice, Xavier is inspired to purchase a set of bongo drums and learn how to play them. But he dreads returning to his empty house, feels pulled southward to Key West, and when last seen has plunged into the ocean and is "swimming home" to Havana "in pursuit of the unattainable." Although it has some funny moments, the book presents a bleak outlook for YUCAs, Young Urban Cuban Americans, as Suarez calls them, those "in haste, no time to waste." Perhaps he intends Xavier to be more broadly representative, that is, the pursuit of the materialistic American dream is pulling everyone under. At any rate, the novel does seem also to be a picture of American life of its time, at the least a satire jabbing at those who neglect self, families, and community to impress others with their success, however defined. In this pared-to-the-bone story, certain avenues are opened but not explored, for example, the negative attitude of Xavier's American wife's father toward Xavier. Does the protagonist's last name, which means caves, have any significance? The open-ended conclusion is also troubling. Altogether the book seems less successful at dealing with men's lives than its predecessor, *Havana Thursdays*, at examining those of Cuban-American women. Lastly, although the protagonist seems foolish, he is still a likable and sympathetic figure. For other books by Suarez, see *Iguana Dreams* and *Latin Jazz*, nos. 371 and 382, also fiction, in *This Land Is Our Land* (1994).

365 Suarez, Virgil, *Havana Thursdays*, Arte Publico, 1995 (hardcover), ISBN 1–55885–143–7, $19.95, 250 pp. Ages 14 up, grades 9 up.

Contemporary, realistic novel of the Torres family, Cuban Americans in the Miami, Florida, area, focusing on the women. Although Zacarias Torres, an eminent agriculturist specializing in seeds, appears only in the first chapter, in which he suffers a fatal heart attack, he is effectively the main character, since his death changes the lives of the rest of his family. His wife, Laura, flies to Sao Paulo, Brazil, brings his body back, arranges the funeral, calls her children together, and defines what the rest of her life must be and what her relationship will be with respect to her alcoholic sister, Maura, and their mother-in-law. Maura, his sister-in-law, resolves once again to stop drinking and hopes for a more focused future, since Norberto, Zacarias's twin and her husband, will be spending more time in Miami on the family business. Sofia, Laura's daughter, leaves her unfaithful Argentine husband and returns to Miami to complete her education. Beatriz draws closer to her Mexican Navy man fiance; and Cristina, the youngest of Zacarias and Laura's daughters, learns that during the funeral her entry in an important photo contest was awarded second place, assuring her of a future in photography, the result of the skill her father had nurtured. Sammy, the only son, having learned from his father's death of the brevity of life, decides to give his marriage with his selfish, almost-estranged wife another chance and moves from Maryland back to Miami to help Norberto with the business. Celia, Norberto and Maura's only child, decides to leave teaching, which she hates, and seek another career, one less stressful, and nurture her relationship with Rafael, an artist and her live-in companion. All anticipate that the matriarchs will revive the Thursday dinners, like the ones they had in Havana. The lives of the women in this extended family, which is trying to maintain Cuban traditions and also adjust to the American way of life, seem credible and convincing, in spite of the many shifts in point of view imposed by the novel's structure of moving from one to another and back again. Each person's crisis is sympathetically handled, even the loneliness and isolation of the family dowager, Eleonor. A list of characters at the beginning of the book is a welcome help in keeping the large cast straight. Suarez has also published *Iguana Dreams* and *Latin Jazz*, nos. 371 and 382, also fiction, described in *This Land Is Our Land* (1994).

366 Talbert, Marc, *A Sunburned Prayer*, Simon & Schuster, 1995 (hardcover), ISBN 0–689–80125–4, $14.00, 108 pp.; (paper), ISBN 0–689–81326–0, $4.50, 128 pp. Ages 9–14, grades 4–9.

Realistic boy's growing-up novel with animal-story aspects set mostly on a recent Good Friday near and in the mountain village of Chimayo, New Mexico, not far from Santa Fe. Mexican-American Eloy, eleven, wishes to emulate the youthful feat of his abuelo (grandfather) and join the Good Friday pilgrimage of seventeen miles from his village of Pedernal to Chimayo. He wishes to secure soil from the Santuario (church) to heal his abuela's (grandmother's) terminal cancer. His busy, cynical parents forbid him to go, unless someone else in the family accompanies him. His older brother, Benito, whom Eloy regards as hard, silent, and interested only in girls and cars, refuses to oblige, and his abuela tells him to obey his parents. With a little food and water, Eloy sneaks out very early in the morning, cutting across foothills to join a pilgrim procession. He soon notices he is being followed by a medium-sized, grayish, spotted female dog just beyond the puppy stage. Although he dislikes dogs, he warms to the spirited, loving, companionable creature and names her Magdalena. One of the book's strengths is its fidelity to Eloy's point of view. He bargains with God, even threatens God, and worries about thinking "dirty" thoughts and using curse words. He associates the acute tension that has developed between his parents recently with his grandmother's failing health and decides that his pilgrimage is also for them and Benito, to restore their previous warm family life. He grows hungry, hot, thirsty, and footsore and tears off his shirt to cool his overheated body. He shares his small supply of water with the dog and also with an aged Indio (Indian). To his surprise, he finds Benito and abuela inside the Santuario at Chimayo. Along with abuela, he prayerfully eats a few pinches of the holy soil. His grandmother compliments him on his perseverance, emphasizing that what he has done cannot change things—she will die soon—but he has made it easier for her to die, since she knows he is growing up to be a good man. She also tells him that he can keep the dog. Home again, his back hurting, Eloy thinks of himself as a sunburned prayer on two legs. The sense of Hispanic-American working-class life, strong Catholicism, and close family ties is vivid. The minimalist style and strictly focused third-person viewpoint project the impression of first person and give the narrative an intensity only occasionally relieved by humor. This is a moving account of a boy's gaining new insights into life and of his efforts to both act upon and define his faith through his relationships to those he loves the most. A glossary gives definitions of the numerous Spanish words and phrases.

367 Velasquez, Gloria L., *Maya's Divided World*, Arte Publico, 1995 (hardcover), ISBN 1–55885–126–7, $12.95, 125 pp.; (paper), ISBN 1–55885–131–3, $7.95. Ages 10–14, grades 5–9.

Novel dealing with the effect of divorce on a teenaged girl, as well as her mother and her psychologist, in the disapproving Hispanic culture. Maya, sixteen, blames her mother when her father leaves Laguna Beach for San Francisco, believing that what her Sante Fe grandmother said must be true, that the fault was in her mother's seeking higher education and not living just to please her husband. Further hurt because her father does not call her, Maya drops out of the tennis team, abandons her school friends, takes up with Shane and his friend Charley, both smoking, drinking toughs, sneaks out of her window at night, and eventually is arrested for shoplifting. In despair, her mother turns to a psychologist friend, Sandra Martinez, who agrees to see Maya if the girl is willing. Not until Maya, after a dispute with her mother, runs away from home and turns to her old friend Juanita does she agree to see Ms. Martinez, who persuades her to go home, talk things out with her mother, stand up to Shane, drop him from her life, and resume her old friends and study habits. Her father invites her to San Francisco for Thanksgiving and assures her that he still loves her and that the divorce was not her mother's fault. About half the chapters are from the point of view of Ms. Martinez, who years before had endured her mother's blame for her divorce after an inappropriate early marriage. At the end both she and Maya's mother have made peace with their own mothers, despite having gone against the traditional strictures of their culture. This book is one in the Roosevelt High School Series, following *Juanita Fights the School Board* (1994).

368 Velasquez, Gloria L., *Tommy Stands Alone*, Arte Publico, 1995 (hardcover), ISBN 1–55885–146–1, $14.95, 135 pp.; (paper), ISBN 1–55885–147–X, $7.95. Ages 10–15, grades 5–10.

Problem novel of a high school–aged Mexican-American boy struggling with his realization that he is homosexual and with his difficulties in admitting it to himself, his friends, and his family. For years, Tommy Montoya has felt that he is different from his friends, but it is only when they start dating that he confronts his own sexual orientation. After first hiding it, drinking heavily, then attempting suicide, he gets help from Sandra Martinez, a professional psychologist, who has been alerted by Tommy's truest friend, Maya, a girl who has recently been seeing Ms. Martinez to work out problems after her parents' divorce. Action is seen partly from the point of view of the psychologist and partly from Tommy's, as he works through his misery and self-loathing, comes out to his family, is thrown out of the apartment by his father, and eventually brought home by his mother. His two little sisters are delighted to have him back, but his father refuses to speak to him. The attitude of his classmates almost defeats him, but soon his long-time friend, African-American Tyrone, and another girl as well as Maya rally to his support. While it is clear that his father will take a long time to accept his son for what he is, in the end he has begun to speak to Tommy again, if only to order him around. The problems of any gay teenager are increased by the macho Chicano culture of Tommy's family and their unfamiliarity with homosexuality. While the treatment of the subject is somewhat simplistic, it is appropriate for the age group at which the novel aims. This is one of a series concerned with racially mixed Roosevelt High School.

369 Wing, Natasha, *Jalapeno Bagels*, illus. Roberta Casilla, Atheneum, 1996 (hardcover), ISBN 0–689–80530–6, $15.00, unp. Ages 5–8, grades K–3.

Pablo, whose mother is Mexican and his father Jewish, puzzles over what to bring to school for International Day, something, the teacher has said, that reflects each child's culture. His mother suggests that he help with the Sunday baking at their *pananderia*, the family bakery, and choose what he wants. As she makes *pan dulce*, Mexican sweet bread, he thinks that may be his choice, then changes his mind as they make *empanadas de calabaza*, pumpkin turnovers, and again as they make chango bars, a favorite dessert with chocolate chips and nuts. Helping his father make bagels and challah, Pablo considers them but rejects his father's lox on pumpernickel bagel with cream cheese. Finally, he decides on *jalapeno* bagels, a recipe his parents have made up themselves that he sees as a mixture of their two cultures, just as he is. The simple family story is enhanced by rich, full-page watercolor illustrations, a brief glossary of both Spanish and Yiddish terms, and recipes for both *chango* bars and *jalapeno* bagels.

370 Ybarra, Ricardo Means, *Brotherhood of Dolphins*, Arte Publico, 1997 (paper), ISBN 1–55885–215–8, $11.95, 288 pp. Ages 14 up, grades 9 up.

Mystery-suspense novel with detective-story aspects set in 1986 mostly in the barrios of East Los Angeles and based on the actual unsolved arson of the Los Angeles Central Library on April 29, 1986. When Sylvia Cruz, Mexican-American firefighter, is heroically injured in the Central Library fire, the close-knit Hispanic community joins together to celebrate her bravery and ability both as a Hispanic American and as a woman. Among these is Pete Escobedo, a long-time family friend and detective with the Los Angeles Police Department, who is soon assigned to the case. With clever deduction, some luck, and a good deal of pluck and perseverance, Escobedo connects the library fire to those involving the strangulation and arson sex-slayings of a woman activist and artist and the murder of Sylvia herself. Realizing that he is dealing with a psychotic personality, Escobedo traces the killer's friends and through them learns of the man's obsession with saving the earth by going back to nature, symbolized by pyramids and schools of dolphins, and his connection with a nature event soon to take place on the gulf coast of Baja California. In a slam-bang, fingernail-biting conclusion, Escobedo corners the murderer, who has kidnapped Escobedo's girlfriend and taken her to the Mexican peninsula and who is killed in the attempt to escape. The warm, close-knit Mexican-American families and neighborhoods; the vividly described valleys and hills, drawn with such highly sensory language that the area becomes palpable; the prejudice toward Hispanics within the LAPD and the fire department; the carefully constructed and well-paced plot filled with action and suspense; the determined, intelligent hero; and the tightly scripted conclusion make this novel both a topnotch thriller and a fine view of a proud and capable element of American life. Explicit sex scenes, including some with deviant sex, appear. Although there are many Spanish words and phrases, attentive readers will have no difficulty following this gripping story.

371 Zaldivar, Raquel Puig, *Women Don't Need to Write*, Arte Publico, 1998 (paper), ISBN 1–55885–25–3, $13.95, 328 pp. Ages 12 up, grades 7 up.

Long family saga, following the life of Rosa from the day she marries Juan Garach in 1900 to her ninety-fifth birthday, which she celebrates in Miami, Florida, in the midst of her now large, extended family that has held together largely through her efforts. On her wedding day she prays for health, healthy children, and someone to teach her to read and write, but her husband meets this request dismissively, saying, "Women don't need to write." From their first years in the province of Castellon, Spain, to the end of her life, Rosa works hard and uncomplainingly with single-minded devotion for her family. She has four sons, Andres, who is partially crippled when he is dropped at his baptism and is thereafter rejected by his father, twins Lucas and Fermin, and Jose, whom they call Pepet as a child, and one daughter, Lucia. Throughout their marriage, Juan is demanding, arbitrary, and unappreciative, and Rosa submits, as a Spanish wife is supposed to do, but she never gives up her desire to learn, and, a few times when she must protect her children, she confronts her abusive husband and wins a small victory. First Lucas, an insensitive, bullying young man with a talent for making money, then his brothers, and finally Juan and Rosa, leave Spain for Cuba. Political changes force them back to Spain, where Juan dies. Rosa feels only relief that her husband is gone and enjoys a short period of autonomy, but her sons soon exert their dominance. Back in Cuba, the family prospers until the revolution, which at first seems hopeful but soon turns sinister. Except for Andres and his wife, Norma, who are caught up in counterrevolutionary action, and their son, who is seized by the police, most of the family manages to leave for the United States, some abandoning everything they have to get away. At the end, Andres has made a harrowing escape, his son has been located and communicated with in the Soviet Union, and his wife, who has been imprisoned for years, is about to be released. Rosa has again collected her family around her and is being taught to read by her once estranged daughter. Although it is easy to become concerned with the well-drawn characters and the adversities suffered are interesting, the novel is strangely without tension, perhaps because the focus is always on the old woman who has survived so much. Still, it is a clear and unsensational picture of Spanish and Cuban history in the twentieth century, and an unsentimental look at Cuban-American life in Florida.

8

Hispanic Americans: Books of Oral Tradition

372 Bernier-Grand, Carmen T., ret., *Juan Bobo: Four Folktales from Puerto Rico*, illus. Ernesto Ramos Nieves, HarperCollins, 1994 (hardcover), ISBN 0–06–023389–3, $14.00, 63 pp. Ages 4–8, grades PS–3.

An early reader with simple sentences and widely spaced lines retelling four noodlehead stories from the oral tradition. Juan Bobo is not a naughty child, but he is not very smart, or at least he does not use his head, and nothing he does turns out as he intends. When he goes to fetch water and, finding the buckets too heavy, substitutes baskets, he is surprised to find a puddle at the door. Left to care for the pig while his mother goes to church, he manages to lose the pig and ruin his mother's clothes. After promising to be on his best behavior when they go on a visit, he gets his mother's signals mixed up, refuses all the good food, and comes home hungry. Trusted to sell his mother's sugar-cane syrup to the widows, whom his mother says he will know by their shiny black dresses, he mistakes flies from the mill for the widows, drinks the syrup himself, and comes home with money he has found. The humor is obvious enough for the youngest listener, and the bright illustrations showing a little brown-skinned boy in settings of rural Puerto Rico should make this a favorite of beginning readers. A Spanish translation is given at the end of the book.

373 Climo, Shirley, ret., *The Little Red Ant and the Great Big Crumb: A Mexican Fable*, illus. Francisco X. Mora, Clarion, 1995 (hardcover), ISBN 0–3957–0732–3, $14.95, 40 pp.; (paper), ISBN 0–3957–2097–4, $5.95. Ages 4–8, grades PS–3.

A Mexican version of a well-known fable with the moral, "You can do it if you think you can." A red ant, smaller than the others in the nest, finds a large, sweet cake crumb, and looks for someone to help her carry it back. She approaches the lizard, the spider, the rooster, the coyote, and even the man, none willing to help and all threatening. When she realizes that she has frightened the man, who scares the coyote, who chases the rooster, who wakes the sun, who warms the lizard, who can destroy the anthill, she declares, "I am the strongest of all!" and she summons strength to carry the crumb home. The illustrations are slightly cartoonish, done in simple, large color blocks outlined in pen, giving the impression that the target audience is the very young. A number of Spanish words are used, the meaning clear from the context, and a page at the end defines them and gives the pronunciation.

374   Espinosa, J. Manuel, coll., and Joe Hayes, trans. and ed., *Cuentos de Cuanto Hay: Tales from Spanish New Mexico*, illus. William Rotsaert, Univ. of New Mexico, 1998 (hardcover), ISBN 0–826–31927–0, $35.00, 235 pp.; (paper), ISBN 0–826–31928–9, $15.95. Ages 8 up, grades 3 up.

Delightfully entertaining collection of fifty-six folktales, selected, translated, and edited by Hayes from the 110 stories folklorist Espinosa collected in the 1930s from Spanish-speaking residents of all levels of society in north-central New Mexico and southern Colorado, written down in Spanish verbatim from the storytellers. Each story is presented in Spanish on the left-hand side of the page and in English on the right, with the teller's name, age, and town given at the end. While characters, plots, motifs, and themes reveal the stories' European origin, they have taken on the color of the region, though surprisingly few involve Indians. "Two Lost Children" is the equivalent of "Hansel and Gretel," "Juan Camison" moves like "Seven at One Blow" with bits of the romance of El Cid, "The Horse of Seven Colors" recalls the story of the crop that is mysteriously devoured every night (see also no. 386), and "I'll See What God Will Give Me" is like "The Donkey, the Table, and the Stick." A version of the "Tar Baby" (the sticky doll motif) story involves a melon-eating rabbit. In the very last tale, "The Cow and the Little Calf," a coyote tricks and gobbles up a calf in the manner of the wolf in "The Wolf and the Seven Little Kids." Six principal classifications appear: tales of magic, religious tales (involving God and saints), picaresque tales (adventurers), romantic tales, animal tales, and anecdotes, according to Espinosa in the introduction. Since the stories are lively and packed with dialogue, with a strong oral aspect, those looking for storytelling material will find this book a treasure. Those who just want good reading entertainment will also delight in it. Black-and-white scratchboard illustrations introduce each story and add interest. For another book by Hayes, see *La Llorona, The Weeping Woman*, in *This Land Is Our Land* (1994), no. 393.

375   Gonzalez, Lucia M., ret., *The Bossy Gallito/El Gallo de Bodas: A Traditional Cuban Folktale*, illus. Lulu Delacre, Scholastic, 1994 (hardcover), ISBN 0–590–46843–X, $15.95, unp.; 1999 (paper), ISBN 0–439–06757–X, $5.99. Ages 4–8, grades PS–3.

A delightfully amusing, colorfully illustrated cumulative tale, presented in both English and Spanish, which winds and unwinds like the story of the old woman who could not get her pig to go over the stile. A handsome, proud, bossy rooster on the way to the wedding of his uncle the parrot cannot resist eating two shiny gold kernels of corn lying near a mud puddle and dirties his beak. He spends the rest of the book trying to get his beak clean so he can go to the wedding. He asks the grass to clean him, but the grass refuses; he asks the goat to eat the unaccommodating grass, but the goat does not like to be bossed either and refuses; he asks the stick to beat the goat; and so on, all unsuccessfully, until at last his good friend the sun, to whom the little rooster always sings in the morning, agrees to help. The beak is cleaned, and the bossy little rooster gets to the wedding on time. The story's good humor is advanced by slightly comic mixed media and watercolor pictures. They show the little rooster as a really natty dresser, with spats on his feet and a rose in his lapel, and many bird and animal friends and some buildings, according to an endnote, of the Little Havana area of Miami, Florida. Another version of this story, by Alma Flor Ada, appears in *This Land Is Our Land* (1994), no. 390, *The Rooster Who Went to His Uncle's Wedding*.

376 Gonzalez, Lucia M., coll. and ret., *Senor Cat's Romance and Other Favorite Stories from Latin America*, illus. Lulu Delacre, Scholastic, 1997 (hardcover), ISBN 0–590–48537–7, $17.95, 48 pp. Ages 4–8, grades PS–3.

Five folktales and one song from Spain and from Africa that are popular among children throughout Hispanic America. In "The Little Half-Chick," the hero sets out to see the king, learns to his sorrow when he arrives that he should have been more helpful to those he met along the way, and ends up as a weathervane. When, in "Juan Bobo and the Three-Legged Pot," the mother of slow-witted Juan Bobo (the equivalent of lazy Jack) sends him to his grandmother's house to get a three-legged pot for making chicken and rice, he orders the pot to walk home. Martina, the little cockroach (in the story of that name) is wooed by a cat, a rooster, and toad, rejects them because their speech displeases her, and finally chooses Ratoncito Perez, Perez the Mouse. A little ant helps an old man and woman whose garden is ravaged by a billy goat in "The Billy Goat and the Vegetable Garden," and in a Brer Rabbit–type story, "How Uncle Rabbit Tricked Uncle Tiger," Tio Conejo outwits his perennial enemy, Tio Tigre. The last offering is a song-story in rhyme, "Senor Cat's Romance," in which Senor Cat comes to grief on his wedding day because he celebrates too exuberantly. Humor, action, and surprise endings combine with the strong folktale plots for lively, exciting stories related in good style for the most part and complemented by full-page and cross-page illustrations in the bright, happy tones of the illustrator's native Puerto Rico. The reteller and the illustrator both contribute notes that contain information about the stories, and notes and a glossary appear after each tale.

377 Hayes, Joe, ret., *A Spoon for Every Bite*, illus. Rebecca Leer, Orchard, 1996 (hardcover), ISBN 0–531–09499–5, $15.95, unp.; (paper), ISBN 0–531–07143–X, $5.95. Ages 4 up, grades PS up.

Amusing retelling in picture-book form of a Hispanic story from the American Southwest, in which the simply told text is perfectly complemented by strongly executed paintings. A young couple are so poor they own only two spoons, one for each of them. Their neighbor, on the other hand, lives extravagantly in a big, elegantly furnished house. When the young couple's baby is born, they decide to invite the rich man to dinner and save up money to buy a spoon for him to use. The rich man makes fun of their sacrifice, pointing out that he has so much money that he could use a different spoon every day of the year. Whereupon the wife points out that they have a friend who uses a different spoon for every bite of food he eats. Not to be outdone, the rich man uses up all his spoons, giving them to the young couple after they have been used once. He buys more and more spoons, until he has squandered all his wealth and the young couple have a mountain of spoons that towers over their tiny hut. They then take the formerly rich man to visit their friend—an elderly Indian who scoops up beans with tortillas, one tortilla piece serving as a spoon for each bite. The rich man has learned a lesson, and the young couple have enough money in spoons to last them the rest of their days. Objects, like pots and wooden dishes, the gray-tan church with rounded spire and Spanish bells, the cacti, the longhorn steers, the grayish mesas, the rusty brown desert, the rich man with his long, waxed mustache—these establish the old Spanish-American period. The funniest pictures are of the humble, rude, flat-roofed dwelling of the young couple, over which towers a mountain of grayish spoons, and of the expression on the rich man's face as he watches the Indian eat beans with his tortilla-chip spoons. A writer's note about sources appears at the end. For another book by Hayes, see no. 393, *La Llorona, The Weeping Woman*, in *This Land Is Our Land* (1994).

378 Hayes, Joe, ret., *Tell Me a Cuento/Cuentame Un Story: 4 Stories in English & Spanish*, illus. Geronimo Garcia, Cinco Puntos, 1998 (paper), ISBN 0–938317–38–5, $11.95, 64 pp. Ages 6–10, grades 1–5.

Four highly entertaining, loosely retold folktales from the Spanish and Hispanic-American traditions, which have counterparts in tales elsewhere. Each story is presented in English at the top of the page and in Spanish below, highly patterned, flamboyant, colorful illustrations occupying the centerfold portions of the pages and extending the humor and action. A proud butterfly marries a mouse, which is gobbled up by a cat whose suit the butterfly had rejected. A poor, hard-working mother is aided by little men who give her a pot of gold, while the selfish, rich woman for whom she has been working receives a pot of scorpions and other poisonous creatures. A bossy rooster named Jose eventually gets someone to help him go to his uncle's wedding, but when he asks if the guests would like him to sing, they unanimously respond, "No way, Jose!" The last story, a Billy Goats Gruff type of narrative, tells how a bee foils a terrible monster. Intended as a bilingual early reader, this is one of several books of lively tales that storyteller Hayes has published. For another book, see *La Llo-rona, The Weeping Woman*, no. 393 in *This Land Is Our Land* (1994).

379 Hayes, Joe, coll. and ret., *Watch Out for Clever Women!/¡Cuidado con las Mujeres Astutas!: Hispanic Folktales*, illus. Vicki Trego Hill, Cinco Puntos, 1995 (hardcover), ISBN 0–938317–21–0, $16.95, 77 pp.; (paper), ISBN 0–938–21720–2, $10.95. Ages 4 up, grades PS up.

Highly engaging retellings of five Hispanic-American underdog folktales pop-ular in the southwestern United States, in which tricksters are undone by the wit and cleverness of women. Each story is told first in English and then in Spanish, the two versions appearing together on each page or on facing pages, and is decorated and amplified by realistic, atmospheric drawings that charac-terize the principals, depict situations, and add greatly to the humor and suspense of the stories. "In the Days of King Adobe," two thieves steal an old woman's ham, which during the night she replaces with a brick. A wealthy rancher, known for his deceit and greed, cheats a peasant boy who has won a bet against him, only to be embarrassed in front of guests by his angry daughter in "This Will Teach You." "The Day It Snowed Tortillas" tells of a clever wife who protects three bags of gold her husband has found by persuading thieves that her husband, who has bragged about the gold, is really a talkative fool who thinks tortillas fall from the sky. In "Just Say Baaaa," a mother similarly assists her son in keeping the lambs he worked hard to acquire. In "Watch Out!," a wife saves the family farm by outwitting a moneylender, who discovers she is more adept at playing the "shell game" than he. These delightful stories have cross-generational appeal and hold the attention for many readings and tellings. An introductory note gives information about the stories. For an earlier book by Hayes, see *La Llorona, The Weeping Woman*, no. 393 in *This Land Is Our Land* (1994).

380 Hayes, Joe, ret., *Where There's A Will, There's A Way/Donde Hay Ganas, Hay Manas*, illus. Lucy Jelinek, Trails West, 1995 (paper), ISBN 0–939729–25–3, $5.95, 27 pp. Ages 4–8, grades PS–3.

Amusing numbskull folktale in which the one thought foolish triumphs through wit over someone who thinks he is far superior in intellect. A jobless, unnamed youth is taken in by a haughty priest to be his servant. The priest requires that the boy call common objects by certain arbitrary, long-winded terms. In the end, the boy obediently recites the entire series of loquacious phrases as he warns the priest that his house is about to be set on fire and then departs, leaving the priest to his own devices. The vigorously told story is ac-companied by full-page and spot black-and-white, whimsical drawings that clev-erly extend the action and characterization. As each new term is prescribed, picture bubbles reveal what the boy really thinks of the pompous priest. The story is told in English at the top of the page and in Spanish at the bottom.

Hayes has also published no. 393, *La Llorona, The Weeping Woman*, in *This Land Is Our Land* (1994).

381   Jaffe, Nina, ret., *The Golden Flower: A Taino Myth from Puerto Rico*, illus. Enrique O. Sanchez, Simon & Schuster, 1996 (hardcover), ISBN 0–689–80469–5, $16.00, unp. Ages 4–8, grades PS–3.

Origin-of-the-world myth from the Taino people, the first inhabitants of Puerto Rico. Before there are any plants or water on the earth, a child finds seeds, floated by the wind, which he plants on the top of a mountain. There a forest grows up, and in the middle is a tall tree with a vine wrapped around it, on which grows a bright flower with golden petals. At the center of the flower appears a globe, from which can be heard strange noises. One day two men approach the globe from different sides of the mountain, both desiring what they now see is a pumpkin. As they fight over it, the vine breaks and the pumpkin rolls down the mountain, crashes into a sharp rock, and bursts apart, releasing a great flood of water. It rises and rises, driving all the people and animals up the mountain to the forest the boy planted. There the water stops, and the people discover small streams, golden beaches, and the sparkling sea. And that is how Boriquen, the original name for Puerto Rico, came to be. The illustrations, done in brilliant acrylic and gouache, are stylized, some of them almost abstract, covering all but the lowest two inches on each page where the text is printed. An afterword tells of the Taino people, who were mostly enslaved and destroyed by the Spanish after Columbus.

382   Mohr, Nicholasa, ret., *The Song of el Coqui and Other Tales of Puerto Rico*, illus. Antonio Martorell, Viking, 1995 (hardcover), ISBN 0–670–85837–4, $15.99, unp. Ages 4 up, grades PS up.

Three folk tales of Puerto Rico, each representing a different segment of the population, the indigenous Tainos, the African people who were brought as slaves, and the conquering Spaniards, who eventually merged with the others to create the present culture of the island. The title story tells of the origin of Boriquen or Puerto Rico. The god Huracan finds the island beautiful, but he is lonely and unhappy, so he creates a million-year storm, then falls asleep. When he awakes, he hears the song "Coqui, coqui," everywhere. In his long search, he discovers it is made by a tiny frog. As he laughs, all the animals begin to sing along, and soon there is music throughout the island. In the second story, "La Guinea, the Stowaway Hen," a guinea hen, terrified by the shots of the slave traders, hides in a basket and is unwittingly transported to Puerto Rico. There, after being chased by a variety of islanders, she comes to the cabin of Don Elias, the mask maker, who sees her striking beauty and treats her kindly, even acquiring a mate for her. The third tale, "La Mula, the Cimarron Mule," is about an overworked and abused mule who escapes her Spanish oppressors with a slave. Together, they make their way to his former home among the

Cimarrones, runaway slaves who live as free people high in the mountains. There, La Mula is treated well and works happily. The striking illustrations covering every page with text overprinted are in brilliant colors, more expressionistic than realistic. Notes at the end explain about the animals and other Spanish words used. For an earlier novel, see *Going Home*, in *This Land Is Our Land* (1994), no. 363.

383 Mora, Pat, ret., *The Race of Toad and Deer*, illus. Maya Itzna Brooks, Orchard, 1995 (hardcover), ISBN 0–531–08777–8, $14.95, unp. Ages 4–8, grades PS–3.

Guatemalan folktale about how clever toad beats much faster deer in a race. With all the jungle watching, Uncle Toad, Tio Sapo, enlists the help of his friends to make Venado, the deer, think he is ahead on the path instead of hopping steadily behind. Confused and exhausted from trying to catch up, Venado approaches the finish line with shaking legs, only to have Sapo hop over first to win. The meaning of the Spanish words used is always clear from context. The brightly colored illustrations, in gouache and casein, are in a semi-primitive style. In *This Land Is Our Land* (1994), a picture-story book by Mora, *A Birthday Basket for Tia*, is no. 365, and a book of poems, *Communion*, is no. 406.

384 Orozco, Jose-Luis, sel., *De Colores and Other Latin-American Folk Songs for Children*, illus. Elisa Kleven, Dutton, 1994 (hardcover), ISBN 0–525–45260–5, $16.99, 56 pp.; Puffin, 1999 (paper), ISBN 0–140–56548–5, $6.99. Ages 4–8, grades PS–3.

Twenty-seven poems, two of them written by the selector but all the others from oral tradition in Mexico, Central, and South America. They include songs for Christmas, birthdays, and other special days, games and finger plays, counting, and nonsense. With the exception of two rhymes, all are accompanied by musical transcription arranged by Orozco. All are given in both Spanish and in English translation, and each is preceded by a short paragraph of explanation describing the meaning of various expressions, how the games are played, and the occasions on which the songs are most likely to be sung. The illustrations are brightly colored, mixed-media collages with decorative strips running down the outside of each page.

385 Pitre, Felix, ret., *Paco and the Witch*, illus. Christy Hale, Lodestar, 1995 (hardcover), ISBN 0–525–67501–9, $13.99, unp. Ages 4–8, grades PS–3.

Puerto Rican folktale of the Rumpelstiltskin type, but with a strong sense of the local culture in both retelling and illustrations. Paco goes to the *bodega* to get the candy his mother has forgotten for the fiesta, but in the heat he stops to rest. An old woman offers him a cool drink, and, although he knows he should not stray from the road, he follows her into the woods to her little house, not realizing that she is a *bruja*, a witch. She makes him gather wood, pick pigeon peas, and fetch water, saying he cannot leave unless he guesses her name. As he weeps beside the river, a crab takes pity on him and tells him the witch's name, *Lampu'a Lentemue*. On his third and last chance, Paco almost forgets the name, but comes out with it on time and is free to run home. The angry witch hunts through the woods for the one who told Paco, accusing first the parrot, then the frog, and at last the crab, who admits he is the one, then scuttles under a rock before she can beat him with her stick. This explains the crab's behavior to this day. The illustrations are bright, slightly cartoon-like, and full of action. Many Spanish words are used, all either defined as they appear or clear from context, but there is also a glossary preceding the story.

386 San Souci, Robert D., ret., *The Little Seven-Colored Horse: A Spanish American Folktale*, illus. Jan Thompson Dicks, Chronicle, 1995 (hardcover), ISBN 0–8118–0412–7, $13.95, unp. Ages 4–10, grades PS–5.

Retelling of a story popular in the Spanish-speaking world and with variants throughout Europe, here set in the illustrations in the Texas–New Mexico area during the late 1700s or early 1800s. A farmer, distraught because something or someone is stealing his corn every night, orders his two eldest sons, Diego and Pedro, to guard the crop. Both fall asleep on the watch, and the *maiz* is eaten. The youngest son, Juanito, although ridiculed, insists on being given a chance, and at midnight captures the culprit, a little horse whose coat seems to be of seven colors that continually change. The horse begs to be let go, promising not to eat corn again and always to help Juanito when he has need. Faced with precarious situations in his quest for fortune in adventures that confront him on land and sea, Juanito several times calls upon the horse, who always saves him, until finally Juanito wins the hand of Maria, the mayor's beautiful daughter, and settles down to splendor. The vibrantly colorful illustrations sweep across the pages, often enclosing the text, and give a vivid sense of the pageantry of the period and the glory of this despised third son's triumph and rise to splendor. A glossary of Spanish terms that appear in the narrative and notes on sources and settings complete the book. Other publications by San Souci include nos. 187, 188, 189, 316, and 317 in *This Land Is Our Land* (1994) (for titles, see entry 155, this book).

9

Hispanic Americans: Books of Poetry

387 Alarcon, Francisco X., *From the Bellybutton of the Moon and Other Summer Poems/Del Ombligo de la Luna y otros poemas de verano: Poems/Poemas*, illus. Maya Christina Gonzalez, Children's Book, 1998 (hardcover), ISBN 0–89239–153–7, $15.95, 32 pp. Ages 4–8, grades PS–3.

Collection of twenty-two short, bilingual poems, successor to *Laughing Tomatoes and Other Spring Poems* (1997; no. 388) and illustrated by the same artist. While the poems in the first book are light, even funny, these are somewhat nostalgic in celebrating the writer's Mexican origins, the landscape of that country, and his relatives as he remembers them from childhood. In the five brief lines of "Morning Yolks," he recalls the shining "suns" his aunt used to place on his plate in the morning. He speaks of his farmer Uncle Vincente resting in his porch rocker after a tough day, still looking forward with gratitude and anticipation to the next morning. He remembers his grandfather teaching his siblings and him the alphabet in Spanish and telling them they had now received the "true keys/to the universe." He speaks of his "bilingual dog" and going barefoot in the grass. The experiences are those that everyone regardless of age can relate to or recall. A couple of poems are extremely short, just one brief image, and two, "Air Wheel" and "Water Wheel," are circular, the ends of the little poems leading right back to the beginnings in the pictorial portrayal. The title of the book (and of two poems) refers to the Aztec name for Mexico City. The bold, dramatic, high-color, poster-like pictures project a splashy quality that enhances the celebratory attitude. Each poem is in both Spanish and English, with, in most instances, the Spanish version being more euphonious and accurate in rhythms than the English version. This is a delightful book, which, although in picture-book format, offers possibilities for pleasure even for those well beyond the picture-book stage.

388 Alarcon, Francisco X., *Laughing Tomatoes and Other Spring Poems/Jitomates Risuenos y otros poemas de primavera*, illus. Maya Christina Gonzalez, Children's Book, 1997 (hardcover), ISBN 0–89239–139–1, $15.95, 32 pp. Ages 4–8, grades PS–3.

Collection of twenty amusing poems, each poem, in almost every case, appearing in English and in Spanish on the same page. Almost all the poems describe growing things or things that occur in nature, like dew, roots, the morning sun, first rain, tomatoes, corn (maiz), and strawberries. Some, like "Cinco de Mayo," celebrate not only the historical triumph but also the products eaten at the modern festival. The poems are light and joyful, mostly very short, filled with images and interesting expressions. Overwhelming them in thought but adding a great deal to the book's fun are full-color, bold, comic pictures, which explode exuberantly around the text and depict characters and situations. Some figures, like a certain cat and dog, reappear from illustration to illustration in various positions and activities. Surrealistic touches add interest, and political, economic, and social commentary appears, for example, on the two pages about strawberries, in which the doublespread picture shows a girl working alongside an adult (of whom only a hand is seen) in a strawberry field. Captions at the bottom of the pages explain Spanish words and phrases used in the poems. In a simple essay aimed at children, Alarcon describes how he came to write poetry.

389 Carlson, Lori Marie, ed., *Barrio Streets Carnival Dreams: Three Generations of Latino Artistry*, Holt, 1996 (hardcover), ISBN 0–8050–4120–6, $15.95, 127 pp. Ages 12 up, grades 7 up.

A collection of various pieces—memoirs, poems, essays, drawings, and photographs—by Hispanic Americans from the early nineteenth through the twentieth century. All are short, many of them excerpts from longer works. The most interesting writings are memoirs, though there are also poems and one Puerto Rican folktale, "The Parrot Who Wouldn't Say 'Catano'," retold by Pura Belpre. Among the poets represented are Raul Nino, David Hernandez, Jaime Manrique, Carlos Cumpian, and Elias Zacklin. The book is divided into three sections: America, Barrio Streets, and Carnival Dreams, in roughly chronological order. The visual art works reproduced are not effective, since the format is small and in black and white, while the originals, according to the descriptions, are mostly in brilliant color. Each section is preceded by an introduction telling something of Latino life in the period, and each piece is introduced by a short note giving biographical information about the artist or writer. This is a scattered sampling rather than a broad overview.

390 Carlson, Lori Marie, ed., *Cool Salsa: Bilingual Poems on Growing Up Latino in the United States*, Holt, 1994 (hardcover), ISBN 0–8050–3135–9, $14.95, 123 pp.; Juniper, 1998 (paper), ISBN 0–4497–0436–X, $4.50. Ages 12 up, grades 7 up.

Anthology of thirty-six poems, all but six of them in both English and Spanish. In cases where a translation is not given, the poems employ a combination of the two languages that is mostly understandable from the context. Although most of them give a flavor of Hispanic or Hispanic-American experience, only six were originally written in Spanish. Almost all are in free verse, and none is in regular rhymed meter. The writers are from a wide variety of countries— Mexico, Puerto Rico, Bolivia, Cuba, Venezuela, and Colombia, among others— as well as a number with a Latino heritage whose families have lived for generations in the United States. Some are well known: Sandra Cisneros, Gary Soto, Amy Castillo, and Pat Mora, for instance. While the poems were not written specifically for children, many are about the writers' childhoods, and they are not too difficult for good readers in later middle school and junior high. A glossary and brief biographical sketches of the poets are included.

391 Cisneros, Sandra, *Loose Woman*, Knopf, 1994 (hardcover), ISBN 0–69–41644–7, $16.00, 115 pp.; Vintage, 1995 (paper), ISBN 0–6797–5527–6, $10.00. Ages 15 up, grades 10 up.

Sixty poems, all in unrhymed, nonmetrical verse, all concerning love from a female point of view. A few are written wholly or partly in Spanish, but in most the meaning of non-English words is clear from context. While some are ethnic-specific, like "Old Maids," which explains why "My cousins and I" do not marry, being "too old by Mexican standards," but actually too aware of what marriage means in a male-dominated culture, more are applicable to women everywhere. Some are obscure, but often an intriguing title gives clues to decipher the meaning, as in "You Bring Out the Mexican in Me," "I Am So Depressed I Feel Like Jumping in the River Behind My House but Won't Because I'm Thirty-Eight and Not Eighteen," and "I Am on My Way to Oklahoma to Bury the Man I Nearly Left My Husband For." In *This Land Is Our Land* (1994), an earlier book of poems, *My Wicked Wicked Ways*, is no. 401, and a book of short stories, *Woman Hollering Creek and Other Stories*, is no. 349.

392 Cruz, Victor Hernandez, Leroy V. Quintana, and Virgil Suarez, eds., *Paper Dance: 55 Latino Poets*, Persea, 1995 (paper), ISBN 0–89255–201–8, $13.95, 242 pp. Ages 12 up, grades 7 up.

Exciting, eclectic, comprehensive anthology of fifty-five Latino and Latina poets, with ethnic origins in Cuba, Colombia, the Dominican Republic, Ecuador, Guatemala, Puerto Rico, and Mexico, arranged in alphabetical order by poet. Almost every poet is represented by at least two poems, most of which are one or two pages long. They range from sophisticated, esoteric pieces better for mature readers to perhaps equally sophisticated but more easily apprehensible work. Most make their point intelligibly and forcefully and then stop. The collection opens with Francisco Alarcon's touching "Shame," in which he presents himself (perhaps remembers himself?) as a boy attempting to wash the brownness from his skin before leaving for school. The short, one- or two-word lines catch the emotion of alienness that is too frequently echoed elsewhere in the collection, belonging to neither culture completely and feeling denigrated by the Anglo. Alarcon's second poem, "L.A. Prayer," deplores the 1992 street violence, in another minimalist description of anguish. The book's last two poems, Rafael Zepeda's "Pony" and "Trans Pacific," continue the somber tone but in more explicit detail, with the first offering an account of a drug dealer, who has been "At the end of the earth, man," and the other a conversation on board a ship during the Vietnam conflict, when a shipmate refers to all Mexicans as "lazy." In addition to tackling stereotypes of Hispanics and examining bicultural experiences, family, friends, school experiences, romance, religion, migrant fieldwork, and the barrio, a myriad of other matters are taken up, many of them nonethnic in stance. Humor is not absent, as for instance in Gina Valdez's "English Con Salsa," about learning English; Leo Romero's "Marilyn Monroe Indian"; and the delightfully rueful "Nobody Knows My Name" by Gustavo Perez Firmat, in which he says he is tired "of getting mail addressed/to all those people I never was" because the addressers never spell his names right. The structures are free, rhythms vary, and the pulsating Afro-Cuban/Caribbean rhythms of Adrian Castro's two poems, "Pulling the Muse from the Drum" and "Herald of Cocos (I)," are enough to send readers back for more. Adding to the book's value are short biographical sketches of the poets. For other books by Suarez, see *Iguana Dreams* and *Latin Jazz*, nos. 371 and 382 in *This Land Is Our Land* (1994).

393 Cumpian, Carlos, *Latino Rainbow: Poems About Latino Americans*, illus. Richard Leonard, Children's, 1994 (hardcover), ISBN 0–516–05153–9, $21.95, 48 pp. Ages 6 up, grades 1 up.

Twenty poems about a page each in length that introduce "the rich heritage of U.S. Latino culture and history" through describing the contributions of major Latino-American figures, most of them recent or contemporary. Included are Louis Agassiz, naturalist; Luis Alvarez, Nobel Prize–winning physicist; Dr. Hector Perez Garcia, civil rights organizer; Ritchie Valens, singer and songwriter; Cesar Chavez, labor organizer; Joan Baez, singer and civil rights activist; Roberto Clemente, baseball player; Antonia Coelho Novello, U.S. Surgeon General; Henry Cisneros, political leader; and Ellen Ochoa, astronaut. One poem deals with a historical event, the Treaty of Guadalupe Hidalgo, and several discuss the collective endeavors and bravery of the California rancheros and Cuban- and Central-American refugees. The poems are prosy, little essays rather than proper, free-verse, rhythmical poems, but they speak clearly and forcefully of the figures' roles and can serve as a valuable avenue to learning about these figures for both Latinos and non-Latinos. Each poem is augmented by a striking, expressive, full-color, full-page portrait, which, taken together, make this a very attractive coffee-table addition to any home reading center and an enticing reading-table volume in school or public library. Spanish words appearing in the poems are translated at the bottom of the page, and a glossary of words and terms concludes the book.

394 Espada, Martin, ed., *El Coro: A Chorus of Latino and Latina Poetry*, Univ. of Massachusetts Press, 1998 (hardcover), ISBN 1–55849–110–4, $30.00, 166 pp.; 1997 (paper), ISBN 1–55849–111–2, $14.95. Ages 12 up, grades 7 up.

Anthology of 100 poems (some in both Spanish and English) by forty-three poets of Hispanic descent from throughout the Western Hemisphere, either born here or arrived here at an early age, "with a special focus on Latino writers living in New England, particularly in Massachusetts and Connecticut." The poets (slightly fewer than half are women) are arranged in alphabetical order. Most poems are free in form, and a few are prose poems. Themes that appear are those that frequently inform Latino/a poetry—loss of homeland and language, yearning for homeland, culture shock, culture erosion, family, assertion of female validity in a machismo culture, poverty, gangs, alienation, and a welfare system that either cannot or refuses to understand the needs and problems of the poor. In their ways, all the poems celebrate Hispanic life and culture, but some tackle other matters, too, for example, going to college, the artistry of a wood sculptor, fishing, and baseball (the poem printed in the form of a diamond, with the excitement cleverly contained in the broader part of the diamond as it faces the reader: "Bases Loaded" by Gloria Vando). Most of the poets are otherwise also anthologized, but collectively they present a chorus or choir (hence the title, *El Coro*) of Hispanic-American poetic voices at the end of the twentieth century. Among the poets represented are Clemente Solo Velez (a Puerto Rican imprisoned for his role in the island Independence Movement), Gary Soto, Dionisio D. Martinez, Victor Cruz, Jack Agueros, Judith Ortiz Cofer, Pat Mora, Sandra Cisneros, Ana Castillo, Pedro Adorno, and Ray Gonzalez. Some of the poems are obscure, and the characteristic Latin surrealism marks many pieces; tones vary from the sad and wistful to angry and polemic, since typically the poets tend to think along political lines, to downright funny, but on the whole the attitudes are serious. Biographical information appears at the end.

395 Espada, Martin, *Imagine the Angels of Bread: Poems*, Norton, 1996 (hardcover), ISBN 0–393–03916–1, $18.95, 107 pp.; 1997 (paper), ISBN 0–393–31686–6, $11.00. Ages 12 up, grades 7 up.

Thirty-six poems varying in length from one-half page to the final and longest one of nine pages, which pays tribute to Clemente Soto Velez, the Puerto Rican poet and political figure, who was imprisoned for advocating independence for Puerto Rico. Politics, justice for the poor, the powerless, immigrants, and workers, violence, deplorable living conditions, greedy landlords, and similar issues occupy the poet's mind in these concisely worded, sharply visual, pithily expressed, not-afraid-to-tell-it-like-he-sees-it pieces, which are sprinkled with Spanish words. His own home life occupies his thoughts in some poems: his grandfather in a nursing home, "hunched and palsied," the old man's mind addled from drink and disease; and his son lying near death from pneumonia at six days of life in a hospital emergency. Remembered scenes form the substance of other poems: "Cada Puerco Tiene Su Sabado" (Every Pig Has His Saturday), in which he remembers a family pig roast; "Rednecks," in which a farmer kisses a woman's terribly scarred face, while the poet pumps gas into his pickup and checks his oil; and "Public School 190, Brooklyn 1963," in which he recalls how the children are herded onto buses on the day Kennedy is shot. Most of the poems are free, but several are more tightly knit, and one is a villanelle, "The Prisoners of Saint Lawrence," about the "island men" (Puertoriquenos) incarcerated in a New York State prison. Other political poems that are especially memorable include "Huelga" (strike), which lists ways that Cesar Chavez helped Latino Americans, and "Sing in the Voice of a God Even Atheists Can Hear," which celebrates the courage and activism of Demetria Martinez, also a poet, who was prosecuted for assisting in the sanctuary movement. While most of the poems require experience for appreciation, those readers who are dedicated to poetry, have an understanding of history, or have a feel for current events, as well as a love for what can be done with language, will appreciate them at the junior high and early high school levels. Espada has also published *City of Coughing and Dead Radiators* (1993).

396 Gonzalez, Ray, ed., *Currents from the Dancing River: Contemporary Latino Fiction, Nonfiction, and Poetry*, Harcourt, 1994 (hardcover), ISBN 0–15–123654–2, $26.95, 573 pp.; Harvest, 1994 (paper), ISBN 0–15–600130–6, $15.05. Ages 14 up, grades 9 up.

Large anthology of prose and poetry by Latino/a writers living and writing today in the United States and speaking on a broad range of contemporary Latino/a concerns. Of the some 130 selections (short stories, excerpts from novels, essays mostly of personal experience, a few stories from oral tradition, and poems), seventy-nine are poems. (The short fiction is discussed in no. 324 in this book.) Most of the poems are short, free, and unpatterned, with subtle rhythms and vivid images, but a few cover several pages. Miguel Pinero contributes "On the Day They Buried My Mother" and "This Is Not the Place Where I Was Born," in speaking about the changes in Puerto Rico that have taken place. Albert Rios says that he has seen "The Vietnam Wall," which is like "a scar / Into the skin of the ground," and in quite a different attitude, ruefully, almost cynically, offers a "Psalm for Your Image" to God, who he says must have a "cigarette cough" since he gave the Indians tobacco and made humans in his image. Humorously, Victor Hernandez Cruz has a campesino (worker) remarking that the "Problem with Hurricanes" is not the wind but flying mangoes and other fruits. Francisco Alarcon's "Sonnets of Dark Love" are filled with provocative imagery and allusions, and Sandra Maria Esteves's "Mambo Love Poem" glides, flows, and hesitates like the mambo cha-cha its rhythms imitate. Luis J. Rodriguez's voice is furious with anger as he speaks "To the police officer who refused to sit in the same room as my son because he's a 'gang' member" (this is the poem's title), and Miguel Algarin describes present-day "Taos Pueblo Indians: 700 strong according to Bobby's last census" (this is the poem's title), and Martin Espada talks about "The Other Alamo," in the San Antonio of 1990. Some of the poems are obscure in meaning and demand a sophisticated, dedicated reader, but most are apprehensible with attention, and the best of them are well worth the effort. Gonzalez has also published an anthology of Latino poets and a collection of his own poetry, both of which are described in *This Land Is Our Land* (1994), nos. 104 and 405 respectively, and an anthology of short fiction, no. 355 in the same book.

397 Gonzalez, Ray, ed., *Touching the Fire: Fifteen Poets of Today's Latino Renaissance*, Anchor, 1998 (paper), ISBN 0–385–4782–3, $12.95, 304 pp. Ages 12 up, grades 7 up.

Comprehensive anthology of fifteen contemporary Latino/a poets, seven of them women, whom the editor regards as "key factors in the larger gains Latino literature has made over the last twenty years." He thinks they have also "changed the course of American writing forever" through "emphasizing poetry as the sound of everyday life." Each poet is represented by ten poems, which constitute a "mini-book" for each and which, Gonzalez says, "amplifies the style and voice of each poet," unlike most anthologies, in which the poets are represented by perhaps two or three pieces. All reveal "a confidence of language in its many forms, a gift for shattering, emotional honesty, and an ear for the rhythms of a vibrant culture." Gonzalez has aptly described this anthology—a range of ideas, voices, and concerns set forth in language that is sure and deft, in most instances, although a few are overly sophisticated, even pretentious, or fail to make the intended point clearly or soon enough. The poets can be found in other anthologies—Judith Ortiz Cofer, Victor Hernandez Cruz, Martin Espada, Juan Herrera, Diana Garcia, Gonzalez himself—but seldom with such a scope of offerings, since in most other anthologies the selections are the couple of poems for which the writer has come to be known. The main concerns here are those that occupy other Latino/a poets—home, family, heritage, continuation of culture, the culture clash, political matters, like the "disappeared," refugees, and the wars in Nicaragua, religion, church, machismo, love, sex, music, and so on. The importance of this collection is that it does just what Gonzalez says it does: brings together enough work by each of these important writers so that the reader/listener can get a good feel for the poets' skills and concerns. Gonzalez has also published *After Aztlan, Twilights and Chants*, and *Mirrors Beneath the Earth*, nos. 404, 405, and 355 in *This Land Is Our Land* (1994).

398 Kanellos, Nicolas, ed., *Hispanic American Literature: A Brief Introduction and Anthology*, HarperCollins, 1995 (paper), ISBN 0–673–46956–5, $19.95, 339 pp. Ages 14 up, grades 9 up.

Anthology of fiction (see no. 332) and poetry by Hispanic Americans of different ethnic backgrounds, with a few autobiographical selections and a play, in the HarperCollins Literary Mosaic Series, of which Ishmael Reed is general editor, intended primarily for college classes. The book includes a history of Hispanic-American writing and a short list of additional works of interest. Each poet's section is preceded by a short introduction that gives biographical information about the writer, predominant themes or interests, and some other titles. Of the nineteen poets represented, arranged by order of birth, eight are Puerto Rican American, eight are Mexican American, and three are Cuban American. Gloria Vando opens the set with a scathing indictment of the Spaniards who invaded Taino territory and obliterated the Indians in "Legend of the Flamboyan," while near the end of the set, Martin Espada, a Puerto Rican American about twenty years younger, speaks of how "The Spanish conquered / with iron and words" in "Colibri," two examples of the anti-conquest theme that often appears in minority writing. Represented also is Miguel Algarin, the Puerto Rican American noted for influencing Hispanic-American letters by providing opportunities for minority poets to perform, a factor that contributed to the strong oral quality of Hispanic-American poetry. This strong orality is evident is his own poetry, for example, "Taos Pueblo Indians," in which the jumble of activity and noise in that ancient pueblo popular with Anglo tourists can be heard as well as visualized. Angela de Hoyas (Mexico) reveals her strong political/feminist bent in "Lesson in Semantics," an anti-macho and anti-male diatribe. Pablo Medina (Cuba) presents the United States as a great whore in "Madame America," and Tato Laviera (Puerto Rico) coins a new term for his generation in "AmeRican." Not all poems are angry, politically motivated, or pessimistic, however; Victor Cruz Hernandez (Puerto Rico) contributes the lightly satirical "The Latest Latin Dance Craze," and Gustavo Perez-Firmat's (Cuba) hilarious "Lime Cure" describes how his life seems to be taken over by limes.

399 Martinez, Dionisio D., *Bad Alchemy*, Norton, 1995 (hardcover), ISBN 0–393–03733–9, $17.95, 109 pp. Ages 14 up, grades 9 up.

A collection of thirty-eight poems by a Cuban-American writer with wide-ranging subject matter—Carl Sandburg, Thoreau, Ed Sullivan and other icons of popular culture, Jackson Pollock, and Michelangelo, for example. Several involve the death of his father. Some are about love and loss. The final poem is about his childhood memory of the revolution, about the newspapers with large blank squares on nearly every page, not a triumph of the people but, with the constantly dwindling rations, too little coffee for his parents. Some of the poems are obscure, but there are moving images of a displaced person, of one who, no matter where he goes, will always "carry foreign currency." None of the poems is in rhymed, tight metrical form, but almost all have pattern and pleasing rhythm.

400 Milligan, Bryce, Mary Guerrero Milligan, and Angela de Hoyos, eds., *Daughters of the Fifth Sun: A Collection of Latina Fiction and Poetry*, Riverhead, 1995 (hardcover), ISBN 1–57322–009–4, $23.95, 284 pp. Ages 12 up, grades 7 up.

Anthology of fifteen poems, two of which are translated, and seventeen short stories by thirty-two contemporary Latina writers (no. 342), "a floricanto offering—the truth of the Latina experience as it is best expressed in fiction and in poetry." Most of the poems are short, but a few go to six or seven pages. The pieces speak of love, religion, ethnic experiences, home, family, food, loss, hope, longings, loneliness, sadness, social problems—a broad span of concerns as seen through women's eyes and recorded as an expression of their emotion. "Night Vigil," by Evangelina Vigil-Pinon, re-creates the night as it describes inward and outward night-watching and night-musings, the "solitude, darkness, quiet" that envelop the speaker and reader/listener; Nicole Pollentier speaks of the "boy with wedgewood eyes" in "Ryan, Thanks for the Offer," a poem that moves as a kind of round; Lorna Dee Cervantes speaks ruefully and angrily of bananas that rot and workers displaced when big business gobbles up fields in "Bananas"; "Dear World," by Alma Luz Villanueva, is a prayer at early morning in gratitude for safety and sufficiency compared to that of the unfortunates in other parts of the world; and Angela de Hoyos celebrates the poetic process, the end being the xochitl, the flower-poem in "Xochitl-Poem: For Paul Perry, Joseph Booker, and the Palo Alto Writers Guild." Verses are free, voices are clear, some poems are narrative, some lyrical, all effective in their ways. A fine foreword, excellent introduction about Latina writing, and notes on the contributors enhance the book's value.

401 Milligan, Bryce, Mary Guerrero Milligan, and Angela de Hoyos, eds., ¡Floricanto Si!: A Collection of Latina Poetry, Penguin, 1998 (paper), ISBN 0–14–058893–0, $14.95, 310 pp. Ages 14 up, grades 9 up.

Anthology of 131 poems, a few in both Spanish and English, by forty-seven contemporary Latina poets from various Western Hemisphere, Hispanic-ethnic backgrounds. The editors indicate that the "term 'floricanto,' which literally translates as flower-and-song, is the Spanish equivalent of the Nahuatl compound meaning poetry" and is "laden with powerful mythic, aesthetic, and political associations, both ancient and modern." The authors of the poems, mostly one page in length and free verse in form, inform these associations, drawing some of their material from myth and legend, continuing the rich, ancient practice of employing colorful nature imagery, and using their poems as an avenue for political and human rights commentary, a practice that is especially strong among Latinos/as. Other topics involve identity, family, cultural and national realities, the world and condition of women, religion and church, and history. The selections vary in tone and attitude, mostly serious, some playful, some funny ("Una pequena contribucion" (sic) by Miriam Bornstein), and some pointed and cynical ("Aliens" by Pina Pipino), and some play with form ("La Buena Pastora: The Good Shepherdess" by Pat Mora). Bilingualism is frequent as the poets move from Spanish to English and back again, and a few Meso-American words from Aztec and Maya appear. A fine introduction on Latina poetry opens the book, and closing it are a glossary of Spanish terms and phrases and notes on historical figures and on the contributors. Here are eloquent voices, among the finest in Hispanic-American letters, who are giving the world of literature much fine reading.

402 Mora, Pat, *Agua Santa: Holy Water*, Beacon, 1995 (hardcover), ISBN 0–8070–6828–4, $17.95, 130 pp.; Beacon, 1997 (paper), ISBN 0–8070–6829–2, $11.00, 160 pp. Ages 14 up, grades 9 up.

Fifty-two sensitive poems, mostly short, divided into six sections, all having to do with water in some form: Old Sea, Rivers, Descent, Where We Were Born, What Falls from the Sky, and Wondrous Wetness. Some of them are about childhood memories, some about the concerns of being a woman. One section, Where We Were Born, is a cleverly revisionist retelling of ancient myths and folk traditions, Aztec and other Mexican, including Christian. A few are about current events or official attitudes, often deeply ironic but not polemic. Others celebrate the beauty of the world and of friendships. Only a few employ rhyme and regular meter, but all are rhythmic and many have striking images. Although some are obscure, despite helpful notes at the end, most are not too difficult for motivated high school students. The occasional Spanish words are mostly understandable from context. In *This Land Is Our Land* (1994), *Communion*, no. 406, is an earlier book of poems by Mora, and *A Birthday Basket for Tia*, no. 365, is a picture-story book.

403 Mora, Pat, *Aunt Carmen's Book of Practical Saints*, Beacon, 1997 (hardcover), ISBN 0–807–07206–0, $20.00, 128 pp.; Beacon, 1999 (paper), ISBN 0–807–07207–9, $17.50. Ages 12 up, grades 7 up.

Thirty-two charming, accessible poems, each directed to a saint or saints by an old woman who cleans the church. The poems are in a wide variety of forms, from free verse and songs ("Saint Pascal Baylon") to simply-rhymed quatrains ("Saint Martin of Porres") to intricate poetic patterns, among them the sonnet ("Saint Joseph"), the sestina ("Saint Gertrude the Great"), the villanelle ("Saint Isidore the Farmer"), and many other variations. One ("The Visitation") is an example of concrete poetry, with the lines arranged on the page in the shape of a pregnant woman's profile. All are handled with skill. Tone varies from devout to fond to scolding to humorous, as eighty-year-old Carmen dusts the statues and talks to her favorites, often complaining about the priests, changes from the Latin service, her aging husband, her sore knees. What emerges is not only a review of the great variety of qualities venerated in the persons of saints but also a picture of a wise and loving old woman who knows and admits her own faults and stubbornly continues her work with naive but genuine understanding. Notes at the end give helpful information about the lives and feast days of the saints. The book is illustrated with photographs of paintings and statues, mostly from the Museum of International Folk Art at the Museum of New Mexico. In

This Land Is Our Land (1994), *A Birthday Basket for Tia*, no. 365, is a picture-story book by Mora, and *Communion*, no. 406, is a book of poetry.

404 Mora, Pat, *Confetti: Poems for Children*, illus. Enrique O. Sanchez, Lee & Low, 1996 (hardcover), 1–8800–0025–3, $15.95, unp.; Lee & Low, 1999 (paper), ISBN 1–8800–0085–7, $6,95. Ages 4 up, grades PS up.

Thirteen short poems about things that occur in a child's ordinary life. Several have regular rhyme, among them "Cloud Dragons" and "Abuelita's Lap." Some others get their rhythm from repetition, as in "Sun Song," where each line ends either "sun's first song" or "morning song," and "Can I, Can I Catch the Wind," in which each line starts with a repetition of the title, and "I Hear, I Hear," with every line starting, "I hear" and every other line repeating "pom, pom." Others are in unpatterned free verse like "Purple Snake," about a wood carver who wakes the animals that he "found asleep in a piece of wood." All are simple but show sensitivity to sounds and image. The frequent Spanish words are re-peated in a glossary at the end. Illustrations are full-page heavily bordered acrylic paintings, predominantly in shades of purple, gold, and orange, with the text printed in blocks of color on the facing pages. In *This Land Is Our Land* (1994), *A Birthday Basket for Tia*, no. 365, is a picture-story book by Mora, and *Communion*, no. 406, is a book of poetry.

405 Mora, Pat, *The Desert Is My Mother: El Desierto Es Mi Madre*, illus. Daniel Lechon, Arte Publico, 1994 (hardcover), ISBN 1–558–85121–6, $14.95, unp. Ages 4–8, grades PS–3.

Highly illustrated poem in both English and Spanish, telling in simple lan-guage the joys, terrors, and benefits of living in desert country. Each text page has the English printed on light green and below it the Spanish on golden-yellow, all enclosed in a varicolored frame, with the illustration on the facing page, mostly with a little dark-haired girl experiencing whatever is described. In these, also, frames are used, with some of the scenes, like that of lightning and dark storm clouds, mounted on a larger, gold-colored oblong, with the child standing partly outside the painting. Other borders employ Southwestern motifs. At the end the poem is reprinted in free-verse couplets in both languages. In *This Land Is Our Land* (1994), no. 365, *A Birthday Basket for Tia*, is a picture-story book by Mora, and *Communion*, no. 406, is a book of poetry.

406 Mora, Pat, *Listen to the Desert/Oye al desierto*, illus. Francisco X. Mora, Clarion, 1994 (hardcover), ISBN 0–395–67292–9, $14.95, unp. Ages 3–8, grades PS–3.

Bilingual poem describing noises of the desert and its animals in lines each starting, "Listen to," repeated to form a couplet in English, then in Spanish. "Listen to the toad / hop, plop, plop, plop." The noises are slightly different in the two languages: "plop" becomes "currucu," the mouse's "scrrt, scrrt" be-comes "criic, criic." The result is a quiet poem with a simple but compelling rhythm, having the effect of breath held to hear the slightest sound. The watercolor illustrations are also deceptively simple, looking almost like cut-paper collages in mostly primary colors, each bordered at the base with a repeated southwestern pattern. More than an English verse with an accompanying translation, this is a poem genuinely conceived bilingually. See also *A Birthday Basket for Tia* and *Communion*, nos. 365 and 406 in *This Land Is Our Land* (1994).

407 Mora, Pat, *This Big Sky*, illus. Steve Jenkins, Scholastic, 1998 (hardcover), ISBN 0–590–37120–7, $15.95, unp. Ages 5–9, grades K–4.

Fourteen poems of the natural world in the Southwest—the landscape, the animals, the weather. Only two of the brief poems have regular rhyme, but all are rhythmical, often using repetition to good effect. Images are especially striking: the horned lizard is a "bellybulge pincushion," the raccoon "pours / herself headfirst into her dark / safe hole." Frequent use of Spanish words is simplified for the English-speaking reader by a pronouncing glossary at the end. The cut-paper collage illustrations are striking, making this an unusually lovely book. In *This Land Is Our Land* (1994), no. 365, *A Birthday Basket for Tia*, is a picture-story by Mora, and *Communion*, no. 406, is a book of poetry.

408 Mora, Pat, *Uno, Dos, Tres: One, Two, Three*, illus. Barbara Lavallee, Clarion, 1996 (hardcover), ISBN 0–395–67294–5, $14.95, unp. Ages 2–8, grades PS–3.

Rhyming counting book, giving numbers up to ten in both Spanish and English. Two little girls go through a Mexican market buying gifts for their mother's birthday. Each number is introduced with a line that rhymes: "dos two Two doves that say coo-coo." At intervals the numbers are repeated in both languages to reinforce the memory. At the end the author adds a note about the lively, colorful markets in border towns and a pronunciation guide, which should help non–Spanish-speaking adults reading the book aloud. Illustrations are watercolor paintings in bright, striking shades, depicting the variety and zest of the market. Another lively bilingual picture-story book by Mora is *Delicious Hullabaloo/Pachanga deliciosa* (1998), about a fiesta prepared by armadillos, lizards, bees, and birds, described in quatrains rhymed in both English and Spanish. In *This Land Is Our Land* (1994), no. 365, *A Birthday Basket for Tia*, is a picture-story book by Mora, and *Communion*, no. 406, is a book of poetry.

409 Orozco, Jose-Luis, sel., *De Colores and Other Latin-American Folk Songs for Children*, illus. Elisa Kleven, Dutton, 1994 (hardcover), ISBN 0–525–45260–5, $16.99, 56 pp.; Puffin, 1999 (paper), ISBN 0–140–56548–5, $6.99. Ages 4–8, grades PS–3.   See entry 384.

410 Ortiz Cofer, Judith, *Reaching for the Mainland and Selected New Poems*, Bilingual, 1995 (paper), ISBN 0–927534–55–X, $9.00, 77 pp. Ages 11 up, grades 6 up.

Fifty-nine, brief, free-verse, short-lined poems of reflection and observation, mostly one page in length. Some treat of her Puerto Rican heritage or background, others of the progress to the United States, while many describe her parents or facets of her family life. Rhythms are subtle, and a ruminative, remembering tone can often be heard. Word pictures are plentiful; for example, she tenderly likens her grandmother's cheek to having lines "like a map to another time" ("Visiting La Abuela"), and on arriving in the United States, she and those traveling with her are "expelled / like fetuses" from the airplane's belly in "Arrival." Some are more sensory, like "Returning from the Maya Ruins," which describes the persona's driving through the night in a town in the Yucatan. The poem exudes the smells of the recent rain, the damp tropical earth, and heaps of trash and concludes by drawing a wry comparison between these sleepy modern-day Maya and their ambitious, accomplished ancestors. The opening poem, "They Say," tells of her own birth, as she remembers it described by "they," those who were there. Other poems speak of the church confessional, fruit vendors, an old mule, who gives his opinion about loyalty, a Caribbean island, which is called a "fat whore lolling," and her mother dancing in the dark to a record playing, while her father is in the Pacific in the service. This is a pleasing, consistent collection, not musical, but vivid, impressive, and often arresting. For other books by Puerto Rico-born Ortiz Cofer, see *The Line of the Sun*, no. 367 (fiction), and *Triple Crown* and *Terms of Survival*, nos. 403 and 407 (poems), in *This Land Is Our Land* (1994).

411 Soto, Gary, *Canto familiar*, illus. Annika Nelson, Harcourt, 1995 (hardcover), ISBN 0–15–200067–4, $17.00, 79 pp. Ages 8 up, grades 3 up.

Twenty-six short-lined, uncomplicated free-verse poems of one to three pages in length about various childhood activities, feelings, and thoughts, many in a family context. While some are ethnic specific, most transcend national origins and speak eloquently and often humorously of matters of concern to most children. The book's title is apt—the poems sing in celebration of the small, familiar things of life. They celebrate parents and grandparents, teachers, and playmates. They examine such common childhood activities as putting one's shoes on the wrong feet to see what happens, misplacing one's eyeglasses, and giving oneself stars for those times when one does not achieve, like spilling milk and not picking up socks, to balance out those one receives for success in school. In a poem both humorous and poignant, the speaker laments having to go to school after locking plastic handcuffs about his wrists and not being able to find the key. Taking ballet lessons, entertaining a baby brother, ironing clothes, and putting up with an exuberant kitten are matters that occupy other poems. Some Spanish words and phrases appear but can be easily understood from context. Full-page, colorful, woodcut-like illustrations picture situations and people and give the book visual as well as auditory attractiveness. This varied, pleasing, skillful collection consistently offers surprises and pleasures and is a worthy companion to the writer's earlier books of poetry for young readers, *Neighborhood Odes*, and *Who Will Know Us?*, described in *This Land Is Our Land* (1994), nos. 409A and 409B.

412   Soto, Gary, *Junior College*, Chronicle, 1997 (hardcover), ISBN 0–8118–1541–2, $22.95, 83 pp.; (paper), ISBN 0–8118–1543–9, $12.95. Ages 12 up, grades 7 up.

Delightfully entertaining, varied collection of forty-nine poems by a leading Hispanic-American poet, few of which are ethnic specific and most of which are light or even downright funny. Many involve remembered scenes at home, as in "Inferior Dog," about the old dog he dearly loves but acknowledges is not the equal intellectually or athletically of his friends' dogs; about the house with his mother in "Guilt and the Iron Lung"; with his brothers, who think he has "evolved" (strayed from his roots) too much in "Evolved People"; or in "Phone Calls," in which he is threatened and worries about the car lingering in the street outside. The most memorable set of poems appears in the last half of the book, where the poems that give the book its title appear. These contain remembered scenes from his days in junior college, for the most part amusing pictures of activity or discussions in different classes, professors, reactions to subject matter, searching for his academic niche, doing odd jobs for spending money, and awareness of his growing sexuality. In "Pompeii and the Uses of Our Imagination," he does what his history professor suggests and allows his imagination to carry him away, to ancient times and to various other places that insist on intruding. In "Statistics," an informal survey indicates the truth of the professor's statement that "Virginity is on the decline." He puts on "Starchy Clothes" and uncomfortably attends a string-quartet concert for extra credit for Music Appreciation, and while he takes "The Essay Examination for What You Have Read in the Course World Religions," his attention strays to the window through which he sees "Two dudes smoking joints, / Yukking it up," while inside his teacher is reading the sports page and he and his classmates "suffered." Soto writes with engaging wit, an accurate eye for detail, and a good understanding of how to make poetry say something of value and entertain at the same time. For other books by Soto, see *This Land Is Our Land* (1994), nos. 376, 377, 378, 379, and 380 (all fiction), and 409A and 409B (poems) (for titles, see entry 355, this book).

413   Soto, Gary, *New and Selected Poems*, Chronicle, 1995 (paper), ISBN 0–8118–0758–4, $12.95, 177 pp. Ages 12 up, grades 7 up.

Rich collection of 119 poems, ninety-six selected from previously published collections, among them *The Elements of San Joaquin* (1977), *The Tale of Sunlight* (1978), *Where Sparrows Work Hard* (1981), and *Black Hair* (1985), and twenty-three more in *Super-Eight Movies* (1996). Mostly short, although a few, like "The Elements of San Joaquin," extend over several pages, tidily constructed with subtle rhythms and skillful repetitions, the poems celebrate the area and society, personal and larger, that have informed the Hispanic-American poet's life. The poems are highly concrete, drawing for images upon the geographical region and upon people in his family and acquaintance. "The Elements of San Joaquin" gives a visual and atmospheric sense of the valley in which Fresno, Soto's hometown, stands: the dirt of the grape fields, the drying winds, the red ants, tumbleweed, sparrows, night stars, the hot sun, the misty fogs, and the "onions that are unplugged from their sleep." He talks about sweethearts, pals, his father dead at an early age, the loss of his grandfather, and his grandmother, her face "streaked/From cutting grapes." Soto talks of the barrio torn down for better things that never materialize in "Braley Street"; the sexual activity initiated in "At the Cantina" and in "Catalina Trevino Is Really from Heaven"; attending a baseball game in "Black Hair," in which in his heart and mind he becomes one with the star; early marriage in "Fair Trade"; memories of being five years old in "Waterwheel"; having a roaring good time in "Drinking in the Sixties"; and the fun of exploring a conglomeration of wares in the amusing "Ode to the Yard Sale." Filled with surprises, not a dud in the lot, these poems offer much good reading, readily accessible, not unsophisticated, but never pretentious. Introducing the volume is an essay by Soto that gives valuable background for the poems. Earlier publications are described in *This Land Is Our Land* (1994), nos. 376, 377, 378, 379, and 380 (fiction), and nos. 409A and 409B (poems) (for titles, see entry 355, this book).

414 Suarez, Virgil, *You Come Singing*, Tia Chucha, 1998 (paper), ISBN 1–882688–19–8, $10.95, 103 pp. Ages 12 up, grades 7 up.

Forty euphonious, emotionally moving, skillfully composed poems by a Cuban-American writer, who speaks of his memories of living in Cuba, Spain, Los Angeles, and Florida, where he now makes his home, and of the immigrant experience. The poems are mostly short and easily understood on at least the surface level, sometimes sad, sometimes angry, occasionally wry, and often nostalgic for what once was and might have been. Rhythms of the free-verse pieces vary, sometimes subtle or even seemingly lacking in rhythm, sometimes in guitar rhythms or conga movement. He speaks often of family matters, and occasionally of observed family matters, as in poems that take place in a Florida hospital. He speaks of getting beaten up in a Los Angeles school because he looks different and knows little English; of political repression in Cuba, of the abiding love of his parents for each other, she who worked in a sweatshop in Los Angeles, he who was a pattern cutter and listens to Cuban music; of his little daughter complaining of his "stinky" feet; of making up sins to satisfy the nuns in the family; of cruising Los Angeles streets; of trying to explain to his daughter that people who leave are not necessarily gone forever; of a wood sculptor at work—a wide variety of interesting poems that cast light on their subjects and human nature. Suarez has also published *Iguana Dreams* and *Latin Jazz*, nos. 371 and 382 in *This Land Is Our Land* (1994).

415 Velasquez, Gloria L., *I Used to Be a Superwoman*, illus. Jose Antonio Burciaga, Brandi Trevino, and Robert John Velasquez Trevino, Arte Publico, 1997 (paper), ISBN 1–558–85191–7, $8.95, 126 pp. Ages 14 up, grades 9 up.

Thirty-five poems, most of them in both Spanish and English, though a few are in English only with occasional Spanish words understandable by context. These verses describe growing up Chicana in poverty, her overworked mother, her alcoholic father, her brother killed in Vietnam, her ambition, her feeling of displacement at Stanford University, and some of her friends. There is no indication of whether these verses were first written in Spanish or English, though she does mention in the acknowledgment paragraph problems in translation. Although some of the poems suffer from polemics and there are few striking images, all are full of energy and reflect the determination and difficulties of a woman breaking from a cultural tradition without giving up the heritage.

416 Zamora, Bernice, *Releasing Serpents*, Bilingual Press, 1994 (paper), ISBN 0–927534–39–8, $11.00, 116 pp. Ages 14 up, grades 9 up.

Eighty-eight poems by a Hispanic-American poet, some previously published in *Restless Serpents* (1976), short one-page, single-idea, tightly constructed, meticulous but not pretentiously so, pieces on a range of subjects, some being women's concerns (but not complaining or whiny), Chicano/a activism, and the illogical behavior and attitudes of Anglos. She is particularly good at giving scenes and moments life, often in haiku-like compression. Such devices as unusual juxtapositions and transpositions of words and using nouns as verbs arrest the reader, forcing thought, while including Spanish commentary within the English lines, or at times double-coding, makes the reader recall the poet's orientation as an educated, American-born Latina. She remarks acidly that "money-changers" are the "gringos' " religious guides; she recalls her first kiss, after which her mother and teacher shame her, but no one reproves the boy; "Restless Serpents" and "Moctezuma's Treasure" hark back to the pre-conquest, glory days; the fieldworker Hispanics' lot occupies her in "Metaphor and Reality," where the bosses exist on "your children's bones." Although there is levity, on the whole the collection is serious. Some Spanish-language poems appear, but most are in English. Those students who appreciate poetry and find satisfaction in writing their own will find much to intrigue them in this collection.

10

Native-American Indians: Books of Fiction

417 Ackerman, Ned, *Spirit Horse*, Scholastic, 1998 (hardcover), ISBN 0–590–39650–1, $15.95, 170 pp. Ages 8–13, grades 3–8.

Historical novel of survival and a boy's growing up, set on the American Plains in the 1770s. Running Crane, a Siksika Blackfoot Indian youth of about fourteen, has been living with his mother and her new husband among the Kainaa Blackfoot. Diffident and poor at riding, he is often the butt of jokes, especially from slightly older, bullying Weasel Rider. Along with Weasel Rider, he rides south with warrior Wolf Eagle and nine other men to steal horses from Snake Indians. Each boy dreams of capturing the Snakes' famous, giant-sized, blue-gray stallion, called the spirit horse for his speed and proud, unyielding nature. When the raid on the Snake village fails, Running Crane is separated from the group. He eludes the Snake dogs and slowly makes his way northward toward Kainaa territory, having various adventures along the way. He spots the spirit horse running loose, trails the stallion, and pens him in a ravine. He tames the powerful creature and is finally able to mount and ride, careful to respect the huge stallion's power and sensibilities. He encounters Wolf Eagle, ill and confused, his memory of events at the village gone, helps the warrior by making a travois of sticks behind the spirit horse, and kills a huge buffalo for meat. About a day and a half from the Kainaa village, Running Crane prevents Weasel Rider from stealing the horse. Wolf Eagle recovers his memory and reveals that Weasel Rider caused the raid to fail. A fight ensues between Running Crane and Weasel Rider, during which Running Crane realizes that he has medicine power from the wind with which he defeats Weasel Rider. Running Crane and Wolf Eagle return to the village and are hailed as heroes. Running Crane has learned to persist, have faith in himself, and remain positive. The plot relies heavily on coincidence, the author's efforts to create "Native American" speech results in ponderous dialogue, and Weasel Rider is too insufferable to be fully credible. Best are the descriptions of the physical surroundings, the preparations for the journey, and life along the way and the suspenseful passages of capturing and taming the horse. Small details are fascinating; for example, tree sap rubbed on arms and hands will calm horses.

418 Alexie, Sherman, *Indian Killer*, Atlantic Monthly, 1996 (hardcover), ISBN 0–87113–652–X, $22.00, 420 pp.; 1998 (paper), ISBN 0–446–67370–6, $12.99. Ages 15 up, grades 10 up.

Complex, large-cast, mystery novel set in Seattle, Washington, mostly among Native Americans of various groups. John Smith was taken at birth from his fourteen-year-old Indian mother and adopted by Olivia and Daniel Smith, an affluent, loving white couple. Conflicted about his background, John becomes a steelworker on a high-rise building. Slowly but inexorably he descends into madness, a state that he seems to recognize and links to the need to kill a white man. Characters who touch John's life include outspoken Marie Polatkin, a Spokane student at the University of Washington, and her cousin Reggie, who are constantly at odds with a Native-American Literature professor, over teaching materials. The mystery begins when a white man is found murdered and scalped on a trail in the university sector. Then a white student is murdered and a little white boy kidnapped while his parents are sleeping. Truck Schultz, a Rush Limbaugh-type talk-show host, sets out to inflame the white community against the Indians by ranting about the Indian Killer. Also appearing is Jack Wilson, an ex-police detective turned novelist, who says he is part Indian and begins a novel based on the murders. Added to the mix are Indian youths who beat up whites and white youths who beat up Indians. The stories of these various figures are explored in subplots. Events so fall out that John Smith takes Jack Wilson up into an unfinished skyscraper, brutalizes him, and then throws himself down forty stories to his death. Although police believe that John Smith was responsible for the murders, the matter is never completely resolved. What comes through loud and clear, however, is the deeply strained relationship between whites and Indians that results in hate crimes and overt racial animosity, along with the alienation, despair, and anger of even rational Indians. In this charged mix, the innocent and most vulnerable, like John and the kidnapped boy, fall prey to disaster, while those who attempt to rectify matters, like Marie, are marginalized. This hefty book is often sexually explicit and earthy in language and demands both subjective and objective reading perspectives. Racial tension obscures the mystery, and the problems that Indians face become the substance of long discourses, probably intended to contribute texture and flesh out characters but preachy and didactic. The book is less effective than Alexie's *Reservation Blues*, no. 419. For other prose and poetry by Alexie see *The Business of Fancy Dancing, The Lone Ranger and Tonto Fistfight in Heaven*, and *Old Shirts and New Skins*, in *This Land Is Our Land* (1994), nos. 411 (also 543), 412, and 544.

419 Alexie, Sherman, *Reservation Blues*, Atlantic, 1995 (hardcover), ISBN 0–87113–594–9, $21.00, 306 pp.; 1996 (paper), ISBN 0–446–677235–1, $13.99. Ages 15 up, grades 10 up.

Often humorous, realistic novel of reservation life by a noted Spokane–Coeur d'Alene Indian writer. Robert Johnson (an actual historical musician, who died in 1938) comes to the Spokane reservation in Washington State in 1992 carrying his strange and powerful guitar. He leaves his guitar in the van of young Thomas Builds-the-Fire, a lonely storyteller, who becomes the lead singer, songwriter, and bassist in a rock-and-roll group, with Junior Palotkin on drums and Junior's best friend, Victor Joseph, a ne'er-do-well mooch, also Spokane, on Johnson's guitar. Although only passable musically and extremely klutzy, they gain attention playing bars and taverns, adding on keyboard and backup two Flathead sisters they pick up at a gig in Montana, Chess and Checkers Warm Water. While playing in a contest in Seattle, they are heard by front men for a recording company in New York City and invited to audition. Before they leave, they are helped in polishing their act by Big Mom, a mythic figure on the reservation. Their act unaccountably self-destructs, and they return dispirited and disorganized, their instruments abandoned. Junior commits suicide, Victor drifts, Chess and Thomas, in love, move to Spokane for a new start, accompanied by Checkers. A subplot concerns the ill-fated romance between Checkers and Father Arnold, a Catholic priest. Big Mom is only one of the novel's extraordinary figures, others being the crazy old Indian known as the-man-who-was-probably-Lakota, who constantly warns of the end of the world, and the tribal leader, who incites the Indians against the group. Dreams, flashbacks, faxes, newspaper articles, journal entries, and letters provide background information and flesh out the characters, and well-utilized surrealistic elements tie events to the tragic history of the Spokane and other Native Americans. The men from the recording company and their boss bear the names of U.S. Army Indian fighters, who slaughtered hundreds of Indian horses and are responsible for metaphorically slaughtering the rock group. Thomas, the only fairly normal (by most people's standards) member of the original group, is abnormal by reservation standards, where the abnormal—constant unemployment, total despair, and chronic alcoholism—is rampant and hence normal. This is an often funny, sometimes sad, always interesting, fast-moving look at modern-day reservation Indian life. For other books by Alexie, see *This Land Is Our Land* (1994), nos. 411, 412, 543, and 544 (for titles, see entry 418, this book).

420 Allen, Paula Gunn, ed., *Song of the Turtle: American Indian Literature, 1974–1994*, Ballantine, 1996 (hardcover), ISBN 0–345–37525–4, $25.00, 353 pp. Ages 15 up, grades 10 up.

Thirty-three stories from as many Native-American Indian writers of different tribal backgrounds, arranged by order of publication by the Laguna-Sioux-Lebanese-American editor. Sequel to *Voice of the Turtle: American Indian Lit-*

erature, 1900–1970 (1995), the anthology examines "the manifold ways in which spirituality and its system of values, attitudes, customs, and manners define the Native world . . . [and] explores some of the consequences of living within . . . [that] particular paradigm." The stories are about evenly distributed between what the editor defines as the second and third "waves" of Native written (in the Anglo sense) literature. The second wave, extending from 1974 to 1990, exhibits a sense of renewal and hope, reasserts Native identity, and incorporates ritual elements drawn from the ceremonial traditions. Stories representing this period include Opal Lee Popkes's wryly humorous "Zuma Chowt's Cave," in which a white man finds refuge of sorts in an Indian family's cave; Mary TallMountain's vivid picture of the Tenderloin area in San Francisco in "Tender Street"; Roxy Gordon's "Pilgrims," which reverses perspectives and the Indians become the Pilgrims; and Louis Owens's "Soul-Catcher," which underscores the point that old beliefs must always be heeded. The third wave, beginning about 1990, features Native writers "as comfortable in literary circles as back home on the Res or traveling the powwow highway," as comfortable in writing about non-Native themes as about Native ones. Michelle T. Clinton explores the horrifying abuse of a child in "Humiliation of the Boy," and Esther Belin examines the irony of Native soldiers in the Gulf War defending a country that has often destroyed and almost always marginalized Native people in "indigenous irony" (sic). Karen Wallace's "Mary" deals with the dilemma of a white wife trying to navigate her husband's Native world and reconcile it with her own and that of her half-white children. Included are excerpts from such novels as Louise Erdrich's *The Bingo Palace* (1994) and N. Scott Momaday's *The Ancient Child* (1989). Most writers are established, among them Sherman Alexie, Joy Harjo, Beth Brant, and Anna Lee Walters, but less well-known and rising ones also appear, like Debra Earling, D. Renville, and Karen Wallace. Moods and themes vary, from the popular trickster mode to the liminal and transformational, and many of the stories are ironic. Some selections are too self-conscious, and some are demanding even for a sophisticated and tenacious reader, but most represent a satisfying sampling of what Native writers have had on their minds during this twenty-year period. A long introduction provides valuable if sometimes overly esoteric background, and a list of supplementary readings and short biographical sketches conclude the book. For other books by Allen, see *Spider Woman's Granddaughters* and *Skins and Bones*, in *This Land Is Our Land* (1994), nos. 413 (also 480) and 545.

421 Bell, Betty Louise, *Faces in the Moon*, Univ. of Oklahoma, 1994 (hardcover), ISBN 0–8061–2601–9, $19.95, 193 pp.; 1995 (paper), ISBN 0–806–12774–0, $14.95. Ages 12 up, grades 7 up.

Novel of a girl's growing up and of family life set in recent years among the Native-American Cherokee Indians in western Oklahoma but covering in retrospect most of the twentieth century. The narrative is told by adult Lucie Evers and involves three generations of Evers women, bits and pieces of whose lives Lucie recalls from stories told to her or overheard by her. When Helen Evers Jeeters, Lucie's grandmother, died, she said she would be watching her descendants from the moon, and Lucie often looks for her and her other maternal relatives there. Helen married young, to a "no-account Scotch preacher," who left her with two small daughters, Gracie (Lucie's mother) and Rozella, called Auney. Lucie describes both Gracie and Rozella as continually hooking up with and being abandoned by no-good, hard-drinking, white men. Both women find comfort after a fashion in alcohol and cigarettes and in attempting to embrace the latest white fashions. Although Gracie is often brutal and disparages Lucie, and her husband of the moment abuses the child sexually, Lucie, four, is not eager to leave her mother. Gracie, however, takes her for a few years to Lucie's forceful, independent Great-Aunt Lizzie Sixkiller Evers, the wife of Uncle Jerry Evers, Helen's brother, on their hardscrabble farm. The girl meets Uncle Henry and Aunt Bertha, Uncle Jerry's brother and his wife through whom, and through Lizzie as well, she learns that there are other life choices than those Gracie and Rozella have made. She gets an education, and goes her way in life, returning when Gracie is dying. She handles arrangements for Gracie and comes to terms with her, at least in memory. The story is almost plotless, the main interest lying in the characters of the women and their attitudes toward their bleak lives. At the end, Lucie even sees some good in her mother's tacky paint-by-numbers pictures, plastic-covered furniture, ill-composed and misspelled letters, and the random clippings Gracie sent her. Stories, words, the circle of generations, the durability of these women—these are some of the motifs that recur. Although the nonlinear movement sometimes baffles and the book needed more careful editing, the mixture of unschooled and schooled speech works, and Lucie's gradual acceptance and growing understanding of her ancestors and culture are well handled.

422 Bowen, Peter, *Wolf, No Wolf*, St. Martin's, 1996 (hardcover), ISBN 0–312–14078–9, $20.95, 213 pp.; 1997 (paper), ISBN 0–312–96103–0, $5.99, 226 pp. Ages 14 up, grades 9 up.

Third in a series of mysteries starring French-Indian Deputy Sheriff Gabriel Du Pre, set in north central Montana near the Wolf Mountains in the fictional small town of Toussaint. To the dismay of many and the fury of a few of the locals, the Fish and Wildlife Service is reintroducing wolves into the mountains nearby, threatening, they think, their cattle, but even more exacerbating their distrust of government and their fear that changes in grazing rights will drive their marginal ranches from business. Du Pre has no personal quarrel with the wolves, but he foresees violence and resents outsiders disturbing the small community—the young environmentalists, the fake Indian who exploits their enthusiasm, the activists who cut fences and shoot cattle and are soon found murdered, the reporters who flock to the area, the FBI agents sent in to solve the murders who antagonize everyone. Before it is all over, there are other deaths, several in an avalanche, a couple of suicides, a female FBI agent shot through her truck's back window, and a friend, driven to a frenzy and shooting wildly with a rifle, whom Du Pre himself must gun down. Although the novel is full of action and suspense, its strength lies in its picture of the close, isolated community, the Metis—Du Pre and his loving, sensible common-law wife, Madelaine, and their many relatives—the ranchers, the genuine Indian wise man, Benetsee, the wealthy recovering alcoholic, Bart, who acts as sheriff through the troubles, and a dozen other memorable characters. As in the earlier books of the series, *Coyote Wind* (1994) and *Specimen Song* (1995), Du Pre fiddles for dances, plays the melancholy songs of his voyageur ancestors, talks in a convincing dialect, and drinks like a true Westerner. Language is earthy but not salacious. Other novels in the series are *Notches* (1997) and *Thunder Horse* (1998).

423 Bruchac, Joseph, *The Arrow Over the Door*, illus. James Watling, Dial, 1998 (hardcover), ISBN 0–803–72078–5, $15.99, 96 pp. Ages 9–12, grades 4–7.

Historical novel based on a real incident during the American Revolution. Stands Straight, an Abenaki Indian boy of about fourteen, travels with his uncle, Sees-the-Wind, and a group from the St. Lawrence River area who have been asked by the British to join in the war against the American Rebels. Unsure that they want to be part of this conflict, they come to decide what their role should be. They arrive at the Saratoga Quaker meeting house just as the Friends are assembling and watch the group which includes Samuel Russell, his parents, and his younger brother, Jonathan, enter the roughly built cabin and sit quietly, with the door partly open. Watching especially Samuel, who has hurt his ankle and carries a stout stick as a cane, Stands Straight sees that none of the other Bostoniaks, as they call the Americans, is armed, and he senses that Samuel will fight with his stick if they attack. Sees-the-Wind, motioning the others to follow him, steps through the door. Samuel hesitates a moment, then lays his stick on the floor in front of him as a sign of peace. Robert Nisbet, a French-speaking Quaker who has traveled to attend the meeting, steps forward and welcomes the Indians to join them. Soon all those present are shaking hands with the strangers. After a meal at a nearby house, the Abenaki leave, having decided that the war is not their business and, like the Quakers, they will not join either side. As a sign of peace, Sees-the-Wind fastens an arrow over the meeting house door. A long note follows the story, telling of Bruchac's research into the historical background and why his novel varies from some other published versions of the same incident. In *This Land Is Our Land* (1994), Bruchac is represented by *Dawn Land*, no. 416 (novel), and *The First Strawberries*; *Flying with the Eagle, Racing the Great Bear*; and *Thirteen Moons on Turtles's Back*, nos. 489, 490, and 491 (all oral tradition).

424 Bruchac, Joseph, *Children of the Longhouse*, Dial, 1996 (hardcover), ISBN 0–8037–1793–8, $14.99, 150 pp.; Puffin, 1998 (paper), ISBN 0–140–38504–5, 160 pp. Ages 9–12, grades 4–7.

Novel of twins, a boy and a girl of the Bear Clan of the Mohawk Indians, set in what is now northern New York State in the late fifteenth century during the dominance of the Great League of Peace of the Iroquois Nations. Now about eleven, the twins are very close and much alike, except that Ohkwa'ri is impulsive, while his sister, Otsi:stia, is careful, always thinking actions through before starting and trying to teach her brother caution. Resting in his secret hideaway, a cave on the hill above their village, Ohkwa'ri overhears four of the older boys, led by Grabber, planning a raid on the Anen:taks, the Abenaki people to their east, although they are at peace with the much larger group. Troubled, he tells his sister, and together they go to their grandmother, She Opens the Sky, who is the oldest Clan Mother and essentially policy director of the village. At the ensuing council meeting the leading men discuss the foolishness of the idea. Under this scorn, Grabber drops his plan but becomes an implacable enemy to the younger boy. Some days later, a Tekwaarathon, a game now called lacrosse, is planned to honor Thunder's Voice, an old man whose health is failing. Because Thunder's Voice can no longer play, he chooses Ohkwa'ri to take his place, where he acquits himself well, but is waylaid by Grabber, who plans to beat or possibly kill him in a stony gully. When Ohkwa'ri swerves out of the way, Grabber falls and breaks his leg. Ohkwa'ri immediately turns back and stems the heavy bleeding, holding pressure on the leg until Otsi:stia appears, bringing with her an Abenaki healer who is visiting. This selfless conduct brings peace between Ohkwa'ri and Grabber and wins much approval of the younger boy in the village. The novel is full of stories told by the elders or repeated in the thoughts of the youngsters, tales that reinforce the morals of the group and give an idea of their beliefs but slow the action. The social organization of the tribe, the relationship of uncle-nephew that is more important than father-son, the arrangement of the longhouse—all these elements dominate the contrived and rather flimsy plot. In *This Land Is Our Land* (1994), Bruchac is represented by nos. 416 (novel) and 489, 490, and 491 (all oral tradition) (for titles, see entry 423, this book).

425 Bruchac, Joseph, *Dog People: Native American Dog Stories*, illus. Murv Jacob, Fulcrum, 1995 (hardcover), ISBN 1–55591–228–1, $14.95, 64 pp. Ages 8–11, grades 3–6.

Five stories, plus an introduction and a glossary, about six Abenaki children and their six dogs, all from the same litter, set in northern New England some ten thousand years ago. Among the children are three girls, Hummingbird, Sweetgrass Girl, and Cedar Girl, and three boys, Muskrat, Keeps-Following-the-Trail, and Rabbit Stick, all about ten to twelve years old. The dogs are referred to by their Abenaki names, which mean Raccoon, Little Bear, Little

Moose, Long Tooth, Squirrel, and Good Nose. Each dog-child pair has an adventure, except for Rabbit Stick and Sweetgrass Girl, who together with their dogs rescue her parents, lost in a storm and waiting, injured, in a cave from which they cannot escape without help. The stories are simply told with some details of life as it must have been for Native Americans of the period. In *This Land Is Our Land* (1994), books by Bruchac are nos. 416, 489, 490, and 491 (for titles, see entry 423, this book).

426 Bruchac, Joseph, *Eagle Song*, illus. Dan Andreasen, Dial, 1997 (hardcover), ISBN 0–803–71918–3, $14.00, 80 pp.; Puffin, 1999 (paper), ISBN 0–141–30169–4, $3.99, 80 pp. Ages 9–12, grades 4–7.

Realistic contemporary novel set in Brooklyn, New York, about the difficulties a Mohawk boy from the Akwesasne Reservation has as the only Indian in his fourth-grade class. After two months of being isolated and teased, Danny Bigtree hopes that a visit to school from his ironworker father will change the attitude of his classmates, and he senses that the story his father tells of the forming of the Iroquois Nation has impressed the other children. Then word comes that his father has been injured in an accident, saving another worker's life but suffering a broken leg and other injuries. Danny and his mother travel to Philadelphia, where he has been working, and visit him in the hospital. When Danny returns to school, he is sustained by his father's faith in peace and his classmates' new support. Because the novel is written simply, with the didactic message overtly stated, it is appropriate for only the younger children in its recommended age group. In *This Land Is Our Land* (1994), Bruchac is represented by a novel, no. 416; a single folktale, no. 489; and two collections of tales from oral tradition, nos. 490 and 491 (for titles, see entry 423, this book).

427 Bruchac, Joseph, *The Waters Between: A Novel of the Dawn Land*, University Press of New England, 1998 (hardcover), ISBN 0–86451–881–4, $22.95, 291 pp. Ages 12 up, grades 7 up.

Third in a trilogy about the Abenaki people of ten thousand years ago, only a few generations after the last ice age, following *Dawn Land* (see *This Land Is Our Land*, no. 416) and *Long River* (Fulcrum, 1995). The hero again is Young Hunter, who, along with his pregnant wife, Willow Woman, and several of the deep-seeing people, elders who are gifted with extrasensory perception, defeats twin menaces and restores his people to their happy life. The first danger is from a sea serpent or "bigger-than-big snake," which has become trapped by an earthquake and landslides in Lake Champlain, known as the Waters Between, where the people are accustomed to do their summer fishing. The second is from a twisted deep-seer named Watches Darkness, a man whose abusive childhood has so warped him that he wants to kill all other people with power and eat their hearts. Both Young Hunter and, to some degree, Willow Woman, are deep-seers, though without the mature power of the older ones. The ability of these people to perform what we call magic, to telecommunicate with certain animals and men, and even to fly, is not questioned in the novel. Much of the wisdom they impart is encapsulated in stories which are inserted, making appropriate points but interrupting the action. Although there are many details showing research into the ways of these ancient people, their lives are romanticized, as is the language they speak. Still, the exciting events should attract a spellbound young adult audience. In *This Land Is Our Land*, Bruchac is represented by a novel, no. 416, and three books from oral tradition, nos. 489, 490, and 491 (for titles, see entry 423, this book).

428 Bunting, Eve, *Cheyenne Again*, illus. Irving Toddy, Clarion, 1995 (hardcover), ISBN 0–396–70364–6, $14.95, 32 pp. Ages 4–8, grades PS-3.

Picture-story book about the forced removal of Native-American children to boarding schools to learn white men's ways and lose their ethnic heritage. Young Bull, a ten-year-old Cheyenne, is taken from his prairie home to the barracks-like school where his braids are cut off and his buckskins exchanged for a scratchy wool uniform. He is forced to speak only English and to learn skills useless to his people, like arithmetic, writing, and carpentry. When he tries to run away, he is recaptured and punished. Only one teacher urges him to remember and retain his Indian ways and memories. To escape the hopelessness of his situation, he draws warriors in full regalia against a bright Cheyenne sky. In double-page spreads the illustrations picture Cheyenne country in rich golds and blues, while the grim school has darker scenes against gray or dull purple background. In *This Land Is Our Land* (1994), *Summer Wheels*, no. 13, is a chapter book by Bunting for early readers, and *How Many Days to America?* no. 344, is a picture-story book.

429 Burks, Brian, *Runs With Horses*, Harcourt, 1995 (hardcover), ISBN 0–15–20064–2, $11.00, 118 pp.; (paper), ISBN 0–15–200994–9, $5.00. Ages 11 up, grades 6 up.

Historical novel set mostly in the Sierra Madre Mountains of northern Mexico in 1886, telling of the last free days of the Chiricahua Apache Indians, whose leader is historical Geronimo. The demise of the Chiricahuas is personalized by presenting events as occurring to diligent warrior-in-training Runs With Horses, sixteen, who has completed two raids and needs two more to be considered a man. Mentored by his father, the much-respected Red Knife, he undergoes training intended to toughen him in body, mind, and spirit so that he can survive any hardship and withstand any pain. When Geronimo decides to lead a raid for supplies, Runs With Horses and Little Face are elated to be allowed to join. The group kills three Mexican miners and takes their mules, supplies, and guns, then moves on to burn and raid a ranch near the Sierra en Medio Mountains. On the return, they are attacked by Mexican soldiers and lose three men before they make it back to their camp. Since they are now too few to continue resisting the combined forces of the Mexicans and White Eyes (Americans), Geronimo accepts the terms of surrender imposed by the American army. Although the two boys know the chances are exceedingly slim, they continue to dream of becoming warriors in the traditional way. An epilogue indicates that the group of thirty-eight is disarmed and variously incarcerated, many of them in Florida, never to return to their homeland. The young people are sent to the Carlisle School in Pennsylvania, where they are educated as whites. The simple, almost laconic style, the ironic earnestness and dreaming of the young protagonist, and the details of training and the ethic of the warriors give this book intensity and emphasize the tragedy of the end of the communal, traditional life of these dignified, stalwart people. A brief bibliography completes the book.

430 Burks, Brian, *Walks Alone*, Harcourt, 1998 (hardcover), ISBN 0–15–201612–0, $16.00, 115 pp. Ages 11 up, grades 6 up.

Historical novel of the Mimbres Apache Indian struggle in the mid 1880s to continue their traditional way of life against the increasing raids and relentless onslaught of white settlers and soldiers. Walks Alone, fifteen, looks forward to marriage with Little Hawk. Resourceful and inventive, she belongs to the group led by historical Victorio. Victorio's Apaches have been on the run, having fled from captivity in Arizona Territory to Warm Springs near the Mescalero Reservation in New Mexico Territory. After a few months of peace at Warm Springs, they flee again when they learn that Victorio is to be arrested. White soldiers and turncoat Apache scouts attack, and many of Walks Alone's people are killed, but Victorio escapes with a few survivors. Walks Alone and her little brother escape by hiding in an arroyo, but Walks Alone is shot in the leg. In spite of her wound, she provides for them by living off the land and steals horses so that they can reach the Mescalero Reservation. When the Mescaleros are imprisoned at the Indian Agency and her brother dies there of malnutrition, Walks Alone runs for Mexico. After terrible hardships, she rejoins her people on their trek to the Lakes of Tres Castillos. She is about to marry Little Hawk, when Victorio's people are attacked by Mexican soldiers, and the few survivors are taken captive. An epilogue gives historical details, indicating that most of the eighty-nine survivors were enslaved in Mexico City and in mines, but a few escaped and joined other Apache bands. This is a stark, dramatic, horrifying account of cruelty and inhumane treatment. Many details of Apache life set the bleak account in relief, evoke admiration for the people, and support the credibility of Walks Alone and her people's story.

431 Carter, Alden R., *Dogwolf*, Scholastic, 1994 (hardcover), ISBN 0–590–46741–7, $13.95, 231 pp.; (paper), ISBN 0–590–46742–5, $4.50. Ages 12 up, grades 7 up.

Realistic boy's growing-up novel set in recent years near a Chippewa (Ojibwa) Indian reservation in the deep forests of northern Wisconsin. Pete LaSavage, fourteen, part Indian, part white, feels trapped "in some terrible nowhere in between," like the neighbor's caged dogwolf whose nightly howling sorely frays local nerves. Pete admires his stepfather, Chuck, a respected Forest Service Officer and firefighter, loves his mother and two small half-sisters, and has enough friends in their little forest enclave to be satisfied. He would like to know more about his real father, a timberman who was maimed on the job and subsequently disappeared. He would like Mona, his sometime girlfriend, to leave him alone and is wary about carousing with rootless Jim Redwing. Mostly he worries about the "big one" that Chuck predicts will come, the fire to end all fires that will be the climax of this long, dry, very hot summer; about how much of him is really Indian; and, increasingly, about whether his secretly releasing the dogwolf, as he has done, is the cause of recent mysterious deaths. The "big one," the dogwolf, and Pete's determination to take responsibility for his action, as he is advised to do by his Metis (French-Indian) grandfather, make for a tense, rapid-action conclusion. A likable, honest-sounding narrator/protagonist; scenes of warm family life; credible interfamily relationships, especially between stepfather and stepson; a well-drawn picture of small-town and rural forest life; sufficient descriptions of firefighting preparations and procedures; and a keen sense of the physical setting of smoldering peat-bog fires, lightning near and far, constant dust, unrelenting heat, and darkness filled with danger make this top-notch suspense and boy's-story reading.

432 Casler, Leigh, *The Boy Who Dreamed of an Acorn*, illus. Shonto Begay, Philomel 1994 (hardcover), ISBN 0–399–22547–1, $15.95, unp. Ages 5–12, grades K–7.

Mood-evoking, coming-of-age, picture-story book set among the Chinook Indians once upon a time. The slightly formal, understated language supports the timeless quality of the story, as do the misty, dark-toned, representational paintings. Three boys set out on their spirit quests. Two receive visions right away, one of a bear, the other of an eagle. The third boy, who has climbed farther up the mountain than the other two, sees only a tiny acorn. Disappointed and worried by so nontraditional a vision, the boy consults the wise, old man of the village, who advises him to be satisfied and make the most of what he has seen. He gives the boy an acorn and tells him to plant it. The boy does, and as the years pass, the acorn develops into a tall, rangy, sturdy oak. The boy, however, remains relatively small in comparison to the other two boys, who become known for strength and hunting ability. After the boy is again advised by the old man to make the most of what he has been given, he notices that animals and birds, even the mighty eagle, come to the tree for shelter and food, and people of the village gather under its spreading arms. Like the tree, the boy, now a man, becomes known for his gentle, kind, generous ways, a helper to all around him. A writer's note and a glossary of Chinook terms precedes the story.

433 Conley, Robert J., *The Peace Chief: A Novel of the Real People*, St. Martin's, 1998 (hardcover), ISBN 0–312–19314–9, $25.95, 339 pp. Ages 14 up, grades 9 up.

Compelling historical novel of sixteenth-century Cherokee Indians in Georgia during early contact with the French, raids of the Spaniards from the south, and uneasy relations with the Seneca Indians to the north. Young Puppy accidentally kills his best friend, Asquani, and flees to Kituwah, a sanctuary town, where he must stay for one year according to tribal rules. At first, Young Puppy can hardly bear his situation. He cannot marry, hunt, fight, or explore the countryside. Mentored by the religious leader, he painstakingly learns the rituals and ceremonies of his people and becomes the next ceremonial leader, or Peace Chief, Comes Back to Life. He marries Guwisti and takes as a second wife the wife of the man he had killed. Oliga, the young man most determined to avenge Asquani's death by killing Young Puppy, makes his way north to the Seneca, assists in expelling a group of Shawnee, and much soberer and more sensible, becomes War Chief and co-leader with Comes Back to Life. Others involved in this multiplotted, broad-canvas story are Uyona, the medicine woman; Jacques Tournier, the leader of a French delegation who truly respects the Cherokees; and Striker, who is captured by the Spaniards to be a slave and who escapes and subsequently frees a hundred other enslaved Indians. This large-cast, action-filled, engrossing story excels in creating the world view and daily and ceremonial life of the Real People, attitudes of the French and Spaniards toward the Indians, and the Indians' attitudes toward these invaders. Best, as is always true with the books of this Cherokee writer, is the sympathy and clarity with which he tackles the Indians' problems. A note about the ceremonies is helpful in building credibility and adding texture, and a glossary appears at the end of the book. For other books by Conley, see *Mountain Windsong, Nickajack,* and *The Witch of Going Snake and Other Stories,* in *This Land Is Our Land* (1994), nos. 418, 419, and 420, all fiction.

434 Conley, Robert J., *War Woman: A Novel of the Real People,* St. Martin's, 1997 (hardcover), ISBN 0–312–17058–0, $25.95, 357 pp.; Griffin, 1998 (paper), ISBN 0–312–19361–0, $15.95. Ages 14 up, grades 9 up.

Broad-span historical novel set from 1580 to 1654 in Cherokee Indian territory in Georgia. Events follow those of *The Peace Chief* (1998; no. 433). Whirlwind, sixteen, has from infancy been independent and imperious. Each of the novel's three sections involves Cherokees in a major event that she inspires. Whirlwind persuades Daksi, a visiting Coyatee, and her twin brother, Little Spaniard, to accompany her to Florida to open up trade with the Spaniards, on the way becoming Daksi's wife. After Daksi is killed, the twins make it home, where for her skill in repulsing the attack Whirlwind is renamed War Woman. Twenty years later, trade flourishes between the Spaniards and the Cherokees, and some Cherokees, like Little Spaniard, suffer from alcoholism. War Woman marries Juan Morales, a Spanish trader and decent, steady man, who respects the Cherokee and with whom she has two children. War Woman and Morales arrange an agreement between the Florida Spaniards and a neighboring Cherokee village to mine gold, proceeds to be shared. The effort produces wealth for all parties until the vein runs out and strife ensues. Morales and War Woman return to New Town wiser for the experience. About fifty years later, now a widow, elder, and wise woman, War Woman leads a group of 700 Cherokees to reestablish a Powhatan Indian town in Virginia destroyed by the English. In trying to repulse the Cherokees, the English are soundly trounced, but War Woman leads the group back to their friends and families, and the new village is abandoned. The three events have their source in history and logic. Although decidedly unlikable in the first part of the book for her selfish, domineering ways, War Woman grows likable. Little Spaniard is a sad, pathetic figure, Morales is admirable, as is the leader of the Virginia expedition, Running Man. After a slow beginning, excitement abounds, and this absorbing story grips and holds. The Spaniards are presented as morally reprehensible for the most part. Best is the detailed picture of the life and times of the Cherokee during this almost 100-year period. Although culture erosion occurs, some, like War Woman and Running Man, seek to maintain their people's respect in themselves and pride in heritage. The gold-mining section sadly foreshadows the removal of the Cherokees about 200 years later. For other books by Conley, see *This Land Is Our Land* (1994), 418, 419, and 420, all fiction (for titles, see entry 433, this book).

435 Curry, Jane Louise, *Dark Shade*, McElderry, 1998 (hardcover), ISBN 0–689–81812–2, $16.00, 168 pp. Ages 12 up, grades 7 up.

Time-slip novel of the period of the French-Indian War, when the British were building a road through the Pennsylvania wilderness to Fort Duquesne, now Pittsburgh. Mary Margaret (Maggie) Gilmour, who works for her veterinarian father and is more at home with animals than other young people, secretly follows her friend, Kip Maclean, up a path high in the mountains and finds herself in the eighteenth century. There she encounters an injured and unconscious young soldier from a Highland regiment and learns from his papers that he is Robert Mackensie. In the next few days she sets his broken arm, brings him food, and when he recovers enough to walk, directs him toward the remains of the trail being built by his troops. In the meantime she discovers that Kip, who has been increasingly withdrawn since a fire that killed his parents and badly burned him, has joined a band of Lenape Indians, who have been healing his burns with bear grease and have welcomed him into their group. When Maggie, who has returned home every afternoon, realizes that Kip plans to stay in the earlier period, she sets out to retrieve him. While she is in the Lenape village trying to persuade him to return, two warriors drag Robert Mackensie into the village, torment him savagely, and force him to run the gauntlet. Shocked by the change in the gentle people he has been with, Kip agrees to go home with Maggie, while the Lenape, impressed by Robert's courage, adopt him into their tribe. Back in the twentieth century, Kip and Maggie learn that they are both descended from Robert and his Lenape wife. Although most of the book is from Maggie's point of view, the picture of the Lenape village and their way of life is the most compelling portion. Myths and tales of the California Indians collected by Curry appear in *Back in the Beforetime*, in *This Land Is Our Land* (1994), no. 497.

436 Dorris, Michael, *Cloud Chamber*, Scribner, 1997 (hardcover), ISBN 0–684–81567–2, $24.00, 316 pp.; 1998 (paper), ISBN 0–684–83535–5, $12.00, 320 pp. Ages 14 up, grades 9 up.

Realistic novel of family life covering some 100 years and several generations of the woman ancestors of Rayona Taylor, the mixed-blood protagonist of Dorris's best-known novel, *Yellow Raft in Blue Water* (1987), and of his more recent *The Window* (no. 439). In late nineteenth-century Ireland, beautiful, black-haired Rose Mannion is forced to flee from the British for her Irish-Republican activities. She and gawky Martin McGarry marry, emigrate to the United States, and settle in western Kentucky, where Martin dies an early death. Andrew, the eldest and his mother's favorite, becomes a priest and Robert, a railroad carpenter. Andrew is killed in a train accident, and Robert takes to drink, becomes an amnesiac, and dies of consumption, leaving two daughters, Edna, his favorite, a staunch Catholic, and Marcella, who becomes Rayona's white grandmother. When Marcella is hospitalized for consumption in Louisville, she meets handsome Earl Taylor, a black deliveryman with whom she falls in love. They move West, where they can legally marry, and have a son, Elgin, who becomes Rayona's father. Later, in World War II, Earl is reported killed in Germany. Elgin, grown up and a soldier himself, meets and marries Native-American Christine, and settles in the Tacoma, Washington, area. Their daughter is Rayona, who maintains ties with her father's family as well as her mother's. At the end of the book, Rayona, motherless and college bound, is the focus of a give-away powwow at which her Grandmother Marcella and Great-Aunt Edna are among the guests and at which she is to assume the name Rose. The novel ambles on, with many period aspects as well as much detail of character. The book's primary concern, however, is with the contribution of these women to the family saga and their condition of being women. Inter- and intragenerational conflicts, resentments, secrets, heartaches, joys, concerns, and domestic ironies drive the story, all of which for this family have their origin with their conniving, domineering Irish ancestress. Tone recalls stories in women's magazines and women-oriented soap operas of the middle part of this century. For another book by Dorris, see *Yellow Raft in Blue Water*, in *This Land Is Our Land* (1994), no. 424.

437 Dorris, Michael, *Guests*, Hyperion, 1994 (hardcover), ISBN 0–7868–0047–X, $16.95, 119 pp.; 1996 (paper), ISBN 0–786–81108–0, $4.50, 128 pp. Ages 8–12, grades 3–7.

Realistic novel set among an unnamed group of Native-American Indians in a village in a forested area, probably New England, at the time of very early contact with whites. Moss, about twelve, resents being treated like a child while expected to act like an adult. His older cousin, Cloud, refuses to tell him what it was like during Cloud's "away time," the period in which boys go alone into the forest to find direction for their lives and receive their adult names. Moss particularly resents his family's having as guests the white strangers, whom his father invited to their annual harvest dinner. Moss impulsively runs into the forest, where he spies a porcupine, with whom he engages in a conversation entirely in his head. Among others, the porcupine leaves him with the puzzling idea that he is who he is. He encounters Trouble, a spirited, independent girl of another clan, a runaway from expectations for a girl. After conversation, the two come to uncertain conclusions about their lives and return to the village, from which they have been gone only a few hours. Moss participates at the dinner and later at another social gathering with the whites, but Trouble has problems with her women relatives and is consoled by Moss's mother. When the matter of the away time comes up, Trouble says that Moss already has an adult name, Thunder. A potboiler, splintered plot, stereotypical characters, and awkward dialogue are among the book's negative features, while good points include Moss's male adolescent rebellion and restlessness, which ring true to the age, and the Indian customs, stories, and sex-role expectations. Dorris has also written an earlier book, *Yellow Raft in Blue Water*, described in *This Land Is Our Land* (1994), no. 424.

438 Dorris, Michael, *Sees Behind Trees*, Hyperion, 1996 (hardcover), ISBN 0–786–890224–3, $14.95, 104 pp.; Disney, 1999 (paper), ISBN 0–786–812542–4, $4.95, 112 pp. Ages 8–12, grades 3–7.

Personal-problem novel set among an unspecified group of woodlands Indians in the sixteenth century. Since partially sighted Walnut, about twelve, cannot hit a moving target with his bow and arrow, he knows he will probably never take his place among the men. His mother wisely urges him to "see" things with his ears. At the coming-of-age ceremony, he identifies with only his ears Gray Fire, a limping elder, and is rewarded by Otter, the female elder, with an adult name, Sees Behind Trees. One day, Gray Fire tells the boy how he and Otter, his twin, years ago found an beautiful "land of water" inside a remote gorge, where he lost the two toes that produced his limp. The boy agrees to help him try to find that extraordinary place. After two days, they arrive at the gorge, where Gray Fire can walk again and Sees Behind Trees can see. Gray Fire sinks into the whirlpool, leaving the boy to make his slow way home alone. He finds an abandoned baby and, bearing the child in his arms, follows the path by touching the moss on rocks and trees and following similar signs that Gray Fire had given him. At home, Otter tells him that, jealous of her twin's ability as a runner, she took him to the wonderful land of water and prepared the trap in which he lost his toes. Realizing that she has lost her beloved brother forever because of her selfishness, she weeps uncontrollably. Sees Behind Trees understands that, when he "received . . . [his] new name, . . . [he] had no idea how many trees there were [in the world], and how much there was to see behind each of them." Although his first-person narrative conveys little evidence of the culture, the pieces of the cliched plot do not mesh well, and the mysticism is puzzling and annoying, Sees Behind Trees tells his story of making the most of what you have in keenly sensory language. The two elders are well if minimally drawn, and the boy is credible. Dorris, deceased, was Native American and published other novels, both individually and with his wife, Louise Erdrich. See *Yellow Raft in Blue Water*, in *This Land Is Our Land* (1994), no. 424.

439 Dorris, Michael, *The Window*, Hyperion, 1997 (hardcover), ISBN 0–786–80301–0, $16.95, 112 pp.; Disney, 1999 (paper), ISBN 0–786–81373–3, $4.99. Ages 8–14, grades 3–9.

Contemporary sociological problem novel set in Tacoma, Washington, and Louisville, Kentucky. When Native American Christine Taylor's "hard nights" with alcohol keep her away from their small apartment for several days at a time and the refrigerator stands bare, her daughter, Rayona, eleven, the self-possessed narrator, reports that her separated African-American father, Elgin, steps in. He takes the girl by plane to stay with Marcella, his mother, Aunt Edna (Rayona's great-aunt), and Rayona's grandmother, Mamaw, in Louisville. All three women are white and have never before seen Rayona. She soon feels very much at home with her loving, independent, self-sufficient forebears. She learns about her ancestors both black and white. When Elgin phones with the news that Christine has joined Alcoholics Anonymous, his mother and Aunt Edna drive Rayona the 2,000 miles to Tacoma. Since Elgin tells them that the counselors feel that Christine is ready to receive Rayona but not other visitors, the two women return to Louisville without meeting Christine. While the window by which Rayona saw life at the beginning of the book was very small, her view of the world has broadened. She decides that she will not betray her father's secrets—that his mother is white, her heritage Irish—since everyone is entitled to have secrets. Intelligent Rayona's perceptions of her parents are astute, and her ambivalent feelings toward them and other adults seem appropriate and credible. Elgin's women relatives are well drawn, lively, and individualized, if nondynamic. The writer catches scenes well with sharply pictorial language. The novel seems foreshortened, however, and underdeveloped, a tantalizing "prequel" to the life of the triracial young woman, whose story is more adequately explored in Dorris's adult novel *Yellow Raft in Blue Water*, which is described in *This Land Is Our Land* (1994), no. 424.

440 Duey, Kathleen, *Celou Sudden Shout, Idaho 1826*, Demco, 1998 (hardcover), ISBN 0–606–13121–3, $9.75, 152 pp.; Aladdin, 1998 (paper), ISBN 0–689–81622–7, $3.99. Ages 8–12, grades 3–7.

Daring rescue novel starring the daughter of a French fur trapper and a Shoshone mother. Taking advantage of her father's absence and a Blackfoot attack on the nearby Shoshone camp, four Crow men capture Celou's mother and her brothers, Jean-Paul and the infant, Mu'umbie. Watching from hiding, Celou sees one Crow, distinguished by red fringe on his sleeves, hunt for his bah-pack, his precious medicine amulet, which he has lost and she has found. When they start north with wounded Jean-Paul, his hands bound, swaying precariously on one horse, and her mother, with the cradle-board on her back, riding behind one of the men, Celou follows on the one horse the Crows did not steal. Along the way, she ties the bah-pack at the top of a slender tree and marks the spot. Creeping into the sleeping camp, she is able to cut her mother's bonds and Jean-Paul's. Her mother is able to retrieve her own horse and scatter the Crow herd, and they ride furiously, Jean-Paul and Celou on one horse, but the Crows are hot after them. Red-fringe, as she calls the man to herself, is able to overtake them and grab Celou's shoulder. To his surprise, she reins in, leaps off, and sends Jean-Paul on. Then she faces Red-fringe, signs that she knows where it is, and touches her neck to indicate the amulet. Cleverly, she tricks him by pretending to fall from the tree where she has tied the bah-pack and slings it away, then jumps from the tree and onto his horse, galloping away toward her own people. Her mixed blood causes her problems as her father's beliefs conflict with her mother's and the full bloods look at her askance, but ultimately her bravery wins their respect.

441 Durrant, Lynda, *The Beaded Moccasins: The Story of Mary Campbell*, Clarion, 1998 (hardcover), ISBN 0–395–85398–2, $15.00, 183 pp. Ages 9–12, grades 4–7.

Biographical novel of Mary Campbell, who was captured on her twelfth birthday from her home in Pennsylvania by Delaware Indians, along with a neighbor, Mrs. Stewart, and her baby son, Sammy. By order of the government, the Indians are moving west to the Cuyahoga River in Ohio Territory. Their leader, Netawatwees Sachem, has lost a much-loved granddaughter in a plague that killed off many of the children, and he plans to replace her with Mary. As Sammy becomes troublesome, refusing to eat and crying continually, one of the men takes him behind a tree and returns with his scalp. Mary realizes that the same thing could happen to her if she does not please her "grandfather," and she bravely makes the best of her situation, gradually learning the language and accepting the kindness of her new mother. The life is very different from what she was accustomed to and the work is hard, but she takes pride in doing her share. When Netawatwees refuses to trade her for muskets to a French trader who wants a wife, she realizes she is important to him. Later he trades Mrs. Stewart, who has never tried to adjust, to the Frenchman, whom she henpecks unmercifully. Thinking back to her earlier life, Mary has ambivalent feelings. She always resented the favoritism shown to her younger brother, and she hated the confinement of women's life. She discovers the Indians are far from the savages she has imagined, and she fears there would be nothing for her to return to if she should be rescued. The novel, based on a real captive in 1759, does a good job of showing her changes and her acceptance of the Delaware way of life.

442 Erdrich, Louise, *The Bingo Palace*, HarperCollins, 1994 (hardcover), ISBN 0–06–017080–8, $23.00, 274 pp.; 1995 (paper), ISBN 0–06–09258–X, $13.00, 288 pp. Ages 15 up, grades 10 up.

Contemporary realistic novel of life among Chippewa (Ojibwa) Indians on the reservation in North Dakota, the fourth in a set of related books that begins with *Tracks* (1988), continues in *Love Medicine* (1984) and *The Beet Queen* (1986), and involves some of the same characters. Like the others, *The Bingo Palace* can stand by itself and reveals Erdrich's hallmarks of shifting perspectives, smooth, fluid, concrete style and linear structure, skillful intermingling of generations, emphasis on family and tradition, use of old story and beliefs for texture, bold confrontation with universal themes, and engaging combination of parody, comedy, tragedy, and absurdity. The main story strand revolves around young ne'er-do-well Lipsha Morrissey's attempts to win beautiful Shawnee Ray Toose, with whom a relative of his, Lyman Lamertine, a big man on the reservation both literally and figuratively, father of her baby son, survivor, and entrepreneur, is also in love. Counterpointing the ups and downs of this love story is Lyman's plan to build a bingo emporium on tribal land, an establishment that becomes a symbol of hope to the impoverished and discouraged Indians as well as additional evidence of how far they will go to give up old ways and adapt to those of whites to achieve some financial well being. Lipsha, in certain ways, is symbolic of the plight of the Indians, in that he often brings his troubles on himself by muffing opportunities for advancement and making poor choices. As common with Erdrich, she distances the reader from the protagonist, evoking sympathy and also poking fun at him. In a particularly hilarious scene, Lyman agrees to help Lipsha achieve a vision on the tribal lands upon which the casino is to be built. After a sweat, Lipsha sleeps outside alone for two nights, and awakens the third morning to find, not a vision, but a skunk confronting him. Lipsha is convinced that the skunk says, "This [the tribal land] ain't real estate." Later, the words haunt him, and, having seen something of bingo life, he wonders whether or not Lyman is leading the tribe in the wrong direction. The novel is demanding but, as with others by Erdrich, worth the effort. *Tales of Burning Love* (1996), which employs some characters from the earlier books, seems less successful. More recent is *The Antelope Wife* (1998), another complex, demanding mixture of characters, some of whom hark back to earlier books, and familiar Erdrich themes, among them, the Native idea of contemporaneous time and the influence of indigenous ideas. Other books by Erdrich appear in *Tracks* (novel) and *Baptism of Desire* (poems), in *This Land Is Our Land* (1994), nos. 425 and 548.

443 Erdrich, Louise, *Grandmother's Pigeon*, illus. Jim LaMarche, Hyperion, 1996 (hardcover), ISBN 0–7868–2137–X, $15.95, unp.; 1999 (paper), ISBN 0–786–81204–4, $6.99. Ages 4–10, grades PS–5.

Picture-story fantasy in a family setting. One year after eccentric Grandmother rides off on a porpoise for Greenland, her family check her room, thinking it may be time to box up her belongings for safe keeping. Father finds a birds' nest made of rough twigs, which contains three eggs. The eggs soon hatch into what an ornithologist identifies as male passenger pigeons, birds extinct since 1914. The discovery causes a sensation among naturalists, and the family gains notoriety because of the birds. Caught between knowing that the birds are important for science and that they will probably be caged for life, the brother and sister release them one moonlit night, after taping messages to their legs. One message, which reaches Grandmother in Greenland, prompts a letter informing the family that she misses them all and will return soon. Although the plot pushes the edge between realism and mysticism too far and Grandmother's behavior is insufficiently motivated, the theme of respecting all living things comes through clearly but nondidactically. The family atmosphere is warm and loving. Diction is mature, direct, and concrete, and although children may not understand all the words, they will surely grasp the intended meaning. Some might classify the full-color, often mystical, framed paintings as popular calendar art, but they complement the story by providing realism through the scenes involving the family. The molded figures are so lifelike that one can almost hear them breathing and feel the warmth of their bodies. The text does not specify race, nor do the pictures indicate a minority race. *The Birchbark House* (1999), about a little girl who lives on an island in Lake Superior, is also a picture-story book. Erdrich, Ojibwa (Chippewa), is better known for her novels for adults about Native Americans, which are described in *Tracks* (novel) and *Baptism of Desire* (poems), in *This Land Is Our Land* (1994), nos. 425 and 548.

444 Fitzpatrick, Marie Louise, *The Long March: The Choctaw's Gift to Irish Famine Relief*, illus. Marie-Louise Fitzpatrick, Beyond Words, 1998 (hardcover), ISBN 1–885223–71–4, $14.95, unp. Ages 8 up, grades 3 up.

Historical fiction in picture-book form based on a real incident in 1847 in Indian Territory, now the state of Oklahoma. The story is told as an old man by Choona, who was a boy of fourteen at the time of the action. The older people never talk about the Long March, the terrible journey west after his Choctaw people were forced from their land in Mississippi. When his father and Uncle Moshi arrive from Skullyville with news of the potato famine devastating the faraway country of Ireland, Choona agrees with those who say, "What has this to do with us?" At the meeting of his mother's family clan, the Potato Eating People, that sentiment is voiced and answered by Talihoyo, his great-grandmother, the oldest member of the tribe. She tells the story of the Long March, when half the people died, all the old ones and the children. She says the Irish are now walking that trail of tears and that what help they can send will be "an arrow shot through time." At first Choona questions why they did not fight rather than be forced out and why they should help a European people now. His great-grandmother says it was not a mistake, but it has been a mistake to hide the truth from the young ones. Understanding some of the adult pain, Choona admits that they should help the Irish. A foreword and notes at the end tell how the very poor Choctaw sent $170 (more than $5,000 in today's money). The illustrations are realistic black-and-white drawings based on actual Choctaw now living, most notably a full-page picture of an ancient, wrinkled woman, the epitome of dignity and survival. The only color in this beautiful book is in dull-gold inset blocks on which the text is printed.

445 Franklin, Kristine L., *The Shepherd Boy*, illus. Jill Kastner, Atheneum, 1994 (hardcover), ISBN 0–689–31809–X, $14.95, 32 pp. Ages 4–8 up, grades PS–3.

Realistic picture-story book about a young Navajo boy named Ben who tends his family's sheep with the help of his two dogs, White-Eye and No-Tail. One evening when he returns home, only forty-nine of the fifty sheep are in the flock. With the dogs, Ben runs back to the pasture, over rocks and through the canyons, past the cliff houses and the pictographs, and finds the ewe lamb safe. Ben carries it home to the security of the family hogan. The very simple story is beautifully illustrated with many panoramic scenes covering more than three quarters of wide double-page spreads, predominately in the oranges and browns of the Southwest, with the spare text printed down the remaining space on what looks like coarsely woven fabric, divided from the pictures by a line of Navajo motifs. Story, paintings, and design have a warm, comforting but not sentimental tone.

446 Garland, Sherry, *Indio*, Gulliver, 1995 (hardcover), ISBN 0–15–238631–9, $11.00, 292 pp.; 1995 (paper), ISBN 0–152–00021–6, $5.00. Ages 12–18, grades 7–12.

Historical novel of Spanish contact with Indian pit-dwelling farmers along the Rio Grande in western Texas in probably the mid-seventeenth century. The small group of Indians to which Ipa-tah-chi belongs are called by the author Otomoacos, one of several riverside bands that have disappeared from history and about whom very little is known. When Ipa is ten and Apaches from the north raid her small village, kill her healer grandmother, and carry off into slavery her older brother, Ximi, the Otomoacoan way of life continues. When the Spaniards raid three years later, however, the invaders kill or carry off most of the people, including Ipa, to northern Mexico to work in the silver mines and in a mission, almost obliterating the group. Ipa proves of value to the Spaniards because she learned healing from her grandmother. A kindly friar also befriends her, but even he is not able to save her when the mine overseer is found knifed to death and she is imprisoned for murder. While Ipa awaits execution, a young

Spanish soldier, Rodrigo, who had been kind to her during the raid, helps her escape and promises to come for her and marry her. Home again, Ipa finds her village and those around it suffering from a smallpox epidemic. More hardships follow, but eventually Ipa leaves for Mexico City, with the expectation of marrying Rodrigo. The plot is familiar and the conclusion overly optimistic and romantic, but there are enough episodes of daily life both at home and at the mission to hold the interest. Characters, too, are the expected ones, but Ipa, small, delicate, plain, and controlled, wins sympathy. This full, highly detailed novel effectively contrasts the way of life and world view of these peace-loving farmers and the invading Spaniards who ruined their culture. In a preface, the author indicates that she has based the novel on comparative archaeology, history, anthropology, and her imagination. Also about early-contact Indians is *Cabin 102* (1995), a fantasy novel, in which an American boy on a Caribbean cruise ship helps an Arawak Indian girl from the sixteenth century return to her island. For other books by Garland, see *The Lotus Seed* and *Why Ducks Sleep on One Leg*, in *This Land Is Our Land* (1994), nos. 231 and 296.

447 Garland, Sherry, *The Last Rainmaker*, Harcourt, 1997 (hardcover), ISBN 0–15–200649–4, $8.40, 320 pp.; (paper), ISBN 0–15–200652–4, $6.00, 324 pp. Ages 10–15, grades 5–10.

Period novel of Native-American/American attitudes in 1900 with aspects of a girl's growing-up novel. After the death of her grandmother Onita Long, Caroline, thirteen, becomes the ward of her great aunt but longs to travel with her dashing, handsome father and to learn about her beautiful Italian mother, who died when Caroline was born. When her father kidnaps her for ransom and takes her to his cousin in St. Louis, Caroline learns that he is a ne'er-do-well gambler and that her mother was an American Indian, a trick horse rider with Shawnee Sam's Wild West Show. The show comes to St. Louis, Caroline runs away to join it, and becomes a hit trick rider, too. Through Crooked Feather, a Kiowa youth her age, she meets aged Billy Big Tree, a Wichita rainmaker and former peace chief, who was her mother's father. He tells her his daughter fell in love with Caroline's father and, abandoned by him, went to Caroline's grandmother's little town to give birth. The predictable plot, stereotypical characters, and mundane style are offset by the cultural aspects and the spunky heroine. Pathetic Billy Big Tree epitomizes the state of the once-proud, self-sufficient Indians, and Crooked Feather, educated at the Carlisle Indian School in Pennsylvania in white ways, is accepted neither by Indians nor by whites. He is, Crooked Feather says, one of the Lost People. Shawnee Sam (patterned after Buffalo Bill) exploits every avenue, no matter how degrading to the Indians, to make money. Caroline's internal conflict fits the times: she is proud of being the daughter of a beautiful Indian performer and the granddaughter of a former peace chief, but she also considers the Indians dirty and ignorant and does not want people to think she is one of them. The book is a potboiler but still a worthwhile read, because the identity problem—being biracial in a society that degrades and belittles the darker half—and the deterioration of the Indians are well presented. Earlier publications, *The Lotus Seed* and *Why Ducks Sleep on One Leg*, are described in *This Land Is Our Land* (1994), nos. 231 and 296.

448 Glancy, Diane, *Flutie*, Moyer Bell, 1998 (hardcover), ISBN 1–55921–212–8, $18.95, 130 pp. Ages 12 up, grades 7 up.

Short, realistic, girl's growing-up and family-life novel, set in the present-day small town of Vini in western Oklahoma. The action, much of it inside half-Cherokee Flutie's head, extends for about seven years, beginning when she is thirteen. Even by the standards of this marginal town, her family is dysfunctional. Flutie's undemonstrative Indian father, who repairs cars at the only garage in town, is often at odds with her rebellious brother, Franklin, five years older than Flutie, who serves a term in prison. Her German-American mother is cold, easily angered, neglectful, and chiefly known for her wild, fast driving and accumulation of speeding tickets. Flutie is known in town for her inability to express herself. She is so shy and inarticulate that speaking in class terrifies her. She yearns for something to ground her life, give her an identity, and often retreats to a room in her head, where she reflects on the story of Philomela from Greek mythology, in which Philomela's tongue is cut out by the man who raped her. She also sees visionary figures, among them some sort of spirit girl and animals. For a while, Flutie derives a kind of peace from alcohol and the bar scene. She attends Southwestern Oklahoma State University some time after high school on borrowed money, but drops out because she cannot bear speaking in class. She returns home, accepts the marriage proposal of Jess Tessman, then changes her mind and returns to the university, where she is last seen doing satisfactorily with the help of a sympathetic geology lab instructor. She is still frightened, but she has decided to become a teacher and help others who are sealed off inside themselves as she is. This short novel is chiefly memorable for its strength in catching Flutie's painful psychic needs, isolation, and inability to express herself. The brief, almost elliptical sentences reinforce her confusion and yearnings. Although published for adults, the book seems more appropriate for adolescents. Glancy has also published *The Only Piece of Furniture in the House* (1996), of the growing up and early marriage of a girl from a conservative southern family. For other books by Glancy, see *Trigger Dance* (short stories) and *Claiming Breath* and *Iron Woman* (poems), in *This Land Is Our Land* (1994), nos. 426, 551, and 552.

449 Glancy, Diane, *Monkey Secret*, Triquarterly, 1995 (hardcover), ISBN 0–8101–5016–6, $19.95, 116 pp. Ages 14 up, grades 9 up.

Three short stories and a novella by an award-winning Cherokee writer noted for her expressive language and her skill at exploring and counterpointing Anglo and Indian ways and beliefs. She tackles discrimination, culture clash and assimilation, familial relationships, generational tensions, growing up in a mixed-racial environment, the conflux of past and present, and the pull of self versus society. The sense of always being the "Lead Horse" and having to pull more than her share of the load recurs for old Nattie as she and her aging cousins gather to celebrate a birthday. Fletch acknowledges that words also constitute architecture in "At the Altar of American Indian Architecture" as he starts life with a new girlfriend and feels not only the pull of his past domestic relationships but also that of his Indian ancestors' moving west to Arkansas. In "Minimal Indian," James visits his sister, Renah, hoping in vain that she and his best friend, Crowbar, will develop a romantic interest in each other. Jean, the narrator of novella "Monkey Secret," observes during her growing-up years that there is some truth in Reverend Stonesifer's dictum that people have gone "haywire" and are "forever hopping like static electricity," like monkeys. Jean's story looks forward and circles backward in tiny chapters like brief movie or TV shots as she describes life in her large, clannish extended family on their Haran, Arkansas, farms and at their summer cabin on the lake at Bull Shoals. She soaks up the rationalistic philosophy of patriarchal Uncle Bently and the nativistic ideas of her Indian mother; falls in love with and loses her college-teacher older cousin, Cedric; and herself goes off to college. Words become increasingly important to her, as she maintains her journals and eventually is published in the local paper. Glancy's stories are not easily apprehended but are well worth the trouble of persisting. Style is minimalistic and imagistic, little action occurs, and one is left with pictures and sensations rather than with stories that can be verbally summarized. Yet the sense of having been for a short time among shared-culture Indians is strong. Other books by Glancy can be found in *This Land Is Our Land* (1994), nos. 426, 551, and 552 (for titles, see entry 448, this book).

450 Glancy, Diane, *Pushing the Bear: A Novel of the Trail of Tears*, Harcourt, 1996 (hardcover), ISBN 0–151–00225–8, $22.00, 237 pp.; 1998 (paper), ISBN 0–156–00544–1, $12.00, 252 pp. Ages 12 up, grades 7 up.

Comprehensive historical novel covering six months in 1838–1839 as told by people who might have participated. U.S. soldiers come into Cherokee country in North Carolina and force the Indians to march 900 miles through Tennessee, Kentucky, Illinois, Missouri, and Arkansas onto land reserved for them in Oklahoma. One family is typical of the 13,000 Indians who were designated for removal, during which about one quarter of the refugees disappeared or died. Maritole has led a settled existence with family and friends. A young mother with a baby girl in arms, she feels as though the very center of her being has been torn away from her, since "we are the land." She endures the death of friends, her daughter, and her younger brother and the inattention, neglect, and coldness of her husband, Knobowtee. He feels strongly the loss of the land he has been farming, resents the political agreements, and feels bitter about being unable to protect and feed his family and fend off the blows, threats, hostility, degrading comments, and general abuse of the soldiers. The relationship between Maritole and Knobowtee reaches its nadir when Maritole sleeps with a soldier who has been especially kind to her. By Oklahoma, their shared misery has restored something of Maritole and Knobowtee's previous commitment to each other, and the future looks less bleak but not welcoming, a situation history verifies. The novel is especially strong in presenting the woman's separation and survival aspects, but passages featuring the men set forth other moral and spiritual issues. The contributions of Cherokee and U.S. leaders are mentioned in contexts not always credible and in a history-book tone. A metaphorical style, with figures drawn from Cherokee beliefs; short, simple sentences that create tension; old, told stories; the irony inherent in the practices of Christianity as compared to Cherokee ways; Cherokee words in Sequoia's syllabary, used "as holes in the text so that the original can show through"; and portraying the soldiers with greater breadth (they are not all faceless evil automatons) than do most stories about the removals—these are good factors. The title comes from an old Cherokee story and refers to maintaining one's integrity however hard the situation. Although not difficult in diction, the book demands emotional commitment and reading perseverance. A Cherokee, Glancy has also written poetry and other fiction; see *This Land Is Our Land* (1994), nos. 426, 551, and 552 (for titles, see entry 448, this book).

451 Harrison, Jim, *The Road Home*, Atlantic Monthly, 1998 (hardcover), ISBN 0–87113–724–0, $25.00, 446 pp. Ages 15 up, grades 10 up.

Long, multigenerational novel of a Nebraska family of mixed Native-American and white heritage, seen from the point of view of those raised in the white culture but showing how their Indian background affects their lives. The first and longest of several rambling, almost stream-of-consciousness monologues is in the voice of John Wesley Northridge II, rancher and land dealer whose mother was a Lakota Sioux, set in the 1950s as he reviews his life for his granddaughter, Dalva, whom he adores. Born in the 1880s, he reflects the violent spirit of the frontier in his cantankerous personality but also the soul of an artist, his great desire in life having been to succeed as a painter. The second major focus of the novel is on his great-grandson, Nelse, the son to whom Dalva gave birth when she was fifteen and gave up for adoption, partly because the departed father may be her half brother, though possibly some other blood relative, her father, uncle, and grandfather all having been involved with his Lakota mother. Nelse's story, as well as those that follow of his grandmother, his uncle, and his mother, is narrated in the 1980s after he has decided to discover his birth mother and come to terms with his mixed heritage. Much like his great-grandfather in his impulsiveness and love of nature, Nelse is not worried especially about the Native-American portion of his makeup, but it confronts him constantly in the perceptions of the white world—nor are the Indians he meets more accepting. A very intelligent, often uncontrollable, restless young man, Nelse is an interesting and appealing character, but its length and the constant time switches in the narration make this a novel only highly motivated students will tackle and fully appreciate. An earlier novel about the same family is *Dalva* (Dutton, 1988).

452 Hausman, Gerald, *Turtle Island ABC*, illus. Cara and Barry Moser, HarperCollins, 1994 (hardcover), ISBN 0–06–021307–8, $15.00, unp. Ages 4 up, grades PS up.

Evocatively illustrated and poetically written picture-story book of pan–Native-American Indian symbols associated with the North American continent, known as Turtle Island. Each page is devoted to a letter of the alphabet, a symbol given in word form that begins with the letter, a picture illustrating the symbol, and a short story, perhaps better described as a paragraph essay, in which the symbol speaks in the "I" person about what it contributes to Native People or why it is important to them. Some of the symbols are objects, like an arrow, a feather, a pueblo, and a quartz crystal. Others are such beings as the Indian, kachina, buffalo, hummingbird, great serpent, and wolf. Some are qualities or elements, like light, lightning, round, and voice. The illustrations are done in soft pastels that flow off the pages and envelope the objects so that what comes through is an impression of the object or the essence of the object. This is a stunning book, one that, although aimed at the picture-story book set, will carry greater meaning for more sophisticated readers and viewers. A writer's note gives background.

453 Henry, Gordon, Jr., *The Light People: A Novel*, Univ. of Oklahoma, 1994 (hardcover), ISBN 0–8061–2586–1, $22.95, 226 pp.; 1995 (paper), ISBN 0–806–12735–X, $19.95. Ages 14 up, grades 9 up.

Often humorous novel, a tour-de-force mixture of literary forms—poems, essays, vision, drama, but mostly narrative—set in recent years in the fictitious village of Four Bears on the Fineday Reservation (the names foreshadow more wordplay to come) in Ojibwa (Chippewa) Indian country of northern Minnesota. When a young boy, Oskinaway, seeks the identity of his father and the whereabouts of his mother, who walked out with her powwow regalia and drove off with a powwow trader, the boy consults an elder, Jake Seed, one of the light people who can heal and discern matters others cannot. This action sets in motion a series of activities described in the stories told by the young magician and wishful light person Arthur Boozhoo and by others whom he encounters and whom those people encounter, stories that unfold in cumulative, episodic fashion, lead into one another, and turn back on themselves to give an impression of life on contemporary reservations, relationships between the Indians and the U.S. government, ecological, environmental concerns, culture erosion, and the ethics of placing Indian artifacts in museums, among other matters. Some of these embedded stories are sad, for example, the degradation into which the young people fall when they go to bars and night spots off the reservation. Many are humorous, and some are downright funny. When Oshawa spots his uncle's amputated leg on display in a Minneapolis museum and the tribe seeks to have it returned for proper burial, the ensuing trial is a masterpiece of hilarity. Some of the mystical parts are hard to follow, and trying to keep track of who is telling the current story and how that person fits into the whole demands attention. The narratives come full circle, however, in proper Indian fashion, and the sheer joy in words (even if occasionally self-indulgent) and understanding of the importance of words and the lifegiving-ness of language are additional indications of Henry's intellectual and psychical kinship with the past and with other younger Indian writers of today.

454 Hillerman, Tony, *The First Eagle*, HarperCollins, 1998 (hardcover), ISBN 0–00–224569–8, $25.00, 278 pp.; Harper Mass Market (paper), ISBN 0–061–09785–3, $6.99, 288 pp. Ages 14 up, grades 9 up.

Mystery-detective novel set on the present-day Navajo and Hopi Indian reservations in northeastern Arizona. Retired Navajo Tribal Police Lieutenant Joe Leaphorn and his former colleague, Jim Chee, now Acting Lieutenant at the Tuba City post, come together to solve two apparently unrelated problems: locate a missing woman scientist, who has been investigating the source of a plague, and find the murderer of a Navajo Tribal Officer, apparently slain while attempting to apprehend an eagle poacher. As in earlier novels featuring the vaunted duo, solid police work, careful deduction, knowledge of the area and Navajo and Hopi ways, and some luck point Leaphorn and Chee to one man, another scientist, and prove him responsible for murdering both people. Providing color and texture are details of Chee's and Leaphorn's private lives, tension between Tribal Police and the Federal Bureau of Investigation and other federal authorities over jurisdiction and procedures, and fascinating scientific information about rodent-borne bacteria and viruses. Best are the respect shown for traditional Hopi and Navajo traditional ways and beliefs and the well-realized Four Corners setting of desert, canyons, and high country. Also featuring this pair of tenacious lawmen is *The Fallen Man* (1996), about the investigation into the death of a wealthy rancher and mountain climber found on Ship Rock Mountain. Although some of the earlier novels about the Legendary Lieutenant (as he has come to be known on the reservations) and the dedicated, conscientious junior officer are better plotted and are more integral to the cultures, for example, *The Skinwalkers* (1988) and *The Blessing Way* (1990), *The First Eagle* and *The Fallen Man* are pleasing additions to the Leaphorn-Chee cycle on both professional and personal levels. For more of Hillerman's books about Navajo and Hopi peoples, see *Sacred Clowns*, in *This Land Is Our Land* (1994), no. 432.

455 Hobbs, Will, *Beardream*, illus. Jill Kastner, Atheneum, 1997 (hardcover), ISBN 0–689–31973–8, $16.00, unp. Ages 4 up, grades PS up.

Picture-story fantasy, loosely based on Ute folklore of the origin of the group's Bear Dance. Even after all the other bears have left their dens, Great Bear is still asleep, dreaming of playing in the snow or eating sweet wildflowers. In the village, young Short Tail, like the rest of his people, wonders where old Honey Paws is and sets out to look for him. After climbing high into the mountains, he lies down to rest and falls asleep. In a dream, he finds himself in front of the Great Bear's den and awakens the animal. Great Bear is surly at first, but when he sees how respectful the boy is and understands that all the boy wants is to see if Great Bear needs help, Great Bear takes the boy to a clearing where all the bears are dancing a carefully patterned line dance and invites the boy to join. After the dance, he instructs the boy to go back and teach his people how to do the bears' dance. Because they understand that the boy has dreamed a great and powerful dream, the people begin the Bear Dance, which then and henceforth celebrates "the end of winter and the awakening of the bears" in the spring. Strong, atmospheric, dark-toned paintings capture the power and majesty of the Great Bear and the physical setting of which he is an integral part. The pictures add details to the story and especially create the landscape of mountains and streams. Panoramic soft-edged views sweep across and off the pages, enclosing the text and heightening the sense of the story's agelessness and its folkloric origin. In one spread, the boy is on all fours in his dream in front of Great Bear's dark cave, while at the same time he is sleeping in the background on the mountain and appears as the mountain itself, a placement that indicates that the story is also a rites-of-passage narrative. This is an all-ages book, one that speaks across the generations and is worthy of a special place on the coffee table for repeated viewings. An author's note at the end gives background. Another book by Hobbs appears in *This Land Is Our Land* (1994), no. 434, *Bearstone*.

456 Hobbs, Will, *Far North*, Morrow, 1996 (hardcover), ISBN 0–688–14192–7, $15.00, 224 pp.; Avon, 1997 (paper), ISBN 0–780–72576–3, $4.99. Ages 11–15, grades 6–10.

Tense, exciting survival novel set one recent winter mostly along the South Nahanni River southeast of Virginia Falls in the rugged Mackenzie Mountains of the Canadian Northwest Territories. Big, burly, half-orphaned Caucasian Texan Gabe Rogers, fifteen, who tells the story, has come to boarding school in Yellowknife to be near his father, Tree, employee of an oil drilling firm. Gabe's roommate, Raymond Providence, is a tall, slim, handsome Slavey Indian from Nahanni Butte, exactly Gabe's age. At the end of October, Tree arranges for Gabe to accompany Clint, a young bush pilot, on a trip to fly homesick Raymond and a frail elder, Johnny Raven, back to Nahanni Butte. When Clint recklessly deviates from the flight plan and lands on the Nahanni River for a closer look at Virginia Falls, the engine stops and refuses to restart, and the radio ceases to function. They paddle fiercely to shore and get supplies out before the mooring rope breaks and Clint and the plane are swept downriver.

Fortunately, the three survivors have warm clothing and such supplies as some food, a rifle with a little ammunition, a butane lighter, an axe, and some cable. Fortunately, too, the old man is woods wise, but it is five months before they see civilization again, and then only after old Johnny has died and they have endured incredible hardships from the weather and the terrain. Gabe eventually manages to pull severely hurt Raymond out on their toboggan to Nahanni Butte. Recovered, they attend a potlach in Johnny's honor on April 2. Raymond pays tribute to his deceased great-uncle by reading the old man's moving last will and testament. Gabe somberly whispers his good-bye and thank you to Johnny, and both boys ceremonially toss straps of bear fat into a fire. The book follows the Robinsonnade formula for the wilderness survival novel in characters and events. The author includes Native beliefs, mostly presented through Johnny, and vivid descriptions of the extremely rugged territory and incredibly demanding environmental conditions. Although the narrator is white, Raymond is equally important to the story. The book reflects the author's experiences in exploring the Nahanni area by canoe and raft. An outline map is helpful. For another book by Hobbs, see *This Land Is Our Land* (1994), no. 434, *Bearstone*.

457 Killingsworth, Monte, *Circle Within a Circle*, McElderry, 1994 (hardcover), ISBN 0–689–50589–1, $14.95, 139 pp. Ages 12 up, grades 7 up.

Environmental novel set mostly in the Pacific Northwest dealing with the proposed usurpation of a beach sacred to the Chinook people by developers planning a resort and golf course. While the primary protagonist is a white boy named Chris, fourteen, who has just run away from the latest in a series of unhappy foster homes, the more interesting and pivotal character is Chopper or, as he comes to be called, Coyote, a Chinook who has lately been a scientist on a NASA project in New Mexico. Traveling in a souped-up Volkswagon bus with a Porsche engine, Chopper picks up the hitchhiking boy, and together they travel back to where they both came from, only gradually revealing something of their backgrounds to each other. At Wahkaikum they visit the grave of Chris's parents, meet with two Native Americans named Cadillac and Slim, attend a hearing where Coyote speaks eloquently but to no avail, and embark on a scheme to thwart the development by breaking down an old earth dam high in the mountains and letting the backed-up water rush down its old path to form a waterfall that washes out the first of the construction and destroys the site for a golf course. This outer conflict is played out against inner conflicts for each character, Coyote fighting his terrible memories of Vietnam and Chris his hopelessness at being labeled worthless by unsympathetic adults. The focus is about equally on Chris and Coyote, but while the boy is a typical alienated adolescent, the Chinook is given to mystical reveries, perhaps too idealistic but moving in the context. The novel is fast paced, with growing tension moving to a satisfying conclusion.

458 Lemieux, Margo, *Full Worm Moon*, illus. Robert Andrew Parker, Tambourine, 1994 (hardcover), ISBN 0–688–12105–5, $15.00, unp. Ages 4–10, grades PS–5.

Realistic, period picture-book story with the flavor of oral tradition. All winter long, Atuk and his sister, Mequin, New England Algonquians, have loved to hear their mother, Monamie, repeat the legend of the Full Worm Moon. This evening, the night of the Full Worm Moon, when their father, Anawan, returns to the wigwam, he suggests that they spend the night outside to see the worms come out. Right after sunset, they position themselves where they can see the moon easily, wrap themselves in robes, and listen to Mother tell the story. Long ago people grew lazy because the earthworms did such a good job of preparing the soil for the crops. Sun became offended and left the earth to grow dark and cold. A wise old man begged the Moon to ask Sun to return, which he did when people promised to do their share of the work. Every year since, after Moon signals to the worms, they wiggle out and dance under the Moon. Sun returns again, and people can begin planting. Near dawn, the family hear the faint sound of drums and see bright patches of light quiver over the ground. The children know the worms are dancing. Proof that they have returned can be seen in the little mounds of overturned soil that lie all around. This legend-like story is both a warm family narrative and an explanation of the seasons. Delicate, soft, dark-toned watercolors, in mostly browns, grays, and gray-blues, project its intimacy and mystery. Red and orange, the sun's colors, are the only bright tones. The children's faces as they wait for the worms to appear reflect their wonder, their hopes and longing making bearable the cold that is seeping into their bones. In the last scene, the little family walks home together, their clothes brown and their hair black as seen against the brilliant red ball of the sun just arisen in very early morning. An author's note explains that each full moon had a name and that Full Worm Moon occurred in March.

459 MacGregor, Rob, *Hawk Moon*, Simon & Schuster, 1996 (hardcover), ISBN 0–689–80171–8, $16.00, 191 pp.; Laurel Leaf, 1998 (paper), ISBN 0–440–22741–0, $4.50, 207 pp. Ages 12 up, grades 7 up.

Contemporary mystery novel with school- and sports-story aspects set in Aspen, Colorado. When Will Lansa, a half-Hopi Indian, half-white high school senior and star football player, meets Myra Hodges in the ghost town of Ashcroft the night before the big game with Leadville, he has no way of knowing that that will be the last time he will see her alive. The next day, he learns that Myra never returned home. During the game, in which he sets a new school rushing record rushing, Will suffers a head injury, and while unconscious, sees a Hopi kiva ceremony involving the god Masau. Later, he crashes a post-game party, where he discovers that some students are on Chill, a fashionable Los Angeles designer drug. Suspicion points to Will as Myra's killer: his knife has blood on it and traces of Chill appear in his bloodstream and in his locker, none of which Will can explain. Taunting messages appear on his e-mail, although theoretically no one else has his code. Will follows clues on his own behalf, determined to prove his innocence, and his grandfather, burly old ex-miner Ed Conners, and Will's divorced father, Pete Lansa, a reservation Hopi law officer, come to Aspen to help unravel the mystery. Complications ensue in abundance, but the breakthrough comes with the discovery by computer hack Corey Ridder, a bi-racial black girl new to Aspen, that police know all the students' e-mail codes. After Will has another Hopi-influenced dream in which a mine plays a prominent role, Will's grandfather Connors recalls that he sold a mine to Tom Burke, a man about town. Will, Corey, Lansa, and Connors drive to the mine, where they discover sophisticated drug-producing paraphernalia and an empty grave. It turns out that a drug ring has been operating there, involving Burke, two crooked Drug Enforcement Agency men, local Sheriff Kirkpatrick, and some students. It comes out that another student knifed Myra because Myra had found out about the drug operation and threatened to inform authorities. The grand climax comes when the "good guys" are captured and imprisoned in the mine, from which they escape before the "bad guys" bomb the place. Exonerated, Will returns with his father to the reservation where he can continue to benefit from the Hopi beliefs that appear to be strengthening him. The book holds the attention, in spite of trite episodes and characters, but one must be attentive to catch the plot pieces and find out what really happened at the mine. The Hopi dream sequences mesh well with the plot, and Will is a strong protagonist, who, if he makes mistakes, never lapses into self-pity or gives way to anger or self-destructive behavior. The title, which refers to the Hopi coming-of-age ceremony at which Masau appears, appropriately supports Will's maturing.

460 MacGregor, Rob, *Prophecy Rock*, Simon & Schuster, 1995 (hardcover), ISBN 0–689–80056–8, $16.00, 207 pp.; Laurel Leaf, 1998 (paper), ISBN 0–440–22738–0, $4.50. Ages 12 up, grades 7 up.

Realistic murder-mystery novel with boy's growing-up aspects set on the Hopi reservation in northeastern Arizona at the time of publication. Half-white Will Lansa, sixteen, flies from his home in Aspen, Colorado, to spend the summer with his Hopi father, Pete, reservation chief of police, whom he barely knows, and to work as an orderly in the reservation hospital. Before long, he has found a full-blooded Hopi girl, Ellie Polongahoya, to whom he is attracted, and has become involved in a murder case his father is investigating, the killing of a research assistant to the university ethnologist working on the reservation, and then of Ellie's grandmother, Abbey, a tribal elder and seer. Both murders, and other untoward happenings, are tied in with tribal religious beliefs, especially that of the Pahana, the Elder White Brother who legend says will return to bring an end to the curent Fourth World and lead the Hopis into the Fifth World. Suspicion points variously, but eventually it is discovered that the murderer is a half-Hopi maintainence man at the hopital, who is convinced he is the personification of the Pahana. Will's romance with Ellie is sweet and credible, and the growing respect and affection between father and son, the keen depiction of the desert region, and Will's gradually acquired appreciation for Hopi ways, beliefs, and homeland are among the book's best assets. The author does not indicate the source of details of certain ceremonies, unfortunately, but includes a helpful glossary of Hopi terms at the end of the book.

461 Martin, Nora, *The Eagle's Shadow*, Scholastic, 1997 (hardcover), ISBN 0–590–36087–6, $15.95, 172 pp. Ages 8–14, grades 3–9.

Realistic sociological and personal problem novel set for several months in 1946–1947 among the Tlingit Indians of the tiny, coastal fishing village of Tahkeen, Alaska. Clearie, 12, tells how, when her divorced Anglo soldier father is ordered to Japan, he sends her to live with her mother's people in Alaska. Although she never really knew her mother, who abandoned the family when Clearie was five, and at first determined not to like her mother's people, she soon finds them warm, welcoming, and understanding: Grandma Martha, Martha's brother, Uncle Samuel, a fisherman and woodworker, and Aunt Ivy, her mother's sister, an expert traditional weaver. Clearie grows to appreciate them, their friends, and the way of life close to the sea, sky, and earth. She attends the tiny village school, learns to paddle Uncle Samuel's canoe, attends church, enjoys the running-fish festival, and makes friends with the village young people, especially Mark, who attends high school in Sitka and takes her for walks on which she observes the magnificent eagles who frequent the region. Three main problems drive the plot: how the villagers will deal with Henry Jonee and his father, Tom, the village storekeeper, who bring a boatload of liquor from Sitka every Friday, making that "devil's night" in the village; whether or not aging Uncle Samuel will allow Aunt Ivy to help with fishing; and whether or not Clearie will come to terms with both her absent mother and her father. All three strands come together when Henry Jonee is arrested for setting fire to Samuel's boat and injuring Samuel. Aunt Ivy and Clearie take his place in the boat, and Clearie is allowed to stay for the summer but must return to live with her father when school starts in the fall. Clearie also discovers that her mother suffered from alcoholism, the disease affecting not only the relationship with her husband but also his relationship with Clearie. Characters are types drawn in broad strokes, and the plot moves much as expected, with Clearie being luckily on the spot to observe Henry in his various nefarious deeds. Descriptions of village life are sufficient to illuminate the way of life and reveal some of the problems that inroads from Anglo civilization are causing. Some traditional stories provide additional texture.

462 Mead, Alice, *Crossing the Starlight Bridge*, Bradbury, 1994 (hardcover), ISBN 0–02–765950–X, $14.95, 122 pp.; Aladdin, 1995 (paper), ISBN 0–689–80105–X, $3.95. Ages 9–11, grades 4–6.

Contemporary realistic novel set in Maine about a dysfunctional Penobscot Indian family. When her father, despondent over losing his job at the local paper mill, leaves home and her mother, in training to become a grocery store manager, cannot meet their bills, her mother and Rayanne Sunipass, 9, leave the Two Rivers Island Reservation and move in with Gram in Springport. Rayanne's grades have slipped, she often feels sick to her stomach, and she has become antisocial and withdrawn. She misses her pet rabbit, Hop, which she has had to leave with her best island friend, Ann Marie. Her new school seems terribly large, and on the first day, a classmate, Scott, taunts her about being one of those "lazy" and "rich" Indians. In addition, Gram's tiny apartment is cramped, and Rayanne misses the openness and freshness of home. Life takes a turn for the better when Miss Pinkham, her fourth-grade teacher, suggests she create an ecological logo for the fourth-grade section of the school. The design Rayanne fashions of Indian motifs of a soaring eagle on a midnight sky with white stars spread out like a bridge attracts attention, and she makes a few friends. Gram's stories from Penobscot oral tradition and Miss Pinkham's suggesting that Rayanne help with a loon-nesting project and allowing her to bring Hop as a class pet are among other aspects that help her to feel more at home and better about herself. When her father appears one day and announces that he is marrying again and moving down state, Rayanne has developed sufficient courage and self-control to contain her rage. She sees that she can create a good life by drawing on the best parts of both her heritage and her new situation. This story tackles the fears of a child in a disintegrating family, who must also adjust to a new environment hostile to Indians. Gram and Miss Pinkham are good figures, and the story is open ended enough to raise the question of whether Rayanne can maintain her equilibrium. A short afternote gives sources of information about the Penobscot.

463 Mitchell, Barbara, *Red Bird*, illus. Todd L. W. Doney, Lothrop, 1996 (hardcover), ISBN 0–688–10859–8, $16.00, unp. Ages 5 up, grades K up.

Realistic picture-story book describing a modern Native-American powwow. Katie's family pack their station wagon and camper with cooking pots and regalia and leave the big city for the Nanticoke Indian powwow in Delaware, which each year repeats the traditional celebration of the group, attracting Native Americans from the United States and Canada. As the drums call Katie's name, Red Bird, she fades away and becomes Red Bird, Nanticoke Daughter. They park the camper and greet Grandma and Grandpa, aunts and uncles, and long-time friends from all over. The chief calls the dancers to the circle, and Red Bird, elegant in her red shawl and beaded dress, takes her place among the other participants. She samples fry bread and other treats and visits the traders, selecting a headband with Nanticoke beaded upon it. At night, Grandpa tells stories by the campfire, and after sleeping the night with her cousins in their grandparents' wigwam, Red Bird joins the dancing and feasting again the next day. Much too soon it is time to leave, and after the going-away ritual, Red Bird becomes Katie again, and she and her family depart. It is back to school and work for them all, but for Katie the heartbeat of the drums will continue until the next powwow. The text is powerful in its simplicity; it tells without flourishes what it is like to participate in a powwow, particularly from the child's point of view—the wonder of the celebration that binds the generations together, the colorful drama of the dancers' regalia, the spirit of the rituals, and the excitement of meeting friends and relatives. Magnificent full-color, deep-toned oils, so realistic they seem like photographs, capture the drama, splendor, and wonder of the event. An author's note at the end tells about the history of the Nanticoke Native Americans and their powwow tradition.

464 Momaday, N. Scott, *The Man Made of Words: Essays, Stories, Passages*, St. Martin's, 1997 (hardcover), ISBN 0–312–15581–6, $22.95, 211 pp.; Griffin, 1998 (paper), ISBN 0–312–18742–4, $12.95, 224 pp. Ages 14 up, grades 9 up.

Collection of writings focusing upon language as a human construct by the writer many consider the dean of Native-American authors and a leader in late twentieth-century American letters, best known for his Pulitzer Prize–winning novel, *House Made of Dawn* (1966). The collection is divided into three sections. The first set includes essays that discuss the concept of words, with stories and poems of his authorship within them; the second set consists of essays about places, in many instances, those in which important historical events occurred; the third set presents nineteen very short stories to show how the intersection of words and places creates stories: "To tell a story in the proper way, to hear a story told in the proper way—this is a very old and sacred business, and it is very good." Most pieces spring from personal experience, to which then Momaday applies imagination in creating dialogue and in fleshing out incidents. Some conclude by inferentially suggesting the difference between what the Native American has done in the story or the Native-American attitude displayed and what an Anglo would do. For example, in the story entitled "The Toll Road," the persona acknowledges without dissent the claim of the old Indian to the road upon which the persona jogs even though he knows the old man possesses no deed. He knows the man has lived there for many, many years and hence has squatter's rights. Some pieces are small vignettes about real people like Jay Silverheels and Billy the Kid, and others ruminate on Momaday's own life or people he has met. While too cerebral for younger or immature readers, all the stories give ample evidence of Momaday's superiority as a stylist. Momaday has also written and illustrated with his own paintings *In the Bear's House* (1999), an exceptionally attractive and masterfully composed collection of two short stories; eight dialogues, which function as short stories; and nineteen poems. For more of Momaday's work, see *The Ancient Child*, no. 448 in *This Is Our Land* (1994).

465 Moore, Christopher, *Coyote Blue*, Simon & Schuster, 1994 (hardcover), ISBN 0–671–88188–4, $21.00, 303 pp.; Avon, 1996 (paper), ISBN 0–380–72523–1, $12.00. Ages 14 up, grades 9 up.

Farcical, facetious fantasy novel set in Santa Barbara, California, the Crow Reservation in Montana, Las Vegas, and a few points in between about a yuppie's search for meaning in life. Samson Hunts Alone, Crow Indian of fifteen, flees the reservation after he kills a thuggish policeman. Twenty years later, as Sam Hunter, he enjoys a comfortable existence in Santa Barbara, until a gorgeous young woman enters his life, followed soon by a handsome, strange young Indian. In short order, mostly through the machinations of the Indian, Sam loses his job, his condo, and his equilibrium through a variety of astonishing experiences; encounters an amazing array of other oddball figures, including a set of violent, drug-dealing bikers, an ancient Crow medicine man named Pokey Medicine Wing, and a seven-foot-tall hotel security guard; falls in love with the young woman and becomes the surrogate father of her son; with the help of the Indian, who he now knows is Coyote the Native-American trickster god, brings the girl, who has been shot dead by a biker, back to life; and returns to the reservation to live, with the girl now his wife. Except for a brief period in the middle, the novel proceeds at breakneck pace, outlandish figures and overwrought incidents soon replaced by others more outrageous. Sex scenes are few, but raunchy talk abounds, although the effect is tempered by truly witty wordplay and serious philosophical and social commentary, particularly on Anglo versus Indian outlooks. This book offers plenty of entertainment for those readers willing to take the risk.

466 Oughton, Jerrie, *Music from a Place Called Half Moon*, Houghton, 1995 (hardcover), ISBN 0–395–70737–4, $13.95, 160 pp.; Laurel Leaf, 1997 (paper), ISBN 0–4402–1999–X, $3.99, 176 pp. Ages 10–14, grades 5–9.

Novel involving prejudice against Native Americans in the small town of Half Moon in the North Carolina Smoky Mountains in the 1950s. A suggestion that the Vacation Bible School be open to all the children of Half Moon sets off a furor, since many of the children are "half breeds," a group of mixed bloods scorned and feared by some of the residents. Edie Jo Houp, whose father made the suggestion, motivated more by the desire for a good fight than for integration, sees her own family life disintegrate as a result. Her mother, who stands behind her husband in public, stops speaking to him at home. Her grandmother, whose house recently burned down, has displaced Edie from her bedroom. As a result, Edie spends more time than previously at the old sawmill site on the mountain, where she has privacy to read and write poems. There she meets Cherokee Fish, a classmate, the only Indian she actually knows. At first she is terrified, but gradually she begins to talk with him and listen to his harmonica, even beginning to dream of him romantically. Then one day she and her friend Mary Grady come upon Cherokee and his older brother, Sierra, arguing and, from their hiding place, learn that Sierra has responded to an unintended insult from her grandmother by setting her house afire and also starting another fire in which a man is killed. When Cherokee says he will not take the rap for his brother, Sierra attacks and kills him. Edie tries to revive him and is terribly shaken. She goes with her mother to the Fish home, an uncomfortable visit, the first time either of them has been in an Indian home. Later, she gives Cherokee's harmonica, which she took from his pocket, to his younger sister. Although the protagonist is white, the focus of the novel is on the prejudice against Native Americans and on how the incident affects Edie's whole family. See *This Land Is Our Land* (1994) for a tale from oral tradition, *How the Stars Fell into the Sky*, no. 525, retold by Oughton.

467 Owens, Louis, *Bone Game: A Novel*, Univ. of Oklahoma, 1994 (hardcover), ISBN 0–8061–2664–7, $19.95, 243 pp.; 1996 (paper), ISBN 0–806–12841–0, $12.95, 256 pp. Ages 14 up, grades 9 up.

Sequel to the Choctaw-Cherokee writer's mystery, *The Sharpest Sight* (1992), and like it combining realism and mysticism. This murder-mystery thriller takes place almost entirely in and near the campus of the university of California at Santa Cruz, where Cole McCurtain, a Choctaw Indian mixed-blood in his mid-forties, has come to teach Native-American literature for a year. He yearns for the home in the New Mexico mountains that he left after being separated from his wife, drinks too much, eats too little, has trouble organizing his thoughts for his lectures, wishes he could go fishing with his daughter, Abby, is indulgent to his teaching assistant, Robert (a young white man seemingly driven by idealistic notions about Indians and Indian culture), and is much bothered by dreams of a Spanish priest, who was murdered by Indian parishioners to whom he was cruel, and of a strange, parti-painted gambler. So abstracted is he that he is only dimly aware of terrible murders, mostly of women, in the Santa Cruz area, the bodies often horribly mutilated and decapitated. Almost by accident, he becomes friends with a new young faculty member, Alex Yazzie, a Navajo Harvard Ph.D. with a penchant for cross-dressing and a strong respect for his culture and the old ways. After Abby arrives, intending to enroll at the university, the dreams continue, and strange sightings become frequent and also are experienced by others. Back in Cole's childhood home in Mississippi, his father and elderly Choctaw relatives, Great-Uncle Luther and an old medicine woman, Onatima, who has dreamed the same dreams, travel to Santa Cruz to help Cole. Tension builds, while among other cultural events, a sweat-lodge ceremony takes place, and even Abby's life is endangered before the serial killer is unmasked and dealt with. Abby and Alex win the attention, Cole is too ineffectual for sympathy, and the Choctaw relatives, clearly types, provide both comic relief and cultural texture. The dreams and sightings produce a murky atmosphere, but the mysticism gets tedious and even frustrating. The concluding pages are sensationalistic, old-fashioned melodramatic nail-biters, and it is not hard for those familiar with the genre to identify the killer. The writer paints word pictures with great skill. Some earthy language and sex occur. For two earlier books, *The Sharpest Sight* and *Wolfsong*, see *This Land Is Our Land* (1994), nos. 452 and 453.

468 Owens, Louis, *Nightland: A Novel*, Dutton, 1996 (hardcover), ISBN 0–525–94073–1, $22.95, 217 pp.; Signet, 1997 (paper), ISBN 2–451–18683–4, $5.00, 320 pp. Ages 14 up, grades 9 up.

Realistic thriller, with mystical aspects drawn from Native-American lore, involving drug running in the drought-ridden mountains of New Mexico in recent years. Middle-aged, Cherokee-white Billy Keene and Will Striker, lifelong friends and failed ranchers on contiguous, parched spreads, while hunting in the mountains observe a man and a packet fall, or thrown, from a plane. The packet contains hundreds of thousands of dollars, which they divide between them and intend to use to realize big dreams, as well as pay off their debts. Then they realize that whoever owns the money, or thinks he owns it, will be searching for them to reclaim it. Trouble starts even before they get back to their ranches. They are attacked by a helicopter, which appears suddenly out of a thunderstorm and explodes under their rifle fire, only the first of a series of frightening events that take place over the next several weeks, during which they must elude both the claimants and the law. Drawn into matters are a scruffy, threatening bunch of hard-drinking, trash-talking bikers; Will's beautiful, estranged lawyer wife; Billy's new girlfriend, exotically beautiful, smart Odessa Whitehawk, Apache; the local sheriff, who knows more than he lets on; Billy's Cherokee Grampa Siquani, who forms an unlikely friendship with the ghost of Arturo, the murdered man, helps to bury him, and, by laying his spirit, brings water to the dry-as-dust area, which, as it turns out, is not to their total advantage; and a cutthroat drug runner named Paco Ortega, who wants more than money from drug sales. Ortega has a grand plan to subvert white society by giving the Anglos the illegal substances they want, and thus ruin their lives, destroy their society, and obliterate the culture that has devastated the Indians. Sex scenes, more of them and more explicit than necessary; humor, for example, Arturo teaches Grampa how to drive a truck so Grampa can bury him and the old man guns the truck through the barn door; violence; plenty of atmospherics in the way of natural phenomena, cawing crows, and close encounters; enough character revelation so that the reader can identify with the good guys, especially Will; enough "tipped hand" situations so that one can guess the outcome; clever plotting from the beginning to the very last, where the reader finally learns what happens to the ill-gotten cash—this is consistently entertaining thriller material, of the sort that Owens does well, along with cultural background information and personal cultural conflicts that blend well with the plot. For earlier novels about Indians by this Chocktaw–Cherokee–Irish-American writer, see *The*

Sharpest Sight and *Wolfsong*, in *This Land Is Our Land* (1994), nos. 452 and 453.

469 Power, Susan, *The Grass Dancer*, Putnam, 1994 (hardcover), ISBN 1–568–95215–5, $23.95, 352 pp.: Berkeley, 1997 (paper), ISBN 0–425–15953–1, $13.00. Ages 15 up, grades 10 up.

Episodic, period novel of Sioux (Dakota) Indians on a North Dakota reservation, combining humor, tragedy, magic, and realism. The book employs a complicated narrative structure that moves gradually backwards in chronologically uneven segments from 1981 to 1864 and then returns gradually to 1984. The novel opens with one powwow and closes with another. Harley Wind Soldier, seventeen at the first powwow and nineteen at the second, searches for his center both literally and figuratively. His father and older brother were killed in an auto accident before Harley was born, leaving the boy with the feeling of a gaping hole in his midsection. Harley romances a visiting grass dancer, a beautiful, redhaired Menominee girl known as Pumpkin, eighteen and on the powwow trail for the summer. Harley gains some sense of self through the relationship, which ends when Pumpkin dies in an auto accident. Harley, however, is closest to his mother, Lydia, who lost her voice and most of her desire to live when her husband and son were killed. These characters are touched by many other figures in a large cast in both past and present: Jeannette McVay, a white anthropologist and high school social studies teacher almost embarrassingly eager to learn Indian ways; Herod Small War, local medicine man; Margaret Many Wounds, widowed when her young husband dies of tuberculosis, who falls in love with a Japanese-American doctor at a relocation camp; and Red Dress, the maternal ancestor of some of these people, who loves Ghost Horse, a heyoka or sacred clown. At the ending powwow, many of these figures and others who appeared previously come to Harley in a vision. He sweats, then enters the ritual pit for a vision quest and sees Dakota warriors and others, who all join in magnificent song. In a final scene of reconciliation, acceptance, and completion, Harley's voice joins and then rises above theirs. It is unclear whether it is Harley or Pumpkin who is the grass dancer of the book's title, but Herod explains to Harley at the end, when the young man dons a grass-dance costume, that the grass represents rebellion (here apparently against the inroads of white culture). Although Harley is the protagonist, the many women are the most interesting and functional figures. The many interrelated and interacting characters and the varying points of view, sometimes third, sometimes first person, support well the Indian concept of contemporaneous time but may make the book difficult for unaware or inattentive readers. Cultural texture is high, with such features as the circle, the spoken word, stories, and song assuming importance, and dreams and visions are frequent and connect the generations and periods. Satire on the ways of both Indians and whites sets the story in relief, and there are some hilariously comic scenes, such as that in which a bull charges the brand-new motorcycle that Archie Iron Necklace won at bingo. Under the often light surface, however, this is a perceptive view of a complex culture.

470 Santiago, Chiori, *Home to Medicine Mountain*, illus. Judith Lowry, Children's Book, 1998 (hardcover), ISBN 0–89239–155–3, $15.95. 32 pp. Ages 4–12, grades PS–7.

Realistic picture-story book of two brothers' search for home, based on a real-life incident in the youth of the illustrator's father and uncle and illuminating a little-known aspect of American history, and set in the 1930s when Indian children were sent to white boarding schools to be shown the futility of their traditional ways and to learn to live as whites. Brothers Benny Len and Stanley, perhaps ten and twelve, travel by train from their Maidu-Pit River people at Medicine Mountain in northern California to the residential school hundreds of miles to the south at Riverside. There they must wear shoes and uniforms, march in line, sleep in dormitories, learn white American history, and live a regimented life under the supervision of a cold matron and an unfeeling, strict teacher. Benny Len's dreams of home with his grandmother and her traditional stories and memories of dances and gatherings comfort his lonely nights and give him strength to get through the tedious days. When summer vacation time comes, many of the students go home, but Benny Len and Stanley's parents do not have money enough to send them tickets. Stanley, promising Benny Len that he will get them home, engineers their escape from the school in the middle of the night. They hop a train and ride on top of a car to upstate California, where in the morning they see their beloved Medicine Mountain loom majestically in the distance and know that their parents and grandmother are not far away to welcome them. The vivid contrast between the arid life of the residential school and the rich life of the village is emphasized by the expressive, dramatic, full-color, earth-toned paintings, which flow across the pages like murals, recreating the landscape, depicting the people as handsome and strong, and contrasting scenes of school and home. The text makes much use of nature imagery, which is also caught in the pictures. Although poignant and moving, the story never becomes sentimental.

471 Schick, Eleanor, *My Navajo Sister*, illus. Eleanor Schick, Simon & Schuster, 1996 (hardcover), ISBN 0–689–80529–2, $16.00, unp. Ages 5–8, grades K–3.

Picture-story book of the friendship between the narrator, a red-haired Anglo child of about eight to ten, and a Navajo girl named Genni. When the narrator's family comes to live on Navajo land, Genni and her family welcome her and soon give her a Navajo name, Sparrow. Together, the two girls climb the cliffs to the caves of the Ancient Ones, and collect shells there. They ride horses, attend a family picnic, and later the wedding of Genni's cousin. The bride's mother gives both girls silver and turquoise bracelets, considering Sparrow part of the family. When she must leave the Navajo country, she takes her shells and her bracelet and her knowledge of the sisterhood that remains with her. The illustrations, covering every other page facing the text, are done in colored pencil and show scenes of the countryside and of Navajo family life and celebrations. Even though the narrator is not Indian, the story and pictures are warmly appreciative of the Native-American life.

472 Scott, Ann Herbert, *Brave as a Mountain Lion*, illus. Glo Coalson, Clarion, 1996 (hardcover), ISBN 0–395–66760–7, $14.95, unp. Ages 5–9, grades 2–4.

Picture-story book about a little Native-American boy who overcomes stage fright at a reservation school. Although Spider does very well in spelling, he is terrified at the thought of being in the school spelling bee to which parents and others of the community are invited. His father tells him to think he is the bravest animal he knows of, and he decides that is the mountain lion. His grandmother tells him to be as clever as coyote. His older brother, Will, tells him to be cool, secret, and silent, and he thinks of his namesake, Spider. At first he tells his teacher he does not want to participate and hopes that the snow will cause the spelling bee to be canceled, but he summons up his courage and agrees to be in it. With the crowd assembled in the school gym, he mounts the stage and keeps the three animals in his mind. Although he misses on the last word and comes in second, he is relieved, and even Will congratulates him. Both the text and the illustrations, done in watercolor and pastel, capture Spider's apprehension and determination. The Indian faces, realistic and varied, are especially well done.

473 Sneve, Virginia Driving Hawk, *The Trickster and the Troll*, Univ. of Nebraska, 1997 (hardcover), ISBN 0–8032–4261–1, 110 pp.; Bison, 1999 (paper), ISBN 0–803–29263–5, $8.00, 124 pp. Ages 5–12, grades K–7.

Fantasy novel employing material from Native-American and Norwegian folklore. Iktomi, the gangly, man-shaped Lakota (Sioux) trickster, is going along on the Plains of the northern United States one day, when he encounters a gigantic man-being with thighs as big as tree trunks. The giant is Troll, who is sad because he has lost his people, three Norwegian immigrants from the same family, and is searching for them. The two walk westward, Iktomi riding on Troll's shoulders, following the tracks of the family's wagon, until they finally locate the family attempting to farm the land they have recently acquired. Leaving Troll with his people, Iktomi walks onward until he discovers what has happened to his Lakota. He sees the men lying dead from the effects of the white people's "firesticks," the buffalo destroyed, and the remaining starving and maimed people leaving for reservations. Neither Troll nor Iktomi remains with his people, however, because both groups have forgotten their traditional ways and no longer feel the need for their ancient helpers. Years later, however, Troll encounters the descendants of his family, who greet him joyfully, the new generation having acquired an appreciation for the old Norwegian traditions and culture. Iktomi, too, eventually finds Lakota who welcome him, also once again having found value in the old ways and beliefs. The tone is congenial and gentle, the plot moves rapidly with enough suspense and comedy to mask the didacticism, dialogue is extensive and carries the story, and the basic characteristics of each major figure are retained, with stress here, of course, upon their beneficial aspects. Other Norwegian folklore figures are referred to, and the effect in both cases is to project a sense of respect and admiration for ethnic heritage. A glossary of Norwegian and Lakota terms completes the book. Sneve has also published an anthology of short poems and prose pieces by young Native Americans, which are described in *This Land Is Our Land* (1994), no. 564, *Dancing Tepees*.

474 Stewart, Elisabeth J., *On the Long Trail Home*, Clarion, 1994 (hardcover), ISBN 0–395–68361–0, $14.00, 106 pp. Ages 8–13, grades 3–8.

Biographical fiction set in 1838 during the United States government removal of the Native-American Cherokee Nation from their ancestral Great Smoky Mountains area to the Indian Territories west of the Mississippi, the trek known as the Trail of Tears. The story focuses on the escape of the author's great-grandmother, Meli (baptized as Mary Eve Miller), nine, and her sturdy older brother, Tahli, from a military stockade in Kentucky and the hard, eventful journey home, mostly by night and against great odds. During the flight from the stockade, Tahli suffers a bullet in the shoulder. Fortunately, the children are found by a friendly Caddo Indian family, who nurse Tahli until he is well enough to travel again. They are subsequently helped by a white settler with food, a small gun, and directions, but are separated while crossing a swift-flowing river. Captured and imprisoned for a week in the cold, dark cellar of a white bounty hunter's cabin, Meli digs her way out and continues her laborious journey, following the moon by night along an old wagon trail, fighting fear, loneliness, despair, and weariness and capturing small animals, which she eats raw. One night she comes upon a lonely campfire and is caught by the wary campers, who turn out to be her now-widower father and Tahli, who has reached home safely and brought their father to help him find her. Meli's memories of her previous, now lost, warm family life, her attempts to grapple with questions of good and evil, and discussions with Tahli about, among other telling matters, why the whites should feel it so important to "draw lines on the ground" (fix boundaries), provide texture and ballast. A note at the end verifies the general historicity of the story, while a longer epilogue gives facts and quotations from archival accounts about the infamous removal.

475 Strauss, Victoria, *Guardian of the Hills*, Morrow, 1995 (hardcover), ISBN 0–688–06998–3, $15.00, 229 pp. Ages 12 up, grades 7 up.

Fantasy novel with girl's growing-up aspects set in the small town of Flat Hills, Arkansas, one hot, dry summer in the early 1930s. Impoverished by the Great Depression, widow Elizabeth Martin of Connecticut travels with her daughter, Pamela, sixteen, to Arkansas to live with her father, a wealthy lawyer, from whom she has been estranged since before Pamela's birth. Elizabeth feels that her white father emotionally abandoned her Quapaw Indian mother, hastening the woman's premature death. Unaccepted by the town young people because she is part Indian, feeling oppressed by the large, opulent house, Pamela wanders through the backyard woods and discovers five mysterious mounds and an unusual piece of mica stone. The discovery spurs her grandfather, an amateur archaeologist long interested in the Mississippian Culture (Mound Builders) of mid-America, to initiate a dig to discover what the hills may hold of scientific importance and also, in his words, to insure that "there will be no legends left." A terrible summer follows, a period of "sickness, injury, equipment failure, [and] morale problems." The death of a workman in the most important discovery, an ancient crypt, causes a riot among the workers, and Pamela's grandfather suffers a stroke, ending the dig. Paralleling the progress of the excavation is Pamela's own discovery of her Indian Great-Aunt Mirabel, the Guardian of the Hills. The old woman instructs Pamela in the traditions and legends of the Quapaw. She also inspires the reluctant girl with the resolve to assume the role of next Guardian and keep the tribe's evil ancient leader known as the Stern Dreamer from awakening and afflicting his people again. Information about archaeological digs and credible imaginative details about the Mound Builders and their present-day descendants give this novel a solidity that many child-destined-to-save-the-people stories lack. Characters are types, and the book's force lies in the brooding atmosphere, anti-Indian sentiment, and skillfully constructed plot, during which tension builds relentlessly to the suspenseful conclusion. An author's note and a short bibliography about the Mississippian Culture appear at the end of the book.

476 Strete, Craig Kee, *Little Coyote Runs Away*, illus. Harvey Stevenson, Putnam, 1997 (hardcover), ISBN 0–399–22921–3, $15.95, unp. Ages 4–8, grades PS–3.

Humorous, talking-animal, picture-book fantasy, in which a little coyote learns that home provides the safe-making magic that always works. When strict Mother Coyote insists that Little Coyote, only "a half a howl long," cannot eat supper until he washes his fur, he runs away, taking with him his special, protective medicine bag. He encounters a "green grass-eating goat," a "black-billed, big-winged buzzard," and a "brown-backed, big-toothed bear," each of which can easily consume a small coyote. Thinking quickly, in each case he uses special magic from his bag to protect himself. When he meets a "horde of honking cars" and trucks, however, his magic bag is empty, and he runs as fast as he can back home, where Mother Coyote has supper ready and where the two cuddle up snugly together, safe from the horrible dangers outside. The illustrations in tawny tones of yellow, brown, and orange, turquoise greens, and the upland purples recreate the southwestern plateau region, characterize Little Coyote and his mother, and picture important episodes in Little Coyote's journey to learn a lesson in life. The humor of story and pictures and the innovative, alliterative, tongue-enticing language relieve the didacticism and play up the action and tension of this charming story. By contrast, the lesson of tolerance in *The Lost Boy and the Monster* (1999) is blatant. Strete has also published *Big Thunder Magic, Death Chants*, and *Death in the Spirit House*, nos. 460, 461, and 462 in *This Land Is Our Land* (1994), the last two fiction for older readers.

477 Strete, Craig Kee, *The World in Grandfather's Hands*, Clarion, 1995 (hardcover), ISBN 0–395–72102–4, $13.95, 136 pp. Ages 10–14, grades 5–9.

Contemporary realistic novel of family life among urban Indians (group unspecified) in the United States Southwest. Jimmy Whitefeather, eleven, is bitter, angry, and lonely living in the city. A year after his father's death, his mother decided to go to live with Grandfather Whitefeather. Now Jimmy feels imprisoned in his small attic room in the sagging, dilapidated house. The boarded-up houses and shops with iron bars across their windows intimidate him, and he has no friends with whom to play. This impersonal, almost hostile society nearly overwhelms him, and he yearns to return to the pueblo where he had lived happily all his life. His mother comes home every night from her dishwashing job overtired, irritable, and sometimes tearful. She and Grandfather seem to live on empty dreams, and they share a secret that they keep from him that he knows is important in understanding why they are in this cold, forbidding place. After he learns that his father made his mother promise to bring him here so that he can get an education and return and help other Native Americans, and after he sees Grandfather put his father's dream in action by spending all their money on food for a woman Jimmy saw grubbing through garbage to feed her tiny daughter, Jimmy decides to trust Grandfather and his mother. He grows confident that although this world holds many bad things, "good things were waiting out there, too." Events and characters seem made to order to make a point, but Jimmy's feelings and reactions seem believable for a boy his age, the culture shock for reservation Indians new to the city is convincingly drawn, and the descriptions of the desert are filled with sensory appeal. Earlier books by Strete are described in *Big Thunder Magic, Death Chants*, and *Death in the Spirit House*, in *This Land Is Our Land* (1996), nos. 460, 461, and 462.

478 Strete, Craig Kee, and Michelle Netten Chacon, *How the Indians Bought the Farm*, illus. Francisco X. Mora, Greenwillow, 1996 (hardcover), ISBN 0688–14130–7, $15.00, unp. Ages 4–8, grades PS–3.

Humorous picture-story fantasy, a mellow underdog satire in which clever Indians outwit presumably superior whites. A government man tells the "great

Indian chief" and his "great Indian wife" that they must move from their home-land to a farm and raise sheep, cows, and pigs. Lacking money to buy the livestock, the great Indian wife tells the great Indian chief to take his canoe down the river and search for some. He does so, and accumulates a willing moose, beaver, and bear, which he brings home and places in the barn. How the great Indian chief persuades the government man and the "green uniforms" with him that these animals are the required ones and gives the government man the scare of his life to boot makes for a delightfully funny conclusion to the story. The tongue-in-cheek humor is aptly extended by slightly cartoonish full-color, mostly full-page illustrations. For earlier books by Strete, see *Big Thunder Magic, Death Chants*, and *Death in the Spirit House*, in *This Land Is Our Land* (1994), nos. 460, 461, and 462.

479 Stroud, Virginia A., *Doesn't Fall Off His Horse*, illus. Virginia A. Stroud, Dial, 1994 (hardcover), ISBN 0–8037–1634–6, $14.99, unp. Ages 5 up, grades K up.

Historical and biographical fiction in picture-book form, telling how a Kiowa boy makes his first coup and earns his warrior name. Several of the boys in a Kiowa village decide to raid a Comanche camp for horses and leave secretly, knowing that their elders might not approve. As they are loosening the horses' hobbles, they are spotted, and in the breathless chase that follows the narrator is shot in the neck. Despite his wound, he hangs on to his horse and the ropes of two he is leading. When he recovers enough to sit up, a group of elders reprimand the boys for bad judgment and for acting without the counsel of the tribal leaders. The wounded boy, however, is commended for bravery and given the name, "Doesn't Fall Off His Horse." The narrator was the author's adopted grandfather. The illustrations are glowing, stylized acrylic paintings, somewhat reminiscent of the artwork of Paul Gobel. They evoke a way of life long gone for the old man telling the story to his great-grandchild.

480 Stroud, Virginia A., *The Path of Quiet Elk: A Native American Alphabet Book*, illus. Virginia A. Stroud, Dial, 1996 (hardcover), ISBN 0–803–71717–2, $14.99, unp. Ages 4–8, grades PS–3.

Set among the Plains Indians in the late 1800s, the alphabet-story told to a young girl, Looks Within, by Wisdom Keeper, encapsulating a kernel of phi-losophy or moral teaching for each letter. As the two walk down the Path of Quiet Elk, a way of looking at life, the old woman tells how various animals and insects illustrate certain qualities. Butterflies remind one of changes in life, Dragonflies of the tradition that light comes from the Creator, Hummingbirds of the sweetness of the natural world, Turtles of protection, Otters of playful happiness. Other letters stand for ceremonies, like the Medicine Wheel and the Vision Quest. The book ends with Zest, the quality achieved when one follows the correct course in life. Although it is highly didactic, the slight storyline and the acrylic paintings that cover at least half of every page in rich color should appeal to an audience broader and older than that of the usual alphabet book.

481 Tapahonso, Luci, *Blue Horses Rush In: Poems and Stories*, Univ. of Arizona, 1997 (hardcover), ISBN 0–8165–1727–4, $25.95, 120 pp.; 1997 (paper), ISBN 0–8165–1728–2, $12.95, 104 pp. Ages 12 up, grades 7 up.

Fifteen short stories and an equal number of poems (see no. 558) by a renowned Navajo writer that celebrate her homeland in northern New Mexico, her family and ancestors, and the Navajo traditional way of life. Although in the introduction to the slender volume Tapahonso says that the pieces need not be taken as autobiographical, their simplicity, strong visual quality, and concrete detail give them an intensity that makes it hard not to take them that way. They speak of naming practices, the importance of such Native foods as mutton and Red Rose flour, canyons streaked by the setting sun, herds of sheep grazing across the sparsely vegetated, desert-tan landscape, a blessing ceremony, and greeting the dawn sitting outside wrapped in blankets. One story retells a myth of how Navajo women learned the art of weaving from Spider Woman, the ageless being who represents the feminine element and helps those who are worthy. Another retells an Acoma Pueblo version of how the custom of lighting luminarias on Christmas Eve started. The simple, straightforward storytelling is very effective at conveying the sense and appearance of Navajo country and warm, loving Navajo family life.

482 Vizenor, Gerald, ed., *Native American Literature: A Brief Introduction and Anthology*, HarperCollins, 1995 (paper), ISBN 0–673–46978–6, $19.95, 372 pp. Ages 14 up, grades 9 up.

Anthology of Native-American fiction and poetry (see no. 559) arranged by order of the writers' birth, with a few autobiographical selections and two plays, in the HarperCollins Literary Mosaic Series, of which Ishmael Reed is general editor, intended primarily for college courses. The book opens with a history of Native-American writing (in the Anglo sense of the word "writing") and concludes with a thematic arrangement, list of readings, an index of authors, titles, and first lines of poems, and acknowledgments. Each selection is preceded by a short introduction with biographical information about the writers. It is unfortunate that in instances the editor either does not specify or does not indicate clearly whether the fiction piece is a short story or an excerpt from a longer work. Sixteen fiction authors who have published throughout the twentieth century are represented, ranging from such early writers as John Joseph Mathews, with a chapter from his novel *Sundown* (1934), and D'Arcy McNickle, with an excerpt from his novel *The Surrounded* (1936). Excerpts appear from such later novelists as James Welch (*Winter in the Blood*, 1974), Thomas King (*Medicine River*, 1990), Leslie Marmon Silko (*Ceremony*, 1977), Louise Erdrich (*Love Medicine*, 1984), and Gordon Henry (*The Light People*, 1994). Among the short stories, "A Good Chance," by Elizabeth Cook-Lynn, wryly describes how Native-American Magpie meets his death from trigger-happy white cops. In "Someday Soon," Paula Gunn Allen facetiously invents a new Maya myth of creation, written in the style of the ancient Maya Book of the People, the *Popol Vuh*. Le Anne Howe deplores the habit Anglos have of telling Indians what they are thinking and feeling in the pointedly amusing "Moccasins Don't Have High Heels." Evelina Zuni Lucero plays with the traditional hostile Deer Woman concept in "Deer Dance"; and in "A Matter of Proportion," Kimberly Blaeser reminds readers that moments, particularly those of love, can be more important than years. A wide range of tones, attitudes, styles, tribal affiliations, and substance distinguishes this anthology, which introduces readers to a broad span of fine Native-American practitioners. For other publications by Vizenor, a noted writer and editor in his own right, see *The Heirs of Columbus, Landfill Meditation*, and *Touchwood*, nos. 469, 470, and 471 (fiction) in *This Land Is Our Land* (1994).

483 Wangerin, Walter, Jr., *The Crying for a Vision*, Simon & Schuster, 1994 (hardcover), ISBN 0–671–79911–8, $16.99, 279 pp. Ages 12 up, grades 7 up.

Historical/fantasy novel set among the Lakota (Sioux) Indians, based upon Lakota legends and including retellings of Lakota myths and legends. Moves Walking, the son of a Lakota woman and a star, is raised by his mother's mother and the chief of their band and trained for manhood by the village crier. He early shows signs of becoming an extraordinary man. He has unusual prowess with the bow, yet refuses to kill on hunts; has a strange affinity with the stars; and arouses the hatred of the most prominent warrior in the band, Fire Thunder, a charismatic, silent giant of a man about whom warriors from all over gather. After the chief's death, Fire Thunder is chosen chief, in spite of the opposition of several leaders and the outspokenness of Moves Walking, who must then flee for his life. A long period of territorial aggression follows, during which, under Fire Thunder's leadership, bands and tribes around suffer greatly, as do eventually Fire Thunder's own people, from famine and starvation, since all nature appears to rebel against the vain carnage of the wars. At the end, Moves Walking, now fifteen, persuades Fire Thunder to kill him as a sacrifice to save the people. All characters are types, moments of high action offset truly poignant scenes, flashbacks provide background for the enmity between the man and the boy, and the interspersed myths and legends give the narrative universality. The basic story of Moves Walking remakes any of several Plains hero stories, which can be found in such sources as George Bird Grinnell's collections. Numerous Lakota motifs, most prominently the star husband, hoop of the nation (circle of the world), basic colors and directions, and symbiosis of humans and nature appear. Echoes of *Black Elk Speaks* (1932), the autobiography of the famous Sioux holy man, can frequently be heard. The mystic strain characteristic of the

Sioux marks the narrative throughout and gives it a strength that it would otherwise lack. A glossary of Lakota words and phrases is a welcome help.

484 Wheeler, Richard S., *Dark Passage*, Tom Doherty, 1998 (hardcover), ISBN 0–312–86526–0, $23.95, 328 pp. Ages 12 up, grades 7 up.

Western adventure novel set in 1831 mostly in what is now Montana and southern Canada, starring Barnaby Skye, British-born frontiersman and trapper, and his Crow wife, Many Quill Woman or Victoria. Lonesome for her people, Victoria persuades Skye to go to live in the village of her people, the Kicked-in-the-Bellies of the Absaroka. There he is a misfit, miserable at his low status, the utter lack of privacy, his inability to speak fluently, and their casual sexual promiscuity, which is repugnant to him. When Victoria leaves him for the sleeping robes of the flamboyant trader Jim Beckworth, Skye departs and makes his way to Fort Union, planning to work his way to St. Louis on a keelboat carrying furs. There the factor, Kenneth McKenzie, persuades him to work for the American Fur Company, rivals to his old outfit, and trade with the Blackfoot, most feared group in the area and longtime enemies of the Crow. Much of the action is seen from the point of view of Victoria, who, jealous of one of Beckworth's other women, insists on joining a war party on a raid and is captured by Bloods, most vicious of the Blackfoot. After months of slavery and abuse, she quite by chance sees Skye and cries out to him but is hustled away. The rest of the novel is devoted to his efforts to rescue her, and, after he is captured, sold to a Hudson Bay Company group, and taken as a prisoner eastward, her successful rescue of him. Although the characters are mostly stock western types, the action is exciting, and the scenes among the Native Americans show thorough research and understanding of the cultural patterns that divide the two lovers and the different groups of Indians. Especially appealing are the descriptions of the country through which they pass, full of recognizable topography and strong sensory detail. *Rendezvous* (1997) tells of Skye's background in London, his impressment into the British navy, his escape, and his initial years on the American frontier. Eight earlier novels in the series are all set in the 1850s and 1860s, after Skye has become a guide and a western legend. Although most of the novels center on non-Indian Skye, in *Dark Passage*, his Crow wife is an equally important protagonist.

485 Wisniewski, David, *The Wave of the Sea-Wolf*, illus. David Wisniewski, Clarion, 1994 (hardcover), ISBN 0–395–66478–0, $16.95, unp. Ages 4 up, grades PS up.

Awe-inspiring picture-story fantasy, set in early and far-off times among the Tlingit Indians of the Pacific Northwest. A Tlingit princess and two friends pick berries near the mouth of the bay, a dangerous place. The trunk of a great fallen tree upon which she climbs gives way, plunging her into a hole from which she cannot climb out. While she awaits rescue, she sees what she is sure is the spirit Gonakadet, the mighty Sea-Wolf. Henceforth, the princess is able to predict when great waves will beat the coast, an ability that earns her the gratitude of the fishermen and brings wealth and power to her people. Then a huge, winged ship with white people aboard arrives. They bombard the village because the Tlingit do not give them the number of furs they desire. Venturing out in a canoe with some of her people, the princess calls upon the Sea-Wolf for help. A mighty wave arises, engulfs the foreign ship, and deposits the canoe high in a great tree. Although the story is dramatic in its portrayal of the devastation the whites created for the coastal people, motivations are not always clear, the conclusion is abrupt and unclear, and the framework device of the canoe in the tree does not work reasonably with the rest of the story. Best are the magnificent illustrations. Three-dimensional, cut-paper, vibrant with color, vigorous in execution, they extend the plot, adding details of setting and action. They show the immensity of the coastal trees and the power of the sea, depict the towering cliffs overhanging the bay, and through the Tlingit motifs that appear around the boxed text and on clothing, recreate the enduringness and solidity of the ancient culture. The book concludes with a detailed author's note. Although the weak text cannot approach the splendor of the pictures, the book is a striking work of art.

11

Native-American Indians: Books of Oral Tradition

486 Bernhard, Emery, ret., *The Tree That Rains: The Flood Myth of the Huichol Indians of Mexico*, illus. Durga Bernhard, Holiday House, 1994 (hardcover), ISBN 0–823–41108–7, $15.95, unp. Ages 4 up, grades PS up.

Retelling of a myth from the Huichol Indians of Mexico about a world-destroying flood, the survival of a peasant and his dog in a boat with the help of Great-Grandmother Earth, and the re-creation of life after the waters recede. The tree of the title is a great fig that releases gentle rains upon the new fields and is said to stand today near Lake Chapala in central Mexico. Bright, detailed, primitive gouaches adorn and extend the story. Since the text is simply and directly related with a minimum of dialogue and the pictures help to interpret the action, the story can be readily comprehended by young listeners. There are undertones of meaning, however, that only older readers will appreciate. Both text and illustrations reflect the particular characteristics of the landscape where the story developed and where it is still in oral tradition. A note at the end of the book provides helpful information. For a Lakota legend Bernhard earlier retold, see *Spotted Eagle and Black Crow*, in *This Land Is Our Land* (1994), no. 483.

487 Bierhorst, John, ed., *The Deetkatoo: Native American Stories About Little People*, illus. Ron Hilbert Coy, Morrow, 1998 (hardcover), ISBN 0–688–14837–9, $16.00, 160 pp. Ages 10 up, grades 5 up.

Twenty-two stories retold from fourteen Native-American groups from Alaska to mid-South America, which Bierhorst terms "memorate," that is, they are not folktales but "memory stories," narratives from the secondhand reports of what were regarded as actual happenings. Little people, called by such names as tlaloque, surem, and deetkatoo, predate the Europeans in the Western Hemisphere. They live in forests, in water, underground, and on mountains; are benevolent spirits that give rain and foods; protect and sometimes act as moral forces; and interact and even intermarry with humans. They are frequently the source of such rituals as rain ceremonies and bring luck to those who are good to them. Some stories about them operate in a pre-world, mythic in atmosphere, others in a kind of half-world, while some seem more realistic, but all make generous use of magic and the supernatural. Some, like "The Rainmaker's Apprentice" (Nahua [Aztec] of Mexico), with its disobedient helper; "How the Dead Came Back" (Cherokee, North Carolina), an Orpheus-type tale that explains the existence of death; and "The Little Ones and Their Mouse Helpers" (Zuni, New Mexico), recall European tales but predate contact. Most, however, have no counterparts in European tale and offer fresh perspectives for American readers. Fine, full, explicit, detailed introductory and copious end material on the tribes and cultures, two guides to the stories by major motifs and distinctive story features, and a list of references add to the value of this book. White-line-on-black-background, primitive illustrations contribute some interest. For other books by Bierhorst, see *The Mythology of North America, The Naked Bear*, and *The Woman Who Fell from the Sky*, in *This Land Is Our Land* (1994), nos. 484, 485, 486.

488 Bierhorst, John, sel., *On the Road of Stars: Native American Night Poems and Sleep Charms*, illus. Judy Pedersen, Macmillan, 1994 (hardcover), ISBN 0–02–709735–8, $15.95, unp. Ages 3 up, grades PS up.

Fifty short, evocative, mostly unfamiliar poems and chants drawn from the oral traditions of twenty-two North, South, and Central American Native tribes, gleaned from such reputable sources as Ruth Underhill, Frances Densmore, Alanson Skinner, and E. S. Curtis. Some are songs to bring the night, while some are intended to soothe children or to encourage good dreams. Some are songs that animals might sing to their young or that celebrate the movements and behavior of animals or birds, like mice, nighthawks, owls, or bats, as night comes on or in the dark, in the voice of the observer or even the creature itself. There are a "Song to Straighten a Bad Dream" and a poem in which a grandfather comforts his grandson, a short creation poem, and a song that the creator sings. Cradle songs, sleep songs and charms, lullabies, healing songs, and even a song that celebrates the shooting star—this is a skillfully selected and carefully arranged collection whose variety avoids the monotony of many tightly thematic collections. Supporting and extending the poems, and adding to their interest, are full- and double-page, mixed-media paintings that flow off the pages and move the reader/viewer along. The opening poem is a charm for sunset that speaks of hills in partial shadow in late afternoon. Opposite the poem is a landscape with hills in shadow on the lee side of the lowering sun. Some paintings are highly patterned with pictographic shapes, some are impressionistic mood pieces, and one shows a tiny baby, swaddled in white, sound asleep on the back of a gray-toned turtle, as they float through the dark, night sky, which is lit only by a few small stars. This is a remarkably beautiful book. A note about Native-American sleep and night songs and a list of sources appear at the beginning of the book, and a list of the tribes represented and their geographical location concludes the book. Other books by Bierhorst appear in *This Land Is Our Land* (1996), nos. 484, 485, and 486 (for titles, see entry 487, this book).

489 Bierhorst, John, ed., *The White Deer and Other Stories Told by the Lenape*, Morrow, 1995 (hardcover), ISBN 0–688–12900–5, $15.00, 160 pp. Ages 9 up, grades 4 up.

Twenty-five mostly short folktales, myths, and legends from the Lenape (Delaware) Indians. Opening the volume are narratives that tell how the Lenape got stories, how the squirrel, originally giant sized, became small, and why hunters use snow in tracking. Other stories explain why the Lenape hate to kill quail; what causes thunder; how fire came to be; why dogs sniff one another; and why dogs and wolves do not get along. Some particularly humorous tales feature Jack, or Crazy Jack, or, more popularly, Wehixamukes, whose predominant mode is that of fool and whose literalness often gets him into trouble but who also at times assumes a heroic mien. One story, "Why the World Doesn't End," is eschatological, a story type of which others are described in a prefatory note. The title story, about an unlikely hero who triumphs repeatedly against great odds, explains why animals roam the world at will. The narrative styles vary from teller to teller, whose names are given for each story. Some stories have been translated, some recorded directly from the tellers in English, and some were written down as they were remembered and then edited. Stories of magic and grotesquerie, morals distilled and conveyed, plucky monster slayers, and lucky encounters, the tales project a conviction that many longer, more detailed retellings lack and have a pleasing storytelling attitude. An introduction gives information about the Lenape, also known as Delaware, who once occupied the Hudson and Delaware valleys and later were located in Ontario, Indiana, Kansas, and Oklahoma, where some still live. Bierhorst also compares the stories to those of other related groups and appends helpful notes, a glossary, and a bibliography of references. Photographs of storytellers add to the sense of authenticity. For other books by Bierhorst, see *This Land Is Our Land* (1996), nos. 484, 484, and 486 (for titles, see entry 487, this book).

490 Bruchac, Joseph, ret., *Between Earth & Sky: Legends of Native American Sacred Places*, illus. Thomas Locker, Harcourt, 1996 (hardcover), ISBN 0–15–200042–9, $16.00, unp.; Voyager, 1999 (paper), ISBN 0–15–202062–4, $7.00. Ages 8 up, grades 3 up.

Descriptions of ten sacred places in North America and their accompanying myths told simply and sometimes poetically, with gorgeous illustrations, full-page oil landscape paintings wider than they are high. Most are explanations of geological features: the islands in Lake Champlain, the Great Smoky Mountains, the whale-shaped headland off Martha's Vineyard in Massachusetts known as Man-shop or Gay Head, the huge stone called El Capitan in the Navaho lands of Arizona. A few have no specific myths, for instance, the Serpent Mound in southern Ohio and the Mesa Verde pueblo in Colorado, since little is known about the people who created them. The Grand Canyon is explained as a reminder to people of the destructive flood that drove them from the land below to our world. All this is enclosed in a didactic frame story of a young Indian boy learning from his uncle, a defect not sufficient to detract from the art that evokes the part of the country depicted and the mood of each tale. A brief list of further readings is given at the book's opening, and a map, showing the location of the sites pictured and of the Native American groups, as well as a pronouncing glossary, is added at the end. In *This Land Is Our Land* (1994), books by Bruchac are nos. 416 (novel) and 489, 490, and 491 (all oral tradition) (for titles, see entry 423, this book).

491 Bruchac, Joseph, *Four Ancestors: Stories, Songs, and Poems from Native North America*, illus. S. S. Burrus, Murv Jacob, Jeffrey Chapman, and Duke Sine, BridgeWater, 1996 (hardcover), ISBN 0–8167–3843–2, $18.95, 96 pp. Ages 8 up, grades 3 up.

Twenty stories and eleven poems from Native American oral tradition, divided into four sections, Fire, Earth, Water, and Air, representing the four elements considered the ancestors of people. The pieces come from a variety of Indian peoples scattered across the continent. Each section is preceded by an introduction discussing the element and the stories and verses included in that portion. Notes at the end list both printed and oral sources. The book is highly illustrated, each section by a different artist yet in a similar pattern with some full-page paintings, numerous smaller ones, and decorative bands down the side of each text page. Some of the stories are familiar from other collections, like the Seneca "The Three Hunters and the Great Bear," about the forming of the Big Dipper, and the Colville "How Coyote Stole Fire," but many are less widely known. See also no. 504. Five other stories from the Native American oral tradition (among others from around the world) appear in Bruchac's *Tell Me a Tale: A Book about Storytelling* (1997), in which he uses them as examples and comments on reasons and ways to tell them. In *This Land Is Our Land* (1994), books by Bruchac are nos. 416 (novel), 489, 490, and 491 (all oral tradition) (for titles, see entry 423, this book).

492 Bruchac, Joseph, ret., *Gluskabe and the Four Wishes*, illus. Christine Nyburg Shrader, Cobblehill, 1995 (hardcover), ISBN 0–525–65164–0, $14.99, unp. Ages 4 up, grades PS up.

Story from the Wabanaki oral tradition of the four men who seek out Gluskabe, known to grant each one a single wish. With great difficulty they cross a big water and make their requests, one for much wealth, one for great height, one for long life, and the last to become a great hunter, so that he can provide for himself and his family. Each man gets his wish: one receives so many possessions that his canoe overturns and he is drowned; one becomes the tallest pine in the forest; one becomes a rock, which will outlast all living men. Only the unselfish man is able to enjoy the fruits of his gift. Similar tales are told in other Native-American groups. The oversized book, wider than it is tall, is beautifully illustrated with double-page paintings in dark hues, with the text overprinted. Other lavishly illustrated single-story books retold by Bruchac include *The Great Ball Game* (1994), a Muskogee tale explaining the migration of the birds, with bright, mostly full-page collages in stylized patterns. In *This Land Is Our Land* (1994), books by Bruchac are nos. 416 (novel), 489, 490, and 491 (all oral tradition) (for titles, see entry 423, this book).

493 Bruchac, Joseph, and Gayle Ross, *The Girl Who Married the Moon*, BridgeWater Books, 1994 (hardcover), ISBN 0–8167–3480–1, $13.95, 127 pp.; S. S. Burrus, 1996 (paper), ISBN 0–8167–3481–X, $5.95, 128 pp. Ages 9 up, grades 4 up.

Collection of sixteen tales, all but two from the oral tradition of Native North America, about girls and women and their place in the culture. The stories are divided into four groups by geographical region of their origin—Northeast, Southeast, Southwest, and Northwest—a convenience for the structure of the book but one that has little or no significance in the type of tale since, except for the Iroquois nations and their neighbors in the Northeast, the peoples of each section have great diversity of culture. In an introduction, Ross points out that women had more independence, self-determination, and a far more important position in the Native-American societies than European reporters understood, as many of these tales illustrate. Each section is preceded by a long note about the four stories to follow and the peoples from which they come. An afterword by Ross and two pages of acknowledgments by Bruchac give more information about the sources of particular stories. The two pieces that are not folktales are "Where the Girl Rescued Her Brother," based on a historical incident shortly before the Battle of the Little Bighorn, where the Cheyenne clashed with the forces of George Armstrong Custer, a story passed down through oral tradition, and "The Beauty Way—The Ceremony of White-Painted Woman," a story with a fictional protagonist about the coming-of-age ceremony for girls among the Apache. Several of the tales are origin stories of customs or natural phenomena, for example, why wild turkeys are scattered through the mountains and do not trust people, why bears are friendly to the Navaho, what causes red flowers to bloom at the foot of Mina-Sauk Falls, and how the Penobscot people learned about medicine plants. In *This Land Is Our Land* (1994), books by Bruchac are nos. 416 (novel), 489, 490, and 491 (all oral tradition) (for titles, see entry 423, this book).

494 Bruchac, Joseph, and Gayle Ross, *The Story of the Milky Way: A Cherokee Tale*, illus. Virginia A. Stroud, Dial, 1995 (hardcover), ISBN 0–8037–1737–7, $15.99, unp. Ages 5 up, grades K up.

When the cornmeal on which the people depend for winter food starts to disappear from the storage bin of his grandparents, a young boy hides out, hoping to catch the thief. In the night a strange light shaped like a great dog appears, noses the lid from the bin, and laps up the cornmeal. The next morning Beloved Woman, a wise old leader of the people, hears the boy's story and examines the huge prints. She says they are of a spirit dog, and she makes a careful plan. That night all the people hide near the storage bin with drums, rattles, and other noise makers. When the great dog spirit begins to eat the cornmeal, they rise up making a fearful racket. The great dog flees to a hilltop and leaps into the air, trailing a band of light across the sky as each grain of cornmeal turns into a star. Authors' notes tell how they became acquainted with the tale, and an illustrator's note says the stiffly patterned pictures, done in bright acrylics, depict the life and costumes of the Cherokees in the early eighteen hundreds, while they still lived in the Smoky Mountains before their forced removal to Oklahoma. In *This Land Is Our Land* (1994), books by Bruchac are nos. 416 (novel), 489, 490, and 491 (all oral tradition) (for titles, see entry 423, this book).

495 Duncan, Lois, ret., *The Magic of Spider Woman*, illus. Shonto Begay, Scholastic, 1996 (hardcover), ISBN 0–590–46155–9, $14.95, unp. Ages 6–9, grades 1–4.

Tale from the Navajo Indian oral tradition, telling about the origin of weaving in the culture and the reason for the imperfection, the "escape path," woven into the border of every blanket and rug. The story starts with the creation of the *Dineh*, the Navajo, then tells how Wandering Girl, herding her sheep, missed out on the instructions from Spirit Being on building hogans and other survival skills. When winter comes and she is cold, Spider Woman takes pity on her and teaches her to weave the wool from her sheep into warm blankets. She also warns her never to weave too long or a terrible thing will happen. Boy With a Dream invites her to share his hogan, and through the cold weather she weaves with the gray and brown wool, but when spring arrives she moves her loom outdoors, makes dyes, and starts to weave the wonderful colors of nature. Obsessed by the beauty of what she is making, she forgets Spider Woman's warning and weaves day and night until her most beautiful blanket is complete and her husband finds her stiff and unconscious. After the Shaman performs a Blessing Ceremony, he tells the husband that she has woven her spirit into the blanket. When both the man and his wife beg Spider Woman to make the blanket less perfect, she pulls a loose strand from the background and through the picture, opening a spirit pathway and releasing the woman's spirit. The book is printed on light beige paper with large, realistic illustrations mostly in soft, muted colors of the Southwest.

496 Dwyer, Mindy, ret., *Coyote in Love*, illus. Mindy Dwyer, Alaska Northwest, 1997 (hardcover), ISBN 0–88240–485–7, $15.95, unp. Ages 3–10, grades PS–5.

Hilarious retelling of a Coquelle Indian tale that explains the origin of Crater Lake in Oregon. "Back in the old days," trickster Coyote was always in trouble, and this story is no exception. Here, he foolishly falls in love with a beautiful blue star. As he watches her move through the sky, he notices that she always comes close to a certain mountain. He painfully climbs to the mountain top, where he begs the radiant star to marry him. When she scornfully turns him down, he leaps up and grabs her. She pulls him high into the sky and then lets go. Yelping like a puppy, he crashes into the top of the mountain so hard that it explodes, and an immense hole forms. Heartbroken, he weeps, and his big, blue tears form the clear water for which Crater Lake is known today. Now, when Coyote howls at night, he may be telling his star he still loves her. The text is filled with mouth-filling action words and onomatopoetic language emphasized by larger, colored print. The exuberant, highly patterned, colorful paintings are filled with shapes and lines that often extend the text. For example, when Coyote watches the progress of the star and howls for her, purple-orange howl lines reach up from his angular, anthropomorphized figure and encircle the blue streak of her progress. Coyote's silliness is everywhere enhanced by his very long pointy nose, long pointy ears, extended pointy legs, and purple-splotched coat. The book is busy, but the effect seems appropriate for this Coyote story. It is a version of a widespread trickster type, in which the trickster longs to fly with the birds and comes to grief, the obvious didacticism relieved by the abundant comedy. A writer's note discusses sources.

497   Ehlert, Lois, ret., *Cuckoo: A Mexican Folktale*, illus. Lois Ehlert, Harcourt, 1997 (hardcover), ISBN 0–15–200274–X, $16.00, unp. Ages 3 up, grades PS up.

Retelling of a Maya Indian folktale, which explains why the cuckoo's feathers are dark, most notable for its stunning illustrations conveyed in an oversized format. Rainbow-hued Cuckoo is beautiful but lazy; she never does her share of the work, leaving everything to more industrious and prudent birds. Once, however, she spots a field fire that threatens to devour the birds' supply of seeds. All night long, she transports the seeds to safety in Mole's tunnel, scorching her feathers and burning her throat, so that now the cuckoo is a nondescript creature with a raspy voice. The story is told twice, with English at the top of each page and Spanish beneath. The text moves well and agreeably to the explanatory, moralistic ending, but the brilliant collages and paper cuts, based on Mexican crafts and folk art, steal the view. Nonprimary silvers, magentas, greens, oranges, and turquoises stand out against equally brilliant off-blue, off-red, green, and black backgrounds. Children will enjoy the story and the brilliant colors. Older readers and viewers will marvel at how the writer-illustrator has extended the story with the interplay of color and pattern.

498   Esbensen, Barbara Juster, ret., *The Great Buffalo Race: How the Buffalo Got Its Hump*, illus. Helen K. Davie, Little, Brown, 1994 (hardcover), ISBN 0–316–24982–3, $13.95, unp. Ages 4–10, grades PS–5.

Retelling of a Seneca tale, which has counterparts among other North American Native Americans. In the midst of a long, dry, hot spell, the buffalo sense that there is rain in the west. Old Buffalo, the aged leader, advises waiting until the rain breaks in their area, but Young Buffalo insists they should travel to meet the rain. They agree to fight for the leadership and to do whatever the winner decides. Young Buffalo wins, and the two buffalo, each leading a group of followers, head westward in search of rain and better pasture. One group, however, headed by Old Buffalo's wise son, Brown Buffalo, decides to stay behind. The two other groups charge ahead, Old Buffalo's group more temperate in behavior, Young Buffalo's full tilt through the grasses, disrupting the homes of many small birds and animals. Finally, only Old Buffalo and Young Buffalo are still in the race, all the other buffalo having died. In punishment for their foolhardiness and lack of consideration for other creatures, Haweniyo, the Great Spirit, causes humps to grow on their shoulders and their heads to bow toward the ground. Henceforth, all buffalo have humps and hang their heads. Old Buffalo is also transformed into the great White Buffalo, which can still be seen in the clouds, and the Young Buffalo is transformed into the Red Buffalo of the under-earth. The story is retold from Arthur C. Parker's collection, *Skunny Wundy* (1926), and is decorated and extended by colorful, action-filled washes. The symbols that appear in some pictures and the costumes are based on traditional beadwork and clothing found in books on the Iroquois (the confederacy to which the Seneca belonged) and in museums. Earlier Native-American tales published by Esbensen and Davie appear in *The Star Maiden*, no. 501 in *This Land Is Our Land* (1994).

499 Gates, Frieda, ret., *Owl Eyes*, illus. Yoshi Miyake, Lothrop, 1994 (hardcover), ISBN 0–688–12471–0, $15.00, unp. Ages 4 up, grades PS up.

Retelling of a myth featuring the Mohawk Indian Everything-Maker Raweno, who creates the world and gives animals their appearances and attributes. A troublesome owl meddles in the work of creating and is punished by being given eyes that see best in the dark, a short neck that restricts his ability to observe what is going on, and a dull, muddy-colored coat. Vibrantly colored, strongly conceived, representational paintings sweep across the pages, enclose the text, and portray the gradually evolving landscape and animals as Raweno develops them. Raweno is depicted as a gentle, strong-muscled, young Indian father-figure. The simple dignity of the narrative, the humorous commentary on human nature, and the powerful illustrations produce a book that spans the viewing and reading generations.

500 Gerson, Mary-Joan, ret., *People of Corn: A Mayan Story*, illus. Carla Colembe, Little Brown, 1995 (hardcover), ISBN 0–316–30854–4, $15.95, unp. Ages 4 up, grades PS up.

The Maya creation story retold in picture book form, with an introductory few pages about the culture's use of corn today. The two great gods of creation, Plumed Serpent and Heart of Sky, make the world from a black void and populate it with animals, birds, and fish. But none of these creatures can speak to thank and praise them. So they make wooden people, who can talk and work, but since they have no hearts, they cannot love their creators. Frustrated, the gods cause a great storm and flood much of the earth. On their next try they create people from corn, the mother-fathers of the Maya. These people praise and thank the gods, but can see and understand so perfectly that the gods fear them as rivals, so they cloud their vision and their minds. In dreams, however, the people can still know some of the secrets of the gods, and they weave these into the many-colored designs of their cloth. Wider than it is high, the book is illustrated with brilliant gouache paintings showing people and gods with facial characteristics typical of the Maya and landscapes rich with green fields and brightly colored birds. Down the side of text pages runs a strip decorated with motifs from the region.

501 Goble, Paul, ret., *Adopted by the Eagles: A Plains Indian Story of Friendship and Treachery*, illus. Paul Goble, Bradbury, 1994 (hardcover), ISBN 0–02–736575–1, $15.95, unp.; Aladdin, 1998 (paper), ISBN 0–68–962086–0, $5.99, 40 pp. Ages 5 up, grades K up.

Two young Lakota men, White Hawk and Tall Bear, are sworn to be kolas, or eternal friends, but they are both in love with beautiful Red Leaf. At the suggestion of White Hawk, they go on foot to enemy land to raid for horses but cannot find camps or horse herds. Determined not to go home empty-handed, they decide to capture two young eagles from a nest. White Hawk lets Tall Bear down the cliff on a rope to the ledge with the nest, then twitches the rope from his hand and abandons him. The eagles adopt Tall Bear, and when the young ones can fly, he seizes both by the legs and leaps out. The eagles carry him to the earth. When he arrives, tired and tattered, back at the village, White Hawk flees, having reported him slain by the enemy. Tall Bear marries Red Leaf, and in the fall they take gifts of meat mixed with berries to the eagles. Although not a translation of a particular version of the legend, this combines elements from several and gives documentation and notes about sources. Illustrations are in India ink and watercolor, highly patterned with brilliant colors in the style of earlier Goble retellings, as in *Iktomi and the Buffalo Skull* and *The Lost Children*, in *This Land Is Our Land* (1994), nos. 503 and 504.

502 Goble, Paul, ret., *Iktomi and the Buzzard: A Plains Indian Story*, illus. Paul Goble, Orchard, 1994 (hardcover), ISBN 0–531–06812–9, $14.95, Ages 4–8, grades PS–3.

One of a series of Iktomi tales starring the trickster-buffoon figure who, though very clever, often trips up on his schemes because of his self-importance. Dressed in his costume for the Eagle Dance, Iktomi starts for the powwow. Not wanting to get his feathers wet, he persuades Buzzard to carry him acoss a wide river. Riding on the bird's back, he makes rude gestures, not realizing that Buzzard can see them in the shadow on the earth below. Annoyed, the bird drops him into a hollow tree where he sticks fast until he tricks two girls into chopping the tree down, then blames them for ruining his house. The story is printed in highly illustrated, oversized format, with the main text in large type, questions for the storyteller in gray italics, and Iktomi's words and thoughts in small type. The author provides a long introductory note and list of references. Goble is also reteller and illustrator of *Iktomi and the Buffalo Skull* and *The Lost Children*, nos. 503 and 504 in *This Land Is Our Land*.

503 Goble, Paul, ret., *The Legend of the White Buffalo Woman*, illus. Paul Goble, National Geographic, 1998 (hardcover), ISBN 0–7922–7074–6, $16.95, unp. Ages 5 up, grades K up.

Highly illustrated version of the sacred legend of the origin of the Sacred Calf Pipe, which figures in ceremonies of the Lakota and other plains Indians. At a time of great change and suffering, possibly the late 1600s when the Lakota were driven out of Wisconsin and Minnesota, a woman appears to two young men. When one would attack her, he is destroyed by lightning, but the other is directed to prepare for an important visit. The next morning the beautiful woman appears to the assembled people and gives them the sacred pipe, which will insure that their prayers reach the Great Spirit. A short distance from the camp, she disappears, and in her place is a white buffalo calf surrounded by a large herd of buffalo. This myth is sandwiched between one telling of the great flood and the remaking of the world and another of the creation, from the flesh and blood of those drowned, of the red stone in what is now Pipestone Quarry National Monument in Minnesota and from which a number of Indian groups peacefully made their pipe bowls. The story is preceded by an author's note concerning Lakota history and followed by drawings of the construction of peace pipes and the meaning of their various elements. A similar use of several myths is employed in Goble's *Remaking the Earth: A Creation Story from the Great Plains of North America* (1996), which tells of the flood, the remaking of the earth, animals, and man, and also of man's near destruction by the buffalo until Earth Maker sends horses to aid people. Both books are brilliantly decorated with Goble's hallmark full-page stylized illustrations drawn with India ink, then filled in with thickly applied watercolors. Goble is also reteller and illustrator of *Iktomi and the Buffalo Skull* and *The Lost Children*, nos. 503 and 504 in *This Land Is Our Land* (1994).

504 Goldin, Barbara Diamond, ret., *Coyote and the Fire Stick: A Pacific Northwest Indian Tale*, illus. Will Hillenbrand, Harcourt, 1996 (hardcover), ISBN 0–15–200438–6, $15.00, unp. Ages 4–12, grades PS–7.

Humorous, picture-book retelling composed from several sources of how Coyote the trickster brings fire to the Pacific Northwest Indians. Tired of winter cold and raw food, the People appeal to Coyote to help them secure fire from the spirits they see on top of a mountain. His ego inflated by their request,

Coyote climbs the mountain and observes three evil spirits guarding their fire. At a loss, he consults the three huckleberry sisters who live in his stomach. They suggest that he enlist the help of Deer, Mountain Lion, Squirrel, and Frog. Coyote does so, returns to the mountain, snatches a fire stick, and flees, the evil spirits in hot pursuit. He passes the stick to Mountain Lion, who passes it to Deer, and so on, until nearly home, Frog spits what is left of the stick into a tree, but leaves his tail in the grip of the evil spirit who clutches him. Ever since that time, frogs lack tails, and people can make fire by rubbing two sticks of wood together. The text is filled with action and fun, and the scrappy, cartoonish, oil-and-pastel paintings catch its spirit perfectly. Coyote is gnarled, bony, and scrubby, and the huckleberry sisters appear as dark spots on his belly. The evil spirits are grotesquely comical ogres, and the Indians look gaunt and a little apprehensive, perhaps not as confident of Coyote's ability as he thinks. This delightful version has counterparts in Indian lore across the continent and indeed in such stories as that of Prometheus in Greek tradition. An author's note at the end gives sources and valuable background about the Coyote figure.

505 Goldin, Barbara Diamond, ret., *The Girl Who Lived with the Bears*, illus. Andrew Plewes, Harcourt, 1997 (hardcover), ISBN 0–15–200684–2, $15.00, unp. Ages 5 up, grades K up.

Retelling of a folktale popular among several Native-American Indian tribes in the Pacific Northwest, which emphasizes the close relationship between animals and humans and the need for humans to respect the natural world about them. The story, presented as though spoken by a storyteller elder, is set in the very early time when animals could shed their shapes and become human. It features Mouse Woman (although she is not so named), the tiny, mouse-shaped ubiquitous and powerful moral force who often assists those in trouble. A beautiful, haughty princess, in the woods picking berries, speaks disdainfully of bears. She is soon joined by two young men who lead her to a village, where she is imprisoned in a small, dark shed without food or water. A tiny mouse explains that she is being punished for insulting the bears, says that the nephew of the Bear People's chief brought her here, and tells her what to do when the bears come. The girl follows instructions and marries the nephew, who is handsome and kind and never appears in his bear form before her. She continues to long for her home and family, even after she gives birth to twin sons, who, like their father, can shapechange. Early one winter, her husband, whom she loves dearly, tells her that her brother, who has been searching for her, is near and will kill him. He instructs her to tell her brother to decorate the bear's head with feathers, sing a certain death song, and burn the bones to release his spirit. She must return to her people and instruct them to do the same thing every time they kill a bear. She does so, teaching them to treat animals with love and respect so that the hunting and fishing will remain good. The story's drama is extended by realistic acrylics, whose up-front scenes are solid and highly textured and backgrounds wispy and soft-edged. Cultural motifs appear on garments, on buildings, and occasionally in clouds or misty backgrounds. Small black-and-white drawings appear here and there to give details of what is going on elsewhere. The bear skins seem so real that one can almost feel them, and the double-page of the bear sons is endearing. A detailed author's note at the end gives background and sources.

506 Greene, Jacqueline Dunbar, ret., *Manabozho's Gifts: Three Chippewa Tales*, illus. Jennifer Hewitson, Houghton, 1994 (hardcover), ISBN 0–395–69251–2, $14.95, 42 pp. Ages 7–11, grades 2–6.

Three freely retold stories of the many hundreds surrounding Manabozho, the culture hero-trickster-buffoon of the Chippewa, or Ojibwa, Indians. The hero acts as a benefactor in all three stories. He suffers considerable discomfort to make people's lives easier in "How Manabozho Stole Fire," one of the most popular and suspenseful of all the tales about the figure; he receives an answer from the Great Spirit to his appeals for food in an unexpected and amusing way in "How Manabozho Found Rice"; and in "How Manabozho Saved the Rose," he is instrumental in rabbits' receiving long ears and cleft upper lips. The stories are dramatically retold, with good pacing, well-built suspense, and lively dialogue. A foreword gives important introductory information, and notes at the end specify sources. The first story is adapted from retellings done for children in the 1960s, instead of from primary sources. The other two narratives rely on primary material, although in the second one, Greene alters the action by combining the tale with buffoon material. The last story relies mainly on the account of the eminent Canadian Ojibwa authority, Basil Johnston. The skillfully executed black-and-white, stylized, woodcut-like illustrations are not only decorative but also catch the spirit and important action of the episodes, although sometimes they are not synchronized with the texts they portray. An erratic bibliography concludes the book.

507 Greger, C. Shana, ret., *The Fifth and Final Sun: An Ancient Aztec Myth of the Sun's Origin*, illus. C. Shana Greger, Houghton Mifflin, 1994 (hardcover), ISBN 0–395–67438–7, $14.95, unp. Ages 4–11, grades PS–6.

Myth telling how five times the Aztec gods attempt to create the sun, finally achieving the feat through the self-sacrifice of the least of them. First Tezcatlipoca, God of the Night, then Quetzalcoatl, jealous God of the Wind, then again Tezcatlipoca becomes the sun, each trying to destroy the other. Finally the other gods, tired of the fighting, chose Tlalloc, God of the Rain, to be the sun, angering the God of the Wind who, in his wrath, covers the entire world with lava. Later, ashamed of the destruction he has caused, he chooses Tlalloc's wife, Chalchihuitlicue, to become the fourth sun. The God of the Night insults this Goddess of the Waters until her tears cover the land and turn all the creatures into fish. Unable to endure the darkness, the gods convene and realize that to get a permanent sun there must be sacrifice. Tecciztecal, God of the Snails, offers himself but is unable to jump into the fire. Then Nanautzin, the scorned Scabby-Pimply One, rushes into the center of the blaze and becomes the fifth and final sun. The myth is written in simple but dignified language. Illustrations are predominately golds and oranges, with borders based on Aztec patterns and initial letters on the hieroglyphics found on a pre-Hispanic calendar stone. An author's note says the story is taken mostly from a sixteenth-century manuscript and the calendar stone.

508 Haley, Gail, ret., *Two Bad Boys: A Very Old Cherokee Tale*, illus. Gail Haley, Dutton, 1996 (hardcover), ISBN 0–525–45311–3, $14.95, unp. Ages 4–8, grades PS–3.

A Cherokee folktale, essentially the equivalent of the Greek Pandora tale. Before humans had to work to survive, Boy lives with his parents, who provide easily all that is needed, his father going out each day and bringing in sufficient game, his mother collecting corn and beans from the storehouse. But Boy is lonely. He looks into the river and sees a boy exactly like him, who says he is his wild brother. After Wild Boy comes to live with the family, he continually draws Boy into mischief. One day they follow their father and see that he rolls a huge stone from the mouth of a cave. After releasing a buck and shooting it, he quickly rolls the stone back in place. At Wild Boy's urging, the brothers go to the cave, roll back the stone, and release all the wild animals and birds. They are unable to replace the stone. Their father chides them, then leaves for the Western Lands of the Darkening Sun. After that the boys must hunt for game, but their mother still provides corn and beans. Again Wild Boy urges his brother to spy on her, then try to imitate her, but because of their interference, Corn Mother will no longer provide, and their mother flies away to the Western Lands. From then on, humans must dig, plant, tend, and harvest to obtain their vegetables. Haley's gouache illustrations picture realistic animals and Indians on light beige backgrounds, each page surrounded by a border featuring Native-American motifs.

509 Harper, Piers, ret., *How the World Was Saved and Other Native American Tales*, illus. Piers Harper, Western, 1994 (hardcover), ISBN 0–307–17507, $14.95, 23 pp. Ages 5–12, grades K–7.

Simple, directly retold versions of eight Native-American myths decorated with bold, bright, dramatic illustrations whose motifs and settings are drawn from the cultures represented. The reader receives a vivid picture of the world of the dead as a young woman travels there in a Nisqualli myth, "The Girl Who Married a Ghost"; the great and powerful spirit Michabo recreates the world after a mighty flood destroys it in the Algonquin "Michabo and the Flood"; Tirawa, the greatest god of the Pawnee, oversees the work of lesser gods in creating such physical features as trees and other plants to accommodate humans, who are then also brought into being; and in "How the World Was

Saved," twin Navajo heroes, Monster-Slayer and Child-of-the-Water, make the world habitable by ridding it of many of the monsters that plague it. A note about the purpose and function of myths introduces this slim, attractive book but deplorably does not indicate the sources of the tales.

510 Harrell, Beatrice Orcutt, ret., *How Thunder and Lightning Came to Be*, illus. Susan L. Roth, Dial, 1995 (hardcover), ISBN 0–803–71749–0, $14.89, unp. Ages 4–8, grades PS–3.

Choctaw tale illustrated in bright paper collages. Sun, wanting to warn people when he is sending wind and rain, turns the job over to two great, silly birds, Heloha, who is big and slow-moving, and her mate, Melatha, much smaller, very fast, and clumsy. They try several plans without success. Then Heloha lays her eggs on the cloud where they live, thinking it suitably soft and fluffy. The giant eggs, however, begin to roll, and Heloha calls loudly to Melatha to come and save them. He runs so fast that he trips over his own feet and falls to earth, hitting a tree and sending out sparks. The eggs keep rolling, bumping and rumbling, but he cannot catch them. Although Melatha thinks he has failed and is sad, Heloha comforts him, saying she can always lay more eggs. And indeed, whenever she lays her eggs and Melatha streaks across the sky to save them, wind and rain always follow. The tale is prefaced by an author's note about her sources.

511 Hausman, Gerald, ret., *Coyote Walks on Two Legs: A Book of Navajo Myths and Legends*, illus. Floyd Cooper, Philomel, 1994 (hardcover), ISBN 0–399–22018–6, $15.95, unp. Ages 5 up, grades K up.

Retellings in large, highly illustrated format of five stories of the trickster-buffoon-culture hero Coyote from Navajo Indian oral tradition. Coyote causes a world-destroying flood from which the animal people escape to a new world, presumably the current one but situated in the sky. The other four stories, more typical of the trickster, tell how Coyote gets his name, First Angry; how he loses his eyes by trying to copy Magpie's trick of throwing them away and recalling them (a widespread trickster story type); how he tries to steal corn from its guardian, Horned Toad; and how he tries to get a spotted coat like the fawn's by letting sparks burn holes in his hair. The illustrations are realistic, full-page paintings that bleed to the edges in southwestern colors of orange, gold, and tan. The text appears in the form of free-verse poems superimposed on the pictures. Despite its picture-book format, older children can benefit from this striking collection.

512 Hausman, Gerald, ret., *Eagle Boy: A Traditional Navajo Legend*, illus. Cara Moser and Barry Moser, HarperCollins, 1996 (hardcover), ISBN 0–06–021101–6, $19.95, unp. Ages 4–12, grades PS–7.

Retelling in highly attractive, picture-story book form of a Navajo Indian legend, a portion of the very long Beadway ceremonial healing chant. A boy, who dreams of soaring with the eagles, is taken by Father and Mother Eagle high into the "country of clouds at the top of the sky" where the Eagle Chief lives. He amuses himself with Eagle Chief's prayer sticks, rattles, and drums, but although instructed not to go outside, he disobeys and is turned by Coyote the trickster into a skinny little coyote. After he performs tasks imposed upon him by Eagle Chief, he is restored to his human form and allowed to return to his people, now bearing the adult name Eagle Boy. He brings with him a sacred eagle feather, which enables him to become a great medicine man. Although the retelling of this old ceremonial legend moves smoothly with tension and characterization, the point that the Eagle Way ceremony rituals and dances were brought back is not made, but must be inferred from the ending statement that the boy becomes a great medicine man. The story follows a common pattern, particularly in the Southwest, in which a youth goes on a journey, endures hardships, meets a figure of tremendous importance, and returns with tribal rituals and ceremonies. A note at the beginning of the retelling indicates the source of the material, and an endnote comments on the significance of eagles to the Navajo and on the sand painting practice associated with the healing ceremonies. The magnificent illustrations capture the sense of the desert country and especially of the clouds and the sky, and also convey something of the sandpainter's art. Done in pastels on board, they project a hazy, ethereal atmosphere. The pictures of the Eagle Chief evoke the sacred bird's majesty and great strength and those of Coyote the slyness of his character.

513 Hausman, Gerald, coll. and ret., *How Chipmunk Got Tiny Feet: Native American Animal Origin Stories*, illus. Ashley Wolff, HarperCollins, 1995 (hardcover), ISBN 0–06–022906–3, $14.95, 41 pp. Ages 4–8, grades PS–3.

Seven origin tales, collected from Navajo and Creek Indian storytellers and from an unspecified Tsimshian source and retold in pleasing style. They explain certain features of animal appearance or behavior and carry moral lessons of obedience, consideration, being oneself, and the like. In particular, they emphasize that all beings live in the world together. Coyote plays the eye-thrower game (a motif common across the continent) in imitation of Magpie and ends up with the yellow eyes that all coyotes have today. Mouse learns how to play football in a distinctive way and is changed by Mother Earth into Bat. Fat Lizard becomes lean and rough skinned and learns how to camouflage himself, Hawk uses one of his distinctively marked tail feathers to halt a flood, Horse receives speed and grace from Butterfly, Possum loses his beautiful plumed tail to Skunk, and Chipmunk acquires his tiny feet because he stole corn from Gila Monster. The stories are fast moving and amusing and are complemented by strongly composed colorful linoleum-block prints painted with watercolors, which picture situations and characters and accent the humor. Pages are bordered with colorful designs incorporating the iconography distinctive to the tribes.

514 Hausman, Gerald, ret., *The Story of Blue Elk*, illus. Kristina Rodanas, Clarion, 1998 (hardcover), ISBN 0–395–84512–2, $15.00, unp. Ages 4 up, grades PS up.

Romantic folktale from the Pueblo Indians of the bond between a magnificent elk and a mute young man. On the day that a baby boy, perfect in all ways except that he can make no sound, is born, a huge elk with a rack "like the branches of a black oak" comes into the village, casting a long blue shadow as it moves. It stops at the home of the newborn child, stamps its foot twelve times deliberately when the baby is shown to it, and then leaves, as silent and magnificent as when it came. Twelve years later, Blue Elk, now a young man, falls in love with a pretty village girl but cannot speak of his affection. In the meadows one day, he encounters the great elk, and, for a long time, the two become inseparable companions, ranging the hills and uplands. One day, the elk says that, when he dies, his horns must be planted in the earth. A hunter later announces that he has slain a great elk. Blue Elk finds where his slain mentor died and sees that the hunter has placed the horns in the earth appropriately. The rack grows and becomes entwined with the trunk of a young red cedar, from which Blue Elk fashions a flute with which he can finally speak to the woman he loves. Strongly composed, richly paletted, highly textured illustrations in colored pencils and watercolors overpower the simply told text. Rounded and sculptured, they depict the southwestern adobe and hillside settings, reveal the characters, and add details to the story. A writer's note gives information about the story and sources.

515 Jackson, Ellen, ret., *The Precious Gift: A Navaho Creation Myth*, illus. Woodleigh Marx Hubbard, Simon & Schuster, 1996 (hardcover), ISBN 0–689–80480–6, $16.00, unp. Ages 4–8, grades PS–3.

Part of the Navaho origin myth, telling how the Dine people, after they emerge from the underworld into this one, obtain water. They swim up through a reed in the ocean and find a land dry and parched. First Man sends Beaver and Otter, then Frog and Turtle back to bring water to the new world, but they all fail. Then Snail volunteers. She, too, almost is defeated, but in the flask she has tied on her back remains one drop of clear water, from which First Man, with chants, creates rivers. In gratitude, First Man fastens the flask permanently onto Snail's back to be her home. The story, only one part of a longer, more complex creation myth, demonstrates the importance of water in a semidesert area of the Southwest. The gouache illustrations, which cover all the oversized pages with the text overprinted, are brilliant semiprimitives, showing First Man, First Woman, and many animals in stylized pictures full of action.

516 Johnston, Basil, coll., ed., and ret., *The Manitous: The Spiritual World of the Ojibway*, illus. David Johnson, HarperCollins, 1995 (hardcover), ISBN 0–06–017199–5, $24.00, 247 pp.; (paperback), ISBN 0–06–092735–6, $12.00, 272 pp. Ages 14 up, grades 9 up.

Collection focusing on manitous, supernatural beings of various degrees of importance and power of the Anishinaubae (the northeastern woodlands) Indians, in this case, the Ojibway, one of several collections by this writer, an Ojibway from the Cape Croker reserve in Ontario, Canada. Johnston gathered and retold these myths, legends, tales, and spiritual teachings from his own recollections and from interviews with tribal elders. The "Introduction" tells about the creation of the world and humans, a flood, and Sky Woman, an important mythological figure. "Muzzu-Kimmik-Quae: Mother Earth" provides background on Mother Earth or Earth Woman and also tells how the prototypical hero, Nana'b'oozoo, recreated the earth after a world-destroying flood. Also about Nana'b'oozoo and his three heroic brothers are "Maudjee-kawiss: The First Son," which, in addition to being a first-rate adventure story, tells of the origin of recording information on sashes, scrolls, and the like, and of stories; "Pukawiss: The Disowned," about the first dancer, actor, and entertainer; "Cheeby-aub-oozoo: The Ghost of Rabbit," about the first holy man or spiritual leader, who originates vision quests and becomes the ruler of the underworld or afterlife; and "Nana'b'oozoo," a detailed version of the life and adventures of the mightiest trickster and warrior of them all. "The Manitous of the Forests and Meadows" explains how fire, tobacco, and evergreen and birch trees came to be and is also a seasonal tale. "The Spirit of Maundau-meen (Maize)" explains how the Ojibway received corn. The book exhibits an authoritative appeal similar to that of Johnston's best-known book, *Ojibway Heritage* (1976), but it is more tightly organized. The stories also have a stronger affinity to the storytelling mode, even though philosophical comments and explanatory information occasionally impede the flow. A preface and an introduction open the book, and an extensive glossary of names and terms concludes it.

517 Johnston, Tony, ret., *The Tale of Rabbit and Coyote*, illus. Tomie dePaola, Putnam, 1994 (hardcover), ISBN 0–399–22258–8, $14.95, unp. Ages 3 up, grades PS up.

Lively retelling of a tale from the Zapotec Indians of Mexico about how clever Rabbit outwits slow-witted Coyote, in a series of episodes that recall the escapades in the Brer Rabbit stories. After Rabbit eats a farmer's chiles, the farmer captures him by making a wax dummy to which Rabbit sticks. The farmer puts him in a sack and hangs him from a nail on the side of his house. Rabbit tricks gullible Coyote into releasing him by pretending that he is to be married to the farmer's daughter, then again in a series of tricks in which he knocks Coyote out with unripe fruit of a jicara tree, persuades Coyote to hold up a huge rock on the side of a mountain that he claims will fall down and crush the world, gets Coyote to wallop a wasps' nest with a stick, and finally persuades Coyote to drink up the water from a pond to acquire the reflection of the moon, which Rabbit claims is cheese. Although Coyote is bloated like a sponge, he chases Rabbit, who hops up a ladder into the sky and onto the moon. Ever since, Coyote howls at the moon because Rabbit is hiding there. The raucous fun is extended by bright greens, oranges, turquoises, and purples; two-dimensional, comic figures whose faces are distorted to amplify the emotion; detailed backgrounds that create the desert, mountainous setting, and occasional Spanish words in the text and interjections similar to voice bubbles in the illustrations. This is a delightfully amusing, action-filled story that will appeal to a wide age range. A writer's note and a glossary are included. Johnston has also published *The Badger and the Magic Fan*, no. 304 in *This Land Is Our Land* (1994).

518 Manitonquat (Medicine Story), ret., *The Children of the Morning Light: Wampanoag Tales*, illus. Mary F. Arquette, Macmillan, 1994 (hardcover), ISBN 0–02–765905–4, $16.95, 72 pp. Ages 8 up, grades 3 up.

Eleven humorous, fast-paced stories from the Wampanoag, or Pokonoket, Indians of the northeastern United States, chiefly Massachusetts, which the reteller, a Wampanoag elder, heard in his youth. The stories are retold with flair and affection, and the style is highly auditory, so that the storyteller's voice and persona come through strongly. The stories are presented in the framework of Old Storyteller's stirring up the fire and passing them on, after instructing his hearers to gather closely and keep each other warm, a device that seems condescending and unnecessary given the intrinsic strength of the tales. The selections are divided into two sections: "The Morning of the World" and "More Tales of Maushop." The opening story appropriately tells of the beginning of the universe, brought out of nothing by the Great Mystery, who sings joyfully to create time, space, and movement in space, stars and other heavenly bodies, the sky, the ocean, and Mother Earth deep inside the ocean. Other stories tell of the origin of humans, the sweat lodge, death, troubles, wisdom, arts, crafts, and the healing arts. Maushop is a special figure, the one of the two heavenly twins responsible for good things coming to be. Maushop creates Turtle Island, which becomes the earth, made from soil brought up from Mother Earth inside the ocean, and fixes the seasons, among other deeds of beneficence. Some trickster tales appear, among them the story of Muckachuck, the baby who puts one over on Maushop. This substantial, consistently interesting collection is filled with action and fast-moving dialogue and reveals cultural values well. The strongly realized, representational, full-page illustrations accompanying each story are by a Mohawk artist. Explanatory notes accompany the sections.

519 McDermott, Gerald, ret., *Coyote: A Trickster Tale from the American Southwest*, illus. Gerald McDermott, Harcourt, 1994 (hardcover), ISBN 0–15–220724–4, $14.95, unp.; Voyager, 1999 (paper), ISBN 0–152–01958–8, $6.00. Ages 4 up, grades PS up.

Traditional tale of the buffoon type, in which Coyote the trickster comes to grief because of his silly desire to emulate others. One of thousands of stories about this Native-American Indian figure, the predominant trickster west of the Mississippi, the tale is representative of a widespread type in which the trickster attempts to fly with the birds. Coyote happens upon a flock of crows, who chant and dance on top of a mesa and then take a spin through the air on their powerful wings. Coyote especially envies their ability to fly and asks them to help him join them. Old Man Crow tells his friends to pluck out their feathers and stick them up and down Coyote's front legs. Delighted with the feathers, Coyote looks forward to going adventuring in the air. He maneuvers in an awkward, lopsided fashion, until, off balance, he plops to the ground. After the crows stick more feathers into Coyote's legs, he becomes rude and boastful and sings off key. When the crows take off again, Coyote with them, the disgusted birds pull their feathers out. Coyote plunges downward so fast that his tail catches fire. He lands in a pool of water atop a mesa, crawls out, and drags himself home. To this day, coyotes are dusty gray, and their tails have burnt tips, in memory of Coyote's unfortunate adventure. The text consists mostly of short, uncomplicated sentences, whose simplicity and staccato rhythm simulates the behavior and attitude of the troublesome trickster. As is usual in trickster tales, the story's slapstick humor relieves the didacticism. Desert-toned illustrations follow the narrative. Their geometric designs, typical of McDermott's work, enhance the humor and simulate the southwest setting. The horizontal mesas and circular cacti contrast with the vertical crows and the anthropomorphically upright Coyote. Coyote is skinny, mangy, and rangy, a figure of fun, his blue color conspicuous against the tans, while the crows are a deep, purply-black, with green ribbons flowing backward from their cocky heads. This is a hilarious book, masterfully executed, one of several Native-American tales that McDermott has retold and illustrated. A note about Coyote as a trickster appears on the reverse of the title page. See *Raven: A Trickster Tale* in *This Land Is Our Land*, no. 521, for a Pacific Northwest tale about the trickster Raven.

520 McDermott, Gerald, ret., *Musicians of the Sun*, illus. Gerald McDermott, Simon & Schuster, 1997 (hardcover), ISBN 0–689–80706–6, $17.00, unp. Ages 5 up, grades K up.

Tersely poetic retelling of a version of the Aztec Indian myth of how people received music. When the Lord of the Night, the King of the Gods, sees that the earth is gray and dark and human life lacks happiness, he orders Wind to fly to Sun's house and bring back to earth the Sun's four musicians, Red, Yellow, Blue, and Green, which the Sun has imprisoned there, so that people may hear their music. Armed with a turquoise shield, a black thundercloud, and the silver lightning that the Lord of the Night gives him, Wind traverses the sky to Sun's realm. When Sun resists, Wind uses his weapons to create a mighty storm that blots out the Sun and makes it possible for the musicians to break away, come back with Wind, and bring the joy of their music to humanity. The drama of the conflict is accentuated by the richly colored, sophisticated, oversized paintings. McDermott's characteristic geometric style is perfect for rendering the angular and circular forms of traditional Aztec art after the fashion of the iconography in the ancient codices. The pictures typically extend like murals across each set of two pages, conveying both the immensity of the conflict and the vastness of the universe of the gods. Particularly striking are those pictures in which the glaring reds and yellows of the rising Sun cut through the blacks and blues of the deep night, until the pages become suffused with rainbow yellows and oranges, and the power and majesty of red Sun dominates the pages. An afternote gives background about the story and indicates sources. In this version of the widespread myth, the Lord of the Night is the god Tezcatlipoca and the Wind god is Ecehatl. In a better-known version, Tezcatlipoca sends Quetzalcoatl, the serpent god, who wears the feathers of the quetzal bird and also represents the wind. In whatever version, however, this is a powerful myth, and this combination of economical, understated text and lavish paintings strong in storytelling ability catches perfectly the mystery and majesty of the story. For another book by McDermott, see *Raven: A Trickster Tale* in *This Land Is Our Land* (1994), no. 521.

521 Normandin, Christine, ed., *The Echoes of the Elders: The Stories and Paintings of Chief Lelooska*, illus. Chief Lelooska, DK, 1997 (hardcover), ISBN 0–7894–2455–X, $24.95, 40 pp. Ages 4 up, grades PS up.

Five myths and tales told by the Northwest Coast Indians, among them the Kwakiutl, and taught by the elders to Chief Lelooska, who was Cherokee-born, named by the Nez Perce, and adopted in a potlach ceremony by James Sewide, an influential hereditary chief of the Southern Kwakiutl, in honor of Lelooska's contribution to the literature and art of Sewide's people. After the children of a village are warned four times by an old forest witch to stop teasing her, she turns them into mice in "The Old Witch Owl." In "The Boy and the Loon," a boy who releases a loon trapped in a noose is cured of a wasting sickness and becomes a tribal shaman. Raven tricks Sea Gull to recover daylight, which Sea Gull has hidden in a chest in his house, in "Raven and Sea Gull." Because fishermen release a merman they have caught in their net, they are rewarded with successful and safe fishing in years to come in "Poogweese"; and in "Beaver Face," an ugly, despised little girl cleverly saves the village children from being eaten by a fearsome monster. The drama and action of the pleasingly retold, fast-moving stories are complemented by bold, full-color paintings in Northwest Indian style. Figures from the stories with the coastal iconography of masks and animals are foregrounded to the viewer's plane on unframed pages, so that it seems loon, witch, monster, Raven, and others are leaping off the page into the viewer's dimension. The effect is starkly realistic. The tiny, black-and-white icons that appear inside the text, at the ends of sentences or at the beginning of paragraphs, are disconcerting and impede the flow of the stories. This exceptionally handsome and culturally respectful book is truly a collector's item. More Kwakiutl stories appear in *The Spirit of the Cedar People* (1998), a *New York Times* Best Illustrated Book of the Year.

522   Nye, Naomi Shihab, sel., *The Tree Is Older Than You Are: A Bilingual Gathering of Poems & Stories from Mexico with Paintings by Mexican Artists*, Simon & Schuster, 1995 (hardcover), ISBN 0–689–80297–8, $19.95, 111 pp.; Aladdin, 1998 (paper), ISBN 0–689–82087–9, $12.00. Ages 8 up, grades 3 up.

A large collection of mostly authored poems and stories from Native-American Indians of Mexico, each of which is presented in both the original Spanish and English translation. Four short prose pieces are from oral tradition. The Zinacantec story "The Three Suns" explains the origin of the pig and the peccary and tells why the moon's glow is fainter than the sun's rays. In "Fire and the Opossum," from the Mazateco Indians, an opossum steals fire from the selfish old woman who had captured it from the stars and planets and in the process burns his tail bare. "The Rabbit's Ears," from the Maya, tells how the God of the Animals enlarged the rabbit's tiny ears. "The Toad and a Buzzard," a Tzotzil tale, explains why toads hop instead of walk as they once did. The stories are told with dignity and verve. Strongly executed, full-palette paintings make this an especially attractive book. An introduction about the writings and illustrations opens the volume, and notes on the writers and stories and lists of titles in Spanish and English, writers and artists, and illustrations appear at the end.

523   Oughton, Jerrie, ret., *The Magic Weaver of Rugs: A Tale of the Navajo*, illus. Lisa Desimini, Houghton Mifflin, 1994 (hardcover), ISBN 0–315–66140–4, $14.95, 32 pp. Ages 7 up, grades 2 up.

Picture-book version of the myth relating how the Navajo learned to weave rugs, a skill that became an important part of their economy. Two women go off by themselves to pray for help in a time of hardship. In a voice that can split rocks, Spider Woman responds, showing them how to build a loom, shear sheep, dye the wool, and weave it into rugs. Although this information seems of dubious use to them, they are so terrified that they follow her instructions and return to teach their people. Not only are the rugs useful to the Navajo themselves, but they also become a major trade item, with designs expressing their love for their land. The rather grim illustrations show Spider Woman as a shapeless female with straight hair standing on end, a figure to evoke fear and distrust, in scenes dominated by browns and dark earth colors. See *How the Stars Fell into the Sky* in *This Land Is Our Land* (1994), for another tale from oral tradition, no. 525.

524 Rodanas, Kristina, ad., *Dance of the Sacred Circle: A Native American Tale*, illus. Kristina Rodanas, Little Brown, 1994 (hardcover), ISBN 0–316–75358–0, $14.95, unp. Ages 8 up, grades 3 up.

The Blackfoot version of the origin of the horse, a creature of major importance to the Indians of the plains. When people suffer because the buffalo disappear, an orphan boy seeks the Great Chief in the Sky, hoping to persuade him to assist them. After an arduous journey, he has a vision of the Great Chief who shapes, from mud, a new animal. He then calls the trees and all the animals to him and asks each to contribute something useful to the creature. Pine and fir trees give it a tail and mane, Hawk, speed, Turtle, hardness of foot, Elk, great size, and Wolf, courage. Finally Fawn contributes gentleness, so that a rider can trust it. They all dance around the statue, until the Great Chief stops their motion and breathes life into the horse. While riding the new animal back to his people, the boy crosses a wide river and is amazed to see horses' heads popping up through the surface until a whole herd is following him back to camp. In the illustrations done in colored pencil over watercolor wash, the boy is pictured as quite young, perhaps limiting the audience to younger readers, but the pictures themselves are rich and dignified. An earlier retelling is described in *Dragonfly's Tale* in *This Land Is Our Land* (1994), no. 528.

525 Rodanas, Kristina, ad., *The Eagle's Song: A Tale from the Pacific Northwest*, illus. Kristina Rodanas, Little Brown, 1995 (hardcover), ISBN 0–316–75375–0, $15.95, unp. Ages 4–8, grades PS–3.

Folktale of how the Native Americans of the coastal Northwest first became acquainted with each other and learned to dance, sing, and appreciate art. At a time when people lived in single, far-separated houses and did not visit, help, or even speak to each other, three brothers lived together. Two were fine hunters, but the youngest, Ermine, preferred to carve bowls and boxes, decorating them with paintings of animals. Once when the older brothers go out, they do not return, and after many days, Ermine sets out to find them. He hears a low, rhythmic throbbing and catches sight of a dark spot in the sky. Down glides a huge eagle, which turns into a strong young man. He tells Ermine that the older brothers tried to claim his feathers as a trophy and were changed into rivers as cold as their hearts. Saying Ermine may learn to free them, he takes the boy to see his mother, an aging eagle-woman, who teaches the boy to listen to her drumming, to dance, and to sing. At home again, Ermine makes a drum from wood and caribou hide. When he starts drumming, children from the distant houses hear, come to investigate, and soon are laughing and dancing. Their elders follow, until there is a festival of merriment and feasting. In the middle of the party, the two older brothers appear, released from the spell. One day, after he has become a venerated artist, Ermine meets the eagle-man and his mother, who has become again youthful from the warmth and joy of the people. The extensive and striking artwork, done in colored pencil over watercolor wash, uses costumes and motifs of the ancient Indians of the Pacific Northwest. An earlier retelling, *Dragonfly's Tale*, is described in *This Land Is Our Land* (1994), no. 528.

526 Rodanas, Kristina, ret., *Follow the Stars: A Native American Woodlands Tale*, illus. Kristina Rodanas, Marshall Cavendish, 1998 (hardcover), ISBN 0–761–45029–7, $15.95, unp. Ages 4–8, grades PS–3.

Tale from the oral tradition of a number of Eastern Woodland peoples, including the Ojibwa, as recorded by Henry Schoolcraft in 1839. In a year of endless winter, the animals, nearly starving, meet to discuss the situation. Only the Fisher has an explanation and a plan: the birds of summer have not returned to bring spring, and the animals must go to find them. He leads them on a long and difficult journey until they look down from a mountain ridge into a valley of green grass, flowers, and strange houses. Two-legged animals walk there, then go into the houses. Led again by Fisher, the animals rush into the sleeping village. When the terrified residents run, the animals release the caged birds of summer, which fly off in a great rainbow of wings. Fisher urges the other animals to flee, but he remains to free a wave of bluebirds. Chased by the humans, he is almost caught, but he leaps into tallest tree, then springs into the sky, where he is turned into the group of stars we call the Big Dipper. The realistic illustrations, done with colored pencil on watercolor wash, cover more than three quarters of the wide-page doublespreads and together with a well-told text form a beautiful book. An earlier retelling, *Dragonfly's Tale*, is described in *This Land Is Our Land* (1994), no. 528.

527 Ross, Gayle, ret., *How Rabbit Tricked Otter and Other Cherokee Trickster Stories*, illus. Murv Jacob, HarperCollins, 1994 (hardcover), ISBN 0–06–021285–3, $16.89, 80 pp. Ages 6 up, grades 1 up.

Fifteen tales of Rabbit, the trickster figure who sometimes is too clever and becomes the butt of his own jokes. Some explain animal appearance—the cleft in Rabbit's nose, his puffy tail, Deer's antlers and blunt teeth, Possum's naked tail. Others explain animal behavior. The widespread distribution of useful stone is the result of Rabbit's attack on sleeping Flint with a wooden wedge. Introduced with phrases like "Long ago in the beginning days of the world," "In the days when people and animals still spoke the same language," or "This is what the old people told me when I was a child," the tales have the relaxed simplicity of oral tradition but also the careful construction of a skilled stylist. Illustrations are full-page paintings in brilliant colors, each in a circle or square framed by a wide band patterned with Indian motifs. Text pages have black-and-white borders of similar motifs, completing an unusually attractive total design.

528   Ross, Gayle, ret., *How Turtle's Back Was Cracked: A Traditional Cherokee Tale*, illus. Murv Jacob, Dial, 1995 (hardcover), ISBN 0–8037–1728–8, $14.99, unp. Ages 4 up, grades PS up.

An old Cherokee story explaining the characteristic pattern on the turtle's shell. Although Possum was really responsible, Turtle takes credit for killing a troublesome wolf and shows off. Captured by the vengeful pack, he escapes death by tricking them into throwing him into a river, where he cracks his shell. This reteller is a professional storyteller descendant of John Ross, the Cherokee chief at the time of the Trail of Tears. The stylized, highly patterned, bright paintings, done by a part-Cherokee artist, incorporate Cherokee motifs and produce a beautiful book.

529   Ross, Gayle, ret., *The Legend of the Windigo: A Tale from Native North America*, illus. Murv Jacob, Dial, 1996 (hardcover), ISBN 0–8037–1897–7, $14.99, unp. Ages 4–8, grades PS–3.

Legend from the northern woodlands Native-American peoples, known in variations from the northwest Tlingit to the eastern Cree, telling of the origin of mosquitoes. When first one, then another and another person disappear in the woods, the people realize that there must be a Windigo, a cannibal giant made of stone, in the area. Some want to leave; some want to fight it. The elders hold a sweat-lodge ceremony, seeking guidance. Young boys are designated to bring the superheated stones to the lodge. When the last stone splits as a boy picks it up with forked antlers, he has an inspiration, and soon the elders agree that great heat is a possible way to defeat the stone creature. The people dig a deep pit and cover it with branches, leaves, and grass. When the Windigo approaches and crashes into the pit, all the people throw dried leaves and branches on top of it, and one old woman drops in a glowing coal. As the fire blazes up, the Windigo vows that he will continue to eat the people. His heart bursts into many tiny pieces, mosquitoes, each stinging like a speck of burning ash. The Windigo keeps his word. The acrylic paintings, covering all the pages, with text superimposed in boxes, are in brilliant colors, even in the night scenes where the flames flare out. This same story is told in another form in no. 543.

530   Rubalcaba, Jill, ret., *Uncegila's Seventh Spot: A Lakota Legend*, illus. Irving Toddy, Clarion, 1995 (hardcover), ISBN 0–395–68970–8, $14.95, unp. Ages 4 up, grades PS up.

Native-American legend showing that security is not worth the loss of freedom and that true wealth comes only through effort. The huge, evil, serpent-like creature, Uncegila, spoils the hunting and terrorizes the people. Any warrior who looks upon it feels his eyes boil, goes mad, and dies. Blind-Twin hears the brush telling him to find Ugly-Old-Woman, whose magic arrows always find their mark, Uncegila's seventh spot. Led by his brother, First-Twin, he does as directed; since he cannot see the serpent, he will be safe. Ugly-Old-Woman asks only the comfort of a man's arms around her. Unable to see her, Blind-Twin complies, and she turns into a beautiful young girl. She gives Blind-Twin the magic arrows and First-Twin a shield of hardened buffalo skin and sends them off. At the lake where Uncegila lies, Blind-Twin shoots all the seven arrows into the seventh spot and kills the monster. Then, as directed by Ugly-Old-Woman, they cut out the heart, refuse its first request, then follow all its other orders, including bathing Blind-Twin's eyes in the blood, thereby restoring his sight and gaining him a new name, One-Who-Sees. Back at the village, they build a sacred lodge to house the heart, and the people devote all their time and energy to following its directives, making the village prosperous and safe, but no longer free to hunt and tell stories. Finally the twins decide to let the people see the heart, knowing that this will destroy its magic but make them stronger and more resourceful. One-Who-Sees watches a woman approach along the path, and though he has never seen her, he knows it is the one he seeks, Ugly-Old-Woman turned Beautiful-Young-Girl. The illustrations, executed in acrylic and oil paint, are dramatic, filling every other page, with additional silhouette designs of bison on the text pages.

531 San Souci, Robert, D., ret., *Sootface: An Ojibwa Cinderella Story*, illus. Daniel San Souci, Doubleday, 1994 (hardcover), ISBN 0–385–3202–4, $14.95, unp.; Bantam, 1997 (paper), ISBN 0–440–41363–X, $6.99. Ages 4–8, grades PS–3.

Retelling of a folktale known widely among the Woodlands (Northeastern and Great Lakes) Native Americans, the Ojibwa (Chippewa) version of a world-wide story type. Two older sisters openly despise their younger sister, force her to do all the work about their house, beat her, singe her hair, and burn her skin. They rub her face with ashes and call her Sootface. Sootface remains meek and patiently enduring in spite of their abuse and the ridicule of the village. A mighty warrior, who lives in a wigwam across the lake and has the power to make himself invisible, says he will marry the woman who can see him. Both of the older sisters attempt to win him and fail. In spite of their derision, Sootface cleans herself up, dresses herself as best she can in birchbark garments, and travels to his house, where she proves that she can see him by identifying his otherwise invisible bow as composed of the rainbow. This story of virtue re-warded is pleasingly told and accompanied by impressionistic, glowing water-colors that, although resembling calendar art, recreate the woodlands life and incorporate northern iconography. The views of animals and landscape are par-ticularly striking. For other books by San Souci, see nos. 187, 188, 189, 316, and 317, all books of oral tradition, in *This Land Is Our Land* (for titles, see entry 155, this book). For another, less satisfactory version of this Ojibwa tale, see *The Rough-Face Girl*, retold by Rafe Martin, no. 519 in *This Land Is Our Land*.

532 San Souci, Robert D., ret., *Two Bear Cubs: A Miwok Legend from California's Yosemite Valley*, illus. Daniel San Souci, Yosemite Association, 1997 (hardcover), ISBN 0–93966–87–1, $14.95, unp. Ages 4–10, grades PS–5.

Retelling of a Native-American Indian Miwok story of how after several animals fail, a tiny measuring worm (inchworm) succeeds in rescuing two grizzly-bear cubs from the top of the rock known as El Capitan. Occasional Indian terms add spice to the plainly but effectively told narrative, which emphasizes the importance of not judging by appearances, a common theme in Native-American story. Although the bears are too cute for grizzlies and the other anthropomorphized animals also strike false notes, the illustrations are for the most part masterly at catching the action and in particular the terrain, the majesty of the rocks and mountains, the towering trees, and the river flowing through the valley. Information about the story and the Miwok and a list of related readings and Internet resources appear at the end. Other books by San Souci appear in *This Land Is Our Land* (1994), nos. 17, 188, 189, 316, and 317 (for titles, see entry 155, this book).

533 Stevens, Janet, ret., *Old Bag of Bones: A Coyote Tale*, illus. Janet Stevens, Holiday House, 1996 (hardcover), ISBN 0–8234–1215–6, $15.95, unp.; 1997 (paper), ISBN 0–8234–1337–3, $6.95. Ages 4–9, grades PS–4.

Retelling of a funny Shoshoni Indian story about the trickster Coyote, whose foolishness gets him into trouble. Old, scraggly Coyote, who describes himself as "nothing but a bag of bones," yearns to be young and vigorous again, like the buffalo calf he sees in the distance. Limping over, he asks the young buffalo to give him some of his youth, strength, and power. The transfer of youth and strength takes place at Bear Butte, with the buffalo snorting and kicking as he circles Coyote. On the fourth go-round, he rams Coyote solidly. To his great joy, Coyote finds that he has youth and strength again. He even looks like the young buffalo, except for his raggedy tail. The Buffalo says that Coyote is now a Buffote and reminds him that he does not have buffalo power, since that belongs to the buffalo kind alone. Vain and paternalistic, Coyote assures three other aged creatures, a rabbit, a lizard, and a kangaroo rat, that he can help them recover their lost youth. At Bear Butte, he goes through the same sort of ritual as the young buffalo, but only succeeds in leaving the creatures dirtier and dustier than before and changing himself back to his old form. The story is retold in the comic, cartoonish illustrations, scrappily composed and filled with color and movement. The shot of Coyote opposite the title page alerts the viewer immediately to his brash and foolish nature. The scenes with the young buffalo bring out the magnificent strength and power of the buffalo kind in contrast to Coyote. Coyote as Buffote carrying the other animals on his back, puffing away with braggadocio, tail hanging down like an old frayed rope from his back side, is hilarious. A note on the frontispiece gives the source of the story. See *Coyote*

Steals the Blanket, in *This Land Is Our Land* (1994), no. 537, for another Coyote tale Stevens has retold and illustrated.

534 Swann, Brian, ed., *Coming to Light: Contemporary Translations of the Native Literatures of North America,* Random House, 1994 (hardcover), ISBN 0679–41816–4, $30.00, 801 pp.; Vintage, 1996 (paper), ISBN 0–679–74358–8, $17.00. Ages 15 up, grades 10 up.

Scholarly compendium of translations of Native-American Indian stories, poems, prayers, and oratory newly collected or gleaned from sources and translated or retranslated. Detailed, informative introductions by different contributors precede the selections, which are also usually heavily footnoted. The anthology opens with a long essay by Swann, in which he presents the rationale behind the book and gives a history of such scholarly work. While the book's format may intimidate some, the collection offers generously, and while few people will want to read all the way through, sampled here and there, the pieces offer much enjoyment. Thirty-nine tribal groups are represented from all over North America, divided into seven geographical regions, from Alaska to the Woodlands of the east, from the American Southwest to the Southeast, the hope being that "through their literatures, Native American cultures can be seen clearer, appreciated not only for their similarities to our own traditions but for their bracing dissimilarities." More than eighty selections appear—Navajo horse songs, Hopi song-poems, several Coyote stories, Nanabush tales, Ghost Dance songs, creation stories—funny tales and serious stories—a wide variety. The book concludes with a list of suggested readings, notes about the contributors, and a copious subject and title index.

535 Swann, Brian, ad., *Touching the Distance: Native American Riddle-Poems,* illus. Maria Rendon, Harcourt, 1998 (hardcover), ISBN 0–15–200804–7, $16.00, unp. Ages 4 up, grades PS up.

Fourteen very brief riddle-poems, most only a short line in length, collected and adapted from the oral tradition of seven Native-American groups from Bolivia to Alaska. Haiku-like in structure, most of the poems refer to something in nature, from corn to a banana to mosquitoes and moths, but one describes a much-loved grandmother's face as having "gullies" where water falls, and the title poem refers to eyesight. The poems have a gentle lilt, and the intellectual aspect of the riddle form is supported by brilliant mixed-media, abstract paintings, brilliant in color, stylized, and surrealistic. Although small children can appreciate the forms and shapes, the book is complex and sophisticated and will probably most appeal to those who have had some experience in life. The groups from which the riddles come and sources are indicated.

536 Swann, Brian, coll. and ad., *Wearing the Morning Star: Native American Song-Poems*, Random House, 1996 (hardcover), ISBN 0–679–44827–6, $23.00, 182 pp. Ages 12 up, grades 7 up.

Pleasing, authoritative anthology of 100 song-poems, a term by which Swan designates "not only songs but recitative, prayer, and ceremony, a whole variety of Native American verbal and musical expression." These retellings of the original translations come from such respected and well-known sources as Franz Boas, Frank Speck, James Mooney, Gertrude Kurath, Henry Rowe Schoolcraft, and H. R. Voth, "a gathering of samples" that reach from Alaska, through Canada, the Pacific Coast, the Plains, and eastward, southward, and southwestward to California. These mostly short pieces include hunting songs, cradle songs, lullabies, love songs, charms, peyote songs, prayers, and planting songs. Here are a song about an eclipse, an eagle ceremony song, Kachina Dance songs, and night chants of the Navajo, which are especially lovely. There are a little boy's mourning song for his drowned mother, Arapaho Ghost Dance songs, a billy goat's farting song, Yaqui Deer Dance songs, and a girl's coming of age ceremony. Also included are scholarly notes that indicate sources and add information, a fine introduction to the literature and about the history of collecting and translating.

537 Taylor, C. J., ret., *Bones in the Basket: Native Stories of the Origin of People*, illus. C. J. Taylor, Tundra Books, 1994 (hardcover), ISBN 0–88776–327–8, $17.95, 32 pp. Ages 6 up, grades 1 up.

Seven origin stories, one of which comes from the Chuckchee of Russian Siberia. All the others are from North American groups in the United States and Canada. The creation of the world and the people in it is the subject of the Zuni story, "Before All Things Began," the Mohawk myth, "Creation," and the Osage story, "A Place to Have Children." The discovery, not the creation, of the world is the subject of a Mandan story, "From Darkness to Light." In the Cree flood story, "The Raft," two creators, Giant Beaver and Wisagatcak, battle over whether the world should be covered by earth or water. In the title myth, from the Modoc of northern California and southern Oregon, Creator and his daughter bring the spirits of people, in the form of dry bones, up from an underworld. Each story is accompanied by at least one full-page, slightly expressionistic painting. The text is clear, but not overly simplified, preventing the book from being limited to the very young. A page at the end describes the various groups from which the stories come.

538 Taylor, Harriet Peck, ret., *Coyote and the Laughing Butterflies*, illus. Harriet Peck Taylor, Macmillan, 1995 (hardcover), ISBN 0–02–788846–0, $15.00, unp. Ages 4–8, grades PS–3.

Lively retelling of a Tewa Indian explanatory story about the trickster Coyote, in which matters turn out fine in spite of Coyote's laziness. Coyote and his wife are living among the hills about a day's journey from a large salt lake. One day, Coyote's wife asks him to go to the lake to get salt for her cooking. Two times Coyote goes there, and tired from his trip, lies down to nap. Each time, mischievous butterflies pick him up, carry him over the hills to his home, and deposit him, still sleeping, beside his empty sack. His wife scolds him for not bringing the salt she needs. The third time he fills the sack before he falls asleep, and the butterflies carry the sack back along with him. When he awakens, Coyote claims credit for having satisfied her wishes. Even today, butterflies remember the trick they played on Coyote those many years ago and fly in erratic patterns, just as they did when they carried the heavy Coyote and his sack over the hills. This is a sprightly version of a widespread trickster tale in which the trickster attempts to fly with the birds and comes to grief. The humor is underscored by the bright colors and comic aspect of the pictures, especially those that show an elongated slanty-eyed, pointy-nosed, tan and brown Coyote, head hanging, eyes tightly closed in sleep, being carted home through the deep blue sky by many tiny, brilliantly colored butterflies. Various species of cactus, the mesas, the rolling hills, and the pottery establish the southwestern desert and plateau setting. The final three-quarter spread brings the book to a fitting close—Coyote and his wife dancing together, their noses pointed upward against a red-gold moon, while their animal friends, including the flitting and fluttering butterflies, are having fun and enjoying a good meal together. A note about the story is included. For another book about Coyote by Taylor, see *Coyote Places the Stars*, in *This Land Is Our Land*, no. 539.

539 Van Laan, Nancy, sel. and ret., *In a Circle Long Ago: A Treasury of Native Lore from North America*, illus. Lisa Desimini, Knopf, 1995 (hardcover), ISBN 0–679–85807–5, $20.00, 128 pp. Ages 4–11, grades PS–6.

Anthology of twenty-five Indian folktales, myths, hero tales, and a few poems. "The Long Winter" is a Slavey seasonal story about how several animals end a long period of frigid weather by securing heat. The Creek "Mother Sun" is a gently told poem about how light and humans originated, and "The Earth on Turtle's Back" is the Lenape account of the creation of the earth. Trickster tales include "Raven, the River Maker" from the Tlingit, in which Raven steals water from greedy Wolf and in the process his feathers turn black; the Nez Perce "How Beaver Stole Fire," in which pine trees possessed but did not share fire; the Tewa "Coyote and the Blackbirds," which explains the origin of war; the Creek "A Tug of War," which shows Rabbit tricking some tie snakes; "How Possum Got His Skinny Tail," a Cherokee story, in which Rabbit changes Possum's elegantly bushy tail to the skinny one Possum has today, a story that also explains why the Possum plays dead; and "Rabbit and the Willow," from the Seneca, in which Rabbit gains the appearance he has today and willows produce their cottonlike balls in the spring. Most are in simple prose that projects the intimacy of storytelling, but a few are poems. The book is attractively designed with pictures that range from bold, bright, and dramatic to subtle and muted tones and black-and-white line drawings. They vary from doublespreads to spots and attempt to capture the sense of the region as well as the spirit of the tale. A colorful, easy-to-read map and an introduction about how Van Laan came to do the book and about the nature of the stories open the book, and short introductions head each of the eight sections. Information about the Native-American groups, notes about the individual stories and their sources, which are mostly long out of print, and a short bibliography with additional, respected, mostly older sources appears at the end of this attractive, useful book. For two more books by Van Laan, see *Buffalo Dance* and *Rainbow Crow* in *This Land Is Our Land* (1994), nos. 540 and 541.

540 Wargin, Kathy-jo, ret., *The Legend of Sleeping Bear*, illus. Gijsbert van Frankenhuyzen, Sleeping Bear, 1998 (hardcover), ISBN 1–886947–35–X, $16.95, unp. Ages 4–10, grades PS–5.

Retelling of a presumably Ojibwe Indian legend explaining the origin of the huge sand dune that forms the Sleeping Bear National Lakeshore and the two Manitoulin Islands in Lake Michigan just west of the Lakeshore. A mother bear and her two cubs are living in the forest in Wisconsin on the west side of Lake Michigan when a terrible fire breaks out, forcing the animals to flee. The mother bear and her cubs swim desperately through the night, the mother repeatedly encouraging her babies to use all their strength. In the morning, the weary mother collapses on the bank of the east side of Lake Michigan but can no longer see her cubs. She sits on the bank, watching and calling for them for many days and nights, until she falls asleep grieving for them. Years of winds blow sands upon her, covering her and forming the present dune. The great spirit of the land recognizes her dedication to her children by turning them into the North and South Manitou islands, just off shore, which she continues to watch over for all time. The story is sentimental and sentimentally told, more fakelore than folklore, and seems even more so because of rather poor poetic verses spoken by the mother. The story has charm, however, because of its connection to one of the most unusual and outstanding natural phenomena in the United States. Strongly composed full-color, deep-toned paintings, present panoramic views of the lake, shore, and wildlife. Although calendar art, they fit the story well, capture something of the majesty of the region, and relieve the sentiment. Endpaper maps show the location of the dune and the islands. Wargin and van Frankenhuyzen have also collaborated on *The Legend of Mackinac Island* (1999).

541 Wood, Audrey, ret., *The Rainbow Bridge: Inspired by a Chumash Tale*, illus. Robert Florczak, Harcourt, 1995 (hardcover), ISBN 0–152–65475–5, $16.00, unp.; 1998 (paper), ISBN 0–152–02106–X, $6.00. Ages 5–11, grades K–6.

Retelling of a Native-American Indian creation myth from the Chumash of California. The goddess Hutash, lonely on her island home off the coast of the North-American continent, creates humans in her image. Sky Snake takes pity upon them and gives them fire so that they can keep warm and cook their food. The story also explains how Indians came to migrate to mainland California and how dolphins originated. Magnificent, romantic, deep-toned, mostly double-spread paintings follow the dignified and respectful narrative. An introductory note gives background on the legend and the people.

542 Wood, Douglas, ret., *Rabbit and the Moon*, illus. Leslie Baker, Simon & Schuster, 1997 (hardcover), ISBN 0–689–80769–4, $15.00, unp. Ages 4–8, grades PS–3.

Cree legend also known in several other Native-American cultures, explaining the appearance of a rabbit-shaped shadow on the moon and also the crane's appearance. In the early days of the world, Rabbit had a tremendous desire to ride upon the moon and look down on the earth. He asks help from all the birds he knows, only to be rejected. Finally, Crane agrees to try. With Rabbit clinging tightly to his legs, Crane reaches the moon, but he is exhausted, and Rabbit's paws are tinged with blood. In thanks for the marvelous beauty he can now see, Rabbit touches the top of Crane's head, turning it red forever. Because Rabbit's weight is so great, Crane's legs are stretched long and thin. The illustrations, done with pencil and transparent watercolor, depict Rabbit somewhat cartoon-ishly, but are lovely, realistic pictures of the birds.

543 Wood, Douglas, ret., *The Windigo's Return*, illus. Greg Couch, Simon & Schuster, 1996 (hardcoveer), ISBN 0–689–80065–7, $16.00, unp. Ages 4–8, grades PS–3.

Tale of the Ojibwe or Anishinabe people explaining the origin of the mos-quito. At a time of ease and plenty for the people, first a hunter and then an old grandmother disappear, and the elders remember stories of the Windigo, a terrible giant of the forest who eats the people and can change form so quickly that he is never seen. One by one they consider and reject plans until a little girl suggests a trap, a deep pit with venison at the bottom and covered with birch bark and long grass. They dig the pit and disguise it, then hide in the nearby forest at night until they hear the heavy T-R-R-R-O-M-P of the Win-digo's footsteps and the crash as he lands in the pit. They throw embers from the council fire into the pit and shudder as the Windigo in the flames vows to come back and eat them and their children forever. When they dare to look into the pit, they find only a pile of ashes. These they carry to the top of a high hill and fling into the night wind. But the next summer, as they fish, they feel stings as if from fire, and the spots where the bits that look like ashes have landed itch and itch. The story, which is suitable for all ages, is made especially ap-propriate for an oral retelling to a very young audience with sound elements like crashes and sniffs spelled out in capital letters. Illustrations are full-page and double-page paintings in acrylic and color pencil, handsome and sufficiently brooding for the scary story. For another version of this same tale, see no. 529, *The Legend of the Windigo*.

544 Young, Richard, and Judy Dockrey Young, colls. and eds., *Race with Buffalo, and Other Native American Stories for Young Readers*, illus. Wendell E. Hall, August House, 1994 (hardcover), ISBN 0–87483–343–4, $19.95, 172 pp.; (paper), ISBN 0–87483–342–6, $12.95. Ages 9 up, grades 4 up.

Thirty-one stories from Native-American groups, all collected from oral retellings and carefully documented in notes at the end. From the Crow comes a creation-of-the-world story. Explanatory stories of animal appearance and behavior come from the Cherokee, the Seneca, the Iroquois, the Kathlamet, the Cheyenne, and the Northern Pueblo. Tales of the formation of constellations and star patterns come from the Kiowa, the Caddo, the Cherokee, and the Seneca. Fabulous animals appear in some stories, in particular Flint Bird from the Acoma Pueblo and the Bloodsucker from the Northern Pueblo people. Tricksters include Skunnee Wundee from the Seneca and Kuloskap from the Micmac. The origin of such important elements as fire, in "Grandmother Spider Steals the Fire" from the Choctaw, thunder and lightning in "The Twin Brothers" from the Caddo, and the change of seasons, in "Blue Corn Maiden and the Coming of Winter" from the Northern Pueblo are retold, as are all the tales, in simple, unadorned storytelling style. Illustrations are attractive line drawings of scenes from the stories and end-pieces with Indian motifs. In general, this is a good collection, respectful and wide ranging. A glossary is included.

12

Native-American Indians: Books of Poetry

545 Begay, Shonto, *Navajo Visions and Voices Across the Mesa*, illus. Shonto Begay, Scholastic, 1995 (hardcover), ISBN 0–590–46153–2, $15.95, 48 pp. Ages 5 up, grades K up.

Collection of twenty poems accompanied by as many strongly executed, full-color paintings of mountains, plateaus, deserts, and wildlife from the American Southwest and of the Native people who live there. According to its Navajo Indian writer and painter, the book is intended to "explore facets of Navajo life that are rarely touched upon in Western literature . . . [and] take you into corners of my world, the Navajo world . . . [to] experience daily life on the mesa in the twentieth century." The book begins with spiritual elements, moves on to told stories, Begay's memories, members of the community, and rituals, and ends with hope for an early spring. Throughout there is a sense of striving to balance the old ways and beliefs with the intrusive outer world and to protect the earth, which is regarded as sacred. The frontispiece is particularly striking, a painting in which Begay's technique of many very small lines combines with the rosy to brown tones to illuminate the mountains, on an outcropping in which a Navajo boy lies reading, while his goats graze and sport below. The free-verse, un-rhymed poems are keen with images. In "In My Mother's Kitchen," her "Strong brown hands caress soft mounds of dough," larkspurs, wild onions, rodents, and snakes wait in warmth within the earth in "Early Spring," while in "Into the New World," his grandfather's early morning prayer and pollen-scattering are disturbed by "smoke not from cookfires" but by trucks rumbling in the distance, and huge machines rip up the earth for the coal mines. "Our Mysteries, His Knowledge" conveys the enduringness of the coyote, as well as his seeming all-knowingness, in a tribute to the common coyote and also to Coyote the trickster. Several selections are more short stories than prose-poems but fit the whole. This is an exceptionally beautiful book, one in which the paintings are so mem-orable that they more than compensate for the poems' occasional lack of poetic integrity. An earlier book of a story from oral tradition retold and illustrated by

Begay, *Ma'ii and Cousin Horned Toad*, is described in *This Land Is Our Land* (1994), no. 482.

546 Bierhorst, John, sel., *On the Road of Stars: Native American Night Poems and Sleep Charms*, illus. Judy Pedersen, Macmillan, 1994 (hardcover), ISBN 0–02–709735–8, $15.95, unp. Ages 3 up, grades PS up.

See entry 488.

547 Bruchac, Joseph, ed., *The Earth Under Sky Bear's Feet: Native American Poems of the Land*, illus. Thomas Locker, Philomel, 1995 (hardcover), ISBN 0–399–22713–X, unp. Ages 5 up; grades K up.

Twelve poems from Native-American people in as many different groups, set in the context of an old woman telling her granddaughter about the beauties and wonders of the night. Poems are all in rhythmic but nonmetrical unrhymed verse, most of them using repetition for their effect. They include "Sky Bear," a Mohawk story of the Big Dipper; "Song of the Firefly," from the Anishinabe; "Flute Song," from the Pima; "The Old Wolf's Song," from the Lakota; and "Spirit Dance Song," from the Pawnee. Each poem is accompanied by a handsome painting taking up more than an oversized page and a half, with the verse printed down the left side of the double-page spread. Sources are listed in a note at the end. In *This Land Is Our Land* (1994), Bruchac is represented by nos. 416 (novel), 489, 490, and 491 (all oral tradition) (for titles, see entry 423, this book).

548 Bruchac, Joseph, ret., *Four Ancestors: Stories, Songs, and Poems from Native North America*, illus. S. S. Burrus, Murv Jacob, Jeffrey Chapman, and Duke Sine, BridgeWater, 1996 (hardcover), ISBN 0–8167–3843–2, $18.95, 96 pp. Ages 8 up, grades 3 up.

See entry 491.

549 Harjo, Joy, *The Woman Who Fell from the Sky: Poems*, Norton, 1994 (hardcover), ISBN 0–393–03715–0, $21.00, 68 pp.; 1996 (paper), ISBN 0–393–31362–X, $10.00. Ages 12 up, grades 7 up.

Twenty-five prose-poems by an eminent Indian poet of Creek ancestry embracing a variety of subjects and in a broad range of tones. Some are observations on life in general or of aspects particular to Native peoples, some are reflections, some are laments, songs, prayers, or odes. Most rely on traditional Native beliefs, customs, or old stories and themes. All are followed by brief, equally poetic commentaries that add vastly to the impact of the poems. In fact, the poet's voice speaks even more personally and forcefully in the afterwords, and when one rereads the poems with the afterwords in mind, they become much more intense. Harjo makes use of an old myth in applying a Native creation story to contemporary life; describes the grandmother who years ago intimidated her, then performs an act of poignant reconciliation by attributing the old woman's actions to the very hard life she suffered; speaks of the northern lights above Lake Superior, during which at a powwow she meets a young man returned from Vietnam, who later "snuffed his confusion between honor and honor with wine" in Kansas bars; associates crows with death, yet admires them in a certain way, since "they aren't afraid to argue about the inarguable"; and sings praises to houses, which forever hold within them all those who ever lived in them. She speaks frequently of the injustices perpetrated against the Indians, of the waning of the old ways, and of attempts to survive and maintain integrity. Animals appear often, wild ones as well as domestic, like horses; and the earth and the heavenly bodies are always close and near in her verses. The final poem packs perhaps the greatest wallop of all, being ironically a celebration of the importance of that mundane, much taken-for-granted-object, the kitchen table, at which, Harjo says, the world both begins and ends. Relying less on sound for impact than on emotion, repetition, and striking visual images and unusual combinations of words, colors, and images, these poems will most appeal to sophisticated readers, those more capable with this literary form and those who are willing to yield to Harjo's way. Other books of poetry, including *Secrets from the Center of the World*, by Harjo are described in *This Land Is Our Land* (1994), no. 553.

550 Hausman, Gerald, ret., *Coyote Walks on Two Legs: A Book of Navajo Myths and Legends*, illus. Floyd Cooper, Philomel, 1994 (hardcover), ISBN 0–399–22018–6, $15.95, unp. Ages 5 up, grades K up.

See entry 511.

551 Highwater, Jamake, *Songs for the Seasons*, illus. Sandra Speidel, Lothrop, 1995 (hardcover), ISBN 0–688–10659–0, $14.95, unp. Ages 4 up, grades PS up.

Free-verse, mood poem that celebrates the particular features of each of the seasons, starting with summer. The lines make much use of sensory imagery to capture the spirit of each period, but sometimes the writer's attempts to see and hear individually are labored. For example, the meadow grass "clicks and clacks in the fierce heat," a transfer from the action of the grasshopper that seems not to come off as it should. The persona's request that the reader "Listen to autumn's tuneless song" and, later, to "Listen to spring's fragrant song" are paradoxes that require too great a stretch. It is unclear whether or not a stanza asking the reader to listen to the voice of the moon "filling the dank night with her light" belongs to autumn or to winter, but in either case the description does not seem to fit. The many animals mentioned provide life and movement to the lines, however, and make the poem celebratory of nature, as it is probably intended to be. Uplifting the poem are magnificent full-color, chalk pastel paintings on watercolor paper, whose graininess shows through and deepens the smudgy, soft-edged, muted, off-the-page pictures. Most of the illustrations are full-color landscapes that depict whatever season is being discussed. Some are close-ups, like one of two rabbits and three mice scurrying to avoid the hawk gliding in the background. Unifying the poem and sequence of pictures are views of red-tailed hawks in various activities. An end note describes the ways, appearance, and habitat of this hawk, accompanied by sketches. Earlier Highwater published *The Ceremony of Innocence* and *Eyes of Darkness*, nos. 429 and 430, novels described in *This Land Is Our Land* (1994).

552 Kenny, Maurice, *On Second Thought: A Compilation*, Univ. of Oklahoma, 1995 (hardcover), ISBN 0–8061–2766–X, $24.95, 265 pp. Ages 13 up, grades 7 up.

Choice collection of memoirs, essays, short stories, and seventy-one poems selected from five books published from 1987 to 1990, along with nine previously unpublished poems, by a Mohawk writer considered a major influence in Native-American literature in the late twentieth century. The poems embrace many topics, some of them simple human experiences, like "In My Sixth Summer," about a boy and father fishing together; going home, in a poem of that name; or celebrating a birthday, in "Deb." Historical events also occupy the writer's mind, in "Canyon de Chelly" and "Ghost Dance," as well as cultural politics and realities, in "Archeologist" and "Dug-Out," the latter about the unearthing of an ancient dugout canoe in New York State, a poem Kenny has said is among his best. Most of the poems are drawn from nature and/or make use of nature imagery, animals, flowers, trees, birds, and situations, often celebrating particular animals, like "Wolf," "Raccoon," "Coyote," and "Bear." "Basho's Pond" is a clever tour de force, being composed of four haikus. Humor appears, as in "April 22, 1985," where the poet observes, "I hawk   the sky / wolf   the mountain" [spaces are the poet's] and so on, imagining himself into various beings or elements in nature. One poem, "Garden," consists only of the names of flowers. Best are the finely honed, shorter, less discursive poems, internally rhyming (although a few are more conventionally rhymed and structured) and pithy— that leave the reader a little breathless from their impact. Most of the pieces, though sophisticated and demanding, are within the reach of later elementary readers, especially of those who appreciate skillful use of words and enjoy using their intellects. An introduction by Joseph Bruchac opens the book.

553 Minty, Judith, *The Mad Painter Poems*, March Street, 1996 (paper), ISBN 1–882983–25–4, $10.00, 24 pp. Ages 14 up, grades 9 up.

Sixteen poems by an eminent part–Mohawk Indian poet, about mostly common objects or people, like houses, animals, and relatives, but in which the element of madness or craziness is a unifying factor. The world view is off-kilter, daft, mad, even terror-stricken, so that a poem may seem to move logically, then take a turn and lose reality. Images are strikingly vivid, and tension is created by careful juxtaposition of sounds and word-pictures to create uncommon ideas and thoughts and awaken ponderings. "Flying People" describes how, after seeing six brightly dressed people zoom about in the air, she flies, too, then discovers that her wings are unreliable. She imagines deceased relatives returning, one of whom, an aunt, is laid out but has not really died. The persona (the writer?) rents out rooms to a strange conglomeration of tenants, rents another to be near the asylum in which her daughter has been placed, celebrates boats on the Great Lakes, and wonders why she has not been receiving mail and about the birds her grandmother raises in the cupboard. Although not esoteric, these poems demand that readers be imaginative. For another book by Minty, *Dancing the Fault*, see *This Land Is Our Land* (1994), no. 557.

554 Ortiz, Simon, *After and Before the Lightning*, Univ. of Arizona, 1994 (hardcover), ISBN 0–8165–1432–2, $39.95, 134 pp.; (paper), ISBN 0–8165–1448–8, $17.95. Ages 12 up, grades 7 up.

One hundred thirty-nine original poems, composed, according to Ortiz, during the winter months of the year he taught on the Rosebud Reservation in South Dakota. An Acoma Pueblo Indian from New Mexico, he found the "reality of a South Dakota winter demanded to be dealt with . . . [and so he] was compelled to write the poetry." The poems are divided into four sets: The Landscape: Prairie, Time, and Galaxy; Common Trials: Every Day; Buffalo Dawn Coming; and Near and Evident Signs of Spring. The poems begin on November 18 and end on March 21, but not every day is represented. Interspersed among the poems are short, italicized essays, like journal entries, which introduce the poems, shed light on them, or grow out of them. They often contribute a lighter note to what on the whole is a bleak perspective, which not only reflects the atmosphere of the season for this transplanted southwesterner but also provides a metaphorical parallel for what Ortiz calls the "oppressive colonialism" under which Native Americans have long suffered and continue to suffer. Most of the poems are short and, although serious in thought, are not ponderous, esoteric, or inaccessible and hence can be enjoyed even by astute pre-teens. The snow, such birds as blue jays and pheasants, animals like deer, vehicles on highways, local roads, and farms, the fog, ice, and repeatedly the strong winds form subject matter. Some poems are prayers, some celebrate the landscape, some talk about residents, some yearn for his home landscape, but all are clearly visualized, free from pretension, subtly metered with repetition and sound devices like alliteration and consonance to move the pieces along. "Sleek pheasants" move across the road in front of the "metal hulk" he is driving. "They hesitate," then move with "velocity" and make it across, in a poem that aptly recreates the movement of the skittering birds. With some humor, he describes the perils of driving on the "slickery" roads. Most poems are free but not unpatterned; a few are concrete. Some are understated but arresting protest poems, and some are very personal, but most simply take the reader through the winter to share thoughts and experiences as Ortiz recorded them.

555 Rose, Wendy, *Bone Dance: New and Selected Poems, 1965–1993*, Univ. of Arizona, 1994 (hardcover), ISBN 0–8165–1412–7, $19.95, 108 pp.; (paper), ISBN 0–8165–5142–3, $10.95. Ages 14 up, grades 9 up.

Collection of fifty-six poems by a prominent Native-American Miwok/Hopi/white writer, mostly short and tightly structured. The poems are seldom allusive and make generous use of visual nature imagery, especially drawn from the fields and mesas of Hopi country, repetition, alliteration, and present participles, so that the rhythmic effect often approximates that of the steady beat of drums at powwows. They are mostly serious, sometimes near-angry, and frequently political. She likens the wars in Cambodia to Wounded Knee in "The Long Root." She bitterly deplores the additional tragedy perpetrated against the Indians by the sale at antique shows of artifacts whites took from the bodies of dead Indians after the battle of Wounded Knee in "I Expected My Skin and My Blood to Ripen," and the purchase of Indian skeletons by a museum in "Three Thousand Dollar Death Song." She pokes fun at "White Poets Who Would Be Indians" and bewails the dead babies in "The Day They Cleaned Up the Border: El Salvador," and the hundreds of Indians whose bodies were interred by the Spaniards in adobe and found by archaeologists in "Excavation at Santa Barbara Mission." While all the poems are highly personal, whether politically inspired or not, and most arise from her personal experience, a pleasant set records her reactions as she travels east of the Mississippi from large city to large city and state to state, particularly in New England and New York State. The closing poem celebrates "Coyote," a prominent Native-American trickster, which leaves the reader pondering what Rose meant by placing this poem last. The collection is cerebral and invites the reader to think about human life and human affairs. For another book of poems by Rose, see *The Halfbreed Chronicles and Other Poems*, no. 562 in *This Land Is Our Land* (1994).

556 Swann, Brian, ad., *Touching the Distance: Native American Riddle-Poems*, illus. Maria Rendon, Harcourt, 1998 (hardcover), ISBN 0–15–200804–7, $16.00, unp. Ages 4 up, grades PS up.

See entry 535.

557 Swann, Brian, coll. and ad., *Wearing the Morning Star: Native American Song-Poems*, Random House, 1996 (hardcover), ISBN 0–679–44827–6, $23.00, 182 pp. Ages 12 up, grades 7 up.

See entry 536.

558 Tapahonso, Luci, *Blue Horses Rush In: Poems and Stories*, Univ. of Arizona, 1997 (hardcover), ISBN 0–8165–1727–4, $25.95, 120 pp.; 1997 (paper), ISBN 0–8165–1728–2, $12.95, 104 pp. Ages 12 up, grades 7 up.

Fourteen poems and an equal number of short stories (no. 481) by a Navajo writer. They celebrate the natural features of her arid, mountainous homeland on the reservation near Shiprock, New Mexico, speak of her family on the reservation, and in particular describe and honor the traditions and old people that form the heart of Navajo life and culture. The forms are free and unrhymed, repetition gives the poems rhythm, and Navajo words appear liberally. The title poem, a gem that closes the slender volume, celebrates the birth of a granddaughter and connects her arrival with horses that are special to the Navajo and represent the directions. "Hills Brothers Coffee" is a humorous, touching tribute to her mother's brother, who remarked that that brand of coffee was the "one that does it for me." "This Is How They Were Placed for Us" re-creates the area visually and culturally as it praises the mountain peaks sacred to the Navajo and links them to practices vital to Navajo daily life. A few pieces talk about the effects of an important Hohokam archaeological discovery near Phoenix, another laments the loss of the feel of the Navajo earth and the elements when the persona is away from the area, and the opening poem, like the closing one, tenderly and lovingly honors a little granddaughter. She-Who-Brings-Happiness runs to the persona, hugging her legs and murmuring, "My gahma." The poems are accessible, revealing, and moving. For other books by Tapahonso, see *Saanii Dahataal*, no. 566 in *This Land Is Our Land*.

559 Vizenor, Gerald, ed., *Native American Literature: A Brief Introduction and Anthology*, HarperCollins, 1995 (paper), ISBN 0–673–46978–6, $19.95, 372 pp. Ages 14 up, grades 9 up.

Anthology of fiction (see no. 482) and poetry by Native Americans arranged by order of birth, with a few autobiographical passages and two plays, in the HarperCollins Literary Mosaic Series, of which Ishmael Reed is general editor, intended primarily for college courses. At the beginning is a history of Native-American writing (in the Anglo sense of the term writing), and at the end are the selections grouped by theme, a list of additional readings, an index of authors, titles, and first lines of poems, and acknowledgments. Each author's poems are preceded by a short introduction with biographical information about the writer and selected publications. The work of thirteen prominent poets who have published in this century appears. Opening the poetry section is one by Mary TallMountain, an Alaskan Athabaskan, now deceased, "There Is No Word for Goodbye," a poignant recollection of her forced departure from her people when she was a child. Sherman Alexie, a clear and powerful voice from the late twentieth century ends the set with "Crazy Horse Speaks," a sharply worded reflection on Custer-period history. In between are largely the best-known poems of such Native-American leaders in letters as Simon Ortiz, Maurice Kenny, Linda Hogan, Roberta Hill Whiteman, Joy Harjo (included is her "She Had Some Horses," among the most reprinted of all recent Native-American poems), Luci Tapahonso, and Louise Erdrich. Eight of the thirteen poets are women, which testifies to the strong contribution Indian women are making to American literature. The subject matter is broad, including old wrongs, Vietnam, racism, family life, and making a living. Most poems are short, which is typical of

Native-American poetry in general, and to the point, and if angry or protesting, the writers speak with a wry humor that engages the reader. This fine collection, drawn almost entirely from commonly anthologized writers, introduces readers to the best of the Native People working in poetry in this century. For other publications by the anthologist, himself a writer and critic, see *The Heirs of Columbus, Landfill Meditation,* and *Touchwood*, nos. 469, 470, and 471 (fiction) in *This Land Is Our Land* (1994).

560 Whiteman, Roberta Hill, *Philadelphia Flowers,* Holy Cow!, 1996 (paper), ISBN 0–930100–64–6, $10.95, 122 pp. Ages 12 up, grades 7 up.

Fifty short (one or two pages), tightly constructed, free-verse poems. The opening poem strikes chords that reverberate throughout this slender volume: respect for the natural world and the heavenly bodies; spirituality and the concept that everything derives from the all-spirit, or prime mover; the importance of all life and manifestations of life; respect for all people and release from such oppressions as poverty and homelessness; the value of words; the intertwining of generations; and the importance for Native People of perpetuating their ways and beliefs, because in those aspects lie their very lives and continuance. Whether or not the poems revolve around an element in nature, nature imagery appears in almost every one. While there is a variety of subject matter and the attitude is life-affirming and upbeat, a static, reflective, pensive tone predominates, fortunately relieved by moments of movement: a hawk dropping from the sky, two Shoshone women galloping on their mounts, and summer clouds colliding and flaring some communication the viewer seeks to understand. These are choice poems, carefully crafted by a respected Oneida Indian of Wisconsin, which are accessible to most mature readers on at least the first level and offer much for reflection for thinking, more sophisticated readers. She is also the author of *Star Quilt* (1999), more poems, and has been anthologized in important collections.

561 Wood, Douglas, ad., *Northwoods Cradle Song: From a Menominee Lullaby*, illus. Lisa Desimini, Simon & Schuster, 1996 (hardcover), ISBN 0–689–80503–9, $15.00, 28 pp.; Aladdin, 1998 (paper), ISBN 0–689–82228–6, $5.99, 32 pp. Ages 6 mo.–5, grades PS–K.

Five brief verses of about fifty words each, printed in white on full pages of dark-hued illustrations. The gentle words tell of creatures of the woods, streams, and swamps preparing for night, and each ends, "Sleep, little warrior, sleep. Go to sleep. Go to sleep." The paintings of the natural world are lovely and soothing, but the mother is wooden and the baby doll-like, not particularly Native American in appearance. Teepees, cradle-board, and other details reflect Menominee life at the turn of the century.

Index of Titles

(Numerals refer to entries.)

Abuelita's Heart (Cordova, Amy), 318

Across the Lines (Reeder, Carolyn), 106

Adopted by Eagles (Goble, Paul), 501

The Adventures of Sparrowboy (Pinkney, Brian), 98

The Adventures of Sugar and Junior (Medearis, Angela), 77, 340

African-American Literature (Worley, Demetrice A., and Jesse Perry, Jr.), 142, 157, 192

African American Literature (Young, Al), 145, 193

After and Before the Lightning (Oritz, Simon), 554

Agua Santa: Holy Water (Mora, Pat), 402

Ain't Gonna Be the Same Fool Twice (Sinclair, April), 120

Alicia's Treasure (Bertrand, Diane Gonzales), 308

American Visa (Wang, Ping), 231

America's Dream (Santiago, Esmeralda)

Amistad Rising (Chambers, Veronica), 20

Angels (Greenfield, Eloise), 172

Angel to Angel (Myers, Walter Dean), 186

An Mei's Strange and Wondrous Journey (Molnar-Fenton, Stephan), 220

Another Way to Dance (Dabydeen, Cyril), 293

The Antelope Wife (Erdrich, Louise), 442

April and the Dragon Lady (Namioka, Lensey), 221

Arias in Silence (Parks, Gordon), 188

The Arrow Over the Door (Bruchac, Joseph), 423

Ashley Bryan's ABC of African American Poetry (Bryan, Ashley), 160

Asian American Literature (Wong, Shawn), 234, 300

Asian Tales and Tellers (Spagnoli, Cathy), 276

Aunt Carmen's Book of Practical Saints (Mora, Pat), 403

Babylon Boyz (Mowry, Jess), 85

Back Home (Pinkney, Gloria Jean), 101

Bad Alchemy (Martinez, Dionisio D.), 399

Barrio Streets Carnival Dreams (Carlson, Lori Marie), 389

The Bat Boy and His Violin (Curtis, Gavin), 30

The Beaded Moccasins (Durrant, Lynda), 441

Beardream (Hobbs, Will), 455

Bebop-A-Do-Walk! (Hamanaka, Sheila), 43, 206

The Beet Queen (Erdrich, Louise), 442

The Beggar's Magic (Chang, Margaret, and Raymond Chang), 247

Belching Hill (Hamilton, Morse), 256

Benito's Dream Battle (Nye, Naomi Shihab), 347

The Best Older Sister (Choi, Sook Nyul), 198

The Best Way to Play (Cosby, Bill), 26

Between Earth and Sky (Bruchac, Joseph), 490

The Big Bike Race (Bledsoe, Lucy Jane), 8

Big Bushy Mustache (Soto, Gary), 355

Big Meeting (Woodtor, Dee Parmer), 141

Bill Pickett (Pinkney, Andrea Davis), 94

Billy (Roybal, Laura), 353

The Bingo Palace (Erdrich, Louise), 442

The Birchbark House (Erdrich, Louise), 443

Black Betty (Mosley, Walter), 84

Blacker Than a Thousand Midnights (Straight, Susan), 126

Black Feeling, Black Talk, Black Judgement (Giovanni, Nikki), 168, 169

Black Hair (Soto, Gary), 413

A Blessing in Disguise (Tate, Eleanora E.), 127

The Blessing Way (Hillerman, Tony), 454

Blood Child and Other Stories (Butler, Octavia), 16

Bloody Secrets (Garcia-Aguilera, Carolina), 323

Bloody Shame (Garcia-Aguilera, Carolina), 323

Bloody Waters (Garcia-Aguilera, Carolina), 323

Blue Horses Rush In (Tapahonso, Luci), 481, 558

Blues (Giovanni, Nikki), 169

Blu's Hanging (Yamanaka, Lois-Ann), 235

Bone Dance (Rose, Wendy), 467, 555

Bones in the Basket (Taylor, C. J.), 537

Border-Crosser with a Lamborghini Dream (Herrera, Juan Felipe), 329

The Bossy Gallito (Gonzalez, Lucia M.), 375

Boys at Work (Soto, Gary), 356

The Boy Who Dreamed of an Acorn (Casler, Leigh), 432

Brave as a Mountain Lion (Scott, Ann Herbert), 472

Breath, Eyes, Memory (Danticat, Edwidge), 319

Brer Tiger and the Big Wind (Faulkner, William J.), 146

Bright Freedom's Song (Houston, Gloria), 52

Brotherhood of Dolphins (Ybarra, Ricardo Means), 370

Brother Rabbit (Ho, Minfong, and Saphan Ros), 258

Brothers and Sisters (Campbell, Bebe Moore), 18

Brown Angels (Myers, Walter Dean), 186

Buddha (Demi), 248

Buddha (Roth, Susan L.), 268

Buddha Stories (Demi), 248

Bug Park (Hogan, James P.), 208

Buried Onions (Soto, Gary), 357

Business As Usual (Haynes, David), 48

Bus Ride (Miller, William), 82

Busy Bea (Poydar, Nancy), 105

By the Dawn's Early Light (Ackerman, Karen), 1

Cabin 102 (Garland, Sherry), 446

Calling the Doves (Herrera, Juan Felipe), 329

Candle in the Wind (Wartski, Maureen), 232

Canto familiar (Soto, Gary), 411

Can You Dance, Dalila? (Kroll, Virginia), 69

The Captive (Hansen, Joyce), 45

Carlos, Light the Farolito (Ciavonne, Jean), 315

Carolina Shout! (Schroeder, Alan), 118

Carol of the Brown King (Bryan, Ashley), 161

Carousel (Cummings, Pat), 28

The Case of the Firecrackers (Yep, Laurence), 237

The Case of the Goblin Pearls (Yep, Laurence), 237

The Case of the Lion Dance (Yep, Laurence), 237

Cast Two Shadows (Rinaldi, Ann), 107

Cat and Rat (Young, Ed), 285

The Cat's Meow (Soto, Gary), 355

Celie and the Harvest Fiddler (Flournoy, Vanessa, and Valerie Flournoy), 37

Celou Sudden Shout, Idaho 1826 (Duey, Kathleen), 440

Cezanne Pinto (Stolz, Mary), 125

Chato's Kitchen (Soto, Gary), 358

Chave's Memories (Delgado, Maria Isabel), 320

Cherish Me (Thomas, Joyce Carol), 190

Cheyenne Again (Bunting, Eve), 428

Chickens! Chickens! (Porte, Barbara Ann), 103

Child of the Owl (Yep, Laurence), 243

Children of the Longhouse (Bruchac, Joseph), 424

The Children of the Morning Light (Manitonquat, Medicine Story), 518

The Ch'i-lin Purse (Fang, Linda), 251

China Boy (Lee, Gus), 213

China's Bravest Girl (San Souci, Robert D.), 271

Chinese Folktales (Giskin, Howard), 253

Circle Within a Circle (Killingsworth, Monte), 457

City Green (DiSalvo-Ryan, DyAnne), 32

City of Coughing and Dead Radiators (Espada, Martin), 395

Cloud Chamber (Dorris, Michael), 436

The Cloudmakers (Rumford, James), 269

Coffee Will Make You Black (Sinclair, April), 120

Comfort Woman (Keller, Nora Okja), 211

Coming to Light (Swann, Brian), 534

Confetti (Mora, Pat), 404

The Cook's Family (Yep, Laurence), 238

Cool Salsa (Carlson, Lori Marie), 390

cotton candy on a rainy day (Giovanni, Nikki), 169

Cousins (Hamilton, Virginia), 44

Coyote (McDermott, Gerald), 519

Coyote and the Fire Stick (Goldin, Barbara Diamond), 504

Coyote and the Laughing Butterflies (Taylor, Harriet Peck), 538

Coyote Blue (Moore, Christopher), 465

Coyote in Love (Dwyer, Mindy), 496

Coyote Walks on Two Legs (Hausman, Gerald), 511, 550

The Crane Wife (Bodkin, Odds), 245

Crazy Weekend (Soto, Gary), 359

The Creation (Johnson, James Weldon), 180

Creativity (Steptoe, John), 124

The Cricket Warrior (Chang, Margaret, and Raymond Chang), 247

Crossing the Starlight Bridge (Mead, Alice), 462

The Crying for a Vision (Wangerin, Walter), 483

The Crystal Heart (Shepard, Aaron), 275

Cuckoo (Ehlert, Lois), 497

Cuentos de Cuanto Hay (Espinosa, J. Manuel, and Joe Hayes), 374

Currents from the Dancing River (Gonzalez, Ray), 324, 396

Daddy, Daddy, Be There (Boyd, Candy Dawson), 159

Dalva (Harrison, Jim), 451

Dance of the Sacred Circle (Rodanas, Kristina), 524

Danger Zone (Klass, David), 66

The Darker Face of the Earth (Dove, Rita), 164

Dark Passage (Wheeler, Richard S.), 484

Dark Shade (Curry, Jane Louise), 435

Daughters of the Fifth Sun (Milligan, Bryce, Mary Guerrero Milligan, and Angela de Hoyos), 342, 400

Dawn Land (Bruchac, Joseph), 427

Da Wei's Treasure (Chang, Margaret, and Raymond Chang), 247

A Day's Work (Bunting, Eve), 310

De Colores and Other Latin-American Folk Songs for Children (Orozco, Jose-Luis), 384, 409

The Deetkatoo (Bierhorst, John), 487

Delicious Hullabaloo (Mora, Pat), 408

The Desert Is My Mother (Mora, Pat), 405

Devil in a Blue Dress (Mosley, Walter), 84

Devil's Gonna Get Him (Wesley, Valerie Wilson), 133

A Different Beat (Boyd, Candy Dawson), 12

A Dime a Dozen (Grimes, Nikki), 174

Doesn't Fall Off His Horse (Stroud, Virginia A.), 479

Dog People (Bruchac, Joseph), 425

Dogwolf (Carter, Alden), 431

Don't Split the Pole (Tate, Eleanora E.), 128

Down in the Subway (Cohen, Miriam), 317

Down the Road (Schertle, Alice), 117

Dragonfly (Gotera, Vince), 294

The Dragon Prince (Yep, Laurence), 282

The Dragon's Tale and Other Animal Fables of the Chinese Zodiac (Demi), 249

Dreamer (Johnson, Charles), 61

Eagle Boy (Hausman, Gerald), 512

Eagle Song (Bruchac, Joseph), 426

The Eagle's Shadow (Martin, Mora), 461

The Eagle's Song (Rodanas, Kristina), 525

The Earth Under Sky Bear's Feet (Bruchac, Joseph), 547

Easier to Kill (Wesley, Valerie Wilson), 133

Easter Parade (Greenfield, Eloise), 41

Ebony Sea (Smalls-Hector, Irene), 121

The Echoes of the Elders (Normandin, Christine), 521

Echoes of the White Giraffe (Choi, Sook Nyul), 199

The Edge of Heaven (Golden, Marita), 39

Egg-Drop Blues (Banks, Jacqueline Turner), 4

El Coro (Espada, Martin), 394

The Elements of San Joaquin (Soto, Gary), 413

Ernestine & Amanda (Belton, Sandra), 6

Ernestine & Amanda: Members of the C.L.U.B. (Belton, Sandra), 6

Ernestine & Amanda: Mysteries on Monroe Street (Belton, Sandra), 6

Ernestine & Amanda: Summer Camp: Ready or Not! (Belton, Sandra), 6

Face of an Angel (Chavez, Denise), 314

Faces in the Moon (Bell, Betty Louise), 421

The Fallen Man (Hillerman, Tony), 454

Fallout (Mori, Kyoko), 297

Fall Secrets (Boyd, Candy Dawson), 12

Fa Mulan (San Souci, Robert D.), 271

The Farmer and the Poor God (Wells, Ruth), 280

Far North (Hobbs, Will), 256

Father's Day Blues (Smalls-Hector, Irene), 122

¡Fiesta! (Guy, Ginger Foglesong), 325

The Fifth and Final Sun (Greger, C. Shana), 507

Finding My Voice (Lee, Marie), 218

Fireflies for Nathan (Oppenheim, Shulamith Levey), 90

Firefly Summer (Belpre, Pura), 305

The First Eagle (Hillerman, Tony), 454

Fishing Sunday (Johnston, Tony), 210

Fitting In (Bernardo, Anilu), 306

Five Heavenly Emperors (Zhang, Song Nan), 290

¡Floricanto Si! (Milligan, Bryce, Mary Guerrero Milligan, and Angela de Hoyos), 401

The Flower in the Skull (Alcala, Kathleen), 302

Flutie (Glancy, Diane), 448

The Folding Cliffs (Merwin, W. S.), 296

Follow the Stars (Rodanas, Kristina), 526

The Foot Warmer and the Crow (Coleman, Evelyn), 22

Foreign Devil (Wang, Ping), 231

The Foreign Student (Choi, Susan), 200

Forged by Fire (Draper, Sharon M.), 33

For the Love of the Game (Greenfield, Eloise), 173

Forty Acres and Maybe a Mule (Robinet, Harriette Gillem), 109

Four Ancestors (Bruchac, Joseph), 491, 548

The Fred Field (Burgess, Barbara Hood), 15

The Freedom Riddle (Medearis, Angela Shelf), 153

Freedom's Gifts (Wesley, Valerie), 134

Frida Marie (Lattimore, Deborah Nourse), 336

From Amigos to Friends (Garcia, Pelayo "Pete"), 322

From the Bellybutton of the Moon and Other Summer Poems/Del Ombligo de la Luna y otros poemas de verano (Alarcon, Francisco X.), 387

From the Notebooks of Melanin Sun (Woodson, Jacqueline), 139

Full Worm Moon (Lemieux, Margo), 458

Gathering of Pearls (Choi, Sook Nyul), 199

Gathering the Sun (Ada, Alma Flor), 301

The Genie in the Jar (Giovanni, Nikki), 167

The Gettin Place (Straight, Susan), 126

The Ghost Fox (Yep, Laurence), 191

Gingerbread Days (Thomas, Joyce Carol), 191

The Girl from Playa Blanca (Lachtman, Ofelia Dumas), 333

The Girl Who Lived with the Bears (Goldin, Barbara Diamond), 505

The Girl Who Married the Moon (Bruchac, Joseph, and Gayle Ross), 493

Glorious Angels (Myers, Walter Dean), 186

The Glory Field (Myers, Walter Dean), 86

Gluskabe and the Four Wishes (Bruchac, Joseph), 492

God's Trombones (Johnson, James Weldon), 180

Going Under (Suarez, Virgil), 364

The Golden Flower (Jaffe, Nina), 381

Gone Fishing (Mosley, Walter), 84

Gone from Home (Johnson, Angela), 57

Good Luck Gold and Other Poems (Wong, Janet S.), 299

Granddaddy's Gift (Mitchell, Margaree King), 83

Grandmother's Pigeon (Erdrich, Louise), 443

The Grass Dancer (Power, Susan), 469

The Great Ball Game (Bruchac, Joseph), 492

The Great Buffalo Race (Esbensen, Barbara Juster), 498

The Greatest Treasure (Demi), 250

The Great Race (Bouchard, David), 246

Greetings, Sun (Gershator, Phillis, and David Gershator), 166

Guardian of the Hills (Strauss, Victoria), 475

Guests (Dorris, Michael), 437

The Gumma Wars (Haynes, David), 48

Gunga Din Highway (Chin, Frank), 197

Hairs: Pelitos (Cisneros, Sandra), 316

Hang a Thousand Trees with Ribbons (Rinaldi, Ann), 108

Hardscrub (Garcia, Lionel G.), 321

Harlem (Myers, Walter Dean), 187

Harvey Potter's Balloon Farm (Nolen, Jerdine), 89

Haunts (Medearis, Angela Shelf), 78

Havana Thursdays (Suarez, Virgil), 365

Hawk Moon (MacGregor, Rob), 459

Heads by Harry (Yamanaka, Lois-Ann), 235

The Healing (Jones, Gayl), 65

Hearsay (Porte, Barbara Ann), 266

Heaven (Johnson, Angela), 58

Heroes (Mochizuki, Ken), 219

Her Stories (Hamilton, Virginia), 147

The Hired Hand (San Souci, Robert D.), 155

Hiroshima (Yep, Laurence), 240

Hispanic American Literature (Kanellos, Nicolas), 332, 398

Hold Christmas in Your Heart (Hudson, Cheryl Willis), 177

Hold Fast to Dreams (Pinkney, Andrea Davis), 95

Home to Medicine Mountain (Santiago, Chiori), 470

Honey, I Love (Greenfield, Eloise), 172

Honor and Duty (Lee, Gus), 213

Hoops (Burleigh, Robert), 162

House Made of Dawn (Momaday, N. Scott), 464

How Chipmunk Got Tiny Feet (Hausman, Gerald), 513

How Rabbit Tricked Otter and Other Cherokee Trickster Stories (Ross, Gayle), 527

How Stella Got Her Groove Back (McMillan, Terry), 76

How Sweet the Sound (Hudson, Wade, and Cheryl Hudson), 151, 178

How the Indians Bought the Farm (Strete, Craig Kee, and Michelle Netten Chacon), 478

How the World Was Saved & Other Native American Tales (Harper, Piers), 509

How Thunder and Lightning Came to Be (Harrell, Beatrice Orcutt), 510

How Turtle's Back Was Cracked (Ross, Gayle), 528

Humming Whispers (Johnson, Angela), 59

The Hundred Secret Senses (Tan, Amy), 230

Hunger (Chang, Lan Samantha), 195

If You Please, President Lincoln (Robinet, Harriette Gillem), 110

I Hadn't Meant to Tell You This (Woodson, Jacqueline), 140

I Have Heard of a Land (Thomas, Joyce Carol), 130

Iktomi and the Buzzard (Goble, Paul), 502

Imagine the Angels of Bread (Espada, Martin), 395

The Imp That Ate My Homework (Yep, Laurence), 241

In a Circle Long Ago (Van Laan, Nancy), 539

Indian Killer (Alexie, Sherman), 418

Indigo (Jenkins, Beverly), 56

Indio (Garland, Sherry), 446

In the Bear's House (Momaday, N. Scott), 464

Into the Fire (Watanabe, Sylvia, and Carol Bruchac), 233

Irene Jennie and the Christmas Masquerade (Smalls-Hector, Irene), 121

The Island-below-the-Star (Rumford, James), 227

An Island Like You (Ortiz Cofer, Judith), 348

I Smell Honey (Pinkney, Brian, and Andrea Pinkney), 100

Is That Josie? (Narahashi, Keiko), 223

I Thought My Soul Would Rise and Fly (Hansen, Joyce), 46

I, Too, Sing America (Clinton, Catherine), 163

It's Raining Laughter (Grimes, Nikki), 175

I Used to Be a Superwoman (Velasquez, Gloria L.), 415

Jalapeno Bagels (Wing, Natasha), 369

Jamaica and Briana (Havill, Juanita), 47

Jamaica and the Substitute Teacher (Havill, Juanita), 47

Jamaica's Blue Marker (Havill, Juanita), 47

Jamaica's Find (Havill, Juanita), 47

Jamaica's Tag-Along (Havill, Juanita), 47

Jazmin's Notebook (Grimes, Nikki), 42

Jenny Reen and the Jack Muh Lantern (Smalls-Hector, Irene), 121

Jesse (Soto, Gary), 360

Jip His Story (Paterson, Katherine), 93

John Henry (Lester, Julius), 152

Jojofu (Waite, Michael P.), 278

JoJo's Flying Side Kick (Pinkney, Brian), 99

Journey to Freedom (Wright, Courtni C.), 143

Juan Bobo (Bernier-Grand, Carmen T.), 372

Juanita Fights the School Board (Velasquez, Gloria), 367

Jubilee Journey (Meyer, Carolyn), 81

Jumping Off to Freedom (Bernardo, Anilu), 307

Jumping the Broom (Wright, Courtni C.), 143

Jungle Dogs (Salisbury, Graham), 228

Junior College (Soto, Gary), 412

The Junior Thunderbird (Yep, Laurence), 284

Just Family (Bolden, Tonya), 9

Just Rewards or Who Is That Man in the Moon & What's He Doing Up There, Anyway? (Sanfield, Steve), 270

Kevin and His Dad (Smalls-Hector, Irene), 122

The Khan's Daughter (Yep, Laurence), 283

Kinship (Krishner, Trudy), 68

Knoxville, Tennessee (Giovanni, Nikki), 168

Kongi and Potgi (Han, Oki S., and Stephanie Haboush Plunkett), 257

La Mariposa (Jimenez, Francisco), 331

The Last Dragon (Nunes, Susan Miho), 224

The Last Rainmaker (Garland, Sherry), 447

The Last Tales of Uncle Remus (Harris, Joel Chandler)

Later, Gator (Yep, Laurence), 242

Latino Rainbow (Cumpian, Carlos), 393

Laughing Tomatoes and Other Spring Poems/Jitomates Risuenos y otros poemas de primavera (Alarcon, Francisco X.), 388

The Legend of Mackinac Island (Wargin, Kathy-jo), 540

The Legend of Sleeping Bear (Wargin, Kathy-jo), 540

The Legend of the Panda (Granfield, Linda), 254

The Legend of the White Buffalo Woman (Goble, Paul), 503

The Legend of the Windigo (Ross, Gayle), 529

Leticia's Secret (Lachtman, Ofelia Dumas), 334

Lift Ev'ry Voice and Sing (Johnson, James Weldon), 181

The Light People (Henry, Gordon, Jr.), 453

Like Sisters on the Homefront (Williams-Garcia, Rita), 137

Lily and the Wooden Bowl (Schroeder, Alan), 273

Ling-Li and the Phoenix Fairy (Greene, Ellin), 255

Listen to the Desert/Oye al desierto (Mora, Pat), 406

Little Coyote Runs Away (Strete, Craig Kee), 476

Little Lil and the Swing-Singing Sax (Gray, Libba Moore), 40

Little Plum (Young, Ed), 286.

The Little Red Ant and the Great Big Crumb (Climo, Shirley), 373

The Little Seven-Colored Horse (San Souci, Robert D.), 386

Live at Five (Haynes, David), 49

The Long-Haired Girl (Rappaport, Doreen), 267

The Long March (Fitzpatrick, Marie Louise), 444

Long River (Bruchac, Joseph), 427

Loose Woman (Cisneros, Sandra), 391

Losing Absalom (Pate, Alexs D.), 92

The Lost Boy and the Monster (Strete, Craig Kee), 476

The Lost Horse (Young, Ed), 287

Louise's Gift or What Did She Give Me That For? (Smalls-Hector, Irene), 122

Love Medicine (Erdrich, Louise), 442

Love Poems (Giovanni, Nikki), 169

Loverboys (Castilla, Ana), 312

The Loyal Cat (Namioka, Lensey), 265

Luka's Quilt (Guback, Georgia), 204

Ma Dear's Aprons (McKissack, Patricia), 73

The Mad Painter Poems (Minty, Judith), 553

The Magic of Spider Woman (Duncan, Lois), 495

The Magic Shell (Mohr, Nicholasa), 343

The Magic Tapestry (Demi), 250

The Magic Weaver of Rugs (Oughton, Jerrie), 523

The Making of Monkey King (Kraus, Robert, and Debby Chen), 262

Mama Provi and the Pot of Rice (Rosa-Casanova, Sylvia), 352

Manabozho's Gifts (Greene, Jacqueline), 506

The Manitous (Johnston, Basil), 516

The Man Made of Words (Momaday, N. Scott), 464

Maples in the Mist (Ho, Minfong), 29

Marco's Monster (Willis, Meredith Sue), 138

Marisol and Magdalena (Chambers, Veronica), 313

The Marks of Birth (Medina, Pablo), 341

A Matter of Pride and Other Stories (Mohr, Nicholasa), 344

Maya's Divided World (Velasquez, Gloria L.), 367

May'naise Sandwiches & Sunshine Tea (Belton, Sandra), 7

The Meanest Thing to Say (Cosby, Bill), 26

Meet Danitra Brown (Grimes, Nikki), 176

Memories of My Ghost Brother (Fenkl, Heinz Insu), 202

Messey Bessey (McKissack, Patricia, and Fredrick McKissack), 183

Messey Bessey and the Birthday Overnight (McKissack, Patricia, and Fredrick McKissack), 183

Messey Bessey's Closet (McKissack, Patricia, and Fredrick McKissack), 183

Messey Bessey's Garden (McKissack, Patricia, and Fredrick McKissack), 183

Messey Bessey's Holidays (McKissack, Patricia, and Fredrick McKissack), 183

Messey Bessey's School Desk (McKissack, Patricia, and Fredrick McKissack), 183

Minty (Schroeder, Alan), 119

Mississippi Chariot (Robinet, Harriette Gillem), 111

Mister and Me (Holt, Kimberly Willis), 51

Mona in the Promised Land (Jen, Gish), 209

Money Troubles (Cosby, Bill), 26

Monkey King (Chao, Patricia), 196

Monkey Secret (Glancy, Diane), 449

Moriah's Pond (Smothers, Ethel Footman), 123

Mother Love (Dove, Rita), 164

Mouse Match (Young, Ed), 288

Mr. Pak Buys a Story (Farley, Carol), 252

Music from a Place Called Half Moon (Oughton, Jerrie), 466

Musicians of the Sun (McDermott, Gerald), 520

My Father's Boat (Garland, Sherry), 203

My Home Is Over Jordan (Forrester, Sandra), 38

My House (Giovanni, Nikki), 169

My Navajo Sister (Schick, Eleanor), 471

Mysterious Tales of Japan (Martin, Rafe), 263

Nappy Hair (Herron, Carolivia), 50

Native American Literature (Vizenor, Gerald), 482, 559

Navajo Visions and Voices Across the Mesa (Begay, Shonto), 545

The Necessary Hunger (Revoyr, Nina), 226

Necessary Roughness (Lee, Marie G.), 216

New and Selected Poems (Soto, Gary), 413

The New One (Banks, Jacqueline Turner), 4

Nightland (Owens, Louis), 468

Night of the Chupacabras (Lee, Marie G.), 217, 337

Night Song (Jenkins, Beverly), 56

Night Visitors (Young, Ed), 289

No Hiding Place (Wesley, Valerie Wilson), 133

No Mirrors in My Nana's House (Barnwell, Ysaye M.), 158

No Physical Evidence (Lee, Gus), 214

No Place (Haugaard, Kay), 326

Northwoods Cradle Song (Wood, Douglas), 561

Off and Running (Soto, Gary), 361

Of Flesh & Spirit (Wang, Ping), 298

Off to School (Battle-Lavert, Gwendolyn), 5

Ojibway Heritage (Johnston, Basil), 516

Old Bag of Bones (Stevens, Janet), 533

The Old Cotton Blues (England, Linda), 35

Older Brother, Younger Brother (Jaffe, Nina), 260

Old Letivia and the Mountain of Sorrows (Mohr, Nicholasa), 345

The Old Man and His Door (Soto, Gary), 362

One Afternoon (Heo, Yumi), 207

One Fall Day (Bang, Molly), 3

One Hand Clapping (Martin, Rafe, and Manuela Soares), 264

One Hot Summer Day (Crews, Nina), 27

The Only Piece of Furniture in the House (Glancy, Diane), 448

On Second Thought (Kenny, Maurice), 552

On the Bus with Rosa Parks (Dove, Rita), 164

On the Long Trail Home (Stewart, Elizabeth J.), 474

On the Road of Stars (Bierhorst, John), 488, 546

Oren Bell (Burgess, Barbara Hood), 15

The Other Side (Johnson, Angela), 179

Our People (Medearis, Angela Shelf), 79

Owl Eyes (Gates, Frieda), 499

Pablo's Tree (Mora, Pat), 346

Paco and the Witch (Pitre, Felix), 385

Papa's Stories (Johnson, Dolores), 62

Papa Tells Chita a Story (Howard, Elizabeth Fitzgerald), 53

Paper Dance (Cruz, Victor Hernandez, Leroy V. Quintana, and Virgil Suarez), 392

Parable of the Sower (Butler, Octavia), 17

Parable of the Talents (Butler, Octavia), 17

Parrot in the Oven (Martinez, Victor), 338

The Path of Quiet Elk (Stroud, Virginia A.), 480

The Peace Chief (Conley, Robert), 433

Pedro and the Monkey (San Souci, Robert D.), 272

People of Corn (Gerson, Mary-Joan), 500

Pepita Talks Twice/Pepita Habla Dos Veces (Lachtman, Ofelia Dumas), 335

Petty Crimes (Soto, Gary), 363

Philadelphia Flowers (Whiteman, Roberta Hill), 560

The Phoenix Gone, The Terrace Empty (Chin, Marilyn), 292

A Picture of Freedom (McKissack, Patricia C.), 74

Pink and Say (Polacco, Patricia), 102

A Place Called Freedom (Sanders, Scott Russell), 115

A Place to Call Home (Koller, Jackie), 67

The Poet's World (Dove, Rita), 164

The Poison Place (Lyons, Mary E.), 72

The Pool Party (Soto, Gary), 356

Poppa's Itchy Christmas (Medearis, Angela Shelf), 80

Poppa's New Pants (Medearis, Angela Shelf), 80

The Precious Gift (Jackson, Ellen), 515

Pretty Brown Face (Pinkney, Brian, and Andrea Pinkney), 100

Prietita and the Ghost Woman/Prietita y la Llorona (Andaldua, Gloria), 304

Project Wheels (Banks, Jacqueline Turner), 4

Prophecy Rock (MacGregor, Rob), 460

Push (Sapphire), 116

Pushing the Bear (Glancy, Diane), 450

Rabbit and the Moon (Wood, Douglas), 542

The Race of Toad and Deer (Mora, Pat), 383

Race with Buffalo, and Other Native American Stories for Young Readers (Young, Richard, and Judy Dockery Young), 544

The Rainbow Bridge (Wood, Audrey), 541

The Rainbow Hand (Wong, Janet S.), 299

Rattlebone (Clair, Maxine), 21

Raven in a Dove House (Pinkney, Andrea Davis), 96

Re: Creation (Giovanni, Nikki), 167, 169

Reaching for the Mainland and Selected New Poems (Ortiz Cofer, Judith), 410

Red Bird (Mitchell, Barbara), 463

A Red Death (Mosley, Walter), 84

Releasing Serpents (Zamora, Bernice), 416

Remaking the Earth (Goble, Paul), 503

Rendezvous (Wheeler, Richard S.), 484

Reservation Blues (Alexie, Sherman), 419

Restless Serpents (Zamora, Bernice), 416

Returning a Borrowed Tongue (Carbo, Nick), 291

Ribbons (Yep, Laurence), 238

The Richer, the Poorer (West, Dorothy), 135

A Ring of Tricksters (Hamilton, Virginia), 148

Rites of Passage (Bolden, Tonya), 10

The River Where Blood Is Born (Jackson-Opoka, Sandra), 55

The Road Home (Harrison, Jim), 451

Roll of Thunder, Hear My Cry (Taylor, Mildred D.), 129

Rum-a-Tum-Tum (Medearis, Angela Shelf), 184

Run Away Home (McKissack, Patricia C.), 75

Run for Your Life (Levy, Marilyn), 71

Running for Our Lives (Turner, Glennette Tilley), 131

Runs With Horses (Burks, Brian), 429

Saturday Night at the Pahala Theatre (Yamanaka, Lois-Ann), 235

Saying Goodbye (Lee, Marie G.), 218

A School for Pompey Walker (Rosen, Michael J.), 114

School Spirit (Hurwitz, Johanna), 330

Second Cousins (Hamilton, Virginia), 44

Second Daughter (Walter, Mildred Pitts), 132

The Secret of Two Brothers (Hernandez, Irene Beltran), 328

The Secret Super Power of Marco (Willis, Meredith Sue), 138

Seeing Calvin Coolidge in a Dream (Derbyshire, John), 201

Sees Behind Trees (Dorris, Michael), 438

The Selected Poems of Nikki Giovanni (Giovanni, Nikki), 169

Seminole Diary (Johnson, Dolores), 63

Senor Cat's Romance and Other Favorite Stories from Latin America (Gonzalez, Lucia M.), 376

Shake Shake Shake (Pinkney, Brian, and Andrea Pinkney), 100

Shark Bait (Salisbury, Graham), 228

The Sharpest Sight (Owen, Louis), 467

The Shepherd Boy (Franklin, Kristine L.), 445

Shimmy Shimmy Shimmy Like My Sister Kate (Giovanni, Nikki), 170

Shipwreck Saturday (Cosby, Bill), 26

A Shroud in the Family (Garcia, Lionel G.), 321

The Simple Truth (Baldacci, David), 2

Singing in the Comeback Choir (Campbell, Bebe Moore), 19

Skin Deep and Other Teenage Reflections (Medearis, Angela Shelf), 185

The Skinwalkers (Hillerman, Tony), 454

Skunny Wundy (Parker, Arthur), 498

Slam! (Myers, Walter Dean), 87

Smiffy Blue, Ace Crime Detective (Myers, Walter Dean), 88

Smoky Night (Bunting, Eve), 13

Snow Falling on Cedars (Guterson, David), 205

Soccer Cousins (Marzollo, Jean), 339

So Far from the Sea (Bunting, Eve), 194

Solo Girl (Pinkney, Angela), 97

Some Love, Some Pain, Sometimes (Cooper, J. California), 25

Something Terrible Happened (Porte, Barbara Ann), 104

Song Lee and the Hamster Hunt (Kline, Suzy), 212

Song Lee and the "I hate you" Notes (Kline, Suzy), 212

Song Lee and the Leech Man (Kline, Suzy), 212

The Song of el Coqui and Other Tales of Puerto Rico (Mohr, Nicholasa), 382

The Song of the Turtle (Allen, Paula Gunn), 420

Songs for the Seasons (Highwater, Jamake), 551

Songs My Mother Taught Me (Yamauchi, Wakako), 236

Songs of Faith (Johnson, Angela), 60

Sootface (San Souci, Robert D.), 531

Soul Look Back in Wonder (Feelings, Tom), 165

Sound the Jubilee (Forrester, Sandra), 38

Spirit Horse (Ackerman, Ned), 417

The Spirit of the Cedar People (Normandin, Christine), 521

Spirits of the Ordinary (Alcala, Kathleen), 303

Spite Fences (Krishner, Trudy), 68

A Spoon for Every Bite (Hayes, Joe), 377

Star Quilt (Whiteman, Roberta Hill), 560

The Stonecutter (Demi), 250

The Stone Lion (Schroeder, Alan), 274

The Story of Blue Elk (Hausman, Gerald), 514

The Story of the Milky Way (Bruchac, Joseph, and Gayle Ross), 494

A Strawbeater's Thanksgiving (Smalls-Hector, Irene), 121

Sugarcane House and Other Stories About Mr. Fat (Bond, Adrienne), 11

A Suitcase of Seaweed and Other Poems (Wong, Janet S.), 299

Summer on Wheels (Soto, Gary), 359

A Sunburned Prayer (Talbert, Marc), 366

The Sunday Outing (Pinkney, Gloria Jean), 101

The Sun Is So Quiet (Giovanni, Nikki), 171

Super-Eight Movies (Soto, Gary), 413

Super-Fine Valentine (Cosby, Bill), 26

Sweet Fifteen (Bertrand, Diane Gonzales), 309

Taft (Patchett, Ann), 91

Tailypo (Medearis, Angela Shelf), 154

Talent Night (Okimoto, Jean Davies), 225

A Tale of Rabbit and Coyote (Johnston, Tony), 517

The Tale of Sunlight (Soto, Gary), 413

Tales of Burning Love (Erdrich, Louise), 442

Tears of a Tiger (Draper, Sharon M.), 33

Tell Me a Cuento/Cuentame Un Story (Hayes, Joe), 378

Tell Me a Tale (Bruchac, Joseph), 491

Ten Suns (Kimmel, Eric), 261

Thief of Hearts (Yep, Laurence), 243

This Big Sky (Mora, Pat), 407

Those Who Ride the Night Winds (Giovanni, Nikki), 169

Through the Storm (Jenkins, Beverly), 56

Tiger's Tail (Lee, Gus), 215

Tiger Woman (Yep, Laurence), 284

Tio Armando (Heide, Florence Parry, and Roxanne Heide Pierce), 327

To a Widow with Children (Garcia, Lionel G.), 321

Tomas and the Library Lady (Mora, Pat), 346

Tommy Stands Alone (Velasquez, Gloria L.), 368

Tonio's Cat (Calhoun, Mary), 311

Topas (Jenkins, Beverly), 56

Tops & Bottoms (Stevens, Janet), 156

The Tortilla Factory (Paulsen, Gary), 350

Tortillas and Lullabies/Tortillas y cancioncitas (Reiser, Lynn), 351

Touching the Distance (Swann, Brian), 535, 556

Touching the Fire (Gonzalez, Ray), 397

Tracks (Erdrich, Louise), 442

Train (Temple, Charles), 189

The Treasure Chest (Wang, Rosalind C.), 279

The Treasure Hunt (Cosby, Bill), 26

A Treasury of African-American Christmas Stories (Collier-Thomas, Bettye), 24

The Tree Is Older Than You Are (Nye, Naomi Shihab), 522

The Tree That Rains (Bernhard, Emery), 486

The Trickster and the Troll (Sneve, Virginia Driving Hawk), 473

True North (Lasky, Kathryn), 70

Tryin' to Sleep in the Bed You Made (DeBerry, Virginia, and Donna Grant), 31

Tsubu the Little Snail (Williams, Carol Ann), 281

Turtle Island ABC (Hausman, Gerald), 452

The Twins, the Pirates, and the Battle of New Orleans (Robinet, Harriette Gillem), 112

Two Bad Boys (Haley, Gail), 508

Two Bear Cubs (San Souci, Robert D.), 532

The Two Brothers (Ho, Minfong), 259

Uncegila's Seventh Spot (Rubalcaba, Jill), 530

Under the Blood-Red Sun (Salisbury, Graham), 229

Uno, Dos, Tres (Mora, Pat), 408

Vivid (Jenkins, Beverly), 56

Voice of the Turtle (Allen, Paula Gunn), 420

The Wagon (Johnston, Tony), 64

Wagon Train (Wright, Courtni C.), 143

Walks Alone (Burks, Brian), 430

Wan Hu Is in the Stars (Armstrong, Jennifer), 244

The Warrior Woman (Kingston, Maxine Hong), 271

War Woman (Conley, Robert), 434

Washington City Is Burning (Robinet, Harriette Gillem), 113

Watch Me Dance (Pinkney, Brian, and Andrea Pinkney), 100

Watch Out for Clever Women!/¡Cuidado con las Mujeres Astutas! (Hayes, Joe), 379

The Waters Between (Bruchac, Joseph), 427

The Watsons Go to Birmingham—1963 (Curtis, Christopher Paul), 29

The Wave of the Sea-Wolf (Wisniewski, David), 485

Wearing the Morning Star (Swann, Brian), 536, 557

The Weather That Kills (Jones, Patricia Spears), 182

The Wedding (West, Dorothy), 136

The Well (Taylor, Mildred D.), 129

What a Woman's Gotta Do (Coleman, Evelyn), 23

What's in Aunt Mary's Room? (Howard, Elizabeth Fitzgerald), 54

When Birds Could Talk & Bats Could Sing (Hamilton, Virginia), 149

When Death Comes Stealing (Wesley, Valerie Wilson), 133

Where Evil Sleeps (Wesley, Valerie Wilson), 133

Where Sparrows Work Hard (Soto, Gary), 413

Where There's A Will, There's A Way/ Donde Hay Ganas, Hay Manas (Hayes, Joe), 380

White Butterfly (Mosley, Walter), 84

The White Deer and Other Stories Told by the Lenape (Bierhorst, John), 489

White Lilacs (Meyer, Carolyn), 81

Wild Meat and the Bully Burgers (Yamanaka, Lois-Ann), 235

Willie Jerome (Duncan, Alice Faye), 34

The Windigo's Return (Wood, Douglas), 543

The Window (Dorris, Michael), 439

The Wise Old Woman (Uchida, Yoshiko), 9

Wolf, No Wolf (Bowen, Peter), 422

The Woman Who Fell from the Sky (Harjo, Joy), 549

The Women and the Men (Giovanni, Nikki), 169

Women Don't Need to Write (Zaldivar, Raquel Puig), 371

The World in Grandfather's Hands (Strete, Craig Kee), 477

The World of Daughter McGuire (Wyeth, Sharon Dennis), 144

Yang the Second and Her Secret Admirers (Namioka, Lensey), 222

Yang the Third and Her Impossible Family (Namioka, Lensey), 222

Yang the Youngest and His Terrible Ear (Namioka, Lensey), 222

Year of Impossible Goodbyes (Choi, Sook Nyul), 199

The Year of Our Revolution (Ortiz Cofer, Judith), 349

Yellow Raft in Blue Water (Dorris, Michael), 436

Yolanda's Genius (Fenner, Carol), 36

You Come Singing (Suarez, Virgil), 414

Your Move (Bunting, Eve), 14

Index of Writers

(Numerals refer to entries.)

Ackerman, Karen, 1
Ackerman, Ned, 417
Ada, Alma Flor, 301
Alarcon, Francisco X., 387, 388
Alcala, Kathleen, 302, 303
Alexie, Sherman, 418, 419
Allen, Paula Gunn, 420
Anzaldua, Gloria, 304
Armstrong, Jennifer, 244

Baldacci, David, 2
Bang, Molly, 3
Banks, Jacqueline Turner, 4
Barnwell, Ysaye M., 158
Battle-Lavert, Gwendolyn, 5
Begay, Shonto, 545
Bell, Betty Louise, 421
Belpre, Pura, 305
Belton, Sandra, 6, 7
Bernardo, Anilu, 306, 307
Bernhard, Emery, 486
Bernier-Grande, Carmen T., 372
Bertrand, Diane Gonzales, 308, 309
Bierhorst, John, 487, 488, 489, 546
Bledsoe, Lucy Jane, 8
Bodkin, Odds, 245
Bolden, Tonya, 9, 10
Bond, Adrienne, 11
Bouchard, David, 246
Bowen, Peter, 422

Boyd, Candy Dawson, 12, 159
Bruchac, Carol, 233
Bruchac, Joseph, 423, 424, 425, 426,
    427, 490, 491, 492, 493, 494, 547,
    548
Bryan, Ashley, 160, 161
Bunting, Eve, 13, 14, 194, 310, 428
Burgess, Barbara Hood, 15
Burks, Brian, 429, 430
Burleigh, Robert, 162
Butler, Octavia, 16, 17

Calhoun, Mary, 311
Campbell, Bebe Moore, 18, 19
Carbo, Nick, 291
Carlson, Lori Marie, 389, 390
Carter, Alden, 431
Casler, Leigh, 432
Castilla, Ana, 312
Chacon, Michelle Netten, 478
Chambers, Veronica, 20, 313
Chang, Lan Samantha, 195
Chang, Margaret, 247
Chang, Raymond, 247
Chao, Patricia, 196
Chavez, Denise, 314
Chen, Debby, 262
Chief Lelooska, 521
Chin, Charlie, 271
Chin, Frank, 197

Chin, Marilyn, 292
Choi, Sook Nyul, 198, 199
Choi, Susan, 200
Ciavonne, Jean, 315
Cisneros, Sandra, 316, 391
Clair, Maxine, 21
Climo, Shirley, 373
Clinton, Catherine, 163
Cohen, Miriam, 317
Coleman, Evelyn, 22, 23
Collier-Thomas, Bettye, 24
Conley, Robert, 433, 434
Cooper, J. California, 25
Cordova, Amy, 318
Cosby, Bill, 26
Crews, Nina, 27
Cruz, Victor Hernandez, 392
Cummings, Pat, 28
Cumpian, Carlos, 393
Curry, Jane Louise, 435
Curtis, Christopher Paul, 29
Curtis, Gavin, 30

Dabydeen, Cyril, 293
Danticat, Edwidge, 319
DeBerry, Virginia, 31
De Hoyos, Angela, 342, 400, 401
Delgado, Maria Isabel, 320
Demi, 248, 249, 250
Derbyshire, John, 201
DiSalvo-Ryan, DyAnne, 32
Dorris, Michael, 436, 437, 438, 439
Dove, Rita, 164
Draper, Sharon M., 33
Duey, Kathleen, 440
Duncan, Alice Faye, 34
Duncan, Lois, 495
Durrant, Lynda, 441
Dwyer, Mindy, 496

Ehlert, Lois, 497
England, Linda, 35
Erdrich, Louise, 442, 443
Esbensen, Barbara Juster, 498
Espada, Martin, 394, 395
Espinosa, J. Manuel, 374

Fang, Linda, 251
Farley, Carol, 252

Faulkner, William J., 146
Feelings, Tom, 165
Fenkl, Heinz Insu, 202
Fenner, Carol, 36
Fitzpatrick, Marie Louise, 444
Flournoy, Valerie, 37
Forrester, Sandra, 38
Franklin, Kristine L., 445

Garcia, Lionel G., 321
Garcia, Pelayo "Pete," 322
Garcia-Aguilera, Carolina, 323
Garland, Sherry, 203, 446, 447
Gates, Frieda, 499
Gershator, David, 166
Gershator, Phillis, 166
Gerson, Mary-Joan, 500
Giovanni, Nikki, 167, 168, 169, 170, 171
Giskin, Howard, 253
Glancy, Diane, 448, 449, 450
Goble, Paul, 501, 502, 503
Golden, Marita, 39
Goldin, Barbara Diamond, 504, 505
Gonzalez, Lucia, 375
Gonzalez, Lucia M., 376
Gonzalez, Ray, 324, 396, 397
Gotera, Vince, 294
Granfield, Linda, 254
Grant, Donna, 31
Gray, Libba Moore, 40
Greene, Ellin, 255
Greene, Jacqueline Dembar, 506
Greenfield, Eloise, 41, 172, 173
Greger, C. Shana, 507
Grimes, Nikki, 42, 174, 175, 176
Guback, Georgia, 204
Guterson, David, 205
Guy, Ginger Fogelsong, 325

Haley, Gail, 508
Hamanaka, Sheila, 43, 206
Hamilton, Morse, 256
Hamilton, Virginia, 44, 147, 148, 149
Han, Oki S., 257
Hansen, Joyce, 45, 46
Harjo, Joy, 549
Harper, Piers, 509
Harrell, Beatrice Orcutt, 510
Harris, Joel Chandler, 150

Harrison, Jim, 451
Haugaard, Kay, 326
Hausman, Gerald, 452, 511, 512, 513, 514, 550
Havill, Juanita, 47
Hayes, Joe, 374, 377, 378, 379, 380
Haynes, David, 48, 49
Heide, Florence Parry, 327
Henry, Gordon, Jr., 453
Heo, Yumi, 207
Hernandez, Irene Beltran, 328
Herrera, Juan Felipe, 329
Herron, Carolivia, 50
Highwater, Jamake, 56
Hillerman, Tony, 454
Ho, Minfong, 258, 259, 295
Hobbs, Will, 455, 456
Hogan, James P., 208
Holt, Kimberly Willis, 51
Houston, Gloria, 52
Howard, Elizabeth Fitzgerald, 53, 54
Hudson, Cheryl, 151, 178
Hudson, Cheryl Willis, 177
Hudson, Wade, 151, 178
Hurwitz, Johanna, 330

Jackson, Ellen, 515
Jackson-Opoku, Sandra, 55
Jaffe, Nina, 260, 381
Jen, Gish, 209
Jenkins, Beverly, 56
Jimenez, Francisco, 331
Johnson, Angela, 57, 58, 59, 60, 179
Johnson, Charles, 61
Johnson, Dolores, 62, 63
Johnson, James Weldon, 180, 181
Johnston, Basil, 516
Johnston, Tony, 64, 210, 517
Jones, Gayl, 65
Jones, Patricia Spears, 182

Kanellos, Nicolas, 332, 398
Keller, Nora Okja, 211
Kenny, Maurice, 552
Killingsworth, Monte, 457
Kimmel, Eric, 261
Kingston, Maxine Hong, 271
Klass, David, 66
Kline, Suzy, 212

Koller, Jackie, 67
Kraus, Robert, 262
Krishner, Trudy, 68
Kroll, Virginia, 69

Lachtman, Ofelia Dumas, 333, 334, 335
Lasky, Kathryn, 70
Lattimore, Deborah Nourse, 336
Lee, Gus, 213, 214, 215
Lee, Marie G., 216, 217, 218, 337
Lelooska, Chief, 521
Lemieux, Margo, 458
Lester, Julius, 150, 152
Levy, Marilyn, 71
Lyons, Mary E., 72

MacGregor, Rob, 459, 460
Manitonquat (Medicine Story), 518
Martin, Nora, 461
Martin, Rafe, 263, 264
Martinez, Dionisio D., 399
Martinez, Victor, 338
Marzollo, Jean, 339
McDermott, Gerald, 519, 520
McKissack, Fredrick, 183
McKissack, Patricia, 183
McKissack, Patricia C., 73, 74, 75
McMillan, Terry, 76
Mead, Alice, 462
Medearis, Angela Shelf, 77, 78, 79, 80, 153, 154, 184, 185, 340
Medina, Pablo, 341
Merwin, W. S., 296
Meyer, Carolyn, 81
Miller, William, 82
Milligan, Bryce, 342, 400, 401
Milligan, Mary Guerrero, 342, 400, 401
Minty, Judith, 553
Mitchell, Barbara, 463
Mitchell, Margaree King, 83
Mochizuki, Ken, 219
Mohr, Nicholasa, 343, 344, 345, 382
Molnar-Fenton, Stephan, 220
Momaday, N. Scott, 464
Moore, Christopher, 465
Mora, Pat, 346, 383, 402, 403, 404, 405, 406, 407, 408
Mori, Kyoko, 297
Mosley, Walter, 84

Mowry, Jess, 85
Myers, Walter Dean, 86, 87, 88, 186, 187

Namioka, Lensey, 221, 222, 265
Narahashi, Keiko, 223
Nolen, Jerdine, 89
Normandin, Christine, 521
Nunes, Susan Miho, 224
Nye, Naomi Shihab, 347, 522

Okimoto, Jean Davies, 225
Oppenheim, Shulamith Levey, 90
Orozco, Jose-Luis, 384, 409
Ortiz, Simon, 554
Ortiz Cofer, Judith, 348, 349, 410
Oughton, Jerrie, 466, 523
Owens, Louis, 467, 468

Parker, Arthur, 498
Parks, Gordon, 188
Patchett, Ann, 91
Pate, Alexs D., 92
Paterson, Katherine, 93
Paulsen, Gary, 350
Perry, Jesse, Jr., 142, 157, 192
Pierce, Roxanne Heide, 327
Pinkney, Andrea, 100
Pinkney, Andrea Davis, 94, 95, 96, 97
Pinkney, Brian, 98, 99, 100
Pinkney, Gloria Jean, 101
Pitre, Felix, 385
Plunkett, Stephanie Haboush, 257
Polacco, Patricia, 102
Porte, Barbara Ann, 103, 104, 266
Power, Susan, 469
Poydar, Nancy, 105

Quintana, Leroy V., 392

Rappaport, Doreen, 267
Reeder, Carolyn, 106
Reiser, Lynn, 351
Revoyr, Nina, 226
Rinaldi, Ann, 107, 108
Robinet, Harriette Gillem, 109, 110, 111, 112, 113
Rodanas, Kristina, 524, 525, 526
Ros, Saphan, 258, 259

Rosa-Casanova, Sylvia, 352
Rose, Wendy, 555
Rosen, Michael J., 114
Ross, Gayle, 493, 494, 527, 528, 529
Roth, Susan L., 268
Roybal, Laura, 353
Rubalcaba, Jill, 530
Rumford, James, 227, 269

Salisbury, Graham, 228, 229
Sanders, Scott Russell, 115
Sanfield, Steve, 270
San Souci, Robert D., 155, 271, 272, 386, 531, 532
Santiago, Chiori, 470
Santiago, Esmeralda, 354
Sapphire, 116
Schertle, Alice, 117
Schick, Eleanor, 471
Schroeder, Alan, 118, 119, 273, 274
Scott, Ann Herbert, 472
Shepard, Aaron, 275
Sinclair, April, 120
Smalls-Hector, Irene, 121, 122
Smothers, Ethel Footman, 123
Sneve, Virginia Driving Hawk, 473
Soares, Manuela, 264
Soto, Gary, 355, 356, 357, 358, 359, 360, 361, 362, 363, 411, 412, 413
Spagnoli, Cathy, 276
Steptoe, John, 124
Stevens, Janet, 156, 533
Stewart, Elizabeth J., 474
Stolz, Mary, 125
Straight, Susan, 126
Strauss, Victoria, 475
Strete, Craig Kee, 476, 477, 478
Stroud, Virginia A., 479, 480
Suarez, Virgil, 364, 365, 392, 414
Swann, Brian, 534, 535, 536, 556, 557

Talbert, Marc, 366
Tan, Amy, 230
Tapahonso, Luci, 481, 558
Tate, Eleanora E., 127, 128
Taylor, C. J., 537
Taylor, Harriet Peck, 538
Taylor, Mildred D., 129

Temple, Charles, 189
Thomas, Joyce Carol, 130, 190, 191
Turner, Glennette Tilley, 131

Uchida, Yoshiko, 277

Van Laan, Nancy, 539
Velasquez, Gloria L., 367, 368, 415
Vizenor, Gerald, 482, 559

Waite, Michael P., 278
Walter, Mildred Pitts, 132
Wang, Ping, 231, 298
Wang, Rosalind C., 279
Wangerin, Walter, Jr., 483
Wargin, Kathy-jo, 540
Wartski, Maureen, 232
Watanabe, Sylvia, 233
Wells, Ruth, 280
Wesley, Valerie Wilson, 133, 134
West, Dorothy, 135, 136
Wheeler, Richard S., 484
Whiteman, Roberta Hill, 560
Williams, Carol Ann, 281
Williams-Garcia, Rita, 137
Willis, Meredith Sue, 138

Wing, Natasha, 368
Wisniewski, David, 485
Wong, Janet S., 299
Wong, Shawn, 234, 300
Wood, Audrey, 541
Wood, Douglas, 542, 543, 561
Woodson, Jacqueline, 139, 140
Woodtor, Dee Parmer, 141
Worley, Demetrice A., 142, 157, 192
Wright, Courtni C., 143
Wyeth, Sharon Dennis, 144

Yamanaka, Lois-Ann, 235
Yamauchi, Wakako, 236
Ybarra, Ricardo Means, 370
Yep, Laurence, 237, 238, 239, 240, 241,
    242, 243, 282, 283, 284
Young, Al, 145, 193
Young, Ed, 285, 286, 287, 288, 289
Young, Judy Dockrey, 544
Young, Richard, 544

Zaldivar, Raquel Puig, 371
Zamora, Bernice, 416
Zhang, Song Nan, 290
Zubizarrata, Rosa, 301

Index of Illustrators

(Numerals refer to entries.)

Alcorn, Stephen, 163
Allen, Thomas B., 115
Andreasen, Dan, 426
Angelo, 174
Arquette, Mary, 518

Baker, Leslie, 542
Bang, Molly, 3
Battle, Eric, 177
Begay, Shonto, 432, 495, 545
Bennett, Nneka, 97, 190
Bernhard, Durga, 486
Bond, Higgins, 177
Bootman, Colin, 122
Brooks, Maya Itzna, 383
Brown, Sterling, 8, 154
Bryan, Ashley, 160, 161, 171
Bryant, Michael, 79, 185
Buehner, Mark, 89
Burciaga, Jose Antonio, 415
Burrus, S. S., 491, 548
Byrd, Samuel, 131

Carpenter, Nancy, 69
Carter, Gail Gordon, 7
Casilla, Robert, 356, 369
Cepeda, Joe, 50, 355, 362
Chapman, Jeffrey, 491, 548
Chief Lelooska, 521

Clair, Donna, 315
Coalson, Glo, 472
Cohen, Lisa, 40
Colon, Raul, 346
Cooper, Floyd, 53, 73, 130, 151, 159, 176, 178, 191, 511, 550
Cordova, Amy, 318
Couch, Grey, 543
Coven, Rosemary Feit, 266
Coy, Ron Hilbert, 487
Crews, Nina, 27
Cummings, Pat, 28

Davie, Helen K., 498
de Krefte, Kees, 222
Delacre, Lulu, 375, 376
DeLange, Alex Pardo, 335
Demi, 248, 249, 250
dePaola, Tomie, 517
Desimini, Lisa, 523, 539, 561
Diaz, David, 13
Dicks, Jan Thompson, 386
Dillon, Diane, 147
Dillon, Leo, 147
DiSalvo-Ryan, DyAnne, 32
Doney, Todd L. W., 274, 463
Dugan, Karen, 330
Dwyer, Mindy, 496

Ehlert, Lois, 497

Feelings, Tom, 165
Fiedler, Joseph Daniel, 275
Fitzpatrick, Marie Louise, 444
Flavin, Teresa, 35
Flesher, Vivienne, 220
Florczak, Robert, 541
Fuchs, Bernie, 118

Garcia, Geronimo, 378
Garnett, Ron, 177
Geter, Tyrone, 34
Gilchrist, Jan Spivey, 41, 172, 173, 181
Goble, Paul, 501, 502, 503
Golembe, Carla, 50
Gonzalez, Christina, 304
Gonzalez, Maya Christina, 387, 388
Greenberg, Melanie Hope, 317
Greger, C. Shana, 507
Grifalconi, Ann, 327
Griffith, Gershom, 5, 143
Guback, Georgia, 204
Guervara, Susan, 358
Gutierrez, Rudy, 343, 345

Hale, Christy, 385
Haley, Gail, 508
Hall, Wendell E., 544
Hamanaka, Sheila, 43, 206
Han, Oki S., 257
Harper, Piers, 509
Hays, Michael, 272
Henry, Greg, 103
Heo, Yumi, 207
Hewitson, Jennifer, 258, 299, 506
Hill, Vicki Trego, 379
Hillenbrand, Will, 279, 504
Himler, Ronald, 310
Honeywood, Varnette P., 26
Hu, Ying-Hwa, 198
Huang, Benrei, 241, 252
Huang, Zhong-Yang, 246
Hubbard, Woodleigh Marx, 515
Hutton, Warwick, 247
Hyman, Trina Schart, 78

Ito, Yoriko, 273, 278

Jacob, Murv, 425, 491, 527, 528, 529, 548
Jelinek, Lucy, 380
Jenkins, Leonard, 51
Jenkins, Steve, 407
Johnson, David, 247, 516
Johnson, Dolores, 62, 63, 141
Johnson, Larry, 83, 168, 189
Johnson, Stephen T., 162

Kastner, Jill, 445, 455
Kiuchi, Tatsuro, 263, 281
Kleven, Elisa, 384, 409

LaMarche, Jim, 443
Lasker, Emily, 270
Lattimore, Deborah Nourse, 336
Lavallee, Barbara, 408
Lechon, Daniel, 308, 405
Lee, Dom, 219
Lee, Jeanne M., 251
Lee, Paul, 20
Leer, Rebecca, 377
Lelooska, Chief, 521
Leonard, Richard, 393
Lewis, E. B., 30, 117, 124
Lockard, Jon Onye, 121
Locker, Thomas, 490, 547
Lowry, Judith, 470
Lucas, Cedric, 54

Ma, Wenhai, 260, 262
Mak, Kam, 282
Martinez, Edward, 311
Martorell, Antonio, 382
Massey, Cal, 177
McDermott, Gerald, 519, 520
McElrath-Eslick, Lori, 247
Ming-Yi, Yang, 267
Minter, Daniel, 22
Miyake, Yoshi, 499
Mora, Francisco X., 373, 406, 478
Morales, Roberta C., 334
Moreno, Rene King, 325
Morimoti, Junko, 264
Moser, Barry, 148, 149, 452, 512

Moser, Cara, 452, 512
Myers, Christopher, 187

Narahashi, Keiko, 223
Nelson, Annika, 411
Nieves, Ernesto Ramos, 372

O'Brien, Anne Sibley, 47

Pak, Yu Cha, 347
Parker, Robert Andrew, 458
Parks, Gordon, 188
Paulsen, Ruth Wright, 350
Pedersen, Judy, 488, 546
Pham, Leuyen, 11
Pinkney, Brian, 94, 98, 99, 100
Pinkney, Jerry, 101, 119, 150, 152, 155
Pinkney, Myles C., 175
Plewes, Andrew, 505
Polacco, Patricia, 102
Poydar, Nancy, 77, 105, 340

Rand, Ted, 203
Ransome, James E., 14, 37, 64, 177, 180, 184
Raschka, Chris, 167
Regan, Dana, 183
Remkiewicz, Frank, 212
Rendon, Maria, 556
Reynolds, James, 24
Rich, Anna, 177
Robinson, Aminah Brenda Lynn, 114
Rodanas, Kristina, 514, 524, 525, 526
Rogers, Forest, 256
Root, Barry, 210, 244
Roth, Robert, 284, 352
Roth, Susan L., 268, 510
Rotsaert, William, 374
Rumsford, James, 227, 269

Saint James, Synthia, 158, 166
Sanchez, Enrique, 404
Sanchez, Enrique O., 381
San Souci, Daniel, 531, 532
Schick, Eleanor, 471
Shrader, Christine Nyburg, 492
Silva, Simon, 301, 331

Simmons, Elly, 329
Sims, David J. A., 88
Sine, Duke, 491, 548
Soentpiet, Chris K., 194, 224
Sogabe, Aki, 265
Speidel, Sandra, 551
Spirin, Gennady, 245
Springett, Martin, 277
Stevens, Janet, 156, 533
Stevenson, Harvey, 476
Stock, Catherine, 1
Stroud, Virginia A., 479, 480, 494
Symank, Yvonne, 320

Taylor, C. J., 537
Taylor, Harriet Peck, 538
Toddy, Irving, 428, 530
Trevino, Brandi, 415
Trevino, Robert John Velasquez, 415
Trivas, Irene, 339
Tseng, Jean, 239, 259, 271, 283, 295
Tseng, Mou-Sien, 239, 259, 271, 283, 295

Valientes, Corazones, 351
Van Frankenhuyzen, Gijsbert, 540
Van Nutt, Robert, 284
Van Wright, Cornelius, 128, 198

Walker, Sylvia, 177
Wang, Zong-Zhous, 255
Ward, John, 80, 82, 90, 153
Watling, James, 423
Wilson, Roberta, 146
Wilson, Sharon, 134
Wisniewski, David, 485
Wolff, Ashley, 513

Xuan, Yongsheng, 261

Ybanez, Terry, 316
Yoshi, 280
Young, Ed, 285, 286, 287, 288, 289

Zhang, Song Nan, 254
Zinn, David, 48

Index of Titles
by Grade Level

(Numerals refer to entries. Symbols refer to ethnic groups: Af = African Americans; As = Asian Americans; H = Hispanic Americans; N = Native-American Indians.)

Preschool:
I Smell Honey, 100 Af
Pretty Brown Face, 100 Af
Shake Shake Shake, 100 Af
Watch Me Dance, 100 Af
Preschool to Kindergarten:
Cherish Me, 190 Af
Northwoods Cradle Song, 561 N
Preschool to Grade 2:
Greetings, Sun, 166 Af
Is That Josie?, 223 As
No Mirrors in My Nana's House, 158 Af
One Afternoon, 207 As
Preschool to Grade 3:
Angels, 172 Af
Bebop-A-Do-Walk!, 43, 206 Af, As
Benito's Dream Bottle, 347 H
Big Bushy Mustache, 355 H
The Bossy Gallito/El Gallo de Bodas, 375 H
Brother Rabbit, 258 As
Bus Ride, 82 Af
Busy Bea, 105 Af
By the Dawn's Early Light, 1 Af
Can You Dance, Dalila?, 69 Af
Carousel, 28 Af
Cat and Rat, 285 As
Chave's Memories, 320 H

Cheyenne Again, 428 N
Chickens! Chickens!, 103 Af
The Cloudmakers, 269 As
Coyote and the Laughing Butterflies, 538 N
Creativity, 124 Af
A Day's Work, 310 H
De Colores and Other Latin-American Folk Songs for Children, 384, 409 H
Delicious Hullabaloo/Pachanga deliciosa, 408 H
The Desert Is My Mother, 405 H
Down in the Subway, 317 H
Down the Road, 117 Af
The Eagle's Song, 525 N
The Farmer and the Poor God, 280 As
Father's Day Blues, 122 Af
¡Fiesta!, 325 H
Fireflies for Nathan, 90 Af
Follow the Stars, 526 N
The Foot Warmer and the Crow, 22 Af
From the Bellybutton of the Moon and Other Summer Poems/Del Ombligo de la Luna y otros poemas de verano, 387 H
The Genie in the Jar, 167 Af
The Golden Flower, 381 H
Hairs: Pelitos, 316 H
Harlem, 187 Af

Hold Christmas in Your Heart, 177 Af
How Chipmunk Got Tiny Feet, 513 N
How the Indians Bought the Farm, 478 N
How Thunder and Lightning Came to Be, 510 N
Iktomi and the Buzzard, 502 N
It's Raining Laughter, 175 Af
Jamaica and Brian, 47 Af
Jamaica and the Substitute Teacher, 47 Af
Jamaica's Blue Marker, 47 Af
Jamaica's Find, 47 Af
Jamaica's Tag-Along, 47 Af
John Henry, 152 Af
Juan Bobo, 372 H
The Junior Thunder Lord, 284 As
Kevin and His Dad, 122 Af
The Khan's Daughter, 283 As
Kongi and Potgi, 257 As
Laughing Tomatoes and Other Spring Poems/Jitomates Risuenos y otros poemas de primavera, 388 H
The Legend of the Windigo, 529 N
Lily and the Wooden Bowl, 273 As
Listen to the Desert/Oye al desierto, 406 H
Little Coyote Runs Away, 476 N
Little Lil and the Swing-Singing Sax, 40 Af
Little Plum, 286 As
The Little Red Ant and the Great Big Crumb, 373 H
The Long-Haired Girl, 267 As
The Lost Boy and the Monster, 476 N
Louise's Gift or What Did She Give Me That For?, 122 Af
Luka's Quilt, 204 As
Ma Dear's Aprons, 73 Af
The Magic Tapestry, 250 As
Messey Bessey, 183 Af
Messey Bessey and the Birthday Overnight, 183 Af
Messey Bessey's Closet, 183 Af
Messey Bessey's Garden, 183 Af
Messey Bessey's Holidays, 183 Af
Messey Bessey's School Desk, 183 Af
Mouse Match, 288 As

Mr. Pak Buys a Story, 252 As
My Father's Boat, 203 As
Nappy Hair, 50 Af
Off to School, 5 Af
The Old Cotton Blues, 35 Af
Older Brother, Younger Brother, 260 As
Old Letivia and the Mountain of Sorrows, 345 H
The Old Man and His Door, 362 H
One Fall Day, 3 Af
One Hot Summer Day, 27 Af
Our People, 79 Af
Pablo's Tree, 346 H
Paco and the Witch, 385 H
Papa Tells Chita a Story, 53 Af
The Path of Quiet Elk, 480 N
Pepita Talks Twice/Pepita Habla Dos Veces, 335 H
Pepita Thinks Pink/Pepita Y El Color Rosado, 335 H
Poppa's Itchy Christmas, 80 Af
Poppa's New Pants, 80 Af
The Precious Gift, 515 N
Rabbit and the Moon, 542 N
The Race of Toad and Deer, 383 H
A Ring of Tricksters, 148 Af
Senor Cat's Romance and Other Favorite Stories from Latin America, 376 H
The Shepherd Boy, 445 N
Soccer Cousins, 339 H
So Far from the Sea, 194 As
Sootface, 54 N
The Stonecutter, 250 As
Tiger Woman, 284 As
Tomas and the Library Lady, 346 H
Two Bad Boys, 508 N
Uno, Dos, Tres, 408 H
When Birds Could Talk & Bats Could Sing, 149 Af
Where There's A Will, There's A Way/Donde Hay Ganas, Hay Manas, 380 H
Willie Jerome, 34
The Windigo's Return, 543 N
Your Move, 14 Af
Preschool to Grade 4:

Abuelita'a Heart, 318 H
The Adventures of Sparrowboy, 98 Af
The Adventures of Sugar and Junior, 77, 340 Af, H
An Mei's Strange and Wondrous Journey, 220 As
The Beggar's Magic, 247 As
Buddha, 268 As
The Cricket Warrior, 247 As
Daddy, Daddy, Be There, 159 Af
Da Wei's Treasure, 247 As
Mama Provi and the Pot of Rice, 352 H
May'naise Sandwiches & Sunshine Tea, 7 Af
Old Bag of Bones, 533 N
Pink and Say, 102 Af
Preschool to Grade 5:
Back Home, 101 Af
The Bat Boy and His Violin, 30 Af
The Birchbark House, 443 N
Chato's Kitchen, 358 H
Coyote in Love, 496 N
Fishing Sunday, 210 As
Frida Maria, 336 H
Full Worm Moon, 458 N
Gingerbread Days, 191 Af
Grandmother's Pigeon, 443 N
The Great Buffalo Race, 498 N
Harvey Potter's Balloon Farm, 89 Af
Honey, I Love, 172 Af
Just Rewards or Who Is That Man in the Moon & What's He Doing Up There Anyway?, 270 As
The Legend of Mackinac Island, 540 N
The Legend of Sleeping Bear, 540 N
The Little Seven-Colored Horse, 386 H
Pedro and the Monkey, 272 As
The Sunday Outing, 101 Af
The Sun Is So Quiet, 171 Af
Tailypo, 154 Af
Train, 189 Af
Two Bear Cubs, 532 N
What's in Aunt Mary's Room?, 54 Af
Preschool to Grade 6:
The Fifth and Final Sun, 507 H
In a Circle Long Ago, 539 N

Preschool to Grade 7:
Calling the Doves/El Canto de las Palomas, 329 H
Coyote and the Fire Stick, 504 N
Eagle Boy, 512 N
Home to Medicine Mountain, 470 N
Preschool up:
Angel to Angel, 186 Af
Ashley Bryan's ABC of African American Poetry, 160 Af
Beardream, 455 N
Brer Tiger and the Big Wind, 146 Af
Brown Angels, 186 Af
Carolina Shout!, 118 Af
Carol of the Brown King, 161 Af
Confetti, 404 H
Coyote, 519 N
The Crane Wife, 245 As
The Creation, 180 Af
Cuckoo, 497 N
The Dragon Prince, 282 As
The Dragon's Tale and Other Animal Fables of the Chinese Zodiac, 249 As
Easter Parade, 41 Af
The Echoes of the Elders, 521 N
For the Love of the Game, 173 Af
Gathering the Sun, 301 H
Glorious Angels, 186 Af
Gluskabe and the Four Wishes, 592 N
The Great Ball Game, 492 N
The Great Race, 246 As
Hoops, 162 Af
How Sweet the Sound, 151, 178 Af
How Turtle's Back Was Cracked, 528 N
Jojofu, 278 As
Knoxville, Tennessee, 168 Af
The Legend of the Panda, 254 As
Lift Ev'ry Voice and Sing, 181 Af
Night Visitors, 289 As
On the Road of Stars, 488, 546 N
Owl Eyes, 499 N
People of Corn, 500 N
Rum-a-Tum-Tum, 184 Af
The Song of el Coqui and Other Tales of Puerto Rico, 382 H
Songs for the Seasons, 551 N
Soul Looks Back in Wonder, 165 Af

The Spirit of the Cedar People, 521 N
A Spoon for Every Bite, 377 H
The Story of Blue Elk, 524 N
The Tale of Rabbit and Coyote, 517 N
Ten Suns, 261 As
Tops & Bottoms, 156 Af
*Tortillas and Lullabies/Tortillas y can-
    cioncitas*, 351 H
Touching the Distance, 545, 556 N
The Tree That Rains, 486 N
Tsubu the Little Snail, 281 As
Turtle Island ABC, 452 N
Uncegila's Seventh Spot, 530 N
*Watch Out for Clever Women!/¡Cui-
    dado con las Mujeres Astutas!*
    379 H
The Wave of the Sea-Wolf, 485 N
Kindergarten to Grade 3:
  The Best Older Sister, 198 As
  Big Meeting, 141 Af
  Jalapeno Bagels, 369 H
  JoJo's Flying Side Kick, 99 Af
  The Last Dragon, 224 As
  The Lost Horse, 287 As
  My Navajo Sister, 471 N
  Papa's Stories, 62 Af
  A Place Called Freedom, 115 Af
  *Prietita and the Ghost Woman/Prietita
      y la Llorona*, 304 H
  Wan Hu Is in the Stars, 244 As
Kindergarten to Grade 4:
  Brave as a Mountain Lion, 472 N
  Minty, 119 Af
  This Big Sky, 407 H
  Wagon Train, 143 Af
Kindergarten to Grade 5:
  Carlos, Light the Farolito, 315 H
  City Green, 32 Af
  Granddaddy's Gift, 83 Af
  The Hired Hand, 155 Af
  The Making of Monkey King, 262 As
  The Rainbow Bridge, 541 N
  Tio Armando, 327 H
  Tonio's Cat, 311 H
  The Wagon, 64 Af
Kindergarten to Grade 7:
  The Boy Who Dreamed of an Acorn,
      432 N

Celie and the Harvest Fiddler, 37 Af
Five Heavenly Emperors, 290 As
*How the World Was Saved & Other
    Native American Tales*, 509 N
La Mariposa, 331 H
The Trickster and the Troll, 473 N
Kindergarten up:
  Adopted by Eagles, 501 N
  Belching Hill, 256 As
  Bill Pickett, 94 Af
  Coyote Walks on Two Legs, 511,
      550 N
  Doesn't Fall Off His Horse, 479 N
  The Earth Under Sky Bear's Feet,
      547 N
  Fa Mulan, 271 As
  The Freedom Riddle, 153 Af
  The Girl Who Lived with the Bears,
      505 N
  The Island-below-the-Star, 227 As
  I, Too, Sing America, 163 Af
  *The Legend of the White Buffalo
      Women*, 503 N
  Ling-Li and the Phoenix Fairy, 255 As
  The Loyal Cat, 265 As
  Maples in the Mist, 295 As
  Meet Danitra Brown, 176 Af
  *Navajo Visions and Voices Across the
      Mesa*, 545 N
  Red Bird, 463 N
  Remaking the Earth, 503 N
  Smoky Night, 13 Af
  The Stone Lion, 274 As
  The Story of the Milky Way, 504 N
  The Tortilla Factory, 350 H
  The Treasure Chest, 279 As
  The Two Brothers, 259 As
  The Wise Old Woman, 277 As
Grades 1 to 4:
  The Best Way to Play, 26 Af
  The Crystal Heart, 275 As
  The Magic of Spider Woman, 495 N
  The Meanest Thing to Say, 26 Af
  Money Troubles, 26 Af
  Shipwreck Saturday, 26 Af
  Super-Fine Valentine, 26 Af
  The Treasure Hunt, 26 Af

Grades 1 to 5:
  Tell Me a Cuento/Cuentame Un Story,
    378 H
Grades 1 to 6:
  I Have Heard of a Land, 130 Af
  The Magic Shell, 343 H
Grades 1 to 7:
  The Ch'i-lin Purse, 251 As
Grades 1 to 8:
  Heroes, 219 As
Grades 1 up:
  Bones in the Basket, 537 N
  Her Stories, 147 Af
  *How Rabbit Tricked Otter and Other
    Cherokee Trickster Stories*, 527 N
  Latino Rainbow, 393 H
Grades 2 to 4:
  Solo Girl, 97 Af
Grades 2 to 5:
  The Cat's Meow, 355 H
  Song Lee and the Hamster Hunt,
    212 As
  Song Lee and the "I hate you" Notes,
    212 As
  Song Lee and the Leech Man, 212 As
Grades 2 to 6:
  Manabozho's Gifts, 506 N
Grades 2 to 7:
  The Big Bike Race, 8 Af
  A School for Pompey Walker, 114 Af
  Seminole Diary, 63 Af
  *Sugarcane House and Other Stories
    About Mr. Fat*, 11 Af
Grades 2 up:
  The Magic Weaver of Rugs, 523 N
Grades 3 to 6:
  Dog People, 425 N
  Moriah's Pond, 123 Af
  Smiffy Blue, Ace Crime Detective,
    88 Af
Grades 3 to 7:
  Across the Lines, 106 Af
  A Blessing in Disguise, 127 Af
  Boys at Work, 356 H
  Bright Freedom's Song, 52 Af
  Buddha, 248 As
  Buddha Stories, 248 As
  Celou Sudden Shout, Idaho 1826,
    440 N

Don't Split the Pole, 128 Af
Egg-Drop Blues, 4 Af
Ernestine & Amanda, 6 Af
*Ernestine & Amanda: Members of the
  C.L.U.B.*, 6 Af
*Ernestine & Amanda: Mysteries on
  Monroe Street*, 6 Af
Ernestine & Amanda: Summer Camp,
  6 Af
Forty Acres and Maybe a Mule,
  109 Af
Guests, 437 N
If You Please, President Lincoln,
  110 Af
The Imp That Ate My Homework,
  241 As
Leticia's Secret, 334 H
Marco's Monster, 138 Af
Mississippi Chariot, 111 Af
The New One, 4 Af
Off and Running, 361 H
The Pool Party, 356 H
Project Wheels, 4 Af
Run Away Home, 75 Af
The Secret Super Power of Marco,
  138 Af
Sees Behind Trees, 438 N
*The Twins, the Pirates, and the Battle
  of New Orleans*, 112 Af
Washington City Is Burning, 113 Af
Grades 3 to 8:
  Business As Usual, 48 Af
  The Gumma Wars, 48 Af
  Night of the Chupacabras, 217, 337
    As, H
  On the Long Trail Home, 474 N
  Spirit Horse, 417 N
Grades 3 to 9:
  Crazy Weekend, 359 H
  The Eagle's Shadow, 461 N
  Haunts, 78 Af
  Just Family, 9 Af
  Summer on Wheels, 359 H
  The Window, 439 N
Grades 3 to 10:
  Fitting In, 306 H
Grades 3 up:
  Amistad Rising, 20 Af

Between Earth & Sky, 490 N
Canto familiar, 411 H
The Children of the Morning Light, 518 N
Cuentos de Cuanto Hay, 374 H
Dance of the Sacred Circle, 524 N
Ebony Sea, 121 Af
Four Ancestors, 491, 548 N
Freedom's Gifts, 134 Af
God's Trombones, 180 Af
Good Luck Gold and Other Poems, 299 As
Irene Jennie and the Christmas Masquerade, 121 Af
Jenny Reen and the Jack Muh Lantern, 121 Af
The Long March, 444 N
One Hand Clapping, 164 As
The Rainbow Hand, 299 As
A Strawbeater's Thanksgiving, 121 Af
A Suitcase of Seaweed and Other Poems, 299 As
Tell Me a Tale, 491 N
The Tree Is Older Than You Are, 522 N

Grades 4 to 6:
Crossing the Starlight Bridge, 462 N
School Spirit, 330 H

Grades 4 to 7:
The Arrow Over the Door, 423 N
The Beaded Moccasins, 441 N
The Captive, 45 Af
Children of the Longhouse, 424 N
Danger Zone, 66 Af
Eagle Song, 426 N
The Ghost Fox, 239 As
Hiroshima, 240 As
Humming Whispers, 59 Af
I Thought My Soul Would Rise and Fly, 46 Af
Later, Gator, 242 As
Marisol and Magdalena, 313 H
Mister and Me, 51 Af
The Other Side, 179 Af
Songs of Faith, 60 Af
True North, 70 Af
The Watsons Go to Birmingham—1963, 29 Af

The World of Daughter McGuire, 144 Af
Yang the Second and Her Secret Admirers, 222 As
Yang the Third and Her Impossible Family, 222 As
Yang the Youngest and His Terrible Ear, 222 As

Grades 4 to 8:
Jungle Dogs, 228 As
Running for Our Lives, 131 Af
Shark Bait, 228 As

Grades 4 to 9:
Cousins, 44 Af
M. C. Higgins, the Great, 44 Af
Second Cousins, 44 Af
A Sunburned Prayer, 366 H
The Well, 129 Af
Yolanda's Genius, 36 Af

Grades 4 to 10:
A Different Beat, 12 Af
Fall Secrets, 12 Af
My Home is Over Jordan, 38 Af
A Picture of Freedom, 74 Af
Sound the Jubilee, 38 Af

Grades 4 up:
Asian Tales and Tellers, 276 As
The Girl Who Married the Moon, 493 N
Mysterious Tales of Japan, 268 As
Race with Buffalo, and Other Native American Stories for Young Readers, 544 N
The White Deer and Other Tales Told by the Lenape, 489 N

Grades 5 to 8:
The Lost Horse, 287 As

Grades 5 to 9:
The Case of the Firecrackers, 237 As
The Case of the Goblin Pearls, 237 As
The Case of the Lion Dance, 237 As
Child of the Owl, 243 As
A Dime a Dozen, 174 Af
The Fred Field, 15 Af
The Girl from Playa Blanca, 333 H
Heaven, 58 Af
Jip His Story, 93 Af

Juanita Fights the School Board,
  367 H
Jubilee Journey, 81 Af
Kinship, 68 Af
Maya's Divided World, 367 H
Music from a Place Called Half Moon,
  466 N
Oren Bell, 15 Af
Petty Crimes, 363 H
A Place to Call Home, 67 Af
Second Daughter, 132 Af
Spite Fences, 68 Af
Thief of Hearts, 243 As
White Lilacs, 81 Af
The World in Grandfather's Hands,
  477 N
Grades 5 to 10:
  Alicia's Treasure, 308 H
  Firefly Summer, 305 H
  Hold Fast to Dreams, 95 Af
  Jumping Off to Freedom, 307 H
  The Last Rainmaker, 447 N
  Raven in a Dove House, 96 Af
  Run for Your Life, 71 Af
  Tommy Stands Alone, 368 H
Grades 5 to 12:
  Echoes of the White Giraffe, 199 As
  Gathering of Pearls, 199 As
  An Island Like You, 348 H
  Year of Impossible Goodbyes, 199 As
  The Year of Our Revolution, 349 H
Grades 5 up:
  Arias in Silence, 188 Af
  The Deetkatoo, 487 N
  Hearsay, 266 As
  The Last Tales of Uncle Remus,
    150 Af
  Musicians of the Sun, 520 N
  Rites of Passage, 10 Af
  Roll of Thunder, Hear My Cry, 129 Af
  Skin Deep and Other Teenage Reflec-
    tions, 185 Af
  Skunny Wundy, 498 N
Grades 6 to 10:
  Far North, 456 N
  Jazmin's Notebook, 42 Af
Grades 6 to 12:

From the Notebooks of Melanin Sun,
  139 Af
I Hadn't Meant to Tell You This,
  140 Af
Necessary Roughness, 216 As
The Secret of Two Brothers, 328 H
Under the Blood-Red Sun, 229 As
Grades 6 up:
  Cezanne Pinto, 125 Af
  From Amigos to Friends, 322 H
  Reaching for the Mainland and Se-
    lected New Poems, 410 H
  Runs With Horses, 429 N
  Walks Alone, 430 N
Grades 7 to 10:
  Billy, 353 H
  Forged by Fire, 33 Af
  Something Terrible Happened, 104 Af
  Tears of a Tiger, 33 Af
Grades 7 to 11:
  The Cook's Family, 238 As
  Ribbons, 238 As
  Sweet Fifteen, 309 H
  Talent Night, 225 As
Grades 7 to 12:
  Cabin 102, 446 N
  Candle in the Wind, 232 As
  Saying Goodbye, 218 As
Grades 7 up:
  After and Before the Lightning, 554 N
  Ain't Gonna Be the Same Fool Twice,
    120 Af
  April and the Dragon Lady, 221 As
  Aunt Carmen's Book of Practical
    Saints, 403 H
  Babylon Boyz, 85 Af
  Barrio Streets Carnival Dreams, 389 H
  Black Feeling, Black Talk, Black
    Judgement, 168, 169 Af
  Black Hair, 413 H
  Bloody Secrets, 323 H
  Bloody Shame, 323 H
  Bloody Waters, 323 H
  Blue Horses Rush In, 481, 558 N
  Blues, 169 Af
  Blu's Hanging, 235 AS
  Buried Onions, 357 H
  Cast Two Shadows, 107 Af

Chinese Folktales, 253 As
Circle Within a Circle, 457 N
City of Coughing and Dead Radiators, 395 H
Coffee Will Make You Black, 120 Af
Cool Salsa, 390 H
El Coro, 394 H
cotton candy on a rainy day, 169 Af
The Crying for a Vision, 483 N
Dark Passage, 484 N
Dark Shade, 435 N
Daughters of the Fifth Sun, 342, 400 H
Dawn Land, 427 N
Dogwolf, 431 N
The Elements of San Joaquin, 413 H
Faces in the Moon, 421 N
Fallout, 297 As
Finding My Voice, 218 As
Flutie, 448 N
The Glory Field, 86 Af
Gone from Home, 57 Af
Guardian of the Hills, 475 N
Hang a Thousand Trees with Ribbons, 108 Af
Hardscrub, 321 H
Hawk Moon, 459 N
Heads by Harry, 235 As
The House on Mango Street, 316 H
Imagine the Angels of Bread, 395 H
Indio, 446 N
Jesse, 360 H
Junior College, 412 H
Like Sisters on the Homefront, 137 Af
Long River, 427 N
Love Poems, 169 Af
My House, 169 Af
New and Selected Poems, 413 H
No Place, 326 H
The Only Piece of Furniture in the House, 448 N
On Second Thought, 552 N
Paper Dance, 392 H
Parrot in the Oven, 338 H
Philadelphia Flowers, 570 N
The Poison Place, 72 Af
Prophecy Rock, 460 N
Pushing the Bear, 450 N
Rattlebone, 21 Af

Re: Creation, 167, 169 Af
Rendezvous, 484 N
Returning a Borrowed Tongue, 291 As
The Richer, the Poorer, 135 Af
The Selected Poems of Nikki Giovanni, 169 Af
Shimmy Shimmy Shimmy Like My Sister Kate, 170 Af
A Shroud in the Family, 321 H
Slam!, 87 Af
Star Quilt, 560 N
Super-Eight Movies, 413 H
A Tale of Sunlight, 413 H
Those Who Ride the Night Winds, 169 Af
To a Widow with Children, 321 H
Touching the Fire, 397 H
A Treasury of African-American Christmas Stories, 24 Af
The Waters Between, 427 N
Wearing the Morning Star, 536, 557 N
The Weather That Kills, 132 Af
Where Sparrows Work Hard, 413 H
The Woman Who Fell from the Sky, 549 N
The Women and the Men, 169 Af
Women Don't Need to Write, 371 H
You Come Singing, 414 H
Grades 9 up:
African-American Literature, 142, 157, 192 Af
African American Literature, 145, 193, Af
Agua Santa, 402 H
American Visa, 231 As
America's Dream, 354 H
Another Way to Dance, 293 As
Asian American Literature, 234, 300 As
Bad Alchemy, 399 H
Blacker Than a Thousand Midnights, 126 Af
The Blessing Way, 454 N
Blood Child and Other Stories, 16 Af
Bone Dance, 555 N
Bone Game, 467 N
Border-Crosser with a Lamborghini Dream, 329 H

Breath, Eyes, Memory, 319 H
Brotherhood of Dolphins, 370 H
Bug Park, 208 As
Cloud Chamber, 436 N
Coyote Blue, 465 N
Coyote Wind, 422 N
Currents from the Dancing River, 324, 396 H
The Darker Face of Earth, 164 Af
Devil's Gonna Get Him, 133 Af
Dragonfly, 294 As
Easier to Kill, 133 Af
The Edge of Heaven, 39 Af
The Fallen Man, 454 N
The First Eagle, 454 N
¡Floricanto Si!, 401 H
The Flower in the Skull, 302 H
The Folding Cliffs, 296 As
Foreign Devil, 231 As
The Foreign Student, 200 As
The Gettin Place, 126 Af
Going Under, 364 H
Havana Thursdays, 365 H
Hispanic American Literature, 332, 398 H
House Made of Dawn, 464 N
How Stella Got Her Groove Back, 76 Af
The Hundred Secret Senses, 230 As
Hunger, 195 As
Indigo, 56 Af
In the Bear's House, 464 N
I Used to Be a Superwoman, 415 H
The Light People, 453 N
Live at Five, 49 Af
The Mad Painter Poems, 553 N
The Manitous, 516 N
The Man Made of Words, 464 N
The Marks of Birth, 341 H
A Matter of Pride and Other Stories, 344 H
Memories of My Ghost Brother, 202 As
Monkey King, 196 As
Monkey Secret, 449 N
Mother Love, 164 Af
Native American Literature, 482, 559 N

The Necessary Hunger, 226 As
Nightland, 468 N
Night Song, 56 Af
No Hiding Place, 133 Af
Notches, 422 N
Of Flesh & Spirit, 298 As
Ojibway Heritage, 516 N
On the Bus with Rosa Parks, 164 Af
Parable of the Sower, 17 Af
Parable of the Talents, 17 Af
The Peace Chief, 433 N
The Phoenix Gone, The Terrace Empty, 292 As
The Poet's World, 164 Af
Releasing Serpents, 416 H
Restless Serpents, 416 H
Saturday Night at the Pahala Theatre, 235 As
Seeing Calvin Coolidge in a Dream, 201 As
The Sharpest Sight, 467 N
The Simple Truth, 2 Af
The Skinwalkers, 454 N
Snow Falling on Cedars, 205 As
Somebody Else's Mama, 49 Af
Some Love, Some Pain, Sometime, 25 Af
Songs My Mother Taught Me, 236 As
Specimen Song, 422 N
Spirits of the Ordinary, 303 H
Through the Storm, 56 Af
Thunder Horse, 422 N
Topaz, 56 Af
Tryin' to Sleep in the Bed You Made, 31 Af
Vivid, 56 Af
The Warrior Woman, 271 As
War Woman, 434 N
When Death Comes Stealing, 133 Af
Wild Meat and the Bully Burgers, 235 As
Wolf, No Wolf, 422 N
Yellow Raft in Blue Water, 436 N
Grades 10 up:
The Antelope Wife, 442 N
The Beet Queen, 442 N
The Bingo Palace, 442 N
Black Betty, 84 Af

Brothers and Sisters, 18 Af
China Boy, 213 As
Comfort Woman, 211 As
Coming to Light, 534 N
Dalva, 451 N
Devil in a Blue Dress, 84 Af
Dreamer, 61 Af
Face of an Angel, 314 H
Gone Fishing, 84 Af
The Grass Dancer, 469 N
Gunga Din Highway, 197 As
The Healing, 65 Af
Honor and Duty, 213 As
Indian Killer, 418 N
Into the Fire, 233 As
Loose Woman, 391 H
Losing Absalom, 92 Af
Love Medicine, 442 N
Loverboys, 312 H

Mona in the Promised Land, 209 As
No Physical Evidence, 214 As
Push, 116 Af
A Red Death, 84 Af
Reservation Blues, 419 N
The Road Home, 451 N
Singing in the Comeback Choir,
  19 Af
Song of the Turtle, 420 N
Taft, 91 Af
Tales of Burning Love, 442 N
Tiger's Tail, 215 As
Trails, 442 N
Voice of the Turtle, 420 N
The Wedding, 136 Af
What a Woman's Gotta Do, 23 Af
White Butterfly, 84 Af
Grades 11 up:
  The River Where Blood Is Born, 55 Af

Index of Subjects

(Numerals refer to entries. Where the ethnic group is not indicated in the subject heading, the following symbols are used: Af = African American; As = Asian American; H = Hispanic American; and N = Native-American Indian.)

Abenaki Indians
  The Arrow Over the Door, 423
  Dog People, 425
  The Waters Between, 427
abolitionists
  Amistad Rising, 20 Af
  Bright Freedom's Song, 52 Af
  A Picture of Freedom, 74 Af
  Second Daughter, 132 Af
  True North, 70 Af
abortions
  Comfort Woman, 211 As
  Like Sisters on the Homefront, 137 Af
Absaroka Indians
  Dark Passage, 484
abuse
  American Visa, 231 As
  America's Dream, 354 H
  The Captive, 45 Af
  The Edge of Heaven, 39 Af
  Faces in the Moon, 421 N
  Forged by Fire, 33 Af
  I Hadn't Meant to Tell You This, 140 Af
  A Matter of Pride and Other Stories, 344 H
  A Place to Call Home, 67 Af
  Push, 116 Af

Run for Your Life, 71 Af
  The Secret of Two Brothers, 328 H
  True North, 70 Af
accidents, causing injuries
  Eagle Song, 426 N
  Forged by Fire, 33 Af
  The Lost Horse, 287 As
Acoma Pueblo Indians
  After and Before the Lightning, 564
  Race with Buffalo, and Other Native American Stories for Young Readers, 554
acorns
  The Boy Who Dreamed of an Acorn, 432 N
actors and actresses
  The Case of the Lion Dance, 237 As
  Fall Secrets, 12 Af
Adams, John Quincy
  Amistad Rising, 20 Af
adoptions
  An Mei's Strange and Wondrous Journey, 220 As
  Billy, 353 H
  Bloody Waters, 323 H
  Heaven, 58 Af
  The Road Home, 451 N
  Something Terrible Happened, 104 Af

adultery
  The Flower in the Skull, 302 H
  Rattlebone, 21 Af
  Seeing Calvin Coolidge in a Dream,
    201 As
adventure fiction
  Dark Passage, 484 N
  Far North, 456 N
  *The Twins, the Pirates, and the Battle
    of New Orleans*, 112 Af
Africa
  Amistad Rising, 20 Af
  The Glory Field, 86 Af
  The Healing, 65 Af
  The River Where Blood Is Born, 55 Af
African Americans
  For books about African Americans,
    see entries 1 through 193.
AIDS
  An Island Like You, 348 H
  Push, 116 Af
  Something Terrible Happened, 104 Af
  The Weather That Kills, 182 Af
Alabama
  Ma Dear's Aprons, 73 Af
  The Other Side, 179 Af
  Run Away Home, 75 Af
  *The Watsons Go to Birmingham—
    1963*, 29 Af
Alaska
  The Eagle's Shadow, 461 N
Alcee Lingo
  *When Birds Could Talk & Bats Could
    Sing*, 149 Af
alcoholism
  America's Dream, 354 H
  The Eagle's Shadow, 461 N
  Flutie, 448 N
  Havana Thursdays, 365 H
  I Used to be a Superwoman, 415 H
  Jazmin's Notebook, 42 Af
  A Place to Call Home, 67 Af
  The Secret of Two Brothers, 328 H
  War Woman, 434 N
  The Window, 439 N
Algonquian Indians
  Full Worm Moon, 458

alphabet, origin of
  Five Heavenly Emperors, 290 As
alphabet books
  *Ashley Brian's ABC of African Ameri-
    can Poetry*, 160 Af
  Gathering the Sun, 301 H
  The Path of Quiet Elk, 480 N
  Turtle Island ABC, 452 N
American Missionary Society
  Sound the Jubilee, 38 Af
American Revolution
  Cast Two Shadows, 107 Af
  Hang a Thousand Trees with Ribbons,
    108 Af
  Second Daughter, 132 Af
Ananse (Anansi)
  A Ring of Tricksters, 148 Af
  The River Where Blood Is Born, 55 Af
Andersonville
  Pink and Say, 102 Af
angels
  Angels, 172 Af
  The Stonecutter, 250 As
animal-human marriages
  The Girl Who Lived with the Bears,
    505 N
animals, carousel
  Carousel, 28 Af
animals, talking, African Americans
  Brer Tiger and the Big Wind, 146
  Don't Split the Pole, 128
  The Foot Warmer and the Crow, 22
  Her Stories, 147
  The Last Tales of Uncle Remus, 150
  A Ring of Tricksters, 148
  Tops & Bottoms, 156
  *When Birds Could Talk & Bats Could
    Sing*, 149
animals talking, Asian Americans
  Cat and Rat, 285
  Chinese Folktales, 253
  *The Dragon's Tale and Other Animal
    Fables of the Chinese Zodiac*, 249
  The Great Race, 246
  Mouse Match, 288
  Pedro and the Monkey, 272
  Tsubu the Little Snail, 281

animals talking, Hispanic Americans
  The Bossy Gallito/El Gallo de Bodas, 375
  Chato's Kitchen, 358
  Cuentos de Cuanto Hay, 374
  The Little Red Ant and the Great Big Crumb, 373
  The Little Seven-Colored Horse, 386
  Old Letivia and the Mountain of Sorrows, 345
  Paco and the Witch, 385
  The Race of Toad and Deer, 383
  Senor Cat's Romance and Other Favorite Stories from Latin America, 376
  The Song of el Coqui and Other Tales of Puerto Rico, 382
  A Sunburned Prayer, 366
  Tell Me A Cuento/Cuentame Un Story, 378
animals talking, Native-American Indians
  Beardream, 455
  Bones in the Basket, 537
  The Children of the Morning Light, 528
  Coming to Light, 544
  Coyote and the Fire Stick, 514
  Coyote and the Laughing Butterflies, 548
  Coyote Blue, 465
  Coyote in Love, 506
  Coyote Walks on Two Legs, 521, 560
  Cuckoo, 507
  Eagle Boy, 522
  The Eagle's Song, 525
  The Echoes of the Elders, 531
  Follow the Stars, 526
  Four Ancestors, 491
  The Girl Who Lived with the Bears, 515
  The Great Buffalo Race, 508
  How Chipmunk Got Tiny Feet, 523
  How Rabbit Tricked Otter and Other Cherokee Trickster Stories, 527
  How the Indians Bought the Farm, 478
  How Turtle's Back Was Cracked, 528
  In a Circle Long Ago, 549

  The Legend of Sleeping Bear, 550
  Little Coyote Runs Away, 476
  The Lost Boy and the Monster, 476
  Manabozho's Gifts, 516
  The Manitous, 526
  Old Bag of Bones, 543
  On the Road of Stars, 556
  Owl Eyes, 509
  Rabbit and the Moon, 542
  Race with Buffalo, and Other Native American Stories for Young Readers, 544
  The Story of Blue Elk, 524
  The Tale of Rabbit and Coyote, 527
  The Tree Is Older Than You Are, 532
  Two Bear Cubs, 542
  Turtle Island ABC, 452
Anishinabe Indians
  The Earth Under Sky Bear's Feet, 557
  The Windigo's Return, 553
ants
  The Little Red Ant and the Great Big Crumb, 373 H
  Night Visitors, 289 As
Apache Indians
  The Flower in the Skull, 302
  Indio, 446
  Run Away Home, 75 Af
  Runs with Horses, 429
  Walks Alone, 430
apples
  Down the Road, 117 Af
aprons
  Ma Dear's Aprons, 73 Af
Arabs
  The Cloudmakers, 269 As
Arawak Indians
  Cabin 102, 446
Archer of Heaven
  Ten Suns, 261 As
Arizona
  The First Eagle, 454 N
  The Flower in the Skull, 302 H
  Prophecy Rock, 460 N
  Walks Alone, 430 N
Arkansas
  Guardian of the Hills, 475 N

arsenic
  The Poison Place, 72 Af
arson
  Brotherhood of Dolphins, 370 H
artifacts, Indian
  The Girl from Playa Blanca, 333 H
  Guardian of the Hills, 475 N
  The Light People, 453 N
artists
  Bebop-A-Do-Walk!, 206 As
  The Last Dragon, 224 As
  Monkey King, 196 As
  The Poison Place, 72 Af
art works
  Arias in Silence, 188 Af
  The Eagle's Song, 535 N
  Little Lil and the Swing-Singing Sax,
    40 Af
  Soul Looks Back in Wonder, 165 Af
Ashantis
  The Captive, 45 Af
Aspen, Colorado
  Hawk Moon, 459 N
Athens, Ohio
  I Hadn't Meant to Tell You This,
    140 Af
Atlanta, Georgia
  What a Woman's Gotta Do, 23 Af
attorneys
  No Physical Evidence, 214 As
  The Simple Truth, 2 Af
  Tiger's Tail, 215 As
aunts and nieces
  The Case of the Lion Dance, 237 As
  Faces in the Moon, 421 N
  Guardian of the Hills, 475 N
  Raven in a Dove House, 96 Af
  The Sunday Outing, 101 Af
  What's in Aunt Mary's Room?, 54 Af
aunts, great, and nephews
  The Last Dragon, 224 As
Australian aboriginal
  Babylon Boyz, 85 Af
avalanches
  Wolf, No Wolf, 422 N
Aztec Indians
  The Fifth and Final Sun, 517
  Musicians of the Sun, 530

baby selling
  Bloody Waters, 323 H
ballads, source of story
  John Henry, 152 Af
ballfield
  The Fred Field, 15 Af
balloons
  Harvey Potter's Balloon Farm, 89 Af
bandits
  Hearsay, 266 As
banks
  Brothers and Sisters, 18 Af
bars
  Taft, 91 Af
baseball
  The Bat Boy and His Violin, 30 Af
  Boys at Work, 356 H
  Parrot in the Oven, 338 H
  Under the Blood-Red Sun, 229 As
basketball
  Danger Zone, 66 Af
  Forged by Fire, 33 Af
  For the Love of the Game, 173 Af
  Hoops, 162 Af
  The Necessary Hunger, 226 As
  Slam!, 87 Af
beaches
  Alicia's Treasure, 308 H
Beadway chant
  Eagle Boy, 522 N
Bear Dance
  Beardream, 455 N
bears
  The Girl Who Lived with the Bears,
    515 N
  The Legend of the Panda, 254 As
  The Legend of the Sleeping Bear, 550 N
  Tops & Bottoms, 156 Af
  Two Bear Cubs, 542 N
"Beauty and the Beast," Chinese version
  The Dragon Prince, 282 As
beauty, hidden
  Lily and the Wooden Bowl, 273 As
beavers
  The Precious Gift, 525 N
bedtime stories
  Northwoods Cradle Song, 571 N
  One Fall Day, 3 Af

beggars
  The Beggar's Magic, 247 As
  Tiger Woman, 284 As
bets
  Tops & Bottoms, 156 Af
Bible
  The Creation, 180 Af
bicycles
  The Adventures of Sparrowboy, 98 Af
  The Big Bike Race, 8 Af
bilingual books, Chinese/English
  Maples in the Mist, 295 As
bilingual books, Spanish/English
  The Bossy Gallito/ El Gallo de Bodas,
    375 H
  *Calling the Doves/El Canto de las Pal-
    omas*, 329 H
  Chave's Memories, 320 H
  Cool Salsa, 390 H
  Cuckoo, 507 N
  Cuentos de Cuanto Hay, 374 H
  *De Colores and Other Latin-American
    Folk Songs for Children*, 384 H
  *The Desert Is My Mother: El Desierto
    Es Mi Madre*, 405 H
  El Coro, 394 H
  ¡Fiesta!, 325 H
  *From the Bellybutton of the Moon and
    Other Summer Poems/Del Ombligo
    de la Luna y otros poemas de ver-
    ano*, 387 H
  Gathering the Sun, 301 H
  Hairs: Pelitos, 316 H
  I Used to Be a Superwoman, 415 H
  Juan Bobo, 372 H
  *Laughing Tomatoes and Other
    Spring Poems/Jitomates Risuenos y
    otros poemas de primavera*,
    388 H
  Listen to the Desert/Oye al desierto,
    406 H
  *Pepita Talks Twice/Pepita Habla Dos
    Veces*, 335 H
  *Prietita and the Ghost/Prietita y la
    Llorona*, 304 H
  Releasing Serpents, 416 H
  Tell Me a Cuento/Cuentame Un Story,
    378 H
  *Tortillas and Lullabies/Tortillas y can-
    cioncitas*, 351 H
  The Tree Is Older Than You Are,
    532 N
  Uno, Dos, Tres: One, Two, Three,
    408 H
  *Watch Out for Clever Woman!/¡Cui-
    dado con las Mujeres Astutas!*,
    379 H
  *Where There's a Will, There's a Way/
    Donde Hay Ganas, Hay Manas*,
    380 H
Bill Pickett
  Bill Pickett, 94 Af
bingo emporiums
  The Bingo Palace, 442 N
biographical fiction
  The Beaded Moccasins, 441 N
  Bill Pickett, 94 Af
  China Boy, 213 As
  Doesn't Fall Off His Horse, 479 N
  Echoes of the White Giraffe, 199 As
  Gathering of Pearls, 199 As
  Hang a Thousand Trees with Ribbons,
    108 Af
  Honor and Duty, 213 As
  Memories of My Ghost Brother,
    202 As
  Minty, 119 Af
  No Physical Evidence, 214 As
  On the Long Trail Home, 474 N
  The Poison Place, 72 Af
  Year of Impossible Goodbyes, 199 As
birds
  The Adventures of Sparrowboy, 98 Af
  Follow the Stars, 536 N
  *How Thunder and Lightning Came to
    Be*, 520 N
  The Island-below-the-Star, 227 As
  See also specific birds.
Birmingham, Alabama
  *The Watsons Go to Birmingham—
    1963*, 29 Af
birthdays
  The Beaded Moccasins, 414 N
  Carousel, 28 Af
  Later, Gator, 242 As

Sweet Fifteen, 309 H
Uno, Dos, Tres, 408 H
birthmarks
    The Marks of Birth, 341 H
Blackfoot Indians
    Dance of the Sacred Circle, 534
    Dark Passage, 484
    Spirit Horse, 417
Blessing Ceremonies
    The Magic of Spider Woman, 505 N
blindness
    Uncegila's Seventh Spot, 540 N
Blue Ridge Mountains
    Bright Freedom's Song, 52 Af
blues festival, Chicago
    Yolanda's Genius, 36 Af
blunders, military
    Across the Lines, 106 Af
board books
    I Smell Honey, 100 Af
boarding schools for Indians
    Cheyenne Again, 428
    Home to Medicine Mountain, 470
    The Last Rainmaker, 447
boars
    *The Dragon's Tale and Other Animal
      Fables of the Chinese Zodiac*,
      249 As
boats
    Bloody Waters, 323 H
    Fishing Sunday, 210 As
    My Father's Boat, 203 As
bodies, assembling piece by piece
    Haunts, 78 Af
bombings
    Hiroshima, 240 As
    Under the Blood-Red Sun, 239 As
    *The Watsons Go to Birmingham—
      1963*, 29 Af
Boriquen
    The Golden Flower, 381 H
Boston, Massachusetts
    Hang a Thousand Trees with Ribbons,
      108 Af
    True North, 70 Af
    The Weather That Kills, 182 Af
bowls, worn on head
    Lily and the Wooden Bowl, 273 As

boxing
    Parrot in the Oven, 338 H
boycotts, bus
    Bus Ride, 82 Af
brides
    The Ch'i-lin Purse, 251 As
Brooklyn, New York
    Eagle Song, 426 N
    From the Notebooks of Melanin Sun,
      139 Af
    The Weather That Kills, 182 Af
brothers, African Americans
    Egg-Drop Blues, 4
    *The Watsons Go to Birmingham—
      1963*, 29
    The Well, 129
    Your Move, 14
brothers, Asian Americans
    Jungle Dogs, 228
    The Stone Lion, 274
    The Two Brothers, 259
brothers, Hispanic Americans
    Jesse, 360
    No Place, 326
    Parrot in the Oven, 338
    The Secret of Two Brothers, 328
    A Sunburned Prayer, 366
brothers, Native-American Indians
    Home to Medicine Mountain, 470
brothers and sisters
    The Best Older Sister, 198 As
    Solo Girl, 97 Af
    Willie Jerome, 34 Af
    Yolanda's Genius, 36 Af
brutality, police
    Black Betty, 84 Af
    Jubilee Journey, 81 Af
Buddha
    Buddha, 268 As
    The Great Race, 246 As
    One Hand Clapping, 264 As
Buddhists
    The Loyal Cat, 265 As
buffalo
    The Great Buffalo Race, 508 N
    *The Legend of the White Buffalo
      Woman*, 513 N
    Old Bag of Bones, 543 N

Buffalo Soldiers
  Gingerbread Days, 191 Af
buffoons, Hispanic Americans
  Cuentos de Cuanto Hay, 374
  Juan Bobo, 372
  Senor Cat's Romance and Other Favorite Stories from Latin America, 376
  Where There's a Will, There's a Way/Donde Hay Ganas, Hay Manas, 380
buffoons, Native-American Indians
  The Children of the Morning Light, 528
  Coyote, 529
  Coyote and the Laughing Butterflies, 538
  Coyote in Love, 506
  Coyote Walks on Two Legs, 521
  How Chipmunk Got Tiny Feet, 523
  In a Circle Long Ago, 539
  Old Bag of Bones, 543
  The Tale of Rabbit and Coyote, 527
  The White Deer and Other Stories Told by the Lenape, 489
Buh Rabby
  A Ring of Tricksters, 148 Af
bulimia
  Breath, Eyes, Memory, 319 H
bulldoggers
  Bill Pickett, 94 Af
butterflies
  Coyote and the Laughing Butterflies, 538 N
  La Mariposa, 331 H
  The Path of Quiet Elk, 480 N
  Tell Me a Cuento/Cuentame Un Story, 378 H
buzzards
  A Ring of Tricksters, 148 Af

Caddo Indians
  On the Long Trail Home, 474
  Race with Buffalo, and Other Native American Stories for Young Readers, 554
California, African Americans
  Brothers and Sisters, 18
  Fall Secrets, 12
  How Stella Got Her Groove Back, 76

Parable of the Talents, 17
Run for Your Life, 71
Singing in the Comeback Choir, 19
Wagon Train, 143
California, Asian Americans
  The Case of the Lion Dance, 237
  The Cook's Family, 238
  Fishing Sunday, 210
  Honor and Duty, 213
  The Imp That Ate My Homework, 241
  Later, Gator, 242
  No Physical Evidence, 214
  So Far from the Sea, 194
  Songs My Mother Taught Me, 236
  Thief of Hearts, 243
California, Hispanic Americans
  Boys at Work, 356
  Brotherhood of Dolphins, 370
  Crazy Weekend, 359
  Frida Maria, 336
  The Girl from Playa Blanca, 333
  Jesse, 360
  Leticia's Secret, 334
  Maya's Divided World, 367
  New and Selected Poems, 413
  No Place, 326
  Off and Running, 361
  Parrot in the Oven, 338
  Tommy Stands Alone, 368
  Tonio's Cat, 311
  The Tortilla Factory, 350
California, Native-American Indians
  Bone Game, 467
  Coyote Blue, 465
  Home to Medicine Mountain, 470
  Two Bear Cubs, 542
call-and-response style
  Nappy Hair, 50 Af
Calvin Coolidge
  Seeing Calvin Coolidge in a Dream, 201 As
Cambodia
  Brother Rabbit, 258 As
  The Two Brothers, 259 As
Cambridge, Massachusetts
  Saying Goodbye, 218 As
Camden, South Carolina
  Cast Two Shadows, 107 Af

cameras
  Spite Fences, 68 Af
Camino Real
  Frida Maria, 336 H
Campbell, Mary
  The Beaded Moccasins, 441 N
cancer
  Leticia's Secret, 334 H
  A Sunburned Prayer, 366 H
cante fable
  When Birds Could Talk & Bats Could Sing, 149 Af
career novels
  A Different Beat, 12 Af
  Fall Secrets, 12 Af
Casas Grande
  Spirits of the Ordinary, 303 H
catastrophe, world
  What a Woman's Gotta Do, 23 Af
caterpillars
  La Mariposa, 331 H
cats
  Cat and Rat, 285 As
  The Cat's Meow, 355 H
  Chato's Kitchen, 358 H
  Da Wei's Treasure, 247 As
  The Loyal Cat, 265 As
  One Fall Day, 3 Af
  Senor Cat's Romance and Other Favorite Stories from Latin America, 376 H
  Smoky Night, 13 Af
  Tell Me a Cuento/Cuentame Un Story, 378 H
  Tonio's Cat, 311 H
  Yang the Third and Her Impossible Family, 222 As
caves
  Abuelita's Heart, 318 H
  My Navajo Sister, 471 N
  Two Bad Boys, 518 N
Central Park
  Bebop-A-Do-Walk!, 43, 206 Af, As
chain gangs
  Mississippi Chariot, 111 Af
  Sugarcane House and Other Stories About Mr. Fat, 11 Af
Charleston, South Carolina
  Carolina Shout!, 118 Af

Charlie Chan
  Gunga Din Highway, 197 As
Cherokee Indians
  Cherokee Woman, 434
  Faces in the Moon, 421
  Flutie, 448
  How Rabbit Tricked Otter and Other Cherokee Trickster Stories, 537
  How Turtle's Back Was Cracked, 538
  Monkey Secret, 449
  Nightland, 468
  On the Long Trail Home, 474
  The Peace Chief, 433
  Pushing the Bear, 450
  Race with Buffalo, and Other Native American Stories for Young Readers, 554
  The Story of the Milky Way, 504
  Two Bad Boys, 518
Cheyenne Indians
  Cheyenne Again, 428
  Race with Buffalo, and Other Native American Stories for Young Readers, 554
Chicago, Illinois
  Coffee Will Make You Black, 120 Af
  Dreamer, 61 Af
  Easter Parade, 41 Af
  The Glory Field, 86 Af
  Yolanda's Genius, 36 Af
child abuse. *See* abuse.
Chimayo, New Mexico
  A Sunburned Prayer, 366 H
China
  American Visa, 231
  An Mei's Strange and Wondrous Journey, 220
  The Beggar's Magic, 247
  Buddha, 268
  Cat and Rat, 285
  The Ch'i-lin Purse, 251
  Chinese Folktales, 253
  The Cloudmakers, 269
  The Cricket Warrior, 247
  Da Wei's Treasure, 247
  The Dragon's Tale and Other Animal Fables of the Chinese Zodiac, 249
  The Foreign Student, 200

The Greatest Treasure, 250
The Great Race, 246
Hearsay, 266
The Hundred Secret Senses, 230
Just Rewards or Who Is That Man in
    the Moon & What's He Doing Up
    There Anyway?, 270
The Legend of the Panda, 254
Ling-Li and the Phoenix Fairy, 255
Little Plum, 286
The Long-Haired Girl, 267
The Lost Horse, 287
The Magic Tapestry, 250
Maples in the Mist, 295
Mouse Match, 288
Night Visitors, 289
Of Flesh & Spirit, 298
One Hand Clapping, 264
Seeing Calvin Coolidge in a Dream,
    201
The Stonecutter, 250
Ten Suns, 261
The Treasure Chest, 279
The Two Brothers, 259
Wan Hu Is in the Stars, 244
"The Chinaman Who Died"
Gunga Din Highway, 197
Chinatown, Honolulu, Hawaii
    The Last Dragon, 224
Chinatown, Sacramento, California
    No Physical Evidence, 214
Chinatown, San Francisco, California
    The Case of the Lion Dance, 237
    The Cook's Family, 238
    The Imp That Ate My Homework,
        241
    Later, Gator, 242
    Thief of Hearts, 243
Chinese Americans
    American Visa, 231
    An Mei's Strange and Wondrous Jour-
        ney; 220
    Another Way to Dance, 293
    April and the Dragon Lady, 221
    The Case of the Lion Dance, 237
    The Cook's Family, 238
    Gunga Din Highway, 197
    Honor and Duty, 213

The Hundred Secret Senses, 230
Hunger, 195
The Last Dragon, 224
Later, Gator, 242
Mona in the Promised Land, 209
Monkey King, 196
No Physical Evidence, 214
The Phoenix Gone, The Terrace
    Empty, 292
Seeing Calvin Coolidge in a Dream,
    201
Tiger's Tail, 215
Chinese-Korean Americans
    Good Luck Gold and Other Poems,
        299
    The Rainbow Hand, 299
    A Suitcase of Seaweed and Other
        Poems, 299
Chinook Indians
    The Boy Who Dreamed of an Acorn,
        432
    Circle Within a Circle, 457
chipmunks
    How Chipmunk Got Tiny Feet, 523
Chippewa (Ojibwa) Indians
    The Bingo Palace, 442
    Dogwolf, 431
    The Earth Under Sky Bear's Feet, 557
    The Legend of Sleeping Bear, 550
    The Light People, 453
    Manabozho's Gifts, 516
    The Manitous, 526
    Sootface, 541
Choctaw Indians
    Bone Game, 467
    How Thunder and Lightning Came to
        Be, 520
    The Long March, 444
    Race with Buffalo, and Other Native
        American Stories for Young Readers,
        554
Christmas
    Blue Horses Rush In, 481 N
    Carlos, Light the Farolito, 315 H
    Carol of the Brown King, 161 Af
    De Colores and Other Latin-American
        Folk Songs for Children, 384 H
    The Freedom Riddle, 153 Af

Hold Christmas in Your Heart, 177 Af
Little Lil and the Swing-Singing Sax,
    40 Af
Poppa's Itchy Christmas, 80 Af
*A Treasury of African-American
    Christmas Stories*, 24 Af
Chumash Indians
    The Rainbow Bridge, 551
church choirs
    Singing in the Comeback Choir, 19 Af
churches
    *Aunt Carmen's Book of Practical
        Saints*, 403 H
    Big Meeting, 141 Af
    *A Treasury of African-American
        Christmas Stories*, 24 Af
Cimarrones
    *The Song of el Coqui and Other Tales
        of Puerto Rico*, 382 H
Cincinnati, Ohio
    Forged by Fire, 33 Af
Cinco de Mayo
    Big Bushy Mustache, 355 H
Cinderella stories
    Kongi and Potgi, 257 As
    Sootface, 541 N
Cinque, Joseph
    Amistad Rising, 20 Af
city life, African Americans
    The Adventures of Sugar and Junior,
        77
    Babylon Boyz, 85
    Carolina Shout!, 118
    City Green, 32
    Danger Zone, 66
    Easier to Kill, 133
    The Fred Field, 15
    The Glory Field, 86
    Harlem, 187
    Jazmin's Notebook, 42
    Just Family, 9
    Little Lil and the Sweet-Singing Sax,
        40
    Live at Five, 49
    One Hot Summer Day, 27
    Push, 116
    The Richer, the Poorer, 135
    Run for Your Life, 71

The Secret Super Power of Marco, 138
Smoky Night, 13
Solo Girl, 97
The Weather That Kills, 182
Willie Jerome, 34
Your Move, 14
city life, Asian Americans
    The Case of the Lion Dance, 237
    The Cook's Family, 238
    The Imp That Ate My Homework, 241
    The Necessary Hunger, 226
    One Afternoon, 207
city life, Hispanic Americans
    The Adventures of Sugar and Junior,
        340
    Buried Onions, 357
    Jesse, 360
    Mama Provi and the Pot of Rice, 352
    No Place, 326
    The World in Grandfather's Hands,
        477
Civil Rights Movement
    The Glory Field, 86 Af
    Granddaddy's Gift, 83 Af
    Spite Fences, 68 Af
    *The Watsons Go to Birmingham—
        1963*, 29 Af
    The Weather That Kills, 182 Af
Civil War, American
    Across the Lines, 106 Af
    Bright Freedom's Day, 52 Af
    Forty Acres and Maybe a Mule, 109 Af
    The Glory Field, 86 Af
    Pink and Say, 102 Af
    Sound the Jubilee, 38 Af
    Through the Storm, 56 Af
    The Wagon, 64 Af
clarinets
    The Old Cotton Blues, 35 Af
cloning
    What a Woman's Gotta Do, 23 Af
Coffin, Levi
    Bright Freedom's Song, 52 Af
colleges, religious
    The Foreign Student, 200 As
colonies, ex-slaves
    If You Please, President Lincoln,
        110 Af

Colorado
  Cuentos de Cuanto Hay, 374 H
  Hawk Moon, 459 N
Colville Indians
  Four Ancestors, 501
comic-book style
  The Adventures of Sparrowboy, 98 Af
communes, African American
  Parable of the Talents, 17 Af
community centers
  Run for Your Life, 71 Af
community life. *See* neighborhood life.
computers
  Hawk Moon, 459 N
  Second Cousins, 44 Af
conch shells
  The Magic Shell, 343 H
constellations. *See* stars.
contests
  Brave as a Mountain Lion, 472 N
  Celie and the Harvest Fiddler, 37 Af
  Egg-Drop Blues, 4 Af
  Ernestine & Amanda, 6 Af
  John Henry, 152 Af
  The Treasure Chest, 279 As
contraband camps
  Through the Storm, 56 Af
convicts
  The Edge of Heaven, 39 Af
  No Physical Evidence, 214 As
  The Secret of Two Brothers, 328 H
  The Simple Truth, 2 Af
cooks
  The Cook's Family, 238 As
Coolidge, Calvin
  Seeing Calvin Coolidge in a Dream,
    201 As
Coquelle Indians
  Coyote in Love, 506
corn
  Coyote Walks on Two Legs, 521 N
  The Little Seven-Colored Horse, 386 H
  The Manitous, 526 N
  People of Corn, 510 N
  The Tortilla Factory, 350 H
corporate intrigue
  Brothers and Sisters, 18 Af
  Bug Park, 208 As

counting books and songs
  *De Colores and Other Latin-American
    Folk Songs for Children*, 384 H
  ¡Fiesta!, 325 H
  Uno, Dos, Tres, 408 H
court scenes
  No Physical Evidence, 214 H
  The Simple Truth, 2 Af
cousins
  Easter Parade, 41 Af
  Freedom's Gifts, 134 Af
  Leticia's Secret, 334 H
  Like Sisters on the Homefront, 137 Af
  Second Cousins, 44 Af
  Soccer Cousins, 339 H
  Something Terrible Happened, 104 Af
Cowboys
  Bill Pickett, 94 Af
  Cezanne Pinto, 125 Af
Cow Island, Haiti
  If You Please, President Lincoln,
    110 Af
Coyatee Indians
  War Woman, 434
Coyote
  Brave as a Mountain Lion, 472 N
  Coming to Light, 534 N
  Coyote, 519 N
  Coyote and the Fire Stick, 504 N
  Coyote and the Laughing Butterflies,
    538 N
  Coyote Blue, 465 N
  Coyote in Love, 496 N
  Coyote Walks on Two Legs, 511,
    550 N
  Eagle Boy, 512 N
  How Chipmunk Got Tiny Feet, 513 N
  In a Circle Long Ago, 539 N
  Little Coyote Runs Away, 476 N
  Old Bag of Bones, 533 N
  The Tale of Rabbit and Coyote,
    517 N
crabs
  Paco and the Witch, 385 H
cranes
  The Crane Wife, 245 As
  Lily and the Wooden Bowl, 273 As
  Rabbit and the Moon, 542 N

Crater Lake
  Coyote in Love, 496 N
crayons (markers)
  Jamaica's Blue Marker, 47 Af
creation stories, Asian American
  Chinese Folktales, 253
  Five Heavenly Emperors, 290
creation stories, Hispanic American
  The Golden Flower, 381
  *The Song of el Coqui and Other Tales
    of Puerto Rico*, 382
creation stories, Native-American Indians
  Bones in the Basket, 537
  The Children of the Morning Light, 518
  Coming to Light, 534
  In a Circle Long Ago, 539
  *The Legend of the White Buffalo
    Woman*, 503
  The Magic of Spider Woman, 495
  The Manitous, 516
  People of Corn, 500
  The Precious Gift, 515
  The Rainbow Bridge, 541
Cree Indians
  Bones in the Basket, 537
  The Legend of the Windigo, 529
  Rabbit and the Moon, 542
Creek Indians
  How Chipmunk Got Tiny Feet, 513
crickets
  The Cricket Warrior, 247 As
  Hearsay, 266 As
crocodiles
  Brother Rabbit, 258 As
Crow Indians
  Celou Sudden Shout, Idaho 1826, 440
  Coyote Blue, 465
  Dark Passage, 484
  *Race with Buffalo, and Other Native
    American Stories for Young Readers*,
    544
crows
  Coyote, 519 N
  Ten Suns, 261 As
Cuba
  Bloody Waters, 323 H
  From Amigos to Friends, 322 H
  Jumping Off to Freedom, 307 H

  The Marks of Birth, 341 H
  Papa Tells Chita a Story, 53 Af
  Women Don't Need to Write, 371 H
Cuban Americans
  Bad Alchemy, 399 H
  Bloody Waters, 323 H
  Fitting In, 306 H
  From Amigos to Friends, 322 H
  Going Under, 364 H
  Havana Thursdays, 365 H
  Jumping Off to Freedom, 307 H
  The Marks of Birth, 341 H
  Women Don't Need to Write, 371 H
  You Come Singing, 414
cuckoos
  Cuckoo, 497 N
Cultural Revolution, China
  American Visa, 231 As
  Seeing Calvin Coolidge in a Dream,
    201
culture erosion, African Americans
  Losing Absalom, 92
culture erosion, Asian Americans
  The Folding Cliffs, 296
  Mona in the Promised Land, 209
  Necessary Roughness, 216
  *The Phoenix Gone, The Terrace
    Empty*, 292
  Returning a Borrowed Tongue, 291
  Songs My Mother Taught Me, 236
culture erosion, Hispanic Americans
  Buried Onions, 357
  Daughters of the Fifth Sun, 342
  El Coro, 394
  From Amigos to Friends, 322
  Going Under, 364
  An Island Like You, 348
  Jesse, 360
  Paper Dance, 392
  Parrot in the Oven, 338
  Petty Crimes, 363
  The Year of Our Revolution, 349
culture erosion, Native-American Indians
  The Bingo Palace, 442
  Bone Dance, 555
  Bone Game, 467
  Crossing the Starlight Bridge, 462
  Dogwolf, 431

The Eagle's Shadow, 461
Faces in the Moon, 421
The Grass Dancer, 469
House Made of Dawn, 464
Indian Killer, 418
Indio, 446
The Last Rainmaker, 447
The Light People, 453
Native American Literature, 559
Navajo Visions and Voices Across the Mesa, 545
Nightland, 468
On Second Thought, 552
Reservation Blues, 419
Runs with Horses, 429
The Trickster and the Troll, 473
Walks Alone, 430
War Woman, 434
The Woman Who Falls from the Sky, 549
The World in Grandfather's Hands, 477
culture shock/culture clash, Asian Americans
April and the Dragon Lady, 221
Hunger, 195
Songs My Mother Taught Me, 236
Yang the Third and Her Impossible Family, 222
culture shock/culture clash, Hispanic Americans
El Coro, 394
Maya's Divided World, 367
You Come Singing, 414
culture shock/culture clash, Native-American Indians
The Beaded Moccasins, 441
Indian Killer, 418
Indio, 446
Monkey Secret, 449
Native American Literature, 559
Runs with Horses, 429
Walks Alone, 430
War Woman, 434
The World in Grandfather's Hands, 477
culture subversion
Cheyenne Again, 428 N

Home to Medicine Mountain, 470 N
The Last Rainmaker, 447 N
Nightland, 468 N
cups, made from crystal heart
The Crystal Heart, 275 As
Curry Island, South Carolina
The Glory Field, 86 Af
Cuyahoga River
The Beaded Moccasins, 441 N

Dallas, Texas
The Secret of Two Brothers, 328 H
dams, destroyed
Circle Within a Circle, 457 N
dancers and dancing
Beardream, 455 N
Can You Dance, Dalila?, 69 Af
Carolina Shout!, 118 Af
The Cook's Family, 238 As
The Genie in the Jar, 167 Af
The Grass Dancer, 469 N
Home to Medicine Mountain, 470 N
Humming Whispers, 59 Af
Little Lil and the Swing-Singing Sax, 40 Af
Red Bird, 463 N
dawn, watching
By the Dawn's Early Light, 1 Af
Full Worm Moon, 458 N
Day of the Dead
Soccer Cousins, 339 H
The Weather That Kills, 182 Af
death marches
The Long March, 444 N
On the Long Trail Home, 474 N
Pushing the Bear, 450 N
Seminole Diary, 63 Af
deaths, African Americans
The Edge of Heaven, 39
Forged by Fire, 33
Like Sisters on the Homefront, 137
True North, 70
deaths, Asian Americans
Blue's Hanging, 235
The Crystal Heart, 275
The Folding Cliffs, 296
The Legend of the Panda, 254
Memories of My Ghost Brother, 202

Necessary Roughness, 216
Night of the Chupacabras, 217
So Far from the Sea, 194
deaths, Hispanic Americans
  Bad Alchemy, 399
  Brotherhood of Dolphins, 370
  Buried Onions, 351
  The Flower in the Skull, 302
  Havana Thursdays, 365
  Leticia's Secret, 334
  Night of the Chupacabras, 337
  Tio Armando. 327
deaths, Native-American Indians
  Bone Game, 467
  Dogwolf, 431
  Faces in the Moon, 421
  Far North, 456
  The First Eagle, 454
  The Grass Dancer, 469
  Guardian of the Hills, 475
  Indian Killer, 418
  Nightland, 468
  Prophecy Rock, 460
  Pushing the Bear, 450
Declaration of Independence
  Second Daughter, 132 Af
  Washington City Is Burning, 113 Af
deer
  The Race of Toad and Deer, 383 H
Delaware (Lenape) Indians
  The Beaded Moccasins, 441
  Dark Shade, 435
  *The White Deer and Other Stories Told
    by the Lenape*, 489
Delaware (state)
  Red Bird, 463 N
Delta region, Mississippi
  Mississippi Chariot, 111 Af
Demeter and Persephone
  Mother Love, 164 Af
demons
  The Imp That Ate My Homework,
    241 As
  The Khan's Daughter, 283 As
deserters, wartime
  Pink and Say, 102 Af
desert life
  Abuelita's Heart, 318 H
  The Desert Is My Mother, 405 H

Listen to the Desert/Oye al desierto,
  406 H
detectives
  Black Betty, 84 Af
  The Blessing Way, 454 N
  Bloody Waters, 323 H
  Brotherhood of Dolphins, 370 H
  Easier to Kill, 133 Af
  The First Eagle, 454 N
  The Simple Truth, 2 Af
  The Skinwalkers, 454 N
  Smiffy Blue, Ace Crime Detective,
    88 Af
  Wolf, No Wolf, 422 N
Detroit, Michigan
  The Fred Field, 15 Af
developers, land
  Circle Within a Circle, 457 N
  The Gettin Place, 126 Af
diabetes
  April and the Dragon Lady, 221 As
diaries
  *I Thought My Soul Would Rise and
    Fly*, 46 Af
  The Parable of the Talents, 17 Af
  A Picture of Freedom, 74 Af
discrimination. *See* prejudice.
disguises, girl as warrior
  Fa Mulan, 271 As
  The Khan's Daughter, 283 As
Dog the dog
  Smiffy Blue, Ace Crime Detective,
    88 Af
dogs
  Chato's Kitchen, 358 H
  Dog People, 425 N
  Dogwolf, 431 N
  Don't Split the Pole, 128 Af
  *The Dragon's Tale and Other Animal
    Fables of the Chinese Zodiac*,
    249 As
  The Great Race, 246 As
  Jojofu, 278 As
  Jungle Dogs, 228 As
  *Pepita Talks Twice/Pepita Habla Dos
    Veces*, 335 H
  The Secret Super Power of Marco,
    138 Af
  The Story of the Milky Way, 504 N

Tailypo, 154 Af
The Tree That Rains, 486 N
dolls
    One Fall Day, 3 Af
dolphins
    Brotherhood of Dolphins, 370 H
    The Rainbow Bridge, 551 N
domestic abuse. *See* abuse.
domestic adventures, African Americans
    The Adventures of Sparrowboy, 98
    The Adventures of Sugar and Junior,
      77
    The Gumma Wars, 48
    I Smell Honey, 100
    Jojo's Flying Side Kick, 99
    Louise's Gift or What Did She Give
      Me That For?, 122
    The Meanest Thing to Say, 26
    Meet Danitra Brown, 176
    One Hot Summer Day, 27
    The Secret Super Power of Marco, 138
domestic adventures, Asian Americans
    Is That Josie?, 223
    Later, Gator, 242
    One Afternoon, 207
    Yang the Third and Her Impossible
      Family, 222
domestic adventures, Hispanic Americans
    The Adventures of Sugar and Junior,
      340
    Alicia's Treasure, 302
    Boys at Work, 356
    Chave's Memories, 320
    Crazy Weekend, 359
    Gathering the Sun, 301
    Jalapeno Bagels, 369
    Pepita Talks Twice, 335
    The Pool Party, 356
    Summer on Wheels, 359
    Tomas and the Library Lady, 346
    Uno, Dos, Tres, 408
domestic adventures, Native-American Indians
    Brave as a Mountain Lion, 472
    Children of the Longhouse, 424
    Dog People, 425
    Eagle Song, 426
    My Navajo Sister, 471
    The Shepherd Boy, 445

Dominican Americans
    The Magic Shell, 343
    A Matter of Pride and Other Stories,
      344
doors
    The Old Man and His Door, 362 H
Dorgon people
    What a Woman's Gotta Do, 23 Af
double Dutch
    Solo Girl, 97 Af
doves
    Calling the Doves/El Canto de las
      Palomas, 329 H
dragonflies
    The Path of Quiet Elk, 480 N
dragons
    Chinese Folk Tales, 253 As
    The Dragon Prince, 282 As
    The Dragon's Tale and Other Animal
      Fables of the Chinese Zodiac,
      249 As
    The Great Race, 246 As
    Hearsay, 266 As
    The Last Dragon, 224 As
dreams
    Benito's Dream Bottle, 347 H
    Bone Game, 467 N
    Carousel, 28 Af
    Night Visitors, 289 As
drinking gourd
    A Place Called Freedom, 115 Af
drought
    Little Plum, 286 As
    The Long-Haired Girl, 267 As
    Wagon Train, 143 Af
    The Well, 129 Af
drug dealers
    Babylon Boyz, 85 Af
    Live at Five, 49 Af
    Losing Absalom, 92 Af
    Slam!, 87 Af
    Taft, 91 Af
drugs, African Americans
    Babylon Boyz, 85
    A Blessing in Disguise, 127
    Forged by Fire, 33
    The Gettin Place, 126
    The Glory Field, 86
    Jazmin's Notebook, 42

The Secret Super Power of Marco,
  138
drugs, Asian Americans
  Blu's Hanging, 235 As
  Tiger's Tail, 215 As
drugs, Hispanic Americans
  Buried Onions, 357
  An Island Like You, 348
  A Matter of Pride and Other Stories, 344
  No Place, 326
drugs, Native-American Indians
  Coyote Blue, 465
  Hawk Moon, 459
  Nightland, 468
dumplings, rice
  Belching Hill, 256 As
Dusky Demon
  Bill Pickett, 94 Af
dwarfs
  The Foot Warmer and the Crow, 22 Af
dyslexia
  Egg-Drop Blues, 4 Af
  The Simple Truth, 2 Af

Eagle Dance
  Iktomi and the Buzzard, 512 N
eagles
  Adopted by the Eagles, 501 N
  Eagle Boy, 512 N
  The Eagle's Song, 525 N
  The First Eagle, 454 N
early contact, Indians and whites
  Guests, 437
  Indio, 446
  Peace Chief, 433
  War Woman, 434
  The Wave of the Sea-Wolf, 485
Earthseed
  Parables of the Talents, 17 Af
Easter
  Easter Parade, 41 Af
East Los Angeles, California
  Brotherhood of Dolphins, 370 H
easy-reading books, African Americans
  The Adventures of Sugar and Junior,
    77
  The Meanest Thing to Say, 26
  Messey Bessey's School Desk, 183

Smiffy Blue, Ace Crime Detective, 88
Solo Girl, 97
easy-reading books, Asian Americans
  The Best Older Sister, 198
  Song Lee and the Hamster Hunt, 212
easy-reading books, Hispanic Americans
  The Adventures of Sugar and Junior,
    340
  The Cat's Meow, 355
  Juan Bobo, 372
  Soccer Cousins, 339
  Tell Me A Cuento/Cuentame Un Story,
    378
Ebos
  Ebony Sea, 121 Af
ecological stories
  City Green, 32 Af
eels, trained
  Hearsay, 266 As
eggs
  Down the Road, 117 Af
  Egg-Drop Blues, 4 Af
  *How Thunder and Lightning Came to
    Be*, 510 N
El Capitan
  Between Earth & Sky, 490 N
Elder White Brother
  Prophecy Rock, 460 N
elections
  No Physical Evidence, 214 As
  Off and Running, 361 H
elk
  The Story of Blue Elk, 514 N
Emancipation Proclamation
  Freedom's Gifts, 134 Af
  *I Thought My Soul Would Rise and
    Fly*, 45 Af
English people, in New World
  War Woman, 434 N
Enola Gay (airplane)
  Hiroshima, 240 As
escape paths, in weaving
  The Magic of Spider Woman, 495 N
escapes, from various threats
  America's Dream, 354 H
  Bloody Waters, 123 H
  Celou Sudden Shout, Idaho 1826,
    440 N

The Farmer and the Poor God, 280 As
The Folding Cliffs, 296 As
Jip His Story, 93 Af
A Matter of Pride and Other Stories,
    344 H
Paco and the Witch, 371 H
Women Don't Need to Write, 371 H
escapes, slave
The Foot Warmer and the Crow, 22 Af
Minty, 119 Af
Running for Our Lives, 131 Af
Seminole Diary, 63 Af
Through the Storm, 56 Af
True North, 70 Af
ethnic cleansing
What a Woman's Gotta Do, 23 Af
euthanasia, attempted
Rattlebone, 21 Af
evacuations, forced
The Long March, 444 N
Seminole Diary, 63 Af
explanatory stories, Asian Americans
Chinese Folktales, 253
*Just Rewards or Who Is That Man in
    the Moon & What's He Doing Up
    There Anyway?*, 270
The Legend of the Panda, 254
Ling-Li and the Phoenix Fairy, 255
Ten Suns, 261
Wan Hu Is in the Stars, 244
explanatory stories, Hispanic Americans
The Golden Flower, 381
*The Song of el Coqui and Other Tales
    of Puerto Rico*, 382
explanatory stories, Native-American In-
    dians
Between Earth and Sky, 490
Bones in the Basket, 537
Children of the Morning Light, 518
Coming to Light, 534
Coyote, 519
Coyote and the Fire Stick, 504
Coyote in Love, 496
Coyote Walks on Two Legs, 511
Cuckoo, 497
Dance of the Sacred Circle, 524
The Deetkatoo, 487
Eagle Boy, 512

The Eagle's Song, 525
The Echoes of the Elders, 521
The Fifth and Final Sun, 507
Follow the Stars, 526
Four Ancestors, 491
The Girl Who Lived with the Bears,
    505
The Great Buffalo Race, 498
How Chipmunk Got Tiny Feet, 513
*How Rabbit Tricked Otter and Other
    Cherokee Trickster Stories*, 527
*How the World Was Saved & Other
    Native American Tales*, 509
*How Thunder and Lightning Came to
    Be*, 510
How Turtle's Back Was Cracked, 528
In a Circle Long Ago, 539
The Legend of Mackinac Island, 540
The Legend of Sleeping Bear, 540
*The Legend of the White Buffalo
    Woman*, 503
The Legend of the Windigo, 529
The Magic of Spider Woman, 495
The Magic Weaver of Rugs, 523
Manabozho's Gifts, 506
The Manitous, 516
Musicians of the Sun, 520
Owl Eyes, 499
The People of Corn, 500
The Precious Gift, 515
Rabbit and the Moon, 542
*Race with Buffalo, and Other Native
    American Stories for Young Readers*,
    544
The Rainbow Bridge, 541
The Story of the Milky Way, 494
The Tale of Rabbit and Coyote, 517
The Tree Is Older Than You Are, 522
The Tree That Rains, 486
Two Bad Boys, 508
*The White Deer and Other Tales Told
    by the Lenape*, 489
The Windigo's Return, 543
extrasensory perception
The Waters Between, 427
eyes
Coyote Walks on Two Legs, 521
How Chipmunk Got Tiny Feet, 523

fables
  Chinese Folktales, 253 As
  *The Dragon's Tale and Other Animal
    Fables of the Chinese Zodiac*,
    249 As
  *The Little Red Ant and the Great Big
    Crumb*, 373 H
factories
  By the Dawn's Early Light, 1 Af
faith healers
  The Healing, 65 Af
Falconman
  The Adventures of Sparrowboy, 98 Af
family history
  Papa Tells Chita a Story, 53 Af
  The Wedding, 136 Af
  What's in Aunt Mary's Room?, 54 Af
family life, African Americans
  Back Home, 101
  Big Meeting, 141
  A Blessing in Disguise, 127
  By the Dawn's Early Light, 1
  A Different Beat, 12
  A Dime a Dozen, 174
  Down the Road, 117
  Easter Parade, 41
  The Edge of Heaven, 39
  Egg-Drop Blues, 4
  Ernestine & Amanda, 6
  Fall Secrets, 12
  Fireflies for Nathan, 90
  Forged by Fire, 33
  Forty Acres and Maybe a Mule, 109
  The Fred Field, 15
  From the Notebooks of Melanin Sun,
    139
  The Gettin Place, 126
  The Glory Field, 86
  Heaven, 58
  Hold Fast to Dreams, 95
  I Hadn't Meant to Tell You This, 140
  I Have Heard of a Land, 130
  I Smell Honey, 100
  Jamaica's Blue Marker, 47
  Just Family, 9
  Knoxville, Tennessee, 168
  Like Sisters on the Homefront, 137

  *Louise's Gift or What Did She Give
    Me That For?*, 122
  *May'naise Sandwiches & Sunshine
    Tea*, 7
  Mister and Me, 51
  Moriah's Pond, 123
  Nappy Hair, 50
  The New One, 4
  Off to School, 5
  Oren Bell, 15
  Papa's Stories, 62
  Poppa's New Pants, 80
  Project Wheels, 4
  Push, 116
  Rattlebone, 21
  Raven in a Dove House, 96
  The Richer, the Poorer, 135
  Run for Your Life, 71
  Running for Our Lives, 131
  Second Cousins, 44
  The Secret Super Power of Marco, 138
  Singing in the Comeback Choir, 19
  Slam!, 87
  Solo Girl, 97
  Sound the Jubilee, 38
  The Sunday Outing, 101
  Wagon Train, 143
  *The Watsons Go to Birmingham—
    1963*, 29
  The Weather That Kills, 182
  The Wedding, 136
  The Well, 129
  What's in Aunt Mary's Closet?, 54
  Willie Jerome, 34
  Yolanda's Genius, 36
family life, Algonquian Indians
  Full Worm Moon, 458
family life, Asian Americans, origin un-
    specified or mixed
  Jungle Dogs, 228
  One Afternoon, 207
  Songs My Mother Taught Me, 236
  See also family life, Asian Americans,
    specific country
family life, Cherokee Indians
  Faces in the Moon, 421
  Flutie, 448
  Pushing the Bear, 450

family life, China and Chinese Americans
  American Visa, 231
  An Mei's Strange and Wondrous Jour-
    ney, 220
  April and the Dragon Lady, 221
  The Cook's Family, 238
  The Hundred Secret Senses, 230
  Hunger, 195
  Later, Gator, 242
  Mona in the Promised Land, 209
  Monkey King, 196
  Thief of Hearts, 243
  Yang the Third and Her Impossible
    Family, 222
family life, Chippewa (Ojibwa) Indians
  Dogwolf, 431
family life, Cuban Americans
  Fitting In, 306
  From Amigos to Friend, 322
  Going Under, 364
  Havana Thursdays, 365
  Jumping Off to Freedom, 307
  The Marks of Birth, 341
  Women Don't Need to Write, 371
family life, Hawaiians
  The Folding Cliffs, 296
family life, Hispanic Americans, origin
    unspecified
  Alicia's Treasure, 308
  Gathering the Sun, 301
  Hairs: Pelitos, 316
  Mama Provi and the Pot of Rice, 352
  Maya's Divided World, 367
  Sweet Fifteen, 309
  Tortillas and Lullabies/Tortillas y can-
    cioncitas, 351
  See also family life, Hispanic Ameri-
    cans, specific country
family life, interracial
  Cloud Chamber, 436
  Flutie, 448
  A Place to Call Home, 67
  Something Terrible Happened, 104
  Thief of Hearts, 243
  The Window, 439
family life, Japan and Japanese Ameri-
    cans
  April and the Dragon Lady, 221

Blu's Hanging, 235
Candle in the Wind, 232
The Farmer and the Poor God, 280
family life, Korean Americans
  The Best Older Sister, 198
  Necessary Roughness, 216
family life, Maidu-Pit River Indians
  Home to Medicine Mountain, 470
family life, Mexican Americans
  Big Bushy Mustache, 355
  Billy, 353
  Buried Onions, 357
  Calling the Doves/El Canto de las
    Palomas, 329
  Chave's Memories, 320
  Face of an Angel, 314
  The Flower in the Skull, 302
  Jalapeno Bagels, 369
  No Place, 326
  Off and Running, 361
  The Old Man and His Door, 362
  Parrot in the Oven, 338
  Petty Crimes, 363
  The Secret of Two Brothers, 328
  Spirits of the Ordinary, 303
  A Sunburned Prayer, 366
  Tio Armando, 327
  To a Widow with Children, 321
  Tommy Stands Alone, 368
  Tonio's Cat, 311
family life, Nanticoke Indians
  Red Bird, 463
family life, Native-American Indians, un-
    specified and of various groups
  Grandmother's Pigeon, 443
  Guests, 437
  The World in Grandfather's Hands, 477
  See also family life, Native-American
    Indians, specific groups,
family life, Navajo Indians
  Blue Horses Rush In, 481, 558
  Brave as a Mountain Lion, 472
family life, Otomoaco Indians
  Indio, 446
family life, Panamanian Americans
  Marisol and Magdalena, 313
family life, Penobscot Indians
  Crossing the Starlight Bridge, 462

family life, Puerto Rico and Puerto Rican Americans
Firefly Summer, 305
The Magic Shell, 343
A Matter of Pride and Other Stories, 344
family life, Spanish-Cuban Americans
Women Don't Need to Write, 371
family life, Tlingit Indians
The Eagle's Shadow, 461
famine relief
The Long March, 444
Fa Mulan
Fa Mulan, 271
fantasies, African Americans
The Adventures of Sparrowboy, 98
Blood Child and Other Stories, 16
Celie and the Harvest Fiddler, 37
Don't Split the Pole, 128
Harvey Potter's Balloon Farm, 89
Haunts, 78
Parable of the Sower, 17
Parable of the Talents, 17
The River Where Blood Is Born, 55
fantasies, Asian Americans
Bug Park, 208
The Imp That Ate My Homework, 241
fantasies, Hispanic Americans
Benito's Dream Bottle, 347
Chato's Kitchen, 358
Down in the Subway, 317
Old Letivia and the Mountain of Sorrows, 345
Prietita and the Ghost Woman/Prietita y la Llorna, 304
fantasies, Native-American Indians
Beardream, 455
Cabin 102, 446
Coyote Blue, 465
The Crying for a Vision, 483
Dark Shade, 435
Grandmother's Pigeon, 443
Guardian of the Hills, 475
How the Indians Bought the Farm, 478
Little Coyote Runs Away, 476
The Lost Boy and the Monster, 476

The Trickster and the Troll, 473
Turtle Island ABC, 452
The Waters Between, 427
The Wave of the Sea-Wolf, 485
farm life
Calling the Doves/El Canto de las Palomas, 329 H
Forty Acres and Maybe a Mule, 109 Af
Gathering the Sun, 301 H
Off to School, 5 Af
Run Away Home, 25 Af
Song My Mother Taught Me, 236 As
The Tortilla Factory, 350 H
The Wagon, 64 Af
The Well, 129 Af
farms and farmers
Chickens! Chickens!, 103 Af
The Farmer and the Poor God, 280 As
Forty Acres and Maybe a Mule, 109 Af
Harvey Potter's Balloon Farm, 89 Af
How the Indians Bought the Farm, 478 N
Moriah's Pond, 123 Af
Off to School, 5 Af
Pedro and the Monkey, 272 As
Run Away Home, 75 Af
Running for Our Lives, 131 Af
Snow Falling on Cedars, 205 As
The Tale of Rabbit and Coyote, 517 N
The Tree That Rains, 486 N
Tsubu the Little Snail, 281 As
The Well, 129 Af
farolitos
Carlos, Light the Farolito, 315 H
fathers and children
Daddy, Daddy, Be There, 159 Af
fathers and daughters, African Americans
Bebop-A-Do-Walk!, 42
A Blessing in Disguise, 127
A Dime a Dozen, 174
Down the Road, 117
Losing Absalom, 92
Off to School, 5
Our People, 79
Papa's Stories, 62

Papa Tells Chita a Story, 53
Tryin' to Sleep in the Bed You Made, 31
The Weather That Kills, 182
fathers and daughters, Asian Americans
    Bebop-A-Do-Walk!, 206
    Hunger, 195
    Monkey King, 196
fathers and daughters, Hispanic Americans
    Marisol and Magdalena, 313
    Women Don't Need to Write, 371
fathers and daughters, Native-American Indians
    Bone Game, 467
    The Window, 439
fathers and sons, African Americans
    The Bat Boy and His Violin, 30
    Mississippi Chariot, 111
    A Place Called Freedom, 115
    Taft, 91
    The Twins, the Pirates, and the Battle of New Orleans, 112
fathers and sons, Asian Americans
    Heroes, 219
    Honor and Duty, 213
    Memories of My Ghost Brother, 202
    My Father's Boat, 203
    Necessary Roughness, 216
    Ten Suns, 261
fathers and sons, Hispanic Americans
    Big Bushy Mustache, 355
    Parrot in the Oven, 338
    The Secret of Two Brothers, 328
fathers and sons, Native-American Indians
    Dogwolf, 431
    Hawk Moon, 459
    Prophecy Rock, 460
fathers, recently deceased
    Sweet Fifteen, 309 H
FBI agents
    Wolf, No Wolf, 422 N
Feast of the Cross
    Firefly Summer, 305 H
festivals
    Carlos, Light the Farolito, 315 H

The Eagle's Song, 525 N
Firefly Summer, 305 H
Frida Maria, 336 H
Soccer Cousins, 339 H
Yolanda's Genius, 36 Af
fiddlers
    Celie and the Harvest Fiddler, 37 Af
    Haunts, 78 Af
    Wolf, No Wolf, 422 N
field glasses
    Across the Lines, 106 Af
fig trees
    The Tree That Rains, 486 N
Filipino Americans
    Dragonfly, 294 As
    Pedro and the Monkey, 272 As
    Returning a Borrowed Tongue, 291 As
Fineday Reservation
    The Light People, 453 N
fingerplays
    De Colores and Other Latin-American Folk Songs for Children, 384 H
fire
    Coyote and the Fire Stick, 504 N
    Manabozho's Gifts, 506 N
    The Manitous, 516 N
    The Rainbow Bridge, 541 N
    The Tree Is Older Than You Are, 522 N
    When Birds Could Talk & Bats Could Sing, 149 Af
fire-bombing
    Candle in the Wind, 232 As
firefighters
    Brotherhood of Dolphins, 370 H
    Dogwolf, 431 N
    The Gettin Place, 126 Af
fireflies
    Fireflies for Nathan, 90 Af
fires
    Forged by Fire, 33 Af
    Music from a Place Called Half Moon, 466 N
    Smoky Night, 13 Af
    The Windigo's Return, 543 N
fireworks
    Wan Hu Is in the Stars, 244 As

First Man
  The Precious Gift, 515 N
fisher (animal)
  Follow the Stars, 526 N
fishermen and fishing
  Alicia's Treasure, 308 H
  The Crystal Heart, 275 As
  Fishing Sunday, 210 As
  My Father's Boat, 203 As
  Snow Falling on Cedars, 205 As
  The Treasure Chest, 279 As
  Under the Blood-Red Sun, 229 As
fishes
  The Ch'i-lin Purse, 251 As
  The Treasure Chest, 279 As
flags
  Under the Blood-Red Sun, 229 As
Flathead Indians
  Reservation Blues, 419 N
Flint
  *How Rabbit Tricked Otter and Other
    Cherokee Trickster Tales*, 527 N
Flint, Michigan
  *The Watsons Go to Birmingham—
    1963*, 29 Af
Flint Bird
  *Race with Buffalo, and Other Native
    American Stories for Young People*,
    544 N
flood stories
  Bones in the Basket, 537 N
  Coyote Walks on Two Legs, 511 N
  The Golden Flower, 381 H
  *How the World Was Saved & Other
    Native American Tales*, 509 N
  *The Legend of the White Buffalo
    Woman*, 503 N
  The Manitous, 516 N
  People of Corn, 500 N
  The Tree That Rains, 486 N
Florida
  Bloody Waters, 323 H
  From Amigos to Friends, 322 H
  Going Under, 364 H
  Havana Thursdays, 365 H
  Jumping Off to Freedom, 307 H
  The Marks of Birth, 341 H
  Monkey King, 196 As

War Woman, 434 N
Women Don't Need to Write, 371 H
flutes
  The Story of Blue Elk, 514 N
folk art
  Chickens! Chickens!, 103 Af
food, ethnic
  I Smell Honey, 100 Af
  Jalapeno Bagles, 369 H
football
  Necessary Roughness, 216 As
foot binding
  Hearsay, 266 As
foster children
  Circle Within a Circle, 457 N
  A Place to Call Home, 67 Af
Four Bears, Minnesota
  The Light People, 453 N
foxes
  The Ghost Fox, 239 As
  A Ring of Tricksters, 148 Af
Franklin, Benjamin
  Hang a Thousand Trees with Ribbons,
    108 Af
Freedman's Bureau
  Forty Acres and Maybe a Mule,
    109 Af
  *I Thought My Soul Would Rise and
    Fly*, 46 Af
Freedomtown, Texas
  Jubilee Journey, 81 Af
French Indians
  Wolf, No Wolf, 422
French-Indian wars
  Dark Shade, 435 N
French people in the New World
  The Peace Chief, 433 N
Fresno, California
  Boys at Work, 356 H
  Crazy Weekend, 359 H
  Jesse, 360 H
  New and Selected Poems, 413 H
  Off and Running, 361 H
  Petty Crimes, 363 H
friendships, African Americans
  The Adventures of Sugar and Junior,
    77
  Babylon Boyz, 85

Bebop-A-Do-Walk!, 43
The Big Bike Race, 8
A Blessing in Disguise, 127
Cezanne Pinto, 125
Ernestine & Amanda, 6
Fall Secrets, 12
The Fred Field, 15
From the Notebooks of Melanin Sun, 139
If You Please, President Lincoln, 110
I Hadn't Meant to Tell You This, 140
Jamaica's Blue Marker, 47
Like Sisters on the Homefront, 137
May'naise Sandwiches & Sunshine Tea, 7
Meet Danitra Brown, 176
Raven in a Dove House, 96
Run for Your Life, 71
A School for Pompey Walker, 114
The Secret Super Power of Marco, 138 Af
Solo Girl, 97
Tryin' to Sleep in the Bed You Made, 31
The Well, 131
friendships, Asian Americans
Bebop-A-Do-Walk!, 206
Blu's Hanging, 235
Bug Park, 208
Cat and Rat, 285
Gathering of Pearls, 199
Heroes, 219
Honor and Duty, 213
Jungle Dogs, 228
Memories of My Ghost Brother, 202
Mona in the Promised Land, 209
Night of the Chupacabras, 217
Saying Goodbye, 218
Song Lee and the Hamster Hunt, 212
Thief of Hearts, 243
Under the Blood-Red Sun, 229
friendships, Hispanic Americans
The Adventures of Sugar and Junior, 340
Aqua Santa, 402 H
Boys at Work, 356
Buried Onions, 357
Crazy Weekend, 359

Firefly Summer, 305
Fitting In, 306
From Amigos to Friends, 322
Jumping Off to Freedom, 307
La Mariposa, 331
Marisol and Magdalena, 313
Night of the Chupacabras, 217
Off and Running, 361
Soccer Cousins, 339
Summer on Wheels, 359
Tonio's Cat, 311
friendships, interracial, African Americans and others
Across the Lines, 106
The Adventures of Sugar and Junior, 77
Bebop-A-Do-Walk!, 43
Bright Freedom, 52
City Green, 32
Creativity, 124
Egg-Drop Blues, 4
Fall Secrets, 12
Forty Acres and Maybe a Mule, 109
Hold Fast to Dreams, 95
I Hadn't Meant to Tell You This, 140
Jamaica's Blue Marker, 47
Moriah's Pond, 123
Pink and Say, 102
The Poison Place, 72
Yolanda's Genius, 36
friendships, interracial, Asian Americans and others
April and the Dragon Lady, 221
Bebop-A-Do-Walk!, 206
The Best Older Sister, 198
Bug Park, 208
The Foreign Student, 200
Gathering of Pearls, 199
Heroes, 219
Honor and Duty, 213
Mona in the Promised Land, 209
Necessary Roughness, 216
Night of the Chupacabras, 217
Saying Goodbye, 218
Song Lee and the Hamster Hunt, 212
Under the Blood-Red Sun, 229
Yang the Third and Her Impossible Family, 222

friendships, interracial, Hispanic Americans and others
The Adventures of Sugar and Junior, 340
¡Fiesta!, 325
Fitting In, 306
The Magic Shell, 343
Night of the Chupacabras, 337
No Place, 326
friendships, interracial, Native-American Indians and others
The Arrow Over the Door, 423
Far North, 456
Hawk Moon, 459
The Last Rainmaker, 447
My Navajo Sister, 471
friendships, Native-American Indians
Adopted by the Eagles, 501
Dog People, 425
The Eagle's Shadow, 461
Far North, 457
Guests, 437
The Last Rainmaker, 447
Nightland, 468
Reservation Blues, 419
Runs with Horses, 429
Sees Behind Trees, 438
The Trickster and the Troll, 473
frogs
The Dragon's Tale and Other Animal Fables of the Chinese Zodiac, 249 As
The Precious Gift, 515
The Song of el Coqui and Other Tales of Puerto Rico, 382 H
frontiersmen
Dark Passage, 484 N
funerals
Jubilee Journey, 81 Af
The Loyal Cat, 265 As
futuristic fiction
Blood Child and Other Stories, 16 Af
The Parable of the Talents, 17 Af

gamblers and gambling
April and the Dragon Lady, 221 As
Bone Game, 467 N

The Foot Warmer and the Crow, 22 Af
The Last Rainmaker, 447 N
games
De Colores and Other Latin-American Folk Songs for Children, 348, 409, H
gardens and gardeners
City Green, 32 Af
A Day's Work, 310 H
gauntlet, running the
Dark Shade, 435 N
Gay Head
Between Earth and Sky, 490 N
gene altering
What a Woman's Gotta Do, 23 Af
Georgia
Ebony Sea, 121 Af
Forty Acres and Maybe a Mule, 109 Af
Like Sisters on the Homefront, 137 Af
Moriah's Pond, 123 Af
The Peace Chief, 433 N
Spite Fences, 68 Af
Through the Storm, 56 Af
War Woman, 434 N
geographical features
Between Earth and Sky, 490 N
Geronimo
Run Away Home, 75 Af
Runs With Horses, 429 N
Ghost Dance
Coming to Light, 534 N
Wearing the Morning Star, 536 N
ghosts
Chinese Folktales, 253 As
The Ghost Fox, 239 As
Hearsay, 266 As
The Hundred Secret Senses, 230 As
Memories of My Ghost Brother, 202 As
Mysterious Tales of Japan, 263 As
Prietita and the Ghost Woman/Prietita y la Llorna, 304 H
giants
The Legend of the Windigo, 529 N
The Windigo's Return, 543 N
gifts
Creativity, 124 Af
Later, Gator, 242 As

Louise's Gift or What Did She Give Me That For?, 122 Af

goats
  The Great Race, 246 As
  Night of the Chupacabras, 217, 337 As, H

gods
  The Children of the Morning Light, 518 N
  Dance of the Sacred Circle, 524 N
  The Farmer and the Poor God, 280 As
  Five Heavenly Emperors, 290 As
  The Great Buffalo Race, 498 N
  How the World Was Saved & Other Native American Tales, 509 N
  The Long-Haired Girl, 267 As
  Manabozho's Gifts, 506 N
  The Manitous, 516 N
  Musicians of the Sun, 520 N
  Owl Eyes, 499
  People of Corn, 500 N
  The Rainbow Bridge, 541 N
  Tiger Woman, 284 As
  Tsubu the Little Snail, 281 As

gold
  Spirits of the Ordinary, 303 H
  War Woman, 434 N

gold coins
  The Stone Lion, 274 As

goldsmiths
  The Stone Lion, 274 As

Good Friday
  A Sunburned Prayer, 366 H

gourds
  Older Brother, Younger Brother, 260 As

Grand Canyon
  Between Earth and Sky, 490 N

granddaughters, replacement for
  The Beaded Moccasins, 441 N

grandfathers
  So Far from the Sea, 194 As

grandfathers and granddaughters
  Granddaddy's Gift, 83 Af
  Guardian of the Hills, 475 N
  JoJo's Flying Side Kick, 94 Af
  Petty Crimes, 363 H
  True North, 70 Af

grandfathers and grandsons
  The Cloudmakers, 269 As
  A Day's Work, 310 H
  Dogwolf, 431 N
  Fishing Sunday, 210 As
  The Fred Field, 15 Af
  The Imp That Ate My Homework, 241 As
  Nightland, 468 N
  Soccer Cousins, 339 H
  A Sunburned Prayer, 366 H
  Tomas and the Library Lady, 346 H
  Under the Blood-Red Sun, 229 As
  The World in Grandfather's Hands, 477 N

grandfathers, great
  Doesn't Fall Off His Horse, 479 N

grandmothers
  Angel to Angel, 186 Af
  Confetti, 404 H
  Grandmother's Pigeon, 443 N

grandmothers and granddaughters
  Abuelita's Heart, 318
  April and the Dragon Lady, 221 As
  The Best Older Sister, 198 As
  Blue Horses Rush In, 558 N
  Busy Bea, 105 Af
  By the Dawn's Early Light, 1 Af
  Candle in the Wind, 232 As
  Can You Dance, Dalila?, 69 Af
  Cast Two Shadows, 107 Af
  The Cook's Family, 238 As
  The Eagle's Shadow, 461 N
  The Earth Under Sky Bear's Feet, 517 N
  Faces in the Moon, 421 N
  Fall Secrets, 12 Af
  Fitting In, 306 H
  The Great Race, 246 As
  Knoxville, Tennessee, 168 Af
  Like Sisters on the Homefront, 137 Af
  Lily and the Wooden Bowl, 273 As
  Luka's Quilt, 204 As
  Mama Provi and the Pot of Rice, 352 H
  Marisol and Magdalena, 313 H
  May'naise Sandwiches & Sunshine Tea, 7 Af

Moriah's Pond, 123 Af
No Mirrors in My Nana's House,
    158 Af
Singing in the Comeback Choir,
    19 Af
*Tortillas and Lullabies/Tortillas y can-
    cioncitas*, 351 H
grandmothers and grandsons
    Benito's Dream Bottle, 347 H
    The Big Bike Race, 8 Af
    The Gumma Wars, 48 Af
    The Marks of Birth, 341 H
    School Spirit, 330 H
    A Sunburned Prayer, 366 H
grandmothers, black, and granddaughters,
    white
    Cast Two Shadows, 107 Af
grandmothers, great
    The Long March, 444 N
    *Sugarcane House and Other Stories
        About Mr. Fat*, 11 Af
    Sweet Fifteen, 309 H
    Thief of Hearts, 243 As
grandparents and grandchildren
    Chave's Memories, 320 H
    Fireflies for Nathan, 90 Af
    Red Bird, 463 N
Grand River, Michigan
    Yolanda's Genius, 36 Af
Great Smoky Mountains
    Between Earth and Sky, 490 N
    On the Long Trail Home, 474 N
greed
    The Crane Wife, 245 As
    Older Brother, Younger Brother,
        260 As
    The Stone Lion, 274 As
growing-up fiction, boy's, African Ameri-
    cans
    From the Notebooks of Melanin Sun,
        130
    The Well, 129
growing-up fiction, boy's, Asian Ameri-
    cans
    China Boy, 213
    Honor and Duty, 213
    Jungle Dogs, 228

Necessary Roughness, 216
    Shark Bait, 228
growing-up fiction, boy's, Hispanic
    Americans
    Buried Onions, 357
    From Amigos to Friends, 322
    Jesse, 360
    Parrot in the Oven, 338
    The Secret of Two Brothers, 328
    A Sunburned Prayer, 366
growing-up fiction, boy's, Native-
    American Indians
    The Boy Who Dreamed of an Acorn,
        432
    The Crying for a Vision, 483
    Dogwolf, 431
    Far North, 456
    Guests, 437
    Prophecy Rock, 450
    Runs With Horses, 429
    Sees Behind Trees, 438
    Spirit Horse, 417
growing-up fiction, boy's and girl's
    An Island Like You, 348 H
    Rites of Passage, 10 Af
growing-up fiction, girl's, African Ameri-
    cans
    A Blessing in Disguise, 127
    Cast Two Shadows, 107
    Coffee Will Make You Black, 120
    Hang a Thousand Trees with Ribbons,
        108
    I Hadn't Meant to Tell You This, 140
    Jazmin's Notebook, 42
    Just Family, 9
    Like Sisters on the Homefront, 137
    Moriah's Pond, 123
    Raven in a Dove's House, 96
    Sound the Jubilee, 38
    Tryin' to Sleep in the Bed You Made,
        31
    The World of Daughter McGuire, 144
    Yolanda's Genius, 36
growing-up fiction, girl's, Asian Ameri-
    cans
    Blu's Hanging, 235
    Heads by Harry, 235

Mona in the Promised Land, 209
Wild Meat and the Bully Burgers,
    235
growing-up fiction, girl's, Hispanic Amer-
    icans
    Alicia's Treasure, 308
    Breath, Eyes, Memory, 319
    Maya's Divided World, 367
    The Year of Our Revolution, 349
growing-up fiction, girl's, Native-
    American Indians
    Cloud Chamber, 436
    Faces in the Moon, 421
    Flutie, 448
    Guardian of the Hills, 475
    Indio, 446
    The Last Rainmaker, 447
    *The Only Piece of Furniture in the
        House*, 448
    Walks Alone, 430
    The Window, 439
    Yellow Raft in Blue Water, 426
Guatemala
    The Race of Toad and Deer, 383 H
guinea hens
    *The Song of el Coqui and Other Tales
        of Puerto Rico*, 382 H
guitars
    Reservation Blues, 419 N
Gulf of Mexico
    My Father's Boat, 203 As
guns
    The Gettin Place, 126 Af
    Raven in a Dove House, 96 Af

hair
    Hair: Pelitos, 316 H
    The Long-Haired Girl, 267 As
    Nappy Hair, 50 Af
hair stylists
    Easier to Kill, 133 Af
    The Glory Field, 86 Af
    The Healing, 60 Af
Haiti
    Breath, Eyes, Memory, 319 H
    If You Please, President Lincoln,
        110 Af

Halloween
    Celie and the Harvest Fiddler, 37 Af
    The Weather That Kills, 182 Af
hamsters
    Song Lee and the Hamster Hunt, 212 As
handicapped persons
    Comfort Woman, 211 As
    Egg-Drop Blues, 4 Af
    If You Please, President Lincoln, 110 Af
    *I Thought My Soul Would Rise and
        Fly*, 46 Af
    Sees Behind Trees, 438 N
    The Simple Truth, 1 Af
    The Story of Blue Elk, 514 N
    Uncegila's Seventh Spot, 530 N
    Women Don't Need to Write, 371 H
hangings
    Cast Two Shadows, 107 Af
Harlem, New York
    Jazmin's Notebook, 42 Af
    Just Family, 9 Af
    *Louise's Gift or What Did She Give
        Me That For?*, 122 Af
    Push, 116 Af
    Slam!, 87 Af
Harlem Renaissance
    The Richer, the Poorer, 135 Af
    *Shimmy Shimmy Shimmy Like My Sis-
        ter Kate*, 170 Af
harmonicas
    Music from a Place Called Half Moon,
        466 N
    The Old Cotton Blues, 35 Af
Harvard University
    Saying Goodbye, 218 As
hate crimes
    Indian Killer, 418 N
    See also prejudice.
Havana, Cuba
    From Amigos to Friends, 322 H
Hawaii
    Blu's Hanging, 235 As
    Comfort Woman, 211 As
    The Folding Cliffs, 296 As
    The Island-below-the-Star, 227 As
    Jungle Dogs, 228 As
    The Last Dragon, 224 As

Luka's Quilt, 204 As
Under the Blood-Red Sun, 229
Hawaiian-Filipino-Chinese-Portuguese
    Americans
Jungle Dogs, 228 As
healers
    Abuelita's Heart, 318 H
    Going Under, 364 H
    Guardian of the Hills, 475 N
    The Healing, 65 Af
    Indio, 446 N
    *Old Letivia and the Mountain of Sor-
        rows*, 345 H
    *Prietita and the Ghost Woman/Prietita
        y la Llorona*, 304 H
    Spirits of the Ordinary, 303 H
Heart of Sky
    People of Corn, 500 N
herbs
    *Prietita and the Ghost Woman/Prietita
        y la Llorona*, 304 H
heroes, folk
    Bill Pickett, 94 Af
    Fa Mulan, 271 As
    John Henry, 152 Af
hired men
    The Hired Man, 155 Af
Hiroshima
    Fallout, 297 As
    Hiroshima, 240 As
historical fiction, African Americans
    Across the Lines, 106
    Amistad Rising, 20
    Bright Freedom's Song, 52
    The Captive, 45
    Cast Two Shadows, 107
    Cezanne Pinto, 125
    Ebony Sea, 121
    Forty Acres and Maybe a Mule, 109
    The Glory Field, 86
    If You Please, President Lincoln, 110
    *I Thought My Soul Would Rise and
        Fly*, 46
    My Home Is Over Jordan, 38
    Papa Tells Chita a Story, 53
    A Picture of Freedom, 74
    Pink and Say, 102
    Run Away Home, 75

Second Daughter, 132
Seminole Diary, 63
Sound the Jubilee, 38
Spite Fences, 68
*The Twins, the Pirates, and the Battle
    of New Orleans*, 112
The Wagon, 64
Washington City Is Burning, 113
historical fiction, Asian Americans
    Hiroshima, 240
    Under the Blood-Red Sun, 229
historical fiction, Hispanic Americans
    The Flower in the Skull, 302
historical fiction, Native-American Indi-
    ans
    The Arrow Over the Door, 423
    Children of the Longhouse, 424
    The Crying for a Vision, 483
    Dark Shade, 435
    Doesn't Fall Off His Horse, 479
    Dog People, 425
    Indio, 446
    The Long March, 444
    On the Long Trail Home, 474
    The Peace Chief, 433
    Pushing the Bear, 450
    Runs with Horses, 429
    Spirit Horse, 417
    Spirits of the Ordinary, 303
    Walks Alone, 430
    The Waters Between, 427
    War Woman, 434
historical figures, African Americans
    Amistad Rising, 20
    Bill Pickett, 94
    Bright Freedom's Song, 52
    Cast Two Shadows, 107
    Dreamer, 61
    Hang a Thousand Trees with Ribbons,
        108
    If You Please, President Lincoln, 110
    The Poison Place, 72
    Second Daughter, 132
    Sound the Jubilee, 38
    *The Twins, the Pirates, and the Battle
        of New Orleans*, 112
    Washington City Is Burning, 113
    Yolanda's Genius, 36

historical figures, Hispanic Americans
  Latino Rainbow, 393
historical figures, Native-American Indians
  The Arrow Over the Door, 423
  The Beaded Moccasins, 441
  Dark Passage, 484
  The Man Made of Words, 464
  A Picture of Freedom, 74
  Reservation Blues, 419
  Run Away Home, 75
  Runs With Horses, 429
  Walks Alone, 430
historical overviews of literature
  African-American Literature, 142
  African American Literature, 145
  Asian-American Literature, 234 As
  Coming to Light, 534 N
  Currents from the Dancing River, 324
  Daughters of the Fifth Sun, 233 H
  ¡Floricanto Si!, 401 H
  Hispanic American Literature, 332 H
  Into the Fire, 233 As
  Native American Literature, 482, 559 N
  Shimmy Shimmy Shimmy Like My Sister Kate, 170 Af
  Song of the Turtle, 420 N
  Voice of the Turtle, 420 N
  Wearing the Morning Star, 536 N
Hollywood images
  The Case of the Lion Dance, 237 As
  Gunga Din Highway, 197 As
holy men
  Buddha, 248 As
  Buddha, 268 As
homeless people
  Babylon Boyz, 85 Af
  Tryin' to Sleep in the Bed You Made, 31 Af
  The Weather That Kills, 182 Af
homosexuals
  Babylon Boyz, 85 Af
  Bone Game, 467 N
  From the Notebooks of Melanin Sun, 139 Af
  An Island Like You, 348 H
  Tommy Stands Alone, 368 H
  See also lesbians.

Hong Kong
  Seeing Calvin Coolidge in a Dream, 201 As
Hopi Indians
  Bone Dance, 555
  The First Eagle, 454
  Hawk Man, 459
  Prophecy Rock, 460
horseman, headless
  Haunts, 78 Af
horse races
  The Healing, 65 Af
horses
  Dance of the Sacred Circle, 524 N
  Doesn't Fall Off His Horse, 479 N
  Frida Maria, 336 H
  The Great Race, 246 As
  The Last Rainmaker, 447 N
  The Legend of the White Buffalo Woman, 503 N
  The Little Seven-Colored Horse, 386 N
  The Lost Horse, 287 As
  My Navajo Sister, 471 N
  A Picture of Freedom, 74 Af
  Spirit Horse, 417 N
hospital scenes
  Danger Zone, 66 Af
  Eagle Song, 426 N
  Jazmin's Notebook, 42 Af
  Monkey King, 196 As
  The Simple Truth, 2 Af
huckleberry sisters
  Coyote and the Fire Stick, 504 N
Hughes, Langston
  Carol of the Brown King, 161 Af
Huichol Indians
  The Tree That Rains, 486 N
humorous fiction, African Americans
  The Adventures of Sugar and Junior, 77
  Don't Split the Pole, 128
  Egg-Drop Blues, 4
  The Fred Field, 15
  The Gumma Wars, 48
  Harvey Potter's Balloon Farm, 89
  Live at Five, 49
  Off to School, 5

Oren Bell, 15
Poppa's Itchy Christmas, 80
Poppa's New Pants, 80
Smiffy Blue, Ace Crime Detective, 88
The Watsons Go to Birmingham—
    1963, 29
humorous fiction, Asian Americans
    Blu's Hanging, 235
    Gunga Din Highway, 197
    The Imp That Ate My Homework, 241
    Later, Gator, 242
    Mona in the Promised Land, 209
    Night of the Chupacabras, 217
    Seeing Calvin Coolidge in a Dream,
      201
humorous fiction, Hispanic Americans
    The Adventures of Sugar and Junior,
      340
    Big Bushy Mustache, 355
    Boys at Work, 356
    Chato's Kitchen, 358
    Crazy Weekend, 359
    Down in the Subway, 317
    Frida Maria, 336
    Mama Provi and the Pot of Rice, 352
    Night of the Chupacabras, 337
    Off and Running, 361
    The Old Man and His Door, 362
    The Pool Party, 356
    School Spirit, 330
    To a Widow with Children, 321
humorous fiction, Native-American Indi-
    ans
    The Bingo Palace, 442
    Coyote Blue, 465
    How the Indians Bought the Farm, 478
    The Light People, 453
    Little Coyote Runs Away, 476
    Reservation Blues, 419
hunters
    The Eagle's Song, 525 N
    Jojofu, 278 As
Huracan, god
    The Song of el Coqui and Other Tales
      of Puerto Rico, 382 H
hurricanes
    Firefly Summer, 305 H
    Fitting In, 306 H

Iktomi
    Iktomi and the Buzzard, 502 N
    The Trickster and the Troll, 473 N
Illinois
    Easter Parade, 41 Af
    Yolanda's Genius, 36 Af
illiteracy
    Papa's Stories, 62 Af
    Push, 116 Af
    Spite Fences, 68 Af
    Women Don't Need to Write, 371 H
illnesses
    Babylon Boyz, 85 Af
    Leticia's Secret, 334 H
    A Place to Call Home, 67 Af
immigrants, Asian Americans
    The Foreign Student, 200
    Hunger, 195
    Necessary Roughness, 216
    Returning a Borrowed Tongue, 291
    Songs My Mother Taught Me, 236
    Thief of Hearts, 243
    Yang the Third and Her Impossible
      Family, 222
immigrants, Hispanic Americans
    Bad Alchemy, 399
    Calling the Doves/El Canto de las
      Palomas, 329
    Currents from the Dancing River, 324
    Daughters of the Fifth Sun, 342
    Going Under, 364
    Havana Thursdays, 365
    Imagine the Angels of Bread, 395
    Jumping Off to Freedom, 307
    La Mariposa, 331
    Mama Provi and the Pot of Rice, 352
    The Marks of Birth, 341
    Off and Running, 361
    Parrot in the Oven, 338
    Petty Crimes, 363
    Tonio's Cat, 311
    The Year of Our Revolution, 349
    You Come Singing, 414
immigrants, Native-American Indians
    The Trickster and the Troll, 473
impersonations
    The Cook's Family, 238 As

Dreamer, 61 Af
Seeing Calvin Coolidge in a Dream,
    201 As
imps, Chinese
    The Imp That Ate My Homework, 241
incest
    Monkey King, 196 As
    A Place to Call Home, 67 Af
    Push, 116 Af
    The Road Home, 451 N
indentured servants
    Bright Freedom's Song, 52 Af
    The Captive, 45 Af
Independence Day, African American
    Spite Fences, 68
India
    Buddha, 248 As
Indiana
    A Place Called Freedom, 115 Af
Indian Territories
    The Long March, 444
    On the Long Trail Home, 474
    Pushing the Bear, 450
insects
    Bug Park, 208 As
International Day
    Jalapeno Bagels, 369 H
internment camps, Japanese American
    Snow Falling on Cedars, 205
    So Far from the Sea, 194
    Songs My Mother Taught Me, 236
Iowa
    Billy, 353 H
    Tomas and the Library Lady, 346 H
Ireland
    Cloud Chamber, 436 N
Irish famine
    The Long March, 444 N
Iroquois Indians
    Eagle Song, 426
    *Race with Buffalo, and Other Native
        American Stories for Young Readers*,
        554
Island Lady
    Down in the Subway, 317 H
Italy
    Danger Zone, 66 Af

Jackson, General Andrew
    *The Twins, the Pirates, and the Battle
        of New Orleans*, 112 Af
Jade Emperor of Heaven
    Cat and Rat, 285 As
jades
    The Ch'i-lin Purse, 251 As
Jamaica
    Easier to Kill, 133 Af
    How Stella Got Her Groove Back,
        76 Af
Japan
    Buddha, 268 As
    The Crane Wife, 245 As
    The Farmer and the Poor God, 280 As
    Hiroshima, 240 As
    Lily and the Wooden Bowl, 273 As
    The Loyal Cat, 265 As
    Mysterious Tales of Japan, 263 As
    One Hand Clapping, 264 As
    The Wise Old Woman, 277 As
Japanese Americans
    Another Way to Dance, 293
    Bebop-A-Do-Walk!, 206
    Candle in the Wind, 232
    Fallout, 297
    Fishing Sunday, 210
    Heroes, 219
    The Necessary Hunger, 226
    Snow Falling on Cedars, 205
    So Far from the Sea, 194
    Songs My Mother Taught Me, 236
    Talent Night, 225
    Under the Blood-Red Sun, 229
Japanese-Hawaiian Americans
    Blu's Hanging, 235
Jataka stories
    Buddha Stories, 248 As
jazz
    Little Lil and the Swing-Singing Sax,
        40 Af
    The Weather That Kills, 182 Af
jellyfish
    Alicia's Treasure, 308 H
Jews, Chinese
    Hearsay, 266 As
Jews, Mexican
    Spirits of the Ordinary, 303 H

Jim Crow Laws
  Granddaddy's Gifts, 83 Af
  Run Away Home, 75 Af
  Running for Our Lives, 131 Af
  True North, 70 Af
Jordan, Michael
  For the Love of the Game, 173 Af
journals
  From the Notebooks of Melanin Sun,
    139 Af
  *I Thought My Soul Would Rise and
    Fly*, 46 Af
  Jazmin's Notebook, 42 Af
jumping rope
  Solo Girl, 97 Af
Juneteenth
  Freedom's Gifts, 134 Af
  Jubilee Journey, 81 Af

Kansas City, Kansas
  Rattlebone, 21 Af
karate
  The Case of the Lion Dance, 237 As
  JoJo's Flying Side Kick, 99 Af
  See also tae kwon do.
Kathlamet Indians
  *Race with Buffalo, and Other Native
    American Stories for Young Readers*,
    544
Kentucky
  Cloud Chamber, 436 N
  Egg-Drop Blue, 4 Af
  On the Long Trail Home, 474 N
  The Window, 439 N
kidnappings
  Billy, 353 H
King, Martin Luther, Jr.
  Dreamer, 61 Af
Kiowa Indians
  Doesn't Fall Off His Horse, 479
  The Last Rainmaker, 447
  *Race with Buffalo, and Other Native
    American Stories for Young Readers*,
    544
kite makers
  The Last Dragon, 224 As
Knoxville, Tennessee
  Knoxville, Tennessee, 168 Af

Kock, Bernard
  If You Please, President Lincoln, 110 Af
Korea
  Comfort Woman, 211 As
  Echoes of the White Giraffe, 199 As
  The Foreign Student, 200 As
  Kongi and Potgi, 257 As
  Mr. Pak Buys a Story, 252 As
  Older Brother, Younger Brother,
    260 As
  Tiger's Tail, 215 As
  Year of Impossible Goodbyes, 199 As
Korean Americans
  Another Way to Dance, 293 As
  The Best Older Sister, 198 As
  Comfort Woman, 211 As
  Finding My Voice, 218 As
  Gathering of Pearls, 199 As
  Memories of My Ghost Brother,
    202 As
  Necessary Roughness, 216 As
  Night of the Chupacabras, 217 As
  Saying Goodbye, 218 As
  Song Lee and the Hamster Hunt,
    212 As
Korean-Chinese Americans
  Good Luck Gold And Other Poems,
    299 As
  The Rainbow Hand, 299 As
  A Suitcase of Seaweed, 299 As
Korean War
  The Foreign Student, 200 As
  Heroes, 219 As
Kuloskap
  *Race with Buffalo, and Other Native
    American Stories for Young Readers*,
    544 N
Kwakiutl Indians
  The Echoes of the Elders, 521
  The Spirit of the Cedar People, 521

lacrosse
  Children of the Longhouse, 424 N
Lafitte, Jean
  *The Twins, the Pirates, and the Battle
    of New Orleans*, 112 Af
Laguna Beach, California
  Maya's Divided World, 367 H

Lake Champlain
  Between Earth & Sky, 490 N
  The Waters Between, 427 N
Lake Michigan
  The Legend of Sleeping Bear, 540 N
Lake Superior
  The Birchbark House, 443 N
Lakota (Sioux) Indians
  Adopted by Eagles, 501
  The Crying for a Vision, 483
  The Grass Dancer, 469
  The Legend of the White Buffalo Woman, 503
  The Road Home, 451
  The Trickster and the Troll, 473
  Uncegila's Seventh Spot, 530
La Llorona
  Prietita and the Ghost Woman/Prietita y la Llorna, 304 H
land rush, Oklahoma
  I Have Heard of a Land, 130 Af
Las Posadas
  Carlos, Light the Farolito, 315 H
laundresses
  Ma Dear's Aprons, 73 Af
legs, amputated
  The Light People, 453 N
Lelooska, Chief
  The Echoes of the Elders, 521 N
Lenape Indians. *See* Delaware Indians.
lepers
  Blu's Hanging, 235 As
  The Folding Cliffs, 296 As
lesbians
  Ain't Gonna Be the Same Fool Twice, 120 Af
  From the Notebooks of Melanin Sun, 139 Af
  The Necessary Hunger, 226 As
  See also homosexuals.
libraries
  Brotherhood of Dolphins, 370 H
  Tomas and the Library Lady, 346 H
Life magazine
  Spite Fences, 68 Af
lightning, origin of
  How Thunder and Lightning Came to Be, 510 N

Lincoln, Abraham, death of
  The Wagon, 64 Af
literacy, for slaves
  I Thought My Soul Would Rise and Fly, 46 Af
  A Picture of Freedom, 74 Af
Little Bill series
  The Meanest Thing to Say, 26 Af
little people
  The Deetkatoo, 487 N
  Little Plum, 286 As
  Old Letivia and the Mountain of Sorrows, 345 H
  Tsubu the Little Snail, 281 As
Little Red Riding Hood, folktale
  Papa's Stories, 62 Af
London, England
  Hang a Thousand Trees with Ribbons, 108 Af
loons
  The Echoes of the Elders, 531 N
looting
  Smoky Night, 13 Af
Los Angeles, California
  Black Betty, 84 Af
  Brothers and Sisters, 18 Af
  Danger Zone, 66 Af
  The Gettin Place, 126 Af
  The Girl from Playa Blanca, 333 H
  Leticia's Secret, 334 H
  The Necessary Hunger, 226 As
  No Place, 326 H
  Singing in the Comeback Choir, 19 Af
  Smoky Night, 13 Af
lost-and-found
  Busy Bea, 105 Af
Louisiana
  Mister and Me, 51 Af
Louisville, Kentucky
  The Window, 439 N
lullabies
  Northwoods Cradle Song, 561 N
  On the Road of Stars, 488, 546 N
luminarias
  Blue Horses Rush In, 481 N
  Carlos, Light the Farolito, 315 H
Lyles Station
  A Place Called Freedom, 115 Af

lynching
  *A Treasury of African-American
    Christmas Stories*, 24 Af

Mackinac Island, Michigan
  The Legend of Mackinac Island, 540 N
Madison, Dolley
  Washington City Is Burning, 113 Af
Madison, President James
  Washington City Is Burning, 113 Af
magic
  The Beggar's Magic, 247 As
  Belching Hill, 256 As
  Bone Game, 467 N
  Celie and the Harvest Fiddler, 37 Af
  Chinese Folktales, 253 As
  Da Wei's Treasure, 247 As
  The Deetkatoo, 487 N
  Down in the Subway, 317 H
  The Grass Dancer, 469 N
  Harvey Potter's Balloon Farm, 89 Af
  Haunts, 78 Af
  The Hired Hand, 155 Af
  Ling-Li and the Phoenix Fairy, 255 As
  Little Coyote Runs Away, 476 N
  The Loyal Cat, 265 As
  *The White Deer and Other Tales Told
    by the Lenape*, 489 N
mah-jongg players
  April and the Dragon Lady, 221 As
  The Last Dragon, 224 As
Maidu-Pit River Indians
  Home to Medicine Mountain, 470
Maine
  Crossing the Starlight Bridge, 462 N
Manabozho
  Manabozho's Gifts, 506 N
Mandan Indians
  Bones in the Basket, 537
man in the moon
  *Just Rewards or Who Is That Man in
    the Moon & What's He Doing There
    Anyway?*, 270 As
  Rabbit and the Moon, 542 N
Manzanar, California
  So Far from the Sea, 194 As
markets, Mexican
  Uno, Dos, Tres, 408 H

marriages, interracial
  Cloud Chamber, 436 N
  Dark Passage, 484 N
  The Wedding, 136 Af
marriages, slave
  Wagon Train, 143 Af
Martha's Vineyard
  The Wedding, Af
Maryland
  Minty, 119 Af
mask makers
  *The Song of el Coqui and Other Tales
    of Puerto Rico*, 382 H
Massachusetts
  Candle in the Wind, 232 As
  The Captive, 45 Af
  Hang a Thousand Trees with Ribbons,
    108 Af
  Saying Goodbye, 218 As
  Second Daughter, 132 Af
Massachusetts Constitution
  Second Daughter, 132 Af
Mau-shop
  Between Earth & Sky, 490 N
  The Children of the Morning Light, 518 N
Maya Indians
  Cuckoo, 497
  People of Corn, 500
  The Tree Is Older Than You Are, 522
Mazateco Indians
  The Tree Is Older Than You Are, 522
medicine men
  Coyote Blue, 465 N
  Eagle Boy, 512 N
  The Light People, 453 N
Medicine Mountain
  Home to Medicine Mountain, 470 N
medicine wheels
  The Path of Quiet Elk, 480 N
medicine women
  Bone Game, 467 N
  Guardian of the Hills, 475 N
  The Peace Chief, 433 N
  *Prietia and the Ghost Woman/Prietia
    y la Llorona*, 304 H
  War Woman, 434 N
mediums, spiritualist
  Comfort Woman, 211 As

memorials
   The Fred Field, 15 Af
Memphis, Tennessee
   Dreamer, 61 Af
   Taft, 91 Af
Mende people
   Amistad Rising, 20 Af
Menominee Indians
   Northwoods Cradle Song, 561
mentally ill persons
   Comfort Woman, 211 As
   Humming Whispers, 59 Af
   Jazmin's Notebook, 42 Af
   Jip His Story, 93 Af
   The Secret Super Power of Marco, 138 Af
merry-go-rounds
   Carousel, 28 Af
Mesa Verde
   Between Earth and Sky, 490 N
Metis (French-Indian)
   Dogwolf, 431
   Wolf, No Wolf, 422
Mexican Americans
   Abuelita's Heart, 318 H
   Billy, 353 H
   Black Hair, 413 H
   Boys at Work, 356 H
   Brotherhood of Dolphins, 370 H
   Buried Onions, 357 H
   Calling the Doves/El Canto de las Palomas, 329 H
   Canto familiar, 411 H
   Carlos, Light the Farolito, 315 H
   Chave's Memories, 320 H
   Crazy Weekend, 359 H
   A Day's Work, 310 H
   The Elements of San Joaquin, 413 H
   Face of an Angel, 314 H
   The Flower in the Skull, 302 H
   Frida Maria, 336 H
   Gathering the Sun, 301 H
   The Girl from Playa Blanca, 333 H
   Jesse, 360 H
   Junior College, 412 H
   La Mariposa, 331 H
   Leticia's Secret, 334 H
   Loose Woman, 391 H
   New and Selected Poems, 413 H

   Night of the Chupacabras, 337
   No Place, 326 H
   Off and Running, 361 H
   Parrot in the Oven, 338 H
   Petty Crimes, 363 H
   Releasing Serpents, 416 H
   Restless Serpents, 416 H
   The Secret of Two Brothers, 328 H
   A Shroud in the Family, 321 H
   Soccer Cousins, 339 H
   Spirits of the Ordinary, 303 H
   A Sunburned Prayer, 366 H
   Super-Eight Movies, 413 H
   Sweet Fifteen, 309 H
   The Tale of Sunlight, 413 H
   Tio Armando, 327 H
   To a Widow with Children, 321 H
   Tommy Stands Alone, 368 H
   Tonio's Cat, 311 H
   The Tortilla Factory, 350 H
   Where Sparrows Work Hard, 413 H
Mexican Indians
   The Flower in the Skull, 302 H
   Spirits of the Ordinary, 303 H
   The Tree Is Older Than You Are, 522 N
Mexico
   The Flower in the Skull, 302 H
   From the Bellybutton of the Moon and Other Summer Poems/Del Ombligo de la Luna y otros poemas de verano, 387 H
   Indio, 446 H
   Night of the Chupacabras, 217, 337 As, H
   Runs with Horses, 429 N
   Soccer Cousins, 339 H
   Spirits of the Ordinary, 303 H
   A Tale of Rabbit and Coyote, 517 N
   Walks Alone, 430 N
Miami, Florida
   Bloody Waters, 323 H
   From Amigos to Friends, 322 H
   Going Under, 364 H
   Havana Thursdays, 365 H
   The Marks of Birth, 341 H
   Women Don't Need to Write, 371 H

mice
  Chato's Kitchen, 358 H
  The Echoes of the Elders, 521 N
  The Girl Who Lived with the Bears,
    505 N
  Mouse Match, 288 As
  Tell Me a Cuento/Cuentame Un Story,
    378 H
Michigan
  The Fred Field, 15 Af
  The Legend of Mackinac Island,
    540 N
  The Legend of Sleeping Bear, 540 N
  *The Watsons Go to Birmingham—
    1963*, 29 Af
  Yolanda's Genius, 36 Af
Micmac Indians
  *Race with Buffalo, and Other Native
    American Stories for Young Readers*,
    544
migrant workers
  *Calling the Doves/El Canto de las Pal-
    omas*, 329 H
  Jesse, 360 H
  La Mariposa, 331 H
  Off to School, 5 Af
  Tomas and the Library Lady, 346 H
Milky Way, origin of
  The Story of the Milky Way, 594 N
millers
  The Hired Hand, 155 Af
ministers
  The Flower in the Skull, 302 H
  Like Sisters on the Homefront, 137 Af
  Spirits of the Ordinary, 303 H
Minnesota
  The Light People, 453 N
  Live at Five, 49 Af
  Necessary Roughness, 216 As
mirrors
  No Mirrors in My Nana's House,
    158 Af
missionaries
  Comfort Woman, 211 As
Mississippi
  Bone Game, 467 N
  Mississippi Chariot, 111 Af
  The Well, 129 Af

Missouri
  Running for Our Lives, 131 Af
Miwok Indians
  Bone Dance, 555
  Two Bear Cubs, 532
mixed-ethnic fiction
  The Adventures of Sugar and Junior,
    77, 340 Af, H
  Don't Split the Pole, 128 Af
  The Flower in the Skull, 302 H
  Night of the Chupacabras, 217, 337
    As, H
  Spirits of the Ordinary, 303 H
mixed-ethnic persons
  Blu's Hanging, 235 As
  Bone Game, 467 N
  Cast Two Shadows, 107 Af
  Celou Sudden Shout, Idaho 1826, 440 N
  Cloud Chamber, 436 N
  The Cook's Family, 238 As
  The Eagle's Shadow, 461 N
  Flutie, 448 N
  Guardian of the Hills, 475 N
  Hawk Moon, 459 N
  Jalapeno Bagels, 369 H
  Jubilee Journey, 82 Af
  Jungle Dogs, 228 As
  The Last Rainmaker, 447
  Nightland, 468
  A Place to Call Home, 67 Af
  Prophecy Rock, 460 N
  The Road Home, 451 N
  Something Terrible Happened, 104 Af
  Talent Night, 225 As
  Thief of Hearts, 243 As
  The Window, 439 N
  Wolf, No Wolf, 422 N
  The World of Daughter McGuire, 144 Af
Modine, New York
  Raven in a Dove House, 96 Af
Modoc Indians
  Bones in the Basket, 537
Mohawk Indians
  Bones in the Basket, 537
  Children of the Longhouse, 424
  Eagle Song, 426
  The Mad Painter Poems, 553
  On Second Thought, 552
  Owl Eyes, 499

moles
Cuckoo, 497 N
monasteries, Buddhist
The Two Brothers, 259 As
Monkey King
The Making of Monkey King, 262 As
monkeys
The Dragon's Tale and Other Animal Fables of the Chinese Zodiac, 249 As
The Great Race, 246 As
The Making of Monkey King, 262 As
Pedro and the Monkey, 272 As
monks
The Treasure Chest, 279 As
monsters
Chinese Folktales, 253 As
The Secret Super Power of Marco, 138 Af
Tailypo, 154 Af
Montana
Coyote Blue, 465 N
Dark Passage, 484 N
Wolf, No Wolf, 422 N
moons
Full Worm Moon, 458 N
Just Rewards or Who Is That Man in the Moon & What's He Doing Up There Anyway?, 270 As
Rabbit and the Moon, 542 N
The Tale of Rabbit and Coyote, 517 N
mosquitoes, origin of
The Legend of the Windigo, 529 N
The Windigo's Return, 543 N
mothers and children
Angel to Angel, 186 Af
By the Dawn's Early Light, 1 Af
The Rainbow Hand, 299 As
To a Widow with Children, 321 H
mothers and daughters
The Edge of Heaven, 39 Af
Faces in the Moon, 421 N
Guardian of the Hills, 475 N
May'naise Sandwiches & Sunshine Tea, 7 Af
Mother Love, 164 Af
Tortillas and Lullabies/Tortillas y cancioncitas, 351 H

The Window, 439 N
Women Don't Need to Write, 371 H
mothers and sons
The Grass Dance, 469 N
Honor and Duty, 213 As
Little Coyote Runs Away, 476 N
Ma Dear's Aprons, 73 Af
The Magic Tapestry, 250 As
The World in Grandfather's Hands, 477 N
mothers, single
Face of an Angel, 314 H
From the Notebooks of Melanin Sun, 139 Af
Live at Five, 49 Af
To a Widow with Children, 321 H
Mound Builders (Mississippian Culture)
Guardian of the Hills, 475 N
mountain lions
Brave as a Mountain Lion, 472 N
Mouse Woman
The Girl Who Lived with Bears, 515 N
movies
Gunga Din Highway, 197 As
mules
The Song of el Coqui and Other Tales of Puerto Rico, 382 H
Sugarcane House and Other Stories About Mr. Fat, 11 Af
multigenerational novels
Cloud Chamber, 436 N
Faces in the Moon, 421 N
The Flower in the Skull, 302 H
The Fred Field, 15 Af
The Glory Field, 86 Af
Guardian of the Hills, 475 N
Havana Thursdays, 341 H
Like Sisters on the Homefront, 137 Af
The River Where Blood Is Born, 55 Af
The Road Home, 451 N
Under the Blood-Red Sun, 229 As
The Watsons Go to Birmingham—1963, 29 Af
murders, African Americans
Black Betty, 84
The Edge of Heaven, 39
The Fred Field, 15
The Gettin Place, 126

The Poison Place, 72
Raven in a Dove House, 96
murders, Asian Americans
    Candle in the Wind, 232
    The Dragon Prince, 282
    Snow Falling on Cedars, 205
murders, Hispanic Americans
    Brotherhood of Dolphins, 370
murders, Native-American Indians
    The Beaded Moccasins, 441
    Bone Game, 67
    The First Eagle, 454
    Hawk Moon, 459
    Indian Killer, 418
    Music from a Place Called Half Moon, 466
    Nightland, 468
    Prophecy Rock, 460
    Wolf, No Wolf, 422
Museum of Modern Art
    Bebop-A-Do-Walk!, 43, 206 Af, As
museums, natural history
    The Poison Place, 72 Af
music, musicians
    The Bat Boy and His Violin, 30 Af
    Carolina Shout!, 118 Af
    Celie and the Harvest Fiddler, 37 Af
    Ernestine & Amanda, 6 Af
    The Genie in the Jar, 167 Af
    Haunts, 78 Af
    Hunger, 195 As
    Little Lil and the Swing-Singing Sax, 40 Af
    Musicians of the Sun, 520 N
    The Old Cotton Blues, 35 Af
    Talent Night, 225 As
    The Weather That Kills, 182 Af
    The Wedding, 136 Af
    Willie Jerome, 34 Af
    Yang the Third and Her Impossible Family, 222 As
    Yolanda's Genius, 36 Af
Muskogee Indians
    Gluskabe and the Four Wishes, 492
mystery novels, African Americans
    Black Betty, 84
    Easier to Kill, 133
    The Edge of Heaven, 39

The Fred Field, 15
The Simple Truth, 2
Smiffy Blue, Ace Crime Detective, 88
What a Woman's Gotta Do, 23
mystery novels, Asian Americans
    Bug Park, 208
    The Case of the Lion Dance, 237
    Honor and Duty, 213
    Night of the Chupacabras, 217
    No Physical Evidence, 214
    Tiger's Tail, 215
mystery novels, Hispanic Americans
    Bloody Waters, 323
    Brotherhood of Dolphins, 370
    Firefly Summer, 305
    The Girl from Playa Blanca, 333
    Night of the Chupacabras, 337
mystery novels, Native-American Indians
    Bone Game, 467
    The Crying for a Vision, 483
    The First Eagle, 454
    Hawk Moon, 459
    Indian Killer, 418
    Nightland, 468
    Prophecy Rock, 460
    Wolf, No Wolf, 422

Nags Head, North Carolina
    Sound the Jubilee, 38 Af
names, changes or true
    Doesn't Fall Off His Horse, 479 N
    My Navajo Sister, 471 N
    Paco and the Witch, 385 H
Nana'b'oozoo, Nanabush
    Coming to Light, 534
    The Manitous, 516 N
    See also Manabozho.
Nanticoke Indians
    Red Bird, 463 N
nature, photographs
    Arias in Silence, 188 Af
Navajo Indians
    Blue Horses Rush In, 481, 558
    Bone Game, 467
    Coyote Walks on Two Legs, 521, 550
    Eagle Boy, 512
    The First Eagle, 454
    How Chipmunk Got Tiny Feet, 513

The Magic of Spider Woman, 505
The Magic Weaver of Rugs, 523
My Navajo Sister, 471
Navajo Visions and Voices Across the Mesa, 545
The Precious Gift, 515
The Shepherd Boy, 445
Nebraska
    The Road Home, 451 N
neighborhood life/community life, African Americans
    The Adventures of Sugar and Junior, 77
    A Blessing in Disguise, 127
    Celie and the Harvest Fiddler, 37
    City Green, 32
    Run for Your Life, 71
    Solo Girl, 97
    The Well, 129
neighborhood life/community life, Asian Americans
    Blu's Hanging, 235
    Jungle Dogs, 228
    Memories of My Ghost Brother, 202
    Necessary Roughness, 216
    Night of the Chupacabras, 217
    Under the Blood-Red Sun, 229
    Yang the Third and Her Impossible Family, 222
neighborhood life/community life, Hispanic Americans
    The Adventures of Sugar and Junior, 340
    Boys at Work, 356
    Brotherhood of Dolphins, 370
    An Island Like You, 348
    No Place, 326
    The Pool Party, 356
    To a Widow with Children, 321
neighborhood life/community life, Native-American Indians
    The Light People, 453 N
Netawatwees Sachem
    The Beaded Moccasins, 441 N
Newark, New Jersey
    Easier to Kill, 133
New England
    The Captive, 45 Af

El Coro, 394 H
New Jersey
    Easier to Kill, 133 Af
    An Island Like You, 348 H
    The Year of Our Revolution, 349 H
New Mexico
    Billy, 353 N
    Blue Horses Rush In, 481, 558 N
    Cuentos de Cuanto Hay, 374 H
    Face of an Angel, 314 H
    Nightland, 468 N
    A Sunburned Prayer, 366 H
    Walks Alone, 430 N
New Orleans, Louisiana
    Rum-a-Tum-Tum, 184 Af
    Through the Storm, 56 Af
    The Twins, the Pirates, and the Battle of New Orleans, 112 Af
    The Weather That Kills, 182 Af
newscasters
    Live at Five, 49 Af
newspaper boys
    The Adventures of Sparrowboy, 98 Af
newspaper men
    Candle in the Wind, 232 As
    Snow Falling on Cedars, 205 As
New York City, African Americans
    Bebop-A-Do-Walk!, 43
    From the Notebooks of Melanin Sun, 139
    The Glory Field, 86
    Harlem, 187
    Just Family, 9
    Push, 116
    Something Terrible Happened, 104
    The Weather That Kills, 182
New York City, Asian Americans
    American Visa, 231
    Bebop-A-Do-Walk!, 206
    Gathering of Pearls, 199
    Honor and Duty, 213
    Mona in the Promised Land, 209
    Monkey King, 196
    Night of the Chupacabras, 217
    Of Flesh & Spirit, 298
New York City, Hispanic Americans
    Breath, Eyes, Memory, 319
    Down in the Subway, 317

The Magic Shell, 343
The Marks of Birth, 341
Night of the Chupacabras, 337
New York State
  Like Sisters on the Homefront, 137 Af
  Raven in a Dove House, 96 Af
night riders
  Forty Acres and Maybe a Mule,
    109 Af
  Run Away Home, 75 Af
nightspots, rough
  A Blessing in Disguise, 127 Af
  The Gettin Place, 126 Af
noodlehead stories
  Juan Bobo, 372 H
North Carolina
  Music from a Place Called Half Moon,
    466 N
  Pushing the Bear, 450 N
  Sound the Jubilee, 38 Af
  The Sunday Outing, 101 Af
  The Wagon, 64 Af
North Dakota
  The Bingo Palace, 442 N
  The Grass Dancer, 469 N
Northern Pueblo Indians
  *Race with Buffalo, and Other Native
    American Stories for Young Readers*,
    544
North Star
  Cezanne Pinto, 125 Af
Northwest Territories
  Far North, 456 N
Norwegians
  The Trickster and the Troll, 473 N
notebooks
  From the Notebooks of Melanin Sun,
    139 Af
  Jazmin's Notebook, 42 Af
nunneries, Cuba
  The Bloody Waters, 323 H

Oakland, California
  Fall Secrets, 12 Af
  Run for Your Life, 71 Af
Oak Ridge, Tennessee
  Something Terrible Happened, 104 Af
Ocean King
  The Treasure Chest, 279 As

ogres
  Belching Hill, 256 As
Ohio
  Gone from Home, 57 Af
  I Hadn't Meant to Tell You This,
    140 Af
  A School for Pompey Walker, 114 Af
  Songs of Faith, 60 Af
Ohio Territory
  The Beaded Moccasins, 441 N
Ojibwa (Chippewa) Indians
  The Bingo Palace, 442
  Dogwolf, 431
  Follow the Stars, 536
  The Legend of Sleeping Bear, 540
  The Light People, 453
  Manabozho's Gifts, 506
  The Manitous, 516
  Sootface, 531
  The Windigo's Return, 543
Oklahoma
  Faces in the Moon, 421 N
  Flutie, 448 N
  I Have Heard of a Land, 130
  The Long March, 444
old persons
  See also grandfathers; grandfathers and
    granddaughters; grandfathers and
    grandsons; grandfathers, great;
    grandmothers;
  grandmothers and granddaughters;
    grandmothers and grandsons;
  grandmothers, black, and granddaugh-
    ters, white; grandmothers,
  great; grandparents and grandchildren.
old persons, African Americans
  City Green, 32
  The Old Cotton Blues, 35
  The Sunday Outing, 101
  What's in Aunt Mary's Room?, 54
old persons, Asian Americans
  April and the Dragon Lady, 221
  The Beggar's Magic, 247
  Candle in the Wind, 232
  The Cricket Warrior, 247
  The Imp That Ate My Homework, 241
  Mr. Pak Buys a Story, 252
  Tiger Woman, 284

old persons, Hispanic Americans
  A Day's Work, 310
  Off and Running, 361
  Tio Armando, 327
old persons, Native Americans
  The Boy Who Dreamed of an Ocean, 432
  Crossing the Starlight Bridge, 462
  Doesn't Fall Off His Horse, 479
  Far North, 456
  Guardian of the Hills, 475
  The Last Rainmaker, 447
  The Light People, 453
  Prophecy Rock, 460
  Sees Behind Trees, 438
  The Window, 439
Olympics
  Run for Your Life, 71 Af
Oneida Indians
  Phildelphia Flowers, 560
onions
  Buried Onions, 357 H
Opata Indians
  The Flower in the Skull, 302
oral tradition, African-American collections
  African-American Literature, 257
  Her Stories, 147
  How Sweet the Sound, 151
  The Last Tales of Uncle Remus, 150
  A Ring of Tricksters, 148
  When Birds Could Talk & Bats Could Sing, 149
oral tradition, African-American single stories
  Brer Tiger and the Big Wind, 146
  The Hired Hand, 155
  John Henry, 152
  Tailypo, 154
  Tops & Bottoms, 156
oral tradition, Asian collections
  Asian Tales and Tellers, 276
  Buddha Stories, 248
  The Ch'i-lin Purse, 251
  Chinese Folktales, 253
  The Dragon's Tale and Other Animal Fables of the Chinese Zodiac, 249
  Five Heavenly Emperors, 290
  Hearsay, 266

  Maples in the Mist, 295
  Mysterious Tales of Japan, 263
  One Hand Clapping, 264
oral tradition, Asian single stories
  The Beggar's Magic, 247
  Belching Hill, 256
  Brother Rabbit, 255
  Buddha, 248
  Buddha, 268
  Cat and Rat, 285
  China's Bravest Girl, 271
  The Cloudmakers, 269
  The Crane Wife, 245
  The Crystal Heart, 275
  Da Wei's Treasure, 247
  The Dragon Prince, 282
  Fa Mulan, 271
  The Farmer and the Poor God, 280.
  The Greatest Treasure, 250
  The Great Race, 246
  Jojofu, 278
  Just Rewards or Who Is That Man in the Moon & What's He Doing Up There Anyway?, 270
  The Khan's Daughter, 283
  Kongi and Potgi, 257
  The Legend of the Panda, 254
  Lily and the Wooden Bowl, 273
  Ling-Li and the Phoenix Fairy, 255
  Little Plum, 286
  The Long-Haired Girl, 267
  The Lost Horse, 287
  The Loyal Cat, 265
  The Magic Tapestry, 250
  The Making of Monkey King, 262
  Mouse Match, 288
  Mr. Pak Buys a Story, 252
  Night Visitors, 289
  Older Brother, Younger Brother, 260
  Pedro and the Monkey, 272
  The Stonecutter, 250
  The Stone Lion, 274
  Ten Suns, 261
  The Treasure Chest, 279
  Tsubu the Little Snail, 281
  The Two Brothers, 259
  Wan Hu Is in the Stars, 244
  The Wise Old Woman, 277

oral tradition, Hispanic collections
  Cuentos de Cuanto Hay, 374
  De Colores and Other Latin-American Folk Songs for Children, 384
  Juan Bobo, 372
  Senor Cat's Romance and Other Favorite Stories from Latin America, 376
  The Song of el Coqui and Other Tales of Puerto Rico, 382
  Tell Me a Cuento/Cuentame Un Story, 378
  Watch Out for Clever Women!/¡Cuidado con las Mujeres Astutas!, 379
oral tradition, Hispanic single stories
  Barrio Streets Carnival Dreams, 389
  The Bossy Gallito/El Gallo de Bodas, 375
  The Golden Flower, 381
  The Little Red Ant and the Great Big Crumb, 373
  The Little Seven-Colored Horse, 386
  Paco and the Witch, 385
  The Race of Toad and Deer, 383
  A Spoon for Every Bite, 377
  Where There's A Will, There's A Way/ Donde Hay Ganas, Hay Manas, 380
oral tradition, Native-American Indian collections
  Between Earth and Sky, 490
  Bones in the Basket, 537
  Children of the Morning Light, 518
  Coming to Light, 534
  Coyote Walks on Two Legs, 511
  The Deetkatoo, 487
  The Echoes of the Elders, 521
  Four Ancestors, 491
  The Girl Who Married the Moon, 493
  How Chipmunk Got Tiny Feet, 513
  How Rabbit Tricked Otter and Other Cherokee Trickster Stories, 527
  How the World Was Saved & Other Native American Tales, 509
  In a Circle Long Ago, 539
  Manabozho's Gifts, 506
  The Manitous, 516
  Ojibway Heritage, 516
  On the Road of Stars, 488

  Race with Buffalo, and Other Native American Stories for Young Readers, 544
  Skunny Wundy, 498
  The Spirit of the Cedar People, 521
  Touching the Distance, 535
  The Tree Is Older Than You Are, 522
  Wearing the Morning Star, 536
  The White Deer and Other Tales Told by the Lenape, 479
oral tradition, Native-American Indian single stories
  Coyote, 519
  Coyote and the Fire Stick, 504
  Coyote and the Laughing Butterflies, 538
  Coyote in Love, 496
  Cuckoo, 497
  Dance of the Sacred Circle, 524
  Eagle Boy, 512
  The Eagle's Song, 525
  The Fifth and Final Sun, 507
  Follow the Stars, 526
  The Girl Who Lived with the Bears, 505
  Gluskabe and the Four Wishes, 492
  The Great Buffalo Race, 498
  How Thunder and Lightning Came to Be, 510
  How Turtle's Back Was Cracked, 528
  The Legend of Mackinac Island, 540
  The Legend of Sleeping Bear, 540
  The Legend of the White Buffalo Woman, 503
  The Legend of the Windigo, 529
  The Magic of Spider Woman, 495
  The Magic Weaver of Rugs, 523
  Musicians of the Sun, 520
  Old Bag of Bones, 533
  Owl Eyes, 499
  People of Corn, 500
  The Precious Gift, 515
  Rabbit and the Moon, 542
  The Rainbow Bridge, 541
  Sootface, 531
  The Story of Blue Elk, 514
  The Story of the Milky Way, 494

The Tale of Rabbit and Coyote, 517
The Tree That Rains, 486
Two Bad Boys, 508
Two Bear Cubs, 532
Uncegila's Seventh Spot, 530
The Windigo's Return, 543
Oregon
   Coyote in Love, 496
orphans
   An Mei's Strange and Wondrous Journey, 220
   Jip His Story, 93
   Tiger's Tail, 215
   The Two Brothers, 259
Osage Indians
   Bones in the Basket, 537
Otomoaco Indians
   Indio, 446
otters
   The Path of Quiet Elk, 480 N
   The Precious Gift, 515 N
The Oval
   The Wedding, 136 Af
owls
   Owl Eyes, 499
oxen
   The Dragon's Tale and Other Animal Fables of the Chinese Zodiac, 249
   The Great Race, 246

Pacific Northwest Indians
   Circle Within a Circle, 457
   Coyote and the Fire Stick, 504
   The Eagle's Song, 525
   The Echoes of the Elders, 521
   The Girl Who Lived with the Bears, 505
Pacific Ocean
   The Island-below-the-Star, 227 As
   The Wave of the Sea-Wolf, 485 N
Pahana
   Prophecy Rock, 460 N
painters
   Chickens! Chickens!, 103 Af
   Jubilee Journey, 81 Af
   The Poison Place, 72 Af
   The Road Home, 451 N
Panamanian Americans
   Marisol and Magdalena, 313 H

pandas
   The Legend of the Panda, 254 As
pan dulce (sweet bread)
   Tomas and the Library Lady, 346 H
pants
   Poppa's New Pants, 80 Af
paper, making of
   The Cloudmakers, 269 As
paper routes
   The Adventures of Sparrowboy, 98 Af
   Jungle Dogs, 228 As
parades, Halloween
   Celie and the Harvest Fiddler, 37 Af
parks
   No Place, 326 H
parties
   Candle in the Wind, 232 As
   Carousel, 28 Af
   ¡Fiesta!, 325 H
   The Gumma Wars, 48 Af
Paterson, New Jersey
   An Island Like You, 348 H
   The Year of Our Revolution, 349 H
pawnshops
   Little Lil and the Swing-Singing Sax, 40 Af
Peale's Museum
   The Poison Place, 72 Af
Pearl Harbor
   Under the Blood-Red Sun, 329 As
pears
   The Beggar's Magic, 247
peddlers
   Hearsay, 266
Pennsylvania
   The Beaded Moccasins, 441 N
   Dark Shade, 435 N
   Singing in the Comeback Choir, 19 Af
   The Sunday Outing, 101 Af
Penobscot Indians
   Crossing the Starlight Bridge, 462 N
period fiction, African Americans
   The Bat Boy and His Violin, 30
   Easter Parade, 41
   Granddaddy's Gift, 83
   Mississippi Chariot, 111
   Moriah's Pond, 123
   Roll of Thunder, Hear My Cry, 129

Rum-a-Tum-Tum, 184
The Sunday Outing, 101
*The Watsons Go to Birmingham—
   1963*, 29
The Well, 129
period fiction, Asian Americans
   Heroes, 219
   Mona in the Promised Land, 209
period fiction, Hispanic Americans
   Firefly Summer, 305
   Frida Maria, 336
   From Amigos to Friends, 322
   Jesse, 360
   To a Widow with Children, 321
   The Year of Our Revolution, 349
period fiction, Native-American Indians
   Cloud Chamber, 436
   The Grass Dancer, 469
   Guardian of the Hills, 475
   Guests, 437
   The Last Rainmaker, 447
Peter Pan Program
   From Amigos to Friends, 322 H
Petersburg, Virginia
   Across the Lines, 106 Af
Philadelphia
   Cezanne Pinto, 125 Af
   Losing Absalom, 92 Af
   Singing in the Comeback Choir, 19 Af
   The Sunday Outing, 101 Af
phoenix
   Ling-Li and the Phoenix Fairy,
      255 As
photographers
   Crazy Weekend, 359 H
   Havana Thursdays, 365 H
   Spirits of the Ordinary, 303 H
photographic illustrations
   Angel to Angel, 186 Af
   Arias in Silence, 188
   It's Raining Laughter, 175 Af
   One Fall Day, 3 Af
   One Hot Summer Day, 27 Af
physiognotrace
   The Poison Place, 72
picnics
   Freedom's Gifts, 134 Af
   Knoxville, Tennessee, 168 Af

My Navajo Sister, 471 N
Nappy Hair, 50 Af
picture-story books, alphabet and count-
   ing
   Ashley Bryan's ABC, 160 Af
   ¡Fiesta!, 325 H
   Gathering the Sun, 301 H
   The Path of Quiet Elk, 480 N
   Turtle Island ABC, 451 N
   Uno, Dos, Tres, 408 H
picture-story books, biographical
   Bill Pickett, 94 Af
   Minty, 119 Af
picture-story books, fantasy, African
   Americans
   The Adventures of Sparrowboy, 98
   Carousel, 28
   Celie and the Harvest Fiddler, 37
   The Foot Warmer and the Crow, 22
   Harvey Potter's Balloon Farm, 89
   One Fall Day, 3
picture-story books, fantasy, Asian Amer-
   icans
   Is That Josie?, 223
picture-story books, fantasy, Hispanic
   Americans
   Benito's Dream Bottle, 347
   Chato's Kitchen, 358
   Down in the Subway, 317
   *Old Letivia and the Mountain of Sor-
      rows*, 345
   *Prietita and the Ghost Woman/Prietita
      y la Llorona*, 304
picture-story books, fantasy, Native-
   American Indians
   Beardream, 455
   Grandmother's Pigeon, 443
   How the Indians Bought the Farm, 478
   Little Coyote Runs Away, 476
   The Lost Boy and the Monster, 476
   The Wave of the Sea-Wolf, 485
picture-story books, historical, African
   Americans
   Ebony Sea, 121
   I Have Heard of a Land, 130
   Our People, 79
   Papa Tells Chita a Story, 53
   Pink and Say, 102

A Place Called Freedom, 115
A School for Pompey Walker, 114
Seminole Diary, 63
The Wagon, 64
Wagon Train, 143
picture-story books, historical, Asian
    Americans
Heroes, 219
So Far from the Sea, 194
picture-story books, historical, Native-
    American Indians
Cheyenne Again, 428
Doesn't Fall Off His Horse, 479
The Long March, 444
picture-story books, in verse, African
    Americans
Angels, 172
Ashley Bryan's ABC, 160
Carol of the Brown King, 161
Cherish Me, 190
The Creation, 180
Daddy, Daddy, Be There, 159
For the Love of the Game, 173
The Genie in the Jar, 167
Greetings, Sun, 166
Harlem, 187
Hoops, 162
Knoxville, Tennessee, 168
Lift Ev'ry Voice and Sing, 181
Meet Danitra Brown, 176
Messey Bessey's School Desk, 183
No Mirrors in My Nana's House, 158
Rum-a-Tum-Tum, 184
The Sun Is So Quiet, 171
Train, 189
picture-story books, in verse, Hispanic
    Americans
The Desert Is My Mother, 405
Listen to the Desert/Oye al desierto,
    406
This Big Sky, 407
Uno, Dos, Tres, 408
picture-story books in verse, Native-
    American Indians
Northwoods Cradle Song, 561
picture-story books, period, African
    Americans
The Bat Boy and His Violin, 30

Bebop-A-Do-Walk!, 43
Easter Parade, 41
Granddaddy's Gift, 83
Ma Dear's Aprons, 73
The Sunday Outing, 101
picture-story books, period, Asian Ameri-
    cans
Bebop-A-Do-Walk!, 206
The Island-below-the-Star, 227
picture-story books, period, Hispanic
    Americans
*Calling the Doves/El Canto de las Po-
    loma*, 329
Frida Maria, 336
picture-story books, period, Native-
    American Indians
Cheyenne Again, 428
Home to Medicine Mountain, 470
picture-story books, realistic, African
    Americans
The Adventures of Sugar and Junior,
    77
Big Meeting, 141
Bus Ride, 82
Busy Bea, 105
By the Dawn's Early Light, 1
Can You Dance, Dalila?, 69
Chickens! Chickens!, 103
City Green, 32
Creativity, 124
Down the Road, 117
Fireflies for Nathan, 90
Freedom's Gifts, 134
Jamaica's Blue Marker, 47
JoJo's Flying Side Kick, 99
*Louise's Gift or What Did She Give
    Me That For?*, 122
*May'naise Sandwiches & Sunshine
    Tea*, 7
Nappy Hair, 50
Off to School, 5
The Old Cotton Blues, 35
One Hot Summer Day, 27
Papa's Stories, 62
Poppa's New Pants, 80
Smoky Night, 13
Your Move, 14

picture-story books, realistic, Asian
Americans
An Mei's Strange and Wondrous Jour-
ney, 220
Fishing Sunday, 210
The Last Dragon, 224
Luka's Quilt, 204
My Father's Boat, 203
One Afternoon, 207
So Far from the Sea, 194
picture-story books, realistic, Hispanic
Americans
Abuelita's Heart, 318
The Adventures of Sugar and Junior,
340
Big Bushy Mustache, 355
Calling the Doves/El Canto de las Po-
lomas, 329
Carlos, Light the Farolito, 315
Chave's Memories, 320
A Day's Work, 310
Gathering the Sun, 301
Hairs, 316
Jalapena Bagels, 369
La Mariposa, 331
Mama Provi and the Pot of Rice, 352
Pepita Talks Twice/Pepita Habla Dos
Veces, 335
Tio Armando, 327
Tomas and the Library Lady, 346
Tonio's Cat, 311
The Tortilla Factory, 350
Tortillas and Lullabies, 351
picture-story books, realistic, Native-
American Indians
The Birchbark House, 443
The Boy Who Dreamed of an Acorn,
432
Full Worm Moon, 458
My Navajo Sister, 471
Red Bird, 463
The Shepherd Boy, 445
pigeons
Grandmother's Pigeon, 443 N
Under the Blood-Red Sun, 229 As
pigs
Belching Hill, 256 As
The Great Race, 246 As

Juan Bobo, 372 H
The Old Man and His Door, 362 H
pilgrimages
A Sunburned Prayer, 366 H
pioneers, black women
I Have Heard of a Land, 130 Af
The Wagon Train, 143 Af
Pipestone Quarry National Monument
The Legend of the White Buffalo
Woman, 513 N
pirates
The Twins, the Pirates, and the Battle
of New Orleans, 112 Af
plastic surgery
Hiroshima, 240 As
playgrounds
The Fred Field, 15 Af
Playing the Dozens
The Meanest Thing to Say, 26 Af
plays
Big Bushy Mustache, 355 H
The Secret Super Power of Marco,
138 Af
Plumed Serpent
People of Corn, 510 N
poetry anthologies, African Americans
African-American Literature, 192
African American Literature, 193
Ashley Bryan's ABC of African Ameri-
can Poetry, 160
Hold Christmas in Your Heart, 177
How Sweet the Sound, 178
I, Too, Sing America, 163
Shimmy Shimmy Shimmy Like My Sis-
ter Kate, 170
Soul Looks Back in Wonder, 165
poetry anthologies, Asian Americans
Another Way to Dance, 293
Asian American Literature, 300
Maples in the Mist, 295
Returning a Borrowed Tongue, 291
poetry anthologies, Hispanic Americans
Barrio Streets Carnival Dreams, 389
Cool Salsa, 390
Currents from the Dancing River, 396
Daughters of the Fifth Sun, 400
De Colores and Other Latin-American
Folk Songs for Children, 384

El Coro, 394
¡Floricanto Si!, 401
Hispanic American Literature, 398
Paper Dance, 392
Touching the Fire, 397
poetry anthologies, Native-American Indians
The Earth Under Sky Bear's Feet, 547
Four Ancestors, 548
Native American Literature, 559
On the Road of Stars, 546
Touching the Distance, 556
Wearing the Morning Star, 557
poetry by individual poets, African Americans
Angels, 172
Angel to Angel, 186
Arias in Silence, 188
Black Feelings, Black Talk, Black Judgement, 168, 169
Blues, 169
Carol of the Brown King, 161
Cherish Me, 190
Cotton Candy on a Rainy Day, 169
The Creation, 180
Daddy, Daddy, Be There, 159
The Darker Face of the Earth, 164
A Dime a Dozen, 174
For the Love of the Game, 173
The Genie in the Jar, 167
Gingerbread Days, 191
God's Trombones, 180
Greetings, Sun, 166
Harlem, 187
Honey, I Love, 172
Hoops, 162
It's Raining Laughter, 175
Knoxville, Tennessee, 168
Lift Ev'ry Voice and Sing, 181
Love Poems, 169
Meet Danitra Brown, 176
Messey Bessey's School Desk, 183
Mother Love, 164
My House, 169
No Mirrors in My Nana's House, 158
On the Bus with Rosa Parks, 164
The Other Side, 179
The Poet's World, 164
Re: Creation, 167, 169

Rum-a-Tum-Tum, 184
The Selected Poems of Nikki Giovanni, 169
Skin Deep and Other Teenage Reflections, 185
The Sun Is So Quiet, 171
Those Who Ride the Night Winds, 169
Train, 189
The Weather That Kills, 182
The Women and the Men, 169
poetry by individual poets, Asian Americans
Dragonfly, 294
Fallout, 297
The Folding Cliffs, 296
Good Luck Gold and Other Poems, 299
Of Flesh & Spirit, 298
The Phoenix Gone, The Terrace Empty, 292
The Rainbow Hand, 299
A Suitcase of Seaweed and Other Poems, 299
poetry by individual poets, Hispanic Americans
Agua Santa, 402
Aunt Carmen's Book of Practical Saints, 403
Bad Alchemy, 399
Black Hair, 413
Border-Crosser with a Lamborghini Dream, 329
Canto familiar, 411
City of Coughing and Dead Radiators, 395
De Colores and Other Latin-American Folk Songs for Children, 409
The Elements of San Joaquin, 413
From the Bellybutton of the Moon and Other Summer Poems/Del Ombligo de la Luna y otros poemas de verano, 387
Imagine the Angels of Bread, 395
I Used to Be a Superwoman, 415
Junior College, 412
Latino Rainbow, 393
Laughing Tomatoes and Other Spring Poems/Jitomates Risuenos y otros poemas de primavera, 388

Listen to the Desert/Oye al desierto,
    406
Loose Woman, 391
New and Selected, 413
*Reaching for the Mainland and Se-
    lected New Poems,* 410
Releasing Serpents, 416
Restless Serpents, 416
Super-Eight Movies, 413
The Tale of Sunlight, 413
This Big Sky, 4007
Uno, Dos, Tres, 408
Where Sparrows Work Hard, 413
You Come Singing, 414
poetry by individual poets, Native-
    American Indians
After and Before the Lightning,
    554
Blue Horses Rush In, 558
Bone Dance, 555
Coyote Walks on Two Legs, 550
In the Bear's House, 464
The Mad Painter Poems, 553
*Navajo Visions and Voices Across the
    Mesa,* 545
Northwoods Cradle Song, 561
On Second Thought, 552
Philadelphia Flowers, 560
Songs for the Seasons, 551
Star Quilt, 560
The Woman Who Fell from the Sky,
    549
poets, Chinese
Wan Hu Is in the Stars, 244 As
poets, youthful
Hang a Thousand Trees with Ribbons,
    108 Af
Jazmin's Notebook, 42 Af
poisons
The Ghost Fox, 239 AS
The Poison Place, 72 Af
Pokonoket (Wampanoag) Indians
The Children of the Morning Light,
    518
political oppression
From Amigos to Friends, 322 H
Jumping Off to Freedom, 307 H
The Marks of Birth, 341 H

Women Don't Need to Write, 371 H
You Come Singing, 414 H
Polynesians
The Island-below-the-Star, 227 As
ponds
Moriah's Pond, 123 Af
poor farms
Jip His Story, 93 Af
porcupines
Guests, 437 N
pornography
No Physical Evidence, 214 As
potato famine
The Long March, 444 N
potlach
Far North, 456 N
Powhatan Indians
War Woman, 434 N
powwows
The Grass Dancer, 469 N
Red Bird, 463 N
prayers
A Sunburned Prayer, 366 H
predestination
The Two Brothers, 259 As
pregnancy, unmarried
America's Dream, 354 H
Babylon Boyz, 85 Af
Like Sisters on the Home Front, 127
    Af
Push, 116 Af
Tryin' to Sleep in the Bed You Made,
    31 Af
prejudice, against African Americans
Brothers and Sisters, 18
Bus Ride, 82
Coffee Will Make You Black, 120
Hold Fast to Dreams, 95
Jubilee Journey, 81
Mississippi Chariot, 111
Moriah's Pond, 123
Run Away Home, 75
Run for Your Life, 71
Slam!, 87
Something Terrible Happened, 104
Spite Fences, 68
The Wedding, 136
The Well, 129

prejudice, against Asian Americans
  Another Way to Dance, 293
  Candle in the Wind, 232
  Good Luck Gold And Other Poems, 299
  Heroes, 219
  The Necessary Hunger, 226
  Necessary Roughness, 216
  The Phoenix Gone, The Terrace Empty, 292
  Returning a Borrowed Tongue, 291
  Saying Goodbye, 218
  Smoky Night, 13
  Snow Falling on Cedars, 205
  Song Lee and the "I hate you" Notes, 212
  Songs My Mother Taught Me, 236
  Under the Blood-Red Sun, 229
prejudice, against dark-skinned by light-skinned people
  The Wedding, 136 Af
prejudice, against females
  April and the Dragon Lady, 221 As
  Brothers and Sisters, 18 Af
  Candle in the Wind, 232 As
  Of Flesh & Spirit, 298 As
prejudice, against Hispanic Americans
  Buried Onions, 357
  Currents from the Dancing River, 324
  Jesse, 360
  You Come Singing, 414
prejudice, against mixed bloods
  Music from a Place Called Half Moon, 466 M
prejudice, against Native-American Indians
  Crossing the Starlight Bridge, 462
  Guardian of the Hills, 475
  Indian Killer, 418
  The Last Rainmaker, 447
  Monkey Secret, 449
  Music from a Place Called Half Moon, 466
  Native American Literature, 559
  The Woman Who Fell from the Sky, 549
prejudice, against whites
  Brothers and Sisters, 18 Af
  Coffee Will Make You Black, 120 Af
  Danger Zone, 66 Af
  The Wedding, 136 Af
prejudice, among African Americans
  Coffee Will Make You Black, 120
  Live at Five, 49
  The Richer, the Poorer, 135
  The Wedding, 136
prejudice, among Asian Americans
  The Case of the Lion Dance, 237
prejudice, among mixed bloods
  The Road Home, 451
prejudice. See also hate crimes.
pride in heritage, African Americans
  Can You Dance, Dalila?, 69
  Cherish Me, 290
  Creativity, 167
  The Genie in the Jar, 167
  Gingerbread Days, 191
  I, Too, Sing America, 163
  Jubilee Journey, 81
  Lift Ev'ry Voice and Sing, 181
  Our People, 79
  Soul Looks Back in Wonder, 165
  The World of Daughter McGuire, 144
pride in heritage, Asian Americans
  Another Way to Dance, 253
  The Cook's Family, 238
  Honor and Duty, 213
  The Last Dragon, 224
  Necessary Roughness, 216
  No Physical Evidence, 214
  Saying Goodbye, 218
  Songs My Mother Taught Me, 236
  Talent Night, 225
  Thief of Hearts, 243
  Tiger's Tail, 215
pride in heritage, Hispanic Americans
  El Coro, 394
  Daughters of the Fifth Sun, 342
  Fitting In, 306
  From the Bellybutton of the Moon and Other Summer Poems/Del Ombligo de la Luna y otros poemas de verano, 387
  I Used to Be a Superwoman, 415
  Latino Rainbow, 393
  Parrot in the Oven, 338

Releasing Serpents, 416
Sweet Fifteen, 309
pride in heritage, Native-American Indians
    Blue Horses Rush In, 481, 558
    Bone Dance, 555
    Cheyenne Again, 428
    Coyote Blue, 465
    Eagle Song, 426
    Faces in the Moon, 421
    Home to Medicine Mountain, 470
    The Light People, 453
    Native American Literature, 559
    *Navajo Visions and Voices Across the
        Mesa*, 545
    On Second Thought, 552
    Philadelphia Flowers, 560
    Prophecy Rock, 460
    Red Bird, 463
    Song of the Turtle, 420
    The Trickster and the Troll, 473
    War Woman, 434
    The Woman Who Fell from the Sky,
        549
priests
    The Last Dragon, 224 As
    The Loyal Cat, 265 As
    A Sunburned Prayer, 366 H
    *Where There's a Will, There's a Way/
        Donde Hay Ganas, Hay Manas*,
        380 H
prime ministers
    The Ch'i-lin Purse, 251 As
prisons, prisoners
    The Cloudmakers, 269 As
    The Edge of Heaven, 39 Af
    Iktomi and the Buzzard, 512 N
    No Physical Evidence, 215 As
    The Secret of Two Brothers, 328 H
    The Simple Truth, 2 Af
professional people
    Bone Game, 467 N
    Brothers and Sisters, 18 Af
    The Edge of Heaven, 39 Af
    The Flower in the Skull, 302 H
    Going Under, 364 H
    Havana Thursdays, 365 H
    Hold Fast to Dreams, 95 Af

How Stella Got Her Groove Back,
    76 Af
Hunger, 195 As
I Hadn't Meant to Tell You This,
    140 Af
Like Sisters in the Homefront, 137 Af
Live at Five, 49 Af
Singing in the Comeback Choir, 19 Af
The Wedding, 136 Af
*Yang the Third and Her Impossible
    Family*, 222 As
prostitutes, prostitution
    Comfort Woman, 211 As
    Easier to Kill, 133 Af
    No Physical Evidence, 214 As
    Tiger's Tail, 215 As
proverbs
    Don't Split the Pole, 128 Af
psychologists
    Maya's Divided World, 367 H
    Tommy Stands Alone, 368 H
Pueblo Indians
    The Story of Blue Elk, 514
    The World in Grandfather's Hands,
        477
Puerto Rican Americans
    Creativity, 124 H
    Down in the Subway, 317 H
    Imagine the Angels of Bread, 395 H
    An Island Like You, 348 H
    Mama Provi and the Pot of Rice,
        352 H
    A Matter of Pride and Other Stories,
        344 H
    Reaching for the Mainland, 410 H
    School Spirit, 330 H
    The Year of Our Revolution, 349 H
Puerto Rico
    America's Dream, 354 H
    Barrio Streets Carnival Dreams, 389 H
    Firefly Summer, 305 H
    The Golden Flower, 381 H
    Juan Bobo, 372 H
    A Matter of Pride and Other Stories,
        344 H
    Old Letivia and the Mountain of Sorrows, 345 H
    Paco and the Witch, 385 H

The Song of el Coqui and Other Tales of Puerto Rico, 382 H
The Year of Our Revolution, 349 H
Puget Sound
    Snow Falling on Cedars, 205 As
pumpkins
    The Golden Flower, 381 H
purses
    The Ch'i-lin Purse, 251 As

Quakers
    The Arrow Over the Door, 423 N
    The Captive, 45 Af
    Jip His Story, 93 Af
Quapaw Indians
    Guardian of the Hills, 475
quarrels, parents'
    The Cook's Family, 238 As
Queens, New York
    Like Sisters on the Homefront, 137 Af
question-and-answer books
    Is That Josie?, 223 As
quilts
    Luka's Quilt, 204 As
    Mister and Me, 51 Af
quinceaneras
    Sweet Fifteen, 309 H

rabbits
    Brer Rabbit and the Big Wind, 146 Af
    Brother Rabbit, 258 As
    The Great Race, 246 As
    How Rabbit Tricked Otter and Other Cherokee Trickster Stories, 537 N
    In a Circle Long Ago, 549 N
    Manabozho's Gifts, 516 N
    Rabbit and the Moon, 552 N
    A Ring of Tricksters, 148 Af
    Senor Cat's Romance and Other Favorite Stories from Latin America, 376
    The Tale of Rabbit and Coyote, 527 N
    Tops & Bottoms, 156 Af
rabbits, energizer
    Talent Night, 225 As
races
    The Big Bike Race, 8 Af
    Cat and Rat, 285 As

Coyote and the Fire Stick, 514 N
Frida Maria, 336 H
The Great Buffalo Race, 489 N
The Great Race, 246 As
The Race of Toad and Deer, 383 H
rafts
    Jumping Off to Freedom, 307 H
raids, horse
    Doesn't Fall Off His Horse, 479 N
    Spirit Horse, 417 N
rainmakers
    The Last Rainmaker, 447 N
rallies, for farm workers
    Jesse, 360 H
ranches
    Chave's Memories, 320 H
    Frida Maria, 336 H
    Nightland, 468 N
    Night of the Chupacabras, 217, 337 As, H
    The Road Home, 451 N
    Wolf, No Wolf, 422 N
"ranking"
    The Meanest Thing to Say, 26 Af
rape, attempted rape
    Breath, Eyes, Memory, 319 H
    The Flower in the Skull, 302 H
    Jazmin's Notebook, 42 Af
    Monkey King, 196 As
    No Physical Evidence, 214 As
    Push, 116 Af
rap music
    Talent Night, 225, As
Rastafarians
    Babylon Boyz, 85 Af
ratings, TV
    Live at Five, 49 Af
    Singing in the Comeback Choir, 19 Af
rats
    Cat and Rat, 285 As
    The Dragon's Tale and Other Animal Fables of the Chinese Zodiac, 249 As
    The Great Race, 246 As
    Lily and the Wooden Bowl, 273 As
Raven
    The Echoes of the Elders, 531 N
    In a Circle Long Ago, 549 N

Reconstruction, post–Civil War
    Forty Acres and Maybe a Mule,
      109 Af
    I Thought My Soul Would Rise and
      Fly, 46 Af
refugees
    Fitting In, 306 H
    From Amigos to Friends, 322 H
    Jumping Off to Freedom, 307 H
    The Marks of Birth, 341 H
religious sects
    Parable of the Talents, 17 Af
relocation camps. *See* internment camps.
removals, Native-American Indians
    How the Indians Bought the Farm, 478
    The Long March, 444
    On the Long Trail Home, 474
    Pushing the Bear, 450
    Runs with Horses, 429
reparations, for World War II internments
    Talent Night, 225 As
rescues
    Celou Sudden Shout, Idaho 1826,
      440 N
    Dark Passage, 484 N
    Dog People, 425 N
    Forged by Fire, 33 Af
    The Glory Field, 86 Af
    Pink and Say, 102 Af
    The Shepherd Boy, 445 N
reservation life
    The Antelope Wife, 442 N
    The Beet Queen, 442 N
    The Bingo Palace, 442 N
    Blue Horses Rush In, 481, 568 N
    Brave as a Mountain Lion, 472 N
    Dogwolf, 431 N
    The First Eagle, 454 N
    The Grass Dancer, 469 N
    House Made of Dawn, 464 N
    The Light People, 453 N
    Love Medicine, 442 N
    Prophecy Rock, 460 N
    Reservation Blues, 419 N
    Tales of Burning Love, 442 N
    Tracks, 442 N
responsibility, for siblings
    Forged by Fire, 33 Af

    Humming Whispers, 59 Af
    A Place to Call Home, 67 Af
restaurant openings
    The Case of the Lion Dance, 237 As
retarded persons
    Jip His Story, 93 Af
    Push, 116 Af
    Rattlebone, 21 Af
reunions, family
    Big Meeting, 141 Af
    Knoxville, Tennessee, 168 Af
    On the Long Trail Home, 474 N
    Running for Our Lives, 131 Af
    Second Cousins, 44 Af
Revolution, Cuban
    Bad Alchemy, 399 H
    Women Don't Need to Write, 371 H
rice
    Lily and the Wooden Bowl, 273 As
    Mama Provi and the Pot of Rice,
      352 H
    Manabozho's Gifts, 506 N
    Night Visitors, 289 As
rice paddles, magic
    Lily and the Wooden Bowl, 273 As
riddles
    The Freedom Riddle, 153 Af
    Touching the Distance, 535 N
Rio Seco, California
    The Gettin Place, 126 Af
riots, race
    The Gettin Place, 126 Af
    Smoky Night, 13 Af
rituals and ceremonies
    Beardream, 455 N
    Bone Game, 467 N
    Coyote Blue, 465 N
    The Deetkatoo, 487 N
    Eagle Boy, 522 N
    Far North, 456 N
    The Girl Who Lived with the Bears,
      515 N
    The Grass Dancer, 469 N
    The Magic of Spider Woman, 495 N
    The Peace Chief, 433 N
    Red Bird, 463 N
    Wearing the Morning Star, 546 N
Riverside, California
    Home to Medicine Mountain, 470 N

Roanoke Island
  Sound the Jubilee, 38 Af
robots
  Bug Park, 208 As
rock carvings
  Abuelita's Heart, 318 H
Rock Hounds
  April and the Dragon Lady, 221 As
rock music performers
  The Healing, 65 Af
  Reservation Blues, 419 N
rodeo riders
  Bill Pickett, 94 Af
  Billy, 358 H
romance novels
  Through the Storm, 56 Af
romances
  How Stella Got Her Groove Back, 76 Af
  Loverboys, 312 H
Roosevelt High School Series
  Maya's Divided World, 367 H
  Tommy Stands Alone, 368 H
roosters
  The Bossy Gallito/El Gallo de Bodas,
    375 H
  The Great Race, 246 As
  Tell Me a Cuento/Cuentame Un Story,
    378 H
Rosa Parks
  Bus Ride, 82 Af
Rosebud Reservation
  After and Before the Lightning, 554 N
roses
  Manabozho's Gifts, 506 N
Royal Highway
  Frida Maria, 336 H
royalty, African
  The Captive, 45 Af
  Through the Storm, 56 Af
Rumplestiltskin
  Paco and the Witch, 385 H
runaways, African American
  Bright Freedom's Song, 53
  The Captive, 45
  Cast Two Shadows, 107
  Cezanne Pinto, 125
  If You Please, President Lincoln, 110
  A Picture of Freedom, 74

Run Away Home, 75
  A School for Pompey Walker, 114
  The Secret Super Power of Marco, 138
  *The Twins, the Pirates, and the Battle
    of New Orleans*, 112
  Washington City Is Burning, 113
  The World of Daughter McGuire, 144
runaways, Asian Americans
  The Folding Cliffs, 296 As
runaways, Hispanic Americans
  America's Dream, 354
runaways, Native-American Indians
  Guests, 427
  Home to Medicine Mountain, 470
  Indio, 446
  Little Coyote Runs Away, 476
  On the Long Trail Home, 474
running, sport
  Run for Your Life, 71 Af
rural life
  Fireflies for Nathan, 90 Af
  Moriah's Pond, 123 Af
  See also farm life.

Sacramento, California
  No Physical Evidence, 214 As
Sacred Calf Pipe
  The Legend of White Buffalo Woman,
    503 N
sacred places, Native-American Indians
  Between Earth and Sky, 490
  Circle Within a Circle, 457
sailmakers
  The Crane Wife, 245 As
St. Louis, Missouri
  The Last Rainmaker, 447 N
St. Paul, Minnesota
  The Gumma Wars, 48 Af
  Live at Five, 49 Af
saints
  *Aunt Carmen's Book of Practical
    Saints*, 403 H
Salem, Massachusetts
  The Captive, 45 Af
Saltillo, Mexico
  Spirits of the Ordinary, 303 H
Samarkand
  The Cloudmakers, 269 As

sandal weavers
  The Farmer and the Poor God, 280 As
sand dunes
  The Legend of Sleeping Bear, 540 N
San Francisco, California
  Babylon Boyz, 85 Af
  The Case of the Lion Dance, 237 As
  The Cook's Family, 238 As
  Honor and Duty, 213 As
  How Stella Got Her Groove Back,
    76 Af
  The Imp That Ate My Homework,
    241 As
  Later, Gator, 242 As
  Thief of Hearts, 243 As
  The Weather That Kills, 182 Af
Santa Barbara, California
  Coyote Blue, 465 N
Santa Cruz, California
  Bone Game, 467 N
saxophones
  Little Lil and the Swing-Singing Sax,
    40 Af
scalps, of child
  The Beaded Moccasins, 441 N
Scarshill, New York
  Mona in the Promised Land, 209 As
schizophrenia
  Humming Whispers, 59 Af
school desks
  Messey Bessey's School Desk, 183 Af
school life, African Americans
  Creativity, 124
  A Different Beat, 12
  Egg-Drop Blues, 4
  Fall Secrets, 12
  Hold Fast to Dreams, 95
  Jamaica's Blue Marker, 47
  Messey Bessey's School Desk, 183
  The New One, 4
  Project Wheels, 4
  Push, 116
  Rattlebone, 21
school life, Asian Americans
  Gathering of Pearls, 199
  Honor and Duty, 213
  Jungle Dogs, 228
  The Necessary Hunger, 226

Saying Goodbye, 218
Song Lee and the Hamster Hunt, 212
Talent Night, 225
Thief of Hearts, 243
school life, Hispanic Americans
  Big Bushy Mustache, 355
  Billy, 353
  Fitting In, 306
  La Mariposa, 331
  No Place, 326
  Off and Running, 361
  Petty Crimes, 363
  School Spirit, 330
  Tommy Stands Alone, 368
school life, Native-American Indians
  Cheyenne Again, 428
  Crossing the Starlight Bridge, 462
  Eagle Song, 426
  Hawk Moon, 459
schools, for African-American ex-slaves
  Forty Acres and Maybe a Mule,
    109 Af
  A School for Pompey Walker, 114 Af
  Sound the Jubilee, 38 Af
schools, performing arts
  Fall Secrets, 12 Af
science fantasy
  Bug Park, 208 As
  What a Woman's Gotta Do, 23 Af
scientists
  The First Eagle, 454 N
  What a Woman's Gotta Do, 23 Af
Scouts, Cub
  So Far from the Sea, 194 As
seamstresses
  Mister and Me, 51 Af
  Sweet Fifteen, 309 H
sea serpents
  The Waters Between, 427 N
seasons
  After and Before the Lightning, 554 N
  Gingerbread Days, 191 Af
  Song of the Seasons, 551 N
  The Sun Is So Quiet, 170 Af
  The Tortilla Factory, 350 H
Seattle, Washington
  April and the Dragon Lady, 221 As
  Bug Park, 208 As

Indian Killer, 418 N
Yang the Third and Her Impossible Family, 222 As
Sea-Wolf Spirit
  The Wave of the Sea-Wolf, 485 N
secondhand dealers
  Spite Fences, 68 Af
seduction, child
  The Foreign Student, 200 As
self-esteem
  Cherish Me, 190 Af
  Fall Secrets, 12 Af
  Like Sisters on the Homefront, 137 Af
  La Mariposa, 331 H
  No Mirrors in My Nana's House, 158 Af
  No Place, 326 H
  Our People, 79 Af
  Soccer Cousins, 339 H
  Song of the Turtle, 420 N
self-mutilation
  Monkey King, 196 As
self-sacrifice, of gods
  The Fifth and Final Sun, 507 H
Seminole Indians
  The Secret of Two Brothers, 328 H
  Seminole Diary, 63 Af
Seneca Indians
  Four Ancestors, 491
  The Great Buffalo Race, 498
  The Peace Chief, 433
  Race with Buffalo, and Other Native American Stories for Young Readers, 544
series fiction
  The Bingo Palace, 442 N
  Black Betty, 84 Af
  Bloody Waters, 323 H
  Cloud Chamber, 436 N
  Easier to Kill, 133 Af
  Ernestine & Amanda, 6 Af
  The First Eagle, 454 N
  The Gumma Wars, 48 Af
  I Smell Honey, 100 Af
  Jamaica's Blue Marker, 47 Af
  Maya's Divided World, 367 H
  The Meanest Thing to Say, 26 Af
  Messey Bessey's School Desk, 183 Af

Song Lee and the Hamster Hunt, 212 As
Through the Storm, 56 Af
Tommy Stands Alone, 368 H
The Well, 129 Af
The Window, 439 N
Wolf, No Wolf, 422 N
servants, slow-witted
  Mr. Pak Buys a Story, 252 As
Sewanee, Tennessee
  The Foreign Student, 200 As
sexual abuse. *See* abuse.
sexual harassment
  Brothers and Sisters, 18 Af
shamans
  The Magic of Spider Woman, 495 N
  The Waters Between, 427 N
  Wolf, No Wolf, 422 N
shape changers
  The Ghost Fox, 239 As
  Tiger Woman, 284 As
sharecroppers
  Mississippi Chariot, 111 Af
  Off to School, 5 Af
sheep
  The Shepherd Boy, 445 N
Sheffield, Massachusetts
  Second Daughter, 132 Af
shekeres
  I Smell Honey, 100 Af
Shiprock, New Mexico
  Blue Horses Rush In, 568 N
ships, *Amistad*
  Amistad Rising, 20 Af
shoes, sneakers
  Creativity, 124 Af
shoplifters
  An Island Like You, 348 H
  Maya's Divided World, 367 H
  Petty Crimes, 363 H
  Your Move, 14 Af
short stories, anthologies, African Americans
  African-American Literature, 142
  African American Literature, 145
  Rites of Passage, 10
  A Treasury of African-American Christmas Stories, 24

short stories, anthologies, Asian Americans
   Asian American Literature, 234
   Into the Fire, 233
short stories, anthologies, Hispanic Americans
   Currents from the Dancing River, 324
   Daughters of the Fifth Sun, 342
   Hispanic American Literature, 332
short stories, anthologies, Native-American Indians
   Native American Literature, 482
   Song of the Turtle, 420
   Voice of the Turtle, 420
short stories, individual authors, African Americans
   Blood Child and Other Stories, 16
   Don't Split the Pole, 128
   Gone from Home, 57
   Haunts, 78
   Rattlebone, 21
   The Richer, the Poorer, 135
   Smiffy Blue, Ace Crime Detective, 88
   Some Love, Some Pain, Sometime, 25
   Sugarcane House and Other Stories About Mr. Fat, 11
short stories, individual authors, Asian Americans
   American Visa, 231
   Hunger, 195
   Saturday Night at the Pahala Theatre, 235
   Songs My Mother Taught Me, 236
short stories, individual authors, Hispanic Americans
   Fitting In, 306
   An Island Like You, 348
   Loverboys, 312
   A Matter of Pride and Other Stories, 344
   Petty Crimes, 363
   The Year of Our Revolution, 349
short stories, individual authors, Native-American Indians
   Blue Horses Rush In, 481
   Dog People, 425
   In the Bear's House, 464
   The Man Made of Words, 464
   Monkey Secret, 449

Shoshone Indians
   Celou Sudden Shout, Idaho 1826, 440
   Old Bag of Bones, 533
Siddhartha
   Buddha, 248 As
Sierra Leone
   Amistad Rising, 20 Af
sight, restored
   Uncegila's Seventh Spot, 530 N
singers
   Singing in the Comeback Choir, 19 Af
single-parent families
   Breath, Eyes, Memory, 319 H
   By the Dawn's Early Light, 1 Af
   Egg-Drop Blues, 4 Af
   From the Notebooks of Melanin Sun, 139
   How Stella Got Her Groove Back, 76
   I Hadn't Meant to Tell You This, 140 Af
   Ma Dear's Aprons, 73 Af
   Marisol and Magdalena, 313 H
   Push, 116 Af
   Raven in a Dove House, 96 Af
   The Window, 439 N
Sioux Indians. *See* Lakota Indians.
sisters
   Fall Secrets, 12 Af
   Humming Whispers, 59 Af
   The Hundred Secret Senses, 230 As
   Jazmin's Notebook, 42 Af
   Just Family, 9 Af
   Like Sisters on the Homefront, 137 Af
   Second Cousins, 44 Af
skunks
   The Bingo Palace, 442 N
Skunnee Wundee
   Race with Buffalo, and Other Native American Stories for Young People, 544 N
slaves, ex
   Cezanne Pinto, 125 Af
   Forty Acres and Maybe a Mule, 109 Af
   Freedom's Gifts, 134 Af
   If You Please, President Lincoln, 110 Af

Pink and Say, 102 Af
A Place Called Freedom, 115 Af
A School for Pompey Walker, 114 Af
Through the Storm, 56 Af
Wagon Train, 143 Af
slaves and slavery, African Americans
Across the Lines, 106
Amistad Rising, 20
Bright Freedom's Song, 52
The Captive, 45
Cast Two Shadows, 107
Cezanne Pinto, 125
Ebony Sea, 121
The Foot Warmer and the Crow, 22
The Freedom Riddle, 153
The Glory Field, 86
Hang a Thousand Trees with Ribbons, 108
I Thought My Soul Would Rise and Fly, 46
Jip His Story, 93
The Last Tales of Uncle Remus, 150
Minty, 119
A Picture Called Freedom, 74
A Place Called Freedom, 115
The Poison Place, 72
The River Where Blood Is Born, 55
Running for Our Lives, 131
A School for Pompey Walker, 114
Second Daughter, 132
Seminole Diary, 63
Second the Jubilee, 38
Through the Storm, 56
True North, 70
The Wagon, 64
slaves and slavery, Arabs
The Cloudmakers, 269 As
slaves and slavery, forced prostitution
Comfort Woman, 211 As
slaves and slavery, Native-American Indians
Dark Passage, 484 N
Walks Alone, 430 N
slaves and slavery, Native-American Indians to Spaniards
Indio, 446
Peace Chief, 433
War Woman, 434

slave smuggling
The Captive, 45 Af
Slavey Indians
Far North, 456
Sleeping Bear National Lakeshore
The Legend of Sleeping Bear, 540 N
sleep talking
The Foot Warmer and the Crow, 22 Af
smallpox
Indio, 446 N
small-town life
Blu's Hanging, 235 As
Firefly Summer, 305 H
Flutie, 448 N
Jungle Dogs, 228 As
Mississippi Chariot, 111 Af
Night of the Chupacabras, 217, 337 As, H
The Other Side, 179 Af
See also neighborhood life.
snails
The Precious Gift, 515 N
Tsubu the Little Snail, 281 As
Snake Indians
Spirit Horse, 417 N
snakes
The Dragon's Tale and Other Animal Fables of the Chinese Zodiac, 249 As
The Great Race, 246 As
Jojofu, 278 As
Wagon Train, 143 Af
soccer
Soccer Cousins, 339 H
social workers
Push, 116 Af
The Richer, the Poorer, 135 Af
Run for Your Life, 71 Af
soldiers
Across the Lines, 106 Af
Comfort Woman, 211 As
Dark Shade, 435 N
Memories of My Ghost Brother, 202 As
Night Visitors, 289 As
The Treasure Chest, 279 As
song and dance, origin of
The Eagle's Song, 525 N

songs
  The Crystal Heart, 275 As
  *De Colores and Other Latin-American
    Folk Songs for Children*, 409 H
  The Genie in the Jar, 167 Af
  Hold Christmas in Your Heart, 177 Af
  How Sweet the Sound, 151, 178 Af
  No Mirrors in My Nana's House,
    158 Af
  On the Road of Stars, 488 N
  Wearing the Morning Star, 536 N
Sonora, Mexico
  The Flower in the Skull, 302 H
  Night of the Chupacabras, 217, 337
    As, H
sorcerers
  Hearsay, 266 As
South Carolina
  A Blessing in Disguise, 127 Af
  Bright Freedom's Song, 52 Af
  Cast Two Shadows, 107 Af
  The Glory Field, 86 Af
  *I Thought My Soul Would Rise and
    Fly*, 46 Af
  The Wagon, 64 Af
South Dakota
  After and Before the Lightning, 554 N
South Korea
  Memories of My Ghost Brother,
    202 As
spacemen as ancestors
  What a Woman's Gotta Do, 23 Af
Spain
  Women Don't Need to Write, 371 H
Spaniards, in New World
  The Peace Chief, 433 N
  War Woman, 434 N
Spanish-American War
  Papa Tells Chita a Story, 53 Af
Spanish California
  Frida Maria, 336 H
Spanish-Cubans
  Women Don't Need to Write, 371 H
Spanish language, learning
  Marisol and Magdalena, 313 H
spelling bees
  Brave as a Mountain Lion, 472 N

spiders
  Brave as a Mountain Lion, 472 N
  A Ring of Tricksters, 148 Af
Spider Woman
  Blue Horses Rush In, 481 N
  The Magic of Spider Woman, 495, N
spirits
  Chinese Folktales, 253 As
  Coyote and the Fire Sticks, 504 N
  The Deetkatoo, 487 N
  The River Where Blood Is Born, 55 Af
Spokane/Coeur d'Alene Indians
  Reservation Blues, 419 N
spoons
  A Spoon for Every Bite, 377 H
sports fiction
  The Bat Boy and His Violin, 30 Af
  The Big Bike Race, 8 Af
  Danger Zone, 66 Af
  For the Love of the Game, 173 Af
  Hoops, 162 Af
  The Necessary Hunger, 226 As
  Necessary Roughness, 216 As
  Run for Your Life, 71 Af
  Saying Goodbye, 218 As
  Slam!, 87 Af
  See also specific sport.
springs
  The Long-Haired Girl, 267 As
stars
  Coyote in Love, 496 N
  The Crying for a Vision, 483 N
  Follow the Stars, 526 N
  The Story of the Milky Way, 494 N
  Wan Hu Is in the Stars, 244 As
statues
  The Long-Haired Girl, 267 As
  The Stone Lion, 274 As
steam drills
  John Henry, 152 Af
steel workers
  Eagle Song, 426 N
  Indian Killer, 418 N
stone creatures
  The Legend of the Windigo, 529 N
  The Windigo's Return, 543 N
stonecutters
  The Stonecutter, 250 As

street cries
  Carolina Shout!, 118 Af
  Rum-a-Tum-Tum, 184 Af
street crime
  A Blessing in Disguise, 127 Af
  Buried Onions, 357 H
  Memories of My Ghost Brother, 202 As
  Raven in a Dove House, 96 Af
street gangs
  Boys at Work, 356 H
  Buried Onions, 357 H
  Jesse, 360 H
  No Place, 326 H
  Parrot in the Oven, 338
  Petty Crimes, 363 H
  Your Move, 14 Af
strong men
  John Henry, 152 Af
subways
  Down in the Subway, 317 H
suicide attempts
  Monkey King, 196 As
  Tommy Stands Alone, 368 H
suicides
  Breath, Eyes, Memory, 319 H
  Ebony Sea, 121 Af
  Indian Killer, 418 N
  Memories of My Ghost Brother,
    202 As
  A Place to Call Home, 67 Af
  Reservation Blues, 419 N
sultans
  The Cloudmakers, 269 As
sun
  Ten Suns, 261 As
Sundays
  Fishing Sunday, 210 As
Supreme Court, United States
  Amistad Rising, 20 Af
  The Simple Truth, 2 Af
survival novels
  Far North, 456 N
  Jumping Off to Freedom, 307 H
  Spirit Horse, 417 N
  Walks Alone, 430 N
swallows, wounded
  Older Brother, Younger Brother,
    260 As

sweat house ceremony
  The Bingo Palace, 442 N
  Bone Game, 467 N
  The Grass Dancer, 469 N
Sweet Honey in the Rock
  No Mirrors in My Nana's House,
    158 Af
syrup, sugarcane
  Juan Bobo, 372 H

Tacoma, Washington
  Bug Park, 208 As
  The Window, 439 N
tae kwon do
  Saying Goodbye, 218 As
  See also karate.
tailors
  The Last Dragon, 224 As
tails
  Tailypo, 154 Af
Taino Indians
  The Golden Flower, 381 H
  *The Song of el Coqui and Other Tales
    of Puerto Rico*, 382 H
tall tales
  Harvey Potter's Balloon Farm, 89 Af
  Papa Tells Chita a Story, 53 Af
Tamaulipas, Mexico
  The Girl from Playa Blanca, 333 H
Tang Dynasty
  Maples in the Mist, 295 As
tapestries
  The Magic Tapestry, 250 As
tasks, impossible
  The Khan's Daughter, 283 As
  The Wise Old Woman, 277 As
Tatars
  Fa Mulan, 271 As
taxidermy
  The Poison Place, 72 Af
teenagers' concerns, poems
  Cool Salsa, 390 H
  *Skin Deep and Other Teenage Reflec-
    tions*, 185 H
Tekwaarathon
  Children of the Longhouse, 424 N
television talk shows
  Easier to Kill, 133 Af

Live at Five, 49 Af
Singing in the Comeback Choir,
    19 Af
Tennessee
    The Foreign Student, 200 As
    Knoxville, Tennessee, 168 Af
    Something Terrible Happened, 104 Af
tent shows
    The Last Rainmaker, 447 N
    *Sugarcane House and Other Stories
        About Mr. Fat*, 11 Af
Tewa Indians
    Coyote and the Laughing Butterflies,
        548 N
Texas
    Alicia's Treasure, 308 H
    Bill Pickett, 94 Af
    Cezanne Pinto, 125 Af
    Chave's Memories, 320 H
    Freedom's Gifts, 134 Af
    Hardscrub, 321 H
    Indio, 446 N
    Jubilee Journey, 81 Af
    *Prietita and the Ghost Woman/Prietita
        y la Llorna*, 304 H
    The Secret of Two Brothers, 328 H
    A Shroud in the Family, 321 H
    Spirits of the Ordinary, 303 H
    To a Widow with Children, 321 H
theaters, Chinese
    The Imp That Ate My Homework,
        241 As
theme parks
    Bug Park, 208 As
thunder, origin of
    *How Thunder and Lightning Came to
        Be*, 510 N
Tibet
    Of Flesh & Spirit, 298 As
    The Stone Lion, 274 As
tigers
    Brer Tiger and the Big Wind, 146 Af
    The Great Race, 246 As
Tlingit Indians
    The Eagle's Shadow, 461 N
    The Legend of the Windigo, 529 N
    The Wave of the Sea-Wolf, 485 N

toads
    The Race of Toad and Deer, 383 H
tortillas
    A Spoon for Every Bite, 377 H
    The Tortilla Factory, 350 H
    *Tortillas and Lullabies/Tortillas y can-
        cioncitas*, 351 H
totalitarian regimes
    From Amigos to Friends, 322 H
    Jumping Off to Freedom, 307 H
    The Marks of Birth, 341 H
track (sports)
    Run for Your Life, 71 Af
trade and traders
    The Beaded Moccasins, 441 N
    War Woman, 434 N
Trail of Tears
    The Long March, 444 N
    On the Long Trail Home, 474 N
    Pushing the Bear, 450 N
    Seminole Diary, 63 Af
trains
    Down in the Subway, 317 H
    The Sunday Outing, 101 Af
    Train, 189 Af
trances
    Comfort Woman, 211 As
transformations
    The Eagle's Song, 525 N
    Tiger Woman, 284 As
    Tsubu the Little Snail, 281 As
    Uncegila's Seventh Spot, 530 N
translators, youthful
    *Pepita Talks Twice/Pepita Habla Dos
        Veces*, 335 H
transvestites
    The Gettin Place, 126 Af
trappers
    Celou Sudden Shout, Idaho 1826, 440 N
treasures
    Night Visitors, 289 As
    The Treasure Chest, 279 As
Treetown
    The Gettin Place, 126 Af
trials
    The Captive, 45 Af
    No Physical Evidence, 214 As

The Simple Truth, 2 Af
Snow Falling on Cedars, 205 As
tricksters, African Americans
  Brer Tiger and the Big Wind, 146
  The Foot Warmer and the Crow, 22
  A Ring of Tricksters, 148
  *Sugarcane House and Other Stories
    About Mr. Fat*, 11
  Tops & Bottoms, 156
tricksters, Asian Americans
  Brother Rabbit, 258
  The Making of Monkey King, 262
  Pedro and the Monkey, 272
tricksters, Hispanic Americans
  Cuentos de Cuanto Hay, 374
  *Senor Cat's Romance and Other Fa-
    vorite Stories from Latin America*,
    376
  *Watch Out for Clever Women!/¡Cui-
    dado can las Mujeres Astutas!*, 379
tricksters, Native-American Indians
  The Children of the Morning Light,
    518
  Coyote, 519
  Coyote and the Fire Stick, 504
  Coyote and the Laughing Butterflies,
    538
  Coyote Blue, 465
  Coyote in Love, 496
  Coyote Walks on Two Legs, 511, 550
  Eagle Boy, 512
  The Echoes of the Elders, 521
  *How Rabbit Tricked Otter and Other
    Cherokee Trickster Stories*, 527
  How Turtle's Back Was Cracked,
    528
  Iktomi and the Buzzard, 502
  In a Circle Long Ago, 539
  Manabozho's Gifts, 506
  The Manitous, 516
  Old Bag of Bones, 533
  The Tale of Rabbit and Coyote, 517
  The Trickster and the Troll, 473
trolleys
  The Sunday Outing, 101 Af
trolls, Norwegian
  The Trickster and the Troll, 473 N

trumpets
  Willie Jerome, 34 Af
Tsimshian Indians
  How Chipmunk Got Tiny Feet, 513 N
Tubman, Harriet
  Minty, 119 Af
  Through the Storm, 56 Af
  True North, 70 Af
Tucson, Arizona
  The Flower in the Skull, 302 H
Tulsa, Oklahoma
  The Gettin Place, 126 Af
turnips
  The Long-Haired Girl, 267 As
turtles
  Don't Split the Pole, 128 Af
  How Turtle's Back Was Cracked,
    528 N
  *Old Letivia and the Mountain of Sor-
    rows*, 345 H
  The Path of Quiet Elk, 480 N
  The Precious Gift, 515 N
  A Ring of Tricksters, 148 Af
Tuskegee Institute
  Run Away Home, 75 Af
tutors
  A Picture of Freedom, 74 Af
twins, African Americans
  Egg-Drop Blues, 4
  The Fred Field, 15
  Solo Girl, 97
  *The Twins, the Pirates, and the Battle
    of New Orleans*, 112
twins, Asian Americans
  Necessary Roughness, 216
twins, Hispanic Americans
  Havana Thursdays, 365
  Spirits of the Ordinary, 303
  Women Don't Need to Write, 371
twins, Native-American Indians
  Children of the Longhouse, 424
  Sees Behind Trees, 438
  Uncegila's Seventh Spot, 530
  War Woman, 434
Two Rivers Indian Reservation
  Crossing the Starlight Bridge, 462 N

tyrants
  The Marks of Birth, 341 H
  The Treasure Chest, 279 As
Tzotzil Indians
  The Tree Is Older Than You Are,
    522

Ugly Old Woman
  Uncegila's Seventh Spot, 530 N
Uncegila
  Uncegila's Seventh Spot, 530 N
Uncle Remus
  The Last Tales of Uncle Remus,
    150 Af
uncles and nephews
  Crazy Weekend, 359 H
  Heroes, 219 As
  Honor and Duty, 213 As
uncles and nieces
  Faces in the Moon, 421 N
  Little Lil and the Swing-Singing Sax,
    40 Af
  Night of the Chupacabras, 337 H
  Tio Armando, 327 H
Underground Railroad
  Bright Freedom's Song, 52 Af
  Cezanne Pinto, 125 Af
  A Picture of Freedom, 74 Af
  Running for Our Lives, 131 Af
  True North, 70 Af
University of California
  Bone Game, 467 N
University of the South
  The Foreign Student, 200 As
Ute Indians
  Beardream, 455 N

vampires
  Night of the Chupacabras, 217, 337
    As, H
vandalism
  Smoky Night, 13 Af
Vermont
  Jip His Story, 93 Af
veterinarians
  Dark Shade, 435 N
Victorio
  Walks Alone, 430 N

Vietnam
  The Crystal Heart, 275 As
Vietnamese Americans
  My Father's Boat, 203 As
Vietnam War
  Heroes, 219 As
  Memories of My Ghost Brother,
    202 As
Vigilance Committee
  Cezanne Pinto, 125 Af
village life, Asian Americans
  American Visa, 231
  The Stone Lion, 274
village life, Hispanic Americans
  The Flower in the Skull, 302
village life, Native-American Indians
  The Eagle's Shadow, 461
  Guests, 437
  Home to Medicine Mountain, 470
  The Peace Chief, 433
  Sees Behind Trees, 438
  War Woman, 434
Village of the Great Beyond
  The River Where Blood Is Born,
    55 Af
violinists
  The Bat Boy and His Violin, 30 Af
  Hunger, 195 As
  *Yang the Third and Her Impossible
    Family*, 222 As
Virginia
  Across the Lines, 106 Af
  Cezanne Pinto, 125 Af
  A Picture of Freedom, 74 Af
  War Woman, 434 N
visions
  The Bingo Palace, 442 N
  The Boy Who Dreamed of an Acorn,
    432 N
  The Crying for a Vision, 483 N
  The Flower in the Skull, 302 H
  The Grass Dancer, 469 N
  People of Corn, 500 N
voting
  Granddaddy's Gift, 83 Af

Wabanaki Indians
  Gluskabe and the Four Wishes, 492

wagons
  The Wagon, 64 Af
waitresses
  Face of an Angel, 324 H
  Taft, 91 Af
Wampanoag (Pokonoket) Indians
  The Children of the Morning Light,
    518
warrior women
  Fa Mulan, 271 As
  War Woman, 434 N
wars, American Civil
  Across the Lines, 106 Af
  Forty Acres and Maybe a Mule,
    109 Af
  Pink and Say, 102 Af
  Sound the Jubilee, 38 Af
  Through the Storm, 56 Af
wars, American Revolution
  The Arrow Over the Door, 423 N
  Cast Two Shadows, 107 Af
  Hang a Thousand Trees with Ribbons,
    108 Af
  Second Daughter, 132 Af
wars, among gods
  The Fifth and Final Sun, 507 N
wars, kingdom of ants
  Night Visitors, 289 AS
wars, son exempt from
  The Lost Horse, 287 As
wars, Spanish American
  Papa Tells Chita a Story, 53 Af
wars, War of 1812
  *The Twins, the Pirates, and the Battle
    of New Orleans*, 112 Af
  Washington City Is Burning, 113 Af
wars, World War II
  Easter Parade, 41 Af
  Heroes, 219 As
  Songs My Mother Taught Me,
    226 As
  Under the Blood-Red Sun, 229 As
Washington, Booker T.
  Run Away Home, 75 Af
Washington, D.C.
  The Big Bike Race, 8 Af
  Cezanne Pinto, 125 Af
  Easter Parade, 41 Af

The Simple Truth, 2 Af
Washington City Is Burning, 113 Af
Washington State
  Bug Park, 208 As
  Indian Killer, 418 N
  Reservation Blues, 419 N
  Snow Falling on Cedars, 205 As
  The Window, 439 N
water, obtaining of
  The Precious Gift, 515 N
waterfalls
  Circle Within a Circle, 457 N
  The Long-Haired Girl, 267 As
watermelons
  *Just Rewards or Who Is That Man in
    the Moon & What's He Doing Up
    There Anyway?*, 270 As
weaving
  The Crane Wife, 245 As
  The Magic of Spider Woman, 495 N
  The Magic Weaver of Rugs, 523 N
weddings
  The Fred Field, 15 Af
  Ling-Li and the Phoenix Fairy,
    255 As
  My Navajo Sister, 471 N
  To a Widow with Children, 321 H
  The Wedding, 136 Af
wells
  The Well, 129 Af
Westchester County, New York
  America's Dream, 354 H
West Indians
  Something Terrible Happened, 104 Af
West Point Military Academy
  Honor and Duty, 213 As
West 7th Wildcats
  The Gumma Wars, 48 Af
White Buffalo Woman
  *The Legend of the White Buffalo
    Woman*, 503 N
white supremacy
  Candle in the Wind, 232 As
  What a Woman's Gotta Do, 23 Af
Wichita Indians
  The Last Rainmaker, 447 N
widows
  To a Widow with Children, 321 H

Wild Boy
  Two Bad Boys, 508 N
Wild West Show
  Bill Pickett, 94 Af
  The Last Rainmaker, 447 N
wind
  Brer Tiger and the Big Wind, 146 Af
  *Old Letivia and the Mountain of Sor-
    rows*, 345 H
Windigos
  The Legend of the Windigo, 529 N
  The Windigo's Return, 543 N
winter, endless
  Follow the Stars, 526 N
Wisconsin
  Dogwolf, 431 N
wishes, granted
  Gluskabe and the Four Wishes, 492 N
  The Stonecutter, 250 As
witches
  The Grass Dancer, 469 N
  Haunts, 78 Af
  Paco and the Witch, 385
wolves
  Wolf, No Wolf, 422 N
women pioneers
  I Have Heard of a Land, 130 Af
women's concerns, African Americans
  Brothers and Sisters, 18
  The Edge of Heaven, 39
  Her Stories, 147
  How Stella Got Her Groove Back, 76
  The River Where Blood Is Born, 55
  Singing in the Comeback Choir, 19
  Some Love, Some Pain, Sometime, 25
  Tryin' to Sleep in the Bed You Made,
    31
women's concerns, Asian Americans
  Of Flesh & Spirit, 298
  Songs My Mother Taught Me, 236
women's concerns, Hispanic Americans
  Agua Santa, 402
  America's Dream, 354
  Breath, Eyes, Memory, 319
  Daughters of the Fifth Sun, 342
  Face of an Angel, 314
  The Flowers in the Skull, 302
  Loose Woman, 391

  A Matter of Pride and Other Stories,
    344
  Sweet Fifteen, 309
  *Tortilla and Lullabies/Tortillas y can-
    cioncitas*, 351
  Women Don't Need to Write, 371
  The Year of Our Revolution, 349
women's concerns, Native-American Indi-
  ans
  Cloud Chamber, 436
  Faces in the Moon, 421
  The Girl Who Married the Moon, 493
  Native American Literature, 559
  Pushing the Bear, 450
wood carvers
  Confetti, 404 H
wooden people
  People of Corn, 500 N
work, origin of
  Two Bad Boys, 508
World War II
  Comfort Woman, 211 As
  Easter Parade, 41 Af
  Heroes, 219 As
  Snow Falling on Cedars, 205 As
  So Far from the Sea, 194 As
  Songs My Mother Taught Me, 236 As
  Under the Blood-Red Sun, 229 As
worms
  Full Worm Moon, 458 N
wounds, in horse raid
  Doesn't Fall Off His Horse, 479 N
Wratten, George
  Run Away Home, 75 Af
wrens
  A Ring of Tricksters, 148 Af
writers, "a dime a dozen"
  A Dime a Dozen, 174 Af
writing, desire to learn
  Women Don't Need to Write, 371 H

Young, Martha
  *When Birds Could Talk & Bats Could
    Sing*, 149 Af
youth centers
  Buried Onions, 357 H
  Run for Your Life, 71 Af

Zapotec Indians
  The Tale of Rabbit and Coyote, 517
Zen
  One Hand Clapping, 264 As
Zincantec Indians
  The Tree Is Older Than You Are,
    522

zodiac, Chinese
  Cat and Rat, 285 As
  *The Dragon's Tale and Other Animal
    Fables of the Chinese Zodiac*, 249 As
  The Great Race, 246 As
Zuni Indians
  Bones in the Basket, 537

About the Authors

ALETHEA K. HELBIG, Professor, and AGNES REGAN PERKINS, Professor Emeritus, both of English Language and Literature at Eastern Michigan University, are coauthors of *This Land Is Our Land: A Guide to Multicultural Literature for Children and Young Adults* (Greenwood 1994) and *Myths and Hero Tales: A Cross-Cultural Guide to Literature for Children and Young Adults* (Greenwood 1997). They have written a series of encyclopedic works on fiction for children including *Dictionary of British Children's Fiction* (Greenwood 1989), *Dictionary of Children's Fiction from Australia, Canada, India, New Zealand, and Selected African Countries* (Greenwood 1992) and *Dictionary of American Children's Fiction* (Greenwood 1996), for which they are currently working on the third supplement. Helbig is also author of *Nanabozhoo: Giver of Life*. She is a past president of the Children's Literature Association.